COMPUTER GRAPHICS

Volume 23 • Number 3 • July 1989
A publication of ACM SIGGRAPH
Production Editor Richard J. Beach

SIGGRAPH '89 Conference Proceedings
31 July-4 August, Boston, Massachusetts
Papers Chair Jeffrey Lane

Sponsored by the Association for Computing Machinery's
Special Interest Group on Computer Graphics

The Association for Computing
Machinery, Inc.
11 West 42nd Street
New York, NY 10036

Sample Citation Information:
... Proceedings of SIGGRAPH '89
(Boston, Mass., July 31-August 4, 1989)
In *Computer Graphics*, 23, 4 (August
1989), ACM SIGGRAPH, New York,
1989, pp. xx-yy.

ORDERING INFORMATION

**Orders from nonmembers of ACM
placed within the U.S. should be
directed to:**

Addison-Wesley Publishing
Company
Order Department
Jacob way
Reading, MA 01867
Tel:1-800-447-2226

Addison-Wesley will pay postage and
handling on orders accompanied by
check. Credit card orders may be placed
by mail or by calling the Addison-Wesley
Order Department at the number above.
Follow-up inquiries should be directed to
the Customer Service Department at the
same number.

Please include the Addison-Wesley
ISBN number with your order:
A-W ISBN 0 201-50434-0

**Orders from nonmembers of ACM
placed from outside the U.S. should
be addressed as noted below.**

Latin America and Asia:
Addison-Wesley Publishing Company
Inc.
Reading, MA 01867, U.S.A
Tel: 617-944-3700;
Cable: ADIWES READING;
Telex: 94-9416

Canada: Addison-Wesley Publishing
(Canada) Ltd.
36 Prince Andrew Place
Don Mills, Ontario M3C2T6
Canada
Tel: 416-447-5101

Australia and New Zealand:
Addison-Wesley Publishing
Company
6 Byfield Street
North Ryde, N.S.W. 2113
Australia
Tel: 888-2733;
Cable: ADIWES SYDNEY;
Telex: AA71919

**United Kingdom, Republic of Ireland,
Africa (excluding North Africa) and
South Africa:**
Addison-wesley Publishers Ltd.
Finchampstead Road
Wokingham
Berkshire RG11 2NZ, England
Cable: ADIWES Wokingham;
Telex: 846136

**Continental Europe, the Near East,
Middle East, and North Africa:**
Addison-Wesley Publishing
Company
De Lairesstraat, 90
1071 PJ Amsterdam
The Netherlands
Tel: 020 76 40-44
Cable: ADIWES AMSTERDAM
Telex: 844-14046

Orders from ACM Members:

A limited number of copies are availabl
at the ACM member discount. Send
order with payment to:

ACM Order Department
P.O. Box 64145
Baltimore, MD 21264

ACM will pay postage and handling on
orders accompanied by check.
Credit card orders only:
1-600-342-6626

Customer service, or credit card orders
from Alaska, Maryland, and outside the
US: 301-528-4261

Credit card orders may also be placed
by mail.

Please include your ACM member
number and the ACM Order number
with your order.

ACM Order Number: 428890
ACM ISBN 0-89791-312-4
ISSN 0097-8930

Contents

Technical Papers Program, Wednesday, 2 August 1989

Technical Papers Program, Wednesday, 2 August 1989

Technical Papers Program, Thursday, 3 August 1989

Technical Papers Program, Thursday, 3 August 1989

Technical Papers Program, Friday, 4 August 1989

Technical Papers Program, Friday, 4 August 1989

Panel Sessions, Wednesday, 2 August 1989

Panel Sessions, Thursday, 3 August 1989

Panel Sessions, Thursday, 3 August 1989

Panel Sessions, Friday, 4 August 1989

Computer Graphics Theater

Preface

These proceedings contain the papers presented during the three days of the Technical Program of the 16th annual ACM Conference on Computer Graphics and Interactive Techniques, SIGGRAPH '89. The conference was held July 31, 1989 through August 4, 1989 in the Hynes Convention Center in Boston, Massachusetts. These proceedings are being published as a special issue of *Computer Graphics*.

The paper selection process began with the publication of the Call for Participation, first distributed at SIGGRAPH '88 in Atlanta, Georgia. 190 papers were submitted, 160 of which arrived on the deadline date of January 10th, 1989. 38 papers were accepted to represent the very best of computer graphics today.

The papers were then distributed by me, with the significant assistance of Rick Beach and Frank Crow of Xerox PARC, to the Technical Papers Committee, which consisted of twenty of the leading researchers in the field. These senior reviewers were responsible for reviewing each paper assigned to them and for obtaining at least two other reviews from experts in the field from two separate institutions. All reveiws had to be completed by March 6, 1989. The Technical Papers Committee met March 4-5 to make the final selection of papers.

I would like to express my appreciation to the Technical Papers Committee and and the reviewers for their very considerable efforts and for a job well done. These people provided well documented and detailed opinions on every paper. These reviews take a great deal of time and effort and result in invaluable information to the authors of both accepted and rejected papers.

I especially express my thanks to Kathy Porter, my assistant in organizing the review process: collecting, sorting, and collating not only the reviews and the papers, but at times, the authors and reviewers themselves. She was absolutely invaluable.

Thanks are also due to John Dill, last years' Technical Papers Chair, who refused to let me underestimate the magnitude of the effort required for a successful Technical Program, and to Rick Beach, SIGGRAPH Editor-in-Chief, who worked long hours with authors and the printer, which resulted in this excellent document.

Jeff Lane
SIGGRAPH '89 Technical Program Chair

Conference Committee

CONFERENCE CO-CHAIRS

Branko J. Gerovac
(Digital Equipment Corporation)
Christopher F. Herot
(Bitstream Inc.)

CONFERENCE COMMITTEE CHAIRS

Jeffrey Lane, *Papers*
(Digital Equipment Corporation)
Robert L. Judd, *Panels*
(Los Alamos National Laboratory)
Gereda B. Pruitt, *Courses*
(Digital Equipment Corporation)
Carolyn Hayes, *Exhibits*
(Sun Microsystems, Inc.)
Sally N. Rosenthal, *Computer Graphics Theater*
(Digital Equipment Corporation)
Mark Resch, *Art Show*
(Rensselaer Polytechnic Institute)
Joan Collins, *Audio/Visual*
(Joan Collins and Associates)
Wendy E. Mackay, *Interactive Multi-Media Message System*
(MIT)
Adele Newton, *International Liaison*
(University of Waterloo)
Gwen Bell, *Local Arrangements*
(The Computer Museum)
James A. Banister, *Materials*
(TRW)
Carol Byram, *Public Relations*
(Cubicomp Corporation)
Brian Herzog, *Registration*
(Sun Microsystems, Inc.)
Diana Tuggle, *Speaker Slides*
(Los Alamos National Laboratory)
John E. French, Jr., *Special Interest Groups*
(GeoQuest Systems, Inc.)
Jeff Yates, *Student Volunteer Coordinator*
(Wavefront Technologies)
Bruce Eric Brown, *Technical Slide Sets*
(Wang Laboratories, Inc.)
Steven M. Van Frank, *Treasurer*
(Lynxys, Inc.)

CONFERENCE PLANNING COMMITTEE

James J. Thomas, *Chair* (Battelle Pacific Northwest Laboratories)
Michael J. Bailey (San Diego Supercomputer Center)
Carol Byram (Cubicomp Corporation)
Branko J. Gerovac (Digital Equipment Corporation)
Andrew C. Goodrich (RasterOps)
Christopher F. Herot (Bitstream, Inc.)
David D. Loendorf (Los Alamos National Laboratory)
Adele Newton (University of Waterloo)
Jacqueline M. Wollner (Convex Computer Corporation)
Robert J. Young (CAD/CAM Management Consultants)

PAPERS COMMITTEE

Alan H. Barr (California Institute of Technology)
Forest Baskett (Silicon Graphics)
Richard J. Beach (Xerox PARC)
Russell Brown (Evans and Sutherland)
Ingrid Carlbom (Digital Equipment Corporation)
Loren Carpenter (Pixar)
Edwin E. Catmull (Pixar)
Elaine Cohen (University of Utah)
Robert L. Cook (Pixar)
Tony D. DeRose (University of Washington)
Nick England (Sun Microsystems, Inc.)
A. Robin Forrest (University of East Anglia)
Alain Fournier (University of Toronto)
Henry Fuchs (University of North Carolina at Chapel Hill)
Donald P. Greenberg (Cornell University)
Leo Guibas (DEC Systems Research Center)
Rob Pike (AT&T Bell Laboratories)
Spencer Thomas (University of Michigan)
Turner Whitted (Numerical Design, Ltd.)
Jane Wilhelms (University of California, Santa Cruz)

PANELS COMMITTEE

Christine Barton (Morgan Guaranty)
George Champine (Digital Equipment Corporation)
Alyce Kaprow (The New Studio)
Michael Keeler (Ardent Computer)
David D. Loendorf (Los Alamos National Laboratory)
Theodore N. Reed (Los Alamos National Laboratory)

COURSES COMMITTEE

Frank Bliss (Electronic Data Systems)
Mark Henderson (Arizona State University)
Dick Phillips (Los Alamos National Laboratory)
Dick Rubinstein (Digital Equipment Corporation)
Connie U. Smith (L & S Computer Technology Inc.)
Maryam Taghdiri (Technology Management Corporation)

ART SHOW JURY

Copper Giloth (University of Mass, Amherst)
Lorne Falk (Independent curator and critic, Canada)
Patric Prince (SIGGRAPH Travelling Art Show Chair)
Christine Schopf (ARS Electronica, Austria)
Dorothy Spencer (Read/Write Press)

COMPUTER GRAPHICS THEATER JURY

Loren Carpenter (Pixar)
Lucy Petrovich (University of Wisconsin, Madison)
Fred Ward (*National Geographic* Magazine)

COMPUTER GRAPHICS THEATER COMMITTEE

Maxine Brown (University of Illinois at Chicago)
Rachel Carpenter, *Animation Screening Room Coordinator* (Cinematrix)
Craig Good (Pixar)
Johnie Hugh Horn, *CG Theater Consultant* (Elektra Design Group)
Vicki Putz (Vickie Putz Design)
Sylvie Rueff (Jet Propulsion Lab and CalTech)
Kathy Tanaka (Independent)

TECHNICAL PROGRAM REVIEWERS

Greg Abram
John Airey
Brian Apgar
William Armstrong
James Arvo
Peter Atherton
John Austin
Norman Badler
Ron Baecker
Brian Barsky
Richard Bartels
Ronen Barzel
Daniel Baum
John Beatty
Marshall Bern
Eric Bier
Gary Bishop
Doug Blewett
Jim Blinn
Jules Bloomenthal
J.E. Bresenham
Erik Brisson
Reyer Brons
Frederick Brooks
Marc Brown
Robert P. Burton
Bill Buxton
Gene Caldwell
Tom Calvert
Luca Cardelli
Richard Carey
Tom Cargill
Jack Carroll
Sheue-Ling Chang
Bernard Chazelle
Eric Chen
Fuhua Cheng
Paul Chew
Richard Chuang
Jim Chung
William S. Cleveland
Beth Cobb
Jim Cobb
Ephraim Cohen
Michael Cohen
Mike Cosman
William B. Cowan
Frank Crow
Anthony DeRose
Robert Dickinson
Mark Dippé
D.A. Dobkin
Bob Drebin
Scott Drysdale
Tom Duff
Herbert Edelsbrunner
Kels Elmquist
Nick England
Rida Farouki
Elliot Feibush
Stephen Feiner
Russell Fish
Scott Fisher
Eugene L. Fiume
Kurt Fleischer
Tom Foley
David Forsey
Alain Fournier
William Randolph Franklin
Mark Friedell

Tom Furness
Don Fussell
Steve Gabriel
Richard Gallagher
Jeffrey Gardner
Erik Geisler
David George
Andrew Glassner
Ronald N. Goldman
Julian Gomez
Eric Grant
Dan Greene
Ned Greene
Robert Haber
Paul Haeberli
Eric Haines
Dan Halbert
Roy Hall
Pat Hanrahan
David Haussler
Charles Haynes
Paul Heckbert
Ralph Hill
Parker Hirtle
John Hobby
Eric Hoffert
Kevin Hussey
Dave Immel
Kenneth Jacob
Tom Jensen
James Kajiya
Michael Kaplan
Ari Kaufman
David Kirk
Fred Kitson
Victor Klassen
Lewis Knapp
G.D. Knott
Keith Knox
Bill Kovacks
John Landsdown
Charled Lang
John Lasseter
Jim Lawson
Adam Levinthal
Marc Levoy
Peter Lipman
Andrew Lippman
James S. Lipscomb
Richard Littlefield
Bart Locanthi
Charles Loop
William Lorensen
Tom Lyche
Jock Mackinlay
Tom Malley
Martii Mantyla
R.R. Martin
Nelson Max
W. Thomas McCollough
Eileen McGinnis
M.D. McIlroy
Leonard McMillen
James Miller
Don P. Mitchell
Fanya Montalvo
Matthew Moore
Chuck Moser
Earll Murman
James Murphy

(TECHNICAL PROGRAM REVIEWERS, continued)

Ken Musgrave
Brad Myers
Bruce Naylor
David Neuhoff
Gregory Nielson
Daniel O'Donnell
Art Olsen
Dan Olsen
Peter Oppenheimer
Eben Ostby
Alan Paeth
James Painter
Fred Parke
Nicholas Patrikachus
Darwyn Peachey
Ken Perlin
John W. Peterson
Rob Pike
Maike Pique
M.L.V. Pitteway
Stephen M. Pizar
John Platt
Tom Porter
Michael Potmesil
Pierre Poulin
Prsemyslaw Prusinkiewicz
Lyle Ramshaw
Rod Recker
Bill Reeves
Craig Reynolds
John Rhoades
Henry Rich
Richard Riesenfeld
George Robertson
John Robinson
Julian Rosenman
David Rosenthal
Jarek Rossignac
Holly Rushmeier
Paola Sabella
M.A. Sabin
Raymond Sarraga
Stuart Sechrest
Thomas Sederberg
Raimund Seidel
Jeffrey Shallit
Mike Shantz
Mark Shepard
Larry Sher

George Sherouse
Mikio Shinya
Ken Shoemake
H.B. Siegel
Rob Skinner
Kenneth Sloan, Jr.
Alvy Ray Smith
Robert F. Sproull
C. Stein
Thomas Stephenson
Rodney Stock
Thomas Stockham
Jorge Stolfi
Maureen Stone
Richard Szeliski
Brice Tebbs
Demitri Terzopolous
Jay Torborg
Lloyd Treinish
Howard Trickey
Ben Trumbore
Edward R. Tufte
Greg Turk
Jim Turner
Craig Upson
Steve Upstill
Tim Van Hook
Brian Von Herzen
Victor Vyssotsky
John Wallace
Gregory Ward
Keith Waters
Gary S. Watkins
Mark Watkins
Louise Watson
Kevin Weiler
Michael Wesley
Turner Whitted
A.R. Wilks
Lance Williams
Andy Witkin
Brian Wyvill
Larry Yeager
Polle Zellweger
David Zeltzer
John Zimmerman
Steve Zimmerman
Michael Zyda

PROFESSIONAL SUPPORT

ACM SIGGRAPH '89 Conference Coordinator
Molly Morgan Kuhns

ACM SIGGRAPH Conference Liaison
Lois Blankstein

Administrative Assistants
Janice Manning, *Courses*
Kathy Porter, *Papers*
Diana Salazar, *Panels*
Deborah Williams, *Art Show*

Audio/Visual Management
Audio Visual Headquarters Corporation
Jim Bartolomucci
Rich Farnham
Vickie Feldkircher
Doug Hunt
George Miller
Nancy Richardson

Conference Accounting
Smith Bucklin and Associates, Inc.
Ruth Kerns
Leo Strock

Conference Management
Smith Bucklin and Associates, Inc.
Susan Argenti
Joy Lee
Deidre Ross
Cynthia Stark

Conference Travel Agency
Heritage Meeting & Incentives
Donna Brannen
Bob Ginsburg
Mary McCann-Day

Decorator/Drayage
Andrews-Bartlett and Associates, Inc.
Bob Borsz
Betty Fuller
Ken Gallagher
Tom Gilmore
John Patronski

Exhibition Management
Robert T. Kenworthy, Inc.
Hank Cronan
Barbara Voss

Graphic Design
Watzman+Keyes
Jane Sullivan
Hayley Tsang
Suzanne Watzman

Organization Development Consultant
Overgard Associates
Jeanette C. Overgard

Public Relations
Smith Bucklin and Associates, Inc.
Leona Caffey
Sheila Hoffmeyer
Kathleen Nilles

Exhibitors

Abekas
Academic Press
Adage, Inc.
Addison-Wesley
Advanced Electronics Design, Inc.
Advanced Imaging
Advanced Micro Devices
Advanced Technology Center
AGC (Atari Games Corporation)
Alias Reasearch, Inc.
Alliant/Raster Technology
Analog Devices, Inc.
Apollo Computer
Apple Computer, Inc.
Ardent Computer
Association for Computing Machinery
AT&T Graphics Software Labs
AT&T Pixel Machines
Autodesk, Inc.
Autographix, Inc.
AV Video (Montage Publishing)
Aztek, Inc.
Barco Electronics, Inc.
Brooktree Corporation
Bruning
Bruning Plotter Supplies
BTS
Cadkey Inc.
Cahners Publishing Company
Canon U.S.A., Inc.
Celco Inc.
Chromatics, Inc.
CIS Graphics Inc.
CMP Publications
Commodore Business Machines, Inc.
Computer Graphics Review (Intertec Publishing)
Computer Graphics World
Computer Pictures
Control Systems, Inc.
Convex Computer Corporation
Covid, Inc.
Crosfield Design Systems
Crosfield Electronics Inc.
Cubicomp Corporation
Cyberware Laboratory
Dainippan Screen Manufacturing Company Ltd.
Dalim
Data Translation
Digital Arts
Digital Equipment Corporation
Dimension Technology
DisplayTEK, Inc.
Dubner Computer Systems
Du Pont Company
Dynair Electronics, Inc.
Eastman Kodak Company
Electrohome Limited
Electronic Systems Products
ESD

ESP Corporation
Evans & Sutherland Computer Corporation
Excom
Expert Graphics Systems
Faroudja Laboratories
Flamingo Graphics
Folsom Research
FOR-A Corporation of America
French Expositions in the U.S.
Gammadata Computer Ltd.
General Electric, PDPO
General Parametrics Corporation
Getris Images
GraphON Corporation
James Grunder & Associates, Inc.
GTCO Corporation
Harris Video Systems
Helios Systems-Division of Dynatech
Hewlett-Packard Company
Hitachi America, Ltd.
Hitachi Denshi America Ltd.
Howtek, Inc.
HTM (hi-tech Marketing Corporation)
IEEE Computer Society
Ikegami Electronics
Ilford Photo Corporation
Image Innovation Limited
Imagraph Corporation
Inmos
Intel Corporation
Intelligent Light, Inc.
Interactive Machines, Inc.
Intergraph Corporation
IRIS Grpahics
Ithaca Software
JRL Systems
Kontron Electronics
Kurta Corporation
Lazerus
Leader Instruments
Levco Sales
Lundy Electronics & Systems
Lyon Lamb Video Animation Systems
Macweek (Ziff-Davis)
Magni Systems, Inc.
Management Graphics, Inc.
Matrox Electronic Systems Ltd.
Measurement Systems Inc.
Media Cybernetics
Media Magic
Megascan Technology
Megatek Corporation
Meiko Scientific
Mercury Computer Systems, Inc.
Microfield Graphics Inc.
Micrografx, Inc.
Microtime Inc.
Minolta Corporation
Mitsubishi Electric Sales America Inc.

Mitsubishi Electronics
Mitsubishi International
Modgraph Inc.
Moniterm Corporation
Morgan Kaufmann Publishers
Motorola
Multiwire Division-Kollmorgen Corporation
National Semiconductor Corporation
National Technical Information Service
NCGA
NEC Home Electronics. Computer Products Division
NEC Professional Systems Division
Nikon Inc.
Nissei Sangyo America, Ltd.
Nth Graphics
Number Nine Computer Corporation
Numonics Corporation
Omnicomp Graphics
Open Software Foundation
Oxberry Division
Panasonic Industrial Company
Pansophic Systems, Inc.
Paragon Imaging
Parallax Graphics
PC Week (Ziff-Davis)
Peritek Corporation
Photron Ltd.
Pixar
Pixelink Corporation
Pixelworks, Inc.
Prime Computer Inc.
Prior Data Sciences
QMS, Inc.
Quantum Data Inc.
Rainbow Technologies
Ramtek Corporation
Rastek Corporation
Real World Graphics Ltd.
RGB Technology
Ricoh Corporation, Peripheral Products Division
Ron Scott Inc.
Sampo Corporation
SAS Institute Inc.
Scientific Computer Systems Corporation
Seiko Instruments
Shima seiki
SIGGRAPH '90
Silicon Graphics
Sky Computers, Inc.
Softimage Inc.
SONY Corporation of America
Spaceward Microsystems
Springer-Verlag
Star Technologies, Graphicon Products Division
Stellar Computer Inc.
Stereographics Corporation
Summagraphics Corporation
Sun Microsystems, Inc.
SuperMAC Technology
Symbolics Graphics Division
TDI Thomson Digital Images
Techexport Inc.
Tech-Source
Tektronix, Inc.
Telebit Corporation
Test & Measurement Systems, Inc.
Texas Instruments
Texas Memory Systems Inc.
Texnai Inc.
Time Arts Inc.
Toshiba America Inc.
Truevision Inc.

Univision Technologies Inc.
Unix World Magazine
Van Nostrand Reinhold
Videomedia S.E.D. Inc.
Visual Information, Inc.
Visual Information Technologies
Wacom Company, Ltd.
Waldmann Lighting Company
Wasatch Computer Technology
Wavefront Technologies
John Wiley & Sons, Inc.
Winsted Corporation

1989 ACM SIGGRAPH Awards

Steven A. Coons Award
for
Outstanding Creative Contributions to Computer Graphics

David C. Evans

The 1989 Steven A. Coons Award for Outstanding Creative Contributions is made to David C. Evans, a truly inspiring leader in computer graphics over a period of nearly three decades.

David Evans began his career in computers around 1950, although his formal education was in physics. His early work involved incremental computers applied to numerical controls for the Bendix Corporation. There he also was Project Engineer for the Bendix G-15 computer, a 1956 personal computer with an interpretive programming system. Evans, however, was dedicated to developing computing systems for interactive personal problem-solving.

Thus, he turned his attention to timesharing and graphics. While a professor at the University of California at Berkeley in the early 60's, he directed a laboratory that pioneered a successful multi-user timesharing system, named "GENIE." Many of that system's ideas were subsequently utilized by Scientific Data Systems in its 900-series computers. The Evans laboratory also explored interactive graphics based upon an IDIOM display attached to a Digital Equipment Corporation PDP-5 computer.

This early foray into computer graphics subsequently led to the golden era of computer graphics at the University of Utah and the founding of the Evans and Sutherland Computer Company in Salt Lake City.

Dr. Evans returned home to Utah to build up the Computer Science Department of the University of Utah. There he assembled faculty including such well-known individuals as Ivan Sutherland, the first recipient of the Coons Award, and Thomas Stockham. Steven Coons was a visiting faculty member at Utah in

1973. William Newman, co-author with Robert Sproull of the well-known textbook, spent several years there. Newman said: "He (Evans) had a particular style of running a department that I now think of as magical, in the sense that everything one could wish for seemed to arrive almost without asking."

The period from 1967 through at least 1975 was an extraordinary time for computer graphics at Utah. There was a rare confluence of faculty, students, staff, facilities and resources to support vision research and hard work that produced remarkable developments in computer graphics. This research was responsible for the birth of continuous-tone computer graphics as we know it today. An amazing constellation of students passed through the University of Utah and their names are to be found throughout the publications of SIGGRAPH and other graphics journals. Among them were Jim Blinn and Jim Clark, previous Achievement Award winners, and this year's Achievement Award Winner John Warnock. Many of his students have remarked that it was David Evans' vision and his commitment to them that made their work possible. His guidance and advice were influential in giving them a sense of self-realization.

Beyond his abilities as an educator are his achievements in the business world. With Ivan Sutherland he founded the Evans and Sutherland Computer Corporation to produce premier computer graphics display equipment. A large part of this company's business concerns real time simulation of scenes associated with aircraft flying and automobiles driving. These real time simulators are a partial expression of David Evans' wish to contribute to all manner of simulation. He has been known to say that engineering design is just another form of simulation of the products to be built.

SIGGRAPH is pleased to present the 1989 Coons award to David C. Evans, technical leader and innovator, an advisor and mentor, who regularly inspires those around him and continues to provide the vision and environment for great accomplishments. We hereby express our recognition and gratitude for his direct and indirect contributions to computer graphics.

Previous award winners:

1987: Prof. Donald P. Greenberg
1985: Dr. Pierre Bézier
1983: Dr. Ivan E. Sutherland

Computer Graphics Achievement Award

John Warnock

The 1989 Computer Graphics Achievement Award is given to John Warnock for PostScript, which embodies a major contribution to imaging models and and to integration of graphics and text.

In the computer graphics field, agreement on conventions for describing and communicating models between workers and computers is of great potential benefit, provided the standards are sufficiently powerful and flexible, and if enough people agree on the conventions.

It is to Dr. Warnock's credit that the PostScript language meets all these requirements. It has not only been accepted by researchers and developers, but, has, by the force of its successful application become the *de facto* standard for many graphics applications. As a means of communication between computers and printers, PostScript's power and flexibility for representing text, shapes, and images as graphical entities helped launch the desktop publishing industry. The innovative technical solution presented in PostScript has freed both suppliers and users from the burdens of conflicting and inadequate device drivers. Suppliers are no longer required to develop distinct drivers for each printer supported by a software package, e.g., word processor. Users are relieved of the burden of selecting and tailoring the supplied drivers for individual configurations. PostScript is now used as a representation for window systems and as a link between graphics applications as well. What appears on the screens and in the printout of modern computers is much more exciting than it once was because of the success of this technical achievement.

PostScript is not the only contribution to computer graphics made by Dr. Warnock. PostScript is the culmination of a series of special purpose languages he has spawned over the years. An early example is the language for specifying geometric databases used in the Evans and Sutherland maritime simulator project. While at the Xerox Palo Alto Research Center, he and his co-workers developed JaM, InterPress, and what later became the imaging model for PostScript.

Warnock's is also known for contributions to display algorithms including one of the first hidden surface algorithms as well as algorithms for anti-aliasing of lines and text.

Warnock obtained his PhD at the University of Utah in the computer science department led by David Evans, who receives this year's Coons Award. For several years he worked at Evans and Sutherland Computer Corporation where he had responsibility for the design and implementation of real-time computer generated imaging systems for ship and flight simulators. He also was responsible for company research in interactive computer aided design. Then he became a Principal Scientist at Xerox Palo Alto Research Center where his work involved interactive graphics research, graphics standards and improving the typographic quality of computer gray-scale displays. In 1982 he and Charles Geschke founded Adobe Systems Incorporated, where Warnock is Chairman of the Board and Chief Executive Officer. They received the NCGA Award for Technical Excellence this year.

John Warnock's contributions to computer graphics, especially PostScript, will benefit huge numbers of people for many years. He is truly a worthy recipient of the 1989 Computer Graphics Achievement Award.

Previous award winners

1988: Alan H. Barr
1987: Robert Cook
1986: Turner Whitted
1985: Loren Carpenter
1984: James H. Clark
1983: James F. Blinn

Keynote:
From Bezel to Proscenium
The Human-Computer Interface
25 Years Hence and Beyond
the Desktop Metaphor

Nicholas Negroponte
Professor of Media Technology
and Director of the MIT Media Lab

Stalking the future is a curious game. More often than not we project our current images, sometimes unwittingly, with mere technological changes which, in the case of computers, include speed, memory, and the exotica of i/o. I have a view of the future not generally held, whichaffects the human interface enormously and is not a mere technological advance, but a fundamental departure from commonly held views.

My view of the future of desktop computing is one where the bezel becomes a proscenium and agents are embodied to any degree of literalness you may desire. In the longer term, as holography prevails, little people will walk across your desk (if you have one) dispatched to do what they know how.

The picture is simple. The stage is set with characters of your own choice or creation whose scripts are drawn from the play of your life. Their expressiveness, character, and propensity to speak out are driven by an event (external) and style (yours). If you want your agents to wear bow ties, they will. If you prefer talking to parallelepipeds, fine.

This highly literal model of agents can be dismissed as a foolish scheme to replace serious *icons* with "Snow White and the Seven Dwarfs". But this begs the question about delegation and speech. In some form we can expect surrogates who can execute complex functions, filter information, and intercommunicate in our interest(s).

Direct manipulation has its place, and in many regards is part of the joys of life: sports, food, sex, and for some, driving. But wouldn't you really prefer to run your home and office life with a gaggle of well trained butlers (to answer the phone), maids (to make the beds), secretaries (to filter the world), accountants or brokers (to manage your money), and on some occasions, cooks, gardeners, and chauffeurs when there were too many guests, weeds, or cars on the road?

Simulation of Object and Human Skin Deformations in a Grasping Task

Jean-Paul Gourret[1]
MIRALab, University of Montreal

Nadia Magnenat Thalmann[2]
University of Geneva

Daniel Thalmann[3]
Swiss Federal Institute of Technology

ABSTRACT

This paper addresses the problem of simulating deformations between objects and the hand of a synthetic character during a grasping process. A numerical method based on finite element theory allows us to take into account the active forces of the fingers on the object and the reactive forces of the object on the fingers. The method improves control of synthetic human behavior in a task level animation system because it provides information about the environment of a synthetic human and so can be compared to the sense of touch. Finite element theory currently used in engineering seems one of the best approaches for modeling both elastic and plastic deformation of objects, as well as shocks with or without penetration between deformable objects. We show that intrinsic properties of the method based on composition/decomposition of elements have an impact in computer animation. We also state that the use of the same method for modeling both objects and human bodies improves the modeling of the contacts between them. Moreover, it allows a realistic envelope deformation of the human fingers comparable to existing methods. To show what we can expect from the method, we apply it to the grasping and pressing of a ball. Our solution to the grasping problem is based on displacement commands instead of force commands used in robotics and human behavior.

keywords: synthetic human animation, grasping task, tactile sensing modeling, simulation, contact, physical interaction, deformation

---

1 on leave from Lab. de Traitement du Signal Numérique, Ecole Nationale Supérieure de Physique, Marseille, France

2 MIRALab, CUI, University of Geneva, Switzerland
   CH 1207 Geneva, phone: 41-22-787-6581
   e-mail: thalmann@CGEUGE51.BITNET

3 Computer Graphics Lab., Swiss Federal Institute of Technology, CH 1207 Lausanne, Switzerland
   phone: 41-21- 693-5214, e-mail: thalmann@elma.epfl.ch

INTRODUCTION

Along with walking and speaking, grasping is an important task to be included in a system for animating synthetic actors. In character animation, the notion of task planning is divided into three phases: world modeling, task specification and code generation. World modeling consists mainly of describing the geometry and the physical characteristics of the synthetic actors and the objects. Task specification and code generation are more language oriented; they are not treated in this paper.

World modeling for synthetic actors frequently uses skeletons made up of segments linked at joints. This is suitable for parametric key-frame animation, kinematic algorithmic animation or dynamic based techniques [23]. The skeleton is generally surrounded by surfaces or elementary volumes [3] [20] whose sole purpose is to give a realistic appearance to body.

The model developed by Komatsu [17] uses biquartic Bezier surfaces, and control points are assigned to the links. Magnenat-Thalmann et al. [24] used a technique based on Joint-Dependent Local Deformations (JLD) to tie skin points to joint points obtaining realistic stretching and inflation of flesh. Catmull used polygons [10], and Badler and Morris [2] used the combination of elementary spheres and B-splines to model the human fingers.

On the other hand, the environment of characters is made up of rigid objects, key-frame deformable objects, mathematically deformable objects [5], soft objects represented by scalar combinations of fields around key points [35] [7], or physically deformable objects based on elasticity theory [27] [30]. With physical models, the objects act as if they had a mind. They react to applied forces such as gravity, pressure and contact. Platt and Barr [27] used finite element software and discuss constraint methods in terms of animator tools for physical model control. The models developed by Terzopoulos et al. [30] are implemented using the Finite Difference Method. Collisions between elastic objects are simulated by creating potential energy around each object, i.e., intersections between deformable bodies are avoided by surrounding the object surfaces with a repulsive collision force. This approach is also developed by Luciani [19] who deals with 2D real time animation of objects and characters based on springs, dampers and masses, controlled by gestural transducers with mechanical feedback.

©1989   ACM-0-89791-312-4/89/007/0021 $00.75

Moore and Wilhems [25] treat collision response, developing two methods based on springs and analytical solutions. They state that spring solutions are applicable to the surface shapes of flexible bodies but do not explain how the shapes are obtained before initiation of contact calculations nor how the shapes are modified as a result of a contact.

Our main objective is to model the world in a grasping task context by using a finite element theory. The method allows simulation of both motion and shape of objects in accordance with physical laws, as well as the deformations of human flesh due to contact forces between flesh and objects. The following two arguments support use of the same method for modeling deformation of objects and human flesh.

First, we want to develop a method which will deal with penetrating impacts and true contacts. For this reason, we prefer to consider true contact forces with possibilities of sliding and sticking rather than only repulsive forces. Our approach based on volume properties of bodies permits calculation of the shape of world constituents before contact, and to treat their shape during contact. When a contact is initiated we use a global resolution procedure which considers bodies in contact as an unique body. Simulation of impact with penetration can be used to model the grasping of ductile objects or to model ballistic problems. It requires decomposition of objects into small geometrically simple objects.

Second, all the advantages of the physical modeling of objects can be transferred to human flesh [13]. For example, we expect the hand grasping an object to lead to realistic flesh deformation as well as an exchange of information between the object and the hand which will not only be geometrical. When a deformable object is grasped, the contact forces on it and on the fingertips will lead to deformation of both the object and of the fingertips, giving rise to reactive forces which provide significant information about the object and more generally about the environment of the synthetic human body.

It is important to note that even if the deformations of the object and of the fingers are not visible, or if the object is rigid, the exchange of information will exist because the fingers are always deformable. This exchange of information using active and reactive forces is significant for a good and realistic grip and can influence the behavior of the hand and of the arm skeleton. For grip, interacting information is as important as that provided by tactile sensors in a robot manipulator. This is a well known problem of robotics called "compliant motion control". It consists of taking into account external forces and commanding the joints and links of the fingers using inverse kinematic or dynamic controls. In the past, authors dealing with kinematic and dynamic animation models oriented towards automatic animation control [1] [4] [9] [33], have often referred to works of roboticians [14] [18] [26]. In the same way, we believe that methods intensively used in CAD systems may improve the control of synthetic human animation. However, the method must be adapted to computer animation because the problems here are not the same as in CAD or robotics.

In robotics, it is impossible to expect a grip controller to perform a complete environmental finite element analysis in real time. Consequently, the adopted solution generally uses well-located fingertip sensors to measure the terms that are difficult to compute. In synthetic human modeling, complete computations are possible, though they represent a gigantic problem. To grasp an object, robots and humans apply a prescribed force to the object, whose intensity is related to environment knowledge. This process will not work in animation because force transducers are not yet used in computer animation systems. Hence, our grasping method for animation is based on prescribed displacements instead of prescribed forces.

In the next section, we emphasize the properties of the numerical method developed for computer animation purposes. In the second part, we show how a global approach can contribute to animation of synthetic actors in their environment, using the same method for modeling deformation of objects and human bodies. We describe in detail the grasping and pressing of a ball, and show envelope deformation during finger flexing. In the last section, we discuss how our numerical approach enhances the HUMAN FACTORY system [23].

NUMERICAL METHOD FOR COMPUTER ANIMATION

This section does not describe the finite element theory in detail, but rather introduces those concepts used for computer animation purposes. A comprehensive study of the finite element theory is given in Bathe [6] and Zienkiewicz [36]. A summary of the theory of elasticity can be found in Timoshenko and Goodier [32].

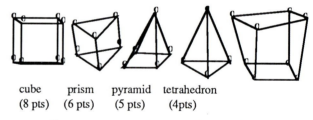

cube   prism   pyramid   tetrahedron
(8 pts)   (6 pts)   (5 pts)   (4pts)

a. linear elements with zero order continu

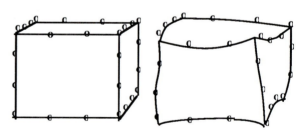

b. cubic element with zero order continu

Figure 1 - elements and their deformations

Solid three-dimensional objects and human flesh are discretized using simple or complex volume elements, depending on the choice of the interpolation function. Zero order simple linear elements and complex cubic elements with their deformations are shown in Figure 1. The finite element approach is compatible with requirements of visual realism because a body surface corresponds to an element face that lies on the body boundary. As with surface patches, it is possible to ensure high order of continuity between elements. However, this procedure is expensive in terms of memory space and CPU time. For this reason, our calculations are based on linear elements with zero order continuity. Nevertheless, the use of complex elements and high order continuity allows us to obtain the same visual effects as with surface patches. Indeed, elements are parametric volumes and the boundary object surface is a parametric surface.

Once the various kinds of elements are defined, the modeled shape is obtained by composition. Each element is linked to other elements at nodal points. In continuum mechanics, the equilibrium of a body presenting a shape can be expressed by using the stationary principle of the total potential or the principle of virtual displacements:

$$wR = wB + wS + wF \qquad (1)$$

where wB represents the virtual work due to the body forces such as gravity, centrifugal loading, inertia and damping, wS represents virtual work of distributed surface forces such as pressure, wF represents the virtual work of concentrated forces and wR represents the internal virtual work due to internal stresses.

In the finite element method, the equilibrium relation (1) is applied to each element e

$$w_{Re} = w_{Be} + w_{Se} + w_{Fe} \qquad (2)$$

and the whole body is obtained by composing all elements

$$\sum_{element=1}^{NBEL} W_{Re} = \sum_{element=1}^{NBEL} W_{Be} + \sum_{element=1}^{NBEL} W_{Se} + \sum_{node=1}^{NBP} W_{Fe} \qquad (3)$$

Our three-dimensional model uses elements with eight nodes and NBDOF = 3 degrees of freedom per node. These elements are easily modified to prismatic or tetrahedral elements to approximate most existing 3D shapes. The composition of NBEL elements with 8 points give NBP points and NB = NBP*NBDOF equations. From the relation (3) we can write the following matrix equation between vectors of size [NB*1] as follows:

$$R + RI = RB + RS + RF \qquad (4)$$

where RB is the composition of body forces, RS is the composition of surface forces and RF represents the concentrated forces acting on the nodes. R + RI is the composition of internal forces due to internal stresses. These stresses are initial stresses which give the RI term, and reactions to deformations created by RB, RS and RF which give the R term.

In the following sections we will use the equilibrium relation (4) under the form (5)

$$K.U = R \qquad (5)$$

where K is the [NB*NB] stiffness matrix, a function of material and flesh constitution, R is the [NB*1] load vector including the effects of the body forces, surface tractions and initial stresses, and U is the [NB*1] displacement vector from the unloaded configuration.

Relation (5) is valid in static equilibrium and also in pseudo-static equilibrium at instant t_i. Instants t_i are considered as variables which represent different load intensities. In this paper, we do not deal with dynamics when loads are applied rapidly. In this case, true time inertia and damping, displacement velocity and acceleration must be added to (5).

Under this form, the body can be viewed as a huge three-dimensional spring of stiffness K and return force R. The equilibrium relation (3) is a function of volume properties because each component is obtained by the summation of integrations over the volume and the area of each element (see [36] for more details).

Since the process used consists of the composition of elements to create a global deformable object, we believe that this property and its inverse, i.e. the decomposition of a global deformable object into two or multiple sub-objects, should be used in computer animation.

The decomposition is very easy to implement because the constitutive properties of each element as well as inter-element forces are memorized and are taken into account during numerical calculations. It is possible for example to create a global object made of different sub-objects; each sub-object would have its own constitutive properties and be composed of one or more elements.

There are several ways to exploit the intrinsic properties of this method:

- The decomposition approach can be exploited to model penetrating shocks between two or more deformable objects. Each object is subdivided into many deformable sub-objects which are able themselves to interact with each other because each inherits its own properties. The decomposition approach may also be used in contact problems when contact is released.

- The composition approach can be used for modeling contacts without penetration between two or more objects. In this case, objects can be considered as sub-objects evolve independently until contact is detected and a global object is composed following contact. In practice this means that relations $K_n.U_n = R_n$ are resolved independently before contact and a unique relation K.U = R is resolved after contact of n bodies. This process works if we take into account the contact forces that prevent overlapping in equation (5). We use the composition approach for the grasping and pressing of a ball described in the following section. A survey of contact problems is given by Bohm [8]. Example of 3D treatments can be found in Chaudary and Bathe [11].

BALL GRASPING AND PRESSING

To show how the physical modeling of deformable objects can contribute to human animation, we present an example of a contact problem dealing with the grasping and pressing of a ball. Starting with the facet-based envelopes of ball and hand obtained from our image synthesis system SABRINA [22], we mesh the volume of the objects to create full 3D bodies or shell bodies depending on the application. After calculations of the deformations using our method based on finite element theory, the facet-based deformed envelopes are extracted from the data base used in our calculations and restored to SABRINA for visualization. In this way, visual realism is always ensured by the image synthesis system. The ball can be modeled by a shell with internal pressure, or can be fully meshed in its volume.

Figure 2 shows the hand and bones used in our calculations. The hand tissue is meshed in a volume around the bones. According to Cutkosky [12], sensory information probes, strategically located on the fingertips and palm seem to provide adequate information on the whole. For example, the fingertip palmar is about ten times more sensitive than the fingertip dorsal. For this reason, the volume mesh may be very loose in poorly sensitive areas and tight in sensitive areas which require accurate calculations. Bones are connected to the segment and joint skeleton animated by the HUMAN FACTORY system. The hand envelope and segment-joint skeleton are sufficient for realistic hand animation without contact but are not able to reproduce skin deformations due to a contact. A mere bone segment is not sufficient to give realistic large deformation of skin under contact forces because, as in human fingers, skin deformations are restricted because of bones. For this reason, we use the realistic bones shown in Figure 2. This has an impact on visual realism and behavior of the hand during grasping, because bone parts are flush against the skin in some regions and are more distant in others. Moreover, in the future, more complex modeling will probably take into account nerves and muscles tied to bones [31].

Consider the equilibrium of the ball and finger shown in Figure 3b, the external forces acting on the ball and finger are surface tractions (such as internal pressure, and external loads representing force contact between ball and support table) and body forces (such as gravity and muscular forces).

Figure 2 - Hand and bones at rest

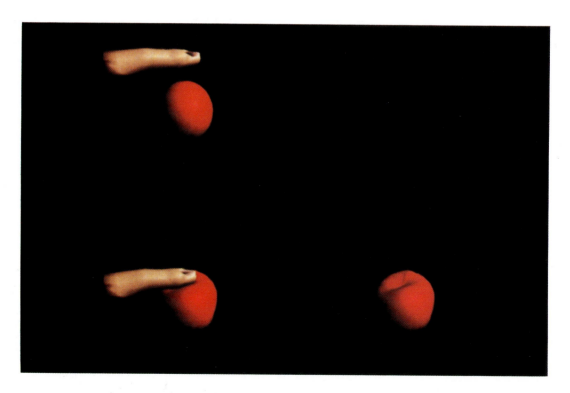

Figure 3 - (a) ball and finger before contact (b) ball and finger after contact (c) deformed ball; this picture presents deformations and fingermarks created by the finger in picture b. It is obviously not a realistic situation because the ball, submitted to internal pressure, will in reality return to its initial shape when the action of the finger is released

We use a composition approach based on the resolution of relation (5) including contact forces between ball and finger. This relation works perfectly in a grasping problem because loads are applied slowly.

However, contact modeling is not easy because the equilibrium equation (5) is obtained on the assumption that the boundary conditions remain unchanged during each time t_i. Two kinds of boundary conditions exist: geometric boundary conditions corresponding to prescribed displacements, and force boundary conditions corresponding to prescribed boundary tractions. We cannot control a single degree of freedom in both position and force; consequently, the unknown displacement will correspond to known prescribed force and conversely known prescribed displacement will correspond to unknown force.

In matrix notation, the problem can be stated in the following way: U_k are known prescribed displacements, U_u are unknown displacements, R_k are known prescribed forces and R_u are unknown forces. In this way, relationship (5) can be written

$$\begin{bmatrix} K_{11} & K_{12} \\ K_{21} & K_{22} \end{bmatrix} \cdot \begin{bmatrix} U_u \\ U_k \end{bmatrix} = \begin{bmatrix} R_k \\ R_u \end{bmatrix} \qquad (6)$$

If NP degrees of freedom are displacement prescribed, NBEQ=NB-NP equations are necessary to find the U_u unknown displacements. Matrix dimensions are [NBEQ*NBEQ] for K_{11}, [NBEQ*NP] for K_{12}, [NP*NBEQ] for K_{21} and [NP*NP] for K_{22}.

Equations for solving U_u are

$$K_{11} . U_u = R_k - K_{12} . U_k \qquad (7)$$

Hence, in this solution for U_u, only the [NBEQ*NBEQ] stiffness matrix K_{11} corresponding to the unknown degrees of freedom U_u need to be assembled. Once U_u is evaluated from (7) the nodal point forces corresponding to U_k can be obtained from (8)

$$R_u = K_{21} . U_u + K_{22} . U_k \qquad (8)$$

Boundary conditions can change during grasping and pressing when prescribed forces or displacements are sufficient to strongly deform the ball and hand skin. This situation creates other contact points between ball and table, and between ball and fingers. Consequently the calculations are more complicated because the number of unknown displacements U_u, and reactive forces R_u, will vary depending upon the number of contact points which prescribe R_k and/or U_k.

When the hand grasps a ball or when a finger presses a ball, the senses of sight and of touch are generally used consecutively.

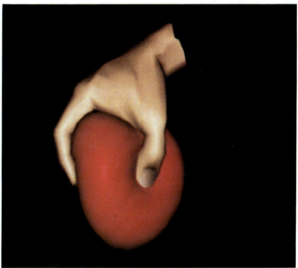

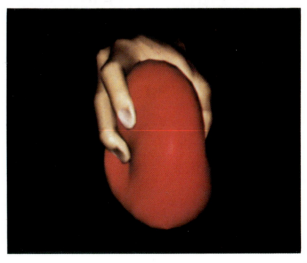

Figure 4 - Grasping of a ball submitted to internal pressure, seen from various viewpoints

In a first step, sight allows us to evaluate certain dimensions, mass, roughness, elasticity etc. i.e. to imagine our position in relation to the ball. In the domain of animation, this information is contained in the ball data base (e.g. volume point coordinates, and physical characteristics such as constitutive law, mass density, and texture which can be related to roughness). The hand grasps or presses the ball applying a prescribed force, whose intensity is dictated by the knowledge acquired by the sense of sight. The prescribed contact force is created by muscular forces acting on bones and using flesh as an intermediary. Generally, the grip is as gentle as possible without letting go of the ball. This can be viewed as a "minimization of the power due to the muscles", as pointed out by Witkin and Kass [34]. A gentle grip not only prevents damage to a fragile object, but also results in a grip that is more stable [12] [29]. In a second step, the sense of touch allows an exchange of information between the ball and the fingers, implying contact forces, sliding contacts, deformations, and internal stresses in the fingers. In computer animation the first step is difficult to implement because the animator does not dispose of force transducers for forces applied directly to the bones. Consequently the first step based on given prescribed forces R_k on bones is not presently possible. For this reason our solution for the grasping problem is different from the robot or human solution. It is displacement-driven rather than force-driven.

In this way, the animator is not concerned with forces but with the hand key position required by the script. For ball grasping, shown in figure 4, the ball is made up of a rubber envelope and is submitted to internal pressure. The animator imposes prescribed displacements U_k on the hand bones using a "classical" method (parametric, kinematic or dynamic) and places the ball between the fingers. During this process the animator can ignore the material of which the ball is built. It can be a very soft ball or a very stiff bowl. The animator positions the fingers (skin and eventually bones) inside the ball. The purpose of calculations is to decide if the chosen finger position is or is not a realistic one and its consequences on skin and ball shapes. This is the reaction of the ball on the fingers which will decide the validity of grasping. Since finger position is prescribed by the animator, the ball must be repelled to prevent overlaps, ignoring, as a first approximation, whether it is stiff or soft. The computational geometry procedure used for determination of repelling points is beyond the scope of this paper.

We show in figure 5 an example of overlap. When a ball node B penetrates the finger and/or palm, it is repelled over the skin surface (point C) in the direction of polygon normal n_F. Ball and hand surface patches are polygon faces of finite elements. With linear elements of zero order continuity, patches are triangular or quadrilateral. The normal direction n_F of each polygon face is calculated at the polygon center. It is a true normal if the patch is triangular and an approximated normal if the patch is quadrilateral because the four surface points are generally not in the same plane. For this reason we use triangular polygons for fingers in our contact calculations.

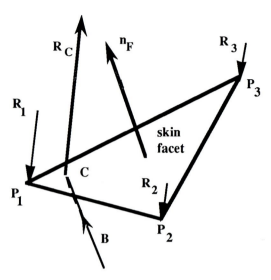

Figure 5 - Overlapping of a ball node. The ball node B is repelled over point C of the skin facet P_1, P_2, P_3 in direction of normal n_F to the facet. The reactive force created by overlapping suppression is shared out among R_1, R_2 and R_3. $R_i = h_i.R_c$ (i=1, 2, 3) where h_i is the interpolation function corresponding to node i, evaluated at point c. Value of h_i is unity at node i and zero at all other nodes.

The overlap suppression creates reactive forces on the ball surface, which are applied to the skin. At equilibrium, these forces maintain compatible surface displacements between the two deformable bodies.

The following is an iterative procedure for obtaining both the contact forces and the displacements under contact:

1 - move links and joints using some "classical" method (parametric, kinematic or dynamic) and calculate new prescribed bone displacements U_k.
While equilibrium between ball and hand is not reached or reactive force on bones has not overrun a threshold force, do:
begin
2 - prescribe displacements U_k of skin; repel ball nodes to prevent overlapping; prescribe displacements U_k of repelled ball nodes;
3 - resolve (7) and (8) to obtain displacements U_u on ball and reactive forces R_u on contact points of the ball;
4 - affect equal and opposite reactive forces R_u on contact points of the skin;
5 - assume the contact forces R_u are prescribed forces R_k, i.e. release all degrees of freedom of ball and skin;
6 - resolve (7) and (8) to obtain displacements U_u of ball and skin, and reactive forces R_u on bones;
end;

Relation (7) is solved using a direct solution (Gauss method). Convergence occurs when for all points the variation between two successive iterations is less than some fixed threshold. In this procedure, relations (7) and (8) represent the global system made up of ball and hand. The first step requires animator manipulation and has been described previously. In the second step all skin displacements, and those ball displacements resulting from overlap suppression are prescribed. In this way, resolution of (7) and (8) in step 3 will give displacements U_u on ball and reacting forces on repelled ball nodes. Step 4 ensures that at equilibrium, contact forces between ball and skin will be equal and opposite to maintain compatible surface displacements. Because ball nodes are not repelled in coincidence with skin nodes, but on skin polygon surfaces, the reacting force calculated in step 4 is distributed among the three nodes constituting the skin facet (Figure 5), with weights depending on the position of the ball node on the facet. In steps 5 and 6, reacting forces are assumed to be known and all degrees of freedom of ball and skin are released. In other words, we rearrange matrix relation (6) because the number of equations is modified in comparison with step 3. The method can be interpreted as a Lagrangian multiplier method that forces the non-penetration condition between the ball and the hand with additional equations. Steps 2 to 6 are repeated until convergence is reached. Otherwise they are stopped when the evaluation of the reacting force on bones overruns a force threshold allowable by the human musculature. Indeed, assume that animator places finger skin and bones into a very stiff bowl. The reacting force R_k on bones obtained in step 6 can then be gigantic and overrun the threshold force attributed to the muscular command of this bone.

In a parametric computer animation system, the reacting force on bones can be used to suggest solutions to the animator as in an expert system.

In a system with inverse dynamics, the position of bones is modified automatically using calculated reacting force.

Calculation of finger deformations are necessary even if fingers and palm deformations are not visible. An exchange of information will take place since the fingers are always deformed. It is finger flexibility and frictional resistance which permit human grasp of rigid objects. This is the reason why actual robot hands are made up of elastic extremities equipped with tactile sensors [16] [28]. Our actual simulation is based on prescribing and releasing the displacement of contact points during each iteration. This allows us to release dynamically the parts of the two bodies. A more sophisticated model, now being developed, must include an evaluation of frictional resistance. For example a Coulomb friction law may be used to simulate the adhesion of papillary ridges. In this law, a coefficient of friction u relates the normal force F_n to the tangential force F_t at contact points. Force $u.F_n$ represents the frictional resistance during contact, and sliding contact is initiated when $F_t \geq u.F_n$.

During the second step of grasping, if the initial prescribed force R_k has been poorly evaluated by the sense of sight, the ball and finger(s) will slide. This information can then be used to increase the prescribed force, or to modify the position of fingers on the ball. The evaluation of sliding and the increase in the prescribed force must be repeated until an equilibrium or an unstable condition is obtained.

Both the tactile sensor model and the command model must be included in a complete automatic motion control, because the stiffness of grip is a function of the stiffness of finger tissue and of the disposition of fingers around the ball. This compliant motion control scheme, which is made to sustain the environmental factors, might be made easier by the fact that kinematic and dynamic models dealing with articulated bodies can be looked upon as a displacement based finite element method applied on trusses and bars.

The global treatment of contact presented here can be applied to inter-deformation of fingers, deformation between fingers and palm, or, more generally, between two synthetic human parts following a compression or a stretching of skin. For this purpose, each part of the body must be considered as an entity able to interact with each other part. An entity cannot interpenetrate itself and some entities cannot reach all others because of joint angle limits imposed on the skeleton [15]. For example, during finger flexing, we consider the third phalanx unable to interpenetrate the second and first phalanges. In the same way we also consider that a foot cannot reach the face unless we are simulating a chubby baby.

FINGER FLEXION WITHOUT CONTACT

The problem of 3D modeling of human skin deformations, during the process of joint flexing, has many different solutions that give a realistic visual appearance to the human body. The skeleton can be surrounded by surfaces of planar or curved patches, or the skin can be modeled by elementary volumes. All the methods have been created to give a realistic appearance to hands and bodies with no concern for the force information exchanged during contact.

In Figure 6, we show the successive steps of finger flexing whose last position can be compared with a JLD result. The starting position was the neutral rest position and the following procedure was applied:

For each time t_i corresponding to link displacement angle less than 10 degrees, do:
begin
1   Move links and joints using some "classical" method (parametric, kinematic or dynamic), and calculate new position of prescribed DOF on bones,
2   from preceding position at time t_{i-1} calculate prescribed DOF displacement U_k on bones
3   calculate stiffness K, erase R_k and solve relation (5) to obtain tissue displacements U_u,
4   update position of tissue points
end

In our calculations, an updated Lagrangian formulation in small strains [32] was used. We also used a classical engineering stress measure (Cauchy stress) and a linear constitutive law for flesh tissue. This formulation is simple, but it gives good visual results, without requiring long calculations. For the displacement of finger links, a variation angle of 10 degrees seems to be a maximum to ensure a small displacement and rotation condition.

Therefore, 30 degrees displacement of the first phalanx and 50 degrees of the second phalanx as shown in Figure 6, needs at least height position calculations corresponding to displacements of 10, 20 and 30 degrees for the first phalanx and displacement of 10, 20, 30, 40 and 50 degrees for the second phalanx; or any combination of these displacements.

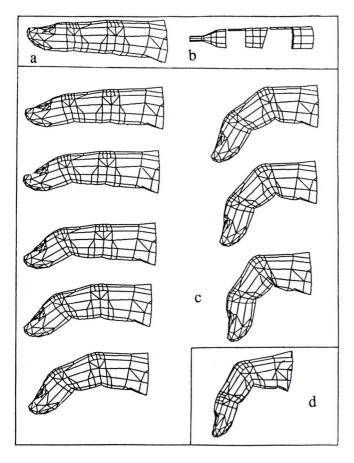

Figure 6 - Successive steps of finger flexing without contact; a. rest position; b. particular bones; c. finger flexing based on FEM deformation d. finger flexing based on Joint-dependent Local deformation (JLD)

It must be noted, however that the final position could be obtained directly from rest position using another formulation which takes into account large displacements and rotations in small strains. In this case, the formulation would be based on the use of a Piola-Kirchhoff stress instead of Cauchy stress, and would require an iterative computation. However, this scheme does not seem very interesting in hand animation because inbetween positions are indispensable for realistic movement decomposition. If more realism, or incompressible material modeling, are desired, increased computation time will be required for material non-linear calculations. When material non-linearities exist, a Newton-Raphson iterative method must be added in step 3 of the procedure for each time t_i. The use of a linear material allows us to obtain inflation of flesh without an iterative calculation and requires less than 1 minute per frame on a VAX 780. But this procedure works only with the particular shape of bones shown in Figure 6. More realistic bones require incompressible material and this increases the computation time.

Although we proved that the calculations described here give realistic deformations of fingers during flexion, in the HUMAN FACTORY system we use a hybrid formulation based on JLD operators when there is no contact, and on FEM calculation when a contact is detected. In a complete grasping task, this method saves CPU time during the reach phase of the task when the hand comes closer to the object.

ANIMATION CONTROL

In this section, we briefly discuss how animation of deformable objects and human bodies has been introduced into the HUMAN FACTORY system. For animation of rigid objects, the HUMAN FACTORY system already contains animation procedures for simple physical movements applied to material points. Examples are movement of pendula, circular movement with acceleration, projectile with initial velocity and so on. It also contains basic animation laws like the Catmull laws (see [20], p.49). These physical or empirical laws are applied to animated variables or state variables. In this way, during the specified interval, state variables are automatically updated to the next value according to the law [21]. Moreover these state variables drive actor transformations. Combining state variables and actor transformations allows a complex animation of actors.

Animation of a physically deformable object can be simply supported in the HUMAN FACTORY system by defining prescribed displacements called U_k in the preceding sections as new state variables. When the three degrees of freedom of some point are prescribed, state variables of VECTOR type are sufficient for defining the movement of prescribed points. When less than three degrees of freedom are displacement prescribed, a new type of state variable has been defined. With this approach deformable bodies are processed as actors. Object points are not only submitted to translations and rotations, but automatically follow the prescribed degrees of freedom according to constitutive laws and other potential constraints such as body forces and surface forces. It should be noted that the use of state variables is not always required and can often be omitted. For example the problem of free fall of a deformable object is implicitly defined and does not require an extra physical law and prescribed degrees of freedom.

We have already discussed the problem of hand animation in the preceding sections. In the system, skeleton animation is based on joint angle definition. A realistic skeleton is linked to animated skeleton segments, and prescribed displacements are fixed on bones surfaces.

We use displacement-based degrees of freedom because displacement transducers (such as mouse, rolling bowl and so on) are more common in computer animation than force transducers (such as remote manipulators in robotics). The procedure based on prescribed displacements is easy to implement in parametric animation systems and can pass information to dynamic animation systems.

Force prescribed systems will be effective when forces transducers are intensively introduced in computer animation. In this case, the animator will be fully engaged in the scene during creation and it will be possible to define a new TYPE OF ACTOR called animator.

CONCLUSION

In this paper we have simulated objects and skin hand deformations in a grasping task. To this end, a finite element module has been developed for modelling both object and synthetic human flesh deformations and their contacts. The method gives information about the synthetic environment of the human. It may be compared to the robot tactile sensor or to the human sense of touch. This information provides a significant contribution to automatic motion control in 3D character animation. We believe that it can be used to improve the behavior of synthetic human grasp and more generally to improve the synthetic human behavior in the synthetic environment. These problems cannot be solved using only geometric solutions, or only force solutions implying gravity and muscular forces based on a single point of contact. In an artist oriented system, the finite element model can be used to define objects in the same way as a sculptor molds his shapes.

The object and human data base contain not only envelope coordinates but also volume point coordinates and information about physical material, tissue characteristics and force threshold. In this way, we take advantage of the intrinsic properties of the numerical method, based on composition-decomposition of elements, for computer animation purposes.

ACKNOWLEDGMENTS

The authors would like to thank Richard Laperrière and Ross Racine for their contribution in producing the images. They are also grateful to referees for their comments and suggestions. The research was supported by the Natural Sciences and Engineering Council of Canada, the FCAR foundation, le Fonds National Suisse pour la Recherche Scientifique and the Institut National de la Recherche en Informatique et Automatique (France).

REFERENCES

[1] Armstrong WW and Green MW. The dynamics of articulated rigid bodies for purpose of animation. The Visual Computer, Vol 1, 1985, pp 231-240

[2] Badler NI and Morris MA. Modeling flexible articulated objects. Proc. Comp. Graphics '82, Online conf., 1982, pp 305-314.

[3] Badler NI and Smoliar SW. Digital representation of human movement. Computing Surveys, Vol 11, No 1, 1979, pp 19-38

[4] Badler NI. Design of a human movement representation incorporating dynamics. Tech. rep., Dept. of computer and infor.science, Univ. of Pennsylvania, Philadelphia 1984

[5] Barr AH. Global and local deformations of solid primitives. Proc. SIGGRAPH '84, pp 21-30

[6] Bathe KJ. Finite element procedures in engineering analysis. Prentice Hall, 1982

[7] Blinn JF. A generalization of algebraic surface drawing. ACM Trans. on graphics, Vol 1 No 3, 1982, pp 235-256

[8] Bohm J. A comparison of different contact algorithms with applications. Comp.Struc., Vol 26 N 1-2, 1987, pp 207-221

[9] Calvert TW, Chapman J, and Patla A. Aspects of the kinematic simulation of human movement. IEEE Computer Graphics and applications, nov 1982, pp 41-52

[10] Catmull E. A System for Computer-generated Movies. Proc. ACM Annual Conference, Vol. 1, 1972, pp.422-431.

[11] Chaudary AB and Bathe KJ. A solution method for static and dynamic analysis of three dimensional contact problems with friction. Comp.Struc. Vol 24 N 6, 1986, pp 855-873

[12] Cutkosky MR. Robotic grasping and fine manipulation. Kluwer Academic Publ., 1985

[13] Gourret JP. Modeling 3D contacts and Deformations using finite element theory in synthetic human tactile perception. in: D. Thalmann et al., SIGGRAPH '88 course notes on synthetic actors, 1988, pp 222-230

[14] Hollerbach JM. A recursive Lagrangian formulation of manipulator dynamics and a comparative study of dynamics formulation. IEEE Trans. on systems, man and cyber., SMC-10 No 11, 1980, pp 730-736

[15] Isaacs PM and Cohen MF. Controling Dynamic simulation with kinematic constraints, behavior functions and inverse dynamics. Proc. SIGGRAPH' 87, pp 215-224

[16] Jacobsen SC, McCammon ID, Biggers KB and Phillips RP. Design of tactile sensing systems for dextrous manipulators. IEEE Control Systems Magazine, Vol 8, N 1, 1988, pp 3-13

[17] Komatsu K. Human skin model capable of natural shape variation. The Visual Computer, No 3, 1988, pp 265-271

[18] Lee CSG, Gonzales RC and Fu KS. Tutorial on robotics. IEEE Comp. Soc. Press, 1983

[19] Luciani A. Un outil informatique de création d'images animées: modèles d'objets, langage, controle gestuel en temps réel. Le système ANIMA. These Docteur-Ing. INP Grenoble 1985

[20] Magnenat-Thalmann N and Thalmann D. Computer animation: Theory and Practice. Springer, Tokyo, 1985

[21] Magnenat-Thalmann N and Thalmann D. 3D Computer Animation: More an Evolution Problem than a Motion Problem, IEEE Computer Graphics and Applications, Vol. 5, No 10, 1985, pp.47-57.

[22] Magnenat-Thalmann N and Thalmann D. Image Synthesis: Theory and practice. Springer, Tokyo, 1987

[23] Magnenat-Thalmann N and Thalmann D. The direction of synthetic actors in the film Rendez-vous à Montréal. IEEE Computer Graphics & applications, Vol 7, No 12, 1987, pp 7-19

[24] Magnenat-Thalmann N, Laperrière R and Thalmann D. Joint-Dependent Local Deformations for hand animation and object grasping. Proc. Graphics Interface '88, Edmonton

[25] Moore M and Wilhelms J. Collision detection and response for computer animation. Proc.SIGGRAPH '88, pp 289-298

[26] Paul RP. Robot manipulators: mathematics, programming and control. The MIT Press, Cambridge, Mass., 1981

[27] Platt JC and Barr AH. Constraint method for flexible models. Proc. SIGGRAPH '88, pp 279-288

[28] Pugh A(ed.). Robot sensors. Vol 2. Tactile and non-vision. IFS publications Ltd (Bedford) and Springer Verlag, 1986

[29] Slotine JJE and Asada H. Robot analysis and control. Wiley, 1986

[30] Terzopoulos D, Platt J, Barr A and Fleischer K. Elastically deformable models. Proc.SIGGRAPH '87, pp 205-214

[31] Thomson DE, Buford WL, Myers LM, Giurintano DJ and Brewer III JA. A hand biomechanics workstation. Proc. SIGGRAPH '88, pp 335-343

[32] Timoshenko S and Goodier JN. Theory of elasticity. 3rd.ed., McGraw-Hill, NY, 1970

[33] Wilhelms J. Toward automatic motion control. IEEE Computer Graphics and applications, Vol 7, No 4, 1987, pp 11-22

[34] Witkin A and Kass M. Spacetime Constraints. Proc. SIGGRAPH '88, pp. 159-168

[35] Wyvill G, McPheeters C, Wyvill B. Data structure for soft objects. The Visual Computer, No 2, 1986, pp 227-234

[36] Zienkiewicz OC. The finite element method. Third edition, McGraw-Hill, London, 1977

Combinatorial Analysis of Ramified Patterns
and Computer Imagery of Trees

Xavier Gérard Viennot [1], *Georges Eyrolles* [1], *Nicolas Janey* [2], *Didier Arquès* [2]

1. LABRI, Département d'Informatique, Université de Bordeaux I, FRANCE
(U.A. CNRS 0726)
2. LIB, Département d'Informatique, Université de Franche-Comté, FRANCE
(U.A CNRS 0822)

Abstract

Herein is presented a new procedural method for generating images of trees. Many other algorithms have already been proposed in the last few years focusing on particle systems, fractals, graftals and L-systems or realistic botanical models. Usually the final visual aspect of the tree depends on the development process leading to this form. Our approach differs from all the previous ones. We begin by defining a certain "measure" of the form of a tree or a branching pattern. This is done by introducing the new concept of ramification matrix of a tree. Then we give an algorithm for generating a random tree having as ramification matrix a given arbitrary stochastic triangular matrix. The geometry of the tree is defined from the combinatorial parameters implied in the analysis of the forms of trees. We obtain a method with powerful control of the final form, simple enough to produce quick designs of trees without loosing in the variety and rendering of the images. We also introduce a new rapid drawing of the leaves. The underlying combinatorics constitute a refinement of some work introduced in hydrogeology in the morphological study of river networks. The concept of ramification matrix has been used very recently in physics in the study of fractal ramified patterns.

CR Categories and Subject Descriptors : I.3.5 [Computer Graphics]: Computational Geometry and Object Modeling. I.3.7.[Computer Graphics]: Three-Dimensional Graphics and Realisms. J.3 [Life and Medical Sciences]: Biology. J.5 [Arts and Humanities]: Arts, fine and performing.

General terms: Trees, plants, algorithms, realistic image synthesis, figurative image synthesis

Additional keywords and phrases: branching patterns in physics, stochastic modeling, analysis of form, fractals, self-similarity, combinatorics, ramification matrix

1. Introduction

Computer Image Synthesis generation of trees and plants has been the subject of many papers in the past few years. Let us mention for example : Marshall, Wilson, Carlson [24], Kawaguchi [16], Reeves, Blau [37], Gardner [11], Aono, Kunii [1], Smith [39], Bloomenthal [4], Niklas [30], Demko,

Hodges, Naylor [7], Oppenheimer [31], Prusinkiewicz [35], Beyer et Friedel [3], Prusinkiewicz, Lindenmayer et Hanan [36], De Reffye, Edelin, Françon, Jaeger, Puech [8].

In these works, tree generation was mainly made at two levels. The first one is the generation of the topological (combinatorial) tree underlying the real tree. In general, this topological tree is binary or ternary. The second level is the generation of the geometrical tree. Each method applies a more or less sophisticated geometrical model to the topological tree. The minimum geometry consists in a 2D-drawing of trees, with width and length choices for each branch and angle choices for each branching node. A more sophisticated geometry consists in a 3D visualization to which are added vegetal elements (leaves, flowers), bark texture on branches and outside constraints such as light, wind or gravity.

In all previous mentioned works, these two topological and geometrical levels are more or less separated during the generation. These methods can be roughly classified as follows :

- Fixed topology methods, like the ones of Kawaguchi [16], Aono & Kunii [1] which only generate perfect trees. Due to the lack of variation of topology, geometry is of great importance in order to create a large diversity of forms.

- Generation methods by development models which include a real growth strategy of trees. For example : generation by fractals of Mandelbrot, Oppenheimer [31], or by stochastic and recursive growth of branching nodes, Niklas [30]; generation by rewriting rules using L-systems theory developed by Lindenmayer, Smith [39], Prusinkiewicz [35], Prusinkiewicz, Lindenmayer, Hanan [36]; generation by a botanical development model De Reffye, Edelin, Françon, Jaeger, Puech [8].

Papers [16],[1],[37],[4], [31] essentially focus on geometry, while papers [3], [8], [35], [36], [39] are mainly interested in the development of topology.

These various methods use geometry in order to obtain the final shape (or form) of the tree. The aim is to realize realistic drawings of plants and trees. All above mentioned methods focus mostly on the parameters involved in the development process, rather than on the direct control of the final shape. The fact that the shape is implicitly contained in its history, is a well known concept : D'Arcy Thompson [6], Hallé, Oldeman and Tomlinson [13]. In this paper a new approach, different from previous ones, is proposed, separating shape from development. In order to obtain better control of the final shape, we first stress on the necessity of defining numerical parameters which allow a certain measure of shape of the tree, i.e. allowing the numerical evaluation of features as thorny, dense, slender, well built or bushy.

Herein, the shape of tree is measured by introducing the new notion of *ramification matrix*. This matrix is a triangular

1. LABRI, Département d'Informatique, Université de Bordeaux I, 33405 Talence, FRANCE - Tél.: (33) 56 84 60 85
2. LIB, département d'Informatique, Université de Franche-comté, 25030 Besançon, FRANCE - Tél.: (33) 81 66 64 63

stochastic one, associated with each tree or ramified structure. Depending only on the underlying topological tree, this matrix is defined from the combinatorial notions of branch *order* and branching node *biorder*. These notions constitute a refinement of some concepts introduced by the hydrogeologists Horton [15] and Strahler [41] in the morphological study of river networks. Our study shows that many visual characteristics connected with the shape of the tree, are reflected in the associated matrix. Very recently, this notion has been used in physical study of fractal ramified structures, Vannimenus, Viennot [43], [44].

Our method consists in the choice of a ramification matrix and then random generation of a combinatorial tree whose ramification matrix is the one chosen (or very similar). At last an elementary 2D geometry is defined. The main idea is to control the width and length of branches, the angles of branching nodes by linear, polynomial or exponential laws in terms of the order and biorder parameters. The advantage is in a better control of the shape. The method is simple and fast while keeping a great variety of possible forms. Although this theoretical model moves away from the botanical ones, a realistic rendering can be obtained. For this purpose, we introduce a fast leaf drawing algorithm. Our method also seems well adapted for obtaining figurative trees as could be painted by artists.

2. Horton-Strahler analysis for binary trees
2.1. Binary trees and botanical trees

In order to avoid confusion between botanical tree, topological tree or geometrical tree, we recall a few concepts from theoretical computer science, see for example Knuth [18]. A *binary tree* is defined by a set of *vertices* or *nodes*, joined by *edges*. There are two kinds of vertices : the *internal nodes* (or *branching nodes*) and the *external nodes* (or *terminal nodes*). Each internal node has two *sons* : a left and a right son, the external nodes having no sons. An internal node is called the *father* of its sons. The edges join a father with each of its sons. The *root* of the tree is the unique node with no father. It will be convenient to add an extra edge from this root, called the *root edge* (see Figure 1).

To each natural branching pattern, one can associate an underlying topological tree. Generally, this tree can be considered as a binary tree. In botany, the binary tree edges are referred to as *branch segments*.

2.2. Order and segments

The vertices of a binary tree are labeled by the following recursive procedure. The terminal nodes are labeled 1. If the two sons of a node v are labeled i and j, then the label of the node v is   ord(v) = max(i,j) if i≠j ;   = i+1 if i=j.

The label ord(e) of an edge e going from the vertex v to one of its sons y is the label of y. The label of a node (resp. edge) is called the *order* of this node (resp. edge) (Figure 1).

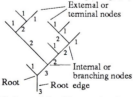

Figure 1. Order and Strahler number in a binary tree.

The order of the root edge (that is the order of the root) is called the *Strahler number* of the tree. A *segment* of order k is a maximal sequence of consecutive edges having order k. The notions of order and segment have been introduced in hydrogeology by Horton [15] (in a slightly different form), and by Strahler [41]. Observe that this concept of order is different from the one usually introduced in the botanical study of trees. In [8] the notion of order is defined from the development history of the tree. When this history is unknown, for each node the distinction between the so-called "straight edge" and "lateral edge", as in [36], is arbitrary. Herein neither development history nor arbitrary convention are required.

2.3. Horton-Strahler analysis in hydrogeology and other sciences.

A river network is supposed to be without islands and triple (or multiple) junction points. Thus, the underlying topological tree is a binary tree. Many studies have been carried out in hydrogeology in order to examine river network morphology. In particular, the concept of bifurcation ratio $ß_k$ of order k has been introduced. If b_k is the number of order k segments, then $ß_k$ is the ratio b_{k-1}/b_k. For example, the binary tree in Figure 1 has bifurcation ratios $ß_2=8/2=4$, $ß_3=2/1=2$. These ratios give certain information about the "shape" of the binary tree. For example the trees in Figures 2, 3 are two extreme cases. The perfect tree of height 3 (each terminal node has the same *height*, Fig. 2) has all segments reduced to the edges: each bifurcation ratio is equal to 2 (this is the minimum possible value). For the very thin tree (Fig. 3) there is one segment of order 2, each terminal edge is a segment of order 1, the bifurcation ratio of order 2 is equal to the number of terminal nodes and can be arbitrarily large.

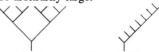

Figure 2. Perfect tree   Figure 3. "Very thin" tree.

Geologists have observed that bifurcation ratios are usually between 3 and 5. We define a *random binary tree* as a binary tree chosen at random with uniform probability among the $C_n = (2n!)/n!/(n+1)!$ binary trees with n branching nodes. In particular, it is known that all the bifurcation ratios of a random binary tree approach 4 as the number of nodes becomes larger, Meier & Moon [25]. Similar studies have been made for other branching patterns in nature as in botany, MacMahon [22] or in anatomy, Woldenberg [47] and neurophysiology, Percheron [33]. Prud'homme and Vigneaux [34] have shown that there exist some correlations between the Horton-Strahler analysis of river networks and the tectonic structure of the subsoil. This analysis has also been made for the valley networks of submarine mountains, Naudin & Prud'homme [27].

Quite unexpectedly, the Strahler number of a tree has also appeared in theoretical computer science in the study of the minimum number of registers required to compute an arithmetical expression, Flajolet et al. [10], Kemp [17], and in molecular biology in the study of the "complexity" of the form and in energy computation of nucleic acids secondary structures (RNA), Vauchaussade de Chaumont & Viennot [45].

3. A new model for tree topology : the ramification matrix.
3.1. Biorder of a branching node.

Consider a branching node of order k in a binary tree, having two sons with order i and j. The *biorder* of this node is the pair (k,i) if j=k and i<k, if not we have i=j=k-1 and the biorder is (k-1,k-1), Fig. 4.

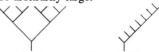

Figure 4. Biorder of order k branching node

3.2. Ramification matrix of a binary tree.

For a binary tree T, we define successively the following quantities :

- for k≥2, a_k is the number of order k branching nodes
- for 1≤i<k, $b_{k,i}$ is the number of nodes of biorder (k,i)
- for k≥2, $b_{k,k}$ is the number of nodes of biorder (k-1,k-1)

- for $1 \leq j \leq k$, $p_{k,j} = b_{k,j} / a_k$.

The number $p_{k,j}$ is then the probability for a branching node of order k to have biorder (k,j). The ramification matrix ram(T) of the binary tree T with Strahler number s is the (s-1)xs stochastic matrix whose (k,j) term ($1 \leq j \leq k \leq s, 2 \leq k \leq s$) is $p_{k,j}$. Adding the entry $p_{1,1} = 1$, this matrix would be a square lower triangular stochastic matrix. The ramification matrix of the

binary tree displayed on Figure 1 is : $\begin{bmatrix} 3/5 & 2/5 \\ 1/2 & 0 & 1/2 \end{bmatrix}$ **Table 1**

The ramification matrix of a real tree is the one of the underlying binary tree associated to it.

3.3. Examples of ramification matrices
3.3.1. Perfect tree

The ramification matrix is $\begin{bmatrix} 0 & 1 \\ 0 & 0 & 1 \\ 0 & 0 & 0 & 1 \\ 0 & 0 & 0 & 0 & 1 \\ & & \cdots & & \end{bmatrix}$ **Table 2**

3.3.2. Random binary tree

Experimental studies have shown that, as the number of nodes tends to infinity, the ramification matrix of a random binary tree (see definition in § 2.3) approaches the matrix of Table 3. This fact has been rigorously proved by Penaud [32].

$\begin{bmatrix} 1/2 & 1/2 \\ 1/2 & 1/4 & 1/4 \\ 1/2 & 1/4 & 1/8 & 1/8 \\ 1/2 & 1/4 & 1/8 & 1/16 & 1/16 \\ & & \cdots & & \end{bmatrix}$ **Table 3**

3.3.3. Random increasing binary tree

One can generate binary trees randomly by the following procedure. Starting from $T_1 = \vee$, the tree having only one branching node and two terminal nodes, we generate a sequence T_n of binary trees by the following iterative process: choose with uniform probability one of the i+1 terminal nodes of T_n, then T_{n+1} is obtained by replacing the chosen node by T_1.

Each tree T_n has n internal nodes, but such a tree is not at all a random binary tree. It is in fact a random *increasing binary tree*. Such a tree is obtained by labelling the internal nodes in the order of substitution. The internal nodes are labelled 1,2,...,n such that the label of the sons are bigger than the label of the father. The number of such trees is in fact n!. Observe that a random increasing binary tree is the same thing as the *binary search tree* associated to a random permutation.

Experimental studies using Monte-Carlo tests show that the ramification matrix for large random increasing binary trees approach the matrix of Table 4 :

$\begin{bmatrix} 0.4 & 0.6 \\ 0.2 & 0.3 & 0.5 \\ 0.1 & 0.2 & 0.3 & 0.4 \\ 0.05 & 0.1 & 0.2 & 0.3 & 0.35 \\ 0.025 & 0.05 & 0.1 & 0.2 & 0.3 & 0.325 \\ & & & \cdots & & \end{bmatrix}$ **Table 4**

3.3.4. Self-similar fern

Figure 5 shows the generation of a *self-similar fern*. At each step of the iteration, each terminal edge is replaced by the elementary self-similar fern obtained after the first iteration, that is by adding p=6 edges to the primitive edges.

For an arbitrary number p, and an arbitrary number of iterations, the ramification matrix has the remarkable form :

$\begin{bmatrix} 1-1/p & 1/p \\ 0 & 1-1/p & 1/p \\ 0 & 0 & 1-1/p & 1/p \\ 0 & 0 & 0 & 1-1/p & 1/p \\ & & \cdots & & \end{bmatrix}$ **Table 5**

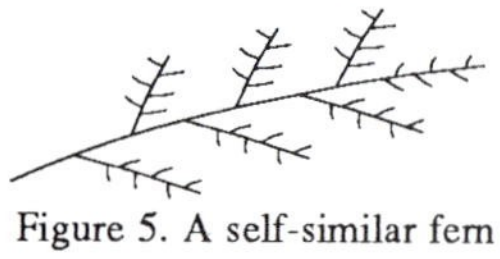

Figure 5. A self-similar fern

3.4. Self-similarity

In the former examples 3.3.1-4, the ramification matrix presents a certain property of self-similarity. By this, we mean that the variation curve of the biorder probability of the kth row looks the same for all the rows. In other words, if we visualize this variation by a curve extrapolating the points ($j,p_{k,j}$) for $1 \leq j \leq k$, all the curves corresponding to each row are statistically correlated. We will say that the binary tree is (statistically) *self-similar* (for the ramification matrix). Note that this notion is different, although related, to the one introduced by Mandelbrot [23]. Ramification matrix of such a statistically self-similar tree can be visualized by a curve. Such curves are displayed on Figure 6.

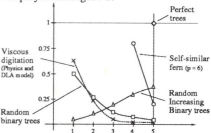

Figure 6. Self-similar ramification matrices

3.5. Ramification matrices in physics

Many studies have recently been made in physics concerning tree-like structures occuring in nature. We will quote for example *electric breakdowns*, Niemeyer, Pietronero, Wiesman [28], *electrolytic metal deposit*, Sawada, Dougherty, Gollub [38], the so-called *viscous fingers*, Nittmann, Daccord, Stanley [29], VanDamme et al. [42] or the well-known *Diffusion Aggregation Process* (DLA) of Witten and Sanders [46], and Ball [2] for a survey.

The patterns are (or approximated by) branching fractal structures. The visual aspect of these patterns is usually measured by physicists with a single number: the *fractal mass dimension* (see Mandelbrot [23]). Very recently, the branching structures of these patterns have been taken into account by applying the ramification matrix model, Vannimenus [43], Vannimenus, Viennot [44]. The *viscous fingers*, the 2D *DLA model* and the so-called 2D *branching Eden model* have been studied. The ramification matrices are again self-similar. The corresponding curves are close to the one corresponding to random binary trees (see Figure 6). It is known that, in high dimension, these models should behave as random increasing binary trees. The difference between the two curves (associated to random binary and random increasing binary trees) of Figure 6 shows the strong influence of the planarity constraint.

4. Generation and visualization of trees using ramification matrices
4.1. Generation of the topological tree

A stochastic triangular (s-1)xs matrix R is given, together with a number $S \leq s$. The algorithm generates randomly a binary tree T having Strahler number S and whose ramification matrix is (almost) the same as the one obtained by taking the rows 2 to S of R. This randomness insures a more natural aspect to the final image.

The generation starts with a tree T_1 reduced to a single edge (its root edge) labelled S. Then, iteratively, a sequence T_n of labelled binary trees will be constructed. The tree T_{n+1} is obtained from T_n by choosing one terminal edge of T_n labelled $k \neq 1$, and by dividing this edge into two edges labelled respectively k and i<k or both k-1. The choice (k,i) or (k-1,k-1) is made from a random selection according to the biorder distribution probability given by the kth row of the matrix R. The algorithm stops when all the terminal edges are labelled 1.

Experiments show that the ramification matrix of the final tree T is close to the given matrix R, especially for the first rows (corresponding to the small orders) and when the size of the tree is sufficiently large (more than a few hundred nodes). The control of the size of the tree is made by choosing the Strahler number S. In the pictures below, the Strahler number is chosen between 5 and 10, with a size of the tree varying from a few hundred branching nodes to several thousand.

4.2. Orientation of the structure

In the algorithm described in 4.1, in the case of a biorder (k,i) with i<k, we have not completely described which edge (left or right son) receives the label k (this edge will be called the *main edge* of the branching). The second step of the method is to make this choice explicit.

There are essentially four options in the program. The first is to make this choice randomly (usually with probability 1/2). The second option is to make this choice such that the main edges alternate (left and right) when moving along a segment of the tree. The third option is to fix the choice such that the main edge is always on the same side; this may give a simulation of a wind effect in the final image of the tree. The last option is to choose the orientation such that the main edge is closer to the vertical direction than the other edge. This choice cannot be decided until the coordinates of the branching nodes on a 2D or 3D image are computed (see below 4.3).

4.3. Generation of the geometrical tree

The third step of our method is the application of an elementary geometry, once the topological tree has been obtained, by determining the position in the space of each node of the tree.

By elementary geometry, we mean the choices (Figure 7):

- for each edge e, a width W(e) and a length L(e),

- for each branching node v, two angles $\theta_1(v)$ and $\theta_2(v)$,

- in the case of a 3D drawing, a third angle $\theta_3(v)$ is necessary, corresponding to the so-called *phyllotaxy* botanical phenomenon.

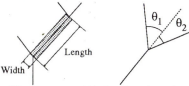

Figure 7. The 2D geometry : width, length and two branching angles.

One of the main ideas of our method is to make the width and length of an edge depend only on the order k of that edge, and the two angles θ_1 and θ_2 relative to a branching node depend only on the biorder of that node.

We have chosen certain arbitrary laws for these four parameters, corresponding to a certain aesthetic effect of the image of the tree, together with a certain realism from the botany; for a more precise study, see Honda [14], Leopold [19], Mendes-France[26], Stevens[40]. Usually, for botanical trees, as for many other natural branching patterns, the width of the branches decreases when moving from the root to the terminal nodes. In general, it is the same for the length of the branches, although the decrease is less important. Thus, it is natural to choose the laws of width and length as non-decreasing functions W(k) and L(k) of the order k. In the pictures presented below, the laws are linear or quadratic for L(k) and polynomial or exponential for W(k) :

$L(k) = c_1 * k$ or $L(k) = c_1 * k^2$; $W(k) = c_2 * k^\alpha$ or $W(k) = c_2 * \beta^k$ with c_1, c_2, α and β some numerical constants. For the choice of α, good visual aspects are obtained with α such that $W(k) = c_3 * L(k)^{S/2}$, that is $\alpha=S$ or S/2 in the quadratic or linear cases for the length.

We also have chosen analog aesthetic effects and a certain amount of realism for the choice of the angle laws θ_1 and θ_2. The principal idea is that the main branches should have a smaller deviation with respect to their mother branches than the less important branches of the tree. In our model, the importance of a branch is measured by its order. We have thus used the following laws :

For a branching node with biorder (k-1,k-1), that is a *fork*, the two resulting branches have the same importance, and we set $\theta_1=\theta_2=\theta_f$, a real constant.

For a branching node with biorder (k,i), i<k, then the respective deviation angles θ_m and θ_s of the main and secondary branches with their mother branch (see Figure 8) are given by

$$\theta_m(k,i) = c_m * i/(k-1), \qquad \theta_s(k,i) = c_s * (k-i)/(k-1)$$

where c_m and c_s are some numerical constants.

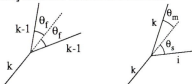

biorder (k-1,k-1)   biorder (k,i), k<i

Figure 8. Angles θ_f, θ_m, θ_s as functions of the biorder.

Good visual effects can be obtained with c_s and θ_f equal 30° and c_m equal 10°. Of course it is possible to adopt any other kind of parameterization, depending on the final visual effects one desires.

For 2D drawing, these definitions are sufficient for defining the (elementary) geometry of the tree. The coordinates of each node of the tree can be computed using length and angle parameterizations. As most of our pictures are given in 2D, we do not insist in the choice of the phyllotaxy angle θ_3. There are no natural reasons to make this angle depend on the order of the mother branch.

4.4. 2D-drawing

For the purpose of quicker drawing, and also for a better understanding of the influence of the choice of the ramification matrix, we have simplified the drawing algorithm.

Once the coordinates of each node have been computed, each edge of the underlying binary tree is represented by a line segment. This edge is visualized on the screen by a rectangle. The junction between the rectangles corresponding to a branching node is organized as shown in Fig 9.

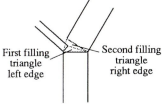

First filling   Second filling
triangle   triangle
left edge   right edge

Figure 9. Jonction between branches represented by rectangles.

In the drawing of Figure 10 (end of the paper), some rectangles have not been filled up. This is to show that, when the length or width of some edges is very small (a few pixels or under the size of a pixel) the tree may have many more branching nodes than those visualized on the screen (more than 1000 for the binary tree related to this figure). Figures 10, 20 give examples of two different geometric laws for the width of the branches: exponential and polynomial.

5. Relationship between form and ramification matrix

The ramification matrix is relative to the topological binary tree underlying the geometrical tree. The "shape" or "form" of

this topological tree, without any geometrical consideration, is obviously a purely abstract concept. The study of the relationship between the ramification matrices and the tree shape can only be made with geometrical trees. It is one of the reasons for which a very simplified geometry (2D geometry, each edge being visualized by a rectangle) has been defined, in order to avoid a too important influence from this geometry upon the relationship study between shapes and matrices. The parameters and geometrical laws chosen for the photos of the trees in this section, are always the same.

5.1. Self-similar matrices

Two typical matrices leading to very different visual results are those given by above given Tables 3 & 4, i.e. the ramification matrices of random binary trees and of random increasing binary trees. In the first case (Figure 11) we obtain rather airy trees with a slender or bushy shape, with a few long segments where many *thorns* are settled, i.e. branching nodes of biorder (k,1) (these thorns are too small to be seen in the photo in Fig. 11). The thorns and the small *subtrees* associated to the biorder (k,2) concentrate 75% of the biorder probabi-lities. The second matrix gives rise to a family of trees which contains many more important branches and are more well balanced (Fig. 12). In this matrix, 60% to 70% of biorder probabilities are concentrated on the 2 last values (diagonal and sub-diagonal).The "well-balanced" aspect is due to the high probability of the biorder (k-1,k-1) giving rise to many forks (however without reaching the totally well-balanced aspect of the perfect tree). Very few thorns or small subtrees appear on high order branches.

The matrix of Table 6 is similar to the one of random increasing binary trees, except for the biorders (k-1,k-1) whose probability has mainly been reduced, while maintaining a high probability for the biorders (k,k-1). This matrix looks like a self-similar one (at least for the orders ≥ 4). This leads to quite well-balanced trees (Fig. 13), with few forks and then long segments of constant order (and then of constant thickness). These long segments appear at all levels of the tree (for all the orders).

$$\begin{bmatrix} 0.5 & 0.5 \\ 0.25 & 0.5 & 0.25 \\ 0.125 & 0.25 & 0.5 & 0.125 \\ 0.0625 & 0.125 & 0.25 & 0.5 & 0.0625 \\ 0.0313 & 0.0625 & 0.125 & 0.25 & 0.5 & 0.0312 \\ 0.0156 & 0.0313 & 0.0625 & 0.125 & 0.25 & 0.5 & 0.0156 \end{bmatrix}$$ Table 6,

$$\begin{bmatrix} 0.2 & 0.8 \\ 0.1 & 0.1 & 0.8 \\ 0.1 & 0.1 & 0.1 & 0.7 \\ 0.1 & 0.1 & 0.1 & 0.6 & 0.1 \\ 0.1 & 0.1 & 0.1 & 0.1 & 0.5 & 0.1 \\ 0.1 & 0.1 & 0.1 & 0.1 & 0.1 & 0.4 & 0.1 \end{bmatrix}$$ Table 7

5.2. Operations on ramification matrices

Two types of operations can be applied to ramification matrices : the *shuffle* and the linear combination of several matrices.

The shuffle consists of forming a matrix whose i_1 first lines are the i_1 first lines of a ramification matrix R_1; then whose i_2 following lines are the lines $i_1+1,...,i_1+i_2$ of a ramification matrix R_2; and so on for the following lines with matrices R_3, ..., R_m. Generally, the matrices R_1, ..., R_m are chosen autosimilar. The shuffle operation allows the generation of non (statistically) autosimilar trees (§ 3.4). An example is given in Figure 14. This tree is generated from a matrix which is the shuffle of three matrices. The lines of order 2, 3, 4 are issued from the perfect tree matrix (Table 2), the lines 5,6 from the random binary tree matrix (Table 3), the lines 7,8 from the random increasing binary tree matrix (Table 4). The generated tree inherits (statistically) features of the three corresponding families of trees, each one at a different level : the important

branches, i.e. of high order, are bushy as in a random increasing binary tree (Figure 12), then the intermediary branches become slender as in a random binary tree, simulating regrowth on old branches (Figure 11), finally the terminal branches become small perfect trees simulating inflorescences. Note that these perfect trees have a random order (2,3 or 4) and that they replace the "thorns" which exist in great quantity on a random binary tree.

The matrix in Table 7 is a shuffle of a matrix similar to the matrix of the tree in Figure 13 and a matrix similar to the one of a perfect tree. Figure 15 shows a tree generated by this matrix, with long main branches, on which grow many almost perfect trees making a bunch effect.

The tree in Figure 16 is generated by the random increasing binary tree matrix of order 6, to which is added the line of order 7 : (0.8;0;0;0;0;0;0.2). This shuffle implies the appearance of many thorns on the *trunk* (i.e. the segment of highest order). The algorithm applying the length branch law, leads to a length increasing effect of the trunk. If the geometrical size of order one branches is under the pixel size, we shall only see the increase of the trunk, without the introduced thorns. Obviously, this effect can be introduced at every branch level in the tree.

A second possible operation on ramification matrices is the *linear combination*. In practice, we limit ourselves to two matrices R and M. If λ and μ are positive reals such as $\lambda+\mu=1$, we introduce the (triangular stochastic) matrix $\lambda R+\mu M$. By continuously varying λ from 0 to 1, we can progressively go from the family of trees associated to the matrix M to the one associated with R.

5.3. Alternative tree generation : constraints related to segments

Most photos in this paper are obtained by the random generation algorithm (cf section 4.1) guided by the given ramification matrix. The final shape results from the combination of two components : the stochastic growth and the start parameters.

It is possible to minimize the importance of the stochastic component, and then to obtain greater control of some parts of the tree. Such an alternative of our generation method is called *constraint by segment* : instead of generating the tree, cf §4.1, by random selection (according to the given matrix probabilities $p_{k,i}$ or $p_{k,k}$), of the biorder (k,i) or (k-1,k-1) of a mother edge labelled k>1, we impose a number of branching nodes on the order k segment associated with this edge. This number is also called *length of the segment*.

One rule is to take the average value of this length as the integer part of the inverse of the fork probability $p_{k,k}$. The selection can be exact or gaussian around this average value. The biorders of branching nodes different from the end branching node of the order k segment are randomly chosen, as in section 4.1, with the help of probabilities $p_{k,i}$ (i<k). The ramification matrix of the generated tree will be quite near the one given initially, but visual effect will be different. More regular structures will appear. An example is given in Figure 17 : the tree contains only one very long segment of order 3, to which join segments of order 2. In fact these segments are themselves composed of a multitude of small line segments representing the edges of the binary tree. The edges of order 1 are too small and do not appear on the screen. This gives the "aerial" effect of floating filaments, although we have not changed geometric laws.

Another strategy consists in choosing segment lengths independently from the ramification matrix. A possible rule is to choose little order segments with lengths equal to 1, i.e. as if fork probability $p_{k,k}$ was equal to 1. This introduces perfect

trees at the branch tips. Obviously, with this method, the ramification matrix of the generated tree could be more different than the one given. An example is visualised in Figure 18 which seems to simulate an herbaceous plant.

6. The leaf model

In order to obtain realistic drawings (Figures 22 to 27), we describe herein a model for drawing leaves. Such an efficient and fast algorithm is primordial to draw trees with hundreds of branches and then thousands of leaves.

6.1 The leaf drawing model

As shown in Figure 19, a leaf is made of an arborescence of "*veins*" immersed in the *limb* (body of the leaf once we have removed the veins). In a first approximation, the leaf is supposed to be flat and the underlying arborescence is a ternary tree except at the leafstalk (or *petiole*) where the arity can take any odd value. Below, we call *main vein* a sequence of central edges issued from the petiole, and *secondary vein*, an edge issued from a main vein. We consider in the following that there is no deeper veins than secondary ones. A *lobe* is then constituted of a main vein, its secondary veins and the border surrounding the part of the limb associated to this main vein (border whose geometry is not specified at this level : polygonal, smoothed, far from or near the terminal nodes).

The topological leaf structure is defined by :
1) The number of lobes;
2) The "size" of the leaf, given by the number n of nodes on the central main vein. The number of nodes on each other main vein issued from the petiole being a simple function (usually decreasing) of n and of the "distance" between this vein and the central one.

The geometrical leaf structure is then obtained by defining:
1) The positions of nodes with the help of 3 parameters : two angles Δ and δ and a length law L for arborescence edges.

Δ is the angle between two successive main veins, and δ is the angle between a secondary nervure and its main vein. The length L(d) of an edge is an increasing function of the "depth" d of the edge (d is the distance between the initial vertex of the edge and the final vertex of the main vein of the lobe). Three laws have been tested (the last one giving the best results) :
(1) $L(d) = Cte$, (2) $L(d) = A*d + B$, (3) $L(d) = A*Log(1 + d)+ B$.
If two veins cross, one of the end segments is deleted.
2) The border of each lobe as a polygon joining the root and points in the continuation of the veins determined from the terminal nodes by a multiplicative factor.

The limb border is then the polygon obtained by joining parts of each lobe border belonging to this limb border (see Figure 19). This polygonal representation is sufficient when the leaves are drawn with a little size on the tree (seen from far, see Figures 22 to 25), allowing a fast drawing algorithm of a tree with its foliage.

In the foliage of a tree, leaves being mixed, it is necessary to distinguish them by various colors. A very realistic aspect is obtained by gradation of colors (see Figure 21). To this aim, each lobe color gradation is obtained by two operations : (1) an affinity whose axis is the lobe main vein, whose direction is the one of the secondary veins and whose ratio varying between 0 and 1 gives the color gradation by a function ; (2) an homothety whose center is the root of the arborescence.

When we need to represent a realistic leaf, the limb border must be smoothed. This is done by interpolation with the help of cubics of each lobe border polygonal segment (each segment is replaced by a cubic which is given by its two extremities and two associated tangent vectors, see Figures 19,21).

Such a method for modeling leaves using an underlying tree has already been introduced by Prusinkiewicz et Al. [36]. They use L-systems. As in our method for generating trees, our leaf drawing algorithm separates growth and topology, the

topology being the dominant feature from which is issued the geometry. Our model differs from the one of P. Lienhardt [21] by using simple combinatorial tree structures instead of planar maps. This allows a faster drawing algorithm issued from an easy leaf topological modeling while obtaining a large diversity of forms (see Figure 21). The method proposed by Bloomenthal [4] allows the visualization and the positioning of a digitalized leaf (the maple leaf) with the help of an added polygonal structure for a 3D aspect simulation. The method is quite different from ours : his aim is not to propose a general leaf model. Other fractal approaches appear, given in Oppenheimer [31], in which the external boundary shape of the leaf is the limit of the recursive fractal growth of the internal veins, and in Demko et al. [7] who generates leaves as fractal sets, using *iterated function systems*.

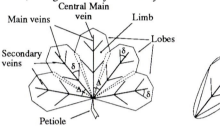

Figure 19. Leaf geometry.

6.2 Spot models

A faster algorithm can be obtained by replacing real leaves by spots. These spots can merely constitute a cloud of color points (two side background trees in Figure 27), or polygonal spots instead of points (the two foreground trees in Figure 27).

7. Realistic rendering

The visualization in two dimensions allows some realism by generating trees with a sufficiently great size if leaves are drawn with a 3D arrangement, see figures 22 to 27.

The leaves are settled on the tree with a rule dependant upon the branch order. They are disposed stochastically with a great density for little order branches and a null density for high order branches. Of course, it is not possible to generate a different leaf each time. The geometrical representation of the wanted leaf is kept in memory and modified by two types of transformations before being drawn in the tree according to the above rule. These two transformations preceding the drawing of a leaf are an homothety of the whole leaf, the final size being chosen along a stochastic law, and a rotation of the leaf in the three dimensions, with possible respect to a certain law (in order to obtain special effects, such as wind or gravity).

The bark texture on the branches in Figures 12, 13, 22 and 24 is obtained by drawing random dotted vector lines of a different color along the direction of the branch.

Irregularities (as dead branches, growth, abnormality, pruned tree effect) can also be simulated, if we stop the generation algorithm in section 4.1 before reaching order one branches, while keeping the geometric laws of §4.3 in the tree geometric drawing (the order k being replaced by the label of the branch which can be different in that case).

Color photos are made on IBM PS/2 8580, screen 8514A, resolution 1024x768 (256 colors). On this computer, the generation time for the topology and the geometry of the tree of Fig. 22 (with 1500 internal nodes) is below one second; the execution time for drawing this tree without foliage is about 20 seconds, with about 3000 polygonal spots is one minute.

A simplified version (without foliage) has been implemented on Apple MacIntosh by Yves Chiricota (UQAM, Montréal).

8. Conclusion

Topology is essential in the herein given method which allows the analysis of a ramified structure, independently from

its history. This leads to a ramification matrix which is the expression of the main features of the ramified structure form. As shown, this matrix allows one a powerful control of the final form and is a tool for image synthesis of ramified structures with such characteristics. This association between image analysis and image synthesis is one of the interesting points of this method.

The association of a geometry depending only on the combinatorial parameters order and biorder, with an easy and fast leaf drawing algorithm, is a good compromise between speed and final rendering, while keeping a great diversity of possible forms. Such an easy and fast method is of practical interest in order to implement an interactive environment for tree creation and animation, in various domains (Botany, arts, architecture,...). The scientific significance occurs then in analysis and synthesis of tree-like structures which are not necessarily botanical ones, for example in physics (electric breakdowns, viscous fingers, DLA,...) and in molecular biology (RNA secondary structures). In particular, the ramification matrix model has been applied recently in physics to branching fractal structures [43] [44].

Further research :
- Development of an interpreter for ramified structure modeling (see [12]). Our method clearly separating the different structure levels (sections 4.1, 4.2, 4.3, 4.4, 5) is well adapted to this aim.

- We could animate the growth algorithm by keeping up to date the orders and biorders of the tree under construction (at each random choice of the biorder of a terminal node, the order changing edges are necessarily on the unique tree-path leading from the root to this node).

- This method seems to be promising for figurative tree drawing with a certain artistic quality.

- Generalization to any arity (e.g. ternary) tree (this is already done in the combinatorial situation by Vauchaussade de Chaumont & Viennot [45]).

Work Partially supported by PRC Mathématiques et Informatique

References
[1]   Aono M., and Kunii T.L. *Botanical tree image generation*, IEEE Computer Graphics & Applications 4,5 (1984),10-34.

[2]   Ball, R.C. *DLA in the real world*, in On growth and form: fractal and non-fractal patterns in Physics, Stanley, H.E., and Ostrowski, N., eds., Martinus Nijhoff, Boston (1986) 69-78.

[3]   Beyer, T., and Friedel. M. *Generative scene modelling*. Proceeding of EUROGRAPHICS '87 (1987),151-158 & 571.

[4]   Bloomenthal, J. *Modeling the Mighty Maple*. Proceedings of SIGGRAPH '85 (San Francisco, CA, July 22-26, 1985). In Computer Graphics 19, 3 (1985), 305-311.

[5]   Cole, V.C. *The artistic anatomy of trees*. Dover Publication, N-Y (1965) (orginally Seely Servi & Co., Lond., 1915).

[6]   D'Arcy Thompson, W. *On growth and form*. University Press, Cambridge, 2nd ed., (1952).

[7]   Demko, S., Hodges, L., and Naylor, B. *Construction of fractal objects with iterated function systems*. Proceedings of SIGGRAPH '85 (San Francisco, CA, July 22-26, 1985). In Computer Graphics 19, 3 (1985), 271-278.

[8]   De Reffye, P., Edelin, C., Françon, J., Jaeger, M., Puech, C. *Plant Models Faithful to Botanical Structure and Development*. Proceedings SIGGRAPH '88 (Atlanta, August 1-15, 1988). Computer Graphics 22, 4(1988),151-158.

[9]   Eyrolles G. *Synthèse d'images figuratives d'arbres par des méthodes combinatoires*. Ph.D. Thesis, Un. Bordeaux I 1986

[10]   Flajolet, P., Raoult, J.C., and Vuillemin, J. *The number of registers required for evaluating arithmetic expressions*. Theor. Computer Science 9 (1979) 99-125.

[11]   Gardner, G., *Simulation of natural scenes using textured quadric surfaces*. Computer Graphics 18, 3 (1984).

[12]   Green, M., and Sun, H. *A langage and system for procedural modeling and motion*. IEEE Comp. Graph. & Ap. , (1988) 52-64.

[13]   Hallé F., Oldeman R., and Tomlinson P. *Tropical trees and forests: an architectural analysis*. Springer Berlin 1978.

[14]   Honda, H. *Description of the form of trees by the parameters of the tree-like body: effects of the branching angle and the branch length of the shape of the tree-like body*, J. Theor. Biol. 31 (1971), 331-338.

[15]   Horton, R.E. *Erosioned development of systems and their drainage basins, hydrophysical approach to quantitative morphology*. Bull. Geol. Soc. America 56 (1945), 275-370.

[16]   Kawaguchi, Y. *A morphological study of the form of nature*. Proceedings of SIGGRAPH '82 (July 1982). In Computer Graphics 16, 3 (1982), 223-232.

[17]   Kemp, R. *The average number of registers needed to evaluate a binary tree optimally*. Acta Infor. 11 (1979), 363-372.

[18]   Knuth, D.E. *The Art of Computer Programming*. vol. 3, Addison-Wesley, Reading (1973).

[19]   Leopold, L.B. *Trees and streams: the efficency of branching patterns*, J. Theor. Biol. 31 (1971), 339-354.

[20]   Lienhardt, P. *Modélisation et évolution de surfaces libres*. Ph.D. Thesis, Univ. Louis Pasteur, Strasbourg (1987).

[21]   Lienhardt P. & Françon J.*Vegetal leaves synthesis*. Proc. COGNITIVA'87 (Paris La Villette,May 18-22,1987)212-18.

[22]   MacMahon, T.A. *The mechanical design of trees*. Scientific American 233 (1975), 92-102.

[23]   Mandelbrot, B. *The fractal geometry of nature*. Freeman & Co., San Francisco (1982).

[24]   Marshall, R., Wilson, R., and Carlson, W. *Procedure models for generating three-dimensional terrain*. SIGGRAPH '80, Computer Graphics 14, 3 (July 1980), 154-162.

[25]   Meier A., Moon J.W. & Pounder J.R. *On the order of random channel networks*. SIAM J. Alg. Disc. Mat.1 (1980) 25-33.

[26]   Mendes-France M., *De l'arbre de Leonardo da Vinci à la théorie de la dimension*. Rev. du Palais de la Découverte, Paris, 10 (1981), 52-60.

[27]   Naudin, J.J., and Prud'homme, R. *Méthodes d'analyse morphologiques et morphostructurales d'interprétation des topogra-phies et des bathymétries dans les domaines continentaux marins*. Bull. de l'Inst. de Géologie du Bassin D'Aquitaine 10 (1971) 111-114

[28]   Niemeyer, L., Pietronero, L., and Wiesmann, A.J. *Fractal structure of dielectric breakdown patterns*. Phys. Rev. Letters 52 (1984) 1033.

[29]   Nittmann, J., Daccord, G., and Stanley, H.E. *Fractal growth of viscous fingers*. Nature 314 (1985) 141-144.

[30]   Niklas, K.J., *Computer-simulated plant evolution*. Scientific American (1986) 78-86.

[31]   Oppenheimer, P. *Real time design and animation of fractal plants and trees*. Proceedings of SIGGRAPH '86 (Dallas, Texas, August 18-22, 1985). In Computer Graph. 20, 4 (1986), 55-64.

[32]   Penaud, J.G. *The ramification matrix of random binary trees*. Research report, LABRI n° 8832 , Département d'Informatique, Université de Bordeaux I (1988).

[33]   Percheron, G., *Principles and methods of the graph theoretical analysis of natural binary arborescences*. J. Theor. Biology 99 (1982) 509-552.

[34]   Prud'homme, R., and Vigneaux, M. *Méthodes morphologiques et morphostructurales appliquées à l'étude des réseaux hydrographiques du Bordelais*. Revue géographique des Pyrénées du Sud-Ouest 41 (1970), 5-14.

[35]   Prusinkiewicz P.*Graphical applications of L-systems*. Proc. of Graphics Interface '86-Vision Interface'86 (1986),247-53

[36]   Prusinkiewicz, P., Lindenmayer, A., and Hanan, J. *Developmental models of herbaceous plants for computer imagery purposes*. Proceedings of SIGGRAPH '88 (Atlanta, August 1-15, 1988).In Computer Graph. 22, 4(1988), 141-150.

[37]   Reeves, W.T. & Blau, R.*Approximate and probabilistic algorithms for shading and rendering structured particle systems* Proceedings of SIGGRAPH '85 (San Francisco, CA, july 22-26, 1985).In Computer Graphics 19, 3 (1985), 313-322.

[38]   Sawada, Y., Dougherty, A., and Gollub, J.P. *Dentritic and fractal patterns in electrolytic metal deposits*. Phys. Review Letters 56 (1986) 1260-1263.

[39] Smith, A.R., *Plants, fractals, and formal languages*. Proceedings of SIGGRAPH '84 (Minneapolis, Minnesota, July 23-27, 1984). Computer Graphics 18, 3 (1984), 1-10.

[40] Stevens, P.S. *Patterns in Nature*. Little, Brown & Co., Boston (1974).

[41] Strahler, A.N.*Hypsometric (area-altitude) analysis of erosional topology*. Bull. Geol. Soc. Amer. 63 (1952) 1117-42.

[42] VanDamme, H., Obrecht, F., Levitz, P., Gatineau, L., Laroche, C. *Nature* 320 (1986), 731.

[43] Vannimenus, J., *On the shape of trees: tools to describe ramified patterns*. Proc. sum. school in Theor. Physics, Les Houches (1987).

[44] Vannimenus, J., and Viennot, X.G. *Combinatorial Tools for the Analysis of Ramified Patterns*. J. Stat. Physics, 54 (1989) 1529-1538.

[45] Vauchaussade de Chaumont, M., and Viennot X.G. *Enumeration of RNAs secondary structures by complexity, in Mathematics in Medecine and Biology*, Lecture Notes in Biomathematics n°57, Capasso, V., Grosso, E., and Paven-Fontana, S.L., eds., Springer-Verlag, Berlin (1985), 360-365.

[46] Witten, T.A., and Sanders, L.M. Phys. Rev. 47 (1981) 1400.

[47] Woldenberg, M.J. *A structural taxonomy of spatial hierarchies*, in Colston papers,v. 22,Butterworth Sci. Publ., London (1970) 147-175.

Figure 10 : Coral like tree

Figure 12 : Random Increasing binary tree

Figure 11 : Random binary tree

Figure 13 : Tree associated with matrix TABLE 6

Figure 14 : Shuffle of 3 matrices associated with :
- Random increasing binary tree
- Random binary tree
- Perfect tree

Figure 15 : Shuffle of 2 matrices

Figure 16 : Length increasing effect of the trunk
by introduicing thorns

Figure 17 : Constraint on segment length
"Feather"

Figure 18 : Constraint on segment length
Perfect tree generation
at extremities

Figure 20

Figure 21 : effect of the length rule on limb shape

Figure 22

Figure
23

Figure
24

Figure
25

Figure
26

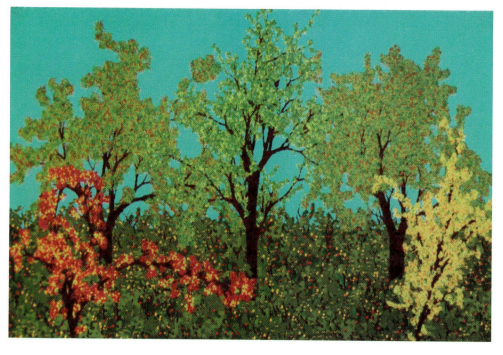

Figure
27

The Synthesis and Rendering of Eroded Fractal Terrains

F. Kenton Musgrave†, Craig E. Kolb† and Robert S. Mace‡

†Yale University Department of Mathematics
Box 2155 Yale Station
New Haven, Connecticut 06520

‡Silicon Graphics, Inc.
2011 N. Shoreline Boulevard
Mountain View, California 94039

Abstract

In standard fractal terrain models based on fractional Brownian motion the statistical character of the surface is, by design, the same everywhere. A new approach to the synthesis of fractal terrain height fields is presented which, in contrast to previous techniques, features locally independent control of the frequencies composing the surface, and thus local control of fractal dimension and other statistical characteristics. The new technique, termed *noise synthesis*, is intermediate in difficulty of implementation, between simple stochastic subdivision and Fourier filtering or generalized stochastic subdivision, and does not suffer the drawbacks of creases or periodicity. Varying the local crossover scale of fractal character or the fractal dimension with altitude or other functions yields more realistic first approximations to eroded landscapes. A simple physical erosion model is then suggested which simulates hydraulic and thermal erosion processes to create global stream/valley networks and talus slopes. Finally, an efficient ray tracing algorithm for general height fields, of which most fractal terrains are a subset, is presented.

CR Categories and Subject Descriptors: I.3.3 [**Computer Graphics**]: Picture/Image Generation, I.3.7 [**Computer Graphics**]: Three-Dimensional Graphics and Realism

General Terms: Algorithms, Graphics

Additional Keywords and Phrases: Fractal, terrain models, stochastic subdivision, fractional Brownian motion, fractal dimension, lacunarity, crossover scale, erosion models, height fields, ray tracing.

1. INTRODUCTION

At first glance, fractal terrains are convincing forgeries of natural mountain terrains. Closer scrutiny, however, reveals an unnatural character in these surfaces as representations of nature. One problem is the fact that if one turns the average "fractal mountain" upside-down and looks at the other side of the surface, it looks (statistically) identical to the "top" side. This is almost never the case in nature, where depressions in the landscape fill up with all manner of detritus, thus acquiring smoother surfaces over the ages of geologic time.

The origin of fractal landscapes in computer graphics is this: some time ago, B. B. Mandelbrot perceived an analogy between a record of Brownian motion over time, and the skyline of jagged mountain peaks.[15] He reasoned that if this process were extended to two dimensions the resulting "Brownian surface" might provide a visual approximation to mountains in nature. He then found it necessary to generalize from Brownian motion to a fractional Brownian surface. Some of Mandelbrot's earliest computer graphics images were of such surfaces.[14] Voss later used Mandelbrot's fractional Brownian surfaces to create some very convincing forgeries of nature.[28] New terrain synthesis methods have since been proposed by Fournier et al.,[4] Miller,[19] and Lewis.[12]

Most fractal terrain surfaces are related to fractional Brownian motion (*fBm*), and can be called more loosely $1/f^{\beta}$ surfaces. Fractal terrains in general have no global erosion features inherently due to isotropy and stationarity, and practically due to the difficulty in implementation and computation of such global processes, which require global communication.

In this paper, we present a flexible approach to the generation of fractal terrain models of varying smoothness and asymmetry in a first-pass surface specification stage, and suggest a second-pass global, physical erosion process for height fields which generates both local and global erosion features through a simplified simulation of natural erosion processes. The terrain generation method features arbitrary local control of *fractal dimension* and *crossover scale*, neither of which was sought in previous methods. It also features arbitrary *lacunarity**, which is not available in common subdivision algorithms. Terrain patches can be compactly represented as height fields; we will also describe a very efficient algorithm for ray tracing regular** height fields. This rendering algorithm can be characterized as the definition of height fields as a new type of primitive (thus joining spheres, planes, polygons, etc.) in the ray tracing paradigm.

2. OTHER WORK

Creating synthetic images of fractal terrains usually involves two distinct procedures: *modelling* and *rendering*. It is well-known that rendering fractal terrains is generally more time-consuming than modelling them, especially if one chooses to ray trace the scene. In our scheme for imaging eroded synthetic terrains, we subdivide modelling into two steps: *terrain generation* and *erosion simulation*. As the latter step is an attempt to simulate the actions of the elements on the landscape over geologic time, it is not surprising to find that it competes with rendering, in the time required to create realistic results.

---

* *Crossover scale* and *lacunarity* will be defined in section 3.1.

** We define a *regular height field* as a two-dimensional array of altitude values where the distance is constant between all rows and between all columns of altitude values.

As all three steps are essential to creating realistic images, we present new results in each area.

First let us review work by other researchers in the fields of fractal terrain synthesis, erosion modelling, and ray tracing of terrain models.

2.1. Fractal Terrain Modelling

Most fractal terrain models have been based on one of five approaches: Poisson faulting,[15, 28] Fourier filtering,[15, 28, 18] midpoint displacement,[4, 12, 19, 25] successive random additions,[28] and summing band-limited noises.[7, 8, 19] The approach presented here is of the last type, which we will refer to as the *noise synthesis* method. We will now briefly review these techniques (for a more detailed review, see Voss and Saupe[25] or Musgrave, Kolb, and Mandelbrot[21]).

The original terrain generation technique employed by Mandelbrot[15] was generation of fBm using Poisson faulting. The Poisson faulting technique involves applying Gaussian random displacements (faults, or step functions) to a plane or sphere at Poisson distributed intervals. The net result is a Brownian surface. This approach has been employed by Mandelbrot to create fractal coastlines and Voss to create fractal planets.[15] It has the advantage of being suitable for use on spheres for creation of planetoids. Its primary drawback is the $O(n^3)$ time complexity of the algorithm.

Midpoint displacement methods are standard in fractal geometry, and were introduced as a fast terrain generation technique by Fournier, Fussell, and Carpenter.[4] We classify the various midpoint displacement techniques by locality of reference: *wireframe* midpoint displacement, *tile* midpoint displacement, *generalized stochastic subdivision*, and *unnested** subdivision. Wireframe subdivision is used only in the well-known triangle subdivision scheme[4] and involves the interpolation between two points in the subdivision process. Tile midpoint displacement involves the interpolation of three or more non-collinear points; it is used in the "diamond-square" scheme of Miller,[19] the square scheme of Fournier et al.,[4] and the hexagon subdivision of Mandelbrot and Musgrave.[25] Generalized stochastic subdivision[12] interpolates several local points, constrained by an autocorrelation function. Miller [19] also proposed an unnested "square-square" subdivision, which is not strictly a *midpoint* subdivision scheme.

Wireframe and tile midpoint displacement methods are generally efficient and easy to implement, but have fixed lacunarity and are nonstationary due to nesting (for illustrations of the resulting artifacts, see Miller[19]). Generalized stochastic subdivision and unnested subdivision schemes are stationary; the former is flexible but not particularly easy to implement, while the latter features fixed lacunarity and is very simple to implement. Note that all midpoint displacement techniques produce true fractal surfaces[23] but simply have an incorrect statistical character to qualify as fractional Brownian motion.[16]

Successive random additions is a flexible unnested subdivision scheme. If points determined in previous stages of subdivision are re-used, they are first displaced by addition of a random variable with an appropriate distribution. Previous points need not be re-used; new grid points to be displaced can be determined from the previous level of subdivision by linear or nonlinear interpolation. Successive random additions features continuously variable level of detail, which is useful for zooms in animation, and arbitrary lacunarity. The lacunarity λ depends on the change of resolution at successive generations; time complexity of the algorithm is a function of λ and the final resolu-

tion R. The successive random additions algorithm is easy to implement.

Fourier filtering generates fBm by taking the Fourier transform of a two-dimensional Gaussian *white noise*, multiplying it in frequency space with an appropriate filter, and interpreting the inverse Fourier transform of the product as a height field.[28] Alternatively, one can simply choose the coefficients of the discrete Fourier transform, subject to the proper constraints, and interpret the inverse Fourier transform as above.[25] Advantages of this approach include the availability of arbitrary lacunarity and precise control of global frequency content. Disadvantages include periodicity of the final surface, which can require that substantial portions of the computed height field patch be discarded, the $O(n \log n)$ time complexity of the FFT algorithm, the level of complexity of implementation, and lack of local control of detail.

What we call *noise synthesis* can be described as the iterative addition of signals with tightly band-limited frequencies, each of which has a randomly varying, or *noisy*, amplitude. Noise synthetic surfaces have been used by Miller,[19] Gardner[7] and Saupe.[8] Miller has used Perlin's procedural "$1/f$ noise"[20] (which is actually $1/f^3$ noise) as a *displacement map*[3] to add detail to the (otherwise straight) edges of polygons tessellating a Brownian surface of similar spectral content. Gardner has introduced a noise function, based on a "poor man's Fourier series"[6] (a variation of the Mandelbrot-Weierstrass function) and interpreted it as a height field. The quantization of altitude values of the height field yields terraced land, such as mesas. Our approach differs from Gardner's in that we exercise local control over frequency content based on the amplitude of existing signal and other functions. The Perlin noise function is notably more isotropic than Gardner's noise function, and is not periodic; Gardner's terrains and textures suffer visible artifacts due to these factors. In addition, the use of Gardner's noise function requires that one subjectively determine critical values for a number of constants. Driven by table lookups, the Gardner noise function is much faster than the Perlin function.

Noise synthesis is a *functional-based modelling* technique. Each point is determined procedurally, independently of its neighbors; no global computation is required. Point-evaluation is a distinguishing property of the noise synthesis method for generating random fractals.

Recently, a parallel and independent research effort by Saupe has developed an approach to noise synthesis similar to that presented here. Saupe's work features an emphasis on mathematical foundations, while the authors' emphasizes applications. For a thorough mathematical treatment of the issues of noise synthesis which is complimentary to this work, see Saupe.[8]

2.2. Erosion Models

The issue of the symmetry of fBm has been addressed by Mandelbrot and Voss[15, 28] through the use of non-linear scaling in a post-processing step, and by Mandelbrot[25] through the use of random variables with non-Gaussian distributions in the displacement process. These approaches yield peaks which are more jagged and valleys which are smoother, but still lack global erosion features. A global river system, created algorithmically at terrain-generation time, has been demonstrated by Mandelbrot and Musgrave,[25] with less-than-satisfactory results (see plate 10).

Kelley et al.[11] have used hydrology data to derive a system for the generation of *stream network* drainage patterns which are subsequently used to determine the topography of a terrain surface. This approach features, by its construction, the global dependence necessary for realistic hydraulic erosion patterns, and has a strong basis in measurements of real physical

---

* *Unnested* here means that successive levels of subdivision retain no points from previous levels.

systems. This approach to modelling hydraulic erosion is relatively efficient; what it lacks is the detail of a fractal surface. While the stream network may be fractal, the "surface under tension" used for the terrain surface is not, and cannot be readily made so without disturbing the drainage basins and stream paths.

A simple hydraulic erosion simulation is proposed here in which water is dropped on each vertex in a fractal height field and allowed to run off the landscape, eroding and depositing material at different locations as a function of the sediment load of water passing over each vertex. It features the global communication necessary to create global features, but is slow despite the $O(n)$ time complexity. We also present a global model for simulation of what we refer to as *thermal weathering*. While hydraulic erosion creates valleys and drainage networks, thermal weathering wears down steep slopes and creates talus slopes at their feet. The thermal weathering simulation can create realistic results in much less computing time than the hydraulic erosion simulation, and is also $O(n)$ in time complexity. Both models are discussed in section 4.

2.3. Ray Tracing Fractal Terrains

Efficient ray tracing of fractal terrains has been addressed by Kajiya,[9,10] Bouville,[2] Miller,[19] and Mastin et al.[18] Kajiya and Miller propose procedural fractal terrain models to save memory and achieve adaptive level of detail; Miller proposes a parallel scheme for rendering terrains which is not specific to ray tracing. Mastin et al. propose a quadtree spatial decomposition for the ray tracing of height fields.

The ray tracing schemes of Kajiya and Bouville rely on invariance of the horizontal position of computed vertices of the terrain height field under subsequent iteration of the midpoint subdivision process used to generate the surface, in order to ensure that the surface is within predictable bounds for ray/surface intersection test culling. This requires that the subdivision scheme *nests*, else the bounding volumes become ill-defined. (Note that nested subdivision schemes suffer most from the *creasing problem*.) The nesting requirement cannot always be met in iterative subdivision schemes, as when subdividing non-nesting polygons such as hexagons (see Mandelbrot[25]). Such limitations led the authors to develop an efficient ray tracing scheme which is not necessarily procedural but is general to all regular height fields. This new method can be implemented hierarchically as an n^2 tree, and in that is similar to the quadtree approach of Mastin et al. It uses a DDA to traverse a spatial subdivision data structure, and in that is reminiscent of the 3DDDA *ARTS* algorithm of Fujimoto.[5] Our "grid tracing"[22] scheme will be described in section 5.

3. TERRAIN SYNTHESIS

3.1. Fractal Dimension, Fractional Brownian Motion, Crossover Scale, and Lacunarity

We now give a very brief description of some of the mathematical terminology associated with the generation of fractal terrains. For greater depth, see Peitgen and Saupe.[25] For this discussion, we define D_f as the *fractal dimension* of the surface, D_E as the *Euclidean dimension* of the surface, and H as the *Holder exponent*. (Note that previous authors have sometimes erroneously referred to H as the fractal dimension.) For terrain models $D_E=2$ and $D_f=3-H$.

The fractal dimension D_f, Euclidean dimension D_E, Holder exponent H, and the *spectral exponent* β of $1/f^\beta$ noise and of fBm are related by

$$D_f = D_E + 1 - H = D_E + \frac{3-\beta}{2}. \qquad (1)$$

It follows that $\beta = 1+2H$ and $H = (\beta-1)/2$. Since $D_E = 2$, for our purposes, $D_f = 3-H = (7-\beta)/2$. H is constrained to the interval $[0,1]$ and β to $[1,3]$; outside this range we do not have formally fractal behavior.

Fractional Brownian motion in one dimension is a *stochastic process* $X(t)$ with a *power spectrum* * $S(f)$ scaling with f as

$$S(f) \sim 1/f^\beta$$

where β again is in the interval $[1,3]$. FBm is itself not a stationary process, but its increments $I(t,\Delta t) = X(t+\Delta t)-X(t)$ are; that is, the expected value of $I(t,\Delta t)$ is zero for all t and Δt and the variance σ^2 of $I(t,\Delta t)$ does not depend on t. In the special case of Brownian motion, $H = 0.5$ and σ^2 varies as Δt^{2H}. Thus for $H = 0.5$ increments are uncorrelated; for $H>0.5$ (as in fractal terrains, where H is approximately equal to 0.8) increments are positively correlated; for $H<0.5$ they are negatively correlated (corresponding to a *very* rough surface). In more than one dimension fBm is a *random field* $X(x,y,...)$ with X on any straight line being a $1/f^\beta$ noise.

Discretized fractional Brownian motion is a stochastic process $X(t)$ with a discrete power spectrum such that each spectral line has the energy

$$\int_{f_i}^{\lambda f_i} S(f)\,df$$

where λ is the logarithmic spacing of the lines. Many fBm surfaces used in computer graphics are discretized fBm's.

A fractal surface changes in character depending on whether it is observed from nearby or from far away. From far away it appears flat or smooth (as the Earth seen from space). The transition from "nearby" to "far away" appearances occurs at the *crossover scale* which is the scale where vertical and horizontal displacements are equal. Thus, for a mountain range rising within one kilometer from sea level to peaks which are one kilometer high, the crossover scale is one kilometer. The crossover scale is not to be confused with the upper and lower frequency cutoffs for a band-limited fBm.

Lacunarity generally refers to gaps in fractals;[15] in this instance it refers to the gap between frequencies composing the discretized fBm of the fractal terrain. Thus when iteratively adding the frequencies composing the discretized fBm, if the frequency f_i added at stage i is a multiple λ of f_{i-1},

$$f_i = \lambda f_{i-1},$$

λ is the spatial lacunarity of the fBm. While spatial lacunarity affects the texture of the fBm, this effect is usually only noticeable for $\lambda > 2$. Therefore we usually let $\lambda = 2$, as lower values involve more computation for a given frequency range of fBm and higher values effect the surface appearance.

3.2. Noise Function

Noise synthetic terrain generation is accomplished by the addition of successive frequencies of tightly band-limited noises. The source of the noise we use is a version of the Perlin[26] noise function. The ideal noise function for our purposes would be *monochromatic* (i.e., single-frequency), *stationary* (invariant under translation), and *isotropic* (invariant under rotation). The Perlin function supplies a band-limited signal of random amplitude variation. It is stationary and nearly isotropic.**

---

* The *power spectrum* $S(f)$ is the power $P(f)$ of the signal at frequency f, or the the mean squared power over interval Δf centered at f, divided by Δf : $S(f) = P(f)^2/\Delta f$.

** It is geometrically impossible to reconcile the three criteria of mono-

The Perlin noise function $N:R^n \to R$ is implemented as a set of random gradient values defined at integer points of a lattice or grid in space (of dimension $n = 1, 2,$ or 3) which are interpolated by a cubic function. At lattice points in space (points in space with integer coordinates), the value of the function is zero (a *zero crossing*) and its rate of change is the gradient value associated with that lattice point. The first derivative of the function is interpolated at non-integer points using the cubic function $3x^2 - 2x^3$, which features second derivative continuity and zero rate of change at the end points, where $x=0$ and $x=1$. Since the gradient might be, for instance, increasing at two consecutive lattice points i and $i+1$, there may also be a zero crossing at a point between i and $i+1$ (see figure 1). This gives rise to frequencies in the noise function higher than the primary frequency, which is defined by the spacing of the integer lattice.

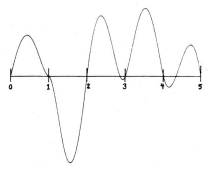

Figure 1   One-dimensional trace of noise function.

The noise function can be modified to have an arbitrary, non-zero value at the lattice points. This increases the variance of the function, but adds low frequency components to the signal which cannot be controlled or subsequently removed.[12] For an analysis of the spectral characteristics of such a noise function see Saupe.[8]

The Perlin noise function $N(\vec{p})$ outputs a signal with a fixed lower frequency f. To generate a signal of lowest frequency uf, one can perform a scalar multiplication $u\vec{p}$ of the coordinate vectors supplied to N. This has the effect of moving the reference points in the noise lattice, producing the desired frequency shift in the output of N. We will see this practice used below.

3.3. Frequency Control

Given the noise function, how do we use it to generate more realistic terrains? Subjective observation of natural landscapes reveals that in certain types of mountain ranges there is a marked change in the statistics of the surface as one moves from the foothills to higher peaks. The foothills are more rounded, while the higher mountains are more jagged. Sometimes, as in the eastern slope of the Sierra Nevada, the entire mountain range rises in a relatively short distance from a nearly flat plain. This change of character can be characterized as a change of fractal dimension D_f, crossover scale, or both.

Using the noise synthesis technique we can easily devise terrain models with such features by modulating the power spectrum of the surface as a function of horizontal position and/or vertical altitude. We give some examples below.

Given a (Perlin) noise function $N:R^n \to R$ with Gaussian distribution in the interval $[-1,1]$, we can generate fBm as fol-

lows: For our lowest frequency offset a_0 we have

$$a_0 = N(\vec{p}_0)$$

where $\vec{p}_0$ is the initial object space coordinate vector of the height field position being calculated. Iterating (discretized) fBm at lacunarity $\lambda > 1$ requires that, at iteration n, the frequency added is proportional to $(f_0\lambda^n)^{-0.5\beta}$. Setting the lowest frequency $f_0=1$ gives a frequency increment at iteration n of $\lambda^{-0.5\beta n}$. Thus for higher frequencies added at iteration $i > 0$ we have

$$a_i = N(\vec{p}_{i-1}\lambda)\omega^i$$

where $\omega = \lambda^{-0.5\beta}$ (a constant) and $\vec{p}_i = \vec{p}_{i-1}\lambda$. Note that for a two-dimensional noise function $N:R^2 \to R$, we have $\vec{p}_i = \vec{p}_0\lambda^i$. For $N:R^3 \to R$, we may have $\vec{p}_i \neq \vec{p}_0\lambda^i$ due to vertical displacement.

For the purposes of terrain modelling we will introduce a number of parameters to the formulae for fBm. We may wish to translate N by a constant c_t so that it is, for instance, always or nearly always positive. We may also wish to scale N by a factor c_s to reduce or expand its range. In the patches shown in plates 3 and 11, we insert the lowest frequency first:

$$a_0 = (N(\vec{p}_0) + c_t) c_s + c_0$$

where a_0 is the initial height of a point in the height field and c_0 is an offset constant which determines the zero value or "sea level" of the terrain. We have for the altitude a_i at stage $i > 0$:

$$a_i = a_{i-1} + a_{i-1} (N(\vec{p}_i) + c_t) c_s \omega^i$$

The procedure used in plates 3 and 11 generates a surface in which the power of the high frequencies is linearly proportional to the (previous) altitude of the surface. This amounts to modulating crossover scale with altitude. In plates 3 and 11, as in the other illustrations of noise-synthetic terrain patches, we set $\lambda = 2$. (The rainbow in plate 11 is from Musgrave.[24])

In plate 4 the crossover scale varies with altitude and horizontal position. Here we have

$$a_0 = F(x) (N(\vec{p}_0) + c_t) c_s + c_0$$

with $F(x) = \min(2x, 2-2x)$, assuming that x varies from 0 to 1. To give the ridge a more natural path than that of a straight line, we add some $1/f^3$ noise to x before calculating $F(x)$. The contribution of higher frequencies is again scaled as

$$a_i = a_{i-1} + a_{i-1} (N(\vec{p}_i) + c_t) c_s \omega^i$$

Fractal dimension can be modulated as easily as the crossover scale by scaling β or H in successive generations. Plate 5 shows a patch which is planar on the left, to space filling on the right (modulo the upper and lower frequency cutoffs, which are approximately at 7 and 1/128 times the patch size, respectively). In this case, we have $\beta = 1/x$ (corresponding to $H = 1/x - 3/2$), and x in the interval $(0,1]$.

In plate 6, we linearly change fractal dimension D_f from 2 ($H=1$, $\beta=3$) to 3 ($H=0$, $\beta=1$) on the right. Note that this is not the same as going from planar ($1/f^\infty$) to filling all of 3 space ($1/f^0$), as in plate 5.

It is interesting to note that experience indicates that modulation of crossover scale is more effective than modulation of fractal dimension for modelling realistic looking terrain. That changing crossover scale alone should have such a dramatic effect is not surprising, for as B. B. Mandelbrot has pointed out,[17] the fractal dimension of the Himalayas is approximately the same as that of the runway at the JFK airport; what is true is simply that the crossover scale of the latter is on the

---

chromaticity, stationarity, and isotropy in a multidimensional Perlin noise function. If the primary (lowest) frequency of an n-dimensional Perlin function is f along the axes of the grid upon which it is defined, then the frequency is $\sqrt{n}\,f$ along the diagonal of that grid.

order of millimeters while that of the former is on the order of kilometers.

It is readily apparent that the global lacunarity λ is subject to precise user control in the noise synthesis scheme. Computational cost for a surface is a function of the number of frequencies used. Thus surfaces generated with small lacunarity will be more expensive to compute than those with large lacunarity. Cost can be reduced by omitting high frequencies when their contribution drops below an arbitrary threshold.

With the noise synthesis method, one may exercise local control over lacunarity. This can be accomplished by displacing the initial coordinate p_0 supplied to the noise function by a vector valued noise function $\vec{N}$ (e. g., Perlin's "Dnoise()"[26]). The effects of such local change of lacunarity are shown in plate 1b, where we modulate intensity on the image plane as

$$intensity = N(\vec{p}_0 + \vec{N}(\vec{p}_0)).$$

(Plate 1a shows the similarly interpreted output of noise $N(\vec{p}_0)$.) Note that local change of lacunarity interferes with the precise local control of frequency. While it is not obvious that this local modulation of lacunarity is particularly useful for terrain synthesis, it may prove useful for the synthesis of other textures, such as clouds, smoke, or flames.

Plates 11 and 12 are details of 100 x 100 patches similar to that in plate 3. Note that the triangles, which are obscured by bump mapping, are quite large in comparison with the overall image. By including only relatively low frequencies in the terrain and leaving high-frequency details to a texture map, we can achieve realistic results using very small height fields.

4. PHYSICAL EROSION MODEL

We have divided erosive processes into two categories: *hydraulic erosion* and *thermal weathering*. Hydraulic erosion is that caused by running water. What we term "thermal weathering" subsumes the non-hydraulic processes which cause rock to flake off steep inclines and form talus slopes at the base. In this section we will illuminate the two erosion simulation algorithms.

4.1. Hydraulic Erosion

The hydraulic erosion model involves depositing water ("rain") on vertices of the height field and allowing the water and sediment suspended in the water to move to any lower neighboring vertices. The erosive power of a given amount of water is a function of its volume and the amount of sediment already carried in the water.

The hydraulic erosion model is implemented by associating with each vertex v at time t an altitude a_t^v, a volume of water w_t^v, and an amount of sediment s_t^v suspended in the water. At each timestep, we pass excess water and suspended sediment from v to each neighboring vertex u. The amount of water passed, Δw, is defined as:

$$\Delta w = min(w_t^v, (w_t^v + a_t^v) - (w_t^u + a_t^u))$$

If Δw is less than or equal to zero, we simply allow a fraction of the sediment suspended in the water at v to be *deposited* at v:

$$a_{t+1}^v = a_t^v + K_d s_t^v$$
$$s_{t+1}^v = (1 - K_d)s_t^v$$

Otherwise, we set

$$w_{t+1}^v = w_t^v - \Delta w$$
$$w_{t+1}^u = w_t^u + \Delta w$$
$$c_s = K_c \Delta w$$

Here, c_s is the *sediment capacity* of Δw. When passing sediment from v to u, we remove at most this amount of sediment from s_t^v and add it to s_{t+1}^u. If c_s is greater than s_t^v, a fraction of the difference is subtracted from a_t^v and is added to s_{t+1}^u, which constitutes the erosion of soil from v. Finally, we allow a fraction of the sediment remaining at v to be deposited as above. Thus, if $s_t^v \geq c_s$, we set

$$s_{t+1}^u = s_t^u + c_s$$
$$a_{t+1}^v = a_t^v + K_d(s_t^v - c_s)$$
$$s_{t+1}^v = (1 - K_d)(s_t^v - c_s)$$

Otherwise,

$$s_{t+1}^u = s_t^u + s_t^v + K_s(c_s - s_t^v)$$
$$a_{t+1}^v = a_t^v - K_s(c_s - s_t^v)$$
$$s_{t+1}^v = 0$$

The constants K_c, K_d, and K_s are, respectively, the *sediment capacity constant*, the *deposition constant* and the *soil softness constant*. K_c specifies the maximum amount of sediment which may be suspended in a unit of water. K_s specifies the softness of the soil and is used to control the rate at which soil is converted to sediment. K_d specifies the rate at which suspended sediment settles out of a unit of water and is added to the altitude of a vertex.

Through the above process, water and, more importantly, soil from higher points on the landscape are transported to and deposited in lower areas. This movement constitutes the communication necessary for modelling the global process of erosion. In a full two-dimensional implementation, one must take care to distribute water and sediment to all neighboring lower vertices in amounts proportional to their respective differences in overall elevation.

Although this model is *ad hoc*, the resulting landscapes bear reasonable resemblance to natural erosion patterns. Further research will concentrate on constructing a more sophisticated, physically accurate model.

Plates 2 and 9 show a terrain patch before and after 2000 time steps of hydraulic and thermal erosion. The erosion simulation required approximately 4 hours of CPU time on a Silicon Graphics Iris 4D/70 workstation. The uneroded patch shows a good first approximation to an eroded landscape with a central stream bed. The uneroded patch was created by weighting the addition of always positive noise values by the distance d of the point from the diagonal of the patch, which diagonal is also "higher" at the far end. The stream bed is made non-linear by the addition of $1/f^3$ noise to the distance d. In this simulation, $K_c = 5.0$, $K_d = 0.1$, and $K_s = 0.3$. Note the gullys, confluences, and alluvial fans that have appeared in the eroded patch, which is rendered as a dry wash, i.e., without water present.

The distribution of rainfall on landscapes in nature is strongly influenced by *adiabatics*, or the behavior of moisture-laden air as it rises and descends in the atmosphere. As air rises, it cools and the relative humidity rises. When the relative humidity exceeds one hundred percent, clouds form; when the clouds become dense, precipitation occurs. Wind blowing over mountains raises air as it passes over the mountains, thus precipitation is much greater at the top and downwind of, mountain peaks. It is easy to include a rough approximation of adiabatic effects in our erosion model by making precipitation a linear function of altitude. This has a significant effect on the erosion patterns produced.

In our use of the hydraulic erosion model, we have simply allowed a fixed amount of rain (approximately one one thousandth of the height of the vertex) to fall at regular intervals (approximately every sixty to one hundred time steps). Mandelbrot and Wallis[13] have pointed out that records of flooding of the Nile river show a $1/f$ noise distribution, i.e., large floods happen with low frequency. Such a noisy distribution in the rainfall would constitute a more realistic simulation of nature; it is probable that it would have a long-term effect on the erosion features created. This is an idea yet to be explored.

4.2. Thermal Weathering

The other erosion process we model is thermal weathering, which is a catch-all term for any process that knocks material loose, which material then falls down to pile up at the bottom of an incline. The thermal weathering process creates talus slopes of uniform angle. Thermal weathering is a kind of relaxation process and is both simple to implement and fast. At each time step $t+1$, we compare the difference between the altitude a_t^v at the previous time step t of each vertex v and its neighbors u to the (global) constant talus angle T. If the computed slope is greater than the talus angle, we then move some fixed percentage c_t of the difference onto the neighbor.

$$a_{t+1}^u = \begin{cases} a_t^v - a_t^u > T: & a_t^u + c_t(a_t^v - a_t^u - T) \\ a_t^v - a_t^u \le T: & a_t^u \end{cases}$$

With care taken to assure the equitable distribution of talus material to all neighboring vertices, the slope to the neighboring vertices asymptotically approaches the talus angle.

Plates 7 and 8 show a patch created with non-uniform lacunarity before and after slumping or thermal weathering. This process has created a rough approximation of sand dunes.

4.3. Discussion of Erosion Models

An interesting extension would be to account for the differing hardnesses of bedrock, silt, and talus. This can be accomplished by adding appropriate fields to the vertex data structure and making the simplifying assumption that silt lies on top of talus, which in turn lies on top of bedrock. Another simple extension will be to add strata of differing hardnesses to the bedrock, as is commonly seen in sedimentary rock. This can be accomplished through the use of a Perlin texture (as in Plate 13) or more efficiently by table lookup of a vertically perturbed one-dimensional array of hardnesses. Finally, it would be desirable to render the water flowing on the landscape. To do this realistically represents a major challenge and will be the aim of future research.

5. RAY TRACING HEIGHT FIELDS

Having created eroded fractal height fields, we now need to render them quickly and realistically. We present a fast ray tracing technique for height fields, termed *grid tracing*.[22]

The basic idea is this: A two-dimensional array of altitude values is traversed in an arbitrary direction by a ray, through the use of a modified *DDA (Digital Differential Analyzer)* algorithm. The array is thought of as composing a *grid* of small square *cells* corresponding to the pixels being illuminated by a DDA algorithm. Each cell has associated with it the height field altitudes at the four corners of the cell. As the ray traverses the array of cells, the altitude of the ray at each cell is compared to the four altitudes associated with the cell. Ray/surface intersection tests need only be performed when the altitude span of the ray over the extent of the cell intersects the interval of altitudes defined by the lowest and highest of the four altitudes associated with the cell. For a ray traveling **above** the surface, the condition can be stated:

$$min(ray_{z_{near}}, ray_{z_{far}}) \le max(h_{i,j}, h_{i,j+1}, h_{i+1,j}, h_{i+1,j+1}) \quad (2)$$

where $ray_{z_{[near,far]}}$ represents the altitudes of the end points of the ray segment within the cell and the $h_{m,n}$ represent the altitudes of the height field H at the four corners of the i,j^{th} cell. As the surface of the terrain within a cell can be represented by exactly two triangles which split the square diagonally, the ray/surface intersection test consists of two ray/triangle intersection tests. These tests are greatly simplified by the shape and orientation of the triangles. Only rays grazing past the surface will fail the intersection tests; most rays will incline directly into the surface at the first cell where surface intersection is tested. Note that the calculation in expression (2) can be simplified by creating an auxiliary array of values for each cell which are equal to the right hand side of (2).

Advantages of this algorithm are manifold. First, only the height field need be calculated and stored as the model. The actual polygon descriptions (i.e., the plane equations of the triangles) need only be calculated when an intersection test is performed. This can save both time and space in the creation of the terrain model, as polygons which are not visible in the rendering are never fully described. Second, the grid traversal can be accomplished with the use of a modified Bresenham DDA[27] algorithm. The Bresenham algorithm is a highly optimized, fast algorithm which uses only floating point addition* in determining the height of the ray and the next cell along the path of the ray. Third, the algorithm is general. Any two-dimensional array of scalar data (i.e., an image) may be interpreted as a height field and ray traced with this algorithm. Fourth, the algorithm performs ray/object intersections in $O(\sqrt{k})$ time with a small constant multiplier, where k is the number of cells in the grid.

Furthermore, the grid tracing algorithm can be made hierarchical and, for fractal terrains which are not post-processed as by an erosion simulation, procedural. The hierarchy is created by having each cell contain another grid rather than two triangles. Each altitude associated with the cell is then equal to the height of the bounding box of the subgrid. Hierarchical decomposition is desirable for ray tracing large grids, as implementation as a hierarchy of $n \times n$ grids (an n^2 tree) reduces the time complexity to $O(\log_n \sqrt{k})$. In renderings of a portion of a 1217 x 1217 grid, grid traversal time was reduced by approximately 50% with a 16^2 tree implementation. Plate 10 is such a rendering, and at one ray per pixel at 1280 x 1024 resolution, it required less than one half of an hour of CPU time times eight CPUs using a parallel ray tracing scheme[22] on an Encore Multimax computer, under the C-Linda parallel programming language.[1]

Grid tracing of procedural terrain models enables adaptive level of detail and efficient memory usage in that no unnecessary height field values need be computed. In the procedural implementation, height field values are calculated and stored when a cell is first traversed by a ray. Measuring divergence of *primary* (first-generation) rays at the far end of a cell determines whether a cell needs to be decomposed into a subgrid; such divergence is a linear function of the distance the ray has traveled. This simple metric breaks down in the face of the bane of ray tracing: rays reflected and refracted by curved or bump-mapped surfaces.

Grid tracing is a memory-bound algorithm. While the grid can be traversed at great speed, page faults generated when a grid is too large to fit into main memory severely compromise the speed of a grid tracing program. A 1000 x 1000 grid com-

---

* The best-known Bresenham DDA is an integer algorithm. The version used for our purposes is not the integer Bresenham DDA, but rather a slightly less optimal floating point version. A simpler alternate scheme could use an ordinary integer DDA for the traversal, but would need to check one cell to either side of the ray path for possible intersections due to imprecision in tracking that path.

posed of two byte integer altitude values comprises two mega-bytes of memory. If one elects to store the plane equation data for triangles when it is calculated for ray/surface intersection tests, the memory usage increases steadily as the image is rendered unless active memory management is implemented. We have found it beneficial to store a small number of triangles in a cache organized as a linked list of triangle data stored in most-recently-used-first order.

Note that height fields tessellated by equilateral triangles, as opposed to right triangles, can be ray traced just as efficiently. A right triangle can be transformed into an equilateral triangle with a skewing and a scaling transformation such as $x = x + y/2$ and $y = y \sqrt{3}/2$. The inverse of the product of these transformations can be applied to the ray, whereupon the ray can traverse a rectilinear grid in "grid space". This is useful because an equilateral triangle tessellation of a surface requires less stored data per unit area of surface and is, upon rendering, often more aesthetically appealing than a right triangle tessellation.

6. CONCLUSION

We have demonstrated a new method for creating fractal terrains which gives a first approximation to erosion features, at terrain generation time. As opposed to previous methods, noise synthesis allows local control over frequencies comprising the surface. We have also suggested two effective erosion algorithms which simulate hydraulic erosion by flowing water and thermal weathering, which chips away steep inclines and forms talus slopes. The hydraulic erosion simulation requires a significant amount of computer time to create extensive, deep drainage systems, while the thermal weathering can be quite fast. Finally, we have described a ray tracing algorithm for height fields which is efficient enough to allow the ray tracing of detailed terrains in a reasonable amount of computer time.

Acknowledgements

The work of Ken Musgrave and Craig Kolb was accomplished in Benoit Mandelbrot's project at Yale University as a part of our ongoing quest for more beautiful and realistic forgeries of nature, using the latest results in fractal geometry. We are deeply grateful to Benoit Mandelbrot, and to Dietmar Saupe, for their comments, corrections, and inspiration in this endeavor. The work at Yale was funded, in part, through the Office of Naval Research contract N00014-88-K-0217, and development was carried out with the invaluable assistance of Nick Carriero, Rob Bjornson, and David Gelerenter of the Yale Computer Science Department, using C-Linda[1] on the Encore Multimax. That system is supported, in part, by NSF grants DCR-8601920 and DCR-8657615. All the authors, particularly Rob Mace, are indebted to Silicon Graphics, Inc. for their generous support.

References

1. Ahuja, S., N. Carriero, and D. Gelerenter, "Linda and Friends," *IEEE Computer*, August, 1986.

2. Bouville, Christian, "Bounding Ellipsoids for Ray-Fractal Intersection," *Computer Graphics*, vol. 19, no. 3, pp. 45-52, July 1985.

3. Cook, Robert L., "Shade Trees," *Computer Graphics*, vol. 18, no. 3, pp. 223-230, July, 1984.

4. Fournier, Alain, D. Fussell, and L. Carpenter, "Computer Rendering of Stochastic Models," *Communications of the ACM*, vol. 25, pp. 371-384, 1982.

5. Fujimoto, A., T. Tanaka, and K. Iwata, "ARTS: Accelerated Ray Tracing System," *IEEE Computer Graphics and Applications*, vol. 6, no. 4, pp. 16-26, April, 1986.

6. Gardner, Geoffrey Y., "Visual Simulation of Clouds," *Computer Graphics*, vol. 19, no. 3, pp. 297-303, July, 1985.

7. Gardner, Geoffrey Y., *Functional Modelling (SIGGRAPH course notes)*, Atlanta, 1988.

8. Jurgens, H., Dietmar Saupe (eds.), and Dietmar Saupe, "Point Evaluation of Multi-Variable Random Fractals," *Visualisierung in Mathematik und Naturissenschaft - Bremer Computergraphik Tage 1988*, Springer-Verlag, Heidelberg, 1989.

9. Kajiya, James T., "New Techniques for Ray Tracing Procedurally Defined Objects," *Computer Graphics*, vol. 17, no. 3, July, 1983.

10. Kajiya, James T., "New Techniques for Ray Tracing Procedurally Defined Objects," *Transactions on Graphics*, vol. 2, no. 3, pp. 161-181, July, 1983.

11. Kelley, Alex D., M. C. Malin, and G. M. Nielson, "Terrain Simulation Using a Model of Stream Erosion," *Computer Graphics*, vol. 22, no. 4, pp. 263-268, August, 1988.

12. Lewis, J. P., "Generalized Stochastic Subdivision," *ACM Transactions on Graphics*, vol. 6, no. 3, pp. 167-190, July, 1987.

13. Mandelbrot, Benoit B. and J. R. Wallis, "Some Long-Run Properties of the Geophysical Records," *Water Resources Research 5*, pp. 321-340, 1969.

14. Mandelbrot, Benoit B., "Stochastic Models for the Earth's Relief, the Shape and the Fractal Dimension of the Coastlines, and the Number-Area Rule for Islands," *Proceedings of the National Academy of Sciences (USA)*, vol. 72, pp. 3825-3828, 1975.

15. Mandelbrot, Benoit B., *The Fractal Geometry of Nature*, W. H. Freeman and Co., New York, 1982.

16. Mandelbrot, Benoit B., "Comment on Computer Rendering of Stochastic Models," *Communications of the ACM*, vol. 25, no. 8, pp. 581-583, 1982.

17. Mandelbrot, Benoit B., *personal communications*, 1988.

18. Mastin, Gary A., P. A. Watterberg, and J. F. Mareda, "Fourier Synthesis of Ocean Waves," *IEEE Computer Graphics and Applications*, vol. 7, no. 3, pp. 16-23, March, 1987.

19. Miller, Gavin S. P., "The Definition and Rendering of Terrain Maps," *Computer Graphics*, vol. 20, no. 4, pp. 39-48, 1986.

20. Miller, Gavin S. P., *personal communications*, 1988.

21. Musgrave, F. Kenton, Craig E. Kolb, and B. B. Mandelbrot, *A Survey of Terrain Synthesis Techniques*, to appear.

22. Musgrave, F. Kenton, "Grid Tracing: Fast Ray Tracing for Height Fields," *Yale Dept. of Computer Science Research Report RR-639*, July 1988.

23. Musgrave, F. Kenton and B. B. Mandelbrot, "About the Cover," *IEEE Computer Graphics and Applications*, vol. 9, no. 1, January, 1989.

24. Musgrave, F. Kenton, "Prisms and Rainbows: a Dispersion Model for Computer Graphics," *Proceedings of the Graphics Interface '89 - Vision Interface '89*, London, Canada, June, 1989.

25. Peitgen, H. O. and Dietmar Saupe (eds.), *The Science of Fractal Images*, Springer-Verlag, New York, 1988.

26. Perlin, Ken, "An Image Synthesizer," *Computer Graphics*, vol. 19, no. 3, pp. 287-296, July, 1985.

27. Rogers, D. F., *Procedural Elements for Computer Graphics,* Mc Graw Hill, New York, 1985.

28. Voss, Richard F., *Random Fractal Forgeries,* Springer-Verlag, Berlin, 1985. (in Fundamental Algorithms for Computer Graphics, R. A. Earnshaw, ed.)

Plates 1a and 1b.

Plate 2.

Plate 3.

Plate 4.

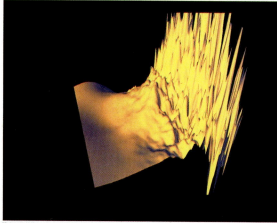

Plate 5.

Plate 6.

Plates 2 through 9 were rendered in real-time on a Silicon Graphics Iris 4D/70 GT workstation. No texture maps have been used.

Plate 7.

Plate 8.

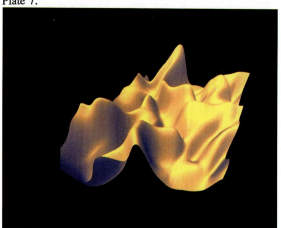

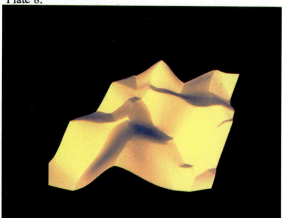

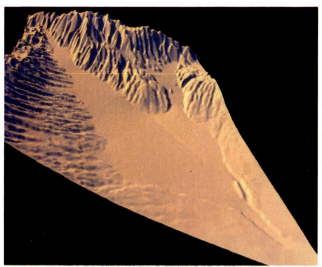

Plate 9. The fractal patch of plate 2 after 2000 time steps of hydraulic erosion and thermal weathering. In this simulation, $K_c = 5.0$, $K_d = 0.1$, $K_s = 0.3$, and $c_t = 0.001$. "Rain" was deposited on each vertex every 65 timesteps in an amount equal to $.001a_t^v$.

Plate 10. A terrain-generation-time erosion model with global drainage system, as described by Mandelbrot.[1] This is a detail of a 1217 x 1217 height field.

Plate 11. "Spirit Lake" is an example of modulation of crossover scale with altitude. High frequency detail is generated with a procedural texture map; triangles tessellating the height field are visible near the peak. The physical rainbow model is from Musgrave.[2]

Plate 12. "Carolina" is a detail of a 100 x 100 height field; note the large triangle size. The series of ridges is a result of a scaling the terrain generation function to compress the terrain along the line of sight. Crossover scale is modulated with altitude.

Plate 13. "Lethe" is a detail of a 407 x 407 height field. Note the procedural texture map simulating sedimentary rock strata. The water is a flat plane with a procedural $1/f^3$ noise bump map.

From Splines to Fractals

Richard Szeliski[†] and Demetri Terzopoulos[‡]

[†]Digital Equipment Corp., Cambridge Research Lab, One Kendall Square, Bldg. 700, Cambridge, MA 02139

[‡]Schlumberger Laboratory for Computer Science, P.O. Box 200015, Austin, TX 78720

Abstract

Deterministic splines and stochastic fractals are complementary techniques for generating free-form shapes. Splines are easily constrained and well suited to modeling smooth, man-made objects. Fractals, while difficult to constrain, are suitable for generating various irregular shapes found in nature. This paper develops *constrained fractals*, a hybrid of splines and fractals which intimately combines their complementary features. This novel shape synthesis technique stems from a formal connection between fractals and generalized energy-minimizing splines which may be derived through Fourier analysis. A physical interpretation of constrained fractal generation is to drive a spline subject to constraints with modulated white noise, letting the spline diffuse the noise into the desired fractal spectrum as it settles into equilibrium. We use constrained fractals to synthesize realistic terrain models from sparse elevation data.

Keywords: Fractals, Splines, Constraints, Scattered Data Interpolation, Digital Terrain Models, Physically Based Modeling, Deformable Models

CR Categories: I.3.5—Object Modeling (Curve, surface, solid, and object representations); I.3.7—Three-Dimensional Graphics and Realism; G.1.1—Interpolation (Spline interpolation); G.1.2—Approximation (Spline approximation)

1 Introduction

Over the years, computer graphics researchers have developed numerous mathematical models capable of generating free-form shapes. Such models come in two varieties—deterministic and stochastic. Spline models, which are deterministic, have established themselves as a convenient and powerful technique for modeling smooth, man-made shapes, such as teapots [2]. By contrast, fractal models have become popular for recreating a wide variety of the shapes found in nature [10]. Most fractal models feature a stochastic component, making them well suited to generating nonsmooth, irregular shapes, such as mountainous terrain [4]. In this paper, we develop a model of shape which combines deterministic splines and stochastic fractals to inherit their complementary features.

1.1 Constraints versus Natural Detail

Splines typically offer precise shape control but they lack natural looking detail. In this paper, we employ a class of variational splines whose positions, slopes, and curvatures are locally controllable though external shape constraints. Furthermore, these variational models can become piecewise smooth, producing local discontinuities such as fractures and creases. However, these splines provide no mechanism for modeling the fine-scale texture of many natural shapes.

By contrast, stochastic fractals provide realistic detail for modeling a wide variety of complex natural phenomena, but they offer little control over shape. This deficiency is most acute in the Fourier based methods [10] which can produce shapes with true fractal distributions but cannot be controlled locally. A common approach for obtaining some control is to first triangulate a given set of points, then add fractal texture by recursively subdividing and randomly perturbing the subtriangles [4]. Unfortunately, this approach produces annoying visual artifacts because the spatial statistics are nonstationary across the original triangle boundaries. Moreover, it makes difficult the imposition of more complicated constraints.

Conventional free-form shape synthesis techniques are therefore inadequate for many graphics applications—splines provide insufficient detail, while fractals provide insufficient shape control. This paper proposes *constrained fractals*, a new shape modeling technique which simultaneously provides both detail and control.

1.2 Overview

Section 2 gives an intuitive explanation of the constrained fractal technique, and discusses fractal terrain generation which serves as our main application area. Section 3 presents the controlled-continuity splines which form the deterministic component of constrained fractals. The main text develops these variational splines in a single variable, and multivariate extensions are relegated to an appendix. We describe how to discretize the spline energy expressions using finite elements, and present examples of spline surfaces constrained by scattered data. Section 4 explains how to associate a probability distribution with variational splines through the Boltzmann distribution, and shows that samples from this distribution have fractal statistics. Section 5 introduces a multiresolution stochastic relaxation algorithm for sampling the Boltzmann distribution to obtain constrained fractals. Because of length limitations, we present a full description of our algorithm in a companion paper [14]. In Section 6 we demonstrate the application of this algorithm, showing how to include local control over smoothness. Finally, Section 7 closes with some conclusions about our work.

2 The Constrained Fractal Approach

2.1 Deterministic Component

A constrained fractal is a physically-based model which makes use of the energy minimization principles underlying variational splines [1].[1] These principles characterize spline curves and surfaces as the "smoothest" shapes consistent with the given constraints; this gives rise to an interesting relationship connecting variational splines to spatial smoothing filters (see [16,13,12]). What is surprising, however, is that "spline smoothing filters" can provide the spatial frequency characteristics of fractal fields [13].

To exploit the filtering property of variational splines in generating constrained fractals, we employ a general class of multivariate spline models called controlled-continuity splines [16]. These splines allow us to create the desired shape by applying local constraints (say, on position and/or orientation) at arbitrary points. Physically, the constraints are interpretable as external forces which shape the spline [15]. Controlled-continuity splines also afford local control over smoothness, which permits us to introduce jump or crease discontinuities at arbitrary points on the spline to yield a piecewise smooth shape.

2.2 Stochastic Component

To introduce fractal detail into the shape, we go one step further. As it minimizes its deformation energy under the influence of constraint forces, we subject the controlled-continuity spline to white noise. Visualize this physically as continually bombarding the spline shape with point masses impacting at random velocities. The impulses imparted by these projectiles randomly perturb the spline as it "relaxes" into a stochastic equilibrium (characterized by minimal time-averaged energy under the random perturbations). During relaxation the spline diffuses the effects of the perturbations spatially, eventually shaping the flat spectrum of the perturbations into the desired fractal spectrum.[2]

2.3 Bayesian Interpretation

We can also motivate our approach by making use of another interesting relationship, first developed in statistical mechanics, which connects energy functionals to random fields via the Boltzmann probability distribution [7]. The relaxing controlled-continuity spline can therefore be interpreted as a "Gibbs Sampler" which draws sample shapes from a Boltzmann distributed ensemble that has fractal statistics due to the spline's internal energy [13]. The constrained fractal is thus a typical sample from the *posterior* distribution, i.e., a random fractal sample consistent with the observations which are provided by the constraints.

2.4 Algorithmic Features

The stochastic equilibrium of the spline is computable by a stochastic relaxation algorithm implemented as a local, iterative, numerical process. We obtain such an algorithm by locally discretizing the continuous spline energy functionals using regular finite difference or finite element grids.[3]

Each relaxation step replaces the values of nodal variables on the grid by a noise-perturbed weighted combination of neighboring variable values, thereby propagating information from node to node across the grid. Because of the local nature of the communication, a large number of iterations may be necessary for the stochastic relaxation process to converge on large, fine grids. If the variational spline problem is discretized on a sequence of successively coarser grids, however, the convergence rates improve dramatically [15]. In this paper we propose a multiresolution stochastic relaxation process which computes the interpolated fractal shape efficiently. The multiresolution process is readily parallelizable, and is therefore suitable for massively parallel computers.

2.5 Fractal Terrain Generation

As an application of our constrained fractal technique, we concentrate on the problem of terrain generation for the synthesis of realistic outdoor scenes.

Fractal terrain generation [10] has traditionally been approached using a variety of stochastic subdivision techniques. Fournier *et al.* [4] employ a technique called random midpoint displacement which creates a tessellated surface by recursively subdividing triangles. The height of each newly created interior point is randomly perturbed away from its original interpolated value, and the magnitude of each perturbation is related to the level of the subdivision. Varying this relationship results in fractals of arbitrary degree. Voss [19] uses successive random additions, which differs in that all of the points are randomly perturbed at each subdivision step (not just the newly cre-

---

[1] Variational splines are simple instances of "deformable models" (see [18,17]); hence, the constrained fractal technique extends to this general class of physically-based models as well.

[2] As Lewis [9] has argued, the spectrum of the random process need not be truly fractal in order to provide realistic detail. We use the term "fractal" to describe a random function whose spectrum we can control.

[3] Regular ("fine-grained") grids are independent of the spatial organization of the data and lead to algorithms that are readily implementable on massively parallel computational structures. These properties account for the prevalent use of regular grids in the computer vision community, as does the massive parallelism of the early human visual system [8]. Our use of regular grids stands in contrast to conventional techniques for interpolating sparse data in computer graphics applications. The latter usually involve irregularly triangulating the domain in a data dependent fashion [5] (techniques have also been developed for the simpler case of interpolating "gridded" data [3]).

ated ones). Lewis [9] proposes generalized stochastic subdivision, a refinement of random midpoint displacement. Instead of displacing each midpoint independently, he adds correlated Gaussian noise, which alleviates the artifacts due to spatially nonstationary statistics across triangles that are sometimes evident with the preceeding methods.

Unlike the above methods, our multiresolution stochastic relaxation algorithm can easily accommodate arbitrary constraints as additional terms in its energy minimization principle. The solution is guaranteed to have spatially stationary statistics, so long as we perform a sufficient number of iterations on the fine level (in practice, this number proves to be quite low).

To apply our constrained fractal technique to terrain modeling, we may begin either with synthetic elevation landmarks selected by a user or with true elevation data acquired in surveys or through aerial photogrammetry. The first step is to create the terrain model from these typically sparse elevation data (e.g., isoelevation contours) by interpolating a dense digital elevation map in the form of a gridded, single-valued surface $f(u, v)$. To do so, we supply these data to our algorithm as elevation constraints d_i, letting the controlled-continuity spline serve as an interpolant whose parameters afford local control over the continuity of the surface and the tightness of fit to the data. At the same time, the stochastic mechanism invents fractal detail that enhances the realism of the interpolated terrain model. Thus our technique solves the surface fitting and detail generation problems simultaneously.

3 Variational Splines

Variational splines are characterized by the minima of energy functionals. To construct a variational spline, we first define a deformation energy functional $\mathcal{E}$ over a suitable class of functions, and then compute a function which minimizes $\mathcal{E}$. In the univariate case, the minimizing functions approximate the steady-state deformations of elastic strings and beams subjected to applied forces.

Suppose that we stretch an elastic string horizontally along the x axis. Let $x = u$ denote the coordinate along the string and let $y = f(u)$ give the shape of the string as a function of u. The (linearized) deformation energy associated with f is given by

$$\mathcal{E}(f) = \frac{1}{2} \int f_u^2 \, du,$$

where f_u indicates differentiation with respect to u.

Next, suppose that $f(u)$ gives the shape of an elastic beam. The (linearized) deformation energy of the beam is

$$\mathcal{E}(f) = \frac{1}{2} \int f_{uu}^2 \, du,$$

where f_{uu} denotes the second derivative. Note that the minimum of this expression characterizes the common cubic spline [1]. Because the string has tension, it defines a continuous curve f. Since the beam resists bending, it defines a smoother curve f that is not merely continuous in position but also in tangent.

3.1 Controlled-Continuity Splines

We can blend the above energies to create a model that combines the properties of the string and beam. Introducing nonnegative rigidity $\rho(u)$ and tension $[1 - \tau(u)]$ parameter functions that take values between 0 and 1 inclusively, the hybrid energy functional is

$$\mathcal{E}_{\mathrm{p}}(f) = \frac{1}{2} \int \rho(u)\{[1 - \tau(u)]f_u^2 + \tau(u)f_{uu}^2\} \, du. \quad (1)$$

Note, that if we restrict $\rho(u) = \rho$ and $\tau(u) = \tau$ to be global constants independent of u, the above spline reduces to the globally continuous "spline under tension" proposed by Schweikert [11].

As functions of u, however, $\rho(u)$ and $\tau(u)$ provide local control over the continuity of the curve. Consequently, the function f which minimizes (1) is a *controlled-continuity spline* [16]. In regions of u where $\rho(u) > 0$ and $\tau(u) > 0$, the spline is continuous in both position and tangent, tending towards the string as $\tau(u) \to 0$ and towards the beam as $\tau(u) \to 1$. In regions where $\tau(u) = 0$, the spline is free to have discontinuous tangents (creases), and in regions where $\rho(u) = 0$, the spline is free to have discontinuous positions (fractures).

The univariate controlled-continuity splines generalize to any number of variables, to any embedding space dimensionality, and to arbitrary order of continuity (see Appendix A), thereby providing a unified treatment of curves, surfaces, solids, or higher-dimensional models (in spacetime) [16]. Since in this paper we concentrate on terrain modeling applications, we make use of the bivariate case—surfaces. Appendix A defines controlled-continuity surface splines based on the membrane and plate, the natural bivariate analogues of the string and beam.

3.2 Fitting Data

To formulate the spline fitting problem, we combine the energy functional of the controlled-continuity spline with a data compatibility constraint. In the univariate case, the data is a collection of values $\{p_i\} = \{(u_i, d_i)\}$. A simple data compatibility constraint measures the squared (weighted Euclidean) distance between the data and the spline $f(u)$ using the constraint functional

$$\mathcal{E}_{\mathrm{d}}(f; \{p_i\}) = \frac{1}{2} \sum_i c_i \left(f(u_i) - d_i\right)^2 \quad (2)$$

where the weights c_i are inversely related to the variance of the uncertainty (noise) in the data ($c_i = \sigma_i^{-2}$).[4]

To find the approximating spline, the functionals (1) and (2) are combined to form the energy functional

$$\mathcal{E}(f) = \lambda \mathcal{E}_{\mathrm{p}}(f) + \mathcal{E}_{\mathrm{d}}(f; \{p_i\}), \quad (3)$$

where λ is known as a regularization parameter. This continuous formulation of the variational spline fitting prob-

---

[4]We can handle orientation (slope) data o_i by adding the term $\frac{1}{2} \sum_i c_i \left(f_u(u_i) - o_i\right)^2$ to (2) [16].

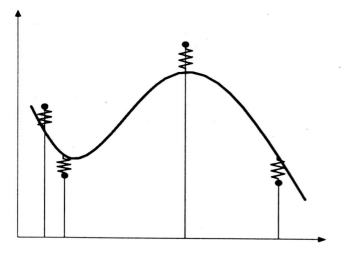

Figure 1: Spline approximation

lem in terms of a functional applies to arbitrarily structured constraint data, whether gridded, contoured, or scattered.

Figure 1 illustrates a physical interpretation of (3) in the univariate case. The first term defines the energy of the spline curve. The second term corresponds to the energy of a collection of zero-length ideal springs (with spring constants c_i) connecting the spline to the data points. The springs apply forces which deflect the spline such that it approximates the data (infinitely stiff springs result in strict interpolation). When (3) is at a minimum, the physical system is at equilibrium, such that the forces exerted by the springs balance the reluctance of the spline to deform.

3.3 Finite Element Discretization

To minimize (3), we apply the finite element method, which provides a systematic approach to the discretization and solution of variational spline problems [15]. We discretize $f(u)$ on a regular "fine grained" mesh of *nodal variables* (see Footnote 1).

When finite element analysis is applied to quadratic functionals such as (1),[5] we obtain a discrete energy function expressible as a quadratic form:

$$E_{\mathrm{p}}(\mathbf{x}) = \frac{1}{2}\mathbf{x}^T \mathbf{A}_{\mathrm{p}} \mathbf{x} \qquad (4)$$

where $\mathbf{x}$ is the vector of nodal variables.[6] The *prior model* matrix $\mathbf{A}_{\mathrm{p}}$ is sparse, having at most 13 entries per row (see [15,12] for details). Similarly, the discrete data constraint in (2) can be written as

$$E_{\mathrm{d}}(\mathbf{x}, \mathbf{d}) = \frac{1}{2}(\mathbf{x} - \tilde{\mathbf{d}})^T \mathbf{A}_{\mathrm{d}} (\mathbf{x} - \tilde{\mathbf{d}}), \qquad (5)$$

---

[5] Actually, (1) is quadratic only if $\rho(u)$ and $\tau(u)$ are fixed functions.

[6] For example, in the univariate case $\mathbf{x} = [f(0), \ldots, f(jh), \ldots, f((M-1)h)]'$, where h is the spacing of a linear M-node mesh.

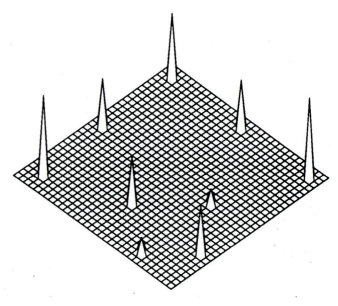

Figure 2: Sparse data points

where $\tilde{\mathbf{d}}$ is a zero-padded vector of data values, and the diagonal matrix $\mathbf{A}_{\mathrm{d}}$ has entries w_i where data points coincide with nodal variables and zeros elsewhere.

Using (4) and (5), we write the combined energy (3) in discrete form as

$$E(\mathbf{x}) = \frac{1}{2}\mathbf{x}^T \mathbf{A}\mathbf{x} - \mathbf{x}^T \mathbf{b} + k \qquad (6)$$

where k is a constant, while

$$\mathbf{A} = \lambda \mathbf{A}_{\mathrm{p}} + \mathbf{A}_{\mathrm{d}} \quad \text{and} \quad \mathbf{b} = \mathbf{A}_{\mathrm{d}}\tilde{\mathbf{d}}.$$

This energy function has a minimum at $\mathbf{x} = \mathbf{x}^*$, the solution to the linear system of algebraic equations

$$\mathbf{A}\mathbf{x} = \mathbf{b}. \qquad (7)$$

In principle, the solution to (7) can be found using either direct or iterative numerical methods. Direct methods are impractical for solving large systems associated with fine meshes because of excessive storage requirements. Alternatively, simple iterative schemes such as Gauss-Seidel relaxation require relatively little storage but can be very slow to converge. We resolve the difficulty using multigrid relaxation, which accelerates convergence by solving the problem at multiple resolution levels [15].

3.4 A Surface Fitting Example

To better visualize the fitting of variational spline models to scattered data, let us consider a small example involving the bivariate controlled-continuity spline model given in Appendix A. Figure 2 shows nine data points. The interpolated thin plate ($\tau = 1$) solution on the finite element mesh is shown in Figure 3. Note that a jump discontinuity ($\rho = 0$) has been introduced along the left edge and an orientation discontinuity ($\tau = 0$) along the right edge.

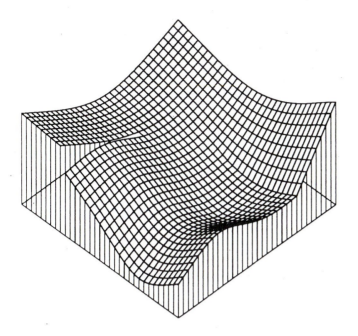

Figure 3: Interpolated piecewise continuous solution

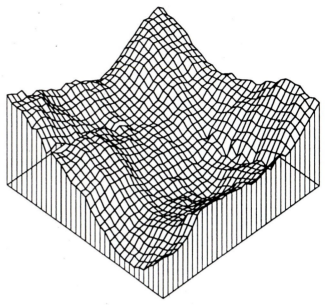

Figure 4: Sample from posterior distribution

4 Converting Energies into Probabilities

The controlled-continuity splines presented in the previous section give us a powerful approach to interpolating (or approximating) data with differing amounts of smoothness. For many graphics applications, however, the resulting shapes have insufficient detail or random texture to look natural. We will now show how to convert our spline energy functions into probability distributions from which we can draw random samples having fractal textures.

The idea of converting an energy function into a probability distribution comes from statistical mechanics. In many stochastic physical systems, the probability of a particular configuration is inversely related to its energy. Many different equations for transforming energies to probabilities are possible. For our application, we will use the Boltzmann distribution, where the energy of a state $E(\mathbf{x})$ is related to its probability $p(\mathbf{x})$ through a negative exponential:

$$p(\mathbf{x}) = \frac{1}{Z} \exp\left(-E_{\mathrm{p}}(\mathbf{x})/T\right) \qquad (8)$$

(the partition function Z is used to normalize the distribution). The temperature parameter T controls how "peaked" the distribution is with respect to its low-energy states. The Boltzmann distribution has properties which make it useful for modeling random fields [7]. For our purposes, the most important of these is that multiplicative interactions between probability distributions can be converted into additive interactions between energies. This becomes particularly useful when we look at fractal generation as sampling from a constrained (conditional) distribution using the Gibbs Sampler algorithm to be presented in the next section.

Interestingly, we can use the energy of the controlled-continuity spline model to define a Boltzmann distribution with a fractal spectrum. A Fourier analysis of this prior model reveals that the resulting distribution is correlated Gaussian noise with a fractal spectrum (i.e., self-affine over scale) for the membrane or string ($\tau = 0$) and for the thin plate or beam ($\tau = 1$) [13] (see Appendix B).

When data $\mathbf{d}$ constrain the fractal shape, we may obtain it by sampling from the conditional distribution $p(\mathbf{x}|\mathbf{d})$. This posterior distribution can be calculated using Bayes' rule

$$p(\mathbf{x}|\mathbf{d}) = \frac{p(\mathbf{d}|\mathbf{x})\, p(\mathbf{x})}{p(\mathbf{d})} \qquad (9)$$

where the distribution $p(\mathbf{d})$ is a normalization factor. The conditional distribution $p(\mathbf{d}|\mathbf{x})$ can be derived from a measurement model which describes how the data $\mathbf{d}$ was acquired from a sample shape $\mathbf{x}$ [12].

For a linear measurement model, the negative logarithm of the posterior distribution $p(\mathbf{x}|\mathbf{d})$ can be written as the sum of two energy functions

$$-\log p(\mathbf{x}|\mathbf{d}) = E(\mathbf{x}; \mathbf{d}) = E_{\mathrm{p}}(\mathbf{x}) + E_{\mathrm{d}}(\mathbf{x}, \mathbf{d}); \qquad (10)$$

i.e., the posterior distribution is itself a Boltzmann distribution. We thus have a correspondence between our Bayesian models and the constraints used in the previous section to fit the generalized spline. The measurement model $p(\mathbf{d}|\mathbf{x})$ corresponds to the constraint data. The prior model $p(\mathbf{x})$ corresponds to the controlled-continuity spline. As shown in Appendix B, we can control the spectrum of this prior model through our choice of the order of the spline.

The posterior distribution $p(\mathbf{x}|\mathbf{d})$ thus defines a class of random shapes which are drawn from a family of fractals and which are also consistent with given shape constraints (observations). The most likely sample from this distribution, the *Maximum a Posteriori* (MAP) estimate, corresponds to the minimum energy solution of (7), as shown in Figure 3. A *typical* sample from this distribution is shown in Figure 4. Devising an efficient method for generating such a random sample is the subject of the next section.

5 Multiresolution Stochastic Relaxation

The explicit evaluation of the Boltzmann distribution given in (8) is very difficult because the computation of the partition function Z requires a summation over all possible states. Fortunately, we can generate random samples from this distribution using a simple algorithm known as the Gibbs Sampler [7]. At each step of this iterative algorithm, a new random state is chosen from the Boltzmann distribution corresponding to the local energy function of the variable being updated. This updating rule is guaranteed to convergence to a random sample from the overall distribution (the ensemble is then said to be at thermal equilibrium).

For our quadratic energy function (6), the local energy function for the node x_i (with all other nodes fixed) is

$$E(x_i) = \frac{1}{2}a_{ii}x_i^2 + \left(\sum_{j \in N_i} a_{ij}x_j - b_i\right)x_i + k, \qquad (11)$$

where a_{ij} are the entries of $\mathbf{A}$, and N_i expresses the fact that the a_{ij} are nonzero only for certain neighbors of node i (see [14] for details). When using Gauss-Seidel relaxation, we choose the new node value which minimizes this local energy

$$x_i^+ = \frac{b_i - \sum_{j \in N_i} a_{ij}x_j}{a_{ii}} \qquad (12)$$

(for pure interpolation, we set $x_i^+ = d_i$ at points coincident with data). We can thus rewrite the local energy as

$$E(x_i) = \frac{1}{2}a_{ii}(x_i - x_i^+)^2 + k'. \qquad (13)$$

For the Gibbs Sampler algorithm, we choose the new value for x_i from the local Boltzmann distribution

$$p(x_i) \propto \exp\left(-E(x_i)/T\right) \propto \exp\left(-\frac{1}{2}\frac{(x_i - x_i^+)^2}{T/a_{ii}}\right) \qquad (14)$$

which is a Gaussian with mean equal to the deterministic update value x_i^+ and a variance equal to T/a_{ii}. Thus, the Gibbs Sampler is equivalent to the usual relaxation algorithm with the addition of some locally controlled Gaussian noise at each step. For instance, the sample surface in Figure 4 exhibits the rough (wrinkled) look of fractals. The amount of roughness can be controlled with the "temperature" parameter T.

5.1 Multiresolution Acceleration

Although the above iterative algorithm will eventually achieve stochastic equilibrium, the convergence may be unacceptably slow in practice. To accelerate convergence, we use coarse-to-fine relaxation on a multiresolution pyramid. The problem is first solved on a coarser mesh, and the solution is used as an initial condition for the next finer level.

The coarse-to-fine technique is thus similar to recursive subdivision and successive addition techniques [4,19,9]. Unlike these approaches, however, we do not just add random detail as the resolution is increased. Instead, we use the coarse (low resolution) solution as an initial condition for the stochastic relaxation algorithm. The iterative nature of this algorithm removes the nonstationarities that are present in the interpolated initial condition, and it also allows us to impose constraints at finer resolutions. The disadvantage of this approach is that the coarse level sample may no longer look like a subsampled version of the fine level sample. This lack of "internal consistency" becomes a problem when we wish to generate renderings at a variety of scales [4].

We can avoid this discrepancy either by limiting the number of iterations at the finer levels, or by "freezing" the points derived from the coarse level and only iterating on the new points (which resembles random mid-point displacement). The second approach is usually preferable, since it allows the fine level shape to relax sufficiently so that "creases" or other artifacts are not visible. However, if this freezing procedure occurs at a resolution much coarser than that of the data, the resulting shape will not fit the data as well as it could. A strategy which allows full relaxation until the data resolution is reached and then freezes coarse level points as more detail is added works well in practice. In [14] we present examples of this approach applied to the generation of "zoom sequences" over fractal terrain.

Using a multiresolution pyramid also gives us additional control over the spectrum of the fractal shape. When we use a membrane (string) or thin plate (beam) model in our stochastic relaxation algorithm, the resulting spectrum is fractal, but it is limited to the form

$$S_f(\boldsymbol{\omega}) \propto |\boldsymbol{\omega}|^{-2m},$$

which corresponds to fractal βs of 2 and 4 respectively (Appendix B). The simplest way to approximate an intermediate fractal degree is to use the controlled-continuity spline. If we choose $w_1 = \omega_0^2 w_2$ in (18), we obtain a power spectrum which behaves as $S_u \propto |\boldsymbol{\omega}|^{-3}$ in the vicinity of ω_0. At lower frequencies, the model behaves as a membrane, while at higher frequencies it behaves like a thin plate.

We can extend the range of intermediate fractal behavior by modifying the coarse-to-fine Gibbs Sampler. Instead of implementing the same energy equation at each level, we modify the algorithm so that a different blend of membrane and thin plate is used at each level [14]. Since the relaxation at a given level mostly affects the short wavelength Fourier components, we can use the coarse levels to shape the low frequencies and the fine levels to shape the high frequencies. The effective power spectrum of the resulting interpolator (or random sample) now depends on the number of iterations performed at each level.

An alternative to the Gibbs Sampler algorithm for generating random samples is diffusion [6]. This approach is closer in spirit to the usual forward difference equations used in physically-based modeling [18]. Instead of adding controlled (spatially varying) Gaussian noise to the result of the relaxation step, we add uniform white noise to a procedure which descends along the energy gradient $\nabla E(\mathbf{x})$:

$$\mathbf{x}_{k+1} = \mathbf{x}_k - \Delta t \nabla E(\mathbf{x}_k) + \sqrt{2T\Delta t}\,\mathbf{g}_k, \qquad (15)$$

where $\mathbf{g}_k$ is a random Gaussian vector with unit variance. We can thus think of the fractal generation process as a dynamic system (with internal and external forces ∇E) driven by small-scale uniform noise. The system eventually diffuses into a stochastic equilibrium which reflects the likelihood of each state as a function of its energy. For this diffusion equation to converge to the correct equilibrium distribution, the time step must be very small. In practice, the Gibbs Sampler is preferred, since it attains equilibrium much faster. Nevertheless, the diffusion equation provides an elegant intuitive model for the generation of constrained fractals.

6   Constrained Fractal Examples

The multiresolution algorithm proposed in the previous section can be used to generate a wide variety of constrained fractals. The controlled-continuity spline models used to generate these fractals include parameters which control the appearance of the final shape. In this section, we will employ cartographic data to show how these and the other parameters of the stochastic relaxation algorithm lend flexibility to our method.

We present an example of fitting constrained fractal surfaces to isoelevation contours [5] extracted from a 256×256 digital terrain map. Figure 5 shows the digital terrain map rendered as a Phong-shaded surface. Aside from the addition of the horizontal blue plane to introduce a "sea level," we forego the usual texture mapping and environmental embellishments in this and subsequent images, using instead a uniform surface reflectance to better reveal the features of the synthesized terrain. We subsampled the digital terrain map using 200m elevation contour lines and we input to our algorithm the resulting sparse contour data rendered in Figure 6.

First we illustrate the reconstruction of smooth controlled-continuity spline surfaces to the contours in Figure 6. The result of using membrane reconstruction (equation (16) with $\tau(u,v) = 0$) on these data is shown in Figure 7. Evidently, the membrane is insufficiently smooth because it has C^0 continuity only. It looks like a "tent"

Figure 5: Original digital terrain map

or "soap film" stretched over the contours, and it flattens peaks and valleys. Figure 8 shows the thin plate reconstruction ($\tau(u,v) = 1$). In this case, the surface is perhaps too smooth, producing a large depression that forms the "lake" at the lower right. The thin plate under tension model (intermediate $\rho(u,v)$ and $\tau(u,v)$) appears to yield a good compromise, as shown in Figure 9.

Next, we invoke the noise process in our multiresolution stochastic relaxation algorithm to synthesize fractal-textured terrain which fits the contour data of Figure 6. Figure 10 shows the result of using the thin plate under tension model with a temperature $T = 50$. If we desire a "rougher" looking surface, we can use a higher temperature; for example, $T = 500$ yields the reconstructed surface shown in Figure 11. The roughness of the surface can also be controlled by changing the fractal degree.

The degree of smoothness and the amount of noise can, of course, be controlled locally to generate spatially varying textures and different kinds of terrain. Figure 12 shows an example of the complicated fractal surfaces that can be generated using our multiresolution Gibbs Sampler algorithm. This fractal scene is constrained by some data points defining the peaks of the mountains and the bottom of the "ravine." Note that it also has a crease coinciding with the "ravine" on the upper right side, and a depth discontinuity on the lower right. Four different parameter value combinations are specified for the controlled-continuity spline in each quadrant of the (u,v) domain—a thin plate under tension in the upper quadrant, a membrane in the right quadrant, a thin plate in the left quadrant, and a very stiff thin plate in the lower quadrant.

7   Conclusion

We have proposed constrained fractals, a new free-form shape modeling technique which combines the complementary features of deterministic spline and stochastic fractal models. This combination enables us to synthesize realis-

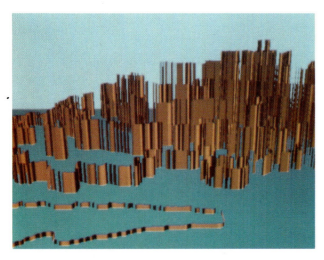

Figure 6: Rendered contour data

Figure 9: Interpolated thin plate under tension surface

Figure 7: Interpolated membrane surface

Figure 10: Fractal surface (thin plate under tension model)

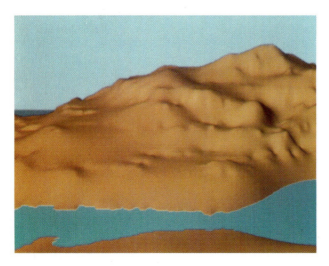

Figure 8: Interpolated thin plate surface

Figure 11: Fractal surface with more noise

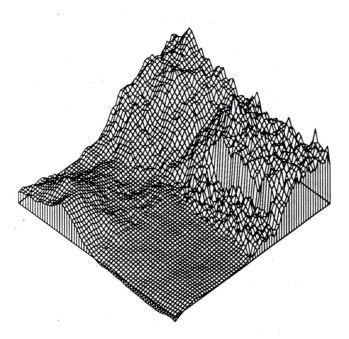

Figure 12: Constrained fractal with spatially varying fractal degree and variance

tically detailed shapes that interpolate data or match prescribed shape constraints. The deterministic component of our technique employs variational splines which can generate piecewise continuous shapes that satisfy sparse, irregular position and orientation constraints. The stochastic component of constrained fractals injects noise into the spline energy minimization procedure in order to imbue the shapes with fractal characteristics. Using the constrained fractal model, we can locally control the continuity of the underlying shape and the amount of random detail added. Such controllability makes our approach extremely flexible.

The constrained fractal computation is performed on a regular, fine-grained mesh using stochastic relaxation; hence, it is amenable to massively parallel implementation. We use a multiresolution pyramid to accelerate the convergence of the relaxation process. This coarse-to-fine procedure bears some similarity to existing recursive subdivision schemes. Unlike these other schemes, however, constrained fractals avoid the artifacts that are introduced during the subdivision process, and they can assimilate constraints at any resolution (instead of merely refining a coarse map).

The ideas developed in this paper are applicable to other deformation energy based models, such as those developed in [18,17]. By augmenting these dynamic models with a closely related method for fractal detailing, we can synthesize a greater variety of realistic, three-dimensional shapes and motions which, in principle, can be readily controlled and constrained. The generality of our approach makes it suitable for a wide range of modeling and computer graphics applications.

Acknowledgements

This research was carried out in part while the authors were at Schlumberger Palo Alto Research, Palo Alto, CA, and while Richard Szeliski was at SRI International, Menlo Park, CA. The digital elevation data was provided courtesy of Jeff Rodriguez of the University of Texas at Austin. The color images were rendered using a modeling testbed system implemented by Kurt Fleischer on Symbolics Lisp Machines.

A Multivariate Spline Interpolation

There exist natural multivariate extensions to the deformation energy functionals given in Section 3 [16]. The bivariate extension of (1) is the "thin plate under tension"

$$
\begin{aligned}
\mathcal{E}_{\mathrm{p}}(f) \;=\; & \frac{1}{2} \iint \rho(u,v)\{[1-\tau(u,v)](f_u^2+f_v^2) \\
& + \tau(u,v)(f_{uu}^2+2f_{uv}^2+f_{vv}^2)\}\,du\,dv, \quad (16)
\end{aligned}
$$

where, the $(f_u^2+f_v^2)$ gives the stretching energy density of a membrane, while the $(f_{uu}^2+2f_{uv}^2+f_{vv}^2)$ term gives the bending energy density of a thin plate. As in the univariate case, the rigidity and tension functions can be used to introduce discontinuities in position and orientation. The bivariate extension of the data compatibility constraint (2) is

$$
\mathcal{E}_{\mathrm{d}}(f; \{p_i\}) = \frac{1}{2}\sum_i c_i \left(f(u_i,v_i)-d_i\right)^2. \quad (17)
$$

The functional (16) is a second-order instance of the general d-variate, p-order controlled-continuity spline model

$$
\mathcal{E}_{\mathrm{p}}(f) = \frac{1}{2}\sum_{m=0}^{p}\int w_m(\mathbf{u})\sum_{j_1+\cdots+j_d=m}\frac{m!}{j_1!\cdots j_d!}\left|\frac{\partial^m f(\mathbf{u})}{\partial u_1^{j_1}\cdots\partial u_d^{j_d}}\right|^2 d\mathbf{u} \tag{18}
$$

where $\mathbf{u}$ is the d-dimensional domain of f. This more general formulation allows us to specify interpolators of arbitrary smoothness. A generalized version of the data compatibility term is

$$
\mathcal{E}_d = \frac{1}{2}\int c(\mathbf{u})|f(\mathbf{u})-d(\mathbf{u})|^2 d\mathbf{u} \tag{19}
$$

where $d(\mathbf{u})$ and $c(\mathbf{u})$ are now continuous functions.

B Fractal Nature of Prior Model

By taking the Fourier transform of the function $f(\mathbf{u})$ and expressing the energy equations in the frequency domain, we can analyze the filtering behavior and the spectral characteristics of the spline model.

Using Rayleigh's energy theorem we can rewrite $\mathcal{E}_p(f)$ in terms of the Fourier transform $F(\omega) = \mathcal{F}\{f(\mathbf{u})\}$ to obtain the new energy function $\mathcal{E}'_p(F)$. Using the general form in (18) with the simplifying assumption that the

weighting functions are constant, $w_m(\mathbf{u}) = w_m$,[7] we obtain

$$\mathcal{E}'_p(F) = \frac{1}{2} \int |G(\boldsymbol{\omega})|^2 |F(\boldsymbol{\omega})|^2 d\boldsymbol{\omega} \qquad (20)$$

where

$$|G(\boldsymbol{\omega})|^2 = \sum_{m=0}^{p} w_m |\boldsymbol{\omega}|^{2m}. \qquad (21)$$

For the membrane interpolator, $|G(\boldsymbol{\omega})|^2 \propto |\boldsymbol{\omega}|^2$ and for the thin plate model, $|G(\boldsymbol{\omega})|^2 \propto |\boldsymbol{\omega}|^4$.

We note that since the Fourier transform is a linear operation, if $f(\mathbf{u})$ is a random variable with a Boltzmann distribution with energy $\mathcal{E}_p(f)$, then $F(\boldsymbol{\omega})$ is a random variable with a Boltzmann distribution with energy $\mathcal{E}'_p(F)$. Thus, $p(F)$ is proportional to $\exp\left(-\frac{1}{2} \int |G(\boldsymbol{\omega})|^2 |F(\boldsymbol{\omega})|^2 d\boldsymbol{\omega}\right)$ from which we see that the probability distribution at any frequency $\boldsymbol{\omega}$ is

$$p(F(\boldsymbol{\omega})) \propto \exp\left(-\frac{1}{2} |G(\boldsymbol{\omega})|^2 |F(\boldsymbol{\omega})|^2\right).$$

Therefore, $F(\boldsymbol{\omega})$ is a random Gaussian variable with variance $|G(\boldsymbol{\omega})|^{-2}$, and the signal $f(\mathbf{u})$ is correlated Gaussian noise with a spectral distribution

$$S_f(\boldsymbol{\omega}) = |G(\boldsymbol{\omega})|^{-2}. \qquad (22)$$

From this analysis, we can conclude that using a controlled-continuity spline is equivalent to using a correlated Gaussian field as the Bayesian prior. The spectral characteristics of this Gaussian field are determined by the choice of spline parameters. For the membrane and the thin plate models, we have

$$S_{\text{membrane}}(\boldsymbol{\omega}) \propto |\boldsymbol{\omega}|^{-2} \qquad (23)$$

and

$$S_{\text{thin-plate}}(\boldsymbol{\omega}) \propto |\boldsymbol{\omega}|^{-4}. \qquad (24)$$

These equations are interesting because they correspond in form to the spectra of Brownian fractals, which can be characterized by the power law

$$S_v(\omega) \propto \omega^{-\beta}. \qquad (25)$$

This spectral density characterizes a fractal Brownian function $v_H(u)$ with $2H = \beta - E$, whose fractal dimension is $D = E + 1 - H$ (where E is the dimension of the Euclidean space) [19]. Comparing (23) or (24) to (25), we can conclude that a random sample drawn from a Boltzmann distribution constructed using the energy model of a membrane or a thin plate is indeed fractal [13].

---

[7] While this assumption does not strictly apply to general piecewise continuous interpolation, it provides an approximation to its local behavior away from boundaries and discontinuities.

References

[1] J. H. Ahlberg, E. N. Nilson, and J. L. Walsh. *The Theory of Splines and their Applications*. Academic Press, New York, 1967.

[2] R. H. Bartels, J. C. Beatty, and B. A. Barsky. *An Introduction to Splines for use in Computer Graphics and Geometric Modeling*. Morgan Kaufmann, Los Altos, CA, 1987.

[3] T. A. Foley. Weighted bicubic spline interpolation to rapidly varying data. *ACM Transactions on Graphics*, 6(1):1–18, January 1987.

[4] A. Fournier, D. Fussel, and L. Carpenter. Computer rendering of stochastic models. *Communications of the ACM*, 25(6):371–384, 1982.

[5] H. Fuchs, Z. M. Kedem, and S. P. Uselton. Optimal surface reconstruction from planar contours. *Communications of the ACM*, 20(10):693–702, October 1977.

[6] D. Geman and Hwang C.-R. Diffusions for global optimization. *SIAM Journal of Control and Optimization*, 24(5):1031–1043, September 1986.

[7] S. Geman and D. Geman. Stochastic relaxation, Gibbs distribution, and the Bayesian restoration of images. *IEEE Transactions on Pattern Analysis and Machine Intelligence*, PAMI-6(6):721–741, November 1984.

[8] B. K. P. Horn. *Robot Vision*. MIT Press, Cambridge, Massachusetts, 1986.

[9] J. P. Lewis. Generalized stochastic subdivision. *ACM Transactions on Graphics*, 6(3):167–190, July 1987.

[10] B. B. Mandelbrot. *The Fractal Geometry of Nature*. W. H. Freeman, San Francisco, 1982.

[11] D. G. Schweikert. An interpolation curve using spline in tension. *J. Math. and Physics*, 45:312–317, 1966.

[12] R. Szeliski. *Bayesian Modeling of Uncertainty in Low-Level Vision*. PhD thesis, Carnegie Mellon University, August 1988.

[13] R. Szeliski. Regularization uses fractal priors. In *AAAI-87: Sixth National Conference on Artificial Intelligence*, pages 749–754, Morgan Kaufmann Publishers, Seattle, Washington, July 1987.

[14] R. Szeliski and D. Terzopoulos. Constrained fractals using stochastic relaxation. Submitted to *ACM Transactions on Graphics*, 1989.

[15] D. Terzopoulos. Multilevel computational processes for visual surface reconstruction. *Computer Vision, Graphics, and Image Processing*, 24:52–96, 1983.

[16] D. Terzopoulos. Regularization of inverse visual problems involving discontinuities. *IEEE Transactions on Pattern Analysis and Machine Intelligence*, PAMI-8(4):413–424, July 1986.

[17] D. Terzopoulos and K. Fleischer. Deformable models. *The Visual Computer*, 4(6):306–331, December, 1988.

[18] D. Terzopoulos, J. Platt, A. Barr, and K. Fleischer. Elastically deformable models. *Computer Graphics (SIGGRAPH'87)*, 21(4):205–214, July 1987.

[19] R. F. Voss. Random fractal forgeries. In R. A. Earnshaw, editor, *Fundamental Algorithms for Computer Graphics*, Springer-Verlag, Berlin, 1985.

HARDWARE ACCELERATION for WINDOW SYSTEMS

Desi Rhoden
Chris Wilcox

Hewlett-Packard Company
Graphics Technology Division
Fort Collins, Colorado, 80525

ABSTRACT

Graphics pipelines are quickly evolving to support multi-tasking workstations. The driving force behind this evolution is the window system, which must provide high performance graphics within multiple windows, while maintaining inter-activity. The virtual graphics system presented by [7] provides a clean solution to the problem of context switching graphics hardware between processes, but does not solve all the problems associated with sharing graphics pipelines.

The primary difficulty in context switching a graphics ac-celerator is the pipeline latency encountered during a pipeline flush. This latency removes the responsiveness and interactivity of the graphics system. As primitives become more complex and pipelines become longer, pipeline latency grows. Hardware solutions are described which further ac-celerate the window system by eliminating the need for pipeline flushing and resynchronization. An overview of the entire system is presented, highlighting the hardware mechanisms which contribute to window acceleration.

CR Category: I.3.1 [Computer Graphics]: Hardware Ar-chitecture - Raster Display Devices.

1. INTRODUCTION

Workstations communicate with their users through an in-terface that allows the user to create and manipulate windows. The primary function of a window system is to provide the user with simultaneous access to multiple processes on the workstation. Each process provides an in-terface to the user through its own area on the display. The result is increased productivity since the user can manage more than one task at a time. An emerging standard for window systems is the X window system [4] developed at MIT. The implementation described in this paper is based on X windows, but the discussion is applicable to any win-dow system.

Each process associated with a window views the workstation resources as if it were the sole owner. This means that resour-ces such as the processing unit, memory, peripherals, and graphics hardware must be shared between these processes in a manner which prevents conflicts. Efficient methods for transparent sharing between processes already exist for con-ventional computing resources; good examples are time-sliced processors and virtual memory systems.

Similar schemes allow processes to share graphics hardware such as framebuffers and graphics accelerators. The goal of our system is to provide a virtual graphics device to each process requesting graphics [7]. Actual implementation of virtual graphics requires extensive hardware support within the graphics system. Many of the difficulties that exist with virtual implementations are a result of the pipeline architec-ture common to most graphics devices. Sharing the graphics accelerator has traditionally required pipeline flushing and resynchronization to maintain the illusion of a virtual device. Unfortunately, these operations are costly and can impact user interactivity, especially when multiple windows are active and context swapping occurs between the host and graphics device. The problem is similar to a virtual memory system thrashing when a majority of CPU time is spent swap-ping pages. To further compound the problem, the current trend of our graphics pipelines is towards higher level, more complex primitives. The complexity of these primitives re-quires more processing time in the pipeline, which increases the penalty for a pipeline flush. Our systems currently sup-port spline primitives that can require several seconds to render, and pipelines can typically contain hundreds of these primitives. Considering the trends toward more complex primitives and longer pipelines, it is clear that alternatives to pipeline flushing are necessary for good system perfor-mance. Allowing the window system to freeze while rendering proceeds can no longer be considered a viable op-tion. Software solutions exist for many of these problems, but are not fast enough. To provide interactivity for a sig-nificant number of windows requires hardware solutions, especially when those windows require the graphics ac-celerator.

©1989   ACM-0-89791-312-4/89/007/0061 $00.75

The goal of the hardware described in this paper is to create a graphics device that can be shared between multiple windows in an efficient manner. Graphics operations within a window should not unduly influence the performance of graphics inside of other windows. To achieve this goal for an unlimited number of windows would require an unconstrained amount of hardware. Since hardware is costly, our solution is to provide acceleration for a reasonable number of windows with a limited amount of resources. The system described in this paper is currently under development. However, many of these features have already been implemented in currently available systems. Each feature will be discussed in detail in the following sections. The key hardware resources provided to accelerate the window system are listed below:

1. *MULTIPLE GRAPHICS CONTEXTS.*
2. *PIPELINE SYNCHRONIZATION.*
3. *PIPELINE BYPASS AND VALVE.*
4. *PIPELINE MARKER CIRCUITRY.*
5. *WINDOW RELATIVE RENDERING.*
6. *WINDOW BLOCK MOVER.*
7. *WINDOW BURST TRANSFER.*
8. *WINDOW COMPARE CIRCUITRY.*
9. *WINDOW CLIPPING PLANES.*
10. *WINDOW DISPLAY MODE PLANES.*
11. *WINDOW OVERLAY PLANES.*
12. *WINDOW OFFSCREEN PLANES.*
13. *MULTIPLE HARDWARE DISPLAY MODES.*
14. *MULTIPLE HARDWARE COLOR MAPS.*
15. *HARDWARE CURSOR SUPPORT.*

The ideal graphics hardware would provide a separate resource for each window, obviously not a practical solution. Instead, enough resources for a reasonable number of windows are added to the system, and these resources are shared in the most efficient manner possible. Window support is integrated into the pipeline at the correct location to minimize interaction of the window system software with graphics rendering. Quick access to window control circuitry is required to allow fast switching, providing the appearance of an unlimited resource. In the sections that follow, the major blocks of our graphics accelerator are presented, with the accompanying modifications for window support.

2 HARDWARE SUPPORT

2.1 System Overview

Support for window acceleration exists in all functional areas of the graphics hardware. Figure 1 shows the graphics accelerator with window support added. The placement of the window support circuitry within the pipeline is especially significant.

A majority of the window support circuitry is placed after the rendering hardware and before the framebuffer. This is the logical location for the window relative and window compare operations, described in a later section. Both of these operations help eliminate the need for pipeline flushing. Another important component is the pipeline bypass, which provides the window system with direct access to various components of the system, including the framebuffer.

2.2 Transform Processor

The transform processor is the core of the accelerated graphics system. On our workstations, the transform processor block is implemented with parallel floating point processors. The transform processors perform many tasks, including graphics context management, matrix transformation calculations, spline tessellation, and lighting model computations. The transform processors also control vector and polygon rendering hardware, implemented with VLSI components as described in [5].

2.2.1 Multiple Graphics Contexts

To accelerate multiple processes the pipeline must be capable of handling multiple contexts [7]. A graphics context consists of the current set of attributes, matrix stack, light sources, shading control, spline basis matrices, and other hardware state information. Our early products supported only a single hardware context, and required the host software to perform all context switching. Software context switching required the host to store context for each active process in virtual memory, writing the context to the device when the process was active, and reading the context back afterwards. Figure 2 shows software context switching.

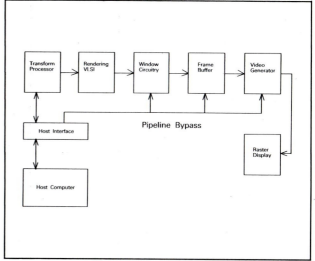

Figure 1 - System Overview

Our current systems store multiple contexts, eliminating the need to constantly pass contexts between the host and graphics device. Our implementation of hardware context switching is shown in Figure 3. The only limitation to the number of contexts stored is the size of memory associated with the transform processor. Our current products, including the system described in this paper, support up to 32 contexts. When all of the hardware contexts are allocated, the least recently used context can be swapped out by the software, using software context switching. Storing contexts in hardware provides high performance context switching, an important step in allowing multiple windows to render simultaneously without degrading performance. Context switches are performed without flushing the pipeline, or interrupting the flow of commands to the device. The hardware context does not contain the window offset, a key factor in the elimination of pipeline flushing.

2.2.2 Pipeline Synchronization

Another area of window support within the graphics pipeline is synchronization hardware. Our system increases the pipeline throughput by using a parallel implementation which contains multiple transform processors. Incoming primitives are divided up and sent to individual transform processors. Load balancing is performed by determining the

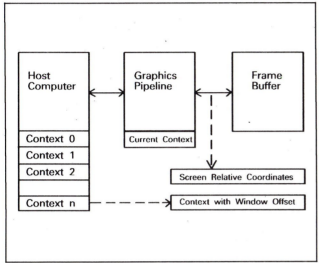

Figure 2 - Software Context Switching

least busy processor, then handing it the current primitive. When a primitive is handed to a transform processor, a sequence marker is stored in the sequence manager. The sequence manager is a circuit that keeps track of the order of primitives, so that the outputs from the transform processors can be restored to their original order before rendering. Large primitives such as polylines, polygon meshes, and splines are split up into segments and sent to separate transform processors to achieve optimum performance from the parallel architecture. Because the sequence manager ensures that these segments are returned to their proper order, results which are order dependent will be consistent [6] and repeatable. This would not be assured if ordering were not maintained. Pipeline synchronization is necessary in the window system environment to assure that primitives from competing processes are rendered in the order requested.

2.2.3 Pipeline Bypass and Valve

Although the pipeline provides good throughput for rendering primitives, it creates some problems for interactive window performance. The primary problem is that complex primitives can require significant processing time, blocking other primitives until they are completely rendered. This means that window operations, which should be interactive, can end up waiting. Another problem that reduces interactivity of the window system is pipeline latency. Pipeline latency is defined as the time required for a single primitive to traverse the pipeline. A pipeline that provides excellent throughput can exhibit a very large latency time.

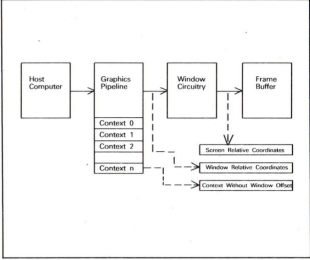

Figure 3 - Hardware Context Switching

Our solution to this problem is to provide a separate path for window primitives that do not require the pipeline. The implementation is via a pipeline bypass, which allows the window system direct access to the framebuffer. The pipeline bypass supports block move, block read, and block write operations in hardware, which will be described later. The pipeline bypass is also used to directly render X window system primitives. The philosophy behind the pipeline bypass is that window systems often require fast access for operations that are comparatively simple. By offering a bypass we can avoid the overhead of the graphics pipeline, while providing the simple services required by the window system. The pipeline offers high performance rendering and other advanced features, while the bypass offers fast block operations and direct framebuffer access. The net result is a system which provides good window system interaction, even in the middle of a complex rendering operation.

Because separate paths are available to the framebuffer, some form of synchronization must be supplied. The system provides explicit control over pipeline access to the framebuffer with a pipeline valve. The pipeline valve turns off data coming from the rendering hardware into the framebuffer. When the pipeline output is stopped, the window system is free to access the framebuffer. The pipeline valve does not stop the transform processors, which continue processing primitives until the entire pipeline backs up. Since the pipeline stages are buffered with FIFOs, significant processing will proceed before the pipeline fills up. While the pipeline valve is closed the window system may move, resize, or otherwise manipulate the windows on the display without regard to the contents of the pipeline. when the pipeline valve is opened, rendering will continue to the modified window structure. The primitives being rendered will appear in the correct location, because they are window relative. Since the window offset is applied after the pipeline valve, window offsets may be changed anytime, even in the middle of drawing a primitive.

2.2.4 Pipeline Marker Circuitry

Another enhancement to the pipeline for window support is the pipeline marker. The pipeline marker is a register that the window system can access via the pipeline bypass without closing the pipeline valve. It is used to keep track of which contexts have primitives still being processed in the pipeline. The purpose is to prevent unnecessary pipeline flushing when changing contexts. A context change often requires swapping of system resources such as window clipping planes or window display mode planes. These must sometimes be swapped during a context switch because they are a limited resource, and are shared between multiple processes. Window system software needs to ensure that all primitives from the context being swapped out are rendered before any swapping is performed. One method for this is to flush the pipeline, which we wish to avoid. A pipeline marker register provides a better method for verifying that the least recently used context is finished rendering, without flushing the pipeline. With enough window clipping planes and display mode planes, it is very unlikely that the least recently used context still has anything in the pipeline, since all windows in the system are rarely active simultaneously.

The mechanism for keeping track of currently active contexts is to send a marker down the pipeline between each context switch. The marker value is incremented each time and a table of contexts currently in the pipeline is maintained. This table shows the context number, window clipping id, and marker number for each active context. As the contexts are processed through the pipeline, the pipeline marker register is automatically updated each time the marker reaches the end of the pipeline. When a context switch occurs, the window system can read the marker register and refer to its table to determine which contexts are still in the pipeline. If the context being swapped is not in the pipeline, the context switch and clipping plane changes can occur immediately. If not, the window system must wait until the marker register indicates that the context has been processed. Under no condition is it necessary to stop the pipeline, or prevent processes from continuing to place commands and data into the pipeline.

2.3 Window Circuitry

Window support circuitry is placed after the rendering hardware and before the framebuffer. The window hardware consists of window relative circuitry, window block mover, window burst transfer, and window compare circuitry.

2.3.1 Window Relative Rendering

Any graphics application will run faster when it views itself as the sole owner of the graphics device. When an application requests a window, the corresponding framebuffer memory is allocated to that application for graphics output. The ideal environment would allow the process to treat the window as a stand alone graphics device. Most systems, however, require the process to be modified to run inside a window. In other words the application needs to be window smart and post process the output of the application to conform to the window environment, by adding window offsets or clipping to window boundaries. Any software that performs this processing will reduce overall system performance considerably. For this reason we have chosen to implement these functions in hardware. In our system, primitives in the pipeline are specified relative to the window origin. Translation to screen relative coordinates occurs after scan conversion, before framebuffer access. This lets the application treat the window as a full screen virtual device.

Of course, the above operations can be included in the transformation matrix. However, if the window offset is included in the matrix stack, the pipeline must be flushed every time the window is moved or changed. After flushing the pipeline, the new window offset is added to the transformation matrix, then the pipeline must be filled up again. This causes a major performance degradation. A better solution is to let the application access the device as if it owned the entire screen, then provide hardware to offset all primitives into the window associated with that process. We have implemented this by rendering primitives in window relative coordinates, and performing the window relative to screen relative conversion downstream from the rendering hardware. The window translation is therefore completely transparent to the application. Because the offset is performed in parallel with other pipeline operations, no performance penalty exists. Figure 4 shows a block diagram of the window support circuitry.

The window relative circuitry consists of a table of offsets with an entry for each window. The window offset is applied to each primitive at the framebuffer, allowing all primitives within the graphics pipeline to remain window relative. Window offsets can be updated asynchronously via the pipeline bypass. This permits windows to be moved or shuffled during rendering by closing the pipeline valve, moving the window, and modifying the window offset entry. When the pipeline valve is opened, rendering will proceed correctly at the new location! This can occur whenever the window system moves or otherwise modifies a window. Applications can therefore run without explicit knowledge of their window location.

2.3.2 Window Block Mover

Block move operations are important for window system performance. These operations support basic window primitives including raster text, icons, and sprites. Window moves, shuffles, and resizes also take advantage of block moves. Block moves can be particularly difficult to handle in the window environment, because window offsets need to be included into an operation that is typically implemented as screen relative. Block move operations inside a window must be window relative, however, forcing all block moves to be window relative is not a good solution. The reason is that many objects such as fonts are stored in offscreen memory, and these objects are identified by screen relative coordinates. The ideal block mover hardware should therefore be able to handle several different kinds of operations. Our implementation of the block mover includes a register with a bit for each operand that specifies whether the operand is window or screen relative. Block moves can be window relative, screen relative, or any combination thereof.

This is useful because it allows the window system to move objects stored offscreen into a window, without explicitly calculating the offset for the destination. Instead, our window relative hardware supplies the window offset for operands that are window relative. To initiate a block move on our system, the driver simply writes the source and destination addresses, block width and height, and a replacement rule.

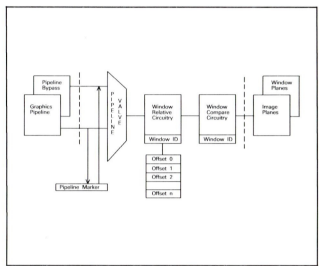

Figure 4 - Window Support Hardware

For efficiency, the hardware handles mixed window and screen relative requests on the fly, and does not require the application to make decisions about the coordinate system used by the various operands. This meets our objective of avoiding extra processing by the window system on top of the application. The mechanism for deciding which requests are window relative and which are screen relative is simple. If an object is offscreen, it is assumed to be screen relative. If an object is displayed, it is assumed to be window relative. These are defaults which can be overridden by explicit commands to the block mover.

2.3.3 Window Burst Transfer

Another feature for window performance is the ability to move large amounts of pixel data to and from system memory. Special hardware to speed up operations like block read and write increase the performance of many window operations. With acceleration, screen redraw, save bitmap, and restore bitmap operations occur very quickly, reducing the need to optimize fonts and bitmaps into offscreen memory.

The actual mechanics of how the burst transfers work are very similar to block moves. The driver just writes registers with a destination address, block width and height, and replacement rule, followed by a stream of data. The burst transfer hardware takes care of getting the data to the right place on the display in the same window relative format as other operations. An additional offset is also included to allow for transfer of data that is not aligned in system memory without performance loss. Block write data is therefore not required to be aligned. The burst transfer hardware supports bit per pixel, byte per pixel, and full pixel

writes. The burst transfer hardware available on our current systems is fast enough to support real time animation using images stored in system memory. Future systems will allow burst transfers in both directions, to speed up block reads and writes inside a window.

2.3.4 Window Compare Circuitry

Another requirement to reduce window system interaction with the application is to provide hardware window clipping. Figure 5 shows overlapping images correctly clipped against the window boundary.

Clipping to window boundaries is a time consuming task for the window system, especially if the window boundaries are arbitrary. The window compare circuitry allows pixels to be clipped to arbitrary boundaries in real time. Pixels come down the pipeline with an associated window clipping id, the same id used for the window relative conversion described above. The window id is written into the compare circuitry and stored for all subsequent operations until a new window id is written. When a pixel is written to the framebuffer, the window id value is compared to the value in the clipping planes to determine whether the pixel should be clipped [1]. The window clipping planes are described in the framebuffer section. Window compare circuitry and window clipping planes work together to provide high performance clipping while rendering complicated objects in a window environment.

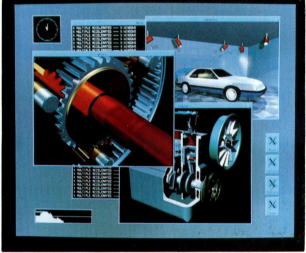

Figure 5 - Overlapping Windows

2.4 Framebuffer

A typical framebuffer contains memory for indices to the color values that comprise an image. Another use of the framebuffer is to store depth and alpha values for rendering with hidden surface removal and transparency. A framebuffer can be divided up into various windows without any special hardware support. However, to allow high speed window clipping and multiple window display modes, extra framebuffer planes have been added. Figure 6 shows a framebuffer organization with window support planes added.

2.4.1 Window Clipping Planes

Window clipping planes contain an id number for the window that currently controls each pixel. When primitives are drawn, the window circuitry compares the window id of the pixel in the framebuffer to the window id of the pixel currently being drawn. If the values match, the primitive lies inside the window, and the pixel is drawn. If the values are different, the primitive must be clipped, so the pixel is discarded [1]. Four window clipping planes provide up to sixteen independent windows, although one value must usually be reserved as a keep out value.

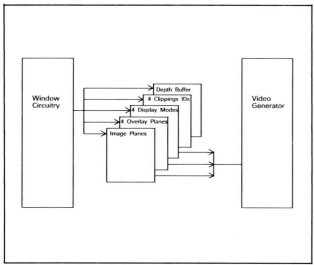

Figure 6 - Framebuffer Organization

2.4.2 Window Display Mode Planes

Window display mode planes work in a similar fashion [7]. The framebuffer values for each pixel are sent in a stream to the video circuitry. At the same time the window display id is also sent. A display processor checks all values simultaneously and reformats the framebuffer data according to the display mode for each pixel. This method allows one window to display from 8 planes, another from 24 planes, another in 12:12 double buffer mode, and so on. Windows which are rendering us ing double buffering can swap buffers asynchronously, a necessity to allow independent processes to render smoothly. Four window display mode planes provide up to sixteen independent display modes. The color map for each window is also chosen based on the display id. Display modes and color lookup tables are discussed in the section on the video generator.

2.4.3 Window Overlay Planes

Another resource that is useful for a window system is overlay planes. These are framebuffer planes that are merged into the display in front of the image planes, allowing windows to coexist with rendered images. Since the actual contents of the framebuffer image planes are not destroyed by overlay data, our system allows rendering to image windows occluded by overlay windows.

2.4.4 Window Offscreen Planes

Offscreen memory is also a valuable resource for window systems. Since many windows use predominantly raster text, raster fonts can be stored in an area of the framebuffer that is not displayed. The advantage is that characters from these fonts can be block moved into the window, a framebuffer to framebuffer copy, faster than they can be written from the host, a system memory to framebuffer copy. The importance of offscreen memory for font storage is reduced if acceleration is available for the system memory to framebuffer path. Our current systems display 1280 by 1024 pixels out of the 2048 by 1024 framebuffer, which provides an offscreen area of 768 by 1024 pixels.

2.5 Video Generator

The video circuitry processes data from the framebuffer and sends it to the raster display. The data is formatted according to the current display mode, mapped through a color lookup table, and converted from digital values to an analog signal. The window support provided by the video generator includes multiple display modes, multiple color maps, and hardware cursors.

2.5.1 Multiple Display Modes

Window support within the video generator is shown in Figure 7. Multiple display modes are provided by the video generator to allow each window to define a unique display mode. The id stored in the window display mode planes in the framebuffer is used as an index into the display mode table, which determines the display mode for all pixels inside the corresponding window. Valid display modes include full 24-bit rgb, 8-bit index, 12-bit index, and many more. Since the display mode selects which framebuffer planes are displayed, double buffering is controlled independently for each window.

The display mode id also determines the color lookup table and other attributes such as blending for each pixel. The four planes for display modes allow for up to 16 different display modes on the display at any one time. Figure 8 shows multiple display modes within separate windows.

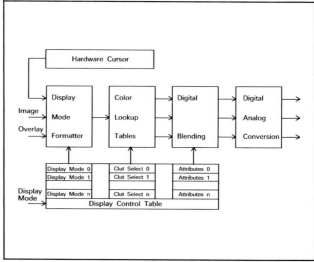

Figure 7 - Video Generator

2.5.2 Multiple Color Maps

Multiple color maps are provided by the video generator to allow each window to define a unique color map. The id stored in the window display mode planes in the framebuffer is used as an index into the hardware color table, allowing up to 16 different color maps. Since there is not an endless supply of storage for color look up tables, there are some restrictions on the types of different display modes in use at the same time. Figure 9 shows that fifteen full 24 bit and fifteen four bit overlay color maps are available for simultaneous use in addition to the one 12 bit index color map. Separate colormap entries are available for cursor color definition.

2.5.3 Hardware Cursor Support

A hardware cursor supplies an important enhancement for window system performance. Software cursor tracking performance does not provide interactivity and can consume valuable CPU cycles. Another problem with software cursors involves synchronization while rendering primitives. Software cursor routines must read the contents of the framebuffer before writing the cursor, and restore the contents when the cursor is moved. If rendering is allowed to proceed during this operation, the integrity of framebuffer data can be lost. Hardware cursors operate by substituting values directly into the pixel stream before digital to analog conversion. Since the cursor is never actually stored in the framebuffer, synchronization of framebuffer data is not a problem. The performance of hardware cursors is excellent, since the only data required to update the cursor is the new screen location.

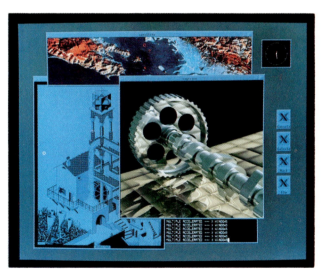

Figure 8 - Multiple Display Modes

3. CONCLUSIONS

Hardware support is a necessity to allow high performance, interactive window systems. Our future systems will emphasize good performance for multiple windows, instead of peak performance for a single device. This will undoubtedly lead to even more hardware support for window systems. By placing window support hardware in the correct stage of the graphics pipeline, increasingly complex primitives can be supported while

preserving and even improving the performance of window operations. Window support hardware will remain a very dynamic area as windows systems and graphics hardware continue to evolve.

4. ACKNOWLEDGMENTS

The authors gratefully acknowledge the Hewlett-Packard Company for supporting this paper. Thanks to the many people within our organization that have contributed their efforts and ideas to the system architecture described in this paper.

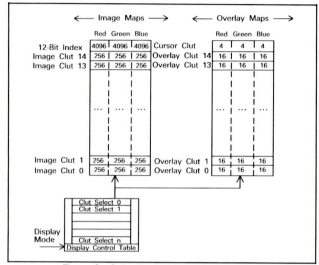

Figure 9 - Color Lookup Table Organization

5. REFERENCES

1. Akeley, Kurt and Jermoluk, Tom. High-Performance Polygon Rendering. Proceedings of SIGGRAPH'88 (Atlanta, Georgia, August 1-5, 1988). In *Computer Graphics* 22,4 (August 1988), 239-246.

2. Foley, James and Van Dam, Andries. *Fundamentals of Interactive Computer Graphics* Addison-Wesley, Reading, Massachusetts, 1982

3. Newman, William and Sproull, Robert. *Principles of Interactive Computer Graphics*. McGraw-Hill, New York, New York, 2cnd edition, 1979

4. Scheifler, Robert and Gettys, Jim. The X-Window System. ACM *Transactions on Graphics* 5,2 (April 1986), 79-109.

5. Swanson, Roger and Thayer, Larry. A Fast Shaded-Polygon Renderer. Proceedings of SIGGRAPH'86 (Dallas, Texas, August 18-22, 1986). In *Computer Graphics* 20,4 (August 1986), 95-101.

6. Torborg, John. A Parallel Processor Architecture for Graphics Arithmetic Operations. Proceedings of SIGGRAPH'87 (Anaheim, California, July 27-31, 1987). In *Computer Graphics* 21,4 (July 1987), 197-204.

7. Voorhies, Douglas, Kirk, David, and Lathrop, Olin. Virtual Graphics. Proceedings of SIGGRAPH'88 (Atlanta, Georgia, August 1-5, 1988). In *Computer Graphics* 22,4 (August 1988), 247-253.

The Pixel Machine: A Parallel Image Computer

Michael Potmesil and Eric M. Hoffert

AT&T Bell Laboratories
Holmdel, New Jersey

Abstract

We describe the system architecture and the programming environment of the Pixel Machine - a parallel image computer with a distributed frame buffer.

The architecture of the computer is based on an array of asynchronous MIMD nodes with parallel access to a large frame buffer. The machine consists of a pipeline of *pipe nodes* which execute sequential algorithms and an array of $m \times n$ pixel nodes which execute parallel algorithms. A *pixel node* directly accesses every m-th pixel on every n-th scan line of an interleaved frame buffer. Each processing node is based on a high-speed, floating-point programmable processor.

The programmability of the computer allows all algorithms to be implemented in software. We present the mappings of a number of geometry and image-computing algorithms onto the machine and analyze their performance.

CR Categories and Subject Descriptors: C.1.2 **[Processor Architectures]**: Multiprocessors - *MIMD processors - parallel processors - pipeline processors*; D.4.2 **[Operating Systems]**: Storage Management - *distributed memories - virtual memory*; I.3.1 **[Computer Graphics]**: Hardware Architecture - *raster display devices*; I.3.3 **[Computer Graphics]**: Picture/Image Generation - *display algorithms*; I.3.7 **[Computer Graphics]**: Three Dimensional Graphics and Realism - *animation - visible line/surface algorithms*; I.4.0 **[Image Processing]**: General - *image displays*.

General Terms: Parallel, Pipeline, Architecture, Algorithms, Geometry and Image Computing, Shared Memory, Distributed Memory, Interleaved Memory, Virtual Memory, Message Passing.

Additional Key Words and Phrases: Active server, passive server, virtual node, virtual shared memory, virtual display lists, virtual volumes, virtual textures, parallel paging.

1. Introduction

As computing technology progressed, it became apparent that even the most powerful computers available, built on principles devised by John von Neumann in the early 1940s, are reaching the limits of their speed imposed by the constraints of physical laws. The single-processor model executing only at most one instruction in every machine cycle is beginning to outlive its usefulness. There is no inherent reason why many calculations cannot be performed simultaneously. Computer graphics is a perfect example of such an application area. Pixels can be read, written and processed simultaneously; in fact, most graphics algorithms impose few limits on the amount of parallelism achievable for pixel processing.

With a parallel architecture, a designer hopes that, instead of the typical linear improvement in performance that is inherent in technology evolution, a quantum leap in performance can be obtained. Such a quantum leap has been *demanded* by the various communities using image computing. The recent report *Visualization in Scientific Computing* [13] stresses the need for innovative high-speed architectures to meet the needs of interpreting large amounts of scientific data. Animators require photorealistic rendering of high scene complexity and image quality with quick turnaround times. Doctors and radiologists must see a 3D reconstruction from an NMR or CT device in seconds. For image computing to be a practical tool in these and other areas, it is not feasible to wait for evolutionary improvements in technology. Instead, a break from traditional architectures must occur and be built. In this paper, we describe such an architecture; what motivated its development, how it works and what it portends for the future of image computing.

The design of the Pixel Machine was inspired and influenced by:

- **speed** - the advent of fast RISC-style digital signal processors that offer a large amount of the functionality found in a microprocessor with an integrated floating-point unit at a fraction of the price [10].

- **parallelism** - parallel architectures, in which processing is performed in parallel by nodes on the contents of their local

Authors' addresses:

Michael Potmesil, AT&T Bell Laboratories, Room 4F-625, Holmdel, NJ 07733; Telephone: (201) 949-4826; Email: mp@vax135.att.com

Eric M. Hoffert, Apple Computer Inc., 20525 Mariani Avenue, Mail Stop 60V, Cupertino, CA 95014; Telephone: (408) 974-0493; Email: emh@apple.com

memories and messages can be exchanged between processors [17,3,9] and local memories can be part of a video frame buffer [7,18].

· **interleaving** - the notion of an interleaved frame buffer, distributed among the processors of a parallel image-computing system, to achieve load balancing as originally developed in [6,14].

· **programmability** - the concept of a programmable graphics machine attached to a host computer as introduced in the *Ikonas* frame buffer and graphics processor and later also used by *Pixar* [11] and *TAAC-1* [19].

· **pipelining** - pipelined operations as applied in the *Geometry Engine* [2] to geometry computing.

· **flexibility** - the value of a rendering and modeling programming environment, such as FRAMES [15], where different computing modules following the old software adage *"small is beautiful,"* can be interconnected in different ways to achieve diverse modeling and rendering functions.

· **partitioning** - image-space or object-space partitioning of data among 2D or 3D arrays of asynchronous, independent processing elements as described in [5].

2. System Architecture

The Pixel Machine was designed as a programmable computer with pipeline and parallel processing closely coupled to a display system [16,1]. The Pixel Machine consists of four major building blocks [Figure 1]: (a) a pipeline of *pipe nodes*, (b) an array of $m \times n$ parallel *pixel nodes* with a distributed frame buffer, (c) a *pixel funnel*, and (d) a *video processor*. The pipeline and pixel-array modules can be incrementally added to a system to build a more powerful computer.

The Pixel Machine functions as an attached processor. In the current configuration the host computer is a high-end workstation, but in principle diverse hosts could be supported, ranging from personal computers to supercomputers.

2.1 Computations

The CPU of the computing nodes is a DSP32 digital-signal processor with an integrated floating-point unit [10]. It consists of a 16-bit integer section and a 32-bit floating point section. The integer section with 21 registers is mainly used to generate memory addresses while the floating-point section with four 40-bit accumulators is used to process geometry and image data.

The DSP32 has a RISC-style instruction set and instruction decoding. Unlike a RISC processor which operates only on data in registers and uses load/store register-memory accesses, the DSP32 uses register pointers to point to arrays of data in memory. The pointers are usually post-incremented during the same instruction. In a typical operation, the DSP32 can read two operands from memory and one from an accumulator, perform a multiply-accumulate operation and write the result to an accumulator and to memory.

The DSP32 has a 16-bit addressing capability, allowing it to address directly only* 64 Kbytes of memory. There are 4 Kbytes of RAM memory on board of the chip. Each pixel and

---

* It should be noted that the next generation of this processor has a 24-bit addressing space allowing it to address directly 16 Mbytes of memory.

pipe node has additional 32 Kbytes of fast static RAM memory. These 36 Kbytes are used for program and scratch data storage.

Pixel nodes also contain a distributed frame buffer and z-buffer. In each pixel node, there are 512 Kbytes of video RAM memory organized as two banks of 256×256 32-bit $rgb\alpha$ pixels and 256 Kbytes of general-purpose dynamic RAM memory which can be organized as a 256×256 32-bit floating-point z-buffer. These additional 3⁄4 Mbytes of memory are addressed via a memory management unit.

The nodes are running at 5 Mips or 10 Mflops which must really be interpreted as 5 million multiply-accumulate operations per second. In typical applications, programmed in C, the overhead of invoking functions, computing data pointers, etc. can reduce the floating-point operations to about 10-25% of the peak rate.

2.2 Communications and Connections

There are a number of different communication paths in the system. Each pixel and pipe node is connected to the VMEbus via a DMA port (*host-to-node connection*). This port can be used by the host to access all memory-mapped locations in a node and for handshaking and synchronization activities by the node.

Pipe nodes are connected with fifos into nine-node pipelines (*downstream pipe node-to-node connection*). The fifo input to the first node is written by the host via the VMEbus, the fifo output of the last node is either broadcast - via a broadcast bus - to all the pixel nodes (*pipe-node to pixel-node connection*) or written to a fifo read back - via the VMEbus - by the host. The pipe nodes in a pipeline are also connected via a unidirectional serial asynchronous link in the direction opposite to the fifos (*upstream pipe node-to-node connection*). Two pipelines can be placed in a system and configured as two parallel pipes or one long serial pipe.

Pixel nodes are connected to their four nearest neighbors, in a closed-torus network, via serial bidirectional asynchronous links (*pixel node-to-node connection*). These pathways allow flexibility for data movement needed in different algorithms. Some pixel-node operations, such as changing display buffers or exchanging messages with adjacent nodes, require all the nodes to be synchronized: they have to wait for the last node to complete its previous computations. There are two hardware semaphores, shared by all the pixel nodes, which allow global synchronization. Pixel nodes can also be synchronized with vertical and horizontal video retrace periods.

2.3 Pixel Mapping and Display

The frame buffer in the Pixel Machine is distributed into the array of the $m \times n$ pixel nodes. The frame buffer is divided into two or more display buffers. One of these buffers is always displayed by the video system, at the selected size and speed, on the screen. When in double-buffered mode, a second buffer is used to draw the next image. Additional buffers may contain other pixel-oriented data such as texture maps. Pixels in the displayed buffer are read by the video processor and mapped on the video screen. This mapping is determined by the position of each pixel node within the array and is fixed. Each pixel node contains the size of the pixel-node array (m,n) and its position within the array (p,q) where $0 \le p < m$ and $0 \le q < n$. The position (p,q) also serves as a unique identification number of each node. Pixel node (p,q) then displays every m-th pixel starting with pixel p on every n-th scanline starting with scanline q, i.e., a processor-space

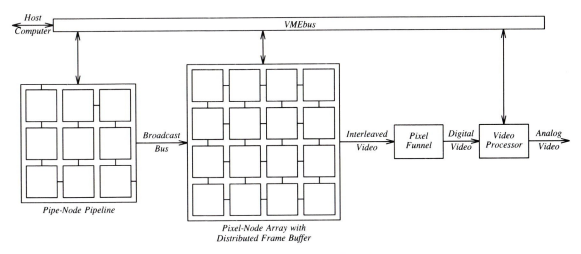

Figure 1 A block diagram of the Pixel Machine.

pixel (i,j) is mapped into a screen-space pixel (x,y) by:

$$x = m \; i + p$$
$$y = n \; j + q \qquad (1)$$

This format requires the display subsystem to collect all of the distributed frame-buffer pixels and assemble them into a contiguous screen image. The device that performs this function is called the video *pixel funnel*. The interleaved format of the frame buffer provides load balancing for image-computing algorithms and matches well the speed limitations of video RAM memories with the speed requirements of a high-resolution display*.

The architecture of the pixel nodes is scalable, using between 16 and 64 nodes [Table 1]. The video processor can be programmed to display two high-resolution formats as well as NTSC and PAL.

To aid in the development of uniform software for all the pixel-node configurations and to allow hardware modularity, the concept of *virtual pixel nodes* was utilized. A virtual node renders into a subset of a buffer, called a *virtual screen*, all within a physical node. The virtual nodes and their virtual screens are also interleaved in an $m' \times n'$ pattern - just as the physical nodes - with each virtual node having a unique screen position (p',q'). The mappings in equation (1) also apply to the virtual nodes. All software is written for one virtual node and is invoked one or more times, depending on the system size, by a physical node. The physical and virtual pixel-node configurations of the Pixel Machine are shown in Table 1.

3. Software Architecture

Software developed to run on the Pixel Machine is always divided into two major conceptual areas: *host software* and *node software*. The latter category is further subdivided into *pipe-node software* and *pixel-node software*. Host software controls interaction with the Pixel Machine, pipe-node software executes sequential-type algorithms and finally pixel-node software executes parallel algorithms.

___
* A pixel is shifted out of a video memory in ≈40 ns while it is displayed on a 1280 × 1024 pixel screen in ≈9 ns. Therefore, at least 5 parallel banks of video memories are required to shift out 5 pixels in ≈40 ns.

3.1 Host Software

Each node in the Pixel Machine is a small autonomous computer, albeit with a number of limitations. The current processor used in each node does not support interrupts and has limited addressing capabilities. These limitations forced the software designers of the Pixel Machine to come up with a number of creative solutions to difficult problems typically not encountered on a conventional computer. A programming environment had to be developed that simulates much of the functionality taken for granted in a standard operating system.

There are two different types of processes which can run on the host computer and interact with or control the Pixel Machine:

- **passive server**

  This process functions as a data-base server for the Pixel Machine. In this capacity, interaction takes place in a linear fashion: the host sends a stream of commands and data to the Pixel Machine, and the Pixel Machine performs various operations on the received data. There is no interaction initiated by the Pixel Machine, it responds only when it is explicitly requested to do so (e.g., to a command to return the current transformation matrix). This server is employed almost exclusively for traditional polygon rendering, where databases and commands are generated by the host and sent to the machine. In this mode the Pixel Machine acts as slave and the host computer as master.

- **active server**

  This process is responsible for responding to all requests for resources that are made by the Pixel Machine. It polls a user-defined set of nodes (pipe *or* pixel) for messages. When a message is received, the active server initiates a host function that supplies needed resources to the requesting node. We have found this to be a very powerful paradigm for host/Pixel Machine interaction. The host needs the Pixel Machine for certain demanding geometry and image computing, and the Pixel Machine needs the host for contiguous large blocks of memory and for access to a file system (among a number of other potential needs). In this mode the Pixel Machine acts as master and the host computer as slave.

Physical			Virtual			V/P
nodes	$m \times n$	pixels/node	nodes	$m' \times n'$	pixels/node	Ratio
16	4×4	256×256*	64	8×8	128×128	4
20	5×4	256×256**	80	10×8	128×128	4
32	8×4	128×256*	64	8×8	128×128	2
40	10×4	128×256**	80	10×8	128×128	2
64	8×8	128×128*	64	8×8	128×128	1
		160×128**			160×128	1

Table 1 Physical and virtual pixel-node configurations.

* Display screen size: 1024×1024 pixels.
** Display screen size: 1280×1024 pixels.

The host process has complete control over all nodes. It can access all memory in each node including program memory and frame-buffer memory in pixel nodes. Such accesses take place, via DMA, even when the nodes are running.

The host software is also responsible for halting, initializing and starting each node as well as for downloading programs into them. It also configures the video processor and accesses the video lookup tables.

3.2 Pixel-Machine Software

Software that runs on the **Pixel Machine** is quite distinct from software that runs on von Neumann machines. The important distinction from the single-processor approach is that software is mapped to different architectural components, each of which has a different *character* and number of nodes. The pipeline (where each pipe node typically contains a distinct program) executes sequential algorithms and the pixel-node array (where each pixel node typically contains the same program*) executes parallel algorithms. In some cases, our algorithm is entirely sequential; such an algorithm would run only in the pipe nodes. Analogously, we have algorithms that are entirely parallel in nature; such an application might not utilize the pipeline at all. We have found that most applications have components that map onto both the pipeline and pixel-node array.

3.3 Pipe-Node Software

Pipe nodes are employed for operations that are intrinsically sequential in nature. Such operations are those that constrain the efficiency of a parallel algorithm. The use of a pipeline is an attempt to remove as much sequential style processing from the parallel pixel-node array as possible.

Pipe-node software requires algorithm partitioning. Each pipe node acts as a distinct computational element in a pipeline. A separate program runs in each node and messages - commands and data - are passed down a pipeline. The last node in a

pipeline has the ability to broadcast messages to all the nodes in a pixel-node array or to return them back to the host.

The **FRAMES** system [15] contains methods for experimenting with pipeline partitioning and how to achieve maximum flexibility in such a scheme. The same philosophy is employed here. Our experience shows that special care must be taken to ensure that software in the pipeline does not become I/O bound.

Pipe-node software can be written to allow the same program to reside in several consecutive nodes and to operate on alternating input messages (e.g., each instance of an n-node transformation program transforms only every n-th polygon). This allows the same software to run efficiently in longer pipelines and to eliminate or reduce bottlenecks by repeating the slowest program in more than one node.

3.4 Pixel-Node Software

This section describes (a) what actions a pixel node performs as a computational element and (b) the general mechanisms available for increasing the amount of data that a pixel node can directly access. There are two approaches to the issue of memory limitation. The first approach is that of message-passing, where nodes exchange portions of distributed data. This approach exploits the ability of a machine to shuffle large amounts of data among its nodes. The second approach utilizes the memory of the host computer, letting it serve as an adjunct memory device for individual nodes.

Support software in the pixel nodes comprises several categories: screen-space to processor-space coordinate mapping, frame-buffer and z-buffer access to pixel-oriented data, display-list access, and optimized mathematical functions.

Mapping functions transfer coordinates from the (x,y) display screen space to the (i',j') virtual screen space of a virtual pixel node (p',q') by:

$$i' = \frac{x - p'}{m'} = \frac{1}{m'} x - \frac{p'}{m'}$$

$$j' = \frac{y - q'}{n'} = \frac{1}{n'} y - \frac{q'}{n'}$$

where the scale multiplication is the same for all the pixel nodes and therefore is actually computed by a pipe node and

---

* However, there is no reason why each pixel node cannot execute a different program.

the offset subtraction is computed individually by each pixel node.

There are four basic mapping functions, used in all image-computing algorithms, which transform screen coordinates to processor coordinates. Function $ilo(x)$ returns the *smallest* integer i' such that $m'i' + p' \geq x$:

$$ilo(x) = \left\lceil \frac{x - p' - 0.5}{m'} \right\rceil$$

Function $ihi(x)$ returns the *largest* integer i' such that $m'i' + p' \leq x$:

$$ihi(x) = \left\lfloor \frac{x - p' + 0.5}{m'} \right\rfloor$$

Similarly, function $jlo(y)$ returns the smallest integer j' such that $n'j' + q' \geq y$, and function $jhi(y)$ returns the largest j' such that $n'j' + q' \leq y$.

The mapping from the screen space to the processor space is not one-to-one: there are more pixels in screen space than in processor space. To be certain that processor-space pixel (i',j') is actually screen-space pixel (x,y), these two conditions must be true:

$$ilo(x) = ihi(x), \text{ and}$$
$$jlo(y) = jhi(y)$$

Each node can independently read or write the contents of its individual frame buffer and z-buffer. Access to these memories is in row and column addressing modes using virtual screens. A 32-bit pixel can be accessed in four instruction cycles (one cycle to read each color component) and a 32-bit z-buffer value in one cycle.

Mathematical functions include routines for frequently used operations in geometry and image computing such as square root (ray-sphere intersection), vector normalization (shading), and dot product (back-face removal). These highly-optimized functions efficiently utilize the floating-point capability of the DSP32 at each node, since many of the operations involve multiply/accumulate instructions.

3.5 Interleave/De-Interleave

Each node in the pixel-node array has a four-way serial I/O switch. This allows a node to communicate directly with its four nearest neighbors. Communications between two nodes occur over a half-duplex serial channel. All nodes must synchronize to exchange data, and message-passing occurs in lock-step fashion, with all nodes sending data in the same direction at the same time. This type of communication scheme is well-suited to problems that map onto a grid or torus architecture.

There are times when it is undesirable to compute on pixels in an interleaved format. Using the current Pixel Machine, this is not possible through hardware due to constraints imposed by video memory access requirements. At this point, the old hardware adage *"do it in software!"* is employed.

Software can take the interleaved frame-buffer format, and using serial I/O message-passing, reconfigure the frame buffer so that each node has a contiguous block of pixels. We call this process *de-interleaving*. Analogously, it is possible to take a frame buffer configured as contiguous blocks and again employing serial I/O message-passing, distribute the pixels so that they are in their correct interleaved position for display. We call this method *interleaving*.

3.6 Virtual Memory

Photorealistic rendering requires large amounts of data. This data is typically geometry information, but can also consist of texture maps, environment maps, etc. Other rendering techniques, such as volume rendering, can also require significant amounts of data storage. We have also found that an efficiently coded implementation of a rendering program (ray or volume tracers, for example) can be very small, in terms of code space. Hence it became apparent that we could develop schemes for virtual memory [4] which would be used only for *data*.

Each node has a page table in its memory along with a set of associated pages. When a memory access is required for data that does not reside in the available pages, a *parallel page-fault* is generated, causing a node to make a request to the host to deliver the required page of memory. The page is broadcast to all nodes in the pixel array from the last node in the pipeline. At this point, the page table in each node is updated, deleting a page based on a page-replacement policy and adding the newly requested page to the table. We call it parallel paging, since typically nodes may request pages from the host concurrently.

The parallel paging scheme is employed for *virtual display lists* in the ray-tracing software implemented on the Pixel Machine. Figure 2 shows a ray-traced image with 17,000 polygons. Each polygon uses 100 bytes, giving a database size of 1.7 Mbytes, substantially more than can fit in one pixel node's local memory. Figure 3 also shows a ray-traced image generated using virtual display lists. This scene contains over 50,000 polygons, area-light sources and is antialiased at 16 samples per pixel.

The active server can store multiple texture maps or volume databases in host's memory. When an individual pixel or voxel is requested by an arbitrary node, the host retrieves a page of adjacent data and routes it to the requesting node. This scheme is especially suitable for either (a) applications with memory requirements that far exceed the collective memory capacity of the pixel nodes, or (b) applications where distribution of memory over the pixel nodes would require an overly complex and/or inefficient algorithm. Because all pixel nodes have access to this memory, we call it *virtual shared memory*.

Figure 4 shows a ray-traced image that uses *virtual texture maps*. There are 13 virtual texture maps requiring a total of 4 Mbytes of texture map data. The scene also contains approximately 2,000 polygons. Figure 5 shows a volume rendering of a nuclear magnetic resonance (NMR) angiography study that uses *virtual volumes*. The size of the data is $256 \times 256 \times 160$ voxels or approximately 10 Mbytes.

3.7 Program Overlays

A node can directly address 64 Kbytes of memory. This constraint coupled with the cost and size of fast static RAM memories dictated the size of program memory at 36 Kbytes in the current Pixel Machine. The solution to this problem of small program size is a classic one, first seen in the early days of computing. If a node does not have enough program or local data memory available for a required function or message processing, we use *program overlays* [8].

A program is manually divided into a static instruction and data segment which resides in a node at all times and several dynamic segments which are swapped-in, one at a time from the host. The host server keeps track of the overlay segments loaded into any of the nodes and ensures that the correct

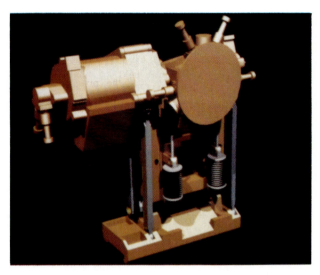

Figure 2 Virtual display lists: *A Stabilized Platform-Deployment Station.*

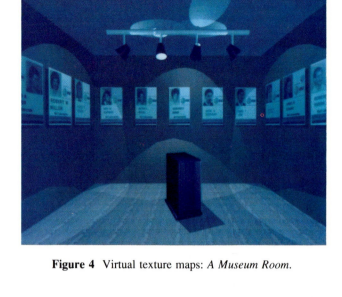

Figure 4 Virtual texture maps: *A Museum Room.*

Figure 3 Virtual display lists: *A Tea Room.*

Figure 5 Virtual volumes: *A Sagittal View of NMR Data.*

segments are loaded into each node before data requiring them arrive. The cost of sending overlays from the host and loading them into a node's program memory is small: the bandwidth from the host to the pipeline is on the order of Mbytes/s and the overlay segments are on the order of single Kbytes.

4. Algorithm Mapping

In this section, we describe the mappings of a few well-known geometry and image-computing algorithms to the Pixel Machine architecture:

- **polygonal rendering**

  Points, lines, polygons and other geometric primitives are transformed, clipped, shaded, projected and broadcast by the pipeline nodes. Complex geometric primitives (patches, superquadrics) are also generated or converted into polygons in the pipeline. The pixel-node array is used for raster

operations, rendering of geometric primitives, z-buffering, texture mapping, image compositing and antialiasing. For polygonal rendering, the passive server is employed, routing large polygonal databases or multiple frames of animation to the Pixel Machine via the pipeline. Image antialiasing is accomplished by supersampling and floating-point convolution with an arbitrary filter kernel.

- **ray tracing**

Ray trees are traced in parallel by the pixel nodes, with each node generating ray trees for pixel sampling points in its unique set of interleaved pixels. Each pixel node contains a copy of the display list of the scene being rendered. If the size of the display list exceeds the local pixel-node memory, the display list is paged from the host computer, using the parallel page-faulting method described earlier. The active server is used to service display list page faults and texture map virtual shared memory requests respectively. The pipeline is used to compute bounding volumes, tessellate geometric primitives and to transform the display list before rendering begins. The floating-point capability of each node is exercised to its maximum for the ray-object intersection tests. Antialiasing is performed by stochastic sampling in multiple passes.

· **volume rendering**

Rays are marched in parallel [12] by the pixel nodes inside volume data. Each node processes its set of interleaved pixels in the image. At each pixel, a ray is cast into the volume and ray-marching incrementally steps along the direction of the ray, sampling the signal inside. The sampled values of a ray are then converted into image intensity according to the application: thresholding, finding maximum, translucency accumulation and integration can be selected. The volume is stored on the host computer, with each pixel node requesting voxel packets that contain voxels along the path of a marching ray. This procedure is accomplished using virtual shared memory via the active server. The pipeline is not utilized in this mapping. Antialiasing is accomplished by sampling very finely along each ray and by interpolating voxel values adjacent to an intersection point.

· **image processing**

An image is processed by the pixel nodes in parallel, with each pixel node computing its set of interleaved pixels. If the image is too large to fit in the local pixel-node memory, it can be distributed over the collective memory of all the nodes in contiguous block fashion and redistributed into interleaved format for a final display using the interleave/de-interleave strategy. The pipeline can be used for run-length decoding and other sequential image functions as an image is being sent to the pixel nodes.

5. Performance Analysis

In this section we attempt to analyze the theoretical performance of the Pixel Machine architecture and then look at some of our actual results.

5.1 Theoretical Performance Analysis

The classic recurrence equation for the *divide-conquer-marry* paradigm is as follows:

$$T(n) = g(n) + M\, T(n/M) + h(n)$$

where $g(n)$ is the cost of dividing up a problem into M subproblems (*divide*), $T(n/M)$ is the cost of running the subproblem (*conquer*), $h(n)$ is the cost of combining the results of the subproblems into a final solution (*marry*) and n is the number of data elements. This generic equation is typically applied to a sequential implementation of a recursive algorithm. Interestingly enough, the equation can also be applied to the analysis of algorithms on parallel machines. In this case, the multiplicative term M would drop out, since the *divided problems* or subproblems are being solved concurrently. The modified equation becomes:

$$T(n) = g(n) + T(n/M) + h(n)$$

The ideal parallel algorithm will have minimal $g(n)$ and $h(n)$ terms; these are the *parallel overhead* costs. The algorithm development efforts for parallel architecture are primarily concerned with ensuring that the $T(n/M)$ term will predominate in the expression above. This ensures that adding more processors to a problem yields a linear improvement in performance. A term that has recently entered into the parlance of parallel

processing is *Non von Neumann bottleneck*. This refers to the costs $g(n)$ and $h(n)$, which are considered bottlenecks if they predominate in the expression above.

The salient difference between the Pixel Machine and other parallel machines is that there is no $h(n)$ term for displaying or animating the image computed by the pixel nodes. This immediately obviates a large amount of the usual parallel overhead. This term is eliminated because the interleaved frame buffer is assembled into a contiguous scan image by the pixel funnel. Only if we read back the computed image from the frame buffer to the host computer does the $h(n)$ term reappear.

The $g(n)$ term represents the cost associated with the screen space to processor space conversion. As an example of how this term affects efficiency, consider the case of rasterizing a geometric primitive in a pixel node. A simple equation describing the rasterization is as follows:

$$T(p) = g(x) + p\, I(x)$$

where p is the number of pixels rasterized, $T(p)$ is the time required to rasterize these pixels, $I(x)$ is the cost per pixel of rasterization for an arbitrary algorithm x and $g(x)$ is the parallel overhead for that algorithm. Let us also define η, the efficiency of a parallel algorithm implementation, to be the slope of the graph of normalized inverted execution time vs. number of pixel nodes. A unity value of η implies exactly linear improvement in performance for linear increases in the number of pixel nodes. This is what we aspire to for all implementations. Values less than unity indicate sublinear improvement for pixel-node increases. If p is small and $g(x)$ is large so that $g(x) > p\, I(x)$, then the parallel overhead predominates and $\eta \ll 1$. Conversely, if p is large and $g(x)$ is small so that $g(x) < p\, I(x)$, then the parallel overhead is small or negligible and $\eta \approx 1$.

The optimal algorithms for the Pixel Machine are those that require a $g(n)$ term only once per *image* as opposed to once per *object*. An example of the former is ray-tracing and of the latter is vector drawing. It is much easier to amortize the cost $g(n)$ once per image than once per object, since there may be many objects in an image.

5.2 Measured Performance Analysis

We have tested the actual efficiency of the machine on a number of different image-computing algorithms:

· **raster operations**

A basic pixel-node function is to modify rectangular regions on the screen in various ways. The pixel-node organization allows $m'n'$ pixels to be processed in parallel by $m' \times n'$ virtual nodes during each iteration. Figure 6 illustrates performance of the machine performing raster operations on 128^2, 256^2, 512^2, and 1024^2 pixel regions. The execution times are plotted as solid lines and the normalized efficiency is shown as dotted lines. The efficiency of the machine, as the slopes of the dotted lines indicate, is very high with almost linear improvement and increases as the size of the region increases.

· **point rasterizing**

A pixel node maps a point into its screen space and then tests if the point actually belongs there and should be drawn. Each pixel node maps and tests all the points but typically draws only $1/m'n'$ of them, giving a very low figure of merit. The graphs in Figure 7 indicate that the sequential part of the algorithm dominates: the bottleneck is a pipe node which converts the host floating-point and integer

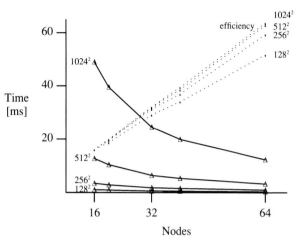

Figure 6 Parallel performance: raster operations.

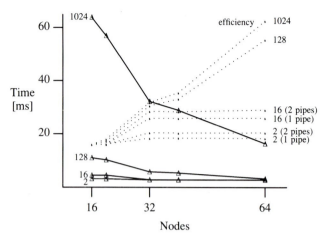

Figure 8 Parallel performance: aliased vectors.

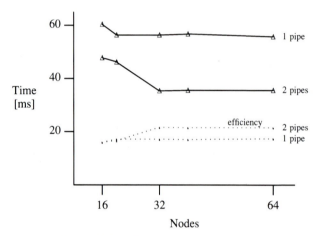

Figure 7 Parallel performance: points.

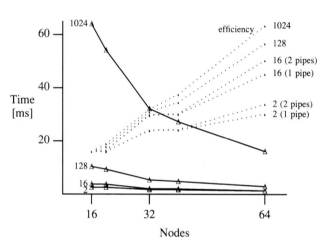

Figure 9 Parallel performance: antialiased vectors.

formats to the DSP32 floating-point format. There is not any speed improvement above 20 pixel nodes when a single pipeline is used. In a system with two parallel pipelines the improvement stops at 32 pixel nodes. Two parallel pipelines improve the speed of this algorithm by about 70% for 32 or more pixel nodes.

- **vector rasterizing**

A parallel version of the Bresenham algorithm rasterizes one-pixel wide aliased vectors. In an $m' \times n'$ array of virtual pixel nodes, the algorithm writes $min(m',n')$ pixels during one iteration. The figure of merit for this algorithm is only $min(m',n')/m'n'$. Line drawing, which is essentially a one dimensional process, cannot be very efficiently implemented on this architecture. Performance for randomly-oriented 2, 16, 128 and 1024 pixel-long vectors is shown in Figure 8. Actual times are again plotted as solid lines while the efficiency of the algorithm is plotted as dotted lines. As expected, the slope of these lines illustrates the low efficiency. For very short vectors the overhead becomes dominant and there is almost no improvement in speed as the number of processors increases.

Antialiased vectors are drawn by a modified version of the above algorithm which computes pixel intensity based on

distance from the vector and blends the intensity with the background. Figure 9 shows the relative performance of this algorithm for the same randomly-oriented vectors as in Figure 8. On absolute time scale, aliased vectors are about twice as fast as antialiased vectors. However, because more processors do more useful work per pixel and per iteration, the antialiased algorithm is more efficiently implemented in this architecture than the aliased algorithm. In both algorithms, a small speed improvement is obtained for short vectors when two parallel pipelines are used.

- **polygon rasterizing**

A pipe node converts polygons into triangles, sorts their vertices in y and computes the slopes of the three edges. The pixel nodes transform the slopes into their processor spaces, compute forward difference in y along the edges and scan-convert the triangle by stepping in y along two active edges and filling the span in x between them. Performance for random triangles within 8^2, 16^2, 64^2, 256^2 and 1024^2 bounding squares is given in Figure 10. For large triangles the performance is similar to raster operations. As the size of the triangles decreases the sequential part (executing in the pipe nodes) and the parallel overhead of the rasterizing algorithm dominates and decreases the efficiency of the architecture.

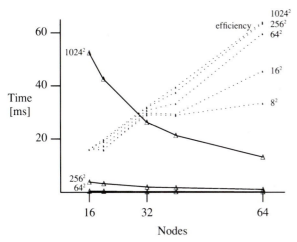

Figure 10 Parallel performance: Gouraud-shaded z-buffered polygons.

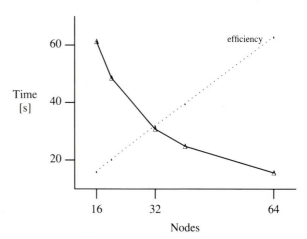

Figure 12 Parallel performance: ray tracing.

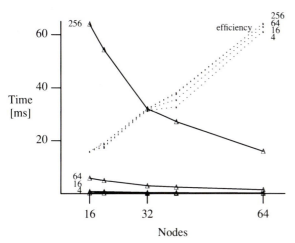

Figure 11 Parallel performance: Phong-shaded z-buffered spheres.

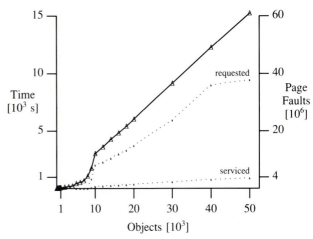

Figure 13 Ray tracing: scene complexity vs. time (solid) and parallel paging (dotted) using virtual data memory.

- **sphere rasterizing**

Phong-shaded z-buffered spheres are rasterized using the approximations described in [7]. Because many computations have to be done at each pixel to evaluate the inside/outside equation, depth, normal vector, and finally the color, the efficiency of this algorithm is high even for small spheres [Figure 11]. Note that the implementation of this algorithm is more efficient then, for example, Gouraud-shaded z-buffered rasterizing of polygons of similar size.

- **ray tracing**

Our first objective was to see if the performance would improve linearly with increases in the number of processing nodes for the case where the object database resides entirely in a node's memory. In these tests, the database size is kept constant while the number of pixel nodes in a system is increased. As can be seen from the dotted graph in Figure 12, our objective of linear improvement was met, and we have had similar experiences with many other object databases. In addition, the actual rendering times for the image are plotted (solid graph) and they are two to three orders of magnitude faster than on typical workstations.

Our second objective was to examine what happens to the performance when the parallel paging is used for virtual display lists. This test was run keeping the number of pixel nodes in the system constant, while increasing the number of objects in a scene. It can be seen from the graph in Figure 13 that the paging begins at about 5,000 objects in the display list. The performance degrades exponentially when the paging begins but becomes again linear above 10,000 objects. The dotted graph labeled "requested" shows the number of page faults generated by all the nodes. Since many nodes request the same page at the same time, the dotted graph labeled "serviced" shows that only about one tenth of the generated page faults had to be serviced. The speed of the algorithm when paging a display list is about five times slower than when all of a display list is in the pixel-node memory.

The measured performance confirms our analysis: the architecture of the machine is best suited for image-computing algorithms which require a parallel overhead only once per image (e.g., ray tracing, fractals, 2D and 3D solid textures) and degenerates as the overhead increases and the number of usefully employed pixel nodes decreases (e.g., line and point rasterizing).

SIGGRAPH '89, Boston, 31 July-4 August, 1989

6. Summary and Conclusions

We have described a parallel image computer designed for fast geometry and image computing. The computer contains a large distributed frame buffer which allows many computing elements, capable of floating-point operations, to access pixel-oriented data in parallel. We have developed software for standard 3D polygonal graphics, 3D volume display and ray tracing, all based on a common programming environment.

To overcome the problems inherent to the architecture of the machine and its current implementation - particularly the limited amounts of program and data memories in each node - we resorted to using established software techniques found in traditional computers such as program overlays for instructions and virtual memory for data. We also found a method to remove the restrictions of the interleaved frame-buffer design using interprocessor communication capabilities. To simplify the development of software for our scalable parallel architecture we have developed a concept of physical and virtual nodes which makes the size of the machine transparent to the programmer.

We have also used the Pixel Machine for real-time playback of compressed audio and video data and as a general-purpose parallel computer.

Acknowledgements and Credits

We would like to thank Bill Ninke, Kicha Ganapathy and Jim Boddie for providing a fertile environment that allowed the exchange of ideas between people involved in graphics, parallel processing and digital signal processing. Leonard McMillan contributed major ideas to both the software and hardware architecture and should be identified as one of the principal architects of the system. Bob Farah should be credited with the design of the pipeline card and for handling enormous numbers of odds and ends. Marc Howard should be thanked for bringing to life very high-quality, reliable video at 2 A.M. on a Friday night. Jennifer Inman should be thanked for writing a great deal of the pipe and pixel-node software. Pete Segal must be credited with much work on the ray tracer. Jon Leech pulled his hair on message-passing and the interleave/de-interleave code. John Spicer and Tom Rosenfeld contributed towards a nice parallel-programming environment.

Miss Piggy was an immense help in the early days when everything great was done at around 4 A.M. and common sense prevailed. Spouses and lovers are most importantly thanked for being understanding at the worst of times. The controversial ghost-writer Tango A. Scampers wrote the original version of this paper.

We would also like to thank NASA for generating the image in Figure 2 and for providing the database for testing purposes. Kamran Manoocheri must be thanked for creating the image *A Museum Room* in Figure 4 and Leonard McMillan for *A Tea Room* in Figure 3.

References

[1] AT&T Pixel Machines, "The Pixel Machine System Architecture," A Technical Report, Holmdel, NJ, November 1988

[2] Clark, J. H., "The Geometry Engine: A VLSI Geometry System for Graphics," *ACM Computer Graphics*, **16**, (3), July 1982, 127-133

[3] DeBenedictis, E. P., *The Bell Laboratories' Hypercube*, personal communication, April 1986

[4] Denning, P. J., "Virtual Memory," *Computing Surveys*, **2**, (3), September 1970, 153-189

[5] Dippé, M., and Swensen, J., "An Adaptive Subdivision Algorithm and Parallel Architecture for Realistic Image Synthesis," *ACM Computer Graphics*, **18**, (3), July 1984, 149-158

[6] Fuchs, H., "Distributing a Visible Surface Algorithm Over Multiple Processors," *Proceedings of ACM 1977*, Seattle, WA, October 1977, 449-451

[7] Fuchs, H., et. al., "Fast Spheres, Shadows, Textures, Transparencies, and Image Enhancements in Pixel-Planes," *ACM Computer Graphics*, **19**, (3), July 1985, 111-120

[8] Heising, W. P., and Larner, R. A., "A Semi-Automatic Storage Allocation System at Loading Time," *Communications of the ACM*, **4**, (10), October 1961, 446-449

[9] Hillis, W. D., *The Connection Machine*, The MIT Press, Cambridge, MA, 1985

[10] Kershaw, R. N., et. al., "A Programmable Digital Signal Processor with 32-bit Floating Point Arithmetic," *Proceedings of IEEE International Solid-State Circuits Conference*, February 1985, 92-93

[11] Levinthal, A., and Porter, T., "Chap - A SIMD Graphics Processor," *ACM Computer Graphics*, **18**, (3), July 1984, 77-82

[12] Levoy, M., "Volume Rendering: Display of Surface from Volume Data," *IEEE Computer Graphics and Applications*, **8**, (3), May 1988, 29-36

[13] McCormick, B. H., DeFanti T. A., and Brown, M. D., "Visualization in Scientific Computing," *ACM Computer Graphics*, **21**, (6), November 1987

[14] Parke, F. I., "Simulation and Expected Performance Analysis of Multiple Processor Z-Buffer Systems," *ACM Computer Graphics*, **14**, (3), July 1980, 48-56

[15] Potmesil, M., and Hoffert, E. M., "FRAMES: Software Tools for Modeling, Rendering and Animation of 3D Scenes," *ACM Computer Graphics*, **21**, (4), July 1987, 85-93

[16] Potmesil, M., McMillan, L., Hoffert, E. M., Inman, J. F., Farah, R. L., and Howard, M., "A Parallel Image Computer with a Distributed Frame Buffer: System Architecture and Programming," *Proceedings of Eurographics '89*, Hamburg, Federal Republic of Germany, September 1989

[17] Seitz, C. L., "The Cosmic Cube," *Communication of the ACM*, **28**, (1), January 1985, 22-33

[18] Sato, H., et. al., "Fast Image Generation of Constructive Solid Geometry Using a Cellular Array Processor," *ACM Computer Graphics*, **19**, (3), July 1985, 95-102

[19] Whitton, M. C., England, N., and DeMonico C., "Manage Design Trade-Offs in High-End Graphics Board," *Electronic Design*, **36**, (6), March 1988, 77-84

Pixel-Planes 5: A Heterogeneous Multiprocessor Graphics System Using Processor-Enhanced Memories[1]

Henry Fuchs, John Poulton, John Eyles, Trey Greer, Jack Goldfeather[2],
David Ellsworth, Steve Molnar, Greg Turk, Brice Tebbs, Laura Israel

Department of Computer Science
University of North Carolina
Chapel Hill, NC 27599-3175

Abstract

This paper introduces the architecture and initial algorithms for Pixel-Planes 5, a heterogeneous multi-computer designed both for high-speed polygon and sphere rendering (1M Phong-shaded triangles/second) and for supporting algorithm and application research in interactive 3D graphics. Techniques are described for volume rendering at multiple frames per second, font generation directly from conic spline descriptions, and rapid calculation of radiosity form-factors. The hardware consists of up to 32 math-oriented processors, up to 16 rendering units, and a conventional 1280x1024-pixel frame buffer, interconnected by a 5 gigabit ring network. Each rendering unit consists of a 128x128-pixel array of processors-with-memory with parallel quadratic expression evaluation for every pixel. Implemented on 1.6 micron CMOS chips designed to run at 40MHz, this array has 208 bits/pixel on-chip and is connected to a video RAM memory system that provides 4,096 bits of off-chip memory. Rendering units can be independently reassigned to any part of the screen or to non-screen-oriented computation. As of April 1989, both hardware and software are still under construction, with initial system operation scheduled for fall 1989.

CR Categories and Subject Descriptors: B.2.1 [Arithmetic and Logic Structures]: Design Styles - parallel; C.1.2 [Processor Architectures]: Multiprocessors - parallel processors; I.3.1 [Computer Graphics]: Hardware Architecture - raster display devices; I.3.3 [Computer Graphics]: Picture/Image generation - display algorithms; I.3.7 [Computer Graphics]: 3D Graphics and Realism - color, shading and texture, visible surface algorithms.

Additional Key Words and Phrases: logic-enhanced memory, ring network, polygon scan-conversion

[1] This work supported by the Defense Advanced Research Projects Agency, DARPA ISTO Order No. 6090, the National Science Foundation, Grant No. DCI-8601152, the Office of Naval Research, Contract No. N0014-86-K-0680, and U.S. Air Force Systems Command, Contract No. F33615-88-C-1848.

[2] Department of Mathematics, Carleton College, Northfield, MN.

1. Introduction

Many computer applications seek to create an illusion of interaction with a virtual world. Vehicle simulation, geometric modeling and scientific visualization, for example, all require rapid display of computer-generated imagery that changes dynamically according to the user's wishes. Much progress has been made in developing high-speed rendering hardware over the past several years, but even the current generation of graphics systems can render only modest scenes at interactive rates.

For many years our research goal has been the pursuit of truly interactive graphics systems. To achieve the necessary rendering speeds and to provide a platform for real-time algorithm research, we have been developing a massively parallel image generation architecture called *Pixel-Planes* [Fuchs 81, 82, 85, Poulton 85]. We briefly describe the basic ideas in the architecture:

Each pixel is provided with a minimal, though general, processor, together with local memory to store pixel color, z-depth, and other pixel information. Each processor receives a distinct value of a linear expression in screen-space, $Ax + By + C$, where A,B,C are data inputs and x,y is the pixel address in screen-space. These expressions are generated in a parallel linear expression evaluator, composed of a binary tree of tiny multiply-accumulator nodes. A custom VLSI chip contains pixel memory, together with the relatively compact pixel processors and the linear expression evaluator, both implemented in bit-serial circuitry. An array of these chips forms a "smart" frame buffer, a 2D computing surface that receives descriptions of graphics primitives in the form of coefficients (A,B,C) with instructions and locally performs all pixel-level rendering computations. Since instructions, memory addresses, and A,B,C coefficients are broadcast to all processors, the smart frame buffer forms a Single-Instruction-Multiple-Datastream computer, and has a very simple connection topology. Instructions (including memory addresses and A,B,C's) are generated in a conventional graphics transformation engine, with the relatively minor additional task of converting screen-space polygon vertices and colors into the form of linear expressions and instructions.

In 1986 we completed a full-scale prototype Pixel-Planes system, Pixel-Planes 4 (*Pxpl4*) [Poulton 87, Eyles 88], which renders 39,000 Gouraud-shaded, z-buffered polygons per second (13,000 smooth-shaded interpenetrating spheres/second, 11,000 shadowed polygons/second) on a 512x512 pixel full-color display. While this system was a successful research vehicle and is extremely useful in our department's computer graphics laboratory, it is too large and expensive to be practical outside of a research setting. Its main limitations are:

- large amount of hardware, often utilized poorly (particularly when rendering small primitives)
- hard limit on the memory available at each pixel (72 bits)
- no access to pixel data by the transformation unit or host computer
- insufficient front-end computation power

This paper describes its successor, Pixel-Planes 5 (*Pxpl5*). *Pxpl5* uses screen subdivision and multiple small rendering units in a modular, expandable architecture to address the problem of processor utilization. A full-size system is designed to render in excess of one million Phong-shaded triangles per second. Sufficient "front end" power for this level of performance is provided by a MIMD array of general-purpose math-oriented processors. The machine's multiple processors communicate over a high-speed network. Its organization is sufficiently general that it can efficiently render curved surfaces, volume-defined data and CSG-defined objects. In addition it can rapidly perform various image-processing algorithms. *Pxpl5*'s rendering units each are 5 times faster than *Pxpl4* and contain more memory per pixel, distributed in a memory hierarchy: 208 bits of fast local storage on its processor-enhanced memory chips, 4K bits of memory per pixel processor in a conventional VRAM "backing store", and a separate frame buffer that refreshes normal and stereo images on a 1280x1024 72Hz display.

2. Background

Raster graphics systems generally contain two distinct parts: a graphics transformation engine that transforms and lights the geometric description of a scene in accordance with the user's viewpoint and a Renderer that paints the transformed scene onto a screen.

Designs for fast transformation units have often cast the series of discrete steps in the transformation process onto a pipeline of processing elements, each of which does one of the steps [Clark 82]. As performance requirements increase, however, simple pipelines begin to experience communication bottlenecks, so designers have turned to multiple pipelines [Runyon 87] or have spread the work at some stages of the pipe across multiple processors [Akeley 88]. Vector organizations offer a simple and effective way to harness the power of multiple processors, and have been used in the fastest current graphics workstations [Apgar 88, Diede 88]. Wide vector organizations may have difficulty with data structures of arbitrary size, such as those that implement the PHIGS+ standard, so at least one commercial offering divides the work across multiple processors operating in MIMD fashion [Torberg 87].

The rendering problem has generally been much more difficult to solve because it requires, in principal, computations for every pixel of every primitive in a scene. To achieve interactive speeds on workstation-class machines, parallel rendering engines have become the rule. These designs must all deal with the memory bandwidth bottleneck at a raster system's frame buffer. Three basic strategies for solving this problem are:

Rendering Pipelines. The rendering problem can also be pipelined over multiple processors. The Hewlett-Packard SRX graphics system [Swanson 86], for example, uses a pipeline of processors implemented in custom VLSI that simultaneously perform 6-axis interpolations for visibility and shading, operating on data in a pixel cache.

The frame buffer bandwidth bottleneck can be ameliorated by writing to the frame buffer only the final colors of the *visible* pixels. This can only be achieved if all the primitives that may affect a pixel are known and considered before that pixel is written. Sorting primitives by screen position minimizes the number that have to be considered for any one pixel. Sorting first by Y, then by X achieves a scan-line order that has been popular since the late 1960's and is the basis for several types of real-time systems [Watkins 70]. The basic strategy has been updated by several groups recently. The SAGE design [Gharachorloo 88] contained a processor for every pixel on a scan-line. Data for primitives active on a scan-line pass by this array, and visible pixel colors are emitted at video rates; no separate frame buffer is required. Researchers at Schlumberger [Deering 88] recently proposed a system in which visibility and Phong-shading processors in a pipeline are assigned to the *objects* to be rendered on the current scan line. The latter two projects promise future commercial offerings that can render on the order of 1M triangles per second with remarkably little hardware, though designs for the front ends of these systems have yet to be published. These machines have each cast one particular rendering algorithm into hardware, enabling a lower-cost solution but one not intended for internal programming by users. New algorithms cannot easily be mapped onto hardware for scan-line ordered pipelines. Finally, a difficulty with these designs is ensuring graceful performance degradation for scenes with exceptional numbers of primitives crossing a given scan-line.

Interlaced Processors. As first suggested a decade ago [Fuchs 77, 79, Clark 80], the frame buffer memory can be divided into groups of memory chips, each with its own rendering processor, in an interlaced fashion (each processor-with-memory handles every *n*th pixel on every *m*th row). The rendering task is distributed evenly across the multiple processors, so the effective bandwidth into the frame buffer increases by a factor of *m•n*. This idea is the basis of several of the most effective current raster graphics systems [Akeley 88, Apgar 88]. Some of these systems, however, are again becoming limited by the bandwidth of commercial DRAMs [Whitton 84]. With increasing numbers of processors operating in SIMD fashion, processor utilization begins to suffer because fewer processors are able to operate on visible pixels, the "write efficiency" problem discussed in [Deering 88]. Raising the performance of interlaced processors by an order of magnitude will probably require more complex organizations or new memory devices.

Processor-Enhanced Memories. Much higher memory bandwidth can be obtained by combining some processing circuitry on the same chip with dense memory circuits. The most widely used example of a "smart" memory is the Video RAM (VRAM), introduced by Texas Instruments. Its only enhancement is a second, serial-access port into the frame buffer memory; nevertheless these parts have had a great impact on graphics system design. The SLAM system, described some years ago in [Demetrescu 85], combines a 2D frame buffer memory with an on-chip parallel 1D span computation unit; it appears to offer excellent performance for some 2D applications but requires external processing to divide incoming primitives into scan-line slices. Recently NEC announced a commercial version of an enhanced VRAM that performs many common functions needed in 2D windowing systems. This approach has been the focus of our work since 1980; in the Pixel-Planes architecture we have attempted to remove the memory bottleneck by performing essentially all pixel-oriented rendering tasks within the frame buffer memory system itself.

The architecture we will describe below employs a MIMD array of processors in its transformation unit and seeks to make more effective use of the processor-enhanced memory approach.

3. Project Goals

We wanted Pixel-Planes 5 to be a platform for research in graphics algorithms, applications and architectures, and a testbed for refinements that would enhance the cost effectiveness of the approach. To this end, we adopted the following goals:

• **Fast Polygon Rendering.** Despite all the interest in higher-order primitives and rendering techniques, faster polygon rendering is still the most often expressed need for many applications: 3D medical imaging, scientific visualization, 'virtual worlds' research. We therefore set a goal of rendering 1 million z-buffered Phong-shaded triangles per second, assuming the average triangle's area is 100 pixels and that it is embedded in a triangle strip. We wanted to achieve this rate without using any special structures for rendering just triangles — we wanted a system for much more than triangles.

• **Generality.** For the system to be an effective base for algorithm development, it needed to have a simple, general structure whose power was readily accessible to the algorithm developer programming in a high-level language. We wanted it to have sufficient generality for rendering curved surfaces, volume data, objects described with Constructive Solid Geometry, for rendering scenes using the radiosity lighting model, and (we hoped) for a variety of other 3D graphics tasks that we have not yet considered. It was essential that the system support a PHIGS+ -like environment for application programmers not interested in the system's low-level details. Further, the hardware platform should be flexible to allow experiments in hardware architectures.

• **Packaging.** A high-performance configuration that met our primary performance goals should fit within a workstation cabinet with no unusual power requirements. We also wanted a system that could be modularly built and flexibly configured to trade cost for performance. The system should drive a 1280x1024 display at >60Hz, and be able to update full scene images at >20 frames/second.

4. Parallel Rendering by Screen-space Subdivision

We now describe the scheme we use in *Pxpl5* to attain high levels of performance in a compact, modular, expandable machine. Our previous work has depended on a single, large computing surface of SIMD parallel processors operating on the entire screen space. In the new architecture, we instead have one or more small SIMD engines, called Renderers, that operate on small, separate 128x128-pixel patches in a virtual pixel space. Virtual patches can be assigned on the fly to any actual patch of the display screen. The system achieves considerable speedup by simultaneously processing graphics primitives that fall entirely within different patches on the screen.

The principal cost of this screen-space subdivision scheme is that the primitives handled in the transformation engine must be sorted into "bins" corresponding to each patch-sized region of the screen space. Primitives that fall into more than one region are placed into the bins for all such regions. The simplest (though expensive) way to support these bins is to provide additional storage in the transformation engine for the entire, sorted list of output primitives. Once transformed, sorted, and stored, a new scene is rendered by assigning all available Renderers to patches on the screen and dispatching to these Renderers primitives from their corresponding bins. When a Renderer completes a patch, it can discard its z-buffer and all other pixel values besides colors; pixel color values are transferred from on-chip pixel memory to the secondary storage system, or "backing store", described below. The Renderer is then assigned to the next patch to be processed. This process is illustrated in Figure 1 for a system configured with only four Renderers.

The general idea of multiple independent groups of pixel processors operating on disjoint parts of the display screen was described in several of our earlier publications as "buffered" Pixel-Planes. What

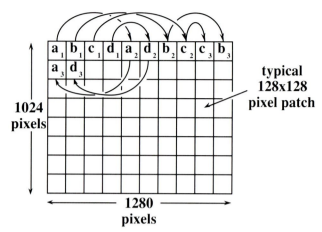

Figure 1: Rendering process for a *Pxpl5* system with 4 Renderers. 1280x1024 screen is divided into 80 128x128 patches. Patches are processed in raster order. Renderers **a-d** are assigned initially to the first four patches. Renderer **a** completes first, and is assigned to the next available patch. Next Renderer **d** completes its first patch and is assigned to the next available patch, and so forth.

is new about this implementation is the idea of flexibly mapping small virtual pixel spaces onto the screen space. It allows useful systems to be built with any number of small rendering units, permits cost/performance to be traded nearly linearly, and can render into a window of arbitrary size with only linear time penalty.

The virtual pixel approach is supported in the *Pxpl5* implementation by a memory hierarchy, whose elements are: (1) 208 bits of fast SRAM associated on-chip with each pixel processor; (2) a "backing store" built from VRAMs, tightly linked to the custom logic-enhanced memory chips; (3) a conventional VRAM frame buffer. The backing store consists of an array of VRAMs, each connected via its video port to one of our custom memory chips; 1MB VRAMs provide 4Kbits of storage per pixel. The backing store memory is available through the VRAM random I/O port to the rest of the system, which can read and write pixel values in the conventional way. A Renderer uses this memory to save and retrieve pixel values, effectively allowing "context switches" when the Renderer ceases operations on one patch and moves to another. A typical context switch takes about 0.4 msec, the time to render a hundred or so primitives, and can be fully overlapped with pixel processing.

In the simple multi-Renderer scheme described above, the backing store is used to store pixel color values for patches of the screen as the Renderer completes them. When the entire image has been rendered, each of these regions is transferred in a block to the (double-buffered) display memory in the Frame Buffer, from which the display is refreshed.

5. Architectural Overview

The major elements of *Pxpl5* are:

• **Graphics Processors** (GPs), floating point engines, each with considerable local code and data storage.

• **Renderers**, each a small SIMD array of pixel processors with its own controller.

• **Frame Buffer**, double-buffered, built from conventional Video RAMs, from which the video display is refreshed.

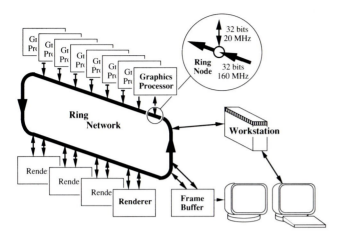

Figure 2: *Pxpl5* block diagram.

- **Host Interface**, which supports communications to/from a UNIX workstation.

- **Ring Network** to interconnect the various processors in a flexible way.

5.1 Ring Network

Pxpl5's multi-processor architecture, motivated by the desire to support a variety of graphics tasks, requires a capable communications network. Rather than build several specialized communications busses to support different types of traffic between system elements, we instead provide a single, flexible, very high performance network connecting all parts of the system.

At rendering rates of 1M primitives per second, moving object descriptions from the GPs to the Renderers requires up to 40 million 32-bit words/second (40 MW/sec), even for relatively simple rendering algorithms. Simultaneously, pixel values must be moved from the Renderers to the Frame Buffer at rates up to 40 MW/sec, for real-time interactive applications. At the suggestion of J. William Poduska of Stellar Computer, Inc., we explored technology and protocols for fast ring networks, and eventually settled on a multi-channel token ring. Ring networks have many advantages over busses in high-speed digital systems. They require only point-to-point communication, thus reducing signal propagation and power consumption problems, while allowing a relatively simple communication protocol. Their major disadvantage, long latency, is not acceptable for many computing systems, but is okay here.

Our network can support eight simultaneous messages, each at 20 MW/sec for a total bandwidth of 160 MW/sec. To avoid deadlock, each transmitting device gains exclusive access first to its intended receiver, then to one of the 8 data channels, before it transmits its data packet. Each Ring Node is a circuit composed of commercial MSI bus-oriented data parts and field-programmable controllers. (At the expense of an expensive development cycle, the Ring Network could be reduced to one or a few ASICs.) The controllers operate at 20MHz, while data is moved at 40MHz (to save wires). Each client processor in the system has one or more of these Nodes, which provides to the client a 20 MW/sec port onto the Ring network.

We have developed a low-level message-passing operating system for the ring devices called the Ring Operating System (ROS). It provides device control routines as well as hardware independent communication. In addition, ROS controls the loading and initialization of programs and data.

5.2 Graphics Processors

The performance goals we have set require sustained computation rates in the "front end" of several hundred MFlops, feasible today only in parallel or vector architectures. We elected to build a MIMD transformation unit; this organization handles PHIGS+ -like variable data structures better than would a vector unit, and supports the "bins" needed for our screen subdivision multi-Renderer.

Much of the system's complexity is hidden by ROS; the programming model is therefore relatively simple. Load sharing is accomplished by dividing a database across the GPs, generally with each GP running the same code. Since the GPs are programmable in the C language, users have access to the machine's full capability without needing to write microcode.

5.3 Renderer

Section 4 describes the essentials of the Renderer design, whose block diagram is shown in Figure 3. It is based on a logic-enhanced memory chip built using 1.6 micron CMOS technology and operating at 40MHz bit-serial instruction rates. In addition to 256 pixel processing elements, each with 208 bits of static memory, the chip contains a quadratic expression evaluator (QEE) that produces the value $Ax+By+C+Dx^2+Exy+Fy^2$ simultaneously at each pixel x,y from global inputs A,B,C,D,E,F [Goldfeather 86]. Quadratic expressions, while not essential for polygon rendering, are very useful for rendering curved surfaces and for computing a spherical radiosity lighting model (see Section 7.6).

A major design issue for the Renderer was choosing the size of the processor array. The effectiveness of the screen-space subdivision scheme for parallel rendering is determined in part by the frequency with which primitives must be processed in more than one region, and this in turn depends on the size of the Renderer's patch. On one hand, economy of use of the fairly expensive custom chips of the processor array and the need to leverage performance by dividing the rendering work across as many processors as possible argue for smaller Renderer patches. A large Renderer patch, on the other hand, reduces the likelihood that primitives will need to be processed more than once. We elected a 128x128 Renderer size; it is fairly efficient for small primitives, and its hardware conveniently fits on a reasonable size printed circuit board.

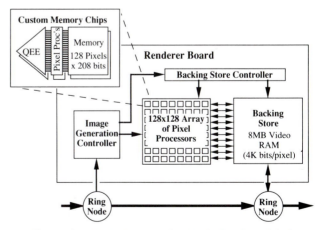

Figure 3: Block diagram of a *Pxpl5* Renderer. Pixel processor array implemented in 64 custom chips, each with 2 columns of 128 pixel processors-with-memory and a quadratic expression evaluator.

5.4 Frame Buffer and Host Interface

The Frame Buffer is built in a fairly conventional way using Video RAMs. It supports a 1280x1024-pixel, 72Hz refresh-rate display, 24-bit true color and a color lookup table. Display modes include stereo (alternating frames) and a hardware 2x zoom. The Frame Buffer is accessed through two Ring Nodes, to provide an aggregate bandwidth of 40 MW/sec into the buffer, allowing up to 24Hz updates for full-size images. *Pxpl5* is hosted by a Sun 4 workstation. Host communication is via programmed I/O, providing up to 4 MBytes/sec bandwidth between *Pxpl5* and its host.

5.5 Performance

Since the transformation engine in *Pxpl5* is based on the same processor used in *Pxpl4*, we estimate, based on the earlier machine's performance, that a GP can process on the order of 30,000 Phong-shaded triangles per second; 32 GPs are therefore required to meet our performance goal. A single Renderer has a raw performance of about 150,000 Phong-shaded triangles per second; actual performance is reduced somewhat by inefficiencies resulting from primitives that must be processed in more than one patch. Simulations predict an actual performance of around 100,000 triangles/sec, so a configuration to meet the performance goals will require 8-10 Renderers.

6. PPHIGS Graphics Library

Pxpl5 may be programmed at various levels. We anticipate users ranging from application programmers, who simply desire a fast rendering platform with a PHIGS+ -style interface [van Dam 88], to algorithm prototypers, who need access to the Renderer's low-level pixel operations and may depart from the PHIGS+ paradigm. To meet these disparate needs, several layers of support software are required. Program initialization and message passing between processors are handled by the Ring Operating System (ROS). A local variation of PHIGS+ (Pixel-Planes PHIGS or *PPHIGS*) provides a high-level interface for users desiring portable code. This section describes PPHIGS.

PPHIGS makes the hardware appear to the "high-level" graphics programmer very much like any other graphics system: the programmer's code (running on the host) makes calls to the graphics system to build and modify a hierarchical data structure. This structure is traversed by the PPHIGS system to create the image on the screen.

6.1 Database Distribution

Since the applications programming library is based on PHIGS, it allows the programmer to create a display list that is a directed acyclic graph of structures. These structures contain elements that are either graphics primitives, state-changing commands, or calls to execute other structures. To take advantage of the multiple graphics processors in *Pxpl5*, we must distribute the database structure graph across the graphics processors in a way that balances the computational load, even in the presence of editing and changes in view. In order to achieve this we must balance the load across GPs for each structure. When a structure is created, some of the primitives are placed on each GP. If the object goes out of view or a new instance is created, the load will remain balanced.

In PHIGS, as in most structured display list systems, child structures inherit information from their parents such as transformation matrices and colors. These state-changing commands as well as structure execution calls must be replicated on each GP since each structure is distributed across multiple GPs. This replication should not be a problem, since we expect the majority of structure elements to be

graphics primitives and not state-changing ones. We have devised other distribution schemes for applications that violate this assumption.

6.2 The Rendering Process

The rendering process is controlled by a designated graphics processor, the master GP, or MGP. By exchanging messages with other GPs and sending commands to other modules when necessary, the MGP synchronizes operations throughout the system.

Before discussing the steps in the rendering process, we first want to emphasize the distinction between pixel operations that take place on a per primitive basis, such as z comparison and storage, and those that can be deferred until the end of all primitive processing or *end-of-frame*. Shading calculations from intermediate values stored at the pixels, for instance, need only be performed once per pixel, rather than once per primitive (assuming there is sufficient pixel storage to hold the intermediate values until end-of-frame). During end-of-frame the final colors can be computed in parallel from the stored values of the visible portions of every polygon that falls within the 128x128 pixel region. For expensive lighting and shading models, such as Phong shading and textures, this speedup is dramatic.

The major steps in the rendering process are:

1. The application program running on the host edits the database using PPHIGS library routines and transmits these changes to the GPs.
2. Application requests a new frame. Host sends this request to the MGP, which relays it to the other GPs.
3. The GPs interpret the database, generating Renderer commands for each graphics primitive. These commands are placed into the local bins corresponding to the screen regions where the primitive lies. Each GP has a bin for every 128x128 pixel region in the window being rendered.
4. The GPs send bins containing commands to Renderers. The Renderers execute commands and compute intermediate results.
5. The GP sending the final bin to a Renderer also sends end-of-frame commands for the region. The Renderers execute these commands and compute final pixel values from the intermediate results.
6. The Renderers send computed pixels to the frame buffer.
7. When all regions have been received, the frame buffer swaps banks and displays the newly-computed frame.

The MGP assigns Renderers to screen regions while the frame is being rendered. It communicates a Renderer assignment to the GPs by sending a message to one GP, which sends its associated bin, and then forwards the message to the next GP, which does the same. At the end, the message is sent back to the MGP, indicating that all the bins have been processed. This method ensures that at most one GP attempts to transmit to a Renderer at a given time. This prevents blocked transmissions, which would slow throughput.

The steps of the rendering process can be overlapped in several ways; at maximum throughput, several frames may be in progress at once. This requires that the bin memory be double buffered. If a GP runs out of bin memory it must send some of its bin data to a Renderer to free up memory. The MGP handles synchronization to keep the frames properly separated [Ellsworth 89].

7. Rendering Algorithms

We now discuss various rendering algorithms in turn. Some of these have been published before, in which case, we review their applica-

bility to *Pxpl5* and give performance estimates. We also report new techniques for efficiently displaying procedural textures and conic spline-defined fonts, for calculating radiosity form-factors, and for displaying volume-defined images at interactive rates.

7.1 Phong Shading

Since *Pxpl5* can evaluate quadratic expressions directly, we can implement Phong shading using Bishop and Wiemer's Fast Phong Shading technique [Bishop 86]. However, the power of the pixel processors allows us to compute the Phong lighting model [Phong 73] directly. This means that the graphics processors do not have to do th₂ extensive computation necessary to compute the quadratic coefficients. We feel that this approach will be faster and more general.

As polygons and other primitives are processed, the x, y, and z components of the surface normal are stored in all the pixels where the primitive is visible. For polygons this is done by simple linear interpolation of each component. When all the primitives for a region have been processed, the pixel-parallel end-of-frame operations are performed. First, the normal vector is normalized by dividing by the square root of its length, which is computed using a Newton iteration; then the color for each pixel is computed using the standard Phong lighting model.

Simulation indicates that the end-of-frame computation for the Phong lighting model with a single light source consumes around 23,000 Renderer cycles or .57 milliseconds. With full screen resolution of 1024 by 1280 and a 16 Renderer system, the total end-of-frame time is .57msec • (80/16) or 2.85msec per frame. At 24 frames per second this is 6.8 percent of the rendering time.

7.2 Spheres

Pxpl5 can render spheres using the same algorithm as on *Pxpl4* [Fuchs 85], but is both faster (taking advantage of the QEE), and can generate higher-quality images (Phong shading with 24-bit color). Phong shading is achieved as follows. The expressions for the coordinates of the surface normal for a sphere are:

$$nx = \frac{x - a}{r}$$

$$ny = \frac{y - b}{r}$$

$$nz = \frac{\sqrt{r^2 - (x - a)^2 - (y - b)^2}}{r^2}$$

The expression for *nz* can be approximated by a parabola:

$$nz = \frac{r^2 - (x - a)^2 - (y - b)^2}{r^2}$$

Then the normals are computed at each pixel by broadcasting two linear expressions and one quadratic expression. Results from simulation indicate that this approximation produces satisfactory shading including the specular highlights. Assuming one light source and 24 frames per second, we estimate the system performance to be 1.8M spheres per second for 100 pixel area spheres and 900K spheres per second for 1600 pixel area spheres.

7.3 Shadows

Pxpl4 was able to generate images with shadows very rapidly — nearly half as fast as images without shadows [Fuchs 85]. Unfortunately we will not achieve similar results with *Pxpl5*. Since a

polygon's shadow volume will cross many screen regions, the speedup we would get from screen-space subdivision will be greatly reduced. A naive approach would be to send the plane equations for the shadow volume to every region. This would greatly increase both the amount of data that would be sent over the ring and the amount of computation that the Renderers would have to do. A simple optimization would be to have the graphics processors compute which regions could possibly be shadowed by a polygon. We have not yet explored these options in depth. Because of the problems mentioned above, we anticipate increasing use of the fast radiosity technique described in Section 7.6.

7.4 Texture Mapping

We have previously reported a technique to compute the *u,v* texture coordinates for polygons in perspective [Fuchs 85]. The speed of this technique is limited by the time to broadcast the individual texture values to the pixels. While 64x64 image textures run at interactive rates on *Pxpl4* (see Figure 4), a more efficient method for *Pxpl5* is to calculate the texture values directly in each pixel. Broadcasting the texture values will be significantly faster on *Pxpl5* than on *Pxpl4*, since texture values can be stored in bins and only broadcast when needed for one or more pixels of a region.

Image-based Textures. We have explored both summed area tables [Crow 84] and mip-maps [Williams 83] for anti-aliasing image

Figure 4: Mandrill mapped onto a plane and hoop on *Pxpl4*. Estimated rendering time on *Pxpl5* is 31 msec.

Figure 5: Procedural earth, water, sky, fire and stars textures (simulated). Estimated rendering time on *Pxpl5* is 5.5 milliseconds.

textures. We feel that mip-maps will work best on *Pxpl5*. During rendering the mip-map interpolation value can be linearly interpolated across the polygon. At end of frame, the mip-map is broadcast to each pixel-processor, and each processor loads the texture elements at its *u,v* coordinate along with neighboring values for interpolation.

Procedural Textures. We have begun to explore procedural textures, as shown by Perlin [Perlin 85] and Gardner [Gardner 88], for use in *Pxpl5*. We have written a program for *Pxpl4* that allows one to explore in real-time the space of textures possible using Gardner's technique. This program and software written by Douglass Turner were used to create the textures shown in Figure 5.

The two-dimensional Gardner spectral functions are calculated using quadratic approximations for the cosine functions. This requires nine multiplies per term plus one multiply to combine the *x* and *y* directions. Different textures for different pixels can be computed simultaneously. The images shown in the figure contains five terms. On *Pxpl5* they would require about 15,000 cycles or 360 microseconds using 10 bits of resolution. These procedural methods can be anti-aliased by eliminating high frequency portions of the texture; terms whose wavelength spans less than one pixel are simply not computed [Norton 82].

7.5 Fonts

Herve Tardif has been developing methods for rapidly rendering fonts. Conic splines, as advocated by several researchers [Pavlidis 83, Pratt 85], are particularly well suited for rendering by *Pxpl5*; with the QEE in the processor-enhanced memories, *Pxpl5* can directly scan convert conic section, from which characters are defined. Initially, a character is represented by a sequence of straight line segments and arcs of conics joined together in the plane. As suggested by Pratt, each arc of a conic is in turn represented by three points M, N, P and a scalar S which measures the departure of the conic from a parabola (Figure 6). Hence, a letter can be represented either by a simple closed polygon or, for letters with holes, two or more polygons. The character is initially converted into the difference between its unique convex hull and the discrepancy with that hull. (Holes are treated the same as other discrepancies.) The process is repeated if the discrepancy region(s) are concave. This process amounts to building a tree whose leaves are convex regions and nodes are set operators [Tor 84]. A character is rendered by traversing its corresponding tree, scan converting each convex region in turn. Since conic sections are invariant under projective maps, this technique can also be applied to the rendering of planar characters embedded in a 3D environment.

Performance estimates have been obtained from a conic representation of a Times Roman font given to us courtesy of Michael Shantz of Sun Microsystems. The average number of convex polygons per character in this set is 8.12, the average number of straight edges per polygon is 4.13, and the average number of conics per character is

8.4. This indicates that the average character can be scan-converted with 36 linear coefficients and 8.4 quadratic coefficients. This suggests that each Renderer can scan-convert over 20,000 letters per second. Assuming each character falls into an average of 1.4 rendering regions, 16 Renderers can draw over 225,000 letters per second. The GPs will have difficulty keeping up with this rendering rate, but they can cache coefficients in 2D applications.

7.6 Fast Radiosity

The realism of indoor scenes is greatly enhanced by the radiosity lighting model [Goral 84, Cohen 85], where the lighting contribution due to diffuse interreflection is taken into account. We believe that Pixel-Planes 5 can be used to speed up the calculations needed to compute radiosity. Initial implementations of radiosity required the lighting of all polygons in a scene to be computed before an image is displayed, and this requires many minutes even for simple scenes. The progressive radiosity method [Cohen 88] allows images of progressively better quality to be displayed as light is being distributed through the scene, thus making radiosity more attractive for interactive applications. The most time-consuming step of this process is in computing the form-factors of a polygon patch, that is, how much a patch "sees" of other patches in the scene. This means that a separate visibility calculation must be performed from each patch in a scene. Two common methods used to compute form-factors are tracing rays from a patch and z-buffer rendering onto five image planes that form a hemi-cube at each patch.

We could use *Pxpl5's* Renderers to compute the five z-buffer images needed for each hemi-cube and then bring this information back to the GPs where the rest of the radiosity calculation can be performed. The quadratic expression tree offers another possibility: one z-buffered image will suffice for the visibility calculation at a patch if the polygons are projected onto a hemisphere. Figure 8 illustrates how the edges of a polygon become sections of ellipses when projected onto a hemisphere and from there onto a plane. To compute such a projected image each edge of a polygon in the scene is scanned using the quadratic expression tree, and then a depth value is computed either by using an approximate depth or by storing special constants at each pixel [Goldfeather 89]. An identifying number for the polygon is stored at all pixels where the polygon is visible. A completed hemisphere image is sent to a GP which uses the image to compute the form-factors, and then this information is used to compute the colors at vertices of the patches in the scene. A radiosity-lit scene is then displayed by the regular scan conversion procedure and by interpolating the vertex colors across each polygon patch. Since the resolution within a single Renderer appears to be more than adequate for each projected image, multiple Renderers can be used independently. Each Renderer should be able to process about 100,000 quadrilaterals per second.

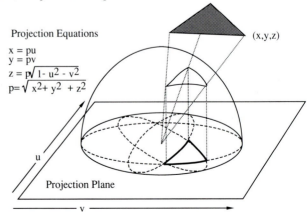

Projection Equations

$$x = pu$$
$$y = pv$$
$$z = p\sqrt{1 - u^2 - v^2}$$
$$p = \sqrt{x^2 + y^2 + z^2}$$

(x,y,z)

u

Projection Plane

v

Figure 7: Hemispherical projection of a triangle.

Figure 6: Conic font constructed by regions bounded by lines and conic sections.

Figure 8: (a) Hemispherical projection of Tebbs and Turk's office, generated on the *Pxpl5* simulator. Estimated rendering time on *Pxpl5* is 2.8 milliseconds. (b) Standard view of the same room as in (a), displayed on *Pxpl4* (radiosity software described in [Airey 89]). The viewpoint in (a) is from the light fixture near the door.

7.7 Volume Rendering

One example of *Pxpl5's* generality is its ability to perform volume rendering. Marc Levoy plans to implement a version of the algorithm described in [Levoy 89a, 89b]. To briefly summarize the algorithm: We begin with a 3D array of scalar-valued voxels. We first classify and shade the array based on the function value and its gradient to yield a color and an opacity for each voxel. Parallel viewing rays are then traced into the array from an observer position. Each ray is divided into equally spaced sample intervals, and a color and opacity is computed at the center of each interval by tri-linearly interpolating from the colors and opacities of the nearest eight voxels. The resampled colors and opacities are then composited in front-to-back order to yield a color for the ray.

For *Pxpl5*, we propose to store the function value and gradient for several voxels in the backing store of each pixel processor. The processor then performs classification and shading calculations for all voxels in its backing store. The time to apply a monochrome Phong shading model at a single voxel using a pixel processor is about 1 msec. For a 256x256x256 voxel dataset, each pixel processor

would be assigned 64 voxels, so the time required to classify and shade the entire dataset would be about 64 msec.

The GPs perform the ray-tracing to generate the image. They are each assigned a set of rays and request sets of voxels from the pixel processors as necessary. The GPs perform the tri-linear interpolation and compositing operations, then transmit the resulting pixel colors to the frame buffer for display. Hierarchical subdivision techniques can be used to reduce the amount of data that must be sent to each graphics processor.

The frame rate we expect from this system depends on which parameters change from frame to frame. Preliminary estimates suggest that for changes in observer position alone, we will be able to generate a sequence of slightly coarse images at 10 frames per second and a sequence of images of the quality of Figure 9 at 1 frame per second.

7.8 Rendering CSG-defined Objects

We and others have developed algorithms to directly render Constructive Solid Geometry (CSG) defined objects on graphics systems with deep frame buffers [Jansen 87, Rossignac 86, Goldfeather 88]. On *Pxpl4* we developed a CSG modeler that displays small datasets at interactive rates.

Pxpl5 provides several opportunities to increase CSG rendering speed: the QEE on *Pxpl5* renders curved-surfaced primitives without breaking them into polygonal facets; having more bits per pixel allows surfaces that are used multiple times to be stored and re-used, rather than being re-rendered, greatly increasing performance; finally, the screen-subdivision technique advocated in [Jansen 87] provides a way to take advantage of *Pxpl5's* multiple Renderers. *Pxpl4* interactively renders CSG objects with dozens of primitives (Figure 10). We expect *Pxpl5* to interactively render objects with hundreds of primitives.

7.9 Transparency

Several methods for rendering transparent surfaces are possible, given the generality and power of *Pxpl5*. The most promising is to enhance the bin sorting in each GP to generate twice as many bins, one for transparent and another for opaque primitives for each region. The transparent primitives are rendered after all the opaque ones. Since we expect relatively few transparent polygons, each of the

Figure 9: Volume-rendered head from CT data, generated by Marc Levoy on a Sun 4. Estimated rendering time on *Pxpl5* is 1 second.

Figure 10: CSG-modeled truck generated on *Pxpl4*. Estimated rendering time on *Pxpl5* is 40 milliseconds.

"transparent" bins can be sorted from back to front and rendered by simple composition. For difficult cases, in which a cluster of transparent polygons cannot be sorted in z (as in a basket-weave of transparent strips), multiple z values can be stored at each pixel to control the compositing step. With this approach, difficult primitives may need to be sent to Renderers several times to ensure correct blending.

8. Current Status of Pxpl5 (April 1989)

Of the three custom CMOS VLSI chips being designed, the backing-store interface chip is being tested and the processor-enhanced memory chip is in fabrication. Layout of the third chip, the Renderer controller, is nearly complete. Detailed simulation of the board-level logic design is well along, and PCBs are being designed. A small version of the Ring Network with a pair of Graphics Processors is expected to become operational by late summer, with a complete system running by year's end. On the software front, a high-level language porting base is running simple code. The Renderer simulator is yielding useful images.

9. Acknowledgments

We wish to thank: our colleagues on the Pixel-Planes team, Michael Bajura, Andrew Bell, Howard Good, Chip Hill, Victoria Interrante, Jonathan Leech, Marc Levoy, Ulrich Neumann, John Rhoades, Herve Tardif, and Russ Tuck for many months of dedicated, creative work; Vernon Chi for the design of a novel clock distribution scheme for the system; J. William Poduska and Andries van Dam for valuable criticism and advice on architecture design; Douglass Turner for the texture rendering program; John Rohlf for implementing textures on *Pxpl4* and computing the radiosity office image; John Airey for writing the radiosity software used for Figure 9b; Randy Brown, Penny Rheingans, and Dana Smith for the office model; UNC Department of Radiation Oncology for the volumetric data set; US Army Ballistic Research Laboratory for the CSG truck data; Sun Microsystems for the Times Roman font data; John Thomas and Brad Bennett for laboratory support; Sharon Walters for engineering assistance.

10. References

[Airey 89] Airey, J. and M. Ouh-young, "Two Adaptive Techniques Let Progressive Radiosity Outperform the Traditional Radiosity Algorithm," University of North Carolina Department of Computer Science Technical Report TR89-020.

[Akeley 88] Akeley, Kurt and T. Jermoluk, "High-Performance Polygon Rendering," *Computer Graphics*, 22(4), (Proceedings of SIGGRAPH '88), pp 239-246.

[Apgar 88] Apgar, B., B. Bersack, A. Mammen, "A Display System for the Stellar Graphics Supercomputer Model GS1000," *Computer Graphics*, 22(4), (Proceedings of SIGGRAPH '88), pp 255-262.

[Bishop 86] Bishop, Gary and David M. Wiemer, "Fast Phong Shading," *Computer Graphics*, 20(4), (Proceedings of SIGGRAPH '86), pp. 103-106.

[Clark 80] Clark, J. and M. Hannah, "Distributed Processing in a High-Performance Smart Image Memory," *LAMBDA (VLSI Design)*, Q4, 1980, pp 40-45.

[Clark 82] Clark, J. July, 1982. "The Geometry Engine: A VLSI Geometry System for Graphics," *Computer Graphics*, 16(3), (Proceedings of SIGGRAPH '82), pp 127-133.

[Cohen 85] Cohen, Michael F., and Donald P. Greenberg, "The Hemi-cube: A Radiosity Solution for Complex Environments," *Computer Graphics*, 19(3), (Proceedings of SIGGRAPH '85), pp. 31-40.

[Cohen 88] Cohen, Michael F., Shenchang Eric Chen, John R. Wallace, and Donald P. Greenberg, "A Progressive Refinement Approach to Fast Radiostiy Image Generation," *Computer Graphics*, 22(4), (Proceedings of SIGGRAPH '88), pp. 75-84.

[Crow 84] Crow, F., "Summed-Area Tables for Texture Mapping," *Computer Graphics*, 18(4), (Proceedings of SIGGRAPH '84), pp. 207-212.

[Deering 88] Deering, M., S. Winner, B. Schediwy, C. Duffy, N. Hunt, "The Triangle Processor and Normal Vector Shader: A VLSI System for High Performance Graphics," *Computer Graphics*, 22(4), (Proceedings of SIGGRAPH '88), pp 21-30.

[Demetrescu 85] Demetrescu, S., "High Speed Image Rasterization Using Scan Line Access Memories," *Proceedings of the 1985 Chapel Hill Conference on VLSI*, Rockville, MD, Computer Science Press, pp 221-243.

[Diede 88] Diede, T., C. Hagenmaier, G. Miranker, J. Rubenstein, W. Worley, "The Titan Graphics Supercomputer Architecture," *Computer*, 21(9), pp 13-30.

[Ellsworth 89] Ellsworth, David, "Pixel-Planes 5 Rendering Control," University of North Carolina Department of Computer Science Technical Report TR89-003.

[Eyles 88] Eyles, J., J. Austin, H. Fuchs, T. Greer, J. Poulton, "Pixel-planes 4: A Summary," *Advances in Computer Graphics Hardware II*, Eurographics Seminars, 1988, pp 183-208.

[Fuchs 77] Fuchs, Henry, "Distributing a Visible Surface Algorithm over Multiple Processors," *Proceedings of the ACM Annual Conference*, 449-451.

[Fuchs 79] Fuchs, H., B. Johnson, "An Expandable Multiprocessor Architecture for Video Graphics," *Proceedings of the 6th ACM-IEEE Symposium on Computer Architecture*, April 1979, pp 58-67.

[Fuchs 81] Fuchs, H. and J. Poulton, "Pixel-planes: A VLSI-Oriented Design for a Raster Graphics Engine," *VLSI Design*, 3rd Quarter, 1981., 2(3),.pp 20-28.

[Fuchs 82] Fuchs, H., J. Poulton, A. Paeth, and A. Bell, "Developing Pixel Planes, A Smart Memory-Based Raster Graphics System," *Proceedings of the 1982 MIT Conference on Advanced Research in VLSI*, Dedham, MA, Artech House, pp 137-146.

[Fuchs 85] Fuchs, H., J. GoldFeather, J.P. Hultquist, S. Spach, J. Austin, F.P. Brooks, Jr., J. Eyles, and J. Poulton, "Fast Spheres, Textures, Transparencies, and Image Enhancements in Pixel-Planes," *Computer Graphics*, 19(3), (Proceedings of SIGGRAPH '85), pp. 111-120.

[Gardner 88] Gardner, G., "Functional Modeling of Natural Scenes, Functional Based Modeling," *SIGGRAPH Course Notes*, vol. 28, 1988, pp. 44-76.

[Gharachorloo 88] Gharachorloo, Nader, S. Gupta, E. Hokenek, P. Balasubramanian, B. Bogholtz, C. Mathieu, C. Zoulas, "Subnanosecond Pixel Rendering with Million Transistor Chips, " *Computer Graphics*, 22(4), (Proceedings of SIGGRAPH '88), pp 41-49.

[Goldfeather 86] Goldfeather, Jack and Henry Fuchs, "Quadratic Surface Rendering on a Logic-Enhanced Frame-Buffer Memory System," *IEEE Computer Graphics and Applications*, 6(1), pp 48-59.

[Goldfeather 88] Goldfeather, Jack, S. Molnar, G. Turk, and H. Fuchs, "Near Real-Time CSG Rendering using Tree Normalization and Geometric Pruning," University of North Carolina Department of Computer Science Technical Report TR88-006. To appear in CG&A, 1989.

[Goldfeather 89] Goldfeather, Jack, "Progressive Radiosity Using Hemispheres," University of North Carolina Department of Computer Science Technical Report TR89-002.

[Goral 84] Goral, Cindy M., Kenneth E. Torrance, Donald P. Greenberg and Bennett Battaile, "Modeling the Interaction of Light Between Diffuse Surfaces," *Computer Graphics*, 18(3), (Proceedings of SIGGRAPH '84), pp. 213-222.

[Immel 86] Immel, D., M. Cohen, and D. Greenberg, "A Radiosity Method for Non-Diffuse Environments," *Computer Graphics*, 20(4), (Proceedings of SIGGRAPH '86), pp. 133-142.

[Jansen 87] Jansen, F. and R. Sutherland, "Display of Solid Models with a Multi-processor System," *Proceedings of Eurographics '87*, Elseviers Science Publications, 1987, pp 377-387.

[Levoy 89a] Levoy, Marc, "Volume Rendering by Adaptive Refinement," *The Visual Computer*, 5(3), June, 1989 (to appear).

[Levoy 89b] Levoy, Marc, "Design for a Real-Time High-Quality Volume Rendering Workstation," *Chapel Hill Workshop on Volume Visualization*, Chapel Hill, North Carolina, May 1989 (to appear)

[Norton 82] Norton, Alan, "Clamping: A Method of Antialiasing Textured Surfaces by Bandwidth Limiting in Object Space," *Computer Graphics*, 16(3), (Proceedings of SIGGRAPH '82), pp 1-8.

[Pavlidis 83] Pavlidis, T., "Curve Fitting with Conic Splines," *ACM Transactions on Graphics*, 2(1), January 1983.

[Perlin 85] Perlin, K., "An Image Synthesizer," *Computer Graphics*, 19(3), (Proceedings of SIGGRAPH '85), pp. 151-159.

[Phong 73] Phong, B.T., "Illumination for Computer-Generated Pictures," Ph.D. Dissertation, University of Utah, Salt Lake City, 1973.

[Poulton 85] Poulton, J., H. Fuchs, J.D. Austin, J.G. Eyles, J. Heinecke, C-H Hsieh, J. Goldfeather, J.P. Hultquist, and S. Spach, "PIXEL-PLANES: Building a VLSI-Based Graphic System," *Proceedings of the 1985 Chapel Hill Conference on VLSI*, Rockville, MD, Computer Science Press, pp 35-60.

[Poulton 87] Poulton, J., H. Fuchs, J. Austin, J. Eyles, T. Greer. "Building a 512x512 Pixel-planes System," *Proceedings of the 1987 Stanford Conference on Advanced Research in VLSI*, MIT Press, pp 57-71.

[Pratt 85] Pratt, V., "Techniques for Conic Splines," *Computer Graphics*, 19(3), (Proceedings of SIGGRAPH '85), pp. 151-159.

[Rossignac 86] Rossignac, J., A. Requicha, "Depth Buffering Display Techniques for Constructive Solid Geometry," *IEEE Computer Graphics and Applications*, 6(9), pp 29-39.

[Runyon 87] Runyon, S., "AT&T Goes to 'Warp Speed' with its Graphics Engine," *Electronics Magazine*, July 23, 1987, pp 54-56.

[Swanson 86] Swanson, R., L. Thayer, "A Fast Shaded-Polygon Renderer," *Computer Graphics*, 20(4), (Proceedings of SIGGRAPH '86), pp 95-101.

[Tor 84] Tor, S. and A. Middleditch, "Convex Decomposition of Simple Polygons," *ACM Transactions on Graphics*, 3(4), October 1984, pp 244-265.

[Torberg 87] Torberg, J., "A Parallel Processor Architecture for Graphics Arithmetic Operations," *Computer Graphics*, 21(4), (Proceedings of SIGGRAPH '87), pp 197-204.

[van Dam 88] van Dam, A., Chairman, PHIGS+ Committee, "PHIGS+ Functional Description, Revision 3.0," *Computer Graphics*, 22(3), July, 1988, pp 125-218.

[Wallace 87] Wallace, J., M. Cohen, and D. Greenberg, "A Two-Pass Solution to the Rendering Equations: A Synthesis of Ray-Tracing and Radisoity Methods," *Computer Graphics*, 21(4) (Proceedings of SIGGRAPH '87), pp. 311-320.

[Watkins 70] Watkins, G., "A Real-Time Visible Surface Algorithm, " University of Utah Computer Science Department, UTEC-CSc-70-101, June 1970, NTIS AD-762 004.

[Whitton 84] Whitton, Mary., "Memory Design for Raster Graphics Displays," *IEEE Computer Graphics and Applications*, 4(3), March 1984, pp 48-65.

[Williams 83] Williams, Lance, "Pyramidal Parametrics," *Computer Graphics* 17(3) (Proceedings of SIGGRAPH '83), pp. 1-11.

Illumination Networks:
Fast Realistic Rendering with General Reflectance Functions

Chris Buckalew

Donald Fussell

Department of Computer Sciences
The University of Texas at Austin
Austin, TX 78712

ABSTRACT

We present a technique for modeling global illumination which allows a wide variety of reflectance functions. Scene coherence is exploited in a preprocessing step in which the geometry is analyzed using iterative techniques. Memory is traded for speed, in anticipation of the high memory capacities of workstations of the future. The algorithm operates well over a wide range of time and image quality constraints: realistic results may be produced very quickly while very accurate results require more time and space. The method can be extended for animation and parallelization.

CR Categories and Subject Descriptors: 1.3.3 [Computer Graphics]: Picture/Image Generation–Display algorithms. 1.3.7 [Computer Graphics]: Three-Dimensional Graphics and Realism.

General Terms: Algorithms

Additional Key Words and Phrases: global illumination, radiosity, ray tracing, memory, specular, diffuse, data structure, incremental, ray space.

1. INTRODUCTION

Most techniques used to model global illumination are well-suited to particular surface reflectance functions. Ray tracing methods built on [14] have been designed to render specular reflection from surfaces, and relatively efficient algorithms for this purpose have been developed [2]. Radiosity methods such as [3] and [10] have been designed to handle diffuse reflection from surfaces, and recent advances have led to relatively efficient algorithms of this type as well [4]. Generalizations of ray tracing techniques to handle diffuse

reflectance functions ([1] [5] [8] [13]) and of radiosity techniques to handle specular reflectance functions ([6]) have been significantly slower. This has led to the development of hybrid methods which capitalize on the strengths of both techniques ([12]) to efficiently render scenes containing both diffuse and specular surfaces.

We have developed a fast algorithm for rendering scenes containing both diffuse and non-diffuse surfaces. The method can produce illumination of arbitrary accuracy, with very realistic results produced in a very short time. The algorithm has been designed to exploit a space-time trade-off, in which the use of large data structures allows a less computation-intensive approach to be used than might otherwise have been possible. In spite of this, the memory requirements of this method are much smaller than the virtual memory capacities of most of today's workstations and well within the real memory capacities of tomorrow's machines. The algorithm can be extended to allow fast animation that saves information between frames, and it can be efficiently parallelized.

2. THE PATCH-LINK MODEL

In diffuse reflection, a surface element interacts with most of the other elements that are visible from its front surface. The usual technique for computing global illumination for diffuse surfaces based on their radiosity solves this problem with virtual frame buffers called hemicubes that represent the scene from each of the elements' points of view [3]. Unfortunately, the hemicubes must be stored at huge memory cost or recalculated frequently, and they represent only that directional information which contributes to the computation of form-factors, or percentage of the energy emitted from each surface element which actually arrives at a given surface element. For non-diffuse reflection, light incident on each surface element reflects in a particular direction, so detailed directional information must be used in modeling this type of reflection. In [6], the hemi-cube approach was generalized to include such information by replacing locally ori-

©1989   ACM-0-89791-312-4/89/007/0089 $00.75

ented hemicubes associated with each surface element with a cube oriented along the coordinate axes for each element. Thus a directionally varying radiosity from any element can be distributed to other elements within the context of a single, global coordinate system providing directional referents. Unfortunately, this method required that an $e \times e$ sparse matrix be replaced by an $ed \times ed$ matrix in solving for the energy balance of the environment, where e surface elements and d directions are being used. In practice, this required on the order of 1.5 to 8 days of CPU time on a small supercomputer to produce images of simple scenes [6].

Ray tracing methods control the high computational cost of global directional illumination by calculating rays from one surface element to another only as they are needed. In specular environments relatively few rays are needed, so the high cost of computing them individually is worthwhile. However, ray tracing diffuse environments requires far more rays to sample the many elements of the scene providing diffuse illumination of each element, and the expense of the ray-object intersection calculations may become significant.

Our algorithm has some of the characteristics of distributed ray tracing and of radiosity techniques. It is based on a data structure called an illumination network (I-net). This data structure implements a model of light and surface interaction which we call the patch-link model. Surfaces in the scene are intersected with a set of rays distributed in orientation and location throughout the scene. Any time a pair of facing surfaces is intersected by a common ray, a "link" between these surfaces is formed. The surfaces are then treated as sets of "patches," each of which is a small neighborhood of links. Light can travel through the scene only by means of these links. The reflectance function associated with each patch consists of a mapping from "incoming" links to "outgoing" links; that is, the input to the function is a collection of incoming light intensities over the set of links, which the function maps to a collection of outgoing light intensities over the same set of links.

The set of links associated with each patch connect it to much of its environment, thus fulfilling the function of hemicubes or the global cubes of [6]. In addition, the links encode the directional relationships of the patches they connect, serving the function of rays in ray tracing methods. The high cost of computing the large number of links necessary is reduced and scene coherence is exploited by calculating all the links incrementally in a preprocessing step.

The collection of links represents a finite subset of all the light rays which pass through the scene. An extreme approach is to select at least one ray which connects each pair of patches and add it to the collection of links. If there are N patches this process will result in at least N^2 links. Another approach is that of [6], in which the projection of a patch onto a global cube element forms a link. Our approach is to choose an "evenly distributed" and geometrically uniform set of rays which intersect the scene. Any of the rays in this set which intersect two objects will become links. Proper choice of this set of rays will allow fast incremental ray-patch intersection computations as a preprocessing step.

The patch-link model clearly works well in the limit, where patch size approaches zero and the number of links approaches infinity, and clearly works poorly where patch size is very large and number of links very small. The correct choice for these sizes depends very much on the reflectance functions of the objects in the scene and the desired resolution and accuracy of the image. Shiny objects and sharp shadows, for instance, require smaller patch sizes, and greater accuracy requires more links.

3. AN OVERVIEW OF THE ALGORITHM

The algorithm consists of three main parts. The first is a preprocessing step in which the objects in the scene are divided into patches and the links between patches in the scene are established. Reflectance functions are set up at this time as well: the reflectance function for a patch is described by an NxN matrix, where the (i,j)th element of the matrix gives the fraction of the light arriving on link i that will leave on link j. The reflectance function, then, is determined by the coefficients of this matrix. For a completely diffuse patch, all the coefficients of the matrix would be equal, with the sums of each of the rows equal to one. In reality a surface will absorb some of the incident radiation, so the sums of each of the rows will actually be less than one–if this were not the case convergence might not be achievable. For a perfect mirror, each row would have one coefficient of 1 with the rest 0, because all the light coming in over link i will leave by the link associated with the reflectance angle of link i.

The second part of the algorithm is the distribution process. Light travels outward over the links associated with the light-emitting patches and arrives at the patches on the other end of these links. For each of these patches, the incoming light is passed through the patch's reflectance function, and the result is passed outward along the patch's links to the patches on the other end of the links, some of which will be the original emitting patches. This process continues until there is no more light incoming to any patch, which occurs when all the light has been reflected out of the scene or absorbed. This strategy resembles the light shooting technique used in the progressive refinement approach to hemi-cube based radiosity computation in [4].

Following convergence, the scene must be rendered; the algorithm gives view-independent results, so viewing parameters are set up and light falling on the screen is determined. The preprocess and the distribution process are cleanly separated, so that once the I-net is set up in the preprocess, it may be reused by multiple passes of the distribution process. Objects' reflectance functions and light source strengths may be changed between passes; the preprocess merely encodes the geometry of the scene into an I-net.

4. LINKS

Links are implemented as pointers; if a ray intersects two patches which face each other, each patch will have a pointer for that link, pointing to the other patch. The geometry thus becomes implicit: the pointer indicates the patch that is hit if light leaves the patch in a certain direction. In our implementation the direction in 3-space associated with a pointer is determined by its location in the patch's array of such pointers.

Some ray-tracing techniques, such as [2] and [11], have used a finite set of rays to partition all the rays intersecting the scene into areas of interest, but our method uses only a predetermined finite set of rays for all light transport throughout the scene. We would like this set to be uniform so that it lends itself to incremental ray-object intersection calculations. To achieve this end we chose a formulation of ray space similar in some respects to that of [2].

The ray space of [2] is 5-dimensional; a ray is represented by a 3-D origin and a 2-D direction. We use a different, 4-dimensional formulation. Rays are represented by lines, each described by two slopes and a two-dimensional intercept. The 2-D intercept gives the line's intersection with an intercept plane (one of $x - y$, $x - z$, or $y - z$ planes) and the slope of the line in each of the intercept plane's two dimensions. There is no ray origin or ray direction as with [2]; origins are built into the data structure (the ray-object intersection points serve as origins) and the ray's direction along the line (plus or minus) is implied by the direction that the object faces.

This formulation of ray space may be visualized more easily by considering the analogous formulation for two-dimensional scenes. In 2-space, lines are described by one intercept (on the $x-$axis or on the $y-$axis) and one slope in the appropriate dimension (dy/dx if intercept is on the $y-$axis or dx/dy if the intercept is on the $x-$axis). Thus this ray space for 2-D scenes is two-dimensional.

However, some rays cannot be described by a $y-$intercept and $y-$slope, just as some rays cannot be described by an $x-$intercept and an $x-$slope. To solve this problem we partition ray space into two regions, one for rays whose $y-$slope is between -1 and $+1$, the other for rays whose $x-$slope is between -1 and $+1$. If we restrict our scene to the first quadrant of the unit square (in 3-space, the first octant of the unit cube), then we can put boundaries on the range of the $x-$ and $y-$intercepts. If $y-$slopes must be less than one, then the lowest possible $y-$intercept is -1. Similarly if $y-$slopes must be greater than -1, the highest possible $y-$intercept is 2. The 2-dimensional version of this situation is shown in Figure 1.

All the rays passing through the first quadrant of the unit square are contained in two areas of ray space, one for each dimension, limited by -1 and $+1$ on the slope axis and -1 and $+2$ on the intercept axis. These areas, and some sample rays, are shown in Figure 2. Our selection of rays that will

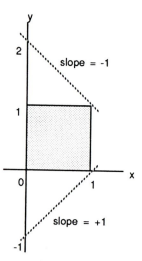

Figure 1: slope and intercept bounds on first quadrant of the unit square

become links is simply a sampling of points in the ray space we have formulated. We choose appropriate intervals for the slope and intercept axes, set up a grid with these intervals, and generate a ray for each grid point.

In 3-space the process is exactly analogous. We have three volumes of ray space, one for each intercept plane, each region bounded by -1 and $+1$ on the slope axes and -1 and $+2$ on the intercept axes. Our finite set of rays is chosen by a uniform point sample in this four-dimensional ray space, just as in the 2-space case. Two things to note: not all the rays inside these limits actually pass through the scene, and the rays are uniform in terms of slopes and intercepts.

They are not uniform in other ways. For example, consider all the rays of this sampling that pass through the origin. The spatial density of the rays decreases as the slopes approach zero. This is shown in the 2-dimensional example in Figure 3. We correct for this error by associating a weighting factor with each slope which is applied to all light traveling along any link having that slope. Each slope accounts for a certain portion of a sphere around the origin of the ray, and the weighting factor is associated with the size of the angle which subtends that portion. For the $k-$th ray counterclockwise from the horizontal about the ray origin, the subtended angle $\theta_k = \arctan((k + 0.5)\Delta y) - \arctan((k - 0.5)\Delta y)$ and the weight associated with that ray is therefore c/θ_k for some constant c.

Another nonuniformity is in the distances between rays with common slopes. Rays orthogonal to their intercept plane are spaced at a distance Δr apart in each of two coordinate directions. Then rays at an angle ϕ with respect to these rays (likewise with respect to the intercept plane normal) are at a distance $\Delta r \cos \phi$ apart (see Figure 4). This nonuniformity in spacing would cause errors if left uncorrected, so an attenuation factor of $\cos \phi$ is associated with all rays at angle ϕ with respect to their intercept plane normal.

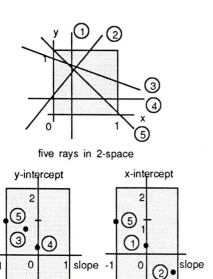

five rays in 2-space

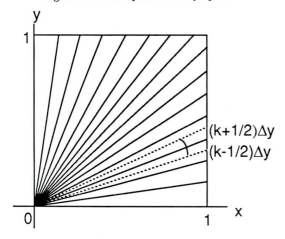

the same rays in ray space

Figure 2: scene space and ray space

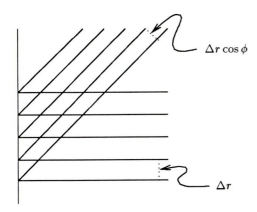

Figure 3: spatial density varies with slope

Figure 4: nonuniform spacing correction

Note that this correction allows Lambert's cosine law for diffuse reflection to be modeled by the intersection densities of rays at various angles to a surface. Given the ray distance correction factor noted above, the density of energy transmitted by a given size set of rays is constant regardless of the slope of the rays. In terms of energy density, this has the same effect as rays with uniform spacing at all slopes with no correction factor. For evenly spaced rays, the density of intersections with rays at angle α with respect to the surface normal varies as $\cos\alpha$ and provides the desired attenuation, therefore our correction for the energy density also provides proper distribution of the incoming energy for Lambertian reflection. As a result, it is not necessary to include this $\cos\alpha$ term in the reflectance functions for surfaces if enough links are involved in the calculation of the intensity at a pixel.

In the current implementation, objects are limited to planar polygons. It is very easy to calculate ray-object intersections incrementally with this set of rays. Once we calculate the intersection point of a given ray and a given object, it is a simple matter to determine the intersection point of the same object and the "next" ray. The planar geometry of the object and the geometry of the relationship of one ray to the next result in very simple incremental calculations, which are described more fully in a later section.

5. PATCHES

Given a uniform set of rays which will become links, the scene is divided into patches. If the patch size is too small, it will not intersect very many rays, and thus will not have very many links. If a patch is too large, one ray for each slope must be chosen as a link out of perhaps many such rays. A bad choice for the link might cause errors. We deal with this problem by dividing each object into rectangular areas each of which is small enough that it can intersect no more than one ray for each slope. This is accomplished by sizing the rectangular areas such that when projected onto the intercept planes the sides of the projected rectangles are equal to the intercept interval.

The I-net data structure is simple. Each patch has an array of pointers, one for each slope, and with each pointer is associated a buffer for incoming light called the in-buffer. Each pointer represents a link, and it points to the patch on the other end of the link. The in-buffer accumulates unprocessed light that has come in over the link, but that has not yet been sent through the reflectance function. The size of the array and the total number of patches depends on the resolution required.

For patches that have only a diffuse component to the reflectance function, the direction of incoming light is not important since it will be evenly distributed. For these patches, then, a great deal of memory may be saved by eliminating their in-buffers and substituting a global in-buffer which receives all the light arriving at the patch, regardless of direction.

6. REFLECTANCE FUNCTIONS

Conceptually, the reflectance function of a patch is described by an $N \times N$ matrix, where N is the number of links connected to the patch. N is usually a large number, so the resulting matrix is very large. For a totally diffuse reflection function, all elements of the matrix are identical, so it may be represented by a scalar constant. In the case of a specular reflectance function, the matrix is very sparse, with entries in each row clustered about the column associated with the reflection direction for that row. For these reflectance functions it is cheaper to store for each link the location of the reflecting link and a small matrix which describes how the light will be distributed around the reflecting link. Usually this small matrix will be the same not only for every link connected to the patch, but for every link connected to the entire object. In this way storage costs are reduced and execution speeds are improved.

Thus diffuse and specular reflectance functions can be stored at modest cost. Other interesting reflectance functions may be stored in this way as well. If the generality of the full matrix representation of a reflectance function is desired, the large matrix need be stored only once for each object (instead of for each patch), since objects are planar.

7. BUILDING THE I-NET STRUCTURE

The preprocess utilizes the slope-intercept format of rays: a ray will intersect an object if its intercept lies inside a polygon formed by projecting the object onto the intercept plane along the ray's slope. This is illustrated in a 3-D example in Figure 5. Basically, then, for each slope S, we project each object onto the intercept plane along S and run a standard scan-conversion algorithm on the resulting polygon. All rays with slope S whose intercepts lie within the polygon intersect the object and those intersection points can be calculated incrementally.

The incremental calculation of ray-object intersections is the key to the speed of the preprocess. Given an object and two slopes, the intercepts are easily determined by scan-converting, as described above. However, we must also determine the coordinates of the ray-object intersections that project to these intercepts in order to find which patches the ray-object intersections are in. Suppose that the plane equation of an object is $Ax + By + Cz + D = 0$ and we wish to find the intersection points of all the rays intersecting the $y - z$ plane with slopes $yslope$ and $zslope$. If the intercept of a particular ray is $(yint, zint)$, then the coordinates of the point (x, y, z) where the ray intersects the object are determined as follows:

$$Ax + By + Cz + D = 0$$

$$Ax + B(yslope * x + yint) + C(zslope * x + zint) + D = 0$$

$$Ax + B * yslope * x + C * zslope * x = -D - B * yint - C * zint$$

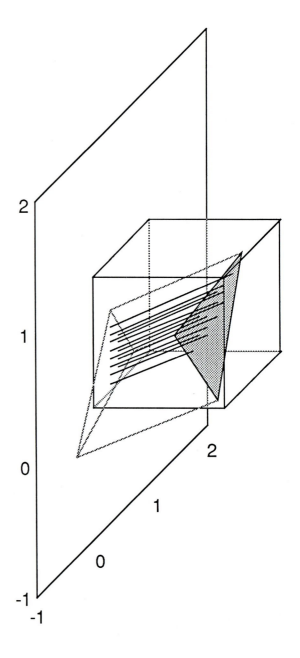

Figure 5: some rays associated with a given slope

Figure 6: a ray and the links it generates

$$x = \frac{(-D - B * yint - C * zint)}{(A + B * yslope + C * zslope)}$$

This is the result for the x-coordinate; y and z are determined from x. If the denominator is zero, then the $y-$ and $z-$slopes are both parallel to the object's plane, and if there is a solution, it will not be unique.

This calculation is not at all fast, and it may be made faster by noticing that the denominator need be calculated only once for each pair of slopes. It is then combined with the numerator coefficients so that

$$D' = D/(A + B * yslope + C * zslope)$$

$$B' = B/(A + B * yslope + C * zslope)$$

$$C' = C/(A + B * yslope + C * zslope)$$

The calculation is now $x = -D' - B' * yint - C' * zint$ which is certainly faster, but if we take advantage of the fact that we are using a scan-conversion algorithm to determine $yint$ and $zint$, it may be made faster yet. Since $zint$ remains constant throughout each scan and at each step of the scan conversion $yint$ is incremented by Δy, then $x_0 = -D' - B' * yint - C' * zint$ at the start of the scan, and $x_{i+1} = x_i - B' * \Delta y$ thereafter. Also, $B' * \Delta y$ is fixed throughout the scan conversion, so each step costs only an addition. The other two coordinates are determined as before.

These intersection points are stored until all intersections have been found for S. At this point each ray with slope S is examined for intersections; links are set up between any pair of patches which have consecutive intersections on the ray and which face each other, as shown in Figure 6. Note that many links may be set up for a single ray if there are multiple pairs of objects facing each other along the ray.

The regularity of the geometry of the patches and links can cause noticeable aliasing. To attenuate the effects of this problem the ray-object intersection points are jittered by a random fraction of the intercept interval amount. This

procedure results in a small perturbation in the slope represented by each link. This loss of regularity is achieved very cheaply, and the resultant noise reduces the effect of the aliasing artifacts. The general problem of aliasing due to uniform point sampling and methods of dealing with it are discussed in [9].

8. THE DISTRIBUTION PROCESS

This part of the algorithm distributes the light throughout the scene until convergence is achieved. Light is first "shot" from the light sources, which have patches and links like any other objects. This light is sent into the scene via the light sources' links, and is accumulated in the recipient patches' in-buffers. Following the light sources' depletion, each patch in the scene is sequentially examined for any unprocessed light in the patch's in-buffers. If any is found, the contents of each of the patch's in-buffers is run through the reflectance function and the result is sent outward over the patch's links into other patches' in-buffers. This process is continued until no patch's in-buffer contains an amount of light larger than a given small threshold value.

The reflectance function calculations consume most of the time used in this process. In the general case, the reflectance function multiplies the array of in-buffers by a matrix of coefficients and the result is mapped back out to the array of links. As mentioned above, we may short-circuit this procedure in the case of diffuse or specular reflectance functions (or a function which is a combination of the two) with a resultant memory savings. For example, if a surface reflects 60% of incoming light in a tight specular pattern and 40% in a diffuse pattern, then 40% of the incoming light will be summed into a global buffer and distributed evenly while the remainder will be distributed around the reflected direction according to a small matrix which describes how the light spreads around the reflected direction. When the patch is totally diffuse only the global buffer need be maintained, and incoming light is processed very rapidly.

9. RENDERING

The algorithm is view-independent; no eyerays need be calculated prior to rendering. Given the standard viewing parameters, eyerays are shot from the eyepoint through each pixel of the image plane. Each eyeray is matched to the "closest" link (in terms of slope and intercept), and the eyeray's intersection point with the nearest object (found with a standard Z-buffer algorithm) determines the patch it hits. The amount of light that the pixel sees is given by the total amount of light reflected from that patch over that link, which has been accumulated in an out-buffer associated with the link.

This procedure is not sufficient to produce good results, however. Sudden jumps in intensity may occur as the eyer-

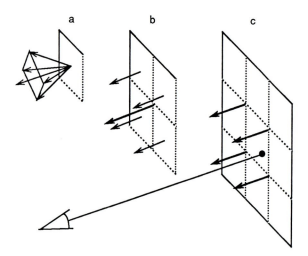

Figure 7: non-diffuse rendering

ays move from patch to patch, or the slope that the eyeray is coerced to changes. To avoid these problems, the light assigned to an eyeray is interpolated in two different ways: the light intensities associated with the rays surrounding the eyeray are interpolated for patches in the intersected patch's 8-neighborhood, and then these values are themselves interpolated. This process is illustrated in Figure 7. A given eyeray is associated with the four slopes that surround it–the $x - z$ slopes immediately to the left and right of the eyeray's $x - z$ slope, and the $x - y$ slopes immediately above and below the eyeray's $x - y$ slope–these are called the bounding slopes. The out-buffers associated with these four slopes are evaluated for each of the patches in the intersected patch's 8-neighborhood. For each of the four patches in each "corner" of the 8-neighborhood, the value associated with the eyeray's slope is bilinearly interpolated from the values of the bounding slopes (a). These four resulting amounts are averaged to get a value for the center of the corner areas (b). This procedure results in four values, one at each corner of the intersected patch. The value for the intersection point is then bilinearly interpolated from these four corner points (c).

A great deal of memory may be saved at the cost of view independence if viewing parameters are determined during the preprocess and out-buffers allocated for only those patches and links that are actually utilized in rendering. For the special case of totally diffuse surfaces, all the out-buffers for a given patch will contain the same value. In this case more memory may be saved by substituting a global out-buffer for each patch, and time may be saved by skipping the first interpolation step.

10. ANALYSIS OF RESULTS

The algorithm was implemented in C on a single processor of an Ardent Titan and on an HP9000 series 300. All time figures are given for the Ardent; the HP workstation figures

were about 5 times slower. Times were measured using the gprof utility in UNIX. All images are 500x500 pixels.

Figure 8 demonstrates the diffuse reflection performance of the algorithm. The light sources are red, green and blue vertical rectangles, which are reflected by a totally diffuse floor. Figure 9 shows the same scene with a specular floor. The irregularities of the reflections are the result of the slight jittering of the ray-object intersections, while the spread of the reflections is a function of the degree of specularity of the floor.

Figures 10 and 11 show the obligatory office scene. This scene was rendered at low resolution, with 2834 patches and 1201 links at each patch. 1.8 million ray-object intersections were calculated in the preprocess, which required 98 seconds for each image. Light sources are the pole lamps, the skylight, the monitor screen, and the tiny lights on the fronts of the machines.

In Figure 10, all the surfaces are diffuse. Memory for the I-net was 15 Mbytes. The distribution process required 24 seconds, and initialization, eyeray calculation, and rendering took 44 seconds. Note the light reflecting from the desk diffusing onto the wall at low center and onto the chair pedestal. The green from the carpet also diffuses onto the lower wall.

In Figure 11, the carpet has been given a heavy coat of wax. The I-net took 18.5 Mbytes. The distribution process jumped to 97 seconds. Initialization, eyeray calculation, and rendering took 69 seconds due to the additional time needed for the non-diffuse rendering. Note the reflections from the light areas of the back wall on the floor foreground and the reflections from the side of the desk on the floor background. The desk front also reflects on the floor, and on the far left the light wall reflects in the floor.

11. EVALUATION OF THE ALGORITHM

While we have only tested diffuse and specular reflectance functions, the method may be used for less ordinary reflectance functions; one example is the reflectance function of an anisotropic surface [7]. Another example is very careful treatment of reflection where different wavelength bands reflect in slightly different directions. This would be implemented with a different reflectance matrix for each color channel.

The method will also handle transparent objects with no modification: instead of a reflectance function, the object's matrix will represent its refractance function. Translucent objects such as frosted glass may be modeled by jittering the outgoing light direction from the incoming direction by an amount determined by the degree of translucence.

This algorithm may be used on other than planar objects with no loss of speed in the distribution process, since the geometry of the scene has been built into the I-net at

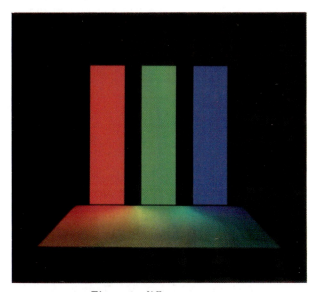

Figure 8: diffuse test scene

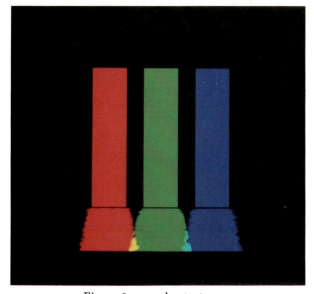

Figure 9: specular test scene

Figure 10: diffuse office scene

Figure 11: "waxed carpet" office scene

that point. The preprocess depends on the incremental calculation of ray-object intersections for much of its speed, however, and unless an efficient method of calculating these intersections is found the advantages of precomputing the I-net may be lost.

One very nice feature of the algorithm is that the time and space it requires are determined primarily by the surface area of all the objects in the scene and by the desired resolution, not the number of objects in the scene. The time required for the preprocess is mainly a function of the number of ray-object intersections to be calculated, and the time required for the distribution process usually depends primarily on the number of patches. There are pathological counterexamples to this generalization–for instance, two mirrors facing each other will result in a very long time for the distribution process–but for most scenes it holds true.

12. FUTURE WORK

Although this technique correctly models both diffuse and non-diffuse interreflections in a scene (to some degree of resolution), often the patch size may be large enough that extremely specular reflections look poor to the eye. Figure 9 shows this well; the floor is almost a mirror, yet the patch size is large enough that "holes" appear near the edge of the reflections where adjacent patches reflect significantly different amounts of light due to discretization. This problem may be fixed in the current implementation by reducing the patch size down to sub-pixel resolution, an expensive solution if the scene has much surface area.

A better approach might be to allow different patch sizes and link densities in different parts of the scene. Very small or highly specular objects will be more accurately rendered if they have been divided into smaller patches, whereas very small patches might result in much unnecessary computation in the case of, for example, a large stretch of blank wall. Sharp shadow boundaries also may require smaller patches. Object size and specularity are known at preprocess time, and objects with appropriate characteristics may be divided into more patches than they would otherwise. Shadows can be detected by noticing when two adjacent links associated with a light-emitting patch are connected to different objects; in this case more links are needed between the two original links.

Another solution is to use ray tracing for the rendering stage of the algorithm. Eyerays are cast into the I-net, and unless the ray hits a specular object, the intensity at the ray-patch intersection is evaluated using bilinear interpolation of the intensities of the patch and its neighbors. If an eyeray hits a specular object, a reflected ray is cast, and a final intensity calculation for that ray performed unless it hits a specular surface. This process continues until the reflected ray hits a diffuse object, a light source, is reflected out of the scene, or a threshold is reached.

Of course, if the environment is completely specular, this process degenerates into standard ray tracing, and the I-net is redundant. What separates this from [1] and two-pass methods ([12]) is that all the illumination of the environment, including both diffuse and nondiffuse interreflection, has been completed at the rendering stage, and the ray tracing merely provides some additional resolution where it matters most. In fact, one can consider this technique to be a form of distributed raytracing, with the I-nets providing a fast way of evaluating the non-specular rays. Since most of the rays will be eyerays whose intersections must be calculated in any case, this procedure will result in little additional work if much of the scene is diffuse.

Since the geometry of a scene is built into a data structure, an interesting extension of this work involves animation. If for each link an accumulator keeps a total of the amount of light that has passed over the link (out-buffers corresponding to the in-buffers mentioned previously) then we can save information between frames. When an object moves between two frames, we determine the links that are affected and negate the light that has traveled over the links; that is, light that previously traveled over the links will be negated and sent down the same links. This "negative light" will be run through the reflectance functions at each patch, and the resulting (smaller) amounts of negative light are dispatched onto the links. This process continues until convergence.

At this point the scene is exactly as it would have looked had the affected links never been there. The links are then removed and new links are established which reflect the geometry of the updated scene. The same light that was negated is now released down these new links and distributed until convergence and the scene is rendered. Note that if the vast majority of the links were unaffected by the change, most of the work done for the first frame will have been saved.

Another area for exploration is the parallelization potential of this algorithm. In the preprocess, the incremental ray-object intersection calculations are both slope-independent and object-independent; slope-object pairs may be taken from a queue by idle processors. In the distribution process, each patch can have its own processor which periodically examines the patch's in-buffers and processes any light it finds there and sends the results out over the patch's links.

Hardware assistance may be useful for the scan-conversion portion of the preprocessing step and the rendering, in the manner of [4].

ACKNOWLEDGMENTS

Our thanks to Emilia Villarreal, A.T. Campbell, and K.R. Subramanian for many helpful technical discussions and suggestions. We would also like to thank the folks at the University of Texas System Center for High Performance Computing, in particular Jesse Driver and Dan Reynolds, for their assistance and the use of their machines.

REFERENCES

[1] Arvo, James, Backward Ray Tracing, Developments in Ray Tracing (SIGGRAPH '86 Course Notes), Vol. 12, August 1986.

[2] Arvo, James and David Kirk, Fast Ray Tracing by Ray Classification, *Computer Graphics* (SIGGRAPH '87 Proceedings), Vol. 21, No. 4, July 1987, pp. 55–64.

[3] Cohen, Michael F., Donald P. Greenberg, A Radiosity Solution for Complex Environments, *Computer Graphics* (SIGGRAPH '85 Proceedings), Vol. 19, No. 3, July 1985, pp. 31–40.

[4] Cohen, Michael F., Shenchang Chen, John Wallace, Donald P. Greenberg, A Progressive Refinement Approach to Fast Radiosity Image Generation, *Computer*

Graphics (SIGGRAPH '88 Proceedings), Vol. 22, No. 4, August 1988, pp. 75–84.

[5] Cook, Robert L., Thomas Porter, Loren Carpenter, Distributed Ray Tracing, *Computer Graphics* (SIGGRAPH '85 Proceedings), Vol. 19, No. 3, July 1985, pp. 111–120.

[6] Immel, David S., Michael F. Cohen, Donald P. Greenberg, A Radiosity Method for Non-Diffuse Environments, *Computer Graphics* (SIGGRAPH '86 Proceedings), Vol. 20, No. 4, August 1986, pp. 133–142.

[7] Kajiya, James T., Anisotropic Reflection Models, *Computer Graphics* (SIGGRAPH '85 Proceedings), Vol. 19, No. 3, July 1985, pp. 15–21.

[8] Kajiya, James T., The Rendering Equation, *Computer Graphics* (SIGGRAPH '86 Proceedings), Vol. 20, No. 4, August 1986, pp. 143–150.

[9] Mitchell, Don P., Generating Antialiased Images at Low Sampling Densities, *Computer Graphics* (SIGGRAPH '87 Proceedings), Vol. 21, No. 4, July 1987, pp. 65–72.

[10] Nashita, Tomoyuki and Eihachiro Nakamae, Continuous Tone Representation of Three-Dimensional Objects Taking Account of Shadows and Interreflection, *Computer Graphics* (SIGGRAPH 85 Proceedings), Vol. 19, No. 3, July 1985, pp. 22–30.

[11] Ohta, Masataka and Mamoru Maekawa, Ray Coherence Theorem and Constant Time Ray Tracing Algorithm, *Computer Graphics 1987* (Proceedings of CG International '87), ed. T. L. Kunii, pp. 303–314.

[12] Wallace, John R., Michael F. Cohen, Donald P. Greenberg, A Two-pass Solution to the Rendering Equation: A Synthesis of Ray Tracing and Radiosity Methods, *Computer Graphics* (SIGGRAPH '87 Proceedings), Vol. 21, No. 4, July 1987, pp. 311–320.

[13] Ward, Gregory J., Frances M. Rubinstein, Robert D. Clear, A Ray Tracing Solution for Diffuse Interreflection, *Computer Graphics* (SIGGRAPH '88 Proceedings), Vol. 22, No. 4, August 1988, pp. 85–92.

[14] Whitted, Turner, An Improved Illumination Model for Shaded Display, *Communications of the ACM*, Vol. 23, No. 6, June 1980, pp. 343–349.

Near Real-Time Shadow Generation Using BSP Trees

Norman Chin
Steven Feiner

Department of Computer Science
Columbia University
New York, NY 10027

Abstract

This paper describes an object-space shadow generation algorithm for static polygonal environments illuminated by movable point light sources. The algorithm can be easily implemented on any graphics system that provides fast polygon scan-conversion and achieves near real-time performance for environments of modest size. It combines elements of two kinds of current shadow generation algorithms: two-pass object-space approaches and shadow volume approaches. For each light source a Binary Space Partitioning (BSP) tree is constructed that represents the shadow volume of the polygons facing it. As each polygon's contribution to a light source's shadow volume is determined, the polygon's shadowed and lit fragments are computed by filtering it down the shadow volume BSP tree. The polygonal scene with its computed shadows can be rendered with any polygon-based visible-surface algorithm. Since the shadow volumes and shadows are computed in object space, they can be used for further analysis of the scene. Pseudocode is provided, along with pictures and timings from an interactive implementation.

CR Categories and Subject Descriptors: I.3.3 [**Computer Graphics**]: Picture/Image Generation—*Display algorithms*; I.3.5 [**Computer Graphics**]: Computational Geometry and Object Modeling—*Curve, surface, solid, and object representations*; I.3.7 [**Computer Graphics**]: Three-Dimensional Graphics and Realism—*Color, shading, shadowing, and texture*

General Terms: Algorithms

Additional Keywords and Phrases: shadows, shadow volumes, BSP, binary space partitioning

©1989   ACM-0-89791-312-4/89/007/0099 $00.75

1 Introduction

One classic problem in 3D computer graphics is that of shadow generation. Areas in shadow are those that are not visible from a light source. The presence of shadows in an image helps viewers to better understand the spatial relationships between objects, is vital for applications such as architectural planning, and, in general, increases the appearance of reality that a picture provides. Unfortunately, current shadow generation algorithms do not run fast enough for interactive performance, except on special hardware [12]. Real-time alternatives to full shadow generation typically involve tricks for transforming polygons to create polygon shadows that are mapped onto one or more infinite planes [4]. These "fake" shadows are not properly clipped to the surfaces that they shadow and are not blocked by intervening surfaces.

We present a shadow algorithm that achieves interactive performance for polygonal environments of modest size when implemented on a graphics system that provides fast polygon scan conversion. After reviewing current shadow algorithms, we describe how the new algorithm is related to them. Next, we provide an overview of previous work on the BSP tree data structure and algorithms on which the shadow algorithm is based, and present a detailed description of how the new algorithm works.

2 Previous Shadow Algorithms

Crow's classic paper on shadow generation [8] describes three basic approaches: scanline shadow computation, the two-pass object-space approach, and shadow volumes. Since Crow's survey appeared, the taxonomy of shadow algorithms has been broadened to include three more basic methods: a two-pass z-buffer method [25], ray tracing [1, 24], and radiosity approaches [7, 17]. Because the algorithm discussed here combines the two-pass object-space approach with the shadow-volume approach, we provide a brief introduction to both.

The two-pass object-space approach, developed by Atherton, Weiler, and Greenberg [2] for arbitrary polygonal environments, applies two passes of an object-space visible-surface algorithm. The first pass, executed from the point of view of the light source, splits polygons into pieces that are visible from the light source (lit) and ones that are invisible from the light source (shadowed). This is accomplished by transforming the polygons from the point of view of the light source and clipping those polygons that are further away against the clip window of those that are closer. Any part of a polygon that lies within a closer polygon, as seen from the light source, is in shadow. Lit polygon fragments are transformed back into their original orientation and attached to the original polygons as surface detail polygons. A second pass through the visible-surface algorithm is then performed from the point of view of the camera.

The shadow-volume approach involves the construction of a ''shadow volume'' for each object facing the light source. The shadow volume of an object is that volume bounded by the object and a set of invisible ''shadow polygons,'' all of which face outward from the volume. A shadow polygon is created by connecting two vectors emanating from the point light source with the two vertices of one of the object's edges. The polygon is bounded by the edge, and the pieces of the two light source vectors that begin at the edge and continue away from the light source. The entire shadow volume is clipped against the view volume to yield a finite volume. Any part of a polygon within another polygon's shadow volume is shadowed. Whether a visible point on a scene polygon is in shadow can be determined by computing the relative number of shadow polygons between it and the eyepoint that are front-facing or back-facing. A number of shadow algorithms have been developed that create shadow volumes as a preprocessing step before rendering with a scan-line or z-buffer visible-surface algorithm [15, 5, 16, 3, 14, 9].

The technique described here combines elements of both these approaches, with some important differences [6]. In the two-pass object-space approach, the scene must be wholly within the light source's view volume and must be transformed by the light source's perspective transformation. While the algorithm described here does clip scene polygons into shadowed and lit parts, it does not require that polygons be transformed in the shadow generation process. The basis of the Atherton, Weiler, and Greenberg algorithm—the Weiler-Atherton polygon clipper [22] (or its more robust descendant [23])—contains a number of implementation subtleties. In contrast, our algorithm uses a simpler clipping algorithm that always clips a polygon against a plane, rather than against another polygon. The new algorithm's second (visible-surface) pass may be conveniently accomplished in image-space. Alternatively, the algorithm may also be used to perform object-space visible-surface determination by placing the light source at the eyepoint and returning the list of the non-overlapping lit (visible) polygon fragments that are computed.

Although the new algorithm generates a shadow volume, the volume does not have to be closed (e.g., by clipping it against the view volume) and does not include the actual scene polygons. Shadow-volume algorithms typically use the shadow volume to compute shadows in the course of performing visible-surface determination. The algorithm described here clips the scene polygons against the shadow volume in object space in the spirit of [16], creating the shadow volume as it proceeds.

Our algorithm benefits from the divide-and-conquer power of the Binary Space Partitioning (BSP) tree [10, 11] and its generalization to modeling polyhedra [20]. It is relatively simple and straightforward to implement and efficient enough to provide interactive performance. In order to understand how the algorithm works it is necessary to review some BSP fundamentals.

3 BSP Fundamentals

The BSP visible-surface algorithm, developed by Fuchs, Kedem, and Naylor, provides an extremely elegant and simple way to determine visibility priority among polygons in a scene independent of the eyepoint [10, 11]. A BSP tree represents a recursive partitioning of n-dimensional space, inspired by the early work of Schumacker [18, 19]. In 3D, the BSP tree's root is a polygon selected from those in the scene. The root polygon is used to partition object space into two half-spaces. One half-space contains all remaining polygons in front of the root polygon, relative to its plane equation, and the other contains all polygons behind it. Any polygon that lies on both sides of the root polygon's plane is split by the plane and its front and back pieces are assigned to the appropriate half-space. One polygon each from the root polygon's front and back half-space become its front and back children. Each child is recursively used to divide the remaining polygons in its half-space in the same fashion. The tree is complete when each leaf node contains only a single polygon whose two half-spaces are empty. A modified inorder traversal of this tree provides for $O(n)$ back-to-front ordering from an arbitrary viewpoint.

Thibault and Naylor [20] introduced the concept of using a BSP tree to represent polyhedral solids. They associate an ''in'' or ''out'' value with each empty region at the leaves. Assuming that a polyhedron's normals point outward, then an ''in'' region corresponds to the half-space on a polygon's back side, and an ''out'' region corresponds to the half-space on a polygon's front side. Each internal node defines a plane and has a list of polygons embedded in the plane. The ''in'' and ''out'' regions form a convex polyhedral tessellation of space. Thus, a BSP tree can represent an arbitrary (possibly concave) solid with holes as a union of convex ''in'' regions. Thibault and Naylor show how to produce a BSP tree from a polygonal boundary representation of a solid and how to perform Boolean set operations on two boundary representations or on a BSP tree and a boundary representation to yield a new BSP tree.

4 The SVBSP Algorithm

The Shadow Volume BSP (SVBSP) tree is a modified version of the BSP tree used by Thibault and Naylor. Each internal node is associated with a ''shadow plane'' defined by a point light source and an edge of a polygon facing the light source. (If a directional light is used, then the shadow plane is defined by the light source's direction vector and the polygon edge.) This is one of the ''shadow polygons'' that Crow refers to as bounding the shadow volume [8]. The direction of the plane's normal is used to determine the half-space in which an object is located. At the leaves are the ''in'' and ''out'' cells indicating whether or not a region is interior to the shadow volume.

There are two basic steps to the Shadow Volume BSP algorithm whose execution is interleaved for each polygon facing the light source:

d down the
shadowed

...me for each
...d to the

...whether a
...h the shadow
... further from
...nnot, however,
... polygons in
...hen each
...he shadow
...en processed
... The front-to-
...regular BSP
...rsing it from the
...s BSP tree
...must be
...ge, not if a light

...e individual
...it is more
...volume that is
...me of each new
...nt-to-back order.
...ons that are closer
to the light than it, there is no need to ... it against those
planes of the merged shadow volume that would have been
defined by these closer polygons. Therefore, these planes may
be left out. (If complete shadow volumes are needed for
subsequent computation, however, the scene polygon planes
must be included.) The resulting merged shadow volume is a
set of semi-infinite pyramids radiating outward from a single
apex at the point light source. Figure 1 (a) shows a merged
SVBSP shadow volume in 2D for a set of lines seen from a
point, while Figure 1 (b) shows the shadow volume with the
lines (planes in 3D) actually included. While Nishita et al. [16]
compare the shadow volumes of two convex polyhedra, BSP
trees make it relatively easy to compare the shadow volume of
one polygon with a typically concave union of shadow
volumes. The union operation is a version of the Boolean set
union for polyhedra described in [20].

The determination of which areas of a polygon are in shadow
is performed by filtering the polygon down the SVBSP tree,

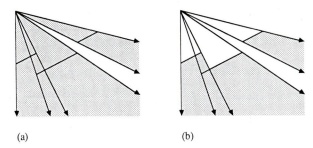

(a)   (b)

Figure 1 SVBSP volume in 2D.

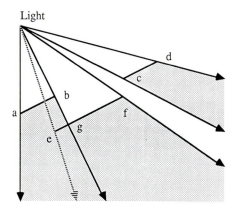

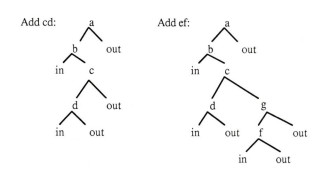

Initial state: out   Add ab:

Add cd: Add ef:

Figure 2 Building an SVBSP volume in 2D.

splitting it whenever it lies in both half-spaces of a node's
plane. Fragments that reach the "in" leaves are in shadow,
while fragments that reach the "out" leaves are lit. Since the
SVBSP tree is built incrementally, each polygon is compared
only with that part of the tree in existence when it is processed.
Note that it is not necessary to filter any polygon that doesn't
face the light source, since it is already entirely in shadow.
Such polygons include any polygon whose plane embeds the
light source.

The SVBSP tree must be augmented to include each lit
fragment's shadow volume. This is accomplished by creating
a set of shadow planes for the fragment's edges and
constructing an SVBSP tree for them, using the algorithm for
building BSP trees presented in [20]. An SVBSP tree node
consists of the shadow plane alone, since the shadow plane
edge is no longer needed. Figure 2 shows the steps in the
construction of an SVBSP tree in 2D. Initially, the tree
contains a single "out" cell. Lines *ab* and *cd* (which would be
polygons in 3D) are both filtered down the SVBSP tree without
any splitting. When line *ef* is filtered down the tree, it is split
into *eg* and *gf* by the shadow plane through *b*. Line *eg* is
wholly inside an "in" cell (the left branch of *b* in Figure 2);

therefore its shadow planes are not inserted. Since each fragment that reaches an "out" cell is lit, it casts a shadow that might fall on fragments added later. Therefore, shadow planes for each edge of a lit polygon fragment are computed and the volume that they define is added to the SVBSP tree, replacing the "out" cell in which the fragment landed.

Figure 3 shows pseudocode for shadowGenerator, the top-level shadow generation loop for the scene polygons. Each scene polygon is processed by the recursive procedure determineShadow (Figure 4), which filters the polygon down the SVBSP tree, splits it when necessary, and augments the SVBSP tree with the shadow volumes of lit fragments. The pseudocode shown here assumes convex polygons and a single light source.

5 Multiple Light Sources

The SVBSP algorithm described above can be easily modified to generate shadows cast by multiple light sources. This can be accomplished by building a separate SVBSP tree for each light source. All processing for one light source is performed before considering the next. Therefore, only one SVBSP tree need be kept in memory at any time. Polygons are processed in front-to-back order with respect to the current light source. Each polygon fragment must keep track of the light sources by which it is lit. If a fragment falls into an SVBSP tree "out" cell, it is marked as lit. If it falls into an "in" cell, it is marked as shadowed. In both cases, the polygon fragment is attached to the regular BSP tree node of the unfragmented polygon with which it is associated. After all the polygons have been

```
; shadowGenerator determines shadow fragments that
; are attached to the appropriate node in the BSP
; tree for subsequent rendering. Alternatively,
; fragments could be written to a file.

procedure shadowGenerator (PLS, BSPtree)

    ; Initialize the SVBSP tree to an OUT cell

    SVBSPtree := OUT

    ; Process all polygons facing light source PLS in
    ; front-to-back order by BSP tree traversal in O(n).

    for each scene polygon p, in front-to-back order
        relative to PLS

        if p is facing PLS

            ; Determine areas of p that are shadowed.
            ; BSPnode is p's node in BSPtree

            SVBSPtree := determineShadow (p, SVBSPtree,
                PLS, BSPnode)
        else
            ; p is not facing PLS or PLS is in p's plane

            mark p as shadowed
        endif
    endfor

    discard SVBSPtree
endproc
```

Figure 3 Pseudocode for shadowGenerator.

```
; determineShadow filters p down SVBSPtree to
; determine shadowed fragments and reattaches shadowed
; fragments to BSPnode.

procedure determineShadow (p, SVBSPnode, PLS, BSPnode)
    returns SVBSPnode

    if (SVBSPnode is an IN cell)
        attach p to BSPnode as a shadowed fragment
    else if (SVBSPnode is an OUT cell)
        attach p to BSPnode as a lit fragment

        ; create shadow volume for p and
        ; append it to the SVBSP tree

        shadowPlanes := planes that form the shadow
            volume of p with PLS
        SVBSPnode :=
            buildSVBSPtree (SVBSPnode, shadowPlanes)
    else
        ; Split p by SVBSPnode.plane, creating
        ; negPart and posPart.

        splitPolygon (p, SVBSPnode.plane, negPart, posPart)

        if (negPart is not null)
            SVBSPnode.negNode :=
                determineShadow (negPart,
                    SVBSPnode.negNode, PLS, BSPnode)
        if (posPart is not null)
            SVBSPnode.posNode :=
                determineShadow (posPart,
                    SVBSPnode.posNode, PLS, BSPnode)
    endif
endproc
```

Figure 4 Pseudocode for determineShadow.

processed in front-to-back order with respect to the current light source, the current SVBSP tree can be discarded and a new one initialized. The polygon fragments created by filtering the scene through the previous SVBSP tree are filtered through the next SVBSP tree in front-to-back order relative to the new light source. Note that the front-to-back order is established by traversing the original BSP tree, which has not gained any nodes due to SVBSP polygon fragmentation.

Shading calculations can be done after the entire scene has been processed for each light source, since each polygon fragment that has passed through the last light source's SVBSP tree is now associated with information indicating which light sources illuminate it. This is ideal for graphics systems that offer hardware shading support for multiple light sources. Alternatively, shading calculations could be performed incrementally as each light source's visibility from a fragment is determined.

6 Discussion

It is highly desirable to keep an SVBSP tree well-balanced, even at the expense of increased size, as is the case when using BSP trees to model polyhedra. This would help in unioning and filtering since each polygon must be filtered down to the tree's leaves. Controlling tree size is also important, however. One major way to accomplish this is to consider only the silhouette edges of the objects of which the polygons are part—a standard shadow algorithm optimization. As well, the edges created by splitting a polygon as it is filtered down the original BSP tree need not be counted. Another way to reduce the size of the tree is to create shadow planes only for polygons that the user marks as being able to cast shadows.

In the special case of one light source, the shadowed fragments may be kept and the lit fragments thrown away, rather than keeping both. In this case, a polygon would be rendered by drawing its shadowed fragments on top of the original unfragmented polygon, as in [2]. There are some cases in which shadows may be known to fall only within a specified region, for example when a light source is defined with cones or flaps [21]. In these cases, the scene can first be clipped to a view volume containing only the region of interest for further processing. This could also be accomplished using a BSP tree.

The fragments produced by filtering down one light's SVBSP tree are pipelined to the next SVBSP tree. Therefore, in processing multiple point light sources, it better to proceed in the order that results in the least amount of polygon fragmentation. One heuristic is to process the light sources in increasing order of the number of polygons facing them. Alternatively, the light sources can be processed in increasing order of the likelihood with which their position will change. If copies of the intermediate fragments produced by each SVBSP tree for each polygon are maintained, then a change in the position of the ith light source will only require sending the fragments from the $i-1$th SVBSP tree through the remaining trees. Therefore, those light sources whose position will change most often can be computed last.

Although a light source's SVBSP tree may be augmented with the shadow volumes of the lit polygon fragments that reach its leaves, these lit portions have already been fragmented by previous SVBSP trees. A smaller tree will result if the SVBSP tree is instead augmented by shadow volumes created from the more coherent lit fragments that result from filtering the original scene polygon down the current SVBSP tree alone. These more coherent fragments cannot be used for multiple light source rendering since they only record the effect of the current light source. They may, however, be used to render the effects of that light source by itself.

As Thibault and Naylor point out, fragmentation could also be reduced if edges were merged when it has been determined that adjacent fragments are both in ''in'' or ''out'' regions. As a special case, if all fragments of the polygon are lit or all are shadowed, then the fragments may be discarded and a copy of the original polygon used, marked accordingly.

7 Implementation

This algorithm has been implemented in C on a HP 9000 350 TurboSRX graphics workstation under HP-UX using the Starbase Graphics Library. To simplify the implementation only convex polygons are handled and polygons are processed individually, so no advantage is taken of the connectivity of polygons in polyhedra to identify silhouette edges. As well, no distinction is made between the original edges of a polygon and those generated by splitting it during creation of the original BSP tree or the SVBSP trees. A bit mask is used to keep track of which light sources illuminate each polygon fragment. Our implementation is able to take advantage of the hardware shading capabilities provided by the graphics system

when rendering the figures. Since the original scene is already represented as a BSP tree, the scene may be rendered with either the BSP visible-surface algorithm (as done in the figures included here) or the hardware z-buffer. Timings for the figures are presented in Table 1 and include only the time needed to generate polygon shadows. Rendering time was an additional fraction of a second.

Figures 5–8 show a scene illuminated by three light sources, shown individually and together. Two versions of the scene are shown in each figure. The first version is shaded using the light sources. The second, fragmented version shows how the scene polygons are split by both the scene BSP tree and the light source SVBSP trees: shadowed fragments are shown in three levels of grey, depending on the number of light sources that illuminate them, while colored fragments are lit by all light sources. Figure 9 shows another scene with only the shadowed fragments outlined. Figures 10 and 11 show additional scenes rendered with the algorithm.

It is important to note that care must be taken to avoid problems posed by limited floating point precision. For example, as polygon fragments get progressively smaller due to fragmentation, the plane equation that would be calculated for each will also get progressively more inaccurate. We currently compute a plane equation for each original scene polygon and assign it to each polygon fragment generated from it. This not only saves computation, but assures that all fragments of the original polygon remain coplanar with each other. A similar approach can preserve the collinearity of edges that are formed by splitting an original scene edge.

8 Conclusions and Future Work

The algorithm that we have presented generates shadows in object space in near real-time for a modest number of polygons. It is simple to implement, and because it generates a set of polygons as output, it may be used as a preprocess to any polygon-based visible-surface algorithm. Since the input and output formats are the same, a pipelined approach for modeling shadows from multiple light sources is easy to implement. No restrictions are placed on the locations of the point light sources and viewer; no transformations are required before visible-surface determination. Our implementation relies on the use of a BSP tree representation of the scene to determine a front-to-back ordering of the scene polygons for each light source in time linear in the number of scene polygons. The algorithm may be easily modified to support a full shadow volume that includes the scene polygons, in which case the scene BSP tree is not necessary. We have recently learned that Naylor (personal communication, 1989) has independently proposed a similar algorithm.

BSP trees not only present a unified framework for visible-surface determination, point classification, and set operations on polyhedra, but, as we have shown, also make possible interactive shadow generation on modern graphics workstations. In addition to pursuing some of the performance improvements mentioned previously, we are also investigating a natural extension to the SVBSP algorithm to support object-space shadow generation for linear and area light sources [6].

Figure	Secs	Lights	Input polygons	Front-facing polygons	Front-facing edges	SVBSP nodes	Fragments
5	.62	1	27	12	49	144	122
6	.68	1	27	15	61	140	108
7	.23	1	27	15	61	31	49
8	5.33	3	27	12,15,15	49,61,61	144,140,32	475
9	1.96	1	126	61	227	88	537
10	4.97	2	65	33,32	132,128	210,169	523
11	7.99	2	106	49,53	196,212	415,191	813
Tetra256	4.15	1	258	130	390	577	723
Tetra1024	25.44	1	1026	514	1542	2894	3345

Table 1 Timings for figures. Figures Tetra256 and Tetra1024 (not shown) are recursive tetrahedra [13] with 256 and 1024 polygons, respectively, casting shadows on themselves and a ground plane.

Acknowledgements

This work is supported in part by the Defense Advanced Research Projects Agency under Contract N00039-84-C-0165, an equipment grant from the Hewlett-Packard Company AI University Grants Program, and the New York State Center for Advanced Technology under Contract NYSSTF-CAT(88)-5. The recursive tetrahedron in Figure 9 was generated using Eric Haines's Standard Procedural Database [13].

References

1. Appel, A. "Some Techniques for Shading Machine Renderings of Solids." *AFIPS SJCC 68*, 32, 1968, 37-45.

2. Atherton, P., Weiler, K., and Greenberg, D. "Polygon Shadow Generation." *Proc. SIGGRAPH '78.* In *Computer Graphics*, 12:3, July 1978, 275-281.

3. Bergeron, P. "A General Version of Crow's Shadow Volumes." *IEEE CG&A*, 6:9, September 1986, 17-28.

4. Blinn, J. "Jim Blinn's Corner: Me and My (Fake) Shadow." *IEEE CG&A*, 8:1, January 1988, 82-86.

5. Brotman, L.S., and Badler, N. "Generating Soft Shadows with a Depth Buffer Algorithm." *IEEE CG&A*, 4:10, October 1984, 5-12.

6. Chin, N. "Shadow Generation Using BSP Trees." M.S. Thesis, Dept. of Computer Science, Columbia University New York (forthcoming), 1989.

7. Cohen, M. and Greenberg, D. "The Hemi-Cube: A Radiosity Solution for Complex Environments." *Proc. SIGGRAPH '85.* In *Computer Graphics*, 19:3, July 1985, 31-40.

8. Crow, F. "Shadow Algorithms for Computer Graphics." *Proc. SIGGRAPH '77.* In *Computer Graphics*, 11:3, July 1977, 242-248.

9. Fournier, A. and Fussell, D. "On the Power of the Frame Buffer." *ACM Trans. on Graphics*, 7:2, April 1988, 103-128.

10. Fuchs, H., Kedem, A., and Naylor, B. "On Visible Surface Generation by A Priori Tree Structures." *Proc. SIGGRAPH '80.* In *Computer Graphics*, 14:3, July 1980, 124-133.

11. Fuchs, H., Abram, G., and Grant, E. "Near Real-Time Shaded Display of Rigid Objects." *Proc. SIGGRAPH '83.* In *Computer Graphics*, 17:3, July 1983, 65-72.

12. Fuchs, H., Goldfeather, J., Hultquist, J., Spach, S., Austin, J., Brooks, Jr., F., Eyles, J., and Poulton, J. "Fast Spheres, Shadows, Textures, Transparencies, and Image Enhancements in Pixel-Planes." *Proc. SIGGRAPH '85.* In *Computer Graphics*, 19:3, July 1985, 111-120.

13. Haines, E. "A Proposal for Standard Graphics Environments." *IEEE CG&A*, 7:11, November 1987, 3-5.

14. Max, N. "Atmospheric Illumination and Shadows." *Proc. SIGGRAPH '86.* In *Computer Graphics*, 20:4, August 1986, 117-124.

15. Nishita, T. and Nakamae, E. "Half-Tone Representation of 3-D Objects Illuminated by Area Sources or Polyhedron Sources." IEEE COMPSAC, November 1983, 237-242.

16. Nishita, T., Okamura, I., Nakamae, E., "Shading Models for Point and Linear Light Sources." *ACM Trans. on Graphics*, 4:2, April 1985, 124-146.

17. Nishita, T. and Nakamae, E. "Continuous Tone Representation of Three-Dimensional Objects Taking Account of Shadows and Interreflection." *Proc. SIGGRAPH '85.* In *Computer Graphics*, 19:3, July 1985, 23-30.

18. Schumacker, R., Brand, B., Gilliland, M., and Sharp, W. "Study for Applying Computer-Generated Images to Visual Simulation." AFHRL-TR-69-14, USAF Human Resources laboratory, September 1969.

19. Sutherland, I., Sproull, R., and Schumacker, R. "A Characterization of Ten Hidden-Surface Algorithms." *ACM Comp. Surv.*, 6:1, March 1974, 1-55.

20. Thibault, W. and Naylor, B. "Set Operations on Polyhedra Using Binary Space Partitioning Trees." *Proc. SIGGRAPH '87.* In *Computer Graphics*, 21:4, July 1987, 153-162.

21. Warn, D. "Lighting Controls for Synthetic Images." *Proc. SIGGRAPH '83.* In *Computer Graphics*, 17:3, July 1983, 13-21.

22. Weiler, K. and Atherton, P. "Hidden Surface Removal Using Polygon Area Sorting." *Proc. SIGGRAPH '77.* In *Computer Graphics*, 11:2, July 1977, 214-222.

23. Weiler, K. "Polygon Comparison using a Graph Representation." *Proc. SIGGRAPH '80.* In *Computer Graphics*, 14:3, July 1980, 10-18.

24. Whitted, T. "An Improved Illumination Model for Shaded Display." *CACM*, 23:6, June 1980, 343-349.

25. Williams, L. "Casting Curved Shadows on Curved Surfaces." *Proc. SIGGRAPH '78.* In *Computer Graphics*, 12:3, August 1978, 270-274.

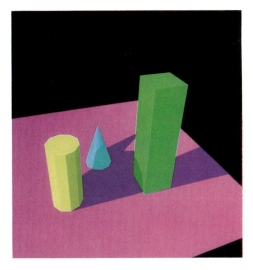 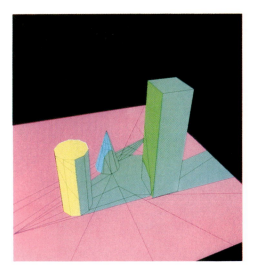

Figure 5 Solids with light source 1.

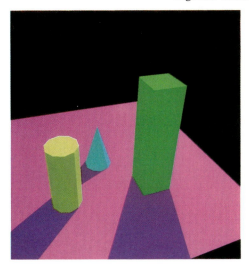 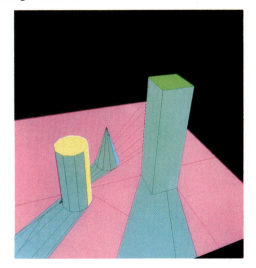

Figure 6 Solids with light source 2.

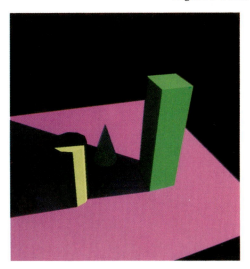 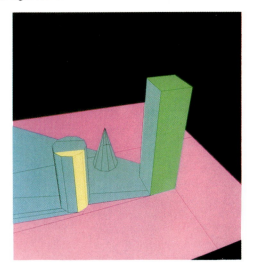

Figure 7 Solids with light source 3.

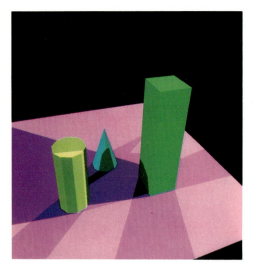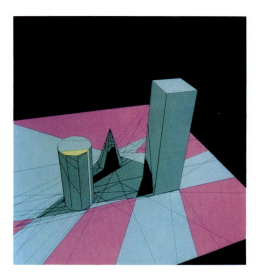

Figure 8 Solids with all three light sources.

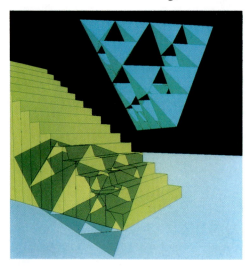

Figure 9 Recursive tetrahedron and staircase with one light source, showing shadow fragments.

Figure 10 Table and chair with two light sources.

Figure 11 Room with two light sources.

Real-Time Rendering of Trimmed Surfaces

Alyn Rockwood
Kurt Heaton
Tom Davis

Silicon Graphics Computer Systems
Mountain View, CA

Abstract

Rational tensor product surfaces, (Bézier, NURBS, Hermite, polynomial, etc.) are rendered in real-time by uniform faceting. The described methods are modular and can be balanced for optimal implementation on different hardware platforms. Discretization anomalies such as angularities, Mach banding, cracking etc. are avoided by tessellating the surface patches and segmenting the trimming curves based on the view.

CR Categories and Subject Descriptors: G.1.5 [Mathematics of Computing]: Roots of Nonlinear Equations - Iterative methods; I.3.3 [Computer Graphics]: Picture/Image Generation - Display algorithms; I.3.5 [Computer Graphics]: Computational Geometry and Object Modeling - Curve, surface, solid and object representations.

Additional Key Words and Phrases: Trimmed NURBS and Bézier surfaces, faceting, roots of nonlinear equations, view-driven tessellation and graphics systems.

1. Introduction

State of the art, 3D graphics systems render over one hundred thousand transformed, lighted and z-buffered polygons per second [Ake88, Apg88]. We expect systems capable of rendering over a million polygons to be available in the future [Dee88, Gha88]. These machines accentuate the need for methods which facet free-form surfaces efficiently for rendering. The display of surfaces such as NURBS (non-uniform rational B-splines), Bézier and polynomial tensor product surfaces is increasingly important in CAD/CAM, animation and scientific visualization.

This paper describes a modular approach to render trimmed surfaces in real-time by a uniform view-driven tessellation per patch. Methods are described to avoid anomalies due to the faceting. The following goals served as guidelines.

- Real-time performance: The surfaces must be trimmed, faceted, transformed, lighted, smooth shaded and z-buffered in real-time.

- High quality images: Discretization anomalies must be minimized regardless of view or motion. Adjacent facets should abut without cracking or overlapping.

- Portability: The algorithms must easily port to different graphics systems. Tasks should be efficiently distributed between CPUs and specialized graphics processors.

Previous algorithms for rendering surfaces [Cat74, Cla79, For79, Kaj82, Lan80, Roc87, Sha88, Swe86] did not fully satisfy our needs. Some methods such as ray-tracing and point sampling do not take advantage of existing polygon rendering abilities. Other methods do not account for trimming or they exhibit too many unwanted visual artifacts. Others are algorithmically too complex.

A new method which satisfies our goals is previewed in Section 2. We discuss in detail each step in Sections 3 through 9. An implementation on an Silicon Graphics GTX Workstation is discussed in Section 10.

2. A Preview

We refer to *object space* as the 3D coordinate system in which the surface is defined. Viewing transformations map object space to *image space*, and *screen space* is the 2D coordinate system defined by projecting image space onto the xy-plane.

Surfaces are defined as a deformation of a (u,v) axis aligned rectangle into object space. The rectangle is called *parameter space*. A surface can be trimmed by restricting the domain to a subset of parameter space called the *trimming region*. The trimming region is defined as the area enclosed by a set of closed loops of directed curves called *trimming curves*.

A region is monotone with respect to an axis if any line perpendicular to that axis has a convex intersection with the region. We refer to a region which is monotone with respect to both the u and the v axes as *uv-monotone*.

Our method converts all surfaces into individual Bézier patches bounded by trimming curves. The patches can be processed in any order or in parallel. The trimming region of each patch is subdivided into *uv*-monotone regions. Each *uv*-monotone region is tessellated in parameter space into a grid of rectangular *tiles* trimmed by triangular *coving* along curve boundaries as shown in Figure 1. The tile size is computed on a per patch basis by transforming the control mesh of the patch into screen space. Step sizes in the u and v directions are determined that guarantee the size of the tiles, when projected to screen space, will be smaller than a user specified tolerance.

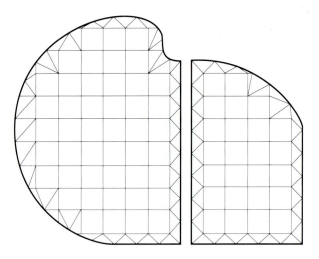

Figure 1. Coving and tiling a trimmed surface patch in parameter space.

Each trimming curve is segmented in parameter space by evaluating points on the curve based on a coving step size which is derived from the tile step size. Triangles are formed between points on the curve and points on the grid. This technique allows the interior of each patch to be tessellated with different size tiles without cracking between edges of abutting patches. Boundary curves of two adjacent patches will generate identical faceting along the edge when rendered, preventing cracking.

The desire for portability led us to organize the method in a modular, tool kit fashion. We decomposed the rendering process into steps with well defined interfaces between them. For many steps we developed competing algorithms, each with different strengths and weaknesses depending upon the implementation chosen, i.e. hardware, software, microcode, VLSI, etc. This enables us to select the best algorithms to distribute processing and balance bandwidth capacities for each system. As a side benefit, code is easier to develop and more maintainable.

The Method

- **Convert to Bézier:** All trimmed surfaces are converted into individual Bézier patches with trimming regions defined by closed loops of Bézier or piecewise linear curves.

- **Calculate Step Sizes:** Step sizes are calculated in parameter space for each curve and surface which guarantee the size of facets in screen space will not exceed a user specified tolerance.

- **Find Extrema:** All points on the trimming curves where the tangents are parallel to the *u* or *v* axes are discovered, i.e. the local minima and maxima.

- **Divide into *uv*-Monotone Regions:** Using extrema, the trimming region of the patch is divided into *uv*-monotone regions. Each region is defined by a closed loop of curves.

- **Cove and Tile:** Using the calculated step sizes, each *uv*-monotone region is uniformly tessellated into a grid of rectangles connected by triangles to points evaluated along the curves.

- **Evaluate Surface Functions:** The polygons defined in (*u,v*) parameter space are transformed into facets in object space by evaluating their vertices with the surface functions. Surface normals are also calculated.

- **Render Facets:** Each facet is transformed to screen space, clipped, lighted, smooth shaded and z-buffered using standard 3D graphics hardware.

The previous steps do not imply a rigid ordering. Specific implementations may change the sequence of steps. In the following sections we discuss the steps in detail.

3. Converting To Trimmed Rational Bézier Patches

Prevalent surfaces in the design of complex sculptured objects are NURBS surfaces or collections of Bézier, polynomial or Hermite patches which are pieced together.

A trimmed surface is obtained by restricting the surface domain to the interior of a region defined by closed loops of directed curves joined end to end. These trimming curves may be either rational or polynomial, and may be NURBS, Bézier etc., or in piecewise linear form.

We convert all trimmed surfaces into a set of trimmed Bézier patches with Bézier or piecewise linear trimming curves. Non-NURBS curves and surfaces can be converted to Bézier form using a change of basis [Far88]; NURBS surfaces and curves are converted to Bézier form by knot insertion [Boe83] and change of basis. A NURBS domain is divided into a set of rectangles which corresponds to domains of Bézier patches. The trimming region must be subdivided along patch boundaries. After conversion, the trimmed Bézier patches may be processed in any order or in parallel. We discuss the NURBS to Bézier conversion in more detail below.

The shape of each NURBS curve or surface depends on a set of control points and on knot vectors (non-decreasing arrays of real numbers). For a NURBS curve or surface of order n, the special case where the first and last knots have multiplicity n and the interior knots have multiplicity n-1 defines a set of Bézier curves or surfaces.

The Boehm knot insertion algorithm [Boe83] inserts a knot, then adds and adjusts control points to yield a new description for the same curve or surface. For example, to convert a NURBS curve of degree 4 with the knot sequence {0, 0, 0, 0, 0, 1, 2, 2, 3, 3, 3, 3, 3} to Bézier form, add five knots with values 1, 1, 1, 2 and 2. The result will be the same curve described as three Bézier curve segments. Closely spaced knots can cause numerical problems. We allow the user to specify a tolerance (1.0E-6 works well); any knots closer than this are coerced to the same value before knot insertion.

The NURBS trimming region is split into patches as illustrated in Figure 2. Trimming curves are split at patch boundaries with additional curves added along patch boundaries to restrict the trim region to individual patches. Piecewise linear curves are split by interpolation. Bézier curves can either be converted to piecewise linear form and split as above, or the root finder algorithm described in Section 5 can be used.

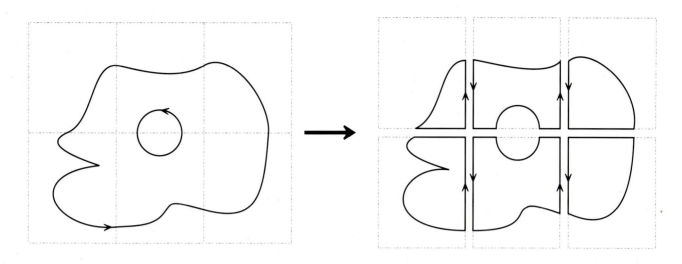

Figure 2. Splitting a NURBS trimming region into patches.

It may be advantageous to further subdivide some Bézier patches, especially those with control points having widely differing weights, or those that come near the eye in a perspective view. Step size calculations explained in Section 4 can be used to determine whether further subdivision is necessary, and if so, the patches can be split [Far88].

Because the Bézier form is our internal representation and is also critical to many of our algorithms, we define it explicitly. A *rational Bézier patch* of degree n in u and degree m in v is defined by R: $[0,1]\text{X}[0,1] \to \mathbf{R}^3$ and

$$R(u,v) = \frac{\sum_{i=0}^{n} \sum_{j=0}^{m} w_{ij} \mathbf{r}_{ij} B_i^n(u) B_j^m(v)}{\sum_{i=0}^{n} \sum_{j=0}^{m} w_{ij} B_i^n(u) B_j^m(v)}, \qquad (1)$$

where w_{ij} are the *weights*, $\mathbf{r}_{ij}$ are the *control points* and the B_i^n are the Bernstein polynomials [Far88]. A *trimming curve* of degree s is defined in the parameter space of a patch by C: $[0,1] \to \mathbf{R}^2$ and

$$C(t) = \frac{\sum_{i=0}^{s} w_i \mathbf{c}_i B_i^s(t)}{\sum_{i=0}^{s} w_i B_i^s(t)}, \qquad (2)$$

where $\mathbf{c}_i = (u_i, v_i)$ are the control points; thus $C(t) = (u(t), v(t))$. $u(t)$ and $v(t)$ are the *component functions*.

If the weights in (1) and (2) are equal to 1 then the denominator disappears (becomes equal to 1) and the patch and curve are just the polynomial Bézier forms.

4. Calculating The Step Sizes Based On View

For each patch, we compute step sizes based on the viewing transformation to ensure the size of facets on the display do not exceed a user specified tolerance. Step sizes for both the u and v directions, as well as step sizes for each trimming curve, are computed.

In the equations below, the control points $\mathbf{r}_{ij}$ and weights w_{ij} are mapped by viewing and perspective transformations to $(W_{ij} X_{ij}, W_{ij} Y_{ij}, W_{ij} Z_{ij}, W_{ij})$ in homogeneous coordinates. Let $\mathbf{R}_{ij} = (X_{ij}, Y_{ij}, Z_{ij})$ be the 3D control point after the perspective division. Let TOL be the user specified tolerance in screen coordinates and π_3 be the projection from image space to screen space. Then the number of steps in the respective u and v directions (between 0 and 1) which guarantee sample points on the patch closer in screen space than TOL are obtained from:

$$n_u = n \sqrt{2} \max(\| W_{ij} \pi_3 \mathbf{R}_{ij} - W_{i+1,j} \pi_3 \mathbf{R}_{i+1,j} \|) / (\text{TOL}^* \min(W_{ij})),$$

for $1 \leq i \leq n\text{-}1$ and $1 \leq j \leq m$. and $\qquad$ (3)

$$n_v = m \sqrt{2} \max(\| W_{ij} \pi_3 \mathbf{R}_{ij} - W_{i,j+1} \pi_3 \mathbf{R}_{i,j+1} \|) / (\text{TOL}^* \min(W_{ij})),$$

for $1 \leq i \leq n$ and $1 \leq j \leq m\text{-}1$.

The formulas in (3) are modifications of those found in [Roc87] (We appreciate one of the referees noting the simple extension to include perspective). The step sizes in parameter space which result in screen space steps less than TOL are given by $\text{STEP}_u = 1/n_u$ and $\text{STEP}_v = 1/n_v$.

The number of steps which partitions a trimming curve of degree s into segments that are smaller in screen space than STEP_u or STEP_v, respectively, can be obtained from:

$$n_t = s \max(\| w_i \mathbf{c}_i - w_{i+1} \mathbf{c}_{i+1} \|) / (\text{STEP}_u {}^* \min(w_i)),$$

for $1 \leq i \leq s\text{-}1$. or $\qquad$ (4)

$$n_t = s \max(\| w_i \mathbf{c}_i - w_{i+1} \mathbf{c}_{i+1} \|)/ (STEP_v \, *\min(w_i)), \qquad (5)$$

for $1 \le i \le s\text{-}1$.

A trimming curve that is either vertical or horizontal should use (4) if it increments in u or (5) if it increments in v. If the curve is a boundary curve, i.e. $u=0$, $v=0$, $u=1$ or $v=1$, then $STEP_u$ in (4) or $STEP_v$ in (5) is derived by using only the control points of the associated boundary edge in (3). Other trimming curves should use the maximum of (4) or (5). The curve step sizes in parameter space which result in screen space steps less than TOL are given by $STEP_t = 1/n_t$.

Note that if the ratio of any two weights is either very large or very small, the formulas will result in wasteful oversampling (oversampling does not produce visible artifacts, but is inefficient). Prior subdivision of the patches or trimming curves can ameliorate this problem. As a rule, weights used for conics or quadric surfaces need not deviate much from 1. If all weights are 1 the formulas simplify to the non-rational form.

5. Finding The Maxima And Minima Of The Trimming Curves

In this section we present a method for finding the intersections of a curve with lines of constant parameter. It is also useful for finding extrema of trimming curves. Local maxima and minima are needed to divide the trimming region of the patch into uv-monotone regions. There are several options to do this. Option 1: If the trimming curves are in piecewise linear form, then finding the relative extrema is easily accomplished by inspection. Option 2: Curves in the Bézier form can be evaluated in increments of $STEP_t$ to form piecewise linear curves.

Option 3: A third option is to use a "root finder" to find the extrema directly. It is equivalent to finding points at which the derivatives of the component functions are zero, that is in (2) find all t such that $u'(t)=0$ or $v'(t)=0$. This option has the advantage that the extrema need only be found when the trimming curve is modified. The other options must find the extrema based on view.

If the trimming curves are non-rational, then the derivative is straightforward [Far88]. If they are rational, the non-rational numerator of Bézier curve of the derivative is used. The conversion from original control points to derivative form is found in [Sed87]. In all instances, one obtains an explicit function $f(t)=\sum f_i B_i(t)$ in Bézier form for which roots are desired (note, the f_i are scalars). We now describe the root finder algorithm.

A reasonable estimate of the smallest root of $f(t)$ is the value of t where the control polygon first crosses the t axis. This is found by testing, in increasing order, successive pairs of f_i for a sign change. If f_i is the smallest value such that $f_i f_{i+1} < 0$, then the estimate of the root is

$$t = \frac{f_i}{n(f_i - f_{i+1})} + i/n \qquad (6)$$

If $i=0$ or $i=n\text{-}1$, then the estimate is exactly the same as in Newton's method. This follows since the Bézier control polygon is tangent to the curve at $t=0$ and $t=1$ [Far88]. In the other cases, the polygon is typically closer to the curve than the tangent and is usually a better estimate of the root.

If all control points are above or below the axis, i.e. there is no sign change in adjacent pairs, then there are no roots of the polynomial in the interval [0,1].

The root finder iterates by subdividing the component curve at the estimate, using the *de Casteljau formula* [Far88]. The de Casteljau formula for evaluating (2) at a point t is given recursively by

$$f_i^{\,j} = (1\text{-}t)\, f_i^{\,j-1} + t\, f_{i+1}^{\,j-1} \qquad (7)$$

for $j=1,...,s$ and $i=1,...,s\text{-}j$, where $f_i^{\,0} = f_i$. The value $f_0^{\,s}$ is $f(t)$. The formula also subdivides the curve at the point t into two curves which are identical to the original curve.

The root finder uses the de Casteljau formula to generate two new sets of control points for the left and right curves, denoted below by L_i's and R_i's respectively. The left curve is investigated for roots by checking the signs of adjacent pairs of values. If there is no root, the right curve is investigated. Convergence is assumed when the function is less in absolute value than a given resolution, RES. To track the root in the original parameter space it is necessary to compute an actual root, ActRoot, and a current root, CurRoot. The latter is relative to the current subdivision. Scale is the scale factor which relates the current subdivision to the original curve.

Our approach resembles one described by Lane and Riesenfeld [Lan81] who begin with binary subdivision and switch to the estimate (6) after a root is isolated. We do not use binary subdivision, but perform a *special subdivision* whenever the estimate approaches a given tolerance ε. The special subdivision is used because (6) loses precision when CurRoot is small. The special guess avoids the precision problem and usually results in a subdivision which significantly contracts the curve and allows greater precision for (6). The precision problem is particularly pronounced when converging to a multiple root. The root finder algorithm is illustrated in Figure 3 and outlined below.

Root Finder Algorithm: Finds the smallest value of t in the interval [0,1] such that the function $f(t) = 0$.

1. **Initialize:** $L_i \leftarrow f_i$, $R_i \leftarrow 1$ for $i = 0,1,...,n$. ActRoot $\leftarrow$ CurRoot $\leftarrow$ Scale $\leftarrow$ OldCRoot $\leftarrow 1$.

2. **Test convergence:** If $|R_0| <$ RES, then output Act Root and End.

3. **Find crossing:** Find k such that $L_k L_{k+1} < 0$ for $k = 0,1,...,n\text{-}1$. If no such k is found then go to step 7.

4. **Guess:** CurRoot $\leftarrow k/n + L_k/(n(L_k - L_{k+1}))$.

5. **Special guess:** If $L_k/(n(L_k - L_{k+1})) < \varepsilon$, then CurRoot $\leftarrow k/n+\varepsilon$.

6. **de Casteljau:** Evaluate L_k's with (7) at CurRoot; new L_k's and R_k's are generated. Scale $\leftarrow$ Scale*OldCRoot, ActRoot $\leftarrow$ ActRoot -Scale* (1-Cur Root). Go to step 2.

7. **Find crossing:** Find k such that $R_k R_{k+1} < 0$ for $k = 0,1,...,n\text{-}1$. If no such k is found, then output "no root" and End.

8. **Guess:** CurRoot $\leftarrow k/n + R_k/(n(R_k - R_{k+1}))$.

9. **Special guess:** If $R_k/(n(R_k - R_{k+1})) < \varepsilon$, then CurRoot $\leftarrow k/n+\varepsilon$.

10. **de Casteljau:** Evaluate R_k's with (7) at CurRoot; new L_k's and R_k's are generated. Scale $\leftarrow$ Scale*(1- OldCRoot), ActRoot $\leftarrow$ ActRoot +Scale* CurRoot. Go to step 2.

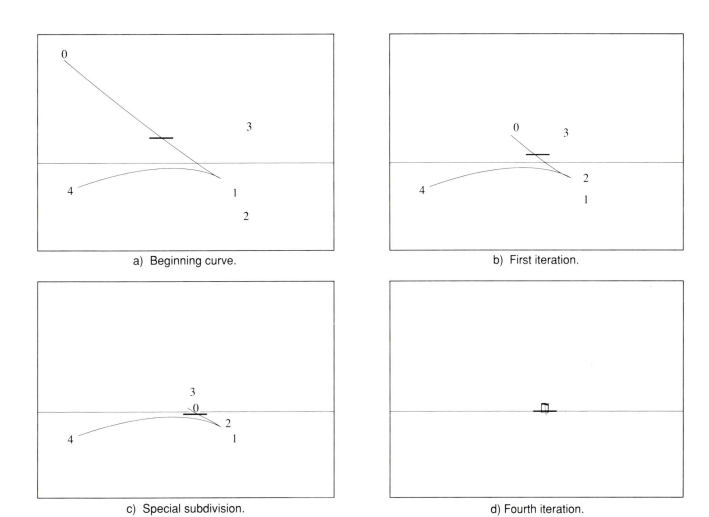

a) Beginning curve.

b) First iteration.

c) Special subdivision.

d) Fourth iteration.

Figure 3. Four iterations of the root finder algorithm. The guesses are indicated by horizontal marks.

Farouki [Faro] notes two deficiencies with the Lane-Riesenfeld algorithm: first, it requires $O(d)$ subdivision stages, each with cost $O(n^2)$ operations for convergence to d binary digits; and second, successive subdivision compounds errors in the coefficients of the successively generated polynomials. It is better to compute roots with a procedure that refers only to the original specification of the polynomial.

As noted before, our root finder converges quadratically as with Newton's method, i.e. $O(\log_2 d)$. This behavior has been confirmed by experience on curves up to degree fifteen; iteration to 32 bits usually occurs in six to seven steps. The occasional special subdivision does not change the overall rate of convergence. The only case experienced in which convergence is less than quadratic is when the root is highly multiple. The time-critical computation is the evaluation of the function and the subdivision of the curve using the de Casteljau algorithm (7). It is an $O(n^2)$ algorithm. It can be adapted as an $O(n)$ algorithm by computing each row of the array in parallel. One such implementation is described by DeRose [DeR87], for instance.

With regard to Farouki's second criticism, the quadratic convergence of the routine minimizes the impact of successive subdivisions "slipping" coefficients. Finally, after convergence, the original curve can be evaluated at ActRoot to test for any slippage and "purified" by another call to the root finder for the appropriate part of the subdivided curve.

To find the next largest root, the original curve must be subdivided at the discovered root (ActRoot) and then the algorithm is applied again in the interval [0,1] for the righthand curve. Repeated application generates an ascending sequence of real roots.

Other options: Sederberg, Zundel and de Boor, and Farouki are considering other approaches to the problem of finding roots of polynomial curves [Sed88].

6. Dividing The Trimming Region Into *UV*-Monotone Regions

The trimming region of a patch is specified by closed loops of trimming curves. Tiling and coving a patch is facilitated if its trimming region is divided into *uv*-monotone regions with a single closed loop of curves enclosing each region.

In Option 1 of this section we discuss a simple technique for generating *uv*-monotone regions. The algorithm is simple but inefficient in that it creates regions that could be combined. As a second option, we present a more complicated algorithm which generates fewer regions.

Option 1: Regions bounded on the left and right by monotone curves and on the top and bottom by horizontal straight lines are *uv*-monotone. As shown in Figure 4, a patch can be decomposed into *uv*-monotone regions by casting a line of constant *v* through curve endpoints and extremal points. The algorithm is outlined below.

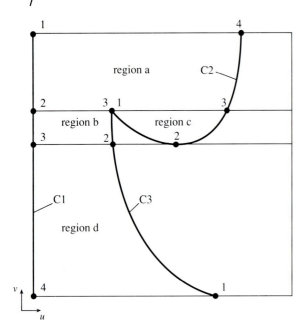

Figure 4. A trimming region divided into *uv*-monotone regions using Option 1.

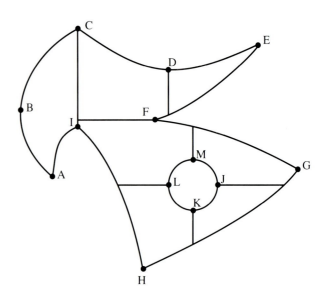

Figure 5. A trimming region divided in *uv*-monotone regions using Option 2.

- **Find intersection points:** Remove trimming curves parallel to the *u* axis if they exist. Cast a line of constant *v* through each extremal point and through the first point and last point of each curve. Find all points on all curves intersected by these lines using either the Root Finder algorithm described in Section 5 or by interpolation.

- **Create lists and sort:** Create a list of points for each trimming curve containing the end points, extremal points entered twice and intersection points entered twice. Sort each list with respect to parameter *t* where C(*t*) defines the curve.

- **Divide into curves:** Divide each list into a collection of pairs of consecutive points. Sort these pairs with respect to *v*. The two points in a pair are the end points of a curve which is monotone in both *u* and *v*.

- **Merge sort into regions:** Create monotone regions by sorting the first point in each pair with the first point in all other pairs with respect to *v* then *u*. If the first elements of two pairs have the same *u* value, determine priority by further sorting with respect to *u* of the second element. After sorting, each two consecutive pairs define a region. Reinsert any horizontal curves removed in the first step. Close each region by inserting additional horizontal curves on the top and bottom of each region as required.

Note that region b and region d can be combined into a single *uv*-monotone region. These regions can be discovered and combined to reduce overhead if desired. However, the cost of creating extra regions may be significant for more complex examples as shown in Figure 5. Option 1 generates nineteen regions from this patch; below we describe an improved algorithm that generates only seven regions.

Option 2: We refer to a point on a trimming curve as *v-critical* if it is a local maximum and the trimming region lies above it or if it is a local minimum and the trimming region lies below. The *u-critical* points are similarly defined. If the region is split vertically at each *v*-critical point and horizontally at the *u*-critical points, the resulting pieces will be *uv*-monotone.

In Figure 5, points D, I, M, and K are *v*-critical and points F, L, and J are *u*-critical. To create *uv*-monotone regions, first we split the trimming region vertically through D, I, M and K. Then we split the resulting trimming regions horizontally through F, L and J. The lines which split the trimming region only extended to the nearest arc rather than across the entire patch. The algorithm is outlined below.

- **Find *v*-critical points:** Find the subset of end points and extremal points that are *v*-critical.

- **Divide vertically:** Through each *v*-critical point, extend a line up or down through the interior of the region until it meets another trimming boundary. Split the region along this segment.

- **Find *u*-critical points:** Find the *u*-critical points in each region generated by the previous step.

- **Divide horizontally:** Through each *u*-critical point, extend a line left or right through the interior of the region until it meets another trimming boundary. Split the region along this segment.

Both options discussed above can be implemented using the same data structure for input and output. We use a list of circular lists of curve segments. Regions are divided and curves inserted in the same fashion that trimming regions are divided at patch boundaries in Section 3, preserving the data structure. The final result is a list of circular lists of curves, where each circular list surrounds a *uv*-monotone region.

Care must be taken in dividing curves to ensure that the new curves segment into exactly the same set of points or cracking may result. Once generated, the *uv*-monotone regions are independent of each other and can be processed in any order or in parallel.

7. Covering And Tiling: Creating Uniform Tessellations That Don't Crack

Coving and tiling tessellates each *uv*-monotone region into three- or four-sided polygons that are defined in (u,v) parameter space and that have edges small enough to satisfy the screen space tolerance. This is done by superimposing a lattice of points a distance $STEP_u$ and $STEP_v$ apart over the *uv*-monotone region as shown in Figure 6. Trimming curves are segmented into points by evaluating them in increments of $STEP_t$. All lattice points that lie within the region and all points on the curves are interconnected to form a mesh of polygons.

Two algorithms for generating this mesh of polygons are discussed in this section. The first algorithm is general purpose and is guaranteed to handle any *uv*-monotone region. The second is more restricted but is faster.

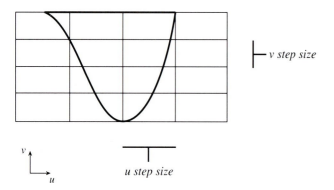

v step size

u step size

Figure 6. A lattice of points is superimposed on the *uv*-monotone trimming region.

Option 1: We refer to horizontal lines through lattice points as *v-lattice lines* and similar vertical lines as *u-lattice lines*. First, the *uv*-monotone regions are divided along *v*-lattice lines into *horizontal slices* $STEP_v$ high as outlined below.

- **Tessellate trimming curves:** If not done previously, segment each trimming curve by evaluating iteratively by $STEP_t$.

- **Subdivide slice boundaries:** Intersect *v* lattice lines with trimming curves by interpolating between two evaluated points. Output a degenerate coving triangle whose vertices are the two evaluated points and the interpolant to avoid cracking.

- **Create slices:** Create each slice by grouping the interpolated points, the evaluated points on the curve between them and any points between the curves on the *v*-lattice lines.

Monotone curves on the left and right edge and horizontal curves top and bottom define each slice. Each horizontal slice is then decomposed into triangles using a general purpose monotone polygon triangulation algorithm such as one described in [Gar78].

- **Triangulate slices:** Each slice is triangulated using a monotone polygon triangulation algorithm.

Option 2: A more efficient algorithm exists for any horizontal slice that contains two points that lie on a *u*-lattice line. The algorithm chops out the rectangular center section of the slice, generating a strip of tiles. The two regions remaining on the left and right ends are triangulated.

An algorithm for triangulating end regions is described below. End Regions are bounded by a *u*-lattice line, a *v*-lattice line and points of a monotone curve. The curve may be increasing or decreasing and may be to the left or right of the *u*-lattice line. Without loss of generality, assume the end region is oriented as shown in Figure 7.

Points B, C, D and the points between C and D are lattice points. Points A, E and the points between them lie on a trimming curve. Assume the points are organized into two lists: TopPoint = {B, A-E} and BottomPoint = {C-D, E}. Next(TopPoint) and Next(BottomPoint) refers to the next point in the top or bottom list respectively. CoveTriangle(p1, p2, p3) means that the points p1, p2, and p3 are output as the vertices of a coving triangle. If p is a point, p.*u* is the *u* coordinate of p. The coving algorithm follows:

1. Top = B; Bottom = C; NextTop = Next(TopPoint); NextBottom = Next(BottomPoint).

2. If NextTop = E and NextBottom = E, then CoveTriangle(Top, Bottom, E) and End.

3. If NextTop.*u* ≥ NextBottom.*u* then go to 7.

4. CoveTriangle(Top, Bottom, NextTop)

5. If NextTop = E then go to 2.

6. Top = NextTop; NextTop = Next(TopPoint); go to 2.

7. CoveTriangle(Top, Bottom, NextBottom).

8. If NextBottom = E then go to 2.

9. Bottom = NextBottom; NextBottom = Next(Bottom); go to 2.

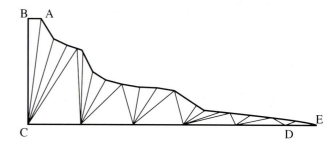

Figure 7. A example of coving an end region of a horizontal slice.

The complete algorithm for coving and tiling a *uv*-monotone regions using Option 2 is summarized below:

- **Divide into slices:** Dividing into horizontal slices as described in the Option 1 above.

- **Test for lattice points:** Check the slice to see if it has two points which lie on a *u*-lattice line. If not, use the general purpose triangulation algorithm and end.

- **Generate tiles:** Output lattice points within the interior of the horizontal slice as a strip of rectangles.

- **Cove left end:** Using the coving algorithm described above, generate a strip of three-side polygons along the left trimming curve.

- **Cove right end:** Using the coving algorithm described above, generate a strip of three-side polygons along the right trimming curve.

8. Generating Surface Facets From Parameter Space Polygons

To generate facets, object space coordinates (x,y,z) and normal vectors (n_x,n_y,n_z) are calculated from (u,v) coordinates of the polygons. The (x,y,z) coordinates are calculated using a polynomial expansion of the Bézier coefficients, or using the de Casteljau algorithm. We compute the normal vector by evaluating the partial derivatives of the surface in the u and v directions, taking their cross product and normalizing the result.

A less expensive way to generate surface normals is first to approximate the surface normals with another patch. This patch interpolates to given analytic surface normals on the original patch. Second, the "surface normals" patch is evaluated exactly as the original patch. This approach requires less computation than forming the cross product from partial derivatives and then normalizing, but it assumes the original patch has no high frequency components. See [Roc87, Sha87] for more details.

9. Rendering Facets By Traditional Techniques

Option 1: The facets are transformed, lighted, smooth shaded and z-buffered using standard 3D polygon rendering techniques [Fol82].

Option 2: A more efficient, but less general way is to derive the facets from the transformed Bézier control mesh instead of transforming each vertex of each facet. The facets are then lighted, smooth shaded and z-buffered using standard techniques. However, this technique requires the surface normals patch approach since the analytic surface normals would otherwise be transformed. Furthermore, distance related local lighting is excluded with this scheme.

The important attribute of Option 1 is that the facets can be treated as standard 3D polygon primitives by the graphics systems. No special handling is required. There is a significant computational savings in Option 2 in transforming the control mesh. However, this benefit may not be as significant if the target graphic system has large rendering capacities in hardware.

10. Implementation Details

The method was successfully implemented on a Silicon Graphics IRIS-4D GTX Workstation. Its architecture comprises multiple RISC-based CPU's interfaced to a high-performance Graphics Subsystem [Ake88]. The Graphics Subsystem contains five identical 20 Mflop processors (Geometry Engines®) which are microcodable.

A user interface was added to the IRIS Graphics Library™ that accepts either NURBS or Bézier surfaces as primitives. The first five steps of the method were programmed in C code to execute on the host CPUs. The algorithmically simple but computationally intensive step of surface evaluation was programmed in microcode and executes on the first Geometry Engine. The microcode evaluates either a single coving triangle, a mesh of coving triangles or a horizontal strip of tiles. Facets are rendered the same as other 3D polygons by the Graphics Subsystem.

We discovered many opportunities to simplify the implementation initially and then improve performance later. For example, the initial implementation used only the general purpose polygon triangulation algorithm [Gar78] and simple microcode that evaluated triangles individually. Adding algorithms to generate and evaluate strips of tiles improved performance substantially.

Our current implementation immediately discretizes the trimming curves and saves the points for use later in coving and tiling. With a complete list of points, finding the local maxima and minima and subdivision into monotone curves becomes trivial. However, since curve tessellation is view dependent, monotone subdivision must be performed each frame. A Root Finder is being added so that monotone subdivision is performed only when a trimming curve is changed.

It is difficult to give meaningful performance values since suitable benchmarks do not exist. Measures such as "surfaces per second" are of little use. The shape of the trimming regions and the perspective viewing parameters can have a substantial effect on the ratio of triangles to rectangles in our method. However, it is not too unreasonable to consider each rectangle to be two triangles and measure triangles per second. We included in our measurement all steps of the method including the conversion from NURBS to internal Bézier form, conversion to monotone regions, coving, tiling and the rendering of the facets.

Using this measure, moderately to extremely complicated trimmed surfaces as shown in Figures 8 and 9 render at about 15,000 triangles per second. Simply trimmed and untrimmed NURBS surfaces as in Figure 10 render up to 60,000 triangles per second. We have observed that coving and tiling is the current bottleneck and is therefore a candidate for microcode in the future. Also, we have yet to take advantage of the multiple CPU's.

As a demonstration of portability, the IRIS-4D GTX implementation was ported to a Silicon Graphics Personal IRIS™ workstation. Although the internal architecture of this machine is significantly different, the port was successfully completed in only two days.

11. Conclusion

We have presented a method that renders trimmed rational tensor product surfaces by view-driven faceting without anomalies. Alternative algorithms were presented for many of the steps to show a method that can be tailored to satisfy the requirements of different graphics systems. A real-time implementation on a high-performance workstation was described.

One feature of the method is that users can readily choose between image quality and rendering speed by specifying a tolerance for on-screen facet size. The speed of the method is due mainly to the fact that we adapt uniform faceting on a per patch basis. The modular architecture of the method makes it quick to implement, portable, maintainable and amenable to incremental improvements.

A notable feature is that trimmed surfaces are decomposed into intermediate forms that are ideally suited for implementation with parallel architectures. With judicious use of hardware, future implementations are feasible which fully utilize the rendering capacities of modern graphics systems.

Figure 8. A stenciled bi-cubic patch.

Figure 9. A patch trimmed with a Peano space filling curve.

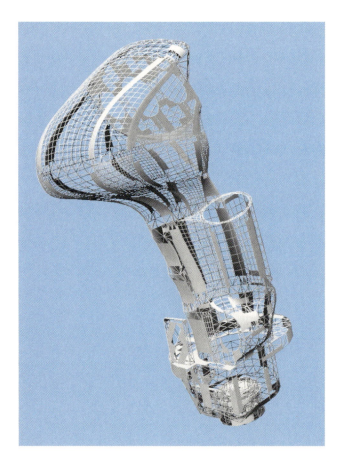

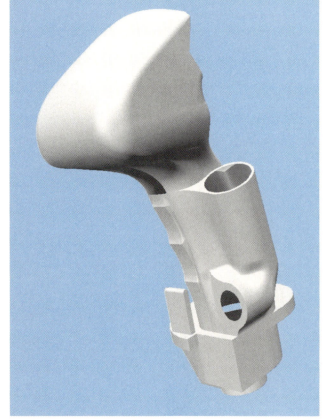

Figure 10. An aircraft joystick showing (left) tiling and coving, and (right) a rendered surface.
(Model courtesy of Lockheed Aircraft Co.)

Acknowledgements

Special thanks to Derrick Burns, Rosemary Chang, Carl Korobkin, Reuel Nash, Ann Sydeman and Vince Uttley for their contributions to the design of the method and its implementation.

We also thank Mark Compton, Paul Haeberli and Monica Schulze for their help in preparing the camera-ready copy and the color images.

References

[Ake88] Akeley, K. and Jermoluk, T. High-Performance Polygon Rendering. Proceedings of SIGGRAPH'88 (Atlanta, August 1-5, 1988). In *Computer Graphics* 22, 4 (August 1988), 239-240.

[Apg88] Apgar, B., Bersack, B. and Mammen, A. A Display System for the Stellar Graphics Supercomputer Model GS1000. Proceedings of SIGGRAPH'88 (Atlanta, August 1-5, 1988). In *Computer Graphics* 22, 4 (August 1988), 255-262.

[Boe84] Boehm, W., Farin, G.E. and Kahmann, J. A Survey of Curve and Surface Methods in CAGD. In *Computer Aidid Geometric Design* 1 (1984) 1-60.

[Cat74] Catmull, E. A Subdivision Algorithm for Computer Display of Curved Surfaces, doctoral dissertation, Univ. of Utah, Salt Lake City (1974).

[Cla79] Clark, J.H. A Fast Algorithm for Rendering Parametric Surfaces. Supplement, proceedings of SIGGRAPH'79. In *Computer Graphics* 13, 2 (1979), 289-299.

[Dee88] Deering, M. et. al. The Triangle Processor and Normal Vector Shader: A VLSI System for High Performance Graphics. Proceedings of SIGGRAPH'88 (Atlanta, August 1-5, 1988). In *Computer Graphics* 22, 4 (August 1988), 21-30.

[DeR87] DeRose, A.D. and Holman, T.J. The Triangle: A Multiprocessor Architecture for Fast Curve and Surface Generation. In TR 87-08-07 University of Washington, Seattle, WA (August 1987).

[Faro] Farouki, R. Concise Piecewise-Linear Approximation. Internal IBM Research Document, Yorktown Heights, NY.

[Far88] Farin, G.E. *Curves and Surfaces for Computer Aided Design*. Academic Press, Inc., Boston (1988).

[Fol82] Foley, J. and Van Dam, A. *Fundamentals of Interactive Computer Graphics*. Addison-Wesley Publishers, 1982.

[For79] Forrest, A.R. On the Rendering of Surfaces. In *Computer Graphics* 13, 2 (August 1979), 253-259.

[Gar78] Garey, M., Johnson, D.S., Preparata, F. P. and Tarjan, R. E. Triangulating a Simple Polygon. In *Info. Proc. Lett.* 7, 4, (1978), 175-180.

[Gha88] Gharachorloo, N. et. al. Subnanosecond Pixel Rendering with Million Transistor Chips. Proceedings of SIGGRAPH'86 (Atlanta, August 1-5, 1986). In *Computer Graphics* 22, 4 (August 1988), 41-49.

[Kaj82] Kajiya, J.T. Ray Tracing Parametric Patches. Proceedings of SIGGRAPH'82. In *Computer Graphics* 16, 3 (1982), 245-254.

[Lan80] Lane, J.M., et. al. Scan Line Methods for Displaying Parametrically Defined Surfaces. Comm. In *ACM* 23, 1 (1980) 23-34.

[Lan81] Lane, J. and Riesenfeld, R.F. Bounds On Polynomials. In *BIT* 21 (1981) 112-117.

[Roc87] Rockwood, A.P. A Generalized Scanning Technique for Display of Parametrically Defined Surfaces. In *IEEE Computer Graphics and its Applications* 7, 8 (August 1987), 15-26.

[Sed88] Sederberg, T. Private communication (1988).

[Sed87] Sederberg, T. and Wang, X. Rational Hodographs. In *CAGD* 4 (1987), 333-335.

[Sha88] Shantz, M. and Chang, S. Rendering Trimmed NURBS with Adaptive Forward Differencing. Proceedings of SIGGRAPH'88 (Atlanta, August 1-5, 1988). In *Computer Graphics* 22, 4 (August 1988), 189-198.

[Sha87] Shantz, M. and Lien, S. Shading Bicubic Patches. Proceedings of SIGGRAPH'87 (Anaheim, July 27-31, 1987). In *Computer Graphics* 21, 4 (July 1987), 189-196.

[Swe86] Sweeney, A.J. and Bartels, R.H. Ray Tracing Free-Form B-Spline Surfaces. In *IEEE Computer Graphics and its Applications* 6, 2 (February 1986) 41-49.

Accurate Color Reproduction
for Computer Graphics Applications

Bruce J. Lindbloom

Crosfield Dicomed, Inc.
Minneapolis, MN

Abstract

A method is presented for accurate color reproduction among a wide variety of display devices. The method is very general, in that it may be applied to virtually any color display device. Its generality has been demonstrated by application to color monitors, film recorders, electronic pre-press systems and color hardcopy devices. The algorithm has been used to accurately translate between device dependent and device independent color specifications and to translate from one device dependent color specification to another.

The method separates the color reproduction process into two distinct components: *device characterization,* which accounts for the colorimetric properties of each class of display device, and *device calibration,* which accounts for local variations from one instance of a device to another.

A *companded* RGB color space is introduced, which is used with trivariate parametric polynomial volumes (i.e. hyperpatches) to perform accurate color transformations.

A color separation algorithm is presented which converts companded RGB to and from the subtractive printing colors (cyan, magenta, yellow, black) using gray component replacement.

CR Categories and Subject Descriptors: I.3.6 [Computer Graphics] Methodology and Techniques – Device independence, I.3.7 [Computer Graphics] Three-Dimensional Graphics and Realism – Color, shading, shadowing and texture.

General Terms: Algorithms.

Additional Key Words and Phrases: color correction, color reproduction, color separation, companding

1. Introduction

Color is becoming increasingly common and available on all computer graphics systems. Once considered a luxury, today even low end PCs are equipped with color and are serving very sophisticated color applications.

Why is accurate color reproduction important?

There are many reasons why color fidelity is of interest to designers and users of systems employing computer graphics as well as researchers in the field.

Observation of industry trends indicates a continuing migration toward higher quality, photorealistic imagery. Sophisticated rendering techniques such as radiosity[5] and ray tracing[18, 9, 6] approximate physical and optical properties with increasing accuracy. However, these images only exist in digital form within the computer until they take on visual meaning by way of display on a display device. This display process must approximate the intended colors with the same degree of accuracy used in the rendering process.

Many commercial applications of computer graphics require consistent and accurate display of color among multiple display devices. Clients often proof a design based on a facsimile of the final output. Most users of computer graphics systems are aware of the oftentimes gross disparities between hardcopy images and screen images.

The interest in accurate color reproduction is further fueled by the plethora of high quality color output devices employing a wide variety of technologies such as dye sublimation, ink jet and thermal transfer. In order to take advantage of these rapid developments, a method is needed which allows accurate color reproduction on new devices without requiring detailed knowledge and expertise of the physics and chemistry of each new display technology.

Finally, there is a growing interest in the integration of device independent color specifications with graphics exchange standards, two examples being the ISO 8613 Colour Addendum and the ANSI IT8. Methods are needed to accurately translate between these color standards and display devices.

The algorithms presented here were initially developed in 1984 and were incorporated into successful commercial applications shortly thereafter. They have proven to be very useful in meeting the needs described above.

2. Design Goals

For a color reproduction algorithm to be general purpose and useful, it should possess certain characteristics set forth as design goals. The following list describes some of the more important goals:

a) It must be able to convert from a device independent color specification to a device dependent color specification.

b) It must be reversible, allowing the conversion from a device dependent color specification to a device independent color specification.

c) The processor and memory requirements must be low enough for implementation in commercial equipment in a high volume, production environment, using general purpose computers including PCs.

d) Colors which lie outside of the color gamut of a device must be handled gracefully and meaningfully.

e) A single method must be applicable to virtually any type of color display device. The operation of this conversion function must be controlled by a relatively small set of characterization parameters for each class of device.

f) It must be applicable to non-RGB color systems such as print (cyan, magenta, yellow and black printers).

g) It must be applicable to color mapped as well as full color raster applications.

h) It must be visually continuous in the sense that no artificial visual discontinuities or anomalies are introduced.

i) It must work with continuous tone devices as well as devices that simulate continuous tones by screening or dithering.

j) It must correctly compensate for imperfect color producing agents, for example 'dye crosstalk' in photographic films caused by unwanted spectral absorption of non-ideal dyes in the processed emulsion and 'additivity failure'[21] that occurs in printing inks.

3. Constraints

Any color reproduction system is faced with many constraints, over which it has little or no control. Among these are:

a) The human visual system is *extremely* complex. Many volumes have been written on this subject alone, and suffice it to say that phenomena such as chromatic adaptation, size and location of visual field, color defective vision, simultaneous contrast and many, many others contribute to the enormous complexity of color perception[7].

b) Display devices require periodic calibration to account for long term drift. In practice, the responsibility of timely and methodical calibration is often neglected.

c) Display devices usually have a fixed set of color producing agents (e.g. dyes, pigments or phosphors). Because of this, the best color match one can reasonably hope for is a *metameric* match, whereby the reproduction will match the original only when viewed with a single, fixed illuminant.

d) All display devices suffer from some degree of inconsistency where fixed inputs produce outputs which vary with time and/or position on the display media. The degree of inconsistency of each class of display device must be recognized when establishing expectation levels of its color matching performance.

Given the ambitious goals described in §2 balanced with the sobering realities of these real world constraints, one is forced to arrive at the humbling conclusion that complete success is simply not achievable. Nevertheless, significant progress towards these goals can be made, as we shall see.

4. Previous Methods

Most previous methods are focused toward a single type of display device, or the matching of colors between two specific display devices (e.g. monitor and print), and therefore cannot be generalized to other types of devices.

An example of this is a color RGB monitor, for which its RGB intensity cube is taken to be a linear transformation of the CIE tristimulus space, (X, Y, Z)[1]. The RGB intensities are then passed through a gamma correction function for accurate display. This method works quite well for a properly calibrated system using high quality components. The validity of the linear transform assumption may be checked by examining color vectors in (X, Y, Z) space. This is done by computing the ratio of the length of the white vector, $\vec{W}$, to the length of the sum of the RGB vectors, $\vec{R}, \vec{G}, \vec{B}$:

$$M = \frac{\left| \vec{W} \right|}{\left| \vec{R} + \vec{G} + \vec{B} \right|}$$

where one would expect M to be unity in a linear system. For a high quality, properly calibrated RGB monitor, the ratio M was computed from experimental measurements to be 1.003. By contrast, the same ratio was computed for a high quality film recorder, for which M was found to be 4.378. It is obvious from this that the linear transformation is a very poor approximation of film recorder behavior, resulting in errors of well over 400%.

Another example of a device specific color reproduction method is the use of the Neugebauer equations in the printing industry, which attempt to predict the red, green and blue reflectances resulting from given dot areas of the overprinted process colors[21]. The Neugebauer equations do not always agree well with measured densities, and therefore have been subjected to various modifications[12]. This method is not readily applicable to other types of display devices.

A recently published method[16] establishes a three dimensional relationship between device color coordinates and XYZ tristimulus space. This relationship is made by numerous spectrophotometric measurements throughout the color gamut of the display device. The color conversion is done by table look up combined with trilinear interpolation.

This method requires many spectrophotometric measurements, which is a tedious process. The relatively coarse sampling array can lead to C^1 discontinuities due to the piecewise linear interpolation function used. The Mach band effect[7] accentuates not only C^0, but also C^1 discontinuities (a common visible defect in the Gouraud shading of a tessellated, curved surface). Figure 1 shows how the Mach band effect can accentuate C^1 discontinuities. The intensity function used here is C^0 continuous everywhere, is horizontally monotonic, and has C^1 discontinuities at the one third and two thirds positions. The bright and dark bands seen in these locations are purely perceptual. Therefore, trilinear interpolation of a coarse sampling array can convert a smoothly blended series of colors into a series of colors with C^1 discontinuities. C^1 discontinuities are particularly troublesome on high quality, continuous tone devices such as film recorders.

Furthermore, as stated by the authors[16], (X, Y, Z) tristimulus space is not conducive to a Newton iteration.

0.00   0.45   0.55   1.00

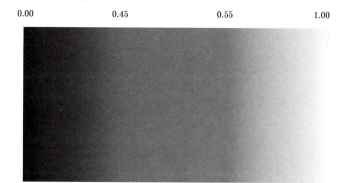

Figure 1: Example of Mach bands

5. Definition of Color Systems

The methods to be described in §6 will use three different color systems, $(L*, u*, v*)$, companded RGB and device color coordinates. In this section each of these color systems will be defined.

5.1. L*, u*, v*

The first is $(L*, u*, v*)$, which is an approximately uniform perceptual color space set forth as a standard by the CIE[20]. It is a non-linear transform of the (X, Y, Z) tristimulus color space:

$$L* = \begin{cases} 116 \, (Y/Y_n)^{1/3} - 16 & \text{for } Y/Y_n > \eta \\ 100 \, \kappa \, (Y/Y_n) & \text{for } Y/Y_n \le \eta \end{cases} \quad (1)$$

$$u* = 13 \, L* \, (u' - u_n')$$

$$v* = 13 \, L* \, (v' - v_n')$$

where

$\eta = 0.008856$

$\kappa = 9.0329$

$u' = 4X / (X + 15Y + 3Z)$

$v' = 9Y / (X + 15Y + 3Z)$

$u_n' = 4X_n / (X_n + 15Y_n + 3Z_n)$

$v_n' = 9Y_n / (X_n + 15Y_n + 3Z_n)$

with (X_n, Y_n, Z_n) being the tristimulus values of the nominally white object color stimulus. Equation (1) transforms luminance into a uniform perceptual lightness scale. Tristimulus values are defined as:

$$X = \int \overline{x}(\lambda) \, \rho(\lambda) \, d\lambda$$

$$Y = \int \overline{y}(\lambda) \, \rho(\lambda) \, d\lambda$$

$$Z = \int \overline{z}(\lambda) \, \rho(\lambda) \, d\lambda$$

for light sources such as CRTs, and as:

$$X = \int S(\lambda) \, \overline{x}(\lambda) \, \tau(\lambda) \, d\lambda$$

$$Y = \int S(\lambda) \, \overline{y}(\lambda) \, \tau(\lambda) \, d\lambda$$

$$Z = \int S(\lambda) \, \overline{z}(\lambda) \, \tau(\lambda) \, d\lambda$$

for transmissive or reflective color samples such as film or paper hardcopy. In these integrals, $\overline{x}(\lambda)$, $\overline{y}(\lambda)$, and $\overline{z}(\lambda)$ are the CIE standard observer functions, $\rho(\lambda)$ is the spectral power distribution of a light producing color sample, $\tau(\lambda)$ is the spectral transmissive or reflective distribution of a transmissive or a reflective color sample and $S(\lambda)$ is the spectral power distribution of a reference white, typically one of the CIE standard illuminants such as D_{65}. The integrals are evaluated over the visible spectrum, approximately 360 to 830 nm.

In practice, the integrals are approximated as the sum of products of discrete samples using the weighted ordinate method with fixed width intervals in λ, usually 1 to 10 nm.

5.2. Companded RGB

The second color system is new and will be called *companded RGB*. This color system is device class dependent in that it is bound to a certain class of display device. In this context, the term *class* refers to a combination of a type of display device with a type of display medium, for example a film recorder type X with film type Y. It includes all instances of this class.

This class dependent color system is called *companded RGB* because the red, green and blue (RGB) intensity components of the display device are passed through a companding (*compressing/expanding*) function. Companding is a technique commonly used in digital signal processing to insure that low amplitude signals are digitized with a minimal loss of fidelity[2]. Two companding function standards used for DSP are 'μ-255 law' and 'A-law', both of which are logarithmic functions.

For companded RGB space, it is suggested here that a normalized version of Equation (1) be used as the companding function. The proposed compression function is:

$$V_c = \begin{cases} 1.16 \, (V_i)^{1/3} - 0.16 & \text{for } V_i > \eta \\ \kappa \, (V_i) & \text{for } V_i \le \eta \end{cases} \quad (2)$$

which converts each of the RGB intensities (V_i, in the range [0, 1]) into companded RGB values (V_c, in the range [0, 1]). This equation is easily inverted to produce the corresponding expansion function:

$$V_i = \begin{cases} \left((V_c + 0.16) / 1.16 \right)^3 & \text{for } V_c > \kappa\eta \\ V_c / \kappa & \text{for } V_c \le \kappa\eta \end{cases} \quad (3)$$

Figure 2a: Data flow without companding

Figure 2b: Data flow with companding

Figures 2a and 2b show the data flow with and without companding.

It is important to note that by definition, the gray scale is represented as equal r, g, b values, which always map onto the $L*$ axis in $(L*, u*, v*)$. Many devices do not have this gray balance property. For example, gray is usually made by unequal RGB values on film recorders and by unequal CMY values on print. The needed gray balance correction is applied in the mapping from companded RGB to device color coordinates, as described in §6.3.

Why use companded RGB? There are three important reasons, which will now be discussed.

Reason 1: Perceived color quantization contours can be eliminated.

Most high quality rendering algorithms such as ray tracing perform shading calculations based on RGB intensities (note the important distinction between *RGB intensities* and *companded RGB values* used throughout this paper). If the intensity of a pixel is quantized to eight bits, contouring becomes visible in colors with any of the RGB components having small values. This is a commonly seen anomaly in computer generated images and is demonstrated in Figure 3a, where color quantization contours are visible near the right and bottom edges. It has been found that companding each of the RGB intensities prior to the 8 bit quantization eliminates all color quantization contouring, as seen in Figure 3b.

The Appendix of this paper contains a brief analysis of this effect. This analysis suggests that in order to eliminate perceived color quantization errors, RGB intensities must be quantized to at least twelve bits, while companded RGB values need only be quantized to eight bits.

Reason 2: Companded RGB provides better user interface color models.

It so happens that companded RGB space is much more perceptually uniform than RGB intensity space. Furthermore, other color models which are derived from RGB (such as HSV) are also more perceptually uniform. Figure 4a shows an RGB cube and an HSV cone computed using RGB intensities. In this figure both models are dominated by pastels, and the dark colors near black occupy a very small volume of the total model. By contrast, Figure 4b shows these same two color models computed using companded RGB values. It is apparent from this figure that the color distribution of both models is much more perceptually uniform.

Clearly, the companded RGB model is not a uniform perceptual color space. The emphasis here is *relative* to RGB intensity space, and the useful properties gained by this relative difference.

The tendency toward perceptual uniformity of companded RGB space also lends itself well to the pseudo color quantization of full color raster images. Companding provides a perceptually based color metric which, as suggested by Heckbert[10], improves the visual quality of the quantized output image.

Figure 3a: Eight bit quantization of RGB intensity

Figure 3b: Eight bit quantization of companded RGB

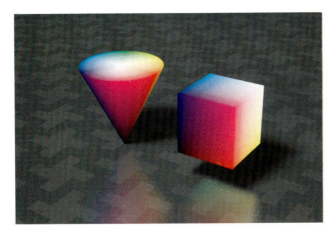

Figure 4a: Color models based on RGB intensity

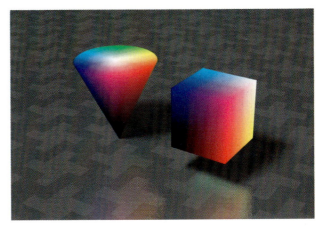

Figure 4b: Color models based on companded RGB

Reason 3: Companding provides a useful convergence criterion.

As we shall see in §6.2, the approximate uniform nature of companded RGB space provides a convenient error measure for the termination of the numerical iteration loop in the $(L*, u*, v*)$ to RGB conversion process.

5.3. Device Color Coordinates

The third and final color space is that of the physical display device. It is dependent, not only on the class of device, but also on each instance of each class. This is the lowest level of color binding. For a film recorder it may be 8 to 12 bit exposure codes for RGB; for an electronic pre-press system it may be dot percentages of the four process color inks; for a thermal transfer printer it may simply be ones and zeros, indicating print or no-print.

6. Algorithm Description

Figure 5 is an overview of the color conversion process. The three color systems described in §5 are depicted by the three boxes. The arrows indicate the algorithms used to convert between color systems. Colors are completely device independent on the far left and become progressively more device dependent toward the right.

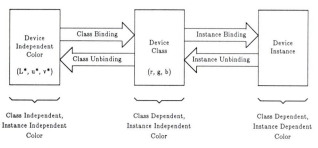

Figure 5: Device dependent binding levels

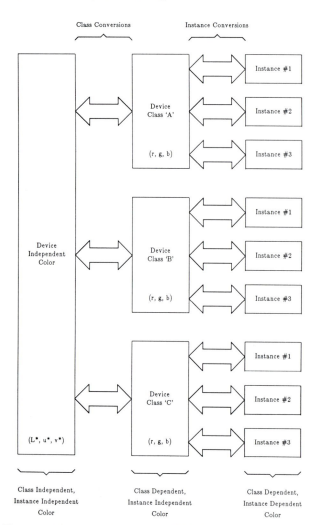

Figure 6: Color conversion among multiple devices

In an environment with multiple display devices, transformations occur as illustrated in Figure 6. In this diagram, the double arrow pairs of Figure 5 are replaced with single, double headed arrows for simplification purposes. As shown, the conversion from one device class to another involves the device independent $(L*, u*, v*)$ color space as a temporary intermediate, through which the exchange is made.

The color transformations indicated by the four arrows in Figure 5 will each be described in §6.1 through §6.4.

6.1. RGB to L*, u*, v* Transformation

The transformation between companded RGB and $(L*, u*, v*)$ is done using trivariate parametric hyperpatches. The degree of the polynomials is arbitrary, with higher degrees providing more accurate color matching at the expense of a longer computation time and a greater effort during the characterization process. In the following discussion, the tricubic case will be used as an example, with the hope that application to other degrees will be obvious. Experience has shown that there is little gained in going beyond degree three, and for many applications triquadratic or even trilinear hyperpatches are adequate.

The process of transforming companded RGB space into $(L*, u*, v*)$ space involves using the companded RGB components ($0 \le r, g, b \le 1$) as the parameters for the polynomials. The hyperpatch therefore applies a free form deformation to the RGB cube, transforming it into $(L*, u*, v*)$ space. This is illustrated in Figure 7, which is an RGB cube in the companded RGB space of a particular class of device, and Figure 8, which shows the cube after transformation to $(L*, u*, v*)$ space.

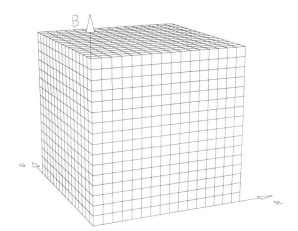

Figure 7: Companded RGB cube in companded RGB space

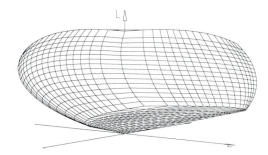

Figure 8: Companded RGB cube in L*, u*, v* space

The mathematical formulation of the tricubic hyperpatch is shown here for the $L*$ component. The $u*$ and $v*$ components are similar.

$$L*(r, g, b) = \begin{bmatrix} r^3 & r^2 & r & 1 \end{bmatrix} \begin{bmatrix} B_{\lambda 3} \end{bmatrix} \begin{bmatrix} f_0(g, b) \\ f_1(g, b) \\ f_2(g, b) \\ f_3(g, b) \end{bmatrix}$$

where

$$f_0(g, b) = \begin{bmatrix} g^3 & g^2 & g & 1 \end{bmatrix} \begin{bmatrix} B_{\lambda 3} \end{bmatrix} \begin{bmatrix} h_0(b) \\ h_1(b) \\ h_2(b) \\ h_3(b) \end{bmatrix}$$

with similar equations for $f_1(g, b)$ through $f_3(g, b)$, and

$$h_0(b) = \begin{bmatrix} b^3 & b^2 & b & 1 \end{bmatrix} \begin{bmatrix} B_{\lambda 3} \end{bmatrix} \begin{bmatrix} L*_0 \\ L*_1 \\ L*_2 \\ L*_3 \end{bmatrix}$$

with similar equations for $h_1(b)$ through $h_{15}(b)$.

In these equations, $(L*_i, u*_i, v*_i)$ are control points derived from spectrophotometric measurements taken during the device characterization process. These control points are interpolated using the basis function, $[B_{\lambda 3}]$. This basis function is derived from the polynomial

$$f(t) = a\ t^3 + b\ t^2 + c\ t + d$$

whose coefficients a, b, c and d we wish to express in terms of control points in $(L*, u*, v*)$ space (P_0 through P_3), which the function will interpolate. We choose the following four conditions:

$$f(0) = P_0$$
$$f(1/3) = P_1$$
$$f(2/3) = P_2$$
$$f(1) = P_3$$

Combining these equations yields

$$\begin{bmatrix} 0 & 0 & 0 & 1 \\ \frac{1}{27} & \frac{1}{9} & \frac{1}{3} & 1 \\ \frac{8}{27} & \frac{4}{9} & \frac{2}{3} & 1 \\ 1 & 1 & 1 & 1 \end{bmatrix} \begin{bmatrix} a \\ b \\ c \\ d \end{bmatrix} = \begin{bmatrix} P_0 \\ P_1 \\ P_2 \\ P_3 \end{bmatrix}$$

which leads to the cubic interpolation basis

$$\begin{bmatrix} B_{\lambda 3} \end{bmatrix} = \begin{bmatrix} 0 & 0 & 0 & 1 \\ \frac{1}{27} & \frac{1}{9} & \frac{1}{3} & 1 \\ \frac{8}{27} & \frac{4}{9} & \frac{2}{3} & 1 \\ 1 & 1 & 1 & 1 \end{bmatrix}^{-1} = \frac{1}{2}\begin{bmatrix} -9 & 27 & -27 & 9 \\ 18 & -45 & 36 & -9 \\ -11 & 18 & -9 & 2 \\ 2 & 0 & 0 & 0 \end{bmatrix}$$

Following a similar process, the quadratic and linear bases are found to be

$$\begin{bmatrix} B_{\lambda 2} \end{bmatrix} = \begin{bmatrix} 2 & -4 & 2 \\ -3 & 4 & -1 \\ 1 & 0 & 0 \end{bmatrix}$$

$$\begin{bmatrix} B_{\lambda 1} \end{bmatrix} = \begin{bmatrix} -1 & 1 \\ 1 & 0 \end{bmatrix}$$

For polynomials of degree N, $(N + 1)^3$ control points are needed. These control points are measured with a spectrophotometer or spectroradiometer from sample colors made on a calibrated output device (calibration is described in §6.3). The colors to be measured are those resulting from all combinations of r, g, b taken from the set $\{i/N\}$, with $i = 0, 1, \cdots, N$.

The hyperpatch exactly interpolates the control points, therefore higher degree polynomials have more control points which are more closely spaced, resulting in a better representation of the actual device properties.

It is noteworthy that not only is the shape of the deformed RGB cube important, but also the locations of the isoparametric curves on its surface and the isoparametric bivariate patches in its interior.

One portion of color space that is particularly sensitive to even small errors is the gray scale. Any hue in an achromatic color is easily perceived. In terms of the color spaces defined here, all colors with equal r, g, b values must map onto the $L*$ axis. Since there are only $N + 1$ control points with this property, the entire gray scale is not guaranteed to map properly. This phenomenon is easily remedied by applying a reparameterization to all r, g, b values prior to substitution into the hyperpatch equations. The effect of this may be seen by comparing Figure 9, which is a transformed gamut without reparameterization, with Figure 8, for which reparameterization was used. This process does not change the shape of the gamut, it only redistributes the isoparametric patches within the gamut such that all $r = g = b$ map onto the $L*$ axis. This redistribution is slight, and in fact no change whatever occurs at any of the control points.

This reparameterization may be implemented using three look up tables, each containing 256 entries. These tables are created once for each class of device by interpolating the $N + 1$ achromatic control points with a parametric polynomial using the $[B_{\lambda N}]$ basis. 256 equal steps in the curve parameter generate 256 $(L*, u*, v*)$ gray scale values, each of which is transformed to RGB parameters using the transformation described in §6.2. Normally, the $(L*, u*, v*)$ values generated this way will be 256 even steps in $L*$, with $u* = v* = 0$. The resulting 256 RGB triplets become the values of the reparameterization look up tables. The reparameterized hyperpatch now interpolates the measured control points with precise gray scale reproduction.

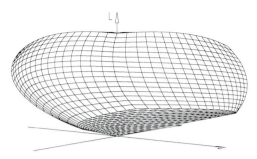

Figure 9: Color gamut without reparmeterization

The information required to characterize a device is

a) the polynomial degree, N, to be used for interpolation,

b) an ordered set of $(N + 1)^3$ control points in $(L*, u*, v*)$ and

c) three reparameterization look up tables, one for each RGB component.

All of this information is measured and computed once for each class of device and is used thereafter for all color conversions between companded RGB and $(L*, u*, v*)$.

To summarize the transformation from RGB to $(L*, u*, v*)$, the companded RGB values are first passed through the reparameterization look up tables and then substituted into the hyperpatch equations, producing a device independent $(L*, u*, v*)$ color.

6.2. L*, u*, v* to RGB Transformation

This transformation is the inverse of the process just described in the previous section. We start with a device independent $(L*, u*, v*)$ color and convert it to a device class dependent, companded RGB color.

There is no closed form solution to the inverse of the hyperpatch equations, so a numerical solution must be employed. Newton's method[3, 13] is used here to transform the color $(L*', u*', v*')$ into companded RGB values. The iteration process obtains guess $n+1$ from guess n as follows:

$$r_{n+1} = r_n + \Delta r_n$$
$$g_{n+1} = g_n + \Delta g_n \qquad (4)$$
$$b_{n+1} = b_n + \Delta b_n$$

where

$$\begin{bmatrix} \Delta r_n & \Delta g_n & \Delta b_n \end{bmatrix} = \begin{bmatrix} \Delta L*_n & \Delta u*_n & \Delta v*_n \end{bmatrix} \begin{bmatrix} J \end{bmatrix}^{-1}$$

$$\Delta L*_n = L*' - L*_n$$
$$\Delta u*_n = u*' - u*_n$$
$$\Delta v*_n = v*' - v*_n$$

and $[J]$ is the Jacobian

$$\begin{bmatrix} J \end{bmatrix} = \begin{bmatrix} \dfrac{\partial L*}{\partial r} & \dfrac{\partial u*}{\partial r} & \dfrac{\partial v*}{\partial r} \\ \dfrac{\partial L*}{\partial g} & \dfrac{\partial u*}{\partial g} & \dfrac{\partial v*}{\partial g} \\ \dfrac{\partial L*}{\partial b} & \dfrac{\partial u*}{\partial b} & \dfrac{\partial v*}{\partial b} \end{bmatrix}$$

where the partial derivatives are evaluated at (r_n, g_n, b_n). The (r, g, b) parameters must always be clamped to the range $[0, 1]$.

As a bit of an historical aside, the first effort in the development of these color reproduction algorithms used a hyperpatch to map the RGB intensity cube to (X, Y, Z) space. This transformed color cube is shown in Figure 10 for a color film recorder (obviously a non-linear transform, as discussed in § 4). The irregular spacing of the RGB intensity points results in very large variations in the partial derivatives, which seriously impairs the stability of the Newton iteration, causing it to take giant steps into oblivion, on its way toward far away roots. Despite considerable effort, this scheme could never be made to work reliably. A comparison of Figure 10 with Figure 8 clearly shows the improvements realized by mapping companded RGB into $(L*, u*, v*)$ space, where the iteration is very well behaved. Furthermore, the use of companded RGB and $(L*, u*, v*)$ gives much better control over perceptual errors than (X, Y, Z) which is very perceptually non-uniform.

The use of Newton's method has three requirements: a sufficiently good initial guess must be available, the functions must be differentiable and some convergence criteria must be available to terminate the iteration process.

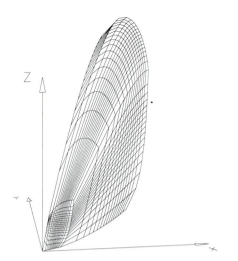

Figure 10: RGB intensity cube in X, Y, Z space

Newton's method has quadratic convergence in the neighborhood of a root, and therefore a good initial guess will be very beneficial in finding a rapid solution. Experimentation has shown the following equation to be easily computed as well as providing an excellent initial guess, shown here for red:

$$r_0 = \frac{\sum_i \dfrac{p_i}{d_i + \epsilon}}{\sum_i \dfrac{1}{d_i + \epsilon}}$$

where the summations occur over all control points, p_i is the red parameter value at control point i, d_i is the square of the distance between $(L*', u*', u')$ and control point i and ϵ is a small constant to prevent divide by zero failures. Initial guesses for the green and blue parameters are similarly computed. These initial guesses are weighted averages of the parameter values associated with the control points based on their distances.

The partial derivatives needed for the Jacobian are easily computed since polynomial functions are used for the interpolation.

There are several criteria which are useful for terminating the iteration process. Since we are iterating in $(L*, u*, v*)$ space, a perceptual color difference may be used to detect convergence[20] :

$$\Delta E*_{uv} = \left(\Delta L*_n{}^2 + \Delta u*_n{}^2 + \Delta v*_n{}^2 \right)^{\frac{1}{2}}$$

However, since we are using companded RGB, a much more convenient and efficient method is available. We can terminate the iteration when maximum($|\Delta r|$, $|\Delta g|$, $|\Delta b|$) $\leq 1/256$.

A maximum iteration count must also be defined. If convergence is not attained after this prescribed number of iterations (say five), the $(L*', u*', v*')$ color is outside the color gamut of the device, and therefore cannot be accurately displayed.

These cases of out of range colors are quite common and may be illustrated by comparing the gamut of Figure 8 (a film recorder with color transparency film) with that of Figure 11 (a press proof from an electronic pre-press system). These two gamuts are quite different, and divide color space into four regions: colors that are only in one gamut, colors that are only in the other gamut, colors that are in both gamuts and colors that are in neither gamut. These regions are easier to visualize by examining Figure 12, which shows the intersecting gamuts.

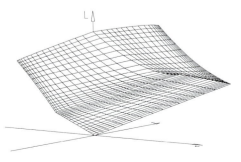

Figure 11: Color gamut for print in L*, u*, v* space

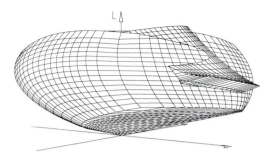

Figure 12: Intersecting gamuts of two devices

This leads to the very complex issue of handling colors which are outside the gamut of the display device[16, 14]. The difficulty arises more from definition than from implementation. The definition of the desired course of action appears to be very dependent on the application context. Mapping to the closest displayable color can result in hue shifts and can introduce discontinuities in a smooth sequence of out of range colors. A method which seems to suit many applications is to treat hue as being more important than saturation, which in turn is more important than lightness. In this case, hue is always maintained. The saturation is altered only if it is greater than 100% in which case it is clamped to 100%. Finally, the lightness is set to 100% only if it is greater than 100%.

This requires ray tracing the outer surfaces of the hyperpatch. These surfaces are bivariate parametric patches for which numerous ray – patch intersection solutions have been devised[11, 17, 18]. However, in this use, there are certain properties of the hyperpatches which make this computation easier than intersecting a ray with an arbitrary patch.

First, it has been found that the three surfaces of the companded RGB cube containing black are always nearly planar after transformation to $(L*, u*, v*)$ space for all device types tested. As an approximation, we may force the $(L*, u*, v*)$ control points to be located on planes fitted through them as part of the characterization process. This reduces the saturation clamping to process to a trivial ray – plane intersection, with the ray originating at $(L*', u*', v*')$ and pointing towards $(L*', 0, 0)$.

However, the same scheme will not work for the lightness clamping because the three surfaces of the companded RGB cube containing white are typically highly curved. Therefore, lightness clamping must be done by ray tracing these three patches. The ray originates at the point $(L*', u*', v*')$ and points toward $(0, 0, 0)$. It will intersect the patch at most only once because these patches are not folded over or grossly distorted (no multiple roots within the parameter range and no silhouette edges). The intersection calculation may be simplified by applying a rotation to the ray (rotating about the $(L*, u*, v*)$ origin) such that the ray lies on the $+L*$ axis. The patch may then be transformed by this same transformation and projected onto the $u*v*$ plane. The 3D ray tracing problem now becomes the 2D problem of intersecting the point $(0, 0)$ with a well behaved 2D bivariate patch. This may be solved by using a simplified version of the Newton's method described earlier. Alternatively, a subdivision scheme may be used by converting from $[B_{\lambda N}]$ basis control points $([G_\lambda])$ to Bézier basis $[B_B]$ control points $([G_B])$:

$$\left[G_B \right] = \left[B_B \right]^{-1} \left[B_\lambda \right] \left[G_\lambda \right] \left[B_\lambda \right]^T \left[B_B \right]^{-1\,T}$$

In many applications, a relative gamut mapping is desired so that no clamping is applied. In such cases, a colorimetric match is not obtained, but rather, pure red for one class of device is mapped onto pure red for a different class of device, green to green, blue to blue, and so on. For example, if colors in the gamut of device Class 'A' (refer to Figure 6) are to be mapped to a Class 'B' device by applying a relative gamut mapping, the $(L*, u*, v*)$ colors are converted to Class 'B' colors using the device characterization information for Class 'A'. The instance mapping that follows uses a Class 'B' instance conversion.

In fact, since the transformation is based on free form hyperpatches, arbitrary mappings may be created by altering the locations of the control points. This allows color gamut mappings based on preference rather than colorimetric principles.

After companded RGB values are determined, they must be reparameterized by the inverse of the function described in §6.1.

To summarize the transformation from $(L*, u*, v*)$ to companded RGB, the input color is first subjected to saturation clamping (if needed) and then passed into the iterative process of Equations 4. If no solution is found, the color must be subjected to lightness clamping. In any event, the resulting parameters are passed backwards through the reparameterization table to arrive at the final companded RGB values. While this seems rather involved, some application examples will be examined in §7 which demonstrate implementation details.

6.3. RGB to Device Color Coordinate Transformation

The companded RGB values are generated for a class of display device. In this context, all instances of this class are identical. Therefore identical RGB data imaged on two different devices of the same class will produce identical results. This is accomplished by processing the RGB data with a local calibration function as part of conversion to device specific coordinates. This calibration process accounts for local variations in a particular instance of a device (e.g. long term drift, new film emulsion batch, new roll of printer ribbon, etc.) as well as differences among devices within the same class.

As we saw in §6.1, the characterization process requires the use of a spectrophotometer or spectroradiometer, which is a very expensive instrument, requiring a skilled operator. However, characterization need only be performed once for each class of device, with the resulting measurements applying forever after to all instances of that class.

Calibration, on the other hand, must be performed at regular intervals by the end user of each instance of the display device, and therefore this process should be simple, requiring less expensive and less sophisticated measurement equipment. In many applications, the end user may have no technical inclination whatever. The simplicity of calibration must be based on this premise.

The method used here is a variant of Catmull's method[4], which used b-splines to establish a linear relationship between $\log_2 i$ and density. One deviation from this scheme is the use of three separate look up tables, one each for red, green and blue. This technique allows gray colors (equal r, g, b values) to be displayed as gray, even on devices which do not exhibit gray tracking properties, such as film recorders and print.

The second deviation from Catmull's method is the linearization of companded RGB values with $L*$, rather than the log of intensity with density. This is in line with our definition of companded RGB and its relationship with the CIE uniform perceptual lightness scale, Equation (1). The conversion from density (D) to $L*$ is done by using intensities (I):

$$I_{white} = 10^{-D_{white}}$$
$$I_{black} = 10^{-D_{black}}$$
$$I_i = 10^{-D_i}$$

where D_i is the density to convert. Relative luminances are then computed as:

$$Y_i = I_i - I_{black}$$
$$Y_n = I_{white} - I_{black}$$

which are then substituted into Equation (1) to produce $L*$.

While the device characterization information is common to all instances of each class of device, the calibration information is unique to each device instance. It is refined periodically at whatever interval seems appropriate. With suitable software support, this calibration process can be made simple enough for non-technical people to perform using relatively inexpensive equipment such as a densitometer. This calibration process involves imaging a stepwedge, measuring the densities of the steps, and using these measurements to refine the calibration tables. This process may be further simplified by using a densitometer with a serial interface.

After the companded RGB values are passed through their respective look up tables, they are transformed into physical device coordinates. This process is, of course, very device specific and may be as simple as scaling the range of the RGB values. Other applications may require conversion to the subtractive printers (CMYK) and possibly screening or dithering.

6.4. Device Color Coordinate to RGB Transformation

This final transformation involves inverting the device specific transformation function to produce RGB components, which are then passed backwards through their look up tables to produce companded RGB values.

7. Application Examples

In this section different types of application examples will be examined. Each example has been chosen to demonstrate a different use of the methods presented in this paper.

7.1. Color Mapped Applications

In a typical color mapped application the user interacts with simple 2D graphics such as lines and polygons. The geometric objects are colored by number, using a color look up table to define the appearance of the relatively small (typically ≤ 256) set of colors. These colors are stored in the graphics file as $(L*, u*, v*)$, although the user interface software presents the user with more useful controls such as companded RGB (using the methods of §6.1 and 6.2) and possibly HSV and HSL[8], which are derivations of RGB. Colors may be mixed specifically for any display device by using the appropriate device characterization parameters during the conversion to and from $(L*, u*, v*)$. When the design session is over, a device independent color table is stored.

Note that the colors in the color table may easily be checked against any device gamut to detect out of range colors. This out of range information is available from the $(L*, u*, v*)$ to RGB conversion process, as any color to

which saturation clamping or lightness clamping has been applied can be so flagged.

When this file is to be displayed on a device, the $(L*, u*, v*)$ to RGB process is applied, using the characterization parameters for the particular display device class, followed by the transformation to the physical device coordinates using local calibration information. The computation time for this small set of colors is acceptable for most commonly used computing platforms in use today.

7.2. Full Color Raster Applications

The computation needed for translation to and from $(L*, u*, v*)$ is too great for use on images with many colors, such as full color raster images. It is suggested here that such images be stored in companded RGB for a certain device class. The conversion of this raster image to the RGB space of a different class of device must use an approximate solution to the processes described in §6.1 and 6.2.

One method of doing this is by tessellating the source RGB space into a large, three dimensional array of points. Each of the source colors associated with these points is transformed to $(L*, u*, v*)$ using the source device class, and then to companded RGB using the destination device class. This process generates a 3D look up table which may be used to transform all colors in the source image, using table look up combined with trilinear interpolation. The size of the look up table is arbitrary. Larger tables will reduce the Mach banding effects discussed earlier, but will require more storage. This trade-off may be changed at will by tessellating at finer or coarser resolutions, thereby allowing optimization for individual applications. Note that the risk of Mach banding is relatively small since continuous functions are being tessellated at points that are approximately uniformly distributed in a perceptual sense.

The compute requirements needed to generate large look up tables suggests that it may be useful to create them off-line for repeated use at later times. When not needed, the look up tables may be discarded, as they may always be exactly recreated at any time and at any resolution from the small set of device characterization information.

7.3. Print Applications

For print applications, companded RGB must be converted to the four process colors: cyan, magenta, yellow and black (CMYK). This process is called *color separation*[15]. The four dimensional CMYK space has an extra degree of freedom which is typically used to control the way in which the black printer is used. Although there is much effort in applying scientific methods to this, there is still a healthy dose of art and craft involved.

One way the extra degree of freedom may be used is in the control of the *gray component replacement* (GCR), which governs the amount of the gray component of a CMY color that is replaced by the black printer. In this simplified case, the specification of a GCR value locks in the extra degree of freedom and establishes a one to one mapping from RGB to CMYK. This implies that different calibration information is needed for every possible GCR value. In practice, it has been found that it is sufficient to calibrate at a few GCR levels and to interpolate this calibration data for other GCR values.

The calibration process is exactly as described in §6.3, with density measurements being taken from a press proof. This correctly compensates for the lack of gray scale tracking in the printing process.

An algorithm is presented here which converts from companded RGB (r, g, b in the range $[0, 1]$) to CMYK (c, m, y, k in the range $[0, 1]$):

$$c' = 1 - r$$
$$m' = 1 - g$$
$$y' = 1 - b$$

$$V_{min} = \min(c', m', y')$$
$$V_{max} = \max(c', m', y')$$
$$V_{rem} = V_{min} G^{\alpha} \left(1 - (V_{max} - V_{min}) \right)^{\beta} \tag{5}$$

$$c = c' - V_{rem}$$
$$m = m' - V_{rem}$$
$$y = y' - V_{rem}$$
$$k = V_{min} G$$

In these equations, G is the GCR value in the range $[0, 1]$. The constant α is used to control the relationship between the black printer and the CMY printers as a function of GCR. Examination of several standard references to good 'blacks'[21, 15] leads to a value for α of about 5. The constant β is used to give further control of the K to CMY relationship as a function of saturation. The value for β is somewhat subjective, but 2 is a good starting point.

The (c, m, y, k) values are generic in the same sense the (r, g, b) values are, and we may think of them as companded CMYK. These values are calibrated for specific output by using the calibration tables:

$$c_{device} = 1 - f_r(1 - c)$$
$$m_{device} = 1 - f_g(1 - m)$$
$$y_{device} = 1 - f_b(1 - y)$$
$$k_{device} = 1 - f_{avg}(1 - k)$$

where f_r, f_g and f_b are the calibration look up tables, and f_{avg} is an average of them. Equation (5) may be implemented as a triangular, two dimensional look up table indexed by V_{min} and V_{max}.

One reason such a simple color separation algorithm works is that the complex non-linearities and crosstalk effects have already been accounted for by the $(L*, u*, v*)$ to RGB transformation described in § 6.2.

This color separation algorithm may be inverted:

$$V_{min} = \min(c, m, y)$$
$$V_{max} = \max(c, m, y)$$
$$V_{rem} = k \; G^{\alpha-1} \left(1 - (V_{max} - V_{min})\right)^\beta \qquad (6)$$
$$V_{rem} = \min(V_{rem}, 1 - V_{max})$$
$$r = 1 - c - V_{rem}$$
$$g = 1 - m - V_{rem}$$
$$b = 1 - y - V_{rem}$$

Equation (6) may be implemented as a rectangular, two dimensional look up table, indexed by k and $(V_{max} - V_{min})$.

Figure 13 shows the effect of gray component replacement on the color separation process, using the algorithm presented above. This demonstrates that as the black increases linearly with GCR, color is removed from the CMY in a non-linear fashion.

A GCR value in the range 0.6 to 0.8 produces a black with the highest density, and therefore offers the greatest dynamic range. Although the maximum GCR value of 1.0 provides the best economy of the more expensive colored printing inks, the resulting printed images suffer from reduced shadow density and increased sensitivity to registration errors between the black and colored printers, causing light outlines to appear on dark picture elements.

Figures 4a, 4b and 13 of this paper were made using this color separation algorithm. Color separation films were made by processing the CMYK output through an electronic pre-press system.

8. Future Work

Some work has begun in applying these techniques to the calibration of color raster scanners. The approach taken involves scanning a monochrome test pattern containing known levels of $L*$. By applying the technique described in §6.3 in reverse, look up tables may be created that map RGB device coordinates from the scanner into companded RGB. This method correctly performs gray scale tracking over the dynamic range of the scanner. However, a method needs to be devised to characterize the scanner gamut in device independent terms.

Preliminary work has also begun on implementing the RGB to CMYK color separation process, combined with optional halftone generation, on a set of four parallel digital signal processors.

9. Conclusions

This paper describes a general framework for device independent color reproduction. Introduced is a companded RGB color space which serves as an important intermediate between physical device color coordinates and device independent color systems. The important issue of color quantization is addressed as part of the development of companded RGB.

The device characterization process is described which generates a relatively small set of parameters used to control the single, general purpose transformation function between companded RGB and $(L*, u*, v*)$ for any type of display device. This transformation function automatically accounts for non-linearities and color crosstalk effects exhibited by various display devices, as well as providing exact gray scale reproduction.

The calibration process is described which is used to map generic, companded RGB values to physical device color coordinates.

These methods have been in use for several years and, although not perfect, have been found to be quite effective in addressing the ambitious design goals set forth in §2.

10. Acknowledgements

In the academic community, the motto is often 'publish or perish'. In the highly competitive industrial segment, a different Boolean function is often used: 'publish *and* perish'.

The author would therefore like to express his appreciation to George Walker and Trevor Haworth of Crosfield Dicomed, Inc. and to Brian Jordan of Crosfield Electronics, Ltd. for allowing this information to be made public.

Thanks is also due to Gerry Baiel, Tom Buck and Jim Dillon for their important liaison roles between research and product development, and to Carey Carlson for his tireless testing, film recorder expertise and many helpful suggestions.

Finally, the author wishes to express sincere gratitude to John Grimaldi for establishing a creative work environment and for his dedicated support of this and other research work.

Appendix

Color Quantization and Companding

Five informal discussions about quantization are presented to support the use of a companded RGB space. Admittedly there is room for more rigor in some of the discussions. However, empirical evidence strongly supports the conclusions drawn.

Discussion 1: Sampling 3D Color Space

Although there is some disagreement among experts as to the exact number, there are approximately ten million detectably different colors[19]. Since color space is three dimensional, this suggests that 215 samples (cube root of ten million) would be sufficient to avoid visible quantization errors, provided the coordinate system axes carried equal perceptual weight and the samples were carefully selected along each axis.

Conclusion 1: It should be possible to define a color system such that three channels of eight bits each should be sufficient to guarantee no perceptible color quantization anomalies.

Discussion 2: Experience with the Companding Function

The companding method described in this paper has been used for many, many pictures. Color quantization problems have never been observed as a result of the companding and quantization processes. Obviously, contours will be visible on display devices lacking adequate color control, but this is a deficiency of the device, not the quantization method.

Companded RGB has three channels of eight bits each, therefore the claim is made that it meets the criteria of Discussion 1.

We can make this claim a little more believable by factoring in two additional safety margins. First, we will use 256 samples per axis rather than 215 to make better use of a binary representation and, second, we realize that no display device is capable of displaying *all* of the ten million perceivable colors. Therefore, we have over 16 million samples to cover fewer than ten million detectably different displayable colors.

Conclusion 2: Eight bit channels of companded RGB are sufficient to guarantee no perceptible color quantization problems.

Discussion 3: Examination of the Companding Function

If we differentiate Equation (3), we find that the part of the function with the minimum slope is $V_c \leq \kappa/100$, where the slope is $1/\kappa$. If we assume that 256 levels are sufficient to avoid quantization errors (Conclusions 1 and 2), the minimum intensity step needed is $1/(256 \times \kappa)$, which in turn means that approximately 2312 evenly spaced intensity levels are required. Therefore, twelve bits of intensity precision are needed ($\lceil \log_2(2312) \rceil = 12$).

Conclusion 3: Twelve bit channels of intensity should be sufficient to guarantee no perceptible color quantization anomalies.

Discussion 4: A Look Up Table Experiment

An experiment was performed using a high quality film recorder with twelve bit exposure control. A look up table was carefully constructed such that 256 equally spaced levels of $L*$ were displayed. Examination of this look up table indicated a minimum slope of about one part in 2793.

Conclusion 4: Same as Conclusion 3. ($\lceil \log_2(2793) \rceil = 12$).

Discussion 5: RGB Interpolation Experiment

Another experiment was performed using the same film recorder. This experiment displayed the 28 unique interpolation paths between all possible pairs of the eight corner colors of the RGB cube. The images were plotted several times, with progressive masking of the least significant bits of the look up table. This simulated display devices with limited control of intensities (12 bit, 11 bit, 10 bit, etc.). The resulting film showed obvious visual quantization breaks in the eight bit simulation, and the discriminating eye could detect subtle breaks even in the 11 bit simulation. No visual quantization defects could be seen on the 12 bit image.

Conclusion 5: Same as Conclusion 3.

Therefore, if RGB channel values are quantized to eight bits in the intensity domain, color quantization defects may be visible. If this is to be avoided, the intensity channels must be quantized to at least 12 bits, resulting in a storage/transmission increase of fifty percent.

On the other hand, companding gives the best of both worlds by guaranteeing no visual quantization problems while maintaining eight bit color channels. Furthermore, referring to Figure 2b, the compression function of Equation (2) combined with the quantization operation may be implemented as a 4096×8 bit look up table, and the scaling operation combined with the expansion function of Equation (3) may be implemented as a 256×12 bit look up table. Therefore, companding becomes a very inexpensive operation.

CMYK CMY C M Y K GCR

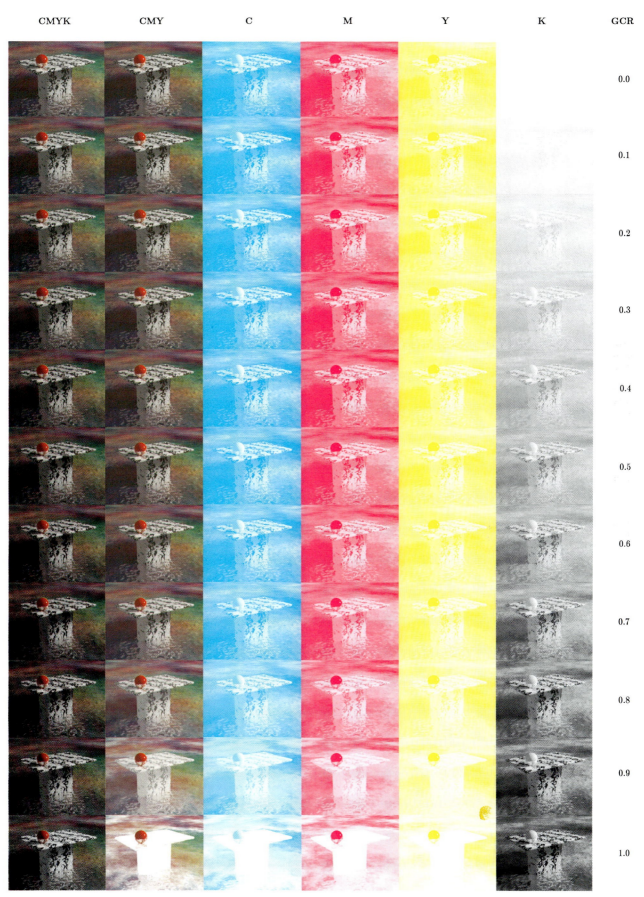

0.0

0.1

0.2

0.3

0.4

0.5

0.6

0.7

0.8

0.9

1.0

Figure 13: Effect of GCR on color separation

References

1. Conrac Corporation, *Raster Graphics Handbook, Second Edition,* Van Nostrand Reinhold Company, 1985.

2. Texas Instruments, *Digital Signal Processing Applications with the TMS320 Family,* 1986.

3. Forman S. Acton, *Numerical Methods That Work,* Harper & Row, 1970.

4. Edwin Catmull, "A Tutorial on Compensation Tables," *Computer Graphics,* vol. 13, no. 2, Association for Computing Machinery, August 1979.

5. Michael F. Cohen and Donald P. Greenberg, "The Hemi-cube, A Radiosity Solution for Complex Environments," *Computer Graphics,* vol. 19, no. 3, Association for Computing Machinery, July 1985.

6. Robert L. Cook, Thomas Porter, and Loren Carpenter, "Distributed Ray Tracing," *Computer Graphics,* vol. 18, no. 3, Association for Computing Machinery, July 1984.

7. Tom N. Cornsweet, *Visual Perception,* Academic Press, 1970.

8. James D. Foley and Andries Van Dam, *Fundamentals of Interactive Computer Graphics,* Addison Wesley Publishing Company, 1982.

9. Roy A. Hall and Donald P. Greenberg, "A Testbed for Realistic Image Synthesis," *Computer Graphics and Applications,* vol. 3, no. 8, IEEE Computer Society, November 1983.

10. Paul Heckbert, "Color Image Quantization for Frame Buffer Display," *Computer Graphics,* vol. 16, no. 3, Association for Computing Machinery, July 1982.

11. James T. Kajiya, "Ray Tracing Parametric Patches," *Computer Graphics,* vol. 16, no. 3, Association for Computing Machinery, July 1982.

12. Irving Pobboravsky and Milton Pearson, "Computation of Dot Areas Required to Match A Colorimetrically Specified Color Using the Modified Neugebauer Equations," 150, Graphic Arts Research Center, Rochester Institute of Technology.

13. Anthony Ralston and Philip Rabinowitz, *A First Course in Numerical Analysis,* McGraw Hill Book Company, 1978.

14. Philip K. Robertson, "Visualizing Color Gamuts: A User Interface for the Effective Use of Perceptual Color Spaces in Data Displays," *Computer Graphics and Applications,* vol. 8, no. 5, IEEE Computer Society, September 1988.

15. Miles F. Southworth, *Color Separation Techniques, Second Edition,* Graphic Arts Publishing, 1979.

16. Maureen C. Stone, William B. Cowan, and John C. Beatty, "Color Gamut Mapping and the Printing of Digital Color Images," *ACM Transactions on Graphics,* vol. 7, no. 3, Association for Computing Machinery, October 1988.

17. Daniel L. Toth, "On Ray Tracing Parametric Surfaces," *Computer Graphics,* vol. 19, no. 3, Association for Computing Machinery, July 1985.

18. Turner Whitted, "An Improved Illumination Model for Shaded Display," *Communications of the ACM,* vol. 23, no. 6, Association for Computing Machinery, June 1980.

19. Gunter Wyszecki and Deane B. Judd, *Color in Business, Science and Industry,* John Wiley & Sons, 1975.

20. Gunter Wyszecki and W. S. Stiles, *Color Science, Concepts and Methods, Quantitative Data and Formulae, Second Edition,* John Wiley & Sons, 1982.

21. J. A. C. Yule, *Principles of Color Reproduction,* John Wiley & Sons, 1967.

Metamouse:
Specifying Graphical Procedures by Example

David L. Maulsby, Ian H. Witten, Kenneth A. Kittlitz

Knowledge Sciences Laboratory, Department of Computer Science
The University of Calgary, 2500 University Drive NW
Calgary, Canada T2N 1N4

Abstract

Metamouse is a device enabling the user of a drawing program to specify graphical procedures by supplying example execution traces. The user manipulates objects directly on the screen, creating graphical tools where necessary to help make constraints explicit; the system records the sequence of actions and induces a procedure. Generalization is used both to identify the key features of individual program steps, disregarding coincidental events; and to connect the steps into a program graph, creating loops and conditional branches as appropriate. Metamouse operates within a 2D click-and-drag drafting package, and incorporates a strong model of the relative importance of different types of graphical constraint. Close attention is paid to user interface aspects, and Metamouse helps the user by predicting and performing actions, thus reducing the tedium of repetitive graphical editing tasks.

CR Categories

I.2.2 [Artificial Intelligence] Automatic Programming – program synthesis; I.2.6 Learning – knowledge acquisition; I.3.6 [Computer Graphics] Methodology – interaction techniques.

Other Keywords and Phrases

Geometric constraints, apprenticeship learning.

1 Introduction

Aesthetically pleasing, visually coherent, meaningful pictures are characterized by the spatial relationships that join components, suggest relative importance, lead the eye through a visual narrative, and reveal subtle connections. These relationships are called "constraints." Often they compete with each other and must be considered as a group, called a "constraint system." With or without the help of a computer, a graphic artist must manage constraints that may be complex and require compromise or careful ordering to be resolved. A drawing evolves as new objects and constraints are added and as some attributes and constraints change while others remain in force. These elements often interact; for example, changing a text font may require enlarging and re-positioning boxes in a flowchart. Despite the features provided by interactive graphics editors to automate constraints, editing still involves repetitive manual work that requires precision and planning.

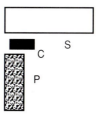

a. Input parameters: spandrel S, capital C, pier P.

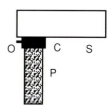

b. Center C on top of P, move S onto C and measure overhang, O.

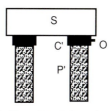

c. Move O to right end of S; put copies of C and P at O.

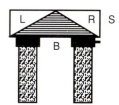

d. Construct triangle LRB inside S.

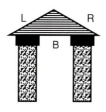

e. Remove S and O.

f. Copy capitals to base of piers.

Figure 1. Constructing an arch from a rough sketch.

This paper describes a system that induces picture-editing procedures from execution traces. It observes the user at work, performs a localized analysis of changes in spatial relations to isolate constraints, and matches action sequences to build a state graph that contains conditional branches and loops. Moreover, it induces variables for objects and distinguishes constants from non-deterministic (ie. run-time input) parameters. The system includes a constraint solver to perform the actions it has learned.

©1989   ACM-0-89791-312-4/89/007/0127 $00.75

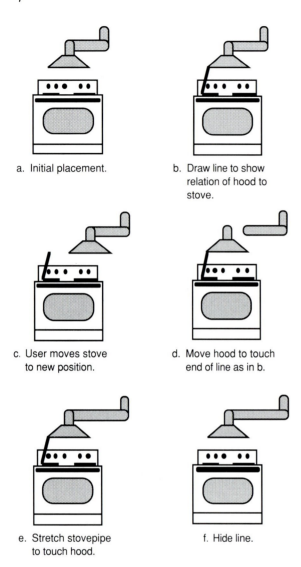

a. Initial placement.

b. Draw line to show relation of hood to stove.

c. User moves stove to new position.

d. Move hood to touch end of line as in b.

e. Stretch stovepipe to touch hood.

f. Hide line.

Figure 2. Maintaining constraints amongst objects.

A key component of the system is its metaphorical apprentice, Metamouse, an icon that follows the user's actions and represents the focus of attention. The metaphor embodies the system's limited model of spatial relations: Metamouse is near-sighted but touch sensitive. The user understands that relations at a distance must be constructed, for example by using a line to demonstrate alignment.

Section 2 describes some example editing tasks that can be taught to Metamouse. Section 3 discusses research issues and related work. Section 4 describes the current implementation. This is followed, in Section 5, by an evaluation of its performance on the sample tasks.

2 Applications

Several types of graphical task are appropriate for automation by a system such as Metamouse. Primary problems for users are 1) achieving precision, 2) maintaining integrity of constraints

throughout the editing process, and 3) coping with the tedium of repetition. Examples of each type of task are described in detail below.

Figure 1 illustrates the construction of an arch from a sketch of its main components. Initially the artist draws one of the piers, a capital, and the spandrel's extents box. The capital is then centered over the pier and the spandrel box is moved down onto it with the desired lateral overhang. After measuring the overhang, the artist duplicates the pier and capital at the other end of the arch. A triangular spandrel is then constructed inside the box. Finally, plinths are added to the base of the piers. This editing sequence specifies a procedure for constructing a type of arch from four graphical inputs: pier, capital, spandrel box, and overhang. The construction requires precision but need only be done once.

Figure 2 illustrates constraints that must be maintained throughout the long-term editing of a picture. If the stove is moved, the ventilation hood must be re-positioned above the burners, and the stove-pipe must be stretched or shortened to reach the hood from the wall exit. The editing sequence proceeds as follows. First, the user expresses the constraint between burners and hood by drawing a tie-line between them. The user then moves the stove to its new position. The constraints are re-established as follows. The tie is moved to touch the burner as before. The hood is moved to contact the tie, and the stove-pipe is stretched to the hood. Finally, the tie-line is removed (or hidden). This task illustrates the use of an auxiliary object (the tie) to express a constraint. Other constraints stem from the role that touches play in terminating actions. This procedure could be invoked manually whenever the stove is moved, but it would be desirable to "attach" it to the operation of moving the stove, which would automatically trigger it.

Figure 3 illustrates a repetitive editing operation or an animation sequence. A teapot moves up and down rows of cups laid out on a buffet, filling them with tea, and then returns to its initial position. Since cups are not perfectly aligned, a row is defined by a line passing through the center of one cup and touching the others. A procedure looping on rows and cups would allow us to change these numbers without re-scripting. Moreover, a constraint-oriented description of the teapot's path (eg. "move rightward to next cup" rather than "move to (x, y)") would tolerate adjustments to the layout. A program for this task is shown in Figure 4.

The teapot's initial position is marked with a slash and the pot moves to the table's nearest corner. For each iteration of the main loop, the row-line advances upwards to the center of some cup — a sweep-selection method [19]. The pot moves to the row-line's near end. For each cycle of the inner loop, the pot advances to meet the following constraints: i) the spout is at the center of some cup, C; ii) C is touching the row-line; and iii) C was not already visited. At the end of a row, some of these constraints fail. Note that the constraints ensure that the pot moves in opposite directions in successive rows. The main loop ends when no cups remain in the row-line's upward path. The teapot then returns to its initial position marker via the buffet's perimeter and, finally, the marker is removed.

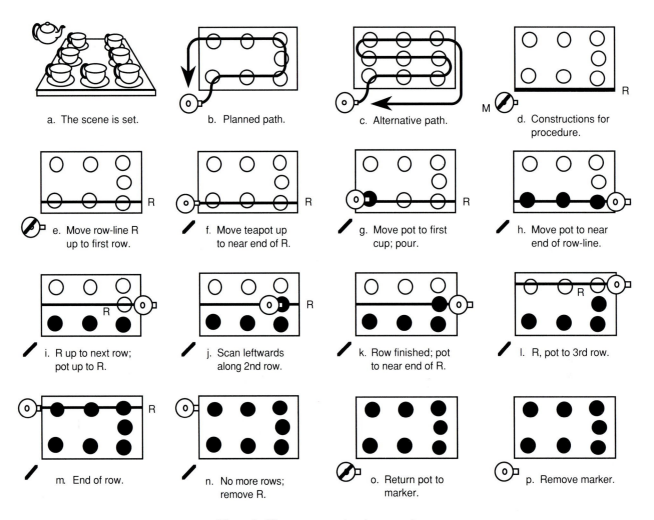

Figure 3. The tea-party animation procedure.

The power of a system like Metamouse lies in its ability to isolate constraints and predict actions. The user performs only a few steps of the tea-party task. Once Metamouse detects repetition, it predicts subsequent actions until it cannot meet the constraints or until the user objects. It observes the teapot move to the second cup and predicts all actions for the rest of row 1. When it fails to find a fourth cup, it asks the user to take over. The user moves the row-line; Metamouse recognizes this action and hence predicts the move-and-pour sequences for the second and third rows.

3 Background and Related Work

Automation of graphical editing tasks has followed two streams of development: interactive tools to help users with constraints; and graphics-oriented programming systems. Interactive help began with SketchPad [22], which used iterative numerical relaxation to resolve several types of constraint among object parameters. A similar approach is adopted in [27], which lets users compose constraints based on least-squares relaxation. Recent research has also produced a system that automatically selects and applies appropriate construction tools [4]. These systems offer simple, appealing interfaces to a restricted set of constraint-satisfaction methods.

End-user programming is one way to support repetitive, customized editing operations and the invention of arbitrary constraint systems. Given that most users are non-programmers, research has focussed on graphical methods, often based on geometric construction [5, 7, 8, 17]. With their graphical interfaces and use of examples, these systems greatly simplify program construction, but users must still work with abstractions. When programming with L.E.G.O. or a macro facility such as [24], the user declares loops and conditional branches, albeit by menu selection. Users of ThingLab must conceive an algebraic model of constraints in order to produce equational networks that define them [5].

An alternative is to observe the user at work and infer loops and branches, constants and variables. A number of systems for programming by demonstration have been produced [2, 9, 11, 16, 21]. Programs are constructed incrementally from several execution traces. Only Noddy, a robot teaching system, relies completely on automatic generalization [2], but it performs an exponentially complex induction of functions and is incapable of coping with errors. SmallStar [9] operates in a very general desktop domain but requires the user to identify variables and their type and value range. Peridot [16] infers value ranges and certain spatial relations (such as "centered within box"), but not loops or branches.

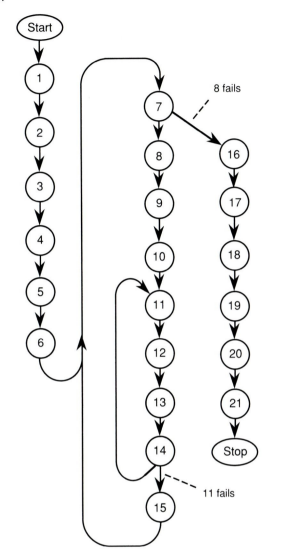

1. move to touch (Table.bottom.left)

2. draw-line R to touch (Table.bottom.right)

3. move to touch (Pot.top.right)

4. draw-line M to touch (Pot.bottom.left)

5. move to grasp (Pot.center)

6. drag Pot to touch (Pot.center : Table.bottom.left)

7. move to grasp (R.midpt)

8. drag R upwards to touch (R.line : F.center),
   where F is first cup found by scanning upwards

9. move to grasp (Pot.center)

10. drag Pot upwards to touch (Pot.center : R.endpt)

11. drag Pot horizontally to touch (Pot.center : C.center),
    where C is first cup found by scanning horizontally

12. move to touch (C.top.right)

13. draw-line to touch (C.bottom.left) ; ie. pour tea!

14. move to grasp (Pot.center)

15. drag Pot to touch (Pot.center : R.endpt)

16. delete R

17. move to grasp (Pot.center)

18. drag Pot to touch (Pot.center : Table.bottom)

19. drag Pot to touch (Pot.center : M.midpt)

20. move to grasp (M.midpt)

21. delete M

Figure 4. Procedure learned for tea-party animation.

Inferring a program is not easy, but induction of complex picture transformations from examples of input and output is intractable [3]. Moreover, systems of equations to represent these transformations would be numerically unstable and difficult to solve. Thus, it is better to induce a sequence of simpler transformations. Drawing is inherently procedural, often systematically ordered with each step governed by very few constraints [26]. Nonetheless, it is hard to induce procedures even from simple steps. Typical users do not always construct (or know how to construct) the relevant measurements and relations, but work instead by visual inspection. In effect, their drawings include invisible objects, as illustrated in Figure 5. Curve-matching methods such as those employed in graphical search and replace [10] are not sufficient for inducing patterns in traces that contain invisible objects. On the other hand, examining the screen for implicit spatial relations clearly involves an enormous amount of search and vastly expands the space of hypotheses for generalization. Therefore the system should isolate a small neighborhood of attention, and restrict itself to explicit relations of touch. It follows that user must specify these constructively.

To worsen matters, a preliminary study of MacDraw users performing a set of graphical tasks [13] revealed that execution traces are riddled with extraneous and erroneous actions. Users not only made mistakes, but were observed performing experiments or simply fidgeting. The order of actions varied greatly within the first several iterations of loops.

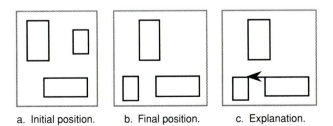

a. Initial position.   b. Final position.   c. Explanation.

Figure 5. An invisible object as a constraint.

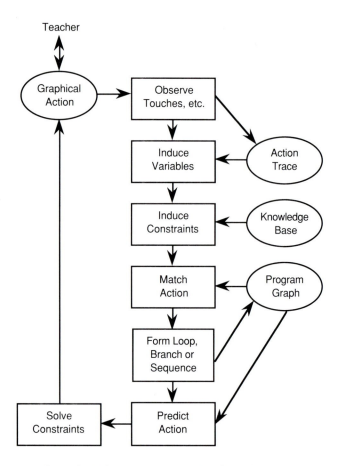

Figure 6. Main components and data flow of system.

only by the presence of the Metamouse icon: there are no special programming commands except to start and stop Metamouse. The flow of data through the system is sketched in Figure 6. When the teacher performs a drawing operation, the system records it and augments it with explanatory features, matching objects with variables and identifying probable constraints on the cursor's new position. Metamouse moves to the point at which the action terminated and highlights object parts involved in constraints. The augmented action is then matched with program steps previously learned. If a match is found, the learning module may conjecture a loop or joining of branches. It then predicts subsequent actions to confirm this. Predicted actions are performed by a constraint solver. Metamouse autonomously moves and highlights objects, and continues to do so until the teacher rejects a prediction or the constraint solver fails.

The next two subsections give brief accounts of the graphics application and the Metamouse interface. Following that we examine individual modules of the learning system.

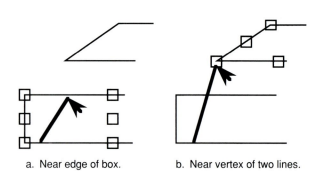

a. Near edge of box. b. Near vertex of two lines.

Figure 7. Highlighting distinguished points near cursor (arrowhead) while rubber-banding a line.

These elicitation problems are well-known in human-human communication, and rules of interaction between human teachers and pupils have been formulated as "felicity conditions" [25], four of which apply when inducing graphical procedures: *correctness, show-work* (demonstrate execution rather than just input and output), *no-invisible-objects* (express constraints by graphical construction), and *focus-activity* (eliminate extraneous actions).

These conditions are difficult for untrained teachers to satisfy. The Metamouse system uses a metaphorical apprentice, intensive interaction, and generalization to help the teacher. The Metamouse is the system's focus of attention; only touch relations involving it or an object it is grasping are examined. The system tries possible generalizations and predicts actions as early as possible during a teaching session, to eliminate free variation and extraneous actions and also to reduce errors. It can learn alternative actions and re-order their precedence in order to overcome errors. It has an internal model of graphical constraints and asks for explanation when an action seems arbitrary, ie. insufficiently constrained. The metaphor encourages the teacher to demonstrate constraints and adopt an intentional stance toward the system [6] rather than understand the details of its constraint and generalization models. Whether or not the metaphor succeeds is an experimental question; some pilot tests have yielded encouraging results [14].

4 The Metamouse System

Our learning system works within an interactive 2D graphics editor. "Teaching mode" is distinguished from normal editing

4.1 A.Sq

Constraints are easier to identify and resolve if primitive operations have few degrees of freedom. Thus a drawing program with a point-and-click user interface, like MacDraw [12], is suitable. Our drawing program, A.Sq (after the protagonist of Flatland [1]), emulates MacDraw but at present includes only box and line primitives. The user draws and transforms primitive objects by moving iconic handles (as in MacDraw). These handles delimit parts of objects distinguished by the learning system. They appear whenever the cursor (or Metamouse) approaches them, as illustrated in Figure 7.

The choice of primitives and operators has a great impact on the user's expression of constraints. Languages such as L.E.G.O. [8] and the primitives of [17] provide a basis for traditional "ruler-and-compass" methods of construction. A.Sq's primitive object types P, auxiliary objects A, modes of operation M, user-interface commands U, and internal operators I, are summarized in Table 1 below.

At present, the drawing program is relatively simple yet rich enough to study programming-by-example issues. No conceptual difficulties are envisaged in extending the learning system to cope with new primitives such as points, polygons, ellipses, and splines, since only an object's distinguished parts have any significance. We also expect to be able to accommodate new operations such as rotation, grouping, and coloring.

P : box (bottom-left, top-right)
     line (endpt$_1$, endpt$_2$)
     point (x, y)
     action (operator, startpt, endpt, object)

A : CurrentPoint : point
     PreviousPoint : point
     CurrentObject : {box, line}
     DisplayList : list of {box, line}
     ActionList : list of actions

M : create-lines
     create-boxes
     transform-objects

U : set-mode (mode ∈ M)
     set-point (PreviousPoint, CurrentPoint, x, y)
     delete-object (CurrentObject)
     undo (ActionList)

I : create-line (CurrentObject, PreviousPoint,
              CurrentPoint, DisplayList)
     create-box (CurrentObject, PreviousPoint,
              CurrentPoint, DisplayList)
     translate-handle-of-object-to-point (handle,
              CurrentObject, CurrentPoint)

Table 1. Elements of the A.Sq drawing program.

4.2 Metamouse

The focus of the teacher's attention is the Metamouse, Basil, a graphical turtle in the tradition of [18]. Prior to working with Basil, teachers skim a bio-sheet, excerpted in Figure 8. When the user of A.Sq senses an opportunity to automate a task, she calls Basil from his den. Rather than follow the cursor continuously, the turtle icon moves to *CurrentPoint* at the closure

of each A.Sq operation. If the system finds no tactile constraint, Basil asks the user whether position or distance are inputs, constants, or should have been constructed. Should the teacher suspend recording temporarily, Basil withdraws into his shell. In all other respects the A.Sq commands operate as usual.

4.3 Touch Relations

Metamouse is described as near-sighted but touch-sensitive; the teacher understands that only touch relations involving Basil or an object in his grasp are analyzed for constraints. The system highlights relevant parts of objects, as illustrated in Figure 9. Touches considered important (see Section 4.5 below) are colored red, others yellow. Associated with each touch is a triangular button; selecting this toggles it from red to yellow or *vice versa*, so the teacher can override the system's decision.

A touch relation is defined as *touch (Object$_1$.Part$_1$: Object$_2$.Part$_2$)*, where *Part$_i$* indicates some part of *Object$_i$*. Distinguished parts are handles (vertices, mid-points) and the line segments between them.

4.4 Variables

The use of variables allows different objects to assume a particular role in successive iterations of actions [20]. The learning system substitutes variables for objects in touch relations. Variables are defined as *variable-definition (Name, Type, Value)* structures maintained in a global symbol table. *Type* is one of {box, line}.

References to variables in touch relations are defined as *variable-reference (Variable, Valuation-flag)* tuples, where Variable points to the definition, and Valuation-flag indicates whether the constraint solver should use the variable's current value or try to assign a new one. The variable inducer looks back through recent steps of the example action trace for previous occurrences of the object; if none is found, the Valuation-flag is set to indicate that the solver must search for it.

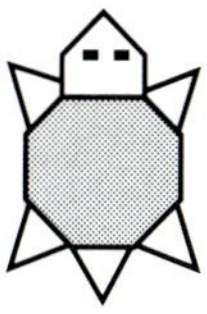

My name is Basil and as you can see I'm a turtle. You teach me repetitive and finicky tasks. I learn by acting as your apprentice — I follow you around till I think I know what you'll do next, then I do it for you.

If I guessed wrong I'll undo it and wait for you to show me what's right. I only predict after I see you do something you've already taught me.

I can draw lines and boxes and carry them by their iconic handles (grasping with my jaws).

Although I have a good memory, I don't see too well. Instead I work mainly by feel. I remember which parts — handles and line segments — are connected.

I'm touch-sensitive only at my snout but I can sense contact between what I'm grasping and anything else.

If I have to find, say a box, I set off in the general direction you've taught me (up, down, left, right) until I bump into one. But if you want me to be more selective, give me a tool to carry and teach me to move until it touches.

I can't learn directly how things should *not* touch — I mean how they should be separated. Instead you should give me tools to separate them.

When you want to teach me, choose "Time for a lesson!" from the Basil menu. If you want to interrupt the lesson say "Take a nap." When you don't agree with what I do, tap me and I'll undo it. When I don't know what to do I'll ask you to show me.

So in general you teach me by doing the task yourself, using some extra tools to help me see patterns by feel.

Hope you enjoy teaching me!

Figure 8. Excerpts from description of Metamouse given to teachers.

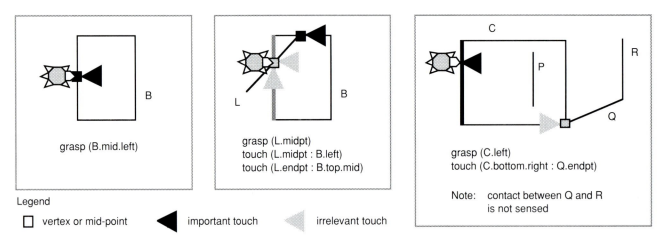

Figure 9. Feedback from Metamouse, highlighting touch relations.

4.5 Constraints

Isolating relevant constraints from the great many that hold in any given situation is, of necessity, a heuristic procedure. When searching for and transforming objects, the constraint solver is governed by touch relations and Basil's path of movement. The constraint inducer examines touch feedback obtained after each step of the trace. It weeds out trivial or irrelevant touches; the survivors comprise the postcondition of a program step.

Although all A.Sq drawing and transformation operators are based on translating *CurrentPoint* in 2-D display space, user actions occur in a model space containing objects with numerous parts, and in the "activity space" in which several alternative actions may be possible at any given time. Thus Basil operates with multiple degrees of freedom (and hence constraint) in the selection of actions and their parameters. Touch relations have 6 degrees of freedom, 3 on each item: selection of object, part, and position within part.

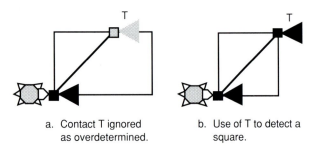

a. Contact T ignored as overdetermined.

b. Use of T to detect a square.

Figure 10. A useful overdetermined constraint.

A constraint is expressed as *constraint (Data, Class, Used)*, where *Data* is a touch relation, path, etc., *Class* is a degree of constraint, and *Used* is a flag indicating whether this constraint is deemed relevant. The constraint inducer assigns each touch relation to one of four classes. "Determining" constraints select a specific object, part and position within it for each item of a touch relation. For example, in Figure 3, contact between Basil's snout (a point) and the teapot's center handle is determining. "Strong" constraints leave one choice free, as in *touch(teapot-spout.endpt$_2$: C.center)*, where *C* is a cup found by scanning along the row. "Weak" relations leave more degrees of freedom.

freedom. "Trivial" touches, like grasping the end-point of the row-line after it is drawn, follow from the definition of A.Sq operators and afford no constraint whatsoever.

If the classifier finds a determining constraint, it marks other touch relations as "overdetermined;" they are not needed to derive a new position for *CurrentPoint*. Such touches may help select an action. They can distinguish otherwise similar situations, as shown in Figure 10. Here, the touch between point T and the rectangle seems irrelevant, since contact between *Box.bottom.left* and Metamouse's snout determines the move. But *touch (Line.endpt : Box.top)* versus *touch (Line.endpt : Box.top.right)* distinguishes a rectangle from a square. The teacher clicks on the relation icon to change its status.

The classifier can detect a lack of sufficient constraint for viable solutions. If all touches are only strong or weak, Basil's path is made a weak constraint with the caveat that the solver may have to relax it. In case of a total lack of touch constraint, Basil asks the user to indicate which of a set of standard tacit constraints, such as input or constant position, applies to this action.

Determining, strong, and weak constraints are considered relevant; overdetermined, trivial and sustained touches are ignored. Such heuristic rules can provide at most a best guess as to the teacher's precise intentions. As mentioned in Section 4.3 and illustrated in Figure 10, the teacher can override Metamouse's decision to ignore a touch relation.

4.6 Actions and Procedures

The learning algorithm takes the linear sequence of steps performed by the teacher and builds a directed graph containing branches and loops. It operates interactively, so that each new step is integrated into the graph as it is performed. If the user's action matches an existing step, the system conjectures a link to that step. A link is verified by predicting its successors.

Each step is a *program-node (Predecessors, Action, Successors)* structure. Its location in the graph is expressed as lists of *Predecessors* and *Successors*. The *Action* is an *action-step (Preconditions, Operation, Postconditions)* tuple. *Operation* is one of the A.Sq operators. *Pre-* and *Postconditions* are lists of *constraints* that must hold before and after executing the action. *Preconditions* are checked by examining Basil's current sensory

state; *Postconditions* are instantiated and verified by the constraint solver.

A program step matches an action demonstrated by the teacher if the operator and constraints are the same. A program step can be generalized by dropping constraints in order to match an action. To avoid over-generalizing, Metamouse drops only weak constraints, like path, and remembers them in case they need to be enforced after all.

At every opportunity the system generates the next action itself. It checks *Successors* of the current node to see if any is executable in the present configuration — that is, its relevant *Preconditions* hold and its *Postconditions* are attainable via constraint satisfaction. If there is none, or if the teacher rejects the prediction, Metamouse asks for a demonstration of the next step and forms a branch to it.

4.7 Constraint Solver

Solving constraints is the process by which actions are predicted — both to test whether a step is performable and to generate specific parameters for the action. Since all A.Sq actions result from translating a single point, the solver is much simpler than most. It examines the list of *Postconditions* in order of strength. It generates a solution to the first and then checks that the rest hold. If not, it backtracks to an alternative solution for the first constraint. The process repeats until all constraints hold or no more solutions exist. Details appear in [15]. The constraint solver is potentially able to generalize the *Postconditions;* at present, only Basil's path is generalized.

5 Evaluation of System

A programming by example system should be evaluated with respect to ease of use, real-time performance, and the correctness and generality of the programs it infers. Ease of use has been tested by measuring potential teachers' ability to predict Basil's behavior [14]. It was found that teachers quickly learned what to expect from their pupil, apart from the occasional surprise.

Real-time performance is governed by the number of program steps and touch relations to be checked by the action matcher and constraint solver. The complexity of a prediction is proportional to the product of these numbers. The number of touch relations is normally quite small, due to the limited range of Basil's touch sense. At most, it is twice the number of object-parts, since every relation involves either Basil or the object in his grasp. The number of program steps is unbounded; hence it may be advisable to limit the search for a matching step.

The current experimental implementation in Lisp on a Macintosh II runs rather slowly, requiring two seconds to make a prediction when joining sequences (subsequent predictions are somewhat faster). Since this delay is invariant with the number of program steps, it is attributable to excessive and inefficient garbage collection.

Metamouse has been tried on a number of example tasks — aligning boxes to arbitrarily rotated axes, distributing boxes at equal spacing along a line, and re-connecting a polyline when one segment is moved. The system learned correct and sufficiently general programs for most of these simple tasks after just one trace. Some examples contained erroneous actions and bizarre coincidences, but errors in the programs were corrected during subsequent lessons.

Table 2 shows performance data for the three tasks presented in this paper. For each execution trace, the number of actions correctly predicted by Metamouse is compared with the total number performed (whether by the user or Metamouse). Task competence is measured as their ratio. The number of predictions rejected by the teacher is also shown. The size and growth of the program graphs is given as the number of edges (ie. transitions between actions).

The Arch task contained some repeated actions, such as asking the user to create three boxes and copying the two capitals to form two plinths. The former actions were distinguished by the prompt strings specified by the teacher after rejecting predicted prompts. The latter were differentiated because the capitals were known as individuals. In a second trace of Arch, the system correctly predicted all actions.

The Stove-hood task was a simple sequence of actions. No predictions could be made during the first trace since the task contains no repeated actions.

The Tea-party task is a two-dimensional iteration on cups within rows. Table 2 shows performance on each row during the first trace. The system was able to generalize direction and number so that covered the second and third rows. In the first row, the teacher moved the row-line into contact with the cups, then moved the teapot to the row-line's nearest end-point, and then rightward to the first cup. After marking the cup (that is, pouring the tea), the teacher advanced the pot to the next cup, which triggered predictions to mark it and repeat for the third. On attempting a fourth iteration, the constraint solver failed to find another cup in Metamouse's path; this failure was the loop's terminating condition. When the teacher advanced the row-line to the next row, the matcher generalized the contact constraints between row-line and cups, since row 2 contained only one cup. The system then successfully predicted that the teapot would advance and thus induced the outer loop. The direction of the teapot's movement along the row was generalized from rightward to horizontal in order to make subsequent predictions. The loops were now general enough to cover the third row.

Task	Trace #	Steps Performed in Task				Edges in Program Graph	
		Total	Predicted	Ratio	Rejected	Total	Growth
Arch	1	41	6	15 %	5	42	42
	2	41	41	100 %	0	42	0
Stove-hood	1	12	0	0 %	0	13	13
	2	12	12	100 %	0	13	0
Tea-party	1	57	34	60 %	5	24	24
	row 1	*18*	*7*	*40 %*	*3*	*7*	*7*
	row 2	*9*	*8*	*90 %*	*0*	*7*	*0*
	row 3	*18*	*18*	*100 %*	*0*	*7*	*0*
	2	65	65	100 %	1	25	1

Table 2. Performance of learning system on example tasks.

6 Further Work

The current implementation is unsuitable for much further research. It is too slow and unreliable; expansion of facilities will only exacerbate these problems. Hence we are re-implementing Metamouse in C++ on Apollo DN4500 workstations. When a prototype is ready, we will conduct studies with casual users. Graphics primitives such as circles, ellipses and splines are planned, as well as object rotation and grouping. Further desirable additions include the ordering of alternative predictions by generality or frequency, and a pattern-matching command to allow the user to specify a pattern without constructing a procedure.

The nature of Metamouse raises several important questions. The system is designed to build a predictive model of human performance by conjecturing intentions behind isolated actions. This focus of attention should be expanded to sequences so that the system might identify free variation on the order of actions, equivalence, ineffectiveness, and so on. Metamouse also facilitates rich interaction. Methods of eliciting constraints from the teacher should be compared with respect to the trade-offs between inductive generalization and explicit indication. Induction of some implicit spatial relations, such as alignment, is not infeasible. On the other hand, graphical gesturing, as in pointing to interesting touch relations, shows promise as a natural technique for teaching.

7 Conclusions

Metamouse demonstrates that it is indeed possible for users to create graphical procedures by direct manipulation. Applications range from producing complex, repetitive drawings, through constructively specifying figures governed by graphical constraint, to generating simple animated algorithms for tasks such as sorting (and pouring tea). Metamouse eagerly reveals its predictions as soon as it can. This has three advantages. First, users reap early benefits when performing repetitive operations. Second, they can correct errors as soon as they occur. Third, they develop confidence in their programs without ever viewing any kind of listing. The principal shortcomings of the current system are its limited repertoire of graphical objects and transformations, the lack of a formal underpinning for the constraint model, and our limited experience of how users react to the new experience of working with Metamouse.

Acknowledgements

This research is supported by the Natural Sciences and Engineering Research Council of Canada. We gratefully acknowledge the key role Bruce MacDonald has played in helping us to develop these ideas. We would also like to thank the referees for their helpful suggestions.

References

1. Abbott, Edwin A. *Flatland — A Romance of Many Dimensions*. Signet Classics edition. New York. 1984.

2. Andreae, Peter. "Justified generalization: acquiring procedures from examples." PhD thesis. Department of Electrical Engineering and Computer Science, MIT. January 1985.

3. Angluin, Dana and Smith, C. H. "Inductive inference: theory and methods." *Computing Surveys 3* (15), pp. 237-269. September 1983.

4. Bier, Eric A. and Stone, Maureen C. "Snap-dragging." Proc. ACM SIGGRAPH '86 (Dallas, August 18–22, 1986), in *Computer Graphics 20, 4*, pp. 233–240.

5. Borning, Alan. "Defining constraints graphically." *Human Factors in Computing Systems: Proc. ACM SIGCHI '86*. Boston. April 1986.

6. Dennett, Daniel C. *The Intentional Stance*. MIT Press. Cambridge MA. 1987.

7. Fuller, Norma and Prusinkiewicz, P. "L.E.G.O.—an interactive graphics system for teaching geometry and computer graphics." *Proc. CIPS Edmonton 1986*.

8. Fuller, Norma and Prusinkiewicz, P. "Geometric modeling with Euclidean constructions," in [23], pp. 379-391.

9. Halbert, Dan. "Programming by example." Research Report OSD-T8402. Xerox PARC. Palo Alto CA. December 1984.

10. Kurlander, David and Bier, Eric A. "Graphical search and replace." Proc. ACM SIGGRAPH '88 (Atlanta GA, August 1–5, 1988), in *Computer Graphics 22, 4*, pp. 113-120.

11. MacDonald, Bruce A. and Witten, Ian H. "Programming computer controlled systems by non-experts." *Proc. IEEE Systems, Man and Cybernetics Annual Conference*. Alexandria VA. October 1987.

12. Cutter, Mark, Halpern, B., Spiegel, J. MacDraw. Apple Computer Inc. 1985, 1987.

13. Maulsby, David. "Inducing procedures interactively." MSc thesis. Department of Computer Science, University of Calgary. December 1988.

14. Maulsby, David and Witten, Ian H. "Inducing procedures in a direct-manipulation environment." *Proc. ACM SIGCHI '89* (in press).

15. Maulsby, David, Kittlitz, Ken and Witten, Ian H. "Constraint-solving in interactive graphics—a user-friendly approach." *Proc. Computer Graphics International 1989* (in press).

16. Myers, Brad. *Creating User Interfaces by Demonstration*. Academic Press. San Diego. 1988.

17. Noma, T., Kunii, T. L., Kin, N., Enomoto, H., Aso, E. and Yamamoto, T. Y. "Drawing input through geometrical constructions: specification and applications," in [23], pp. 403-415.

18. Papert, Seymour. *Mindstorms*. Basic Books. New York. 1980.

19. Preparata, Franco P. and Shamos, Michael I. *Computational Geometry*. Springer-Verlag. New York. 1985.

20. Rich, Charles and Waters, Richard. "The programmer's apprentice: a research overview." *IEEE Computer 21* (11), pp. 11–25. November 1988.

21. Smith, David C. "Pygmalion: a creative programming environment." Report STAN-CS-75-499. Stanford U. 1975.

22. Sutherland, Ivan E. "Sketchpad: a man-machine graphical communication system." *Proc. AFIPS Spring Joint Computer Conference*, vol. 23, pp. 329-246. 1963.

23. Magnenat-Thalmann, Nadia and Thalmann, Daniel, eds. *New Trends in Computer Graphics: Proc. CG International '88.* Geneva. June 1988.

24. Tempo. Affinity MicroSystems Ltd. Boulder CO. 1986.

25. van Lehn, Kurt. "Felicity conditions for human skill acquisition: validating an AI-based theory." Research Report CIS-21. Xerox PARC. Palo Alto CA. 1983.

26. van Sommers, Peter. *Drawing and Cognition.* Cambridge Univ. Press. Cambridge UK. 1984.

27. White, R. M. "Applying direct manipulation to geometric construction systems." in [23], pp. 446-455.

A Two-View Approach to Constructing User Interfaces

Gideon Avrahami
Kenneth P. Brooks
Marc H. Brown

DEC Systems Research Center
130 Lytton Avenue
Palo Alto, CA 94301

Abstract

This paper describes a system for constructing graphical user interfaces following a two-view paradigm: one view contains a textual representation of the interface in a special-purpose, "little" language, and the other view contains a direct manipulation, interactive editor for the user interface. The user interface can be edited in either view, and the changes are reflected in the other view. The language allows dialog boxes to be expressed in a simple and natural way, and has a well-defined mapping into the interactive editor. A base set of interactors is currently available, but the system can be easily extended with more interactors. We believe this approach to building user interfaces combines the advantages of the direct manipulation, WYSIWYG approach with the advantages of the textual, descriptive approach, and does not suffer from the limitations of either approach.

CR Categories and Subject Descriptions: D.2.2 [**Software**] Tools and Techniques – *user interfaces*; I.3.4 [**Computer Graphics**] Graphics Utilities – *software support*; I.3.6 [**Computer Graphics**] Methodology and Techniques – *interactive techniques*

General Terms: User Interface Management Systems (UIMS)

Additional Keywords and Phrases: TEX, Multiple Views

1 Preliminaries

Tools for constructing interactive graphical user interfaces are becoming increasingly important as more and more applications exhibit such interfaces. Indeed, most contemporary workstation and personal computer software environments provide such a tool, typically called a user interface management system, a dialog manager, or an interface builder. While these tools share the goal of making it easier for programmers to create user interfaces, they differ significantly in the model and facilities they offer [7, 12].

The oldest approach to building graphical user interfaces (and one that is still in common use) is to provide a library, or toolkit, of routines to be called from within the application [9]. Although programming languages are inherently expressive, they are not very well tuned to the task of specifying and modifying graphical elements and arrangements.

There are systems that provide a special-purpose descriptive language for specifying the user interface [15]. They provide a concise description of the interface, and also separate an application's source code from its user interface description. However, they still share with the programming approach the disadvantage that the interface designer cannot see the effects of changes to the interface immediately.

A growing trend is to use a direct manipulation editor for constructing user interfaces [1, 2, 6]. The direct manipulation approach has the nice feature that the designer always sees what the interface will look like and can readily change its properties. It has the disadvantage that it is typically difficult to make consistent changes throughout a large collection of interface objects.

Recent research in related areas suggests that the best aspects of a descriptive language and an interactive editor can be combined in a "two-view" editor that provides access to both representations simultaneously. Such editors have been built for documents [5] and for illustration graphics [3, 13].

This paper describes FormsVBT, a system we are implementing that supports a two-view approach to constructing user interfaces from an extensible library of interactor objects. One view contains an interactive editor and the other view contains a textual description of the user interface in a special-purpose "little" language [4]. The interface designer can edit the user interface in either view, and the effects of the editing are displayed in the other view as well. A third, non-editable view shows exactly how the interface will appear at runtime, with proper sizing characteristics. Figure 1 shows the system in action. Our approach for constructing user interfaces combines the virtues of the interactive approach with those of the textual description approach, but without suffering the limitations of either. (FormsVBT also allows user interfaces to be constructed by direct programming, but that is not a focus of this paper.)

The next section presents an overview of the entire FormsVBT system. Actually, there are two parts to the system: a textual language with its runtime support library, and a two-view editor, FormsEdit, for building interface descriptions in this language. Section 3 presents the language. Section 4 describes the runtime aspects of using the system, that is, how a user interface description is "interpreted" into calls on the underlying workstation environment, and how application code communicates with the runtime library. Sections 5 and 6 are devoted to describing the two-view editor for constructing user interfaces: we first describe how an interface designer uses the two-view editor, and then we give an overview of how the editor is actually implemented. The final sections outline some future directions and offer some concluding remarks.

©1989   ACM-0-89791-312-4/89/007/0137 $00.75

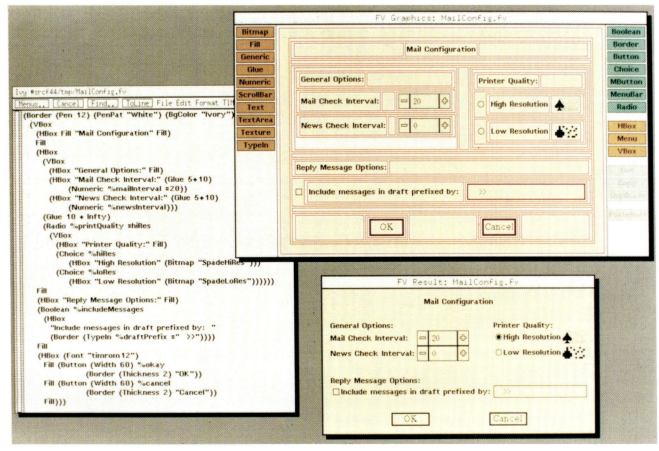

Figure 1: FormsEdit in action.

2 System Overview

We follow the common paradigm that an application's user interface is composed of *dialog* boxes containing various *interactors*. Interactors include buttons, text areas, numeric fields, scrollbars, and so on. Typically the application's window is filled by one dialog, the *base dialog*. Other *popup dialogs* may appear above it from time to time, under program control. Figure 2 shows a typical application with its base dialog and two popup dialogs.

The FormsVBT language is a textual representation for dialogs. An application designer may create dialogs simply by writing FormsVBT-language files using any text editor. Our system, however, provides a more user-friendly option. A separate application, FormsEdit, provides two editable views side by side, allowing the user to use text editing and direct-manipulation graphical editing in any combination, rapidly switching from one view to the other and seeing the results in both. A third, non-editable view displays the dialog in its true size and shape, and exhibits the interactive behavior that will be present at runtime. Dialogs created by the editor are stored as FormsVBT-language text files.

A dialog is specified as a hierarchical organization of *components*. Among these are passive visual elements, basic interactors, and modifiers that add interactive behavior to other components. There are also layout operators that take groups of low-level components and organize them geometrically into vertical and horizontal boxes. A modified form of the boxes-and-glue paradigm from TEX is used to control sizing and placement. Thus the components form a tree structure, with a top-level box representing the entire dialog.

Various information, or *properties*, can be attached to a component to govern its appearance or interactive behavior. These include a *name* for communication with the application, *size* information, and for suitable kinds of components, a default *value*. The type of the value depends upon the *class* of the component. For example, the value of a scrollbar is a number representing the current location of the "thumb," while the value of an editable text field is a character string.

As well as having these universally relevant properties, a component class may have class-specific properties. A border has texture and thickness; a numeric interactor has bounds on its range. All interactors that display text have a font. Some widely-used visual properties, such as font and color, are inherited. Such a property, when set for one component, applies not only to it but to all its descendants in the hierarchy, except where a different value is explicitly specified. This makes it convenient to build groups of components within a dialog that have similar visual characteristics.

An application typically initializes a dialog by loading a FormsVBT-language file at startup time. Thereafter it interacts with

the dialog by referring to the names of its components. Procedures are provided to read and set the values of value-containing components such as numerics and text fields, and to store the values of all value-containing components in a dialog to a file for later retrieval.

Some components can generate *events* in response to user action, and the application can attach to such interactors a procedure that will be called whenever the event is generated. Events insulate the application from the particulars of interactors.

An application is typically structured as an initialization routine and a collection of event-handling procedures. When an application is run, it initializes dialogs and then transfers control to the FormsVBT package. Control is returned to the application when specifed by a event-handling procedure, usually just before the application terminates.

3 The User Interface Language

The FormsVBT language syntax takes the form of symbolic expressions (s-expressions). We chose this for flexibility, and because our software environment, like many others, has a number of utilities for processing s-expressions. Every component of the dialog is described by an s-expression. For example,

```
(Numeric (Name temp)
  (Value 48) (Min 32) (Max 212))
```

represents an interactor that displays an integer and allows the user to modify it using up and down arrow buttons or by typing. The interactor has a default value of 48, and will only display numbers between 32 and 212 inclusive.

In general, every s-expression defines one component of the dialog box. The first element of an s-expression is a keyword that identifies the type of the component. Subsequent subexpressions specify properties of the component: its name, default value, size, and class-specific parameters, as mentioned above.

Figure 3 describes the standard components provided in FormsVBT. These come in five varieties. Passive components influence appearance only; they have no interactive behavior. Basic interactors are building blocks that embody a value, displayed to the user and modifiable by user action. Interactive modifiers take a child component (of arbitrary complexity) and add some interactive behavior to that child. That is, size and appearance are usually specified by the child, whereas response to the mouse is controlled by the modifier. Grouping components define a "group context" within which certain types of descendants (such as radio buttons) will function. Layout components specify geometric constructs; they take an arbitrary number of children and lay them out horizontally or vertically.

Geometric layout uses a model similar to TEX's paradigm of boxes and glue. Details of layout are governed by the size information implicitly present or explicitly specified for the children. This size information includes *stretchability*, which comes into play if the parent box is made larger than the sum of its children's sizes. Size information in general is given by an expression *size + stretchability*. The word `Infty` specifies infinite stretchability.

In TEX, only glue is stretchable (and shrinkable); in FormsVBT, any component may be stretchable (but not shrinkable)—both horizontally and vertically. The `Glue` interactor is only a shorthand for specifying white space with size information given for the horizontal and/or vertical directions. A common glue is one with a zero

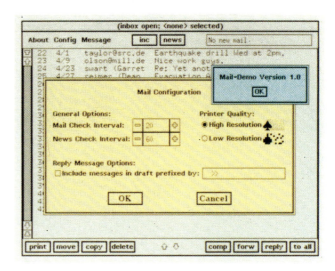

Figure 2: An application interface developed using FormsVBT.

natural size and infinite stretchability, `(Glue 0 +Infty)`; we abbreviate it with the keyword `Fill`. Judicious use of `Fill` can produce very natural layouts that behave well when stretched to various sizes and aspect ratios, as illustrated in Figure 4.

The FormsVBT language has a few more abbreviations. Because the `Name` and `Value` properties are used so frequently, we abbreviate them with single characters. The example above would typically be written as

```
(Numeric %temp =48 (Min 32) (Max 212))
```

There is also an abbreviation for Text components. Rather than requiring `(Text (Value "zzz"))` we allow `"zzz"` instead.

3.1 A Simple Example

Consider the following s-expression:

```
(Border (PenSize 4) (PenPat "Grey")
  (Border (PenSize 8) (PenPat "White")
    (VBox (Width 200)
      (HBox Fill "* General Options *" Fill Fill)
      (HBox "Mail Check:"
            Fill (Numeric %mailInterval))
      (HBox "News Check:"
            Fill (Numeric %newsInterval))))))
```

which results in the following dialog:

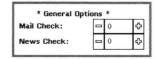

There is a border of 4 pixels, drawn using a texture named `Grey`, and a margin of 8 pixels surrounding a vertical stack of three horizontal rows of components. The horizontal rows will all be 200 pixels wide. In the top row, the text is two-thirds of the way toward the left. In each of the bottom two rows, all white space will appear between the text and the numeric interactor. It is worth noting that the name `Grey` is not a part of the FormsVBT language—it is passed as a parameter to the `Border` drawing code, which assigns it meaning in a manner unknown to FormsVBT.

Passive Elements	`Bitmap`	A bitmap image.
	`Border`	A border of a specified thickness and texture around some other component.
	`Text`	A line of text. Optionally, multiple lines of text with built-in scrollbars.
	`Texture`	A textured rectangle.
Basic Interactors	`Browser`	A list of items, specified at runtime, from which the user can make a selection.
	`Generic`	A place-holder in which the application program can take control. For example, a generic would be used as the main window of a graphics editor.
	`Glue`	Blank space.
	`Null`	A placeholder (displayed while editing as a rectangle textured with "chickenwire").
	`Numeric`	An editable integer value.
	`ScrollBar`	A horizontal or vertical scrollbar.
	`TypeIn`	An editable text field. Optionally, multiple lines of editable text with built-in scrollbars.
Interactive Modifiers	`Boolean`	A binary state variable with visual feedback (usually a checkbox, which can be empty or checked).
	`Button`	Generates an event when it is clicked. Options are available for Guarded, Repeating, UpClick, and DownClick styles of buttons.
	`Choice`	One of a collection of binary state variables within a `Radio` group of which, like pushbuttons on old car radios, only one can be on at a time. Visual feedback is usually a round circle, which can be either empty or filled.
	`Menu`	Displays its first child normally, and its second child when it is clicked and the mouse button stay down. The two children may be any component of any complexity. Menus belonging to the same `MenuBar` group will pass the activation along as the mouse rolls from one to the next.
	`MenuItem`	The basic component of menus. Highlights when the mouse rolls into it with the button down; generates an event if the mouse button is released while inside it.
Grouping	`MenuBar`	Defines a group for descendants that are of class `Menu`.
	`Radio`	Defines a group for descendants that are of class `Choice`. The value of this interactor is the name of its member that is currently set.
Layout	`HBox`	A horizontal arrangement of subordinate components.
	`VBox`	A vertical arrangement of subordinate components.

Figure 3: Standard FormsVBT components.

3.2 A Larger Example

Figure 4 shows a dialog from a color editor whose textual description appears at the right. This dialog allows the user to specify a color by adjusting each color component by the appropriate scrollbar. The high, medium, or low quality options determine how many colors are dithered together to form the desired color. The dialog components are specified so that all components are aligned nicely, and behave reasonably when stretched.

Note that the `Generic` component whose name is `colorArea` is taken over at runtime by the application, which controls its appearance and its interactive behavior, if any. The medium quality option will be selected when the dialog first appears, unless changed by the application. Also, the scrollbars will have default values and ranges unless the application specifies otherwise at runtime.

```
(Border (BgColor "LightGrey")
        (PenSize 8) (PenPat "White")
  (VBox
    (HBox (HBox (Width 60) "Red")  (Scrollbar %red))
    (HBox (HBox (Width 60) "Green")(Scrollbar %grn))
    (HBox (HBox (Width 60) "Blue") (Scrollbar %blu))
    (Glue 10)
    (HBox (Width 200 + Infty) (Height 75 + 200)
      (Radio %quality =med
        (VBox Fill
          (Choice %high "High")   (Glue 10)
          (Choice %med  "Medium") (Glue 10)
          (Choice %low  "Low")    Fill))
      (Generic %colorArea))
    (Glue 10)
    (HBox Fill
      (Button %okay (Border (Width 60) "OK"))
      Fill
      (Button %cancel (Border (Width 60) "Cancel"))
      Fill)))
```

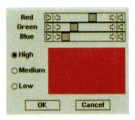
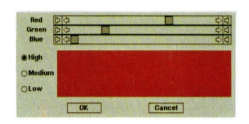
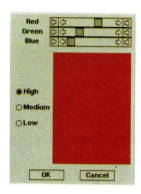

Figure 4: Stretching a dialog.

3.3 Extensibility

The FormsVBT language is extensible. An application may, before initializing any dialogs, add new component classes and properties to the language. A component class is defined by providing its keyword, its syntactic type, the names and syntax of any class-specific properties, and a set of procedures for creating and accessing components of this class. Syntactic type specifies how many children a component of the class may take: zero, one, or any number. All the standard components described in this paper are initialized into the language by the same means that are available to other programmers for extension.

4 Runtime Support

For an application to make use of a FormsVBT-language textual description, the following activities must take place:

- Convert the textual description into a window-system object.

- Attach procedures to the interactors. The procedures will be called when the interactor generates an event.

- Display a dialog on the screen and remove it when it is no longer required.

- Communicate with interactors to examine and set their values.

These services are all provided by the runtime support package. All code is written in Modula-2+, a version of Modula-2 enhanced for building large, integrated, concurrent programs [14]. The system runs on a Firefly multiprocessor workstation [16] running the Topaz operating system [11].

The FormsVBT language and its supporting code are based on the Trestle window system [10]. In Trestle the screen is organized in terms of Virtual Bitmap Terminals, or VBTs. Every window is a VBT, but windows are routinely subdivided into smaller units, also described by VBTs, so that a typical window is actually a hierarchical tree structure of VBTs. VBTs are object-oriented. Each VBT class is expected to implement certain standard procedures to handle events (mouse click, keystroke, reformat of the window, etc.), and does so in a class-specific way.

The Trestle environment is richly supplied with VBT classes designed to serve as building blocks. The concept of horizontal and vertical boxes exists in Trestle in the form of HSplits and VSplits, VBT classes which can take an arbitrary number of children and lay them out in order horizontally or vertically. A BorderVBT, which is used to implement the FormsVBT Border object, takes one child

and puts a border of specified width, and texture around it. A ButtonVBT takes one child, of any class, and makes it into a button which will generate an event when clicked (subject to options such as guarded, transition type, and so on).

These facilities were already in our environment, and the FormsVBT language was designed to take advantage of them. Our language is nearly isomorphic to the VBT structure it describes: with the exception of subexpressions that specify properties, each expression corresponds to one VBT. The keyword at the head of an expression specifies a VBT's class, and every other element either specifies some of the VBT's parameters (such as size, font, range, etc.) or defines a child VBT.

The first task of the runtime system is to convert an s-expression into a tree structure of VBTs, returning a pointer to the top-level VBT of that structure. This is performed by the "scan" procedures:

```
PROCEDURE NewFromFile(fileName: Text): VBT:
PROCEDURE NewFromText(format:   Text): VBT;
```

The top-level VBT returned by these procedures becomes a handle, which is passed to later FormsVBT calls to interact with this structure.

A high-level view of the conversion algorithm is:

1. Create a VBT of the type specified by the keyword of the current s-expression.

2. Scan the rest of the elements in the expression. For each one of them:

3. If it is a property, read its value and set the VBT's corresponding parameter accordingly.

4. Otherwise, it must be a description of a child VBT. Use this algorithm recursively to create that child, and attach it to the current VBT.

While the syntax is uniform, allowing quick and simple parsing, each class must enforce its own semantic constraints—for example, the fact that a `Choice` must occur within a `Radio` group

After reading the description of a dialog box, the application may initialize the values of interactors either directly or by restoring a previously saved set of values from a file (see Section 4.3).

4.1 Events

An application can make itself responsive to user actions in the dialog by attaching procedures to named interactors. The interactor

VBTs respond to user actions by calling the runtime package to generate events. The exact nature of the actions reported is part of the definition of each interactor class. The current set of interactors report the following events:

- Clicking on a `Button`, `Boolean`, or `Choice` interactor.
- Hitting the return key in a `TypeIn` interactor.
- Clicking the plus or the minus buttons on `Numeric` interactor, or hitting the return key while typing into it.
- Clicking in a `Scrollbar`.
- Clicking on an item in a `Browser`.

A procedure is attached to an event by calling `AttachProc`:

```
PROCEDURE AttachProc(v:VBT;
  name:Text; p:Proc; arg:REFANY);

TYPE Proc = PROCEDURE(VBT, Text, REFANY, Time);
```

`AttachProc` binds a procedure to a named interactor within the specified top-level VBT. It takes an extra argument, a `REFANY` (a generic pointer), which is later passed as the last argument when the attached procedure is called. This argument may be used by the application for any purpose, and provides a means of approximating object-oriented programming in a Modula environment.

Once a procedure is attached to an interactor, it will be called whenever a reportable event occurs within that interactor. The arguments to an attached procedure are the top-level VBT, the name of the interactor, the `REFANY` argument passed to `AttachProc`, and the time (for synchronized action in a concurrent environment).

4.2 Communication

Communication between a dialog and its application may be initiated by either of them. In generating events, the dialog takes the initiative. The application, however, can also initiate communication to examine and change the values of interactors. The following procedures provide access to interactors of various types:

```
PROCEDURE GetText    (v:VBT; name:Text):Text
PROCEDURE GetInteger(v:VBT; name:Text):INTEGER
PROCEDURE GetBoolean(v:VBT; name:Text):BOOLEAN
PROCEDURE GetChoice (v:VBT; name:Text):Text

PROCEDURE PutText    (v:VBT; name:Text;
                              text:Text)
PROCEDURE PutInteger(v:VBT; name:Text;
                              num:INTEGER)
PROCEDURE PutBoolean(v:VBT; name:Text;
                              value:BOOLEAN)
PROCEDURE PutChoice (v:VBT; groupName: Text;
                              choiceName:Text)
```

The different classes of interactors handle only the calls that apply to them. For instance, `GetBoolean` and `PutBoolean` apply to `Boolean` and `Choice` interactors, while `GetText` and `PutText` apply to `Text`, `TypeIn` and `Text` interactors. For convenience, we expect text interactors to handle `GetInteger` and `PutInteger`, too, by performing the conversion to and from string representation.

Our underlying window manager provides routines to control the appearance, position, and disappearance of dialogs.

4.3 Snapshot

The FormsVBT runtime library can return to the application programmer an s-expression containing the current values of all value-containing, named interactors, and can restore the interactor values from an s-expression.

For example, the s-expression of values for the color editor example from Section 3.2 is as follows:

```
(CurrentValues
  (quality med)
  (red 70) (grn 23) (blu 0))
```

The value of the `Radio` component (`quality` is the symbolic name of the `Choice` component that is currently selected. The other named components in the example dialog are each of the three scrollbars. Note that the named interactors without values, `colorArea`, `okay`, and `cancel`, are not saved. The `Choice` interactors are not recorded since their grouping `Radio` interactor records their values implicitly.

The ability to "snapshot" and "restore" a dialog has turned out to be quite handy as a way of maintaining state between invocations of an application and storing configuration files for applications. In the latter case, it is desirable that the snapshot be a textual file so that system administrators can use familiar text-based tools for system management.

5 Two-View Editor: User Interface

Figure 1 shows a typical screen during two-view editing with FormsEdit. There are two editable views of the user interface: the *Text* view at the left and the *Graphics* view at the upper right. The Text view uses a standard text editor to display and edit s-expressions. The Graphics view shows the user interface, with its internal structure completely visible. There are also two columns of buttons. A third view, the *Result* view, is located in the lower right. The user does not edit in this view, but sees how the dialog will actually look, stretch, and to some extent, interact.

Editing in the Text view is straightforward. The Result and Graphics views are not updated after each keystroke, but only when the user issues the Reparse command to the editor. The time necessary for updating the graphical views depends on how drastic were the changes to the Text view. By and large, changes that do not involve creating new components happen almost instantaneously, whereas complex editing involving the creation of new components may take several seconds for large dialogs.

Selecting an item in the Graphics view is done in the obvious way: click on an object. Mouse commands exist for traversing the hierarchical structure of the Graphics, either to change the selected object, or to extend or contract the selection. In particular, it is possible (and useful) to select objects without selecting their children. For example, one might select (in order to delete or replace) a box or the border of an object.

The simplest and most common type of editing in the Graphics view is to modify the properties of an existing component. One does this by double-clicking on the component. This causes a dialog to be popped up showing all the properties of that component. Figure 5 shows the dialog for editing the properties of a `Numeric` interactor.

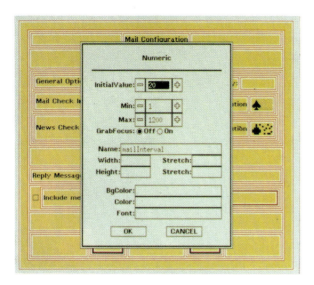

Figure 5: Editing the parameters of a `Numeric` interactor.

One replaces an existing interactor or the selection by dragging a new interactor from the menu (or from the dialog itself) and dropping it on the item to be replaced. If an interactor is dropped on any part of the selection, it replaces the whole selection rather than just the item under the mouse. A new interactor can be inserted in a similar fashion, by dropping it into the divider between two children (or at the beginning or end) of a box. Because only `HBox` and `VBox` interactors support an arbitrary number of children, all insertions are made within them.

The gray and green buttons represent components that can take a child object as an argument. When such an item is inserted anew, or replaces an existing component as described above, it has an initial argument of `Null`. Presumably, the `Null` interactor will eventually be replaced by a more appropriate one.

These items may also be dragged in with the shift key held down. In this case, a new component of the specified class is added, but instead of replacing the target component it becomes its parent. Thus to put a border around a piece of text, one would press the shift key, click on the `Border` button, and drag to the targeted text.

The green buttons represent components that can have an arbitrary number of children. The shifted forms of these commands can operate not only on a single item, but also on a selection consisting of several adjacent siblings of the same existing interactor. These then become members of a new interactor.

The system must take care to ensure that all editing commands are syntactically valid. For example, the parent of an object being deleted must allow as many children as the object being deleted has. When an object is deleted, copied, or duplicated, it is put into a global *paste buffer*. The `PasteBuf` button allows the current contents of the paste buffer to be dragged into the dialog and inserted just like any interactor, subject of course to the constraints of syntactic validity.

6 Two-View Editor: Implementation

FormsEdit is organized around one central data structure, the parse tree. This tree is very closely tied to the syntax of the s-expression language, having one node for each component in the dialog. Figure 7 shows the parse tree for the Mail Configuration example seen in many of the previous figures. The tree is stored in child-sibling format with uplinks as well, from each node to its parent. Each node contains information telling the kind of component, its default value, and any properties that were specified for this component. Each node also contains three pointers (one for each view) to information that is managed by the views for their own private use.

Figure 6 illustrates the overall structure of FormsEdit. One central module maintains the parse tree and communicates with the three modules that manage the three views. Change requests, arising from user action in either of the two editable views, are issued by a call from the view module to the appropriate routine in the parse tree module. This routine makes the change to the tree itself, then calls a similar routine in each view to update that view and its data structures. Here we make use of our workstation's multiprocessing capability: the updates to views are forked and proceed in parallel, though the operation does not complete until they have all completed.

There are noteworthy differences between the two types of editing. Graphics view actions take effect immediately, transforming the parse tree and all views. Text view operations change only the text, leaving the parse tree and the other views untouched until the user gives an explicit Reparse command. This delay is necessary because at many moments, the text is not syntactically valid, and a mapping between the text and the parse tree is impossible. Therefore we update the parse tree and the other views only when the user indicates that it is appropriate. At that time the Text view rechecks the syntax and, if it is correct, issues the appropriate change requests to the parse tree. When the text has been edited and not reparsed, editing operations in the Graphics view are locked out, since it would be impossible to update the text in a meaningful way.

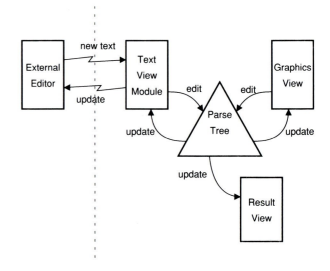

Figure 6: The structure of FormsEdit.

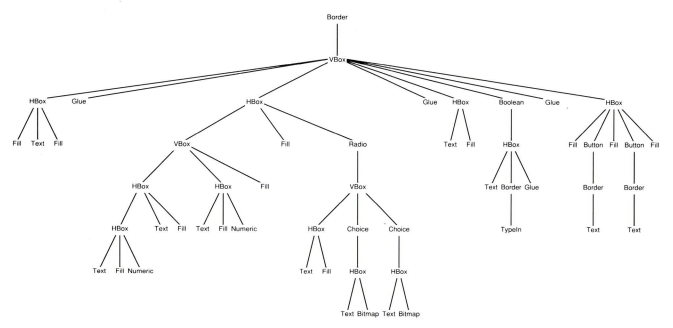

Figure 7: Parse tree corresponding to the Mail Configuration dialog box of Figures 1, 2, and 5.

6.1 The Text View

The text view module is designed to make use of an external editor running as a separate process. It can also be configured to use an internal editor, built from the text-editing tools in our toolkit, but users generally prefer to edit text with the editor they normally use. So we connect to an external text editor, using pipes or any other inter-process communication mechanism that may be available. This editor must provide us at least the ability to read and to change the current contents of its buffer, and to add a user command, Reparse, which will notify the two-view editor process when it is invoked. It is highly desirable that we also have access to the "modified" flag, so dialog-view edits can be locked out when the text is in a modified state.

The use of an external editor has significant consequences for our design. To reparse the full text, and thus fully rebuild the contents of the other views, would be too slow to be acceptable. What we want is to translate textual changes into the smallest possible changes to the parse tree, which in turn will lead to the smallest disruption in the other views. This task would be much easier if we could find out, at the time of a Reparse, what regions of the text have been modified since the last Reparse. However, many editors, including the one we use in our working environment, do not maintain such information or do not make it available to clients.

Our approach is to take the entire modified text and compare it with the old version, computing the differences. For an application with huge volumes of data, such as a document editor, this strategy would be prohibitively time-consuming. However, because there seems to be a natural limit to the useful size and complexity of dialogs (roughly 5K, in our description language), full-text comparison is feasible.

The strategy is centered around the use of a character array containing the text and a token stream describing it. Our lexical analyzer makes a complete pass through the text, discovering tokens and storing them in an array. Each token contains three indices into the character buffer describing the beginning of whitespace prior to the token, the beginning of the token itself, and the end of the token,

as well as other information useful to the parser. The parse tree, in turn, contains information linking it to the token stream. Each node contains a count of all the tokens in the expression describing it and its children. It is thus a simple tree-walking computation to find a node from a token index, or a token index from a node.

A character buffer and token stream corresponding to the current parse tree are stored at all times. When a Reparse command is given, a new character buffer and token stream are created corresponding to the new text. (We refer to a token stream together with its character buffer as a *generation*.) Then we compare the two token streams, using a modified form of Heckel's algorithm [8]. This algorithm finds an island of certainty of matching wherever it finds a token that occurs exactly once in each view. These islands are expanded forward and backward as long as corresponding adjacent neighbors continue to match. We end up with each token in the old and new generations marked as Matched or Probable, with an index linking it to the corresponding token in the other generation, or marked as Unmatched. Groups of adjacent Unmatched tokens are noted as *cores of difference*.

The next phase of the algorithm examines each core of difference in turn to see what change it represents. The simple regularity of s-expressions serves us very well here—it is easy to expand a core to include a complete expression (or several neighboring subexpressions) by looking for a surrounding pair of matching parentheses. During this expansion we determine the actual status of Probable tokens in that vicinity. The cross-link fields of adjacent Matched or Probable tokens allow us to find the corresponding point or region in the other token stream. Given this we can compute a tree-transforming operation. The core in the old generation can be mapped to one or more nodes in the parse tree. The core in the new generation is parsed (a much smaller task than a full-text parse) to generate one or more new nodes. Thus we have the specification for an add, delete, or replace operation on the parse tree. When all differences have been translated into parse tree operations, we then perform them, yielding an updated parse tree and updated Graphics and Result views.

Responding to edits in the Graphics view, we must translate changes in the other direction. The parse tree module calls the Text view, describing the change in terms of parse tree nodes. Using the token count information, we can map from a node to a sequence of tokens in the current token stream. Using the character indices stored in tokens, we can determine the number of characters in each token, and thus determine the group of characters in the text view that will need to be replaced. For newly introduced nodes, we traverse each node and its descendants and synthesize new tokens and text to correspond to them. New tokens are inserted at the appropriate point in the token array; new text is added at the end of the character buffer, for simplicity. White space is generated by a simple algorithm. Once the new text is available, we perform a replacement of the relevant region of text in the editor buffer, to produce an updated text view.

The strategy for comparing token streams interacts well with prettyprinting. Although newly generated text is unformatted and quite difficult to read, the user can invoke a prettyprinter or clean it up as desired. And since tokens are compared based on their content and not on the associated white space, an ensuing Reparse will generate no updates at all to the parse tree.

6.2 The Result View

The Result view displays the dialog as it would actually appear at runtime, with the proper size and stretchability characteristics. No editing is supported; instead, the interactors respond to mouse actions with the same interactive feedback they would give at runtime. (Of course, nothing further happens because no application code is invoked.) The Result view changes in response to parse tree changes initiated by the other views.

The Result view is closely associated with the parse tree. For each node in the parse tree, there is a VBT in the Result view. A field of the node points to the VBT, and to each VBT we attach a pointer to the corresponding node. When a parse tree transformation takes place, it is reported to all the views in terms of nodes; the pointers allow us to find the VBTs involved. Where a new node has been introduced (having no associated Result view VBT), we create the corresponding VBT structure using the same method used to initialize a dialog at runtime, and then add it as a new child of the appropriate parent VBT.

6.3 The Graphics View

The Graphics view resembles the Result view in its implementation, but with some added complications. Where the Result view translates the parse tree directly into a tree of VBTs, the Graphics view adds a border around each VBT, thus making all levels of structure explicitly visible and accessible. The Graphics view also intercepts all mouse actions and translates them into editing operations, rather than allowing them to be received by the interactors.

The Graphics view editor uses the parse tree as its underlying data structure. All selections are represented in terms of nodes in the parse tree, and all editing actions are executed directly as transformations on that tree. User actions, expressed by clicking and dragging with the mouse, are mapped to the indicated VBTs; these are translated into nodes using pointers that were stored when the VBTs were created.

Editing actions lead to tree transformations, such as direct replacement of a node (a new object is dragged onto an interactor), adding a child to a node (a new object is dragged into an HBox or VBox), inserting a level into the tree (an existing object is given a Border, for example), or deleting one or more levels (a Border is deleted). After the tree transformation has taken place, the parse tree module notifies each of the views, including the Graphics view itself. The Graphics view updates its appearance in response to this notification, just as it would if the change had been initiated from the Text view. The updating process is the same as for the Result view, except that new VBTs are given borders.

7 Future Work

A feature we intend to add is a restricted form of macros. Currently our extensibility mechanism allows one to add new interactors by programming, but macros could provide a way to create new component classes derived from existing classes, simply by writing a definition within the FormsVBT language. For example, if one frequently uses black-bordered buttons 60 pixels wide, one might write:

```
(Define (Button60 name label)
   (Border (Width 60)
      (Button %name (Text label))))
```

It is tempting to replace the FormsVBT descriptive "little" language with a general-purpose programming language (LISP is an obvious choice), but the additional expressiveness beyond the macros we do plan to implement does not seem warranted for dialog layout. Also, using a general-purpose programming language would complicate two-view editing significantly.

Another goal is to add dynamic loading to FormsEdit. At present, the language is extensible, but FormsEdit can handle only those components whose implementations have been linked into it. To handle extensions, it must be relinked. However, if it is told what object modules are needed to implement the extensions (perhaps by a preamble to the dialog description), then with dynamic loading it could bring in those modules, whose initialization procedures will add the necessary definitions to the language. By this mechanism, in fact, simple applications could be entirely loaded into the editor and tested, using the Result view as a rapid prototyping testbed.

8 Conclusions

The work we have described here was initiated by our desire to make it as easy to get graphical input within a dialog framework as it is to get textual input today (say, by using scanf in C). And indeed, the programming interface to FormsVBT has led to surprisingly simple programs. For simple types of interactions (integers, reals, strings, choices, booleans), the application is only slightly more complicated than it would be if written using scanf, and it has a much nicer user interface with much better typechecking of the input.

The FormsVBT language has proven to be expressive and well suited to dialog construction. Even before the Graphics view was functional, we were usually able to construct user interfaces more rapidly with FormsVBT than with a pure direct-manipulation editor we had been using. Its advantages were particularly striking whenever modifications were needed to a large collection of interators, and wherever regular sizing, spacing, or alignment of several related components was desired. By using a layout model similar to TEX, it is easy to describe complex tiling configurations without getting bogged down in the details, and with simple and predictable positioning and stretching properties.

Being based on symbolic expressions, the language is simple to learn and can be easily extended to accommodate new building blocks. Not only the language, but also the two-view editor, is entirely independent of the specific set of building blocks provided (except the few that the Graphics view uses in its own user interface), and would merely require relinking to support new contributions to the set.

Because the language provides a level of separation between the application and the actual building blocks used, it would be straightforward to provide a different set of building blocks, accessed by the same syntax but based upon an entirely different window system (or different toolkit in the same window system. Thus it can be a tool for enhancing portability of applications, and particularly of their user interfaces. (As with most UIMS, FormsVBT can also be viewed a mechanism to both give a single application multiple "looks and feels" as well as to provide a single "look and feel" across multiple applications.)

The ability to store and retrieve a dialog's values provides an attractive alternative to many existing "configuration"-type files (now stored either as a binary version of a data structure, or in an arbitrary text file). It removes entirely the need for the programmer to design and support a special file format.

When we set out, it was open to question whether a two-view editor for building user interfaces might combine the disadvantages of the two editing approaches rather than the advantages. Now, even with only preliminary experience, we are no longer worried: FormsVBT appears to combine the advantages of the two approaches while eliminating the disadvantages of each approach. With more experience and with some understanding of why users prefer which view for what purposes, we hope to learn just how much of an advantage the multi-view editing paradigm provides, and gain some insight as to what other domains may benefit from this approach.

Acknowledgements

Many of the interactors we use were developed by Luca Cardelli as part of his DialogEditor project here at SRC. Thanks to Greg Nelson and Mark Manasse, who, unknowingly, made our implementation job much easier than it would have been had we been using any other window system with which we're familiar. Thanks also to Luca, Paul McJones, and John Hershberger for feedback on earlier drafts of this paper.

References

[1] *Interface Builder.* NeXT, Inc., Palo Alto, CA.

[2] *Prototyper.* SmetherBarnes, Portland, OR.

[3] Paul J. Asente. *Editing Graphical Objects Using Procedural Representations.* PhD thesis, Dept. of Computer Science, Stanford University, Stanford, CA, 1987. Also available as Research Report #87/6 from DEC Western Research Laboratory, 100 Hamilton Avenue, Palo Alto, CA 94301.

[4] Jon Bentley. Little Languages. *Communications of the ACM,* 29(8):711–721, August 1986.

[5] Kenneth P. Brooks. *A Two-view Document Editor with User-definable Document Structure.* PhD thesis, Dept. of Computer Science, Stanford University, Stanford, CA, 1988. Also available as Research Report #33 from DEC Systems Research Center, 130 Lytton Avenue, Palo Alto, CA 94301.

[6] Luca Cardelli. Building User Interfaces by Direct Manipulation. In *Proc. ACM SIGGRAPH Symp. on User Interface Software,* pages 152–166, October 17–19 1988.

[7] H. Rex Hartson and Deborah Hix. Human-Computer Interface Development: Concepts and Systems. *ACM Computing Surveys,* 21(1):5–92, March 1989.

[8] Paul Heckel. A Technique for Isolating Differences Between Files. *Communications of the ACM,* 21(4):264–268, April 1978.

[9] Mark A. Linton, John M. Vlissides, and Paul R. Calder. Composing User Interfaces with InterViews. *IEEE Computer,* 22(2):8–22, February 1989.

[10] Mark S. Manasse and C. Greg Nelson. *A Performance Analysis of a Multiprocessor Window System.* Technical Report, DEC Systems Research Center, Palo Alto, CA, (to appear).

[11] Paul R. McJones and Garret F. Swart. Evolving the UNIX System Interface to Support Multithreaded Programs. In *Proc. Winter 1989 USENIX Technical Conference,* pages 393–404, USENIX Association, Berkeley, CA, 1989.

[12] Brad A. Myers. User-Interface Tools: Introduction and Suvery. *IEEE Software,* 6(1):15–23, January 1989.

[13] Greg Nelson. Juno, a constraint-based graphics system. *Computer Graphics,* 19(3):235–243, July 1985.

[14] Paul Rovner. Extending Modula–2 To Build Large, Integrated Systems. *IEEE Software,* 3(6):46–57, November 1986.

[15] Andrew J. Schulert, George T. Rogers, and James A. Hamilton. ADM – A Dialog Manager. In *Proc. ACM SIGCHI '85 Conf. on Human Factors in Computing Systems,* pages 177–183, April 1985.

[16] Charles P. Thacker, Lawrence C. Stewart, and Edwin H. Satterthwaite Jr. Firefly: A Multiprocessor Workstation. *IEEE Transactions on Computers,* 37(8):909–920, August 1988.

Scan Line Display
of
Algebraic Surfaces

Thomas W. Sederberg
Alan K. Zundel
Engineering Computer Graphics Lab
Brigham Young University
Provo UT 84602

Abstract

A robust algorithm is presented for scan line display of algebraic surfaces of arbitrary degree and topology. The algorithm correctly displays singularities of any complexity, even those missed by ray tracing or polygonization, and (for surfaces of degree less than eight) offers a significant speed improvement over ray tracing. Antialiasing can generally be accomplished very quickly. In addition to its typical function of shaded raster display, the algorithm is particularly adept at quickly plotting silhouette and intersection curves. A practical use for the algorithm is to display boolean combinations of algebraic half spaces, including blend surfaces.

A new polynomial basis is introduced, referred to as the Bernstein pyramid polynomial basis, which enhances numerical stability and which simplifies several computations such as scan plane-surface intersection and silhouette detection.

CR Categories and Subject Descriptors: G.1.5 [**Numerical Analysis**]: Roots of Nonlinear Equations - *Polynomials, methods for*; I.3.3 [**Computer Graphics**]: Picture/Image Generation - *Display algorithms*; J.6 [**Computer-Aided Engineering**]: Computer-aided design.

Additional Key Words and Phrases: Algebraic surfaces, blend surfaces.

1 INTRODUCTION

An algebraic surface is one which is given by an implicit equation $f(x, y, z) = 0$ where $f(x, y, z)$ is a polynomial. Interest is growing in the use of algebraic surfaces for geometric modeling. Notable examples include the use of algebraic surfaces for blending between other algebraic surfaces [12, 15, 19,26] and schemes for modeling free-form objects directly with algebraic surfaces [17,21]. This trend motivates the need for robust solutions to the problem of computer graphics display of algebraic surfaces.

The topology of a general algebraic surface can be very difficult to analyze. Indeed, no current algorithm can robustly display all singularities and topological components of a general algebraic surface. (Arnon's algorithm [2] under current development is an exception.) Even ray tracing can miss components such as double lines[1].

This paper presents a *robust* scan line algorithm for displaying algebraic surfaces. It works directly from the implicit equation of the surface, without splitting it into polygons. The algorithm gains its robustness by relying on the algebraic tools of resultants and discriminants, reducing all questions of visibility, topology and singularity to univariate polynomials in the Bernstein basis. The algorithm is equally robust in its display of boolean combinations of algebraic half spaces.

An early version of this algorithm was used to create the pictures of cubic algebraic surfaces in reference [21]. No discussion of the rendering algorithm was made in [21] because power basis polynomials were involved and problems with numerical accuracy were experienced for quartic (and higher degree) surfaces, especially in the presence of singularities. These floating point problems were remedied by basing the algorithm entirely on Bernstein polynomials, which are much more numerically stable than power basis polynomials.

The remarkable numerical stability of polynomials in Bernstein form has been thoroughly discussed by Farouki and Rajan [6,7]. It was also documented in [22] that in computing the intersection points of planar curves using algebraic methods, cases occurred in which the intersection algorithm produced zero digits of accuracy when analyzing two degree five curves expressed in power basis polynomials. The same problem expressed in the Bernstein basis yielded ten digits of accuracy.

This paper assumes a basic familiarity with Bézier curves and surfaces. An excellent review is [8].

1.1 Previous work

Previous publications on the general problem of rendering algebraic surfaces take three basic approaches: Direct computation of silhouette points using discriminants, ray tracing, and polygonization.

The earliest algorithm for computer graphics display of algebraic surfaces, Weiss' BE VISION, appeared over two decades ago [27]. BE VISION plotted the silhouette and intersection curves for a boolean combination of quadric surfaces and planes, computing these curves directly using discriminants and resultants. Mahl used

---

[1] See, for example, the Steiner surface in Figure 6 with its three double lines which avoid detection by ray tracing

similar techniques in developing a scan line algorithm for shaded images of quadric surfaces [14]. Owen and Rockwood have used a related approach, but instead of finding silhouette points by computing discriminants (a univariate polynomial problem), they intersect the surface with its polar surface (see section 4 herein) at each scan plane by solving two polynomials in two unknowns [16]. They had good success with this method, although for algebraic surfaces of unknown topology it would be difficult to assure that all silhouette points had been computed.

Hanrahan showed that algebraic surfaces lend themselves well to ray tracing [11]. The ray-surface intersection equation is reduced to a univariate polynomial of the same degree as the surface. Drawbacks include speed and difficulty in displaying some singularities.

Polygonization algorithms approximate an algebraic surface with a set of polygons, which can then be rendered using traditional methods. An early such algorithm is described in [4], and has been included in the MOVIE.BYU software since 1983. It samples $f(x, y, z)$ function values over a three dimensional rectangular grid of points and linearly interpolates polygons in regions where the function values change sign. Figures 11-13 in this paper were created using this algorithm.

More recently, Tindle [25] based a similar polygonization algorithm on a tetrahedral subdivision of space. Nice improvements are discussed by Bloomenthal [3] and Hall and Warren [10] involving an adaptively refined sample grid to generate more polygons in regions of greater surface complexity. These algorithms are excellent for most cases, but can miss singularities and small, unwanted components. Petersen takes advantage of special polynomial properties in his adaptive polygonization scheme for algebraic surfaces [18].

Arnon [2] is addressing the singularity problem by applying the cylindrical algebraic decomposition algorithm [1] to obtain a polygonization which does not have gaps at singularities and which is topologically correct.

A virtue of polygonization algorithms is that they work on any implicit surface, not just on algebraic ones. Also, they interface well with existing polygon rendering systems. A current limitation is that none of the existing papers address the polygonization of boolean combinations of algebraic half spaces. This is akin to the singularity problem, because tangent discontinuity occurs where surfaces intersect.

1.2 Paper Outline

The major steps in our algorithm are surveyed in section 2. We mentioned that the Bernstein polynomial basis is essential for robust computation of silhouette points for surfaces of degree greater than three. A problem of trivariate polynomials in Bernstein form is that they can be very awkward and expensive to manipulate. This problem is addressed in section 3, wherein a new variation of trivariate Bernstein polynomials is introduced, dubbed Bernstein pyramid polynomials, which lend themselves ideally to the rendering problem. Silhouette computation is described in section 4. Section 5 discusses how to convert from power polynomial basis to Bernstein pyramid basis. Implementation details are provided in section 6, and section 7 gives some examples and makes timing comparisons with ray tracing.

2 ALGORITHM OVERVIEW

We here provide a brief overview of our scan line algorithm. Details follow in subsequent sections.

A key feature of our algorithm is its robust, numerically stable capability of quickly computing *critical points*. Critical points along a scan line consist of the x coordinates of all silhouette points and surface intersection points. Surface intersection points can be generated by two surfaces involved in a boolean operation, by a surface and a z clipping plane, or by a surface intersecting itself. The importance of critical points is that they define changes in visibility: *between two critical points, the same surface is continuously visible.* This enables our scan line algorithm to operate several times faster than a ray tracing algorithm.

Figure 7 shows a partially painted sphere along with the silhouette points of the unpainted portion, and Figure 9 shows the sphere within its viewing pyramid (ignore the control points for now). On the next scan line to be painted, there are two critical points (in addition to $x = 0$ and $x = 1$, which are always critical points). The intersection curve between the scan plane and the sphere is shown in Figure 1. The critical points are marked with a symbol $\vee$. The shading for that entire scan line can be determined by performing a small number of ray-surface intersections – three, in this case. Between each pair of critical points, an "exploratory" ray is cast (see Figure 2). If no surface is intersected (as in rays 1 and 3 in Figure 2), all pixels in the interval between those two critical points are painted with background color. If a surface is intersected (as in ray 2), then rays are cast every ten or twenty pixels within that interval (see Figure 3) to determine shading values, and the color of intermediate pixels is assigned by interpolation.

This underscores the need for numerical stability: If a single critical point is overlooked, an entire interval of pixels will be in error. Using power basis polynomials, it is possible for the silhouette computation to be completely wrong (zero digits of accuracy) for surfaces of degree as low as five.

Furthermore, some algebraic surfaces have extremely complicated critical points. Consider the Steiner surface in Figure 6. This surface has three double lines, one along each of the Cartesian coordinate axes. Since a double line has no thickness, each scan plane that intersects a double line creates two coincident critical points. By using the Bernstein polynomial forms described below, our algorithm can robustly (and more quickly than ray tracing) display the Steiner surface, double lines and all. It should be noted that [11] rendered the same Steiner surface with ray tracing, but failed to detect the double lines.

3 BERNSTEIN PYRAMID BASIS

Most commonly, the equation of an algebraic surface is given in power basis with Cartesian coordinates:

$$f(X, Y, Z) = \sum_{i+j+k \leq n} X^i Y^j Z^k c_{ijk} = 0 \qquad (1)$$

As will be shown, there are compelling advantages for our application to instead express the equation of an algebraic surface in terms of a new variation of trivariate Bernstein polynomials which we will refer to as the Bernstein Pyramid Polynomial (BPP) basis.

The BPP (x,y,z) coordinate system might be referred to as a *projective eye coordinate system*. It is actually defined by the viewing pyramid. The z coordinate of the viewing plane is zero and the z coordinate of the eye is one. The (x, y) coordinates range from $(0, 0)$ in the lower left corner to $(1, 1)$ in the upper right corner. *All points on any line going through the eye position have the same (x, y) coordinates*, except the (x, y) coordinates of the eye are not defined. Formulae for converting from BPP coordinates to Cartesian coordinates are given in equations 16 - 18.

Notation: We will use upper case (X,Y,Z) for Cartesian coordinates and lower case (x,y,z) for BPP coordinates.

A degree n polynomial in BPP form is defined:

$$f(x,y,z) = \sum_{k=0}^{n}\sum_{j=0}^{n-k}\sum_{i=0}^{n-k}\binom{n}{k}\binom{n-k}{j}\binom{n-k}{i}\times \qquad (2)$$

$$(1-z)^{n-k}z^k(1-y)^{n-k-j}y^j(1-x)^{n-k-i}x^i f_{ijk}$$

Two pieces of information are required to define a surface in BPP form: The Cartesian coordinates of the pyramid vertices $\mathbf{P}_{000}$, $\mathbf{P}_{n00}$, $\mathbf{P}_{0n0}$, $\mathbf{P}_{00n}$ (see Figure 4) and the scalar coefficient values f_{ijk} (see Figure 5). Unlike the coefficients of power basis implicit equations, the BPP coefficients f_{ijk} can be thought of as control point values positioned in a regular lattice about the pyramid as shown in Figure 5. The position of coefficient f_{ijk} is denoted $\mathbf{P}_{ijk}$ where

$$\mathbf{P}_{ijk} = \frac{n-i-j-k}{n}\mathbf{P}_{000} + \frac{i}{n}\mathbf{P}_{n00} + \frac{j}{n}\mathbf{P}_{0n0} + \frac{k}{n}\mathbf{P}_{00n}; \quad i+j+k \le n \qquad (3)$$

Figure 9 shows a sphere in BPP form.

Parenthetical point of interest: Unlike the power basis, the BPP coefficients f_{ijk} assume some geometric meaning. Each control point f_{ijk} influences the function $f(x,y,z)$ most heavily in its immediate neighborhood. Thus, there is some amount of geometric intuition connected with these control points, making it possible to anticipate the shape of simple BPP surfaces by considering the values of the control points. This property is reminiscent of piecewise algebraic surfaces, a discussion of which can be found in [21].

3.1 Degree and Redundancy

Section 5 discusses how to convert the power basis equation of an algebraic surface into BPP form. A degree n surface in power basis converts to a degree n BPP equation. However, there is some redundancy in the BPP equation. A degree n power basis equation has $(n+1)(n+2)(n+3)/6$ terms, whereas a degree n BPP equation has $(n+1)(n+2)(2n+3)/6$ terms. The redundancy is due to the fact the a *general* BPP equation of degree n converts to a very special case of a power basis equation which is degree $3n$. However, if a degree n power basis equation is converted to BPP form, the terms in the BPP equation of degree higher than n would cancel out if the equation were converted back to power form.

This redundancy actually facilitates the quick set up critical point equations. We investigated all existing forms of trivariate Bernstein polynomials (such as the tetrahedral "pure degree" case used in [21], which does not involve redundancy) and discovered that the silhouette equations are tremendously awkward and expensive to set up using those existing forms. That awkwardness motivated the development of BPP form.

4 SILHOUETTE DETECTION

A fundamental task in our display algorithm is to compute the silhouette points of the surface. This is a job for which BPP form is perfectly suited.

Classical analytic geometry teaches that silhouette points can be computed as the intersection of the surface and its *polar* surface

with respect to the eye position [20]. A sphere and its polar surface are shown in Figure 8, along with the viewing pyramid. For a degree n surface defined in homogeneous power basis:

$$F(X,Y,Z,W) = \sum_{i+j+k+l=n} X^i Y^j Z^k W^l F_{ijkl} = 0 \qquad (4)$$

its polar surface $P(f)$ is degree $n-1$ and is given by:

$$P(f) = X_{eye}f_X + Y_{eye}f_Y + Z_{eye}f_Z + W_{eye}f_W. \qquad (5)$$

Recall that the homogeneous coordinates (X,Y,Z,W) are equivalent to the Cartesian coordinates $(X/W, Y/W, Z/W)$. Therefore, $W_{eye} = 0$ for orthographic views (eye at ∞) and 1 otherwise.

It turns out that the polar of a degree n BPP surface is trivial to compute[2]. Figure 9 shows the control points for the sphere, and Figure 10 shows the control points for its polar. *Note that the control points for the polar are identical to the control points of the sphere, except the first plane of control points is discarded.* It is simply a BPP surface of degree $n-1$ which is obtained by discarding the first plane of control points (the white control points).

Figures 11-13 show a torus with its polar surface, the control points for the torus and the control points for its polar. We could not label all of the control point values, but emphasize that *the polar of any algebraic surface in BPP form has the same control point values as the surface itself except that all control points lying on the viewing plane are discarded.* Thus, in the case of the torus, its polar is obtained by eliminating the plane of light blue control points.

4.1 Discriminants and Resultants

The intersection curve of two surfaces $f(x,y,z) = 0$ (degree n) and $g(x,y,z) = 0$ (degree m) can be projected to the plane $z = 0$ by computing the *resultant* of the two surfaces. Essentially, the resultant eliminates the variable z from the two equations $f(x,y,z)$ and $g(x,y,z)$, creating a two dimensional curve $h(x,y) = 0$ of degree mn. Any point (x,y,z) which lies on the intersection of the two surfaces projects to a point $(x,y,0)$ on the $z = 0$ plane which lies on the curve $h(x,y) = 0$.

The resultant of a surface and its polar is called the *discriminant* of the surface. For our purposes, the discriminant is a curve in the viewing plane (that is, the $z = 0$ plane) which contains all of the silhouette points.

The two most commonly used resultants are Bezout's and Sylvester's. Bezout's is most efficient. Here we spell out the details of Bezout's resultant for surfaces up to degree four. Don't despair of the following cold equations; there is an example in section 4.3. For a thorough discussion on how to apply Bezout's resultant to polynomials in Bernstein form of higher degree, see [7,9].

In order to form the resultant, we must group the terms of the BPP equations such that $f(x,y,z)$ and $g(x,y,z)$ are univariate polynomials in z with coefficients that are polynomials in x and y. Thus, write

$$f(x,y,z) = \sum_{i=0}^{n}(1-z)^{n-i}z^i f_i(x,y) \qquad (6)$$

---

[2] The complete derivation of the polar of a BPP surface fills a couple of pages. It is accomplished by expanding equation 5 in BPP form.

where

$$f_i(x,y) = \binom{n}{i}\sum_{j=0}^{n-i}\sum_{k=0}^{n-i}\binom{n-i}{j}\binom{n-i}{k}\times$$
$$(1-x)^{n-i-j}x^j(1-y)^{n-i-k}y^k f_{jki}$$

and

$$g(x,y,z) = \sum_{i=0}^{m}(1-z)^{m-i}z^i g_i(x,y) \qquad (7)$$

where

$$g_i(x,y) = \begin{cases} 0 & \text{if } m < i \le n \\ \binom{m}{i}\sum_{j=0}^{m-i}\sum_{k=0}^{m-i}\binom{m-i}{j}\binom{m-i}{k}\times \\ (1-x)^{m-i-j}x^j(1-y)^{m-i-k}y^k g_{jki} & \text{if } 0 \le i \le m \end{cases}$$

Note that $f_i(x,y)$ is a tensor product polynomial in Bernstein form whose coefficients are simply the coefficients of the ith plane of control points in its pyramid, scaled by $\binom{n}{i}$ (and likewise for $g_i(x,y)$). Adopting Salmon's shorthand for a 2×2 determinant:

$$(i,j) = f_i g_j - f_j g_i,$$

the resultant of f and g (which we denote $R(f,g)$) for degrees $n = 1,2,3,4$ are as follows.

n=1:
$$R(f,g) = (1,0) \qquad (8)$$

n=2:
$$R(f,g) = \begin{vmatrix} (2,1) & (2,0) \\ (2,0) & (1,0) \end{vmatrix} \qquad (9)$$

n=3:
$$R(f,g) = \begin{vmatrix} (3,2) & (3,1) & (3,0) \\ (3,1) & (3,0)+(2,1) & (2,0) \\ (3,0) & (2,0) & (1,0) \end{vmatrix} \qquad (10)$$

n=4:
$$\begin{vmatrix} (4,3) & (4,2) & (4,1) & (4,0) \\ (4,2) & (4,1)+(3,2) & (4,0)+(3,1) & (3,0) \\ (4,1) & (4,0)+(3,1) & (3,0)+(2,1) & (2,0) \\ (4,0) & (3,0) & (2,0) & (1,0) \end{vmatrix} \qquad (11)$$

$R(f,g)$ is a tensor product polynomial in Bernstein form, as in equation 12.

4.2 Bernstein Polynomial Arithmetic

For the sake of completeness, we include a brief discussion of Bernstein polynomial multiplication, needed to compute resultants and discriminants. A more thorough treatment can be found in [7] (along with much other relevant material).

Addition of two polynomials in Bernstein form of the same degree (the only case we encounter) is done by simply adding like coefficients.

One Variable: Given two univariate polynomials in Bernstein form,

$$f(t) = \sum_{i=0}^{n}\binom{n}{i}(1-t)^{n-i}t^i f_i$$

$$g(t) = \sum_{i=0}^{m}\binom{m}{i}(1-t)^{m-i}t^i g_i$$

the coefficients h_i of their product

$$h(t) = f(t) \times g(t) = \sum_{i=0}^{m+n}\binom{m+n}{i}(1-t)^{m+n-i}t^i h_i$$

can be found using the algorithm:

$$h(i) = 0; \qquad i = 0,\ldots,m+n.$$

$$h(i+j) = h(i+j) + \frac{\binom{n}{i}\binom{m}{j}}{\binom{m+n}{i+j}}f(i)g(j);$$
$$i = 0,\ldots,n; \quad j = 0,\ldots,m.$$

Two Variables: Given two bivariate polynomials in tensor product Bernstein form,

$$f(x,y) = \sum_{i=0}^{n}\sum_{j=0}^{n}\binom{n}{i}\binom{n}{j}(1-x)^{n-i}x^i(1-y)^{n-j}y^j f_{ij} \quad (12)$$

$$g(x,y) = \sum_{i=0}^{m}\sum_{j=0}^{m}\binom{m}{i}\binom{m}{j}(1-x)^{m-i}x^i(1-y)^{m-j}y^j g_{ij}$$

the coefficients h_{ij} of their product

$$h(x,y) = \sum_{i=0}^{m+n}\sum_{j=0}^{m+n}\binom{m+n}{i}\binom{m+n}{j}\times$$
$$(1-x)^{m+n-i}x^i(1-y)^{m+n-j}y^j h_{ij}$$

can be found using the algorithm:

$$h(i,j) = 0; \qquad i,j = 0,\ldots,m+n.$$

$$h(i+j,k+l) = h(i+j,k+l) +$$
$$\frac{\binom{n}{i}\binom{n}{j}\binom{n}{k}\binom{n}{l}}{\binom{m+n}{i+j}\binom{m+n}{k+l}}f(i,j)g(k,l);$$
$$i,k = 0,\ldots,n; \quad j,l = 0,\ldots,m.$$

BPP: While we're at it, here's how to multiply two trivariate polynomials in BPP form (as in equation 2). This is used in section 5. Given two polynomials in BPP form, $f(x,y,z)$ (degree n, with coefficients f_{ijk}) and $g(x,y,z)$ (degree m, with coefficients g_{ijk}), their product $h(x,y,z)$ is a BPP of degree $m+n$ with coefficients h_{ijk} computed as follows:

$$h(i,j,k) = 0; \qquad k = 0,\ldots,m+n; \; i,j = 0,\ldots,m+n-k.$$

$$h(i_1+i_2,j_1+j_2,k_1+k_2) = h(i1+i2,j1+j2,k_1+k_2) +$$
$$\frac{\binom{n}{k_1}\binom{n-k_1}{j_1}\binom{n-k_1}{i_1}\binom{m}{k_2}\binom{m-k_2}{j_2}\binom{m-k_2}{i_2}}{\binom{m+n}{k_1+k_2}\binom{m+n-k_1-k_2}{j_1+j_2}\binom{m+n-k_1-k_2}{i_1+i_2}}f(i_1,j_1,k_1)g(i_2,j_2,k_2)$$

$$k_1 = 0,\ldots,n; \qquad i_1,j_1 = 0,\ldots,n-k_1;$$
$$k_2 = 0,\ldots,m; \qquad i_2,j_2 = 0,\ldots,m-k_2.$$

4.3 Example

To illustrate how straightforward and algorithmic the resultant computation is, we demonstrate by computing the discriminant of a sphere whose implicit equation is $-x^2 - y^2 - z^2 + 1 = 0$ (our convention is that points inside a half space have positive function values). This example is simple enough that you can follow it through with by hand.

We will use the sphere shown in Figure 9 and its polar shown in Figure 10. Denote the equation of the sphere by $f(x, y, z)$ and the equation of its polar by $g(x, y, z)$. Then, using the definition of f_i and g_i from section 4.1,

$$f_0 = \begin{bmatrix} y^2 & 2y(1-y) & (1-y)^2 \end{bmatrix} \begin{bmatrix} -31 & -6 & -31 \\ -6 & 19 & -6 \\ -31 & -6 & -31 \end{bmatrix} \times$$

$$\left\{ \begin{matrix} (1-x)^2 \\ 2x(1-x) \\ x^2 \end{matrix} \right\} ; \tag{13}$$

$$f_1 = \binom{2}{1} \begin{bmatrix} y & (1-y) \end{bmatrix} \begin{bmatrix} 14 & 14 \\ 14 & 14 \end{bmatrix} \left\{ \begin{matrix} 1-x \\ x \end{matrix} \right\}$$

$$f_2 = -16$$

and for the polar, we have

$$g_0 = \begin{bmatrix} y & (1-y) \end{bmatrix} \begin{bmatrix} 14 & 14 \\ 14 & 14 \end{bmatrix} \left\{ \begin{matrix} 1-x \\ x \end{matrix} \right\} \tag{14}$$

$$g_1 = -16; \quad g_2 = 0 .$$

Substituting these equations for f_i and g_i into equation 9, and using the multiplication algorithm in section 4.2, the resultant $R(f, g) = h(x, y)$ (which in this case is the discriminant of the sphere) is

$$R(f, g) = 25600 \times \begin{bmatrix} y^2 & 2y(1-y) & (1-y)^2 \end{bmatrix} \times$$

$$\begin{bmatrix} -3 & 1 & -3 \\ 1 & 5 & 1 \\ -3 & 1 & -3 \end{bmatrix} \left\{ \begin{matrix} (1-x)^2 \\ 2x(1-x) \\ x^2 \end{matrix} \right\} \tag{15}$$

There is a useful geometric interpretation of equation 15. It can be viewed as a biquadratic Bézier surface patch $z = h(x, y)$. The intersection of this surface patch with the plane $z = 0$ is the discriminant (that is, silhouette) curve $h(x, y) = 0$. Figure 14 shows the surface $z = h(x, y)$ (scaled by $1/25600$), interpreted as a biquadratic tensor product Bézier surface patch.

5 POWER TO BPP CONVERSION

Most algebraic surfaces in use in the computer aided geometric design world are expressed in power basis (equation 1). A preprocess is required in our display algorithm to convert power basis equations to BPP basis. The BPP equation is "view dependent" – it changes as the viewing pyramid changes.

Pyramid to Cartesian Coordinate Conversion. We must first observe how to convert from pyramid coordinates (x, y, z) to homogeneous Cartesian coordinates (X, Y, Z, W). We apologize for the slight complication of introducing the homogeneous variable W, but it really pays off shortly. We can simply set it to one and ignore it, except we will need to compute the partial derivative of F with respect to W.

If the corners of the pyramid have the homogeneous Cartesian coordinates $\mathbf{P}_{000} = (X_{000}, Y_{000}, Z_{000}, 1)$, $\mathbf{P}_{100} = (X_{100}, Y_{100}, Z_{100}, 1)$, $\mathbf{P}_{010} = (X_{010}, Y_{010}, Z_{010}, 1)$, $\mathbf{P}_{110} = (X_{110}, Y_{110}, Z_{110}, 1)$, $\mathbf{P}_{001} = (X_{001}, Y_{001}, Z_{001}, 1)$, where $\mathbf{P}_{110} = \mathbf{P}_{100} + \mathbf{P}_{010} - \mathbf{P}_{000}$, then

$$X(x, y, z) = \sum_{k=0}^{1} \sum_{j=0}^{1-k} \sum_{i=0}^{1-k} (1-z)^{1-k} z^k (1-y)^{1-k-j} y^j$$

$$(1-x)^{1-k-i} x^i X_{ijk} \tag{16}$$

$$Y(x, y, z) = \sum_{k=0}^{1} \sum_{j=0}^{1-k} \sum_{i=0}^{1-k} (1-z)^{1-k} z^k (1-y)^{1-k-j} y^j$$

$$(1-x)^{1-k-i} x^i Y_{ijk} \tag{17}$$

$$Z(x, y, z) = \sum_{k=0}^{1} \sum_{j=0}^{1-k} \sum_{i=0}^{1-k} (1-z)^{1-k} z^k (1-y)^{1-k-j} y^j$$

$$(1-x)^{1-k-i} x^i Z_{ijk} \tag{18}$$

$$W(x, y, z) = 1 \tag{19}$$

Note that $X(x, y, z)$, $Y(x, y, z)$ and $Z(x, y, z)$ are degree one polynomials in BPP form that return Cartesian coordinates as functions of BPP coordinates (x, y, z).

Conversion algorithm. A succinct "high level" trick for converting from power basis to BPP basis (or to any other basis) can be derived from Euler's law for homogeneous polynomials as follows. $F(X, Y, Z)$ (a power basis equation in Cartesian coordinates) can be converted to BPP form $f(x, y, z)$ using the following recursive algorithm:

$$f(x, y, z) = \mathbf{C2B}(0, 0, 0, 0)$$

where the function **C2B** returns a polynomial in BPP form and is defined:

```
FUNCTION C2B(i, j, k, l)
    IF i + j + k + l = n, THEN
†       C2B = i! j! k! l! F_ijk
    ELSE
‡       C2B = [X(x, y, z) × C2B(i + 1, j, k, l) + Y(x, y, z) ×
              C2B(i, j + 1, k, l) + Z(x, y, z) × C2B(i, j, k + 1, l) +
              C2B(i, j, k, l + 1)]/(n − i − j − k − l)
    ENDIF
END C2B
```

Some explanation is in order for statements † and ‡. Recall that for $i + j + k + l = n$,

$$\frac{\partial^n F}{\partial X^i \partial Y^j \partial Z^k \partial W^l} = i! j! k! l! F_{ijk}.$$

In C2B, the arguments i, j, k, l indicate how many times the function F has undergone partial differentiation with respect to X, Y, Z and W respectively. We actually don't differentiate F at all, except to keep track that if it has been differentiated n times, it's equal to the constant $i! j! k! l! F_{ijk}$; hence, statement †.

Statement ‡ is where Euler's law comes in. Euler's law states that for a degree n homogeneous polynomial,

$$F(X, Y, Z, W) = \frac{X \times F_X + Y \times F_Y + Z \times F_Z + W \times F_W}{n}$$

where F_X, etc., indicates partial differentiation. Statement ‡ is simply the implementation of Euler's law: The $\times$ operator is BPP multiply and $X(x, y, z), Y(x, y, z), Z(x, y, z)$ are the degree one BPP functions in equations 16-19.

This conversion algorithm is not the most efficient, but it is easily implemented.

6 IMPLEMENTATION DETAILS

6.1 Critical Point Computation

As a preprocess, the discriminant of each surface is computed. If boolean operations are performed, the resultant of each pair of intersecting surfaces is also computed.

Recall that discriminants and resultants are tensor product polynomials of the form

$$h(x,y) = \sum_{i=0}^{n} \sum_{j=0}^{n} \binom{n}{i} \binom{n}{j} (1-x)^{n-i} x^i (1-y)^{n-j} y^j h_{ij}. \quad (20)$$

For each scan line $y = y_s$, each discriminant and resultant is evaluated at $y = y_s$, producing in each case a univariate polynomial in Bernstein form. All roots of such a polynomial in the $[0, 1]$ interval are critical points, and all critical points are roots of such an equation. Thus, the robustness of this rendering algorithm is due primarily to the robustness of polynomial root finders.

6.2 Polynomial Root Finding

The Bernstein polynomial basis is ideally suited to polynomial root finding [6]. Indeed, our rendering algorithm has proven to be an excellent test bed for the robustness of a root finder in Bernstein basis.

We have refined a root finder which follows the lines suggested by Lane and Riesenfeld [13]. First, roots are isolated, using the variation diminishing property as a test for isolation. Isolated roots are refined using the modified regula falsi method. Additional enhancements to handle multiple roots are discussed in [24]. In most cases, this root finder is much faster than global root finders such as the Jenkins-Traub algorithm.

The root finder finds all roots in the unit interval, and none others. The roots are found in ascending order, and the root finder can optionally stop after finding the first root – ideal for ray tracing. Coherence is harnessed by using roots from preceding polynomials as starting points for Newton iteration. Robustness is then checked using the variation diminishing property.

A good example of the robustness of our root finder is the Steiner surface in Figure 6. The critical points for this surface require the solution of a degree 12 polynomial at each scan line, each having three double roots and four single roots.

6.2.1 Degree limitations

The degree of the discriminant grows quadratically with the degree of the surface. A degree 6 surface has a degree 30 discriminant. This is probably the practical limit for the solution of critical points using discriminants and univariate polynomials.

For degree higher than 6, the answer is to use an algorithm for robustly computing roots of two Bernstein form polynomials in two unknowns. Thus, silhouette points are found by evaluating the surface BPP equation and its polar BPP equation at $y = y_s$ (creating two Bernstein form polynomials in the unknowns x and z) and finding all solutions in the unit interval. Again, robustness is required, and again the Bernstein form comes to the rescue. The first author recently developed an algorithm for dealing with just that problem [23], and the algorithm does robustly find *all* solutions and should in theory work for surfaces at least of degree 25. However, speed suffers dramatically as the degree rises. After about degree 8, raw ray tracing becomes just as fast, although we repeat that ray tracing can miss singularities which our algorithm won't.

6.3 Shading

The reason our algorithm is generally much faster than ray tracing is that we don't need to fire a ray at each pixel. To get smooth shading, we have found it generally sufficient to fire rays every 15 pixels. Surface normals and shading values are obtained basically as in [11]. If there are no highlights, we simply interpolate colors between sample pixels. Otherwise, we interpolate the normals.

The ray-surface intersection equation reduces to a univariate polynomial in Bernstein form whose roots are easily found using our Bernstein root finder.

6.4 Antialiasing

Our algorithm can usually reduce aliasing to an acceptable level with little expense. Critical points are computed to floating point accuracy, and the slope of the silhouette curve is easily obtained. This makes it possible to obtain a good first order approximation to the percent of a pixel being filled by the silhouetting surface. Coloring such a pixel using ratios so determined has worked nicely. All edges but those sloping less than about 5 degrees from the horizontal require no further antialiasing.

6.5 Boolean Operations

The algorithm handles boolean operations efficiently. Figures 18-20 show two intersecting tori. All of the critical points – silhouette (in yellow and blue) and intersection (in black) – are shown in Figure 20. Figure 19 shows a partial picture of the boolean difference of the tori, along with the remaining *visible* critical points. Note that the visible critical points are ultimately the only important ones. In between each pair of visible critical points, the same surface is visible.

7 EXAMPLES AND TIMINGS

Figure 15 shows how our algorithm rendered a cone-cone blend due to Middleditch and Sears [15]. Figure 16 shows a degree 4 blend between two elliptical cylinders, from a paper by Hoffmann and Hopcroft [12], and Figure 17 shows a cubic blend (that's right, it's *not* a torus) between two circular cylinders, devised by Joe Warren [26]. Figures 16 and 17 actually required several boolean operations to trim away unwanted portions of surfaces. Figures 22 and 23 are degree four Kummer surfaces.

We implemented our algorithm on a Macintosh II using Lightspeed C version 2.15, from which all of our photographs were taken. We also ran the algorithm on a VAX 8600 to obtain timings. The VAX typcially ran five times faster than the Macintosh. We didn't have a state-of-the-art ray tracing program to race against. To be objective in comparing our algorithm with ray tracing, we devised a ray tracing algorithm by setting our scan line algorithm to fires a ray at every non-background pixel. In other words, we provided critical point information to the ray tracer so that it knew, to the pixel, where to trace. We felt that no spatial indexing scheme could improve on that.

We ran time tests on five examples:

1. a sphere (Figure 7) - 60.4 % background pixels

2. the Steiner surface (Figure 6) - 77.1% background

3. the degree four blend (Figure 15) - 89.7% background

4. a torus (as in Figure 12) - 62.1% background

5. Torus-torus boolean difference (Figure 19) 84.3% background

Images were computed both at 128×128 resolution and 512×512 resolution. We collected times for silhouette plot (as in Figure 21), shaded image using our algorithm, and ray tracing. Times are in VAX 8600 cpu seconds, with the times for 128×128 resolution and 512×512 resolution seperated by a slash.

	Surface Number				
	1	2	3	4	5
Silhouette	1/4	7/27	4/16	3/14	11/44
Shaded	4/45	18/82	9/40	10/67	29/136
Ray Trace	18/251	36/372	15/137	38/461	49/482

Our algorithm provides images that are pretty well antialiased. For equivalent quality, a ray tracer probably needs to fire four rays per pixel.

Note that execution times do not grow quadratically with the resolution. The critical point computation grows roughly linearly with resolution.

8   CONCLUSIONS

Our primary goal in developing this algorithm was robustness, and we are confident that we have met that goal. Also, for as little time as we have spent optimizing our code, we think that the algorithm is very competitive in execution speed.

We have tried to condense the most essential information into this paper. More detail can be found in [28].

Acknowledgements: This work was supported in part by the National Science Foundation under grant number DMC-8657057. We are appreciative of valuable discussions with Alyn Rockwood and Dennis Arnon.

References

1. Arnon, D.S., Topologically reliable display of algebraic curves, *Computer Graphics*, **17**, 1983, 219-228.

2. Arnon, D.S. and Rauen, J., On the display of cell decompositions of algebraic surfaces, XEROX Technical Report, 1988.

3. Bloomenthal, J., Polygonization of implicit surfaces, *Computer Aided Geometric Design*, **5**, 1988, 341-355.

4. Bradshaw, C.B., Surfaces of functions of three variables, M.S. Thesis, Department of Civil Engineering, Brigham Young University, 1982.

5. Farouki, R.T., The characterization of parametric surface sections, *Computer Vision, Graphics and Image Processing*, 1986, **33**, 209-236.

6. Farouki, R.T. and Rajan, V.T., On the numerical condition of polynomials in Bernstein form, *Computer Aided Geometric Design*, **4**, 1987, 191-216.

7. Farouki, R.T. and Rajan, V.T., Algorithms for polynomials in Bernstein form, *Computer Aided Geometric Design*, 1988, **5**, 1-26.

8. Farin, G., *Curves and Surfaces for Computer Aided Geometric Design*, Academic Press, 1988.

9. Goldman, R.N., Sederberg, T.W. and Anderson, D.C., Vector elimination: A technique for the implicitization, inversion, and intersection of planar parametric rational polynomial curves, *Computer Aided Geometric Design*, **1**, 1984, 327-356.

10. Hall, M. and Warren, J., Adaptive tessellation of implicitly defined surfaces, Rice COMP TR88-84, 1988, Rice University.

11. Hanrahan, P., Ray tracing algebraic surfaces, *Computer Graphics*, **17**, 3, 1983, 83-90.

12. Hoffmann, C.M. and Hopcroft, J.E., Automatic surface generation in computer aided design, *The Visual Computer*, **1**, 1985, 95-100.

13. Lane, J.M. and Riesenfeld, R.F., Bounds on a polynomial, *BIT*, **21**, 1, 1981, 112-117.

14. Mahl, R., Visible surface algorithms for quadric patches, *IEEE Transactions on Computers*, **C-21**, 1, 1972, 1-4.

15. Middleditch, A.E. and Sears, K., Blend surfaces for set theoretic volume modeling systems, *Computer Graphics*, **19**, 1985, 161-170.

16. Owen, J.C. and Rockwood, A.P., Intersection of general implicit surfaces. In *Geometric Modeling: Algorithms and New Trends*, G. Farin, editor, SIAM, Philadelphia, 1987, 335-346.

17. Patrikalakis, N.M. and Kriezis, G.A., Piecewise continuous algebraic surfaces in terms of B-splines, MITSG 88-5, Massachusetts Institute of Technology, August 1988.

18. Petersen, C.S., Adaptive contouring of three-dimensional surfaces, *Computer Aided Geometric Design*, **1**, 1984, 61-74.

19. Rockwood, A.P. and Owen, J.C., Blending surfaces in solid modeling. In *Geometric Modeling: Algorithms and New Trends*, G. Farin, editor, SIAM, Philadelphia, 1987, 335-346.

20. Salmon, G. *Analytic Geometry of Three Dimensions*, Longmans, Green and Co., 1912.

21. Sederberg, T.W., Piecewise algebraic surface patches, *Computer Aided Geometric Design*, **2**, 1985, 53-59.

22. Sederberg, T.W. and Parry, S.R., Comparison of three curve intersection algorithms, *Computer-Aided Design*, **18**, 1, (1986), 58-63.

23. Sederberg, T.W., An algorithm for algebraic curve intersection, to appear in, *Computer-Aided Design*.

24. Sederberg, T.W., Spencer, M.R. and de Boor, C., Real root approximation of polynomials in Bernstein form, in preparation.

25. Tindle, G.L., Tetrahedral triangulation, in, R.R. Martin, ed., *The Mathematics of Surfaces II*, Clarendon Press, Oxford, 1987, 387-394.

26. Warren, J.D., On algebraic surfaces meeting with geometric continuity, Ph.D. Thesis, Cornell University, 1986.

27. Weiss, R.A., BE VISION, A package of IBM 7090 FORTRAN programs to draw orthographic views of combinations of plane and quadric surfaces, *JACM*, **13**, 2, 1966, 194-204.

28. Zundel, A.K., Scan line rendering of algebraic surfaces and half spaces, M.S. Thesis, Department of Civil Engineering, Brigham Young University, 1989.

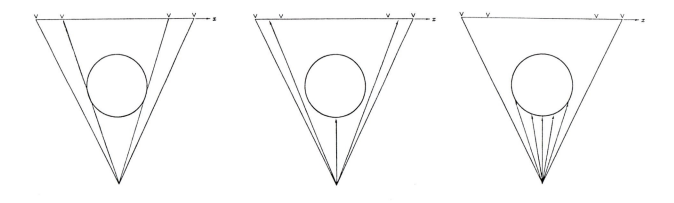

Figure 1. Critical points. **Figure 2.** Exploratory rays. **Figure 3.** Shading rays.

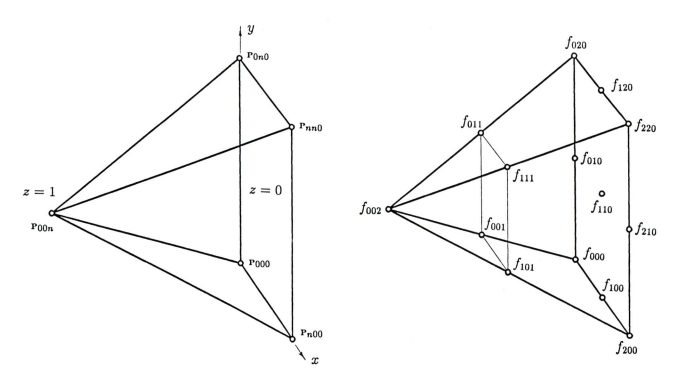

Figure 4. Pyramid vertices. **Figure 5.** BPP coefficients.

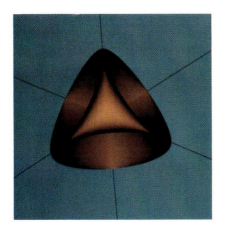

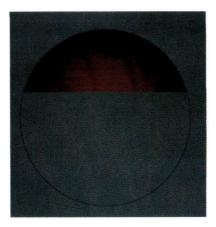

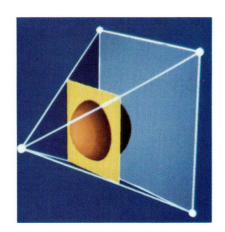

Figure 6. Steiner surface with double lines.   **Figure 7.** Half painted sphere.   **Figure 8.** Sphere and its polar.

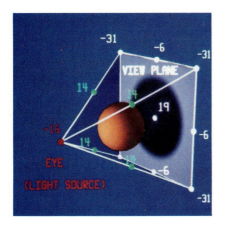

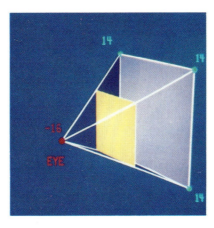

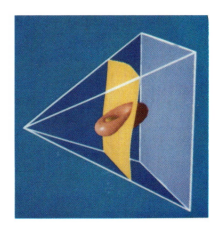

Figure 9. Sphere and control points.   **Figure 10.** Polar of sphere.   **Figure 11.** Torus and its polar.

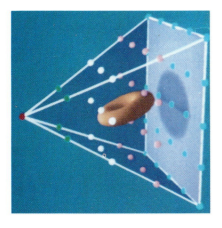

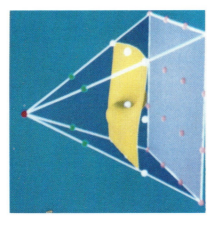

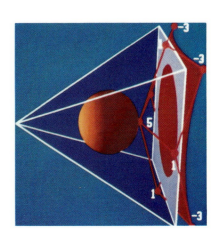

Figure 12. Torus and control points.   **Figure 13.** Polar of torus.   **Figure 14.** Sphere discriminant.

Figure 15. Middleditch-Sears cone blend.

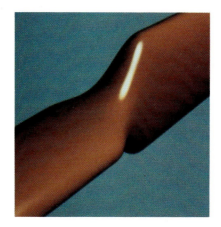

Figure 16. Hoffmann-Hopcroft cylinder blend.

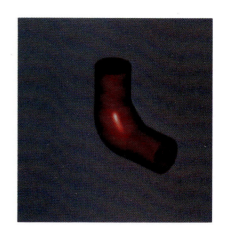

Figure 17. Warren blend.

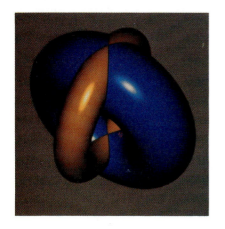

Figure 18. Union of tori.

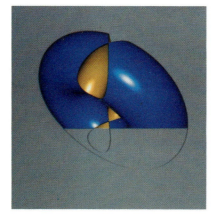

Figure 19. Difference of tori.

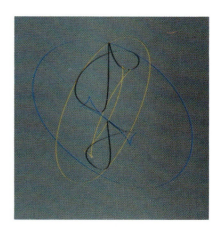

Figure 20. Critical points of tori.

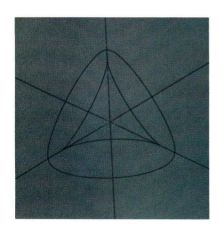

Figure 21. Critical points of Steiner.

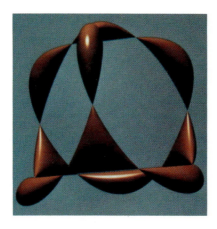

Figure 22. Kummer surface.

Figure 23. Kummer surface.

Rendering Cubic Curves and Surfaces with Integer Adaptive Forward Differencing

Sheue-Ling Chang, Michael Shantz and Robert Rocchetti

Sun Microsystems, Inc.
2500 Garcia Avenue
Mountain View, CA 94043

Abstract

For most compute environments, adaptive forward differencing is much more efficient when performed using integer arithmetic than when using floating point. Previously low precision integer methods suffered from serious precision problems due to the error accumulation inherent to forward differencing techniques. This paper proposes several different techniques for implementing adaptive forward differencing using integer arithmetic, and provides an error analysis of forward differencing which is useful as a guide for integer AFD implementation. The proposed technique using 32 bit integer values is capable of rendering curves having more than 4K forward steps with an accumulated error of less than one pixel and no overflow problems. A hybrid algorithm employing integer AFD is proposed for rendering antialiased, texture-mapped bicubic surfaces.

CR Categories and Subject Descriptors:
I.3.3 [**Computer Graphics**]: Picture/Image Generation - Display algorithms;
I.3.5 [**Computer Graphics**]: Computational Geometry and Object Modelling - Curve, surface, and Geometric algorithms.

Additional Key Words and Phrases: adaptive forward differencing, parametric curve, and texture.

©1989   ACM-0-89791-312-4/89/007/0157 $00.75

Introduction

Much progress has been made in recent years on techniques for computer aided geometrical design. Parametric curves and surfaces including non-uniform rational B-splines are commonly used to describe surfaces of objects being designed. Such objects have typically been rendered by tesselating to bilinear quadrilaterals or triangles which are then rendered using widely available special purpose hardware for polygons. Alternatively, isoparametric curves across the surface are rendered by tesselating to polylines which are rendered using special purpose hardware. These simple piecewise linear approximations are also used to drive numerically controlled milling machines.

Research has focused largely on subdivision methods for rendering and modelling [4, 11]. Less progress has been made on hardware techniques for direct rendering of higher order curves and surfaces. Recursive subdivision is expensive for hardware implementation due to the high speed stack memory requirements and the computational complexity increase over polygon rendering methods. Incremental solutions of the implicit equations have been developed for conics [2, 5, 13, 14], and a few hardware curve generators have been built.

Adaptive forward difference (AFD) is an incremental technique proposed previously for rendering parametric curves and surfaces [12, 17]. Abi-Ezzi [1] adapted the AFD technique to a new basis which has a convex hull property yet retains much of the efficiency of the forward difference basis. AFD is an extension of forward differencing and is similar to adaptive subdivision in its dynamic step size adjustment. AFD differs from recursive subdivision or ordinary forward differencing by generating points sequentially along the curve while adjusting the parametric increment to give pixel sized steps. AFD allows a surprisingly simple hardware implementation, and is compatible with frame buffer memory interleaving for high performance. With special purpose hardware for rendering these curves and surfaces directly, the overhead of subdivision and stack memory is eliminated and the quality of the rendered surface is as good.

AFD in software, with its high speed and low cost, is also attractive for parametric curve and surface rendering. Various implementation methods for integer adaptive forward differencing are discussed in this paper. One 32-bit scheme is proposed which offers advantages in performance, precision, and output format.

The error accumulation in forward differencing is analyzed, including a comparison of the error accumulation in different integer AFD schemes. Integer AFD may also be used for fast rendering of antialiased texture-mapped bicubic surfaces.

Integer Adaptive Forward Differencing

A parametric curve can be tesselated into n segments using equal parametric increments at $1/n$ spacing (assuming that the parameter of the function ranges from 0.0 to 1.0). This is done by first converting a polynomial function into the forward difference basis [8]. The points along the curve can then be generated incrementally with three additions per cycle in the case of a cubic.

The authors described three operators in adaptive forward differencing in the previous paper. Adjust-down is an operator for reducing the parametric increment by half and reducing the step size to approximately one pixel per step when the x,y screen step size is more than one pixel. The adjust-up operation doubles the parametric increment to increase the change in x,y coordinates when the step size is less than 1/2 pixel. The two adjustment operations are performed by transforming the coefficients of the coordinate functions by the the adjust-up matrix $[U]$ or the adjust-down matrix $[D]$:

$$U = \begin{bmatrix} 1 & 0 & 0 & 0 \\ 0 & 2 & 1 & 0 \\ 0 & 0 & 4 & 4 \\ 0 & 0 & 0 & 8 \end{bmatrix} \quad \begin{cases} c' = (c<<1)+b; \\ b' = (a+b)<<2; \\ a' = a<<3; \end{cases}$$

$$D = \begin{bmatrix} 1 & 0 & 0 & 0 \\ 0 & 1/2 & -1/8 & 1/16 \\ 0 & 0 & 1/4 & -1/8 \\ 0 & 0 & 0 & 1/8 \end{bmatrix} \quad \begin{cases} a' = a>>3; \\ b' = (b>>2)-a'; \\ c' = (c-b')>>1; \end{cases}$$

where a, b, c, and d are the coefficients of the curve represented in forward difference basis. The notations "$a<<3$" and "$a>>3$" indicate a left or right shift of coefficient a by three bits. When the step size is within the desired range, the forward-step matrix $[F]$ is applied to move one step forward.

$$F = \begin{bmatrix} 1 & 1 & 0 & 0 \\ 0 & 1 & 1 & 0 \\ 0 & 0 & 1 & 1 \\ 0 & 0 & 0 & 1 \end{bmatrix} \quad \begin{cases} output\ (d); \\ d' = d+c; \\ c' = c+b; \\ b' = b+a; \end{cases}$$

Adaptive forward differencing can be implemented in either floating point or fixed point arithmetic. Floating point implementation offers more precision, but is usually more expensive. Higher performance can be achieved if AFD is performed using integer additions and shifts. There are two straight forward integer AFD implementations. The 64-bit integer AFD, with two 32-bit integers, provides adequate precision for most displays, but the computational cost is more than doubled over 32 bit integer operations due to the carry. The 32-bit integer AFD shown in Figure 1 has an advantage in performance but a disadvantage in precision. It can handle only a very small number of forward steps. Subdivisions are required for large curves to avoid excessive error accumulation. In the error

analysis section we show that this scheme can only handle cubic curves involving up to 100 forward steps on a 1Kx1K screen. The overflow protection bit is used here to avoid clipping a curve exactly to the display window boundary which is quite expensive compared to vector clipping.

a	12.20
b	12.20
c	12.20
d	12.20

Figure 1. An integer forward difference implementation with a sign bit, an overflow-protection bit, 10 integer and 20 fractional bits.

The approach in Figure 2 has the a, b, and c registers aligned and the d register in a 16.16 fract format. A forward step is performed by outputing (d>>16) where

$$d' = d + (c>>8); \quad c' = c + b; \quad b' = b + a;$$

Compared to the first method where all registers are aligned, this approach provides eight more fractional bits which increases the maximum number of forward steps to be 512, at a cost of one extra shift per forward step.

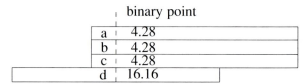

Figure 2. An integer forward difference implementation with the a, b, and c registers aligned and the d register in 16.16 format. Register a has 28 fractional bits.

Bartels etc. [3] discussed using successive guard bits in the forward difference registers to achieve higher precision with less bits. Each register except a contains n successive guard bits for processing up to 2^n forward steps, Figure 3.

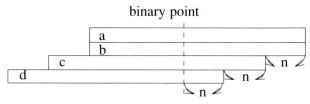

Figure 3. Forward difference registers with n guard bits.

A forward step operation is performed with n guard bits truncated before adding a register:

$$F_i = \begin{bmatrix} 1 & 2^{-n} & 0 & 0 \\ 0 & 1 & 2^{-n} & 0 \\ 0 & 0 & 1 & 1 \\ 0 & 0 & 0 & 1 \end{bmatrix} \quad \begin{cases} output\ (d>>n); \\ d' = d + (c>>n); \\ c' = c + (b>>n); \\ b' = b + a; \end{cases}$$

The constant 2^{-n} indicates a truncation of n guard bits. The use of guard bits significantly increases the number of forward steps allowable with 32-bit integer forward differencing. Register initialization is also simpler with guard bits. A parametric curve $f(t) = At^3 + Bt^2 + Ct + D$ is converted to the forward difference basis with the following transformation where A, B, C, and D are the control points in polynomial basis, a, b, c, and d are the control points in forward difference basis, $\delta = 1/n$ is the parametric increment:

$$\begin{bmatrix} d \\ c \\ b \\ a \end{bmatrix} = \begin{bmatrix} 1 & 0 & 0 & 0 \\ 0 & \delta & \delta^2 & \delta^3 \\ 0 & 0 & 2\delta^2 & 6\delta^3 \\ 0 & 0 & 0 & 6\delta^3 \end{bmatrix} \begin{bmatrix} D \\ C \\ B \\ A \end{bmatrix}$$

The forward difference basis functions are

$$B_3 = \frac{t(t-1)(t-2)}{6}, \quad B_2 = \frac{t(t-1)}{2}, \quad B_1 = t, \quad B_0 = 1$$

This transformation can be performed using integer additions and shifts if the tesselation number is a power of two, ie., the scaling factor $\delta = 2^{-n}$ as follows:

$$\begin{cases} d = D \\ c = (C + (B + (A >> n)) >> n) >> n \\ b = (2B >> 2n) + (6A >> 3n) \\ a = 6A >> 3n \end{cases}$$

With n successive guard bits in each register, the c coefficient is scaled by 2^n and the a and b coefficients are scaled by 2^{2n}. The initialization is simplied as follows:

$$\begin{bmatrix} d \\ c \\ b \\ a \end{bmatrix} = \begin{bmatrix} 1 & 0 & 0 & 0 \\ 0 & 1 & \delta & \delta^2 \\ 0 & 0 & 2 & 6\delta \\ 0 & 0 & 0 & 6\delta \end{bmatrix} \begin{bmatrix} D \\ C \\ B \\ A \end{bmatrix} \quad \begin{cases} d = D \\ c = C + (B + (A >> n)) >> n \\ b = 2B + (6A >> n) \\ a = 6A >> n \end{cases}$$

To utilize a forward difference register set with n successive guard bits in integer AFD the adjust-up $[U]$ and adjust-down $[D]$ operators can be modified as follows

$$U_i = \begin{bmatrix} 1 & 0 & 0 & 0 \\ 0 & 2 & 2^{-n} & 0 \\ 0 & 0 & 4 & 4 \\ 0 & 0 & 0 & 8 \end{bmatrix} \quad \begin{cases} c' = (c << 1) + (b >> n); \\ b' = (a+b) << 2; \\ a' = a << 3; \end{cases}$$

$$D_i = \begin{bmatrix} 1 & 0 & 0 & 0 \\ 0 & 1/2 & -2^{-n}/8 & 2^{-n}/16 \\ 0 & 0 & 1/4 & -1/8 \\ 0 & 0 & 0 & 1/8 \end{bmatrix} \quad \begin{cases} a' = a >> 3; \\ b' = (b >> 2) - a'; \\ c' = (c - (b' >> n)) >> 1 \end{cases}$$

to reflect the alignment of the binary points of the registers. The factor 2^{-n} indicates the existence of the guard bits. The number of guard bits remains unchanged throughout the process.

Victor Klassen [9, 10] extended this pseudo floating concept to the integer AFD implementation. He modified the adjust-up and adjust-down operators $[U_K]$ and $[D_K]$ to incorporate the usage of guard bits in the AFD registers and thus to vary the number of

guard bits following each adjustment operation. One guard bit is added before an adjust down and eliminated after an adjust up:

$$U_K = \begin{bmatrix} 1/2 & 0 & 0 & 0 \\ 0 & 1/2 & 2^{-n-2} & 0 \\ 0 & 0 & 1/2 & 1/2 \\ 0 & 0 & 0 & 1 \end{bmatrix} \quad D_K = \begin{bmatrix} 2 & 0 & 0 & 0 \\ 0 & 2 & -2^{-n} & 2^{-n-1} \\ 0 & 0 & 2 & -1 \\ 0 & 0 & 0 & 1 \end{bmatrix}$$

When the registers acquire one extra guard bit after an adjust-down and lose one guard bit after an adjust-up, matrix $[U_K]$ can be derived from $[U_i]$ by scaling the first row of $[U_i]$ by 1/2, the second row by 1/4, and the third and fourth rows by 1/8. Similarly, $[D_K]$ can be derived by scaling the first row of $[D_i]$ by 2, the second row by 4, and the third and fourth rows by 8. We notice that this technique keeps the a register constant and only shifts the contents of b, c and d registers during an adjustment.

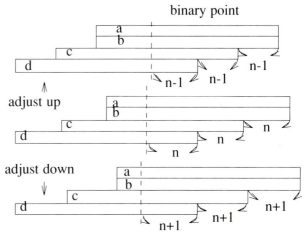

Figure 4. The re-alignment of forward difference registers in Klassen's technique associated with an adjust-up or adjust-down operation. The contents of the a register remains constant during the entire process.

There are different pseudo floating implementations for integer AFD depending on the application. Figure 5 illustrates the register format of our technique where the d register stays constant in an adjustment, and the a, b and c registers are shifted instead.

The new adjust-up matrix $[U_C]$ is derived from $[U_i]$ by scaling the first row of the matrix by 1, the second row by 1/2, and the third and fourth rows by 1/4.

$$U_C = \begin{bmatrix} 1 & 0 & 0 & 0 \\ 0 & 1 & 2^{-n-1} & 0 \\ 0 & 0 & 1 & 1 \\ 0 & 0 & 0 & 2 \end{bmatrix} \quad \begin{cases} c' = c + (b >> (n+1)); \\ b' = b + a; \\ a' = a << 1; \\ n' = n - 1; \end{cases}$$

The adjust-down matrix $[D_C]$ is derived from $[D_i]$ by scaling the first row by 1, the second row by 2, and the third and fourth rows by 4.

$$D_C = \begin{bmatrix} 1 & 0 & 0 & 0 \\ 0 & 1 & -2^{-n-2} & 2^{-n-3} \\ 0 & 0 & 1 & -1/2 \\ 0 & 0 & 0 & 1/2 \end{bmatrix} \quad \begin{cases} a' = a >> 1; \\ b' = b - a'; \\ c' = c - (b' >> (n+2)); \\ n' = n + 1; \end{cases}$$

These transformations preserve the contents of the d register in an adjustment while eliminating one guard bit successively from the a, b and c registers during an adjust-up, and adding one guard bit successively to the a, b and c registers during an adjust-down.

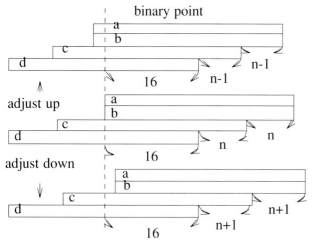

Figure 5. The re-alignment of the forward difference registers in our technique during an adjust-up or adjust-down operation. The binary point of the d register remains fixed.

Pseudo floating point is very important in order to make the most effective use of fixed point arithmetic and fixed width registers. Both methods described above vary the number of guard bits in an adjustment thus giving the effect of a floating binary point. Since single float variables in computers contain only 24 bits of mantissa, these 32-bit pseudo floating point AFD implementations could actually provide more precision than single precision float implementation when the registers are initialized with double precision floating point values.

Figure 6. A comparison of the register layout of the two methods.

By comparing Figures 4 and 5, we can see that the difference between the two methods is that Klassen's method produces an output with a floating binary point while our method produces a fixed point 16.16 fract format output. The new method also offers several advantages including

(1) an easier and less expensive initialization computation for fract format inputs and outputs,

(2) fewer operations in the adjust up and down operations,

(3) a 16.16 fract format output which better suits subsequent integer instructions, and

(4) higher precision when the velocity of a curve decreases and the parametric step size is adjusted severely upward.

When the curve velocity is approximately 4.0 and the parametric increment is at 2^{-2}, Klassen's registers are shifted so far to the left that only few fractional bits remain, whereas the registers in our technique always retain at least 16 fractional bits even in regions of minimum curve velocity, as shown in Figure 6.

Error Analysis on Forward Differencing

While forward differencing has been a popular and inexpensive method for incrementally evaluating points along a parametric function, its rapid error accumulation has been a problem. The user must carefully analyze the error accumulation characteristics of the method to ensure accuracy. In this section the error accumulation properties of forward differencing are analyzed and guide lines are presented for evaluating the error bounds of various implementation schemes.

1. Error analysis on registers without guard bits

For a cubic, the points on the curve can be computed incrementally using three additions per cycle. The contents accumulated in the registers at each cycle are shown in the table. We first assume that the registers are aligned as shown in Figure 1 and that each register has n fractional bits.

cycle	Contents of Forward Difference Register			
0	a	b	c	d
1	a	a+b	b+c	c+d
2	a	2a+b	a+2b+c	b+2c+d
3	a	3a+b	3a+3b+c	a+3b+3c+d
4	a	4a+b	6a+4b+c	4a+6b+4c+d
5	a	5a+b	10a+5b+c	10a+10b+5c+d
6	a	6a+b	15a+6b+c	20a+15b+6c+d
⋮	⋮	⋮	⋮	⋮
k	a	ka+b	ak(k-1)/2+ kb+c	ak(k-1)(k-2)/6 + bk(k-1)/2 + kc+d

The error accumulation problem can then be analyzed by examining the data in the d register after k iterations:

$$d = a\frac{k(k-1)(k-2)}{6} + b\frac{k(k-1)}{2} + kc + d$$

The error accumulated in the d register is approximately

$$e_d = E_a\frac{k(k-1)(k-2)}{6} + E_b\frac{k(k-1)}{2} + kE_c + E_d$$

which is dominated by the initial error in the a register. The initial errors in the registers are $E_a = E_b = E_c = E_d = 2^{-n}$.

The error accumulated in the d register after k cycles is approximately

$$e_d \approx E_a \frac{k(k-1)(k-2)}{6} + O(k^2)$$

A rough estimation on the error accumulation for cubic functions with $k=2^m$ forward steps is approximately $3m-2$ bits:

$$\frac{2^m(2^m-1)(2^m-2)}{6} < \frac{2^{3m}}{4}$$

Therefore, the minimum number of fractional bits required for 2^m forward steps is $n \geq 3m-2$. Based on this analysis, using 32-bit integer layout as shown in Figure 1 one can handle curves in a 1Kx1K grid up to $k=100$ forward steps. This assumes that the 32 bits are used for one sign bit + one overflow bit + 10 integer bits + 20 fractional bits. The a register in this case contains only twenty fractional bits. Or it can handle curves on a 512x512 grid up to $k=128$ forward steps, by assuming one sign bit, one overflow bit, 9 integer bits and 21 fractional bits.

2. Error analysis on registers with guard bits

With successive guard bits in the forward differencing registers as in Figure 3, the error accumulation is similar to the previous analysis except that additional error is introduced through the truncation of the guard bits. Again we analyze the error problem by examining the forward difference process and the contents accumulated in the registers. Each register has a different number of fractional bits, i.e., the a and b registers each have $3n$ bits, the c register has $2n$ bits, and the d register has n bits. The initial errors in the registers are $E_d = 2^{-n}$, $E_c = 2^{-2n}$ and $E_a = E_b = 2^{-3n}$. The content of the d register shown in the table indicates that the error accumulated in the d register after k cycles is dominated by three terms:

$$e_d \approx E_b \frac{k(k-1)(k-2)}{6} + E_c \frac{k(k-1)}{2} + k E_d + O(k^2)$$

	Contents of Forward Difference Register		
0	b	c	d
1	a+b	b+c+E_c	c+d +E_d
2	2a+b	a+2b+c+2E_c	b+2c+d +E_c+ 2E_d
3	3a+b	3a+3b+c+3E_c	a +3b+3c+d+3E_c+3E_d
4	4a+b	6a+4b+c+4E_c	4a +6b+4c+d+6E_c+4E_d
5	5a+b	10a+5b+c+5E_c	10a +10b+5c+d+10E_c+5E_d
6	6a+b	15a+6b+c+6E_c	20a +15b+6c+d+15E_c+6E_d
:	:	:	:
k	ka+b	ak(k-1)/2+kb +c+k E_c	ak(k-1)(k-2)/6 + bk(k-1)/2 +kc+d+E_c k(k-1)/2+kE_d

* The a register column is not shown in this table.

A rough estimate of the error accumulated with this method is approximately $3m+1$ bits for 2^m forward steps. In this case the minimum number of fractional bits required for 2^m forward steps is $3n \geq 3m+1$.

This method offers a dramatic improvement in precision handling when implemented in 32-bit integers even though addi-

tional error is introduced through the truncation of guard bits. Using 32-bit integer layout as shown in Figure 7, a register contains up to forty two fractional bits. One can process curves in a $2^{16}x2^{16}$ screen space up to 2^{13} forward steps. This precision is more than adequate for the display screen sizes currently available on the market. This is, therefore, a much more useful and powerful technique than the previous method which gives only 100 forward steps in a 1Kx1K space.

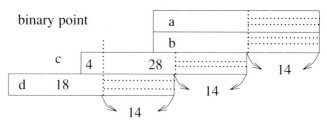

Figure 7. An integer forward difference implementation which can handle curves with up to 2^{13} forward steps.

3. Subpixel accuracy

For rendering antialiased curves, two or three additional bits of subpixel accuracy are desirable. In this case error propagation can be controlled, and higher subpixel accuracy can be achieved by subdividing to reduce the total number of forward steps in the curve. Error accumulation can be analyzed, and the maximum number of forward steps can be estimated by scaling up both the screen space and the curve, and then rendering the curve in this larger screen space. For example, an antialiased curve rendered in a 1Kx1K screen with 3 bits of subpixel address accuracy, is equivalent to a curve scaled up by a factor of eight and rendered in an 8Kx8K screen. The three least significant bits of the x,y coordinates are used as the subpixel address. The guidelines provided above can thus be used to analyze the error accumulation for a given application requirement and to calculate the limitations of a specified implementation.

4. Estimating the number of forward steps

Rockwood [15] derived a formula for estimating the number of forward difference steps required for a given Bezier curve with a specified minimum step size:

$$pmax = maximum \; |p_{i+1}-p_i| \quad \text{for } 0 \leq i \leq n-1$$

$$|f(t+\delta)-f(t)| \leq n \; \delta \; pmax$$

$$tesselation = \frac{1}{n \; pmax}$$

where n is the degree and the p_i's are the control points of the Bezier function. This formula is more intuitively clear by looking at the properties of Bezier functions:

(1) the derivative of a Bezier function $f(t)$ of degree n

$$f(t) = \sum_{i=0}^{i=n} p_i \frac{n!}{i!(n-i)!} t^i (1-t)^{n-i}$$

is a degree $n-1$ Bezier function $f'(t)$ using the vectors of the original polygon as its control points.

$$f'(t) = \sum_{i=0}^{i=m} n(p_{i+1}-p_i) \frac{m!}{i!(m-i)!} t^i (1-t)^{m-i} , \quad m=n-1;$$

(2) the derivative $f'(t)$ is the velocity of $f(t)$, (3) the magnitude of the derivative $|f'(t)|$ is bounded by the convex hull of its own control points, and is equal to maximum $(|n \ (p_{i+1}-p_i)|)$.

When using forward differencing to render a curve with no missing pixels, the step sizes in both the x and y directions should be no greater than one pixel step. Since the x and y coordinates of a Bezier curve are defined by two independent Bezier functions, the tesselation number can be computed in terms of the maximum convexhull of the x coordinate and the y coordinate instead of the convexhull of the length of the polygon:

$$xmax = maximum(x_{i+1} - x_i)$$

$$ymax = maximum(y_{i+1} - y_i)$$

$$pmax = maximum(xmax, ymax).$$

This tesselation number is less expensive to compute and is on the average 30% smaller than the number computed using vector length. However, it is big enough to ensure no x or y step size is more than one pixel.

5. Error bound on AFD without guard bits

In a previous paper the authors observed that the error accumulated using OFD gives an upper bound on the error accumulated using AFD. OFD uses a fixed parametric increment sufficiently small so as to prevent missing pixels in the highest velocity region of the curve. AFD, on the other hand, increases its parametric increment whenever the step size is too small. The parametric step size used in AFD is always greater than or equal to that used in OFD. Thus, the total number of forward steps in AFD is considerably smaller than that in OFD if the velocity of the curve is not constant. In the case of OFD, $2k$ forward steps can accumulate an error of approximately

$$e_d \ (OFD) \approx \frac{2k(2k-1)(2k-2)}{6}$$

With an adjust-up operation in AFD $2k$ forward steps is reduced to k forward steps which consequently introduces an error of approximately

$$e_d \ (AFD) \approx 2^3 \ \frac{k(k-1)(k-2)}{6}$$

The 2^3 factor is due to the left shift 3-bits in an adjust-up operation. The result shows that the error accumulated in AFD is always less than or equal to the error accumulated in OFD:

$$\frac{2k(2k-1)(2k-2)}{6} > 2^3 \ \frac{k(k-1)(k-2)}{6}$$

6. Error bound on AFD with guard bits

When using registers with successive guard bits, the error accumulated in the d register, as discussed previously, is dominated by three terms:

$$E_b \frac{k(k-1)(k-2)}{6} + E_c \frac{k(k-1)}{2} + kE_d$$

The initial errors in the registers with n guard bits are $E_d = 2^{-16}, E_c = 2^{-n} E_d$ and $E_b = 2^{-2n} E_d$. The error accumulated in the d register after 2^n forward steps is

$$e_d \ (OFD) \approx (\frac{2^n(2^n-1)(2^n-2)}{6}2^{-2n} + \frac{2^n(2^n-1)}{2}2^{-n} + 2^n) \ E_d$$

In the case of AFD, there are only $n-1$ successive guard bits in the registers after an adjust-up operation is performed. Ordinarily the initialization errors in registers with $n-1$ guard bits would be $E_d = 2^{-16}$, $E_c = 2^{-n+1} E_d$ and $E_b = 2^{-2n+2} E_d$. However, the initial errors in the a, b and c registers are magnified by two due to the adjust-up operation $[U_C]$, which results in

$$E_c \approx 2^{-n+2} E_d \quad and \quad E_b \approx 2^{-2n+3} E_d$$

The error accumulated after one adjust-up operation followed by 2^{n-1} forward steps is $e_d \ (AFD) \approx$

$$(\frac{k(k-1)(k-2)2^{-2n+3}}{6} + \frac{k(k-1)2^{-n+2}}{2} + 2^{n-1}) \ E_d$$

where $k = 2^{n-1}$. The result shows that $e_d(AFD) \leq e_d(OFD)$, i.e. the error accumulated in AFD through an adjust up operation and 2^{n-1} forward steps is no greater than the error accumulated in OFD through 2^n forward steps.

7. Overflow control

The issues of precision control and estimation of the number of forward steps have been discussed above. Overflow is another issue of great concern when using integer AFD. The following section will analyze this issue using cubic Bezier curves and the convex hull property of Bezier functions. A cubic Bezier curve is defined by four control points, p_a, p_b, p_c, and p_d which reside in a screen size of $2^{13}x2^{13}$:

$$|p_a| < 2^{13}, \ |p_b| < 2^{13}, \ |p_c| < 2^{13}, \ |p_d| < 2^{13}$$

Three times the convexhull of the curve is bounded by 2^n

$$3|p_a - p_b| < 2^n, \ 3|p_b - p_c| < 2^n, \ 3|p_c - p_d| < 2^n$$

Here the notation "$3|p_a - p_b| < 2^n$" implies the x coordinate $3|p_a(x) - p_b(x)| < 2^n$ and the y coordinate $3|p_a(y) - p_b(y)| < 2^n$. The Bezier control points can be transformed into polynomial basis by

$$\begin{cases} D = p_d \\ C = 3(p_c - p_d) \\ B = 3(p_b - p_c) - 3(p_c - p_d) \\ A = (p_a - p_b) - 2(p_b - p_c) + (p_c - p_d) \end{cases}$$

The coefficients in polynomial basis are then converted into forward difference basis. Under the assumptions above, the polynomial coefficients A, B, C, and D are bounded by

$$|D| < 2^n, \ |C| < 2^n, \ |2B| < 2^{n+2}, \ |6A| < 2^{n+3}.$$

Using the register layout shown in Figure 7, the d register contains 18 integer bits and 14 fractional bits. The maximum value the registers can hold at initialization time is less than 2^{17}. If the Bezier control points satisfy the following constraints the maximum number of forward steps required is 2^{13} and there will be no overflow problem at the initialization stage.

$$3|p_a - p_b| < 2^{13}, \ 3|p_b - p_c| < 2^{13}, \ 3|p_c - p_d| < 2^{13}$$

Next we look at the possibility of overflowing during the forward differencing process. We first extend a given curve $f(t) = t^3 p_a + 3t^2(1-t)p_b + 3t(1-t)^2 p_c + (1-t)^3 p_d$ by drawing an extension to the curve for the parameter range $t=1.0$ to $t=2.0$, as shown in Figure 8.

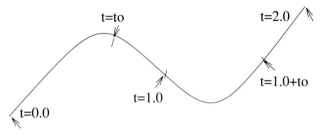

Figure 8. A segment of curve with the parameter ranging from $t = t_o$ to $t = 1.0 + t_o$.

At any instant during the process when the parameter is at $t = t_o$, the contents in the four registers, a, b, c, and d, are the forward difference coefficients of the portion of the extended curve with parameter ranging from $t = t_o$ to $t = 1.0 + t_o$ and scaled by the current tesselation δ :

$$\begin{cases} d = f(t_o) \\ c = f'(t_o) + f''(t_o)\delta/2 + f'''(t_o)\delta^2/6 \\ b = f''(t_o) + f'''(t_o)\delta \\ a = f'''(t_o)\delta \end{cases}$$

The derivatives $f'(t)$, $f''(t)$ and $f'''(t)$ are lower order Bezier functions.

$$f'(t) = 3[t^2(p_a - p_b) + 2t(1-t)(p_b - p_c) + (1-t)^2(p_c - p_d)]$$

$$f''(t) = 6[t(p_a - 2p_b + p_c)] + (1-t)(p_b - 2p_c + p_d)]$$

$$f'''(t) = 6[(p_a - p_b) - 2(p_b - p_c) + (p_c - p_d)]$$

The bound on the convex hull of functions $|f'(t)|$ is 2^{13}, on functions $|f''(t)|$ is 2^{15}, and on functions $|f'''(t)|$ is 2^{16}. Therefore, the magnitude of the derivatives satisfy the constraints at any instant $0.0 \le t_o \le 1.0$

$$|f(t)|, |f'(t)|, |f''(t)|, |f'''(t)| < 2^{16}$$

With the integer AFD implementation we proposed in Figure 5, the d register has 16 integer bits and 16 fractional bits. The maximum number of forward steps this scheme can handle is 2^{12}. In this case, the constraints on the convexhull of the control polygon is

$$3|p_a - p_b| < 2^{12}, 3|p_b - p_c| < 2^{12}, 3|p_c - p_d| < 2^{12}$$

Integer AFD for Surfaces

AFD can be used to render shaded, textured, and trimmed surfaces. Texture and imagery can be mapped onto a surface as a function of the parameters s and t. Shading and image mapping on a bicubic surface is performed by drawing many isoparametric curves very close together so that no pixel gaps exist

in between. Each isoparametric curve is a cubic function of parameter t defined by a constant $s = s_i$. The spacing δs from one curve to the next is measured to decide whether the next curve should be drawn closer to or farther from the current curve.

A polynomial bicubic function can be converted into forward difference basis by the transformation:

$$\begin{bmatrix} 1 & 0 & 0 & 0 \\ 0 & \delta & \delta^2 & \delta^3 \\ 0 & 0 & 2\delta^2 & 6\delta^3 \\ 0 & 0 & 0 & 6\delta^3 \end{bmatrix} \begin{bmatrix} f_{00} & f_{01} & f_{02} & f_{03} \\ f_{10} & f_{11} & f_{12} & f_{13} \\ f_{20} & f_{21} & f_{22} & f_{23} \\ f_{30} & f_{31} & f_{32} & f_{33} \end{bmatrix} \begin{bmatrix} 1 & 0 & 0 & 0 \\ 0 & \beta & 0 & 0 \\ 0 & \beta^2 & 2\beta^2 & 0 \\ 0 & \beta^3 & 6\beta^3 & 6\beta^3 \end{bmatrix}$$

where the $f_{i,j}$'s are the control points in polynomial basis, and δ and β are the parametric increments in the s and t directions, respectively. A surface can be tesselated using ordinary forward differencing into $m*n$ four-sided polygons or m and n isoparametric curves by choosing the scaling factors to be $\delta=1/m$ and $\beta=1/n$. After basis conversion, a surface is described by three coordinate functions, $f_x(s,t)$, $f_y(s,t)$, and $f_z(s,t)$, each being a bicubic function of s and t. An isoparametric curve at a constant $s = s_i$ is a cubic function

$$f(s = s_i, t) = dB_0(t) + cB_1(t) + bB_2(t) + aB_3(t)$$

where the four coefficients a, b, c, d can be computed from the surface matrix $[A]$ using two dimensional AFD. These coefficients are stored in the first row of matrix $[A]$, i.e. a_{00}, a_{01}, a_{02}, and a_{03}. In the curve-to-curve outer loop, a forward-step $[F]$ operation is applied to the surface matrix $[A]$ to produce the coefficients of the next isoparametric curve :

$$\begin{bmatrix} a_{00}+a_{10} & a_{01}+a_{11} & a_{02}+a_{12} & a_{03}+a_{13} \\ a_{10}+a_{20} & a_{11}+a_{21} & a_{12}+a_{22} & a_{13}+a_{23} \\ a_{20}+a_{30} & a_{21}+a_{31} & a_{22}+a_{32} & a_{23}+a_{33} \\ a_{30} & a_{31} & a_{32} & a_{33} \end{bmatrix}$$

After a forward-step operation is applied, the first row of $[A]$, $a_{00}+a_{10}$, $a_{01}+a_{11}$, $a_{02}+a_{12}$, and $a_{03}+a_{13}$ are the coefficients of the next isoparametric curve. These coefficients are then used in the pixel-to-pixel inner loop for computing the address of the pixels on the isoparametric curve. If the spacing between the current curve and the next curve is too small, an adjust-up operation is performed to increase the spacing before a forward step takes place. If the spacing is too large, it is reduced with the $[D]$ operator before $[F]$ is applied:

$$\begin{bmatrix} a'_{0j} \\ a'_{1j} \\ a'_{2j} \\ a'_{3j} \end{bmatrix} = [U] \begin{bmatrix} a_{0j} \\ a_{1j} \\ a_{2j} \\ a_{3j} \end{bmatrix} \quad \text{and} \quad \begin{bmatrix} a'_{0j} \\ a'_{1j} \\ a'_{2j} \\ a'_{3j} \end{bmatrix} = [D] \begin{bmatrix} a_{0j} \\ a_{1j} \\ a_{2j} \\ a_{3j} \end{bmatrix}$$

The two initial parametric increments of AFD can be estimated based on the initial velocity of a surface, i.e. $\delta \approx \partial f/\partial s(0,0)$, $\beta \approx \partial f/\partial t(0,0)$. By choosing these factors to be powers of two, $\delta = 2^{-m}$ and $\beta = 2^{-n}$, the initialization can be greatly simplified.

1. Hybrid integer AFD for surfaces

AFD surface rendering technique can also be implemented in integer arithmetic as long as the precision limitation is carefully considered. When using forward differencing for surface rendering, the error accumulates during both the curve-to-curve and pixel-to-pixel procedures. The curve-to-curve outer loop generates the coefficients of the next isoparametric curve and the pixel-to-pixel inner loop computing the pixel addresses. If 2^m forward steps are spent in the curve loop and 2^n steps in the pixel loop, the error in the a register is magnified by a factor of $2^m(2^m-1)(2^m-2)/6$ in the curve outer loop and a factor of $2^n(2^n-1)(2^n-2)/6$ in the pixel inner loop. The error can accumulate as much as 2^{m+n} forward steps have accumulated. As shown in the analysis section, the 32-bit integer AFD is adequate for rendering curves in a 4Kx4K space up to 2^{12} forward steps. Using 32-bit integer AFD for surface rendering, the maximum number of forward steps of the scheme is limited to $m+n \leq 12$, i.e. approximately 64 curves each no longer than 64 pixels. Surfaces requiring more than 64x64 forward steps must be subdivided.

Alternatively, one can implement the curve outer loop in 64-bit AFD to compute the coefficients of the isoparametric curves and pixel inner loop in 32-bit AFD to compute the pixel addresses. This hybrid scheme provides more precision and uses proper operators in each loop, for example, $[F]$, $[U]$, and $[D]$ in the outer loop and $[F_C]$, $[U_C]$, and $[D_C]$ in the inner loop. Matrix $[F_C]$ is the same as $[F_i]$ except that the d register is in 16.16 fixed point format. A forward step in the curve outer loop can be performed with twelve 64-bit-integer additions (a 64-bit-integer is stored in two 32-bit integers). A forward step in the pixel inner loop can be done with three additions and two register shifts.

The cost of register realignment before entering a pixel inner loop can be eliminated by properly scaling the coefficients of matrix $[A]$ in the t direction at the initialization time so that the first 32 bits of the coefficients a_{00}, a_{01}, a_{02}, and a_{03} can be input directly to the 32-bit integer AFD pixel inner loop:

$$\begin{bmatrix} 1 & 0 & 0 & 0 \\ 0 & \delta & \delta^2 & \delta^3 \\ 0 & 0 & 2\delta^2 & 6\delta^3 \\ 0 & 0 & 0 & 6\delta^3 \end{bmatrix} \begin{bmatrix} f_{00} & f_{01} & f_{02} & f_{03} \\ f_{10} & f_{11} & f_{12} & f_{13} \\ f_{20} & f_{21} & f_{22} & f_{23} \\ f_{30} & f_{31} & f_{32} & f_{33} \end{bmatrix} \begin{bmatrix} 1 & 0 & 0 & 0 \\ 0 & 1 & 0 & 0 \\ 0 & 2^{-n} & 2 & 0 \\ 0 & 2^{-2n} & 6\,2^{-n} & 6\,2^{-n} \end{bmatrix}$$

While rendering a surface, the decision to adjust up or down, or to forward step is made based on the distance between two adjacent isoparametric curves, $d(t) = |f(s+\delta s, t) - f(s, t)|$. The distance is a cubic function of t. The maximum distance between the two curves can be estimated using the Bezier convex hull property if the distance function $d(t)$ is converted into Bezier basis [6]. Converting $d(t)$ into Bezier basis at every curve is quite expensive. Instead of converting $d(t)$ at every curve, one can maintain a dual matrix $[B]$ to minimize this overhead. Matrix B is transformed into Bezier basis in the t direction and forward difference basis in the s direction. Matrix B and the surface matrix A are operated on synchronously in the curve-to-curve outer loop. The first row of A stores the coefficients of the current isoparametric curve. The second row of B stores the distance to the next isoparametric curve. The Bezier convex hull property can be applied directly to the second

row of B to find the maximum distance between two consecutive isoparametric curves.

2. Dicing with integer AFD

An anti-aliasing technique [7] was proposed based on *dicing* to produce micropolygons followed by skittered subsampling and averaging for fast high-quality rendering of complex images. Micropolygons are the basic geometric unit of the technique. They are flat shaded quadrilaterals approximately 1/2 pixel on a side in screen space. Screen space derivatives of a surface are used to estimate how finely to dice, and subdivision and ordinary forward differencing are used to do the actual dicing.

The algorithm presented by Cook for dicing, shading, clipping, and rendering micropolygons is as follows:

> Dice the primitive into a grid of micropolygons;
> Compute normals and tanget vectors for the
>   micropolygons in the grid;
> Shade the micropolygons in the grid;
> Break the grid into micropolygons;
> For each micropolygon
>   Bound the micropolygon in eye space;
>   If the micropolygon is outside the hither-yon range,
>   cull it;
>   Convert the micropolygon to screen space;
>   Bound the micropolygon in screen space;
>   For each sample point inside the screen space bound
>   If the sample point is inside the micropolygon
>   Calculate the z of the micropolygon at the
>   sample point by interpolation;
>   If the z at the sample point is less than the z
>   in the buffer
>   Replace the sample in the buffer
>   with this sample;

Integer AFD can be a much more efficient method for dicing in screen space since the screen space step size is the threshold which controls adjust up, adjust down, or forward step.

A similar algorithm is proposed here using integer AFD to dice a surface.

> AFD a primitive into strips of isoparametric curves;
> AFD an isoparametric curve into a sequence of points;
> Form a chain of micropolygons in between
>   two consecutive isoparametric curves
> For each micropolygon
>   Bound the micropolygon in eye space;
>   Cull the micropolygon if outside the hither-yon range;
>   Bound the micropolygon in screen space;
>   Cull the micropolygon if outside the viewport range;
>   For each sample point inside the screen space bound
>   If the sample point is inside the the micropolygon
>   Interpolate the z at the sample point;
>   If the z at the sample point is less than the z
>   in the buffer
>   Shade the micropolygon if not yet done;
>   Replace the sample in the buffer
>   with this sample;

A surface is first sliced into many strips of isoparametric curves using 64-bit integer AFD. Two consecutive isoparametric curves are no more than 1/2 pixel apart. Each isoparametric curve is then tesselated into a sequence of points using 32-bit integer AFD with two consecutive points lying no more than 1/2 pixel apart. When the tesselation is done, two consecutive isoparametric curves form a chain of micropolygons. Each micropolygon is a triangle with two vertices on one isoparametric curve and one vertex on the other isoparametric curve. Micropolygons are approximately 1/2 pixel on a side in screen space, and flat shaded.

Using synchronized AFD technique, different components of a surface can be computed in difference spaces. For example, the forward difference coefficients of the coordinate functions can be computed in the screen space while the shading functions are calculated in the eye space.

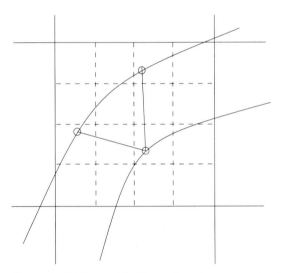

Figure 9. Dicing a bicubic surface into microtriangles with integer AFD in subpixel grid.

The techniques proposed in the shading paper [16] can be used for calculating the shading function N_x, N_y, N_z, $N.L$ and $N.H$ of a bicubic surface. Functions N_x, N_y, and N_z are the components of the normalized or un-normalized normal vector functions, and $N.L$ and $N.H$ are the inner products of the normal vector function with the light source vector L and the high light vector H

$$N.L(s,t) = L_x N_x(s,t) + L_y N_y(s,t) + L_z N_z(s,t)$$

$$N.H(s,t) = H_x N_x(s,t) + H_y N_y(s,t) + H_z N_z(s,t)$$

The coordinate functions and the shading functions are bicubic function of parameters s and t. These functions can be stepped along synchronously using integer AFD. The adjustment decision is made based on the screen step size information. The coordinate functions are diced directly in screen space, thus, the overhead of dicing a primitive in eye space and transforming the micropolygons into screen space is eliminated. The shading functions are computed and then diced in the eye space. The normal vector of each micropolygon is generated by AFD instead of computed at every micropolygon. The overhead of computing the inner products $N.L$ and $N.H$ per micropolygon is also eliminated in this method at the cost of AFDing two bicubic functions. The shading value of a pixel is computed in the inner most loop after the z buffer depth comparison, thus, the no cost is spent on computing the shading of hidden pixels.

For point light source, the un-normalized normal vector functions are used and two inner products and one normalization per pixel are required to calculate the sahding values $N.L$ and $N.H$.

Discussion

The threshold for adjustment in AFD may be set to 0.5 and 1.0, i.e. adjusting up when x and y steps are less than .5 pixel and adjusting down when x or y step is greater than 1 pixel. This ensures no missing pixels and reduces the pixel overpainting rate. Alternatively, one can use 1.0 and 2.0 as the thresholds, filling in a missing pixel whenever x or y takes a two-pixel step. The difference between the two is that in the former case redundant pixels are eliminated and in the latter, missing pixels are filled. The advantage of using a higher threshold, such as 10 to 20 pixels, is to reduce the number of forward steps and to improve the performance by rendering a curve with a polyline.

An adjust-down operation performed on a step size of greater than 1.0 can sometimes result in a step size of less than 0.5. To avoid getting into an infinite loop of adjust-ups and adjust-downs, it is helpful to enforce a forward step before an adjust-up in the implementation.

The computational complexity of the two surface rendering algorithms described in the previous section may be compared by assuming that a bicubic surface is diced into n^2 vertices constituting n^2 quadrilaterals or $2n^2$ triangles. It takes 16 multiplies and 12 additions to do a 4x4 point transformation. Computing the normal vectors of a quadrilateral takes 6 multiplies and 9 additions. The inner product computation for shading values $N.L$ and $N.H$ costs 6 multiplies and 4 additions per quadrilateral. The overhead of dicing a primitive in eye space, computing the shading values on every micropolygon, and transforming the micropolygons into screen space totals to 28 multiplies and 25 additions per quadrilateral. For a total of n^2 micropolygons, the overhead is $28n^2$ multiplies and $25n^2$ additions per surface.

Using the synchronized AFD technique, a forward-step in the curve outer loop costs 12 additions (or 48 additions when using 64-bit integer AFD) and a forward-step in the pixel inner loop costs 3 additions. Dicing a function into n isoparametric curves each with n vertices takes a total of $48n$ additions in the curve loop and $3n^2$ additions in the pixel loop. Computing five shading functions N_x, N_y, N_z, $N.L$ and and $N.H$ costs a total of $15n^2 + 240n$ additions per surface. The AFD method costs a total of $18 n^2 + 288n$ additions. AFD has the overhead of computing the coefficients of the $N.L(s,t)$ and $N.H(s,t)$ shading functions. AFD has the advantages that (1) primitives are diced in screen space with better control of the micropolygon size; (2) the shading values of hidden pixels are not computed, which may account for a large savings in computation when the depth order of the scene is not optimized; (3) the computational complexity is significantly lower.

Acknowledgements

The authors are very grateful to Lewis Knapp for many helpful discussions and inputs to this project and for reviewing early drafts of this paper. Special thanks to John Recker for helping with the implementation and profiling. We thank Victor Klassen for several enlightening email conversations about his technique.

References

1. Salim Abi-Ezzi, "The Graphical Processing of NURB Surfaces," *Industrial Associate Review Summary*, November 1988. Rensselaer Design Research Center, Rensselaer Polytechnic Institute

2. Jerry Van Aken and Mark Novak, "Curve-Drawing Algorithms for Raster Displays," *ACM Transactions on Graphics*, vol. 4, no. 2, pp. 147-169, April 1985.

3. Richard Bartels, John Beatty, and Brian Barsky, *An Introduction to Splines for use in Computer Graphics & Geometric Modeling,* pp. 400-406, Morgan Kaufmann Publishers, 1987.

4. Edwin Catmull, *A Subdivision Algorithm for Computer Display of Curved Surfaces,* Thesis in Computer Science, University of Utah, UTEC-CSc-74-133, 1974.

5. George M. Chaikin, "An Algorithm for High Speed Curve Generation," *Computer Graphics and Image Processing*, vol. 3, pp. 346-349, 1974.

6. Robert Cook, *Patch Work,* Tech. Memo 118, Computer Div., Lucasfilm Ltd., June 1985.

7. Robert Cook, Loren Carpenter, and Edwin Catmull, "The Reyes Image Rendering Architecture," *Proceedings of SIGGRAPH '87, Computer Graphics*, vol. 21, 1987.

8. James Foley and Andries Van Dam, "Fundamentals of Interactive Computer Graphics," *Addison-Wesley Publishers*, p. 533, 1982.

9. Victor Klassen, "Drawing Antialiased Cubic Spline Curves Using Adaptive Forward Differencing," *ACM Transactions on Graphics, under revision*, 1989.

10. Victor Klassen, "Integer Forward Differencing of Cubic Polynomials: Analysis and Algorithms," *ACM Transactions on Graphics, under revision*, 1989.

11. Jeffrey M. Lane and Richard F. Riesenfeld, "A Theoretical Development for the Computer Generation of Piecewise Polynomial Surfaces," *IEEE Transactions on Pattern Analysis and Machine Intelligence*, vol. PAMI-2, pp. 35-46, 1980.

12. Sheue-Ling Lien, Michael Shantz, and Vaughan Pratt, "Adaptive Forward Differencing for Rendering Curves and Surfaces," *Proceedings of SIGGRAPH '87, Computer Graphics*, vol. 21, 1987.

13. M. L. V. Pitteway, "Algorithm for drawing ellipses or hyperbolae with a digital plotter," *Computer Journal*, vol. 10, no. 3, pp. 282-289, Nov. 1967.

14. Vaughan Pratt, "Techniques for Conic Splines," *Proceedings of SIGGRAPH '87, Computer Graphics*, vol. 19, 1985.

15. Alyn Rockwood, *A Generalized Scanning Technique for Display of Parametrically Defined Surfaces,* 7, IEEE Computer Graphics and Applications, August 1987.

16. Michael Shantz and Sheue-Ling Lien, "Shading Bicubic Patches," *Proceedings of SIGGRAPH '87, Computer Graphics*, vol. 21, 1987.

17. Michael Shantz and Sheue-Ling Chang, "Rendering Trimmed NURBS with Adaptive Forward Differencing," *Proceedings of SIGGRAPH '88, Computer Graphics*, vol. 22, 1988.

Curve-to-Curve Associations in Spline-Based Inbetweening and Sweeping

Richard H. Bartels
and
Ronald T. Hardock

University of Waterloo
Department of Computer Science
Computer Graphics Laboratory
Waterloo, Ontario
Canada N2L 3G1

Abstract

We are concerned in this paper with associations between spline curves that will hold at all inbetween positions when the control points of these curves are used as key points for animation or sweeping. It is established that any association between two spline curves that can be expressed as the equality of two linear mappings will hold throughout an inbetweening process provided the inbetweening trajectories are coordinated splines that uniquely interpolate the contol-point key positions. Multiple associations are possible, so long as the basic requirements of linearity and coordination are observed.

Introduction

This is **not** a paper about animation. It is about a property of splines that has applications in the fields of animation and computer-aided geometric design. The terminology of key-frame animation is convenient, however, and we will use it to present our results. We will give our results in terms of *xy*-curves with trajectories in *t*. Again, this is a presentational convenience. The observations we make can easily be applied to higher dimensions, e.g. to the movement of spline surfaces through time or the sweeping of volume densities.

We take the paper by Reeves [8] as a starting point. Reeves describes a means of controlling, throughout inbetweening, relationships that hold between curves in keyframes. He does this by introducing auxiliary curves, from key to key, that enforce the relationships in the temporal domain. Reeves calls these temporal curves *moving point constraints*. These were introduced to provide control over both position and dynamics in an animation, whereas we are concerned only with positional associations in this paper. Such things as the point contact of two curves, the tangency of two curves, the translational or angular orientation of one curve to another are the associations that interest us here.

Since the creation of surfaces by sweeping and extrusion also corresponds to a process of the keyframing type, where the trajectories are in space rather than in time, what we learn here can be useful in computer-aided geometric design as well as in animation. (More precisely, the correspondence that can

be drawn is between keyframe inbetweening and *generalized cylinders* or *non-rigid sweeps* as surveyed by Pegna [7]. The difference between animation and sweeping is in the rendering. In animation, curves are swept through trajectories along the *t* axis, and a sequence of cross sections of the resulting "surface" is presented as the inbetweens. In sweeping, the trajectory axis is *z*, and the interest is in the surface itself, rather than in cross sections of it.)

While the mechanism of moving point constraints may be necessary to ensure that certain forms of association between key curves are maintained throughout the temporal domain, we felt that there ought to be some forms of useful association that would hold automatically throughout the inbetweening process without the complication of imposing constraints. For animation a desirable situation would be one in which the positional and dynamic aspects of an animation were unbundled, with positional relationships on inbetween frames proceeding automatically from the key frames and with dynamics available for independent adjustment by such techniques as [9] or [2]. For computer-aided design dynamics play no role, and positional aspects are all that matter.

A naive hope on our part was that we could express the curves in a key frame as spline curves in a desired association, and that inbetweening the control points would provide inbetween versions of the curves in the same state of association. This was put to the test. One spline curve, which we referred to as "Mickey's snout," was placed tangent to a another spline curve, which we referred to as "Mickey's nose," in a sequence of keyframes that could be loosely described as "Mickey nodding his head." The positions of each given control point of a curve in each keyframe were interpolated by the simplest method described in [6] to provide a trajectory for that control point. The inbetween curves were constructed from the inbetween positions of the control points. The result of doing this is sometimes acceptable and is sometimes not.

The curve-to-curve association that exists within each keyframe may or may not be maintained throughout the inbetween frames. In particular, Mickey's nose may or may not separate from his snout. In Figure 1 we show two keyframes and an inbetween frame for which a curve-to-curve association is maintained. Figure 2 shows a similar situation for which the association is broken in the inbetween frame. Why some configurations showed difficulties while others did not came to be known among us as "the Mickey's nose problem."

In this paper we present conditions ensuring that associations will hold between spline curves under straightforward trajectory interpolation for their control points. The result will be that, if the trajectory interpolation satisfies a few

Research supported by Canada's NSERC Operating, Strategic, and Infrastructure programs, Province of Ontario's ITRC program, and grants from General Motors, Digital, and Silicon Graphics.

straightforward properties, and if the curve-to-curve association likewise satisfies a few properties, then the association will hold automatically throughout all inbetweens. No additional constraints need be imposed. Admittedly, there will be many associations that will not satisfy the properties we set out. One of our fundamental requirements will involve *linearity*, and an association such as: "the arc length of curve R should be a certain multiple of the area enclosed by curve S," to give a wild example, would not fill the bill. However, as we will see, associations that relate a point or a derivative on one curve with a point or derivative on another, possibly through a modeling transformation, will satisfy our requirements.

Representing Curves and Trajectories

Each curve under consideration is to be expressed parametrically in *control-point/basis-function format:*

$$R(u) = \sum_i U_i B_i(u).$$

We make no restrictions on the basis functions B_i, so this format will equally well describe B-spline curves, Bézier curves, Beta-spline curves, Cardinal-spline curves, or NURBS among others ([1] and [4]).

The chief item of interest is some form of association between one curve $R(u)$ and a second curve

$$S(v) = \sum_j V_j C_j(v).$$

The second curve is to be expressed in the same general format, but there is no requirement that the basis functions C_j be related in any way to the basis functions B_i. Hence, we can study associations between B-spline curves and Cardinal curves, for example, or between Bézier curves of one degree and those of another.

We will not be presenting a list of specific associations. Such a list is open ended. Instead, we will be establishing a set of conditions, and any association that conforms can be added to the list. However, we will give examples to show that contact, tangency, fixed separation, and angular orientation are among the associations that can be established to hold throughout sweeping and inbetweening.

The kth *key* of one of the curves, for example $R(u)$, is formed when the control points U_i of the curve are located in some chosen positions $U_{i,k}$ for $k = 0, ..., n$, and the curve is defined relative to those positions. This gives us the kth *instance* of the curve R, which we denote by $R_k(u)$:

$$R_k(u) = \sum_i U_{i,k} B_i(u).$$

A *trajectory* is formed for one of the control points U_i when the sequence of positions $U_{i,0}, ..., U_{i,n}$ is interpolated by a parametric curve, also to be given in control-point/basis-function format,

$$U_i(t) = \sum_l P_{l,i} D_l(t).$$

The values $t_0, ..., t_n$ of the parameter t are those that provide the key positions of the control points U_i for any i, that is

$$U_{i,k} = U_i(t_k) = \sum_l P_{l,i} D_l(t_k).$$

The basis functions D_l are not required to be the same as the basis functions used to represent either of the curves R or S.

To establish curve-to-curve coordination between $R(u)$ and $S(v)$, we first require *conformity of trajectories*. This means that a common interpolation scheme must be applied to all the control points of both curves. Consequently, the control points of $S(v)$ will satisfy equations of the form

$$V_j(t) = \sum_m Q_{m,j} D_m(t)$$

for the same basis functions D that were used for the control points U, and we will recover the key positions of V_j as we did for those of the U_i,

$$V_{j,k} = V_j(t_k) = \sum_m Q_{m,j} D_m(t_k).$$

This establishes the kth instance of the curve S,

$$S_k(u) = \sum_j V_{j,k} C_j(u).$$

If we substitute the interpolation curves for U and V into the definitions of R and S this provides us with *swept versions* of these curves that very in t as well as in their parametric variables,

$$R(u,t) = \sum_i U_i(t)B_i(u) = \sum_i \sum_l P_{l,i} D_l(t)B_i(u)$$

$$S(v,t) = \sum_j V_j(t)C_j(v) = \sum_j \sum_m Q_{m,j} D_m(t)C_j(v).$$

We can recover the kth instance of R or S from these swept versions by substituting the values of t given by $t_0, ..., t_n$:

$$R_k(u) = R(u,t_k) = \sum_i U_{i,k} B_i(u)$$

$$S_k(v) = S(v,t_k) = \sum_j V_{j,k} C_j(v).$$

In addition to the requirement of *conformity of trajectories*, we will also require the interpolation process to be *unique* and *linearly dependent on the data*. By this we mean that all the trajectories derive from a nonsingular system of equations, for example

$$\begin{bmatrix} D_0(t_0) & \cdots & D_n(t_0) \\ \vdots & \vdots & \vdots \\ D_0(t_n) & \cdots & D_n(t_n) \end{bmatrix} \begin{bmatrix} P_{0,i} \\ \vdots \\ P_{n,i} \end{bmatrix} = \begin{bmatrix} U_{0,i} \\ \vdots \\ U_{n,i} \end{bmatrix}.$$

This means that the coefficients $P_{l,i}$ and $Q_{m,j}$ that define the trajectories will be unique linear combinations of the control points of the corresponding key curves

$$P_{l,i} = \sum_\lambda d_{l,\lambda} U_{i,\lambda}$$

and

$$Q_{m,j} = \sum_\lambda d_{m,\lambda} V_{j,\lambda},$$

where the coefficients d are the elements of the inverse of the matrix $\left[D_\alpha(t_\beta) \right]$ of the trajectory system.

Common methods of interpolation that are used to provide trajectories in animation and computer-aided geometric design are, in fact, unique and linearly dependent on the data.

Specific methods of this type worth mentioning are Catmull-Rom spline interpolation and some of its variations [6], natural cubic spline interpolation [5], and trajectories in B-spline format [9] found by solving a system of interpolation equations [3].

Key Associations that Hold for Inbetweens

The result of the previous section is that the swept versions of R and S can be given in the following forms:

$$R(u,t) = \sum_i \sum_l \sum_\lambda d_{l,\lambda} U_{i,\lambda} D_l(t) B_i(u)$$

and

$$S(v,t) = \sum_j \sum_m \sum_\lambda d_{m,\lambda} V_{j,\lambda} D_m(t) C_j(v).$$

The kth instance of each curve is given by

$$R(u,t_k) = \sum_i \sum_l \sum_\lambda d_{l,\lambda} U_{i,\lambda} D_l(t_k) B_i(u)$$

and

$$S(v,t_k) = \sum_j \sum_m \sum_\lambda d_{m,\lambda} V_{j,\lambda} D_m(t_k) C_j(v).$$

To finish our development, we will require that the association that holds between $R_k(u) = R(u,t_k)$ and $S_k(v) = S(v,t_k)$ for each key k be expressible as a *mapping equality*, that is

$$F\left(\sum_i U_{i,k} B_i(u)\right) = G\left(\sum_j V_{j,k} C_j(v)\right),$$

and that the maps F and G be *linear*, that is,

$$\sum_\mu \alpha_\mu F\left(\sum_i U_{i,k} B_i(u)\right) = F\left(\sum_\mu \alpha_\mu \sum_i U_{i,k} B_i(u)\right)$$

$$\sum_\mu \alpha_\mu G\left(\sum_j V_{j,k} C_j(v)\right) = G\left(\sum_\mu \alpha_\mu \sum_j V_{j,k} C_j(u)\right)$$

for any collection of scaler values α_μ. If this is the case, then using $d_{l,k} D_l(t)$ for α and l for μ with each fixed k and t gives us , on the left side of the mapping equality,

$$\sum_l d_{l,k} D_l(t) F\left(\sum_i U_{i,k} B_i(u)\right)$$

$$= F\left(\sum_l d_{l,k} D_l(t) \sum_i U_{i,k} B_i(u)\right),$$

and repeating the process with $\alpha = 1$ and k used in place of μ gives

$$\sum_k F\left(\sum_l d_{l,k} D_l(t) \sum_i U_{i,k} B_i(u)\right)$$

$$= F\left(\sum_k \sum_l d_{l,k} D_l(t) \sum_i U_{i,k} B_i(u)\right)$$

$$= F(R(u,t)).$$

Likewise, on the right side of the mapping equality,

$$\sum_m \sum_k d_{m,k} D_m(t) G\left(\sum_j V_{j,k} C_j(v)\right)$$

$$= G\left(\sum_m \sum_k d_{m,k} D_m(t) \sum_j V_{j,k} C_j(v)\right)$$

$$= G(S(v,t)).$$

This means that, if association F (or G) holds at key k for all k, it will also hold for all possible inbetween positions.

To summarize, when the curves and trajectories under consideration are in control-point/basis-function format, when the trajectories conform and derive from a unique interpolation process that depends linearly on the data, and when the key associations are expressible as mapping equalities with linear maps, then the associations between curves that hold in the keys will hold throughout the trajectories.

This is a general statement about inheritance. We emphasize that it is unnecessary to know the details of any of the formulas. Constants like $d_{m,k}$, which are not the normal output of the trajectory interpolation, do not have to be dealt with. The formulas we have given were used for the sake of advancing the presentation. Only the properties of our summary, which are quite broadly stated, need to be verified. Inheritance proceeds automatically from *format*, *conformity*, and *nonsingular-linear-system interpolation*, and inheritance holds for all associations that can be expressed as *linear mapping equalities*. This covers a great number of practical cases. We give some examples in the next section, but they do not, by any means, exhaust the possibilities.

Examples

One simple example of maps F and G that satisfy the requirements of linearity is given by *evaluation at a point*. Let

$$F(f(u)) = f(u')$$

for any function of u, and let

$$G(g(v)) = g(v')$$

for any function of v. It is easily verified that evaluation at a point is a linear map, and it corresponds to the key association that

$$R_k(u') = S_k(v')$$

at all keys k for given, fixed parameter values u' and v', as is shown in Figure 3.

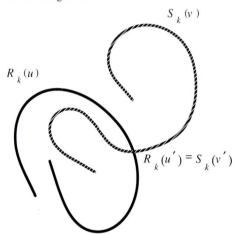

Figure 3. The association at key k is given by evaluation at a point. This will ensure that the point association shown will be maintained for all inbetweens.

This is enough to keep Mickey's nose connected to his snout, but not enough to keep his nose from rotating around the point of contact. To prevent that, we need to control tangency.

Let F and G correspond to *differentiation at a point*, that is

$$F(f(u)) = \frac{d}{du} f(u')$$

for any function of u and

$$G(g(v)) = \frac{d}{dv} g(v')$$

for any function of v. Differentiation at a point is also a linear map, and it corresponds to the key association that the tangent vector of $R_k(u)$ at $u = u'$ corresponds to the tangent vector of $S_k(v)$ at $v = v'$. In fact, nothing would be changed if F and G were multiplied by any nonzero scaling constants. This would mean that, if the tangent vector of $R_k(u)$ at $u = u'$ were equal to a fixed multiple of the tangent vector of $S_k(v)$ at $v = v'$, then the same tangent-vector association would hold for all possible keys, as is indicated by Figure 4.

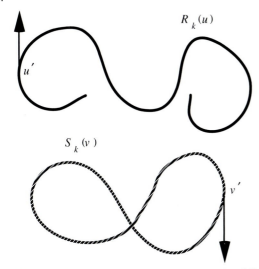

Figure 4. The association at key k is given by differentiation at a point. This means that the tangent vector to R at the chosen value of u is parallel to the tangent vector to S at the chosen value of v. The orientation of one tangent vector with respect the the other will depend upon the sign of the scaling constants.

This is enough to keep Mickey's nose oriented consistently with the end of his snout, but it does not prevent the nose from floating free.

We need one more observation to retire the problem of Mickey's nose. That observation is that several associations can hold simultaneously between R and S, so long as one association's formula is independent of the other. In brief, if F and $\bar{F}$ are independent maps (that is, if F is not defined in terms of $\bar{F}$, or conversely), if the same holds for G and $\bar{G}$, and if

$$\bar{F}\left(\sum_i U_{i,k} B_i(u)\right) = \bar{G}\left(\sum_j V_{j,k} C_j(v)\right)$$

as well as

$$F\left(\sum_i U_{i,k} B_i(u)\right) = G\left(\sum_j V_{j,k} C_j(v)\right),$$

then

$$\bar{F}(R(u,t)) = \bar{G}(S(v,t))$$

as well as

$$F(R(u,t)) = G(S(v,t)).$$

An example of such independence would come by taking F and G to be evaluation at the points u' and v', respectively, and by taking $\bar{F}$ and $\bar{G}$ to be differentiation, also at the points u' and v', respectively. Since the operation of

taking a derivative value at a point is independent of the operation of evaluating at a point, this is a valid example. This means that, at every key, if Mickey's nose touches his snout, and if his nose and snout have a common tangent direction at the point of contact, and if the point of contact occurs at the same parametric value u' and v' in all keys, then Mickey may move his head as he pleases and keep his features together. This was the pair of associations that made Figure 1 successful.

A further example of a suitable mapping is given by any of the familiar modeling transformations applied to the results of evaluation or differentiation at a point. That is, we may let F correspond to the evaluation of R at a fixed value $u = u'$ followed by a translation of the resulting point $R_k(u')$ by a fixed displacement Δ. This composition of mappings will be linear. We may let G correspond to the evaluation of S at a fixed value $v = v'$. Equating the result of F and G will amount to establishing the association between R and S that keeps a chosen point on R at a fixed offset from a known point on S. Figure 5 illustrates this association.

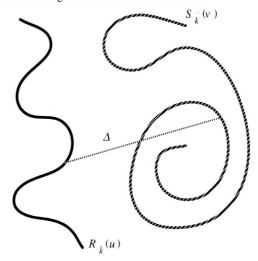

Figure 5. The point evaluation of R is translated to a fixed offset from the point evaluation of S.

If we change F to differentiation and the subsequent transformation to rotation by a fixed angle, and change G to differentiation, then the association that is produced is that of a fixed angular orientation between the tangent vector at a point on R with the tangent vector at a point on S, as is illustrated by Figure 6.

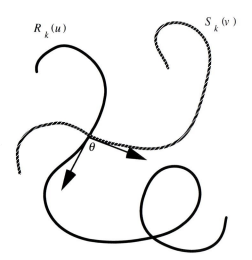

$R_k(u)$ $S_k(v)$

θ

Figure 6. At each key k the tangent to R at a chosen point u is specified to conform to the tangent to S at a chosen point v rotated about a fixed angle.

Finally, just as independent mappings can be used to hold a multiplicity of associations between two curves simultaneously, it is possible to consider simultaneous associations between multiple curves as well. Thus, for example, we could arrange that R and S join at given $u = u'$ and $v = v'$, that curves S and T maintain a given angle between tangents at fixed $v = v''$ and $w = w''$, and that T keep a specified offset from M at a fixed $w = w'''$ and $q = q'''$, all simultaneously. A possible application of multiple associations to computer-aided design is that of *filleting* or smoothly blending between two swept surfaces, as is shown in Plate 2.

Plates 1 through 4 show samples of some associations used to construct a variety of swept surfaces.

References

1.   Bartels, Richard, Beatty, John, and Barsky, Brian. **An Introduction to Splines for Use in Computer Graphics and Geometric Modeling**. Morgan Kaufmann Publishers (1987).

2.   Bartels, Richard and Hardtke, Ines. "Speed Adjustment for Key-Frame Interpolation." Proceedings of Graphics Interface '89. Morgan Kaufmann Publishers (1989) [to appear].

3.   de Boor, Carl. **A Practical Guide to Splines**. Springer-Verlag (1978).

4.   Farin, Gerald. **Curves and Surfaces for Computer Aided Geometric Design**. Academic Press (1988).

5.   Forsythe, George, Malcolm, Michael, and Moler, Cleve. **Computer Methods for Mathematical Computations**. Prentice-Hall (1977).

6.   Kochanek, Doris, and Bartels, Richard. "Interpolating Splines with Local Tension, Continuity and Bias Control." Proceedings of SIGGRAPH'84 (Minneapolis, Minnesota, July 23-27, 1984). In *Computer Graphics 18*, 3 (July, 1984), 33-41.

7.   Pegna, Joseph. *Variable Sweep Geometric Modeling*. PhD Thesis, Stanford University, Stanford, California 94305 (1987).

8.   Reeves, William. "Inbetweening for Computer Animation Utilizing Moving Point Constraints." Proceedings of SIGGRAPH'81 (Dallas, Texas, August 3-7, 1981). In *Computer Graphics 15*, 3 (August, 1981), 263-269.

9.   Steketee, Scott, and Badler, Norman. "Parametric Keyframe Interpolation Incorporating Kinetic Adjustment and Phrasing Control." Proceedings of SIGGRAPH'85 (San Francisco, California, July 22-26, 1985). In *Computer Graphics 19*, 3 (July 1985), 255-262.

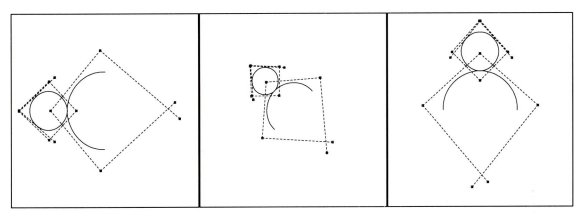

Figure 1. Two spline curves whose key association (tangency at one point) is preserved. The key frames are the first and the last; the inbetween frame is in the middle. A trajectory was computed separately for each control vertex of each curve. Each such trajectory was formed by simple Catmull-Rom interpolation [Kochanek 1984] by regarding each key to be doubled. This corresponds to setting the beginning and final tangent vector on the trajectory to half the chord between the initial and final key positions. The inbetween frame represents the parametric midpoint of the trajectory.

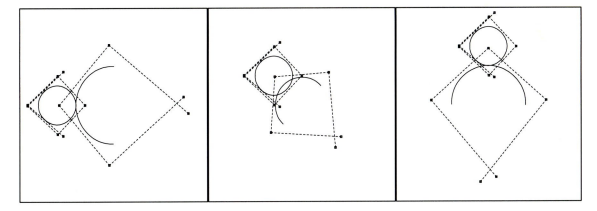

Figure 2. A two splines curves whose key association (tangency at one point) is not preserved on an inbetween frame. The inbetweening was done exactly as in Figure 1. The inbetween frame is, as in Figure 1, the parametric midpoint of the trajectory.

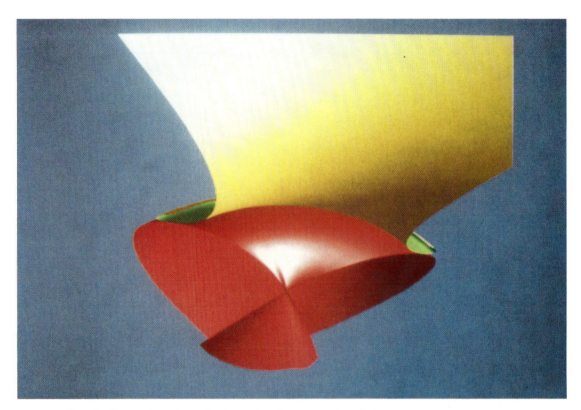

Plate 1. Two surfaces that maintain a point of contact and parallel tangents.

Plate 2. The top and bottom surfaces are independent of each other but are joined by a ''fillet'' surface that has contact and tangency association with both.

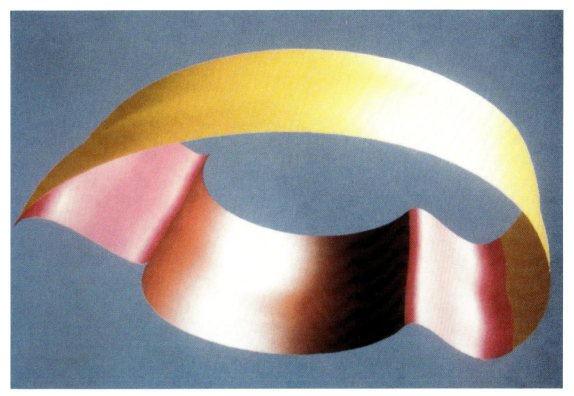

Plate 3. The top surface has a parallel tangency with the left surface, forming a cusp join, and an opposing tangency with the right surface, forming a smooth blend. These associations are mirrored with the bottom surface.

Plate 4. Two surfaces that maintain a point of contact at right angles to each other.

VOXEL SPACE AUTOMATA:
MODELING WITH STOCHASTIC GROWTH
PROCESSES IN VOXEL SPACE

Ned Greene

NYIT Computer Graphics Lab†
Old Westbury, New York

Abstract

A novel stochastic modeling technique is described which operates on a voxel data base in which objects are represented as collections of voxel records. Models are "grown" from predefined geometric elements according to rules based on simple relationships like intersection, proximity, and occlusion which can be evaluated more quickly and easily in voxel space than with analytic geometry. Growth is probabilistic: multiple trials are attempted in which an element's position and orientation are randomly perturbed, and the trial which best fits a set of rules is selected. The term *voxel space automata* is introduced to describe growth processes that sense and react to a voxel environment.

Applications include simulation of plant growth, for which voxel representation facilitates sensing the environment. Illumination can be efficiently estimated at each plant "node" at each growth iteration by casting rays into the voxel environment, allowing accurate simulation of reaction to light including heliotropism.

CR Categories: I.3.5 [Computer Graphics]: Computational Geometry and Object Modeling - Curve, surface, solid and object representation. I.3.7 [Computer Graphics]: Three-Dimensional Graphics and Realism. I.6 [Simulation and Modeling]: Applications.

Additional Keywords and Phrases: Voxel, automata, stochastic processes, illumination, heliotropism, radiosity

† Author's current address:
Apple Computer, 20525 Mariani Ave., Cupertino, CA 95014

1. Voxel Space

By a *voxel space* we mean a region of three dimensional space partitioned into identical cubes (volume elements or *voxels*), typically a region bounded by a rectangular solid so that it can be represented as an array or octree of voxel records. Modeling and rendering techniques which operate on a voxel space are the subject of increasingly active research. Various volume rendering techniques have been developed to visualize data produced by 3D medical imaging devices and computational simulation [5], [19], [21]. In the synthesis domain, voxel spaces have been employed to create surfaces defined by implicit functions [2], [13], [22].

Alternatively, arbitrary three dimensional shapes can be represented in voxel space by marking the voxels that they intersect as "occupied" [11]. This representation is necessarily approximate, since it only indicates which voxels are intersected by the object, not the object's actual surface. Multiple objects can be distinguished from each other by assigning each a unique voxel value, so any collection of non-intersecting objects can be represented. Although partitioning space into voxels makes geometric calculations only approximate and puts a lower limit on the size of objects that can be distinguished, for many applications these disadvantages are outweighted by convenience and speed.

Suppose we wish to initialize voxel space with an environment modeled as a collection of geometric primitives such as lines, polygons, and polyhedra. The process of identifying and labeling voxels that are intersected by a primitive object is referred to as *tiling*. Kaufman has outlined incremental techniques for tiling various primitives [11], although his criterion for tiling a voxel is somewhat different than the simple intersection criterion employed herein: a voxel is tiled if the cube representing its extent is intersected. Figure 1 shows voxel representations of a line and a polygon.

Voxel representation of an environment simplifies geometric operations such as intersection testing and measuring the relative proximity of objects. Whether an object intersects another object already represented in voxel space may be determined by testing each voxel that it intersects to see if it's already occupied. This method of sensing intersection is only approximate in the sense that two non-intersecting objects can

©1989   ACM-0-89791-312-4/89/007/0175 $00.75

intersect the same voxel, in which case intersection will be falsely detected. But it is faster and more convenient than the conventional method of intersecting one geometric element with all other elements in its vicinity using analytic geometry. The conventional approach can be difficult to implement, particularly if a model is constructed from different surface types (polygons, quadric surfaces, patches, etc.). With the voxel method, tiling is the only geometric operation which must be performed, and testing an element of one surface type against an element of another surface type only requires the ability to tile voxel space with each. In addition, performance is independent of scene complexity and does not depend on the number of nearby objects.

Voxel representation also simplifies determining proximity relationships. Given a point in space we may identify the nearest object by scanning voxels in the neighborhood and comparing distances to occupied voxels encountered. Alternatively, the process may be facilitated by adding "boundary layers" of voxels to objects in the environment. According to this scheme, voxels adjacent to voxels which are part of object N are marked as being in boundary layer 1 of object N, voxels one additional layer removed from object N are marked as being in boundary layer 2, and so forth up to some specified number of boundary layers. If L boundary layers have been added to all objects, for any point in voxel space we may immediately determine whether it lies within L voxels of an object, and if so, the identity of the nearest object.

As the discussion will show, voxel representation also facilitates ray casting and a variety of other geometric operations.

2. Growth Systems

The computer graphics literature includes a variety of approaches to simulating plant growth including particle systems [17],[20], graftals [20], and fractals [14]. Recently, Prusinkiewicz et al. and de Reffye et al. have approached the problem with empirically based models of plant development, producing relatively realistic models of actual plant species [16], [18].

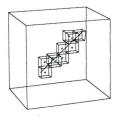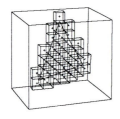

Figure 1.

An 8x8x8 voxel space with voxel
representations of a polygon and a line

Less attention has been paid to the problem of simulating the effects of environmental factors on plant development, which are particularly important in complex environments where plants interact as they compete for space and light. To faithfully mimic a natural growth process which senses and reacts to the environment, a simulated growth process must sense and react to the environment. In crude terms, growth is affected by conditions within the local environment: obstacles should be avoided, proximity to objects or other organisms may inhibit or promote growth, and growth is modulated by available light. At a minimum, simulated growth processes should be aware of these conditions.

Arvo and Kirk have described growth processes capable of sensing the environment which they refer to as "environment-sensitive automata" [1]. Their method performs ray casting to test for intersection and proximity, and they have applied the technique to simulate clinging vines and patches of grass which avoid obstacles. They mention that the method could be extended to simulate heliotropism (sun seeking) and other effects. Their sole means of sensing the environment is ray-object intersection, which limits the type of information that can be obtained.

This article argues that voxel representation simplifies sensing of the environment by growth processes. In particular, it is easier to obtain geometric information by scanning or sampling a voxel environment than by ray casting a conventional model. From any point in voxel space the size, shape, and proximity of neighboring objects can be determined by inspecting the records of nearby voxels. Voxel records may include information about material properties, making it straightforward to confine growth to appropriate regions of the environment. A variety of statistics about the local environment such as "center of mass" and "density" are readily obtained.

Illumination, which depends on the global environment, can be estimated by sampling with ray casting. In this context, ray casting means tiling a ray in voxel space; a ray is occluded if it intersects an occupied voxel. While this means of estimating illumination isn't as accurate or general as ray tracing, it is sufficient to estimate exposure to sunlight and "skylight" in an outdoor scene, and it can be performed very efficiently since it does not require ray-object intersection or any substantial analytic geometry. Fujimoto et al. discuss incremental methods for tiling rays in the context of using uniform spatial subdivision (like a coarse voxel space) to enhance ray tracing performance [6] . The efficiency of ray casting in voxel space makes it feasible to build an illumination table at each active plant "node" at each iteration, allowing accurate simulation of reaction to light including heliotropism.

A paradigm for growth in voxel space may be outlined as follows. The initial state of voxel space is specified, either "empty" or tiled with a three dimensional model of an environment. Beginning at specified seed points, models are grown from predefined geometric elements, added one by one to the model subject to satisfying a set of rules. Typically, rules con-

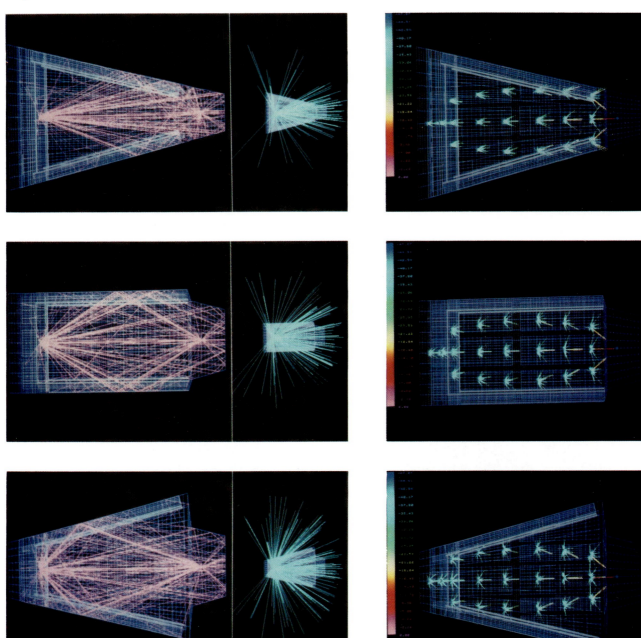

Figure 9: Dummy-head Ray Diagrams in Planar Projection for Fan, Box and Reverse Fan Designs - One is able to see from both the ray path and the ray source diagrams on the left column that the early reflected sound (within the first 50 milliseconds after the direct sound) is least lateral in the fan shaped hall (top), and gets increasingly more lateralized from the box (center) to the reverse fan configuration (bottom). In the fan shaped hall and to some extent in the box shaped hall, sound which can reflect specularly from the side walls and reach the observer at the position shown, must reflect very near the source, thus limiting the possible lateralization. The increased lateralization of the reverse fan shape results from the existence of surfaces on the sides of the hall away from the stage, positioned to specularly reflect sound to the listener.

Figure 10: Dummy-head Soundrose Diagrams in Planar Projection for Fan (top right), Box (center right) and Reverse Fan (bottom right) designs - The relative magnitudes of the rays making up the soundrose icons are displayed using length and color. One is able to see the improved lateralization at numerous positions in the box and reverse fan shaped halls verses the fan shaped one. One is also able to see the general directional characteristics of the lateralized sound which indicates its geometric genesis. Note, the superior lateralization of the box and reverse fan designs for positions in the rear of the hall are consistent with the visualization results of Figure 8 and Figure 9.

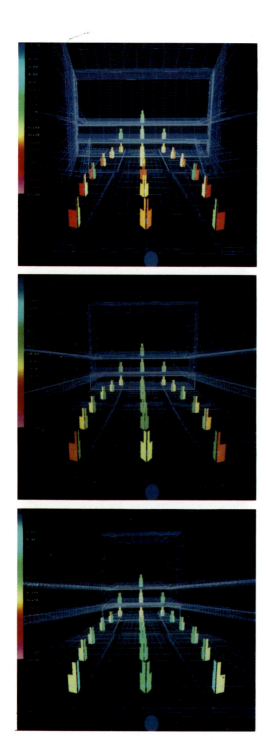

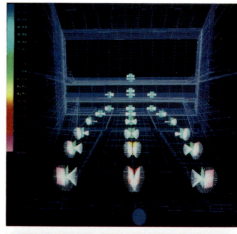

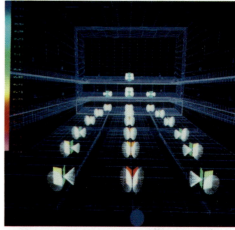

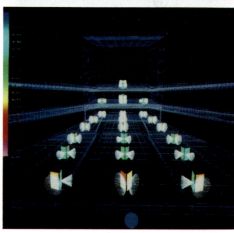

Figure 7: Dummy-head Icon and Color C_{80} in SPL for Fan, Box and Reverse Fan Designs - The fan shaped hall (top left) has improper C_{80} values since the top sections of the icon are so small, and the variation of the values on the dummy-heads is high. The box shape (center left) has both better C_{80} values and less variation between heads. The reverse fan shape (bottom left) clearly has both the best C_{80} values and the least within-hall variation. As a cross-reference, each surface has been assigned a color to represent its C_{80} energy level. Proper values of C_{80} correspond to colors on the gradient starting with a minimum of light blue to a maximum of yellowish green. An analysis of the colors on the listening surfaces of each hall confirms the results shown by the icons.

Figure 8: Dummy-head Icon and Color Lateral Fractions for Fan, Box and Reverse Fan Designs - From the cone angles, one is clearly able to see that the fan shaped hall (top right) has much poorer lateralism at listener positions than the other halls, especially as one moves from the middle to the rear of the hall. The box shape (center right) improves on the lateralism as does the reverse fan shape (bottom right). The reverse fan has better lateralization at the rear of the hall and the box has superior lateralization in the middle of the hall.

Images on this page represent views of the concert hall as seen from the source position looking towards the back wall.

measurements. Figure 26 shows one such combined visualization. The combined visualization is important in a generic sense since it is capable of communicating many parameters simultaneously. Dummy-heads can be placed at any position specifying an x,y,z coordinate. Two ears representing a particular listening orientation specify two more dimensions. Upon each of the ear-like surfaces, the parameters of clarity, spatial impression (lateral fraction), and the direction and magnitudes of the cause of the resultant spatial impression can be conveyed. The overall strength of the sound energy reaching each ear is also shown. By also choosing to show the dynamic propagation of the energy through the environment over time, a dozen or more parameters can be simultaneously imparted to the viewer.

In addition, although not shown, a two-dimensional echogram for any particular receiver position could be concurrently displayed in a separate window to show the time dependence of the energy received there. One could then choose time intervals within the echogram to simultaneously visualize the ray paths responsible for the energy level displayed. This would allow for further analysis into the relationship between the room's reflective characteristics and the sound at a particular position.

Conclusions

A visualization of acoustical measurements allows for the simultaneous assimilation of much of the information necessary to evaluate the acoustical nature of a space. The acoustical analysis of the three performance halls serves as a good example of the visualization of multi-dimensional information in a generic sense. The intuitive use of three-dimensional images, color, animation and abstract representation allows for the comprehension of the complex results of a scientific simulation. Specifically, the simultaneous display of particular icons familiar to the discipline enabled the simultaneous presentation of up to twelve parameters. From a more general point of view, the procedures demonstrate how computer graphics can be utilized for the portrayal of multi-dimensional time dependent data. Thus, the visualization techniques are potentially useful for the display of three-dimensional vector fields in many scientific and design applications.

Acknowledgements

The research was conducted under two National Science Foundation grants entitled, "Interactive Input and Display Techniques" (#DCR8203979) and "Visualization for Scientific Computing" (#ASC8715478). Simulation and displays were performed on equipment generously donated by Digital Equipment Corporation and Hewlett Packard Corporation. Special thanks to Holly Rushmeier, Roy Hall and Michael F. Cohen for their helpful discussions and input into this research and to Carl Rosenberg of Bolt Beranek and Newman for his contribution and encouragement. Lastly, thanks go to Ben Trumbore, Tim O'Conner, Filippo Tampieri, Rod Recker, David Baraff, Jim Ferwerda, Stuart Feldman, Eric Chen, Rich Eaton, Julie O'Brien, Ellen French, and Emil Ghinger for their general assistance.

References

1. Allred and Newhouse. "Applications of the Monte Carlo Method to Architectural Acoustics," *Journal Acoustic Society America*, Vol. 30, No.10, Oct 1958, pages 903-904.

2. Barron M. and A. H. Marshall."Spatial Impression Due to Early Lateral Reflections in Concert Halls: The Derivation of a Physical Measure," *Journal of Sound and Vibration*, Vol. 77 No.2, 1981, pages 211-232.

3. Borish, J. "Extension of the Image Model to Arbitrary Polyhedra," *Journal Acoustic Society America*, Vol. 75, No.6, June 1984, pages 1827-1836.

4. Bradley, J. S. "Experience With New Auditorium Acoustic Measurements," *Journal Acoustic Society America*, Vol. 73, No.6, June 1983, pages 2051-2058.

5. Cremer, L. and H. A. Muller. *Principles and Applications of Room Acoustics*, Vol. 2, Applied Science, London, 1978.

6. Edwards, N. A. "Music Performance Acoustics and Room Shape: An Investigation Employing an Images Model of Room Acoustics," Presented to the Acoustical Society of America Meeting, San Diego, Nov 1983.

7. Edwards, N. A. "Considering Concert Acoustics and the Shape of Rooms," *Architectural Record*, Vol. 172, No.9, Aug 1984, pages 133 - 138.

8. Haviland, J. K. and B. D. Thanedar. "Monte Carlo Applications to Acoustical Field Solutions," *Journal Acoustic Society America*, Vol. 54, No. 54, 1973.

9. Hedeen, Robert A., *Compendium of Materials For Noise Control*, US Dep. HEW, NIOSH Technical Report, Washington, D.C. May 1980.

10. Jordan, V. L. *Acoustical Design of Concert Halls and Theatres*, Applied Science, London, 1980.

11. Keller, J.B. "Geometrical Theory of Diffraction," *Journal Optitcal Society America*, Vol. 52, No. 2,1962, pages 116-130.

12. Kuttruff H. *Room Acoustics*, Wiley, New York, 1973

13. Krokstad, A. and S. Strøm and S. Sørsdal. "Calculating the Acoustical Room Response by the use of a Ray Tracing Technique," *Journal Sound Vibration*, Vol. 8 No. 1, 1968, pages 118-125.

14. London, "The Determination of Reverberant Sound Absorption Coefficients from Acoustical Impedance Measurements," *Journal Acoustic Society America*, Vol. 22, 1950, pages 263-269.

15. Reichardt, W. and W. Schmidt. "Die Wahrnehmbarkeit der Veränderung von Schallfeldparametern bei der Darbeitung von Musik," *Acoustica*, Vol. 18, 1967.

16. Reichardt, W. and U. Lehman. "Optimierung von Raumeindruck und durchsichtigkeit von musikdarbietungen durch auswertung von impulshalltests," *Acoustica*, Vol. 48, 1981, pages 174-185.

17. Sabine, Wallace C. *Collected Papers on Acoustics*, Harvard University, Cambridge, MA 1927. Reprinted Dover 1964.

18. Sekiguchi, K. and Sho Kimura and Tomoyuki Sugiyama, "Approximation of Impulse Response Through Computer Simulation Based on Finite Sound Ray Integration," *Journal Acoustical Society Japan*, Vol. 6, No. 2, 1985.

19. Schroeder, M. R. "Digital Simulation of Sound Transmission in Reverberant Spaces (Part 1)," *Journal Acoustic Society America*, Vol. 47, No. 2, 1970, pages 424-431.

20. Stettner, A. S. *Computer Graphics for Acoustic Simulation and Visualization*, Master's thesis, Program of Computer Graphics Lab, Cornell University, Ithaca, NY, January 1989.

21. Walsh, J. P. "The Design of Godot: a System for Computer-aided Room Acoustic Modeling and Simulation," *Proceeding 10th International Congress on Acoustics*, Sydney, 1980.

22. Wayman, J. L. and J. P. Vanyo. *Computer Simulation of Sound Fields Using Ray Methods*, PhD dissertation, University of California, Santa Barbara, July 1980.

given listener position. Ray source diagrams show the positions of real and virtual sources which would be apparent at a receiver position at a given time interval. A virtual source is an image of a real source whose position has shifted from the real source's position because its sound arrived through indirection.

Ray path diagrams can be investigated and used for comparison with other positions in a hall or similar positions in another design. From examining the lateralization of the ray paths of the sound incident at two receiving surfaces representing ears during the critical first 50 milliseconds or so after the direct sound, one is able to see what room features contribute to that incident sound energy. (Figure 5a and 9)

Ray source diagrams give a graphic representation of the envelopment and lateralization of the sound reaching a listener through time. For each ray which hits the surface or surfaces under scrutiny, a line is drawn in the direction opposite to the ray's incident direction, and is given a length equal to the total distance traveled by the ray on its journey from the source to the surface. (Figure 5b and 9)

While a ray diagram for a surface or receiver position may give directional incident energy information, it may not give an accurate description of the energy reaching a surface through a particular direction. Since many rays, each of which deposit their bundle of energy to a surface, may be traveling over the same or nearly the same path as seen in the visualization, the ray diagram will not accurately indicate the magnitude of the sound incident through particular directions, and thus may give an incorrect indication of lateralization. Furthermore, only the energy incident at one listener position can be analyzed at a time.

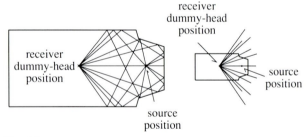

receiver
dummy-head
position

receiver
dummy-head
position

source
position

source
position

Plan View

Figure 5a (left): Sample Ray Path Diagram:
Figure 5b (right): Sample Ray Source Diagram:

As an alternative to these diagrams, the rays incident within a chosen time interval can be sorted through subtended solid angles of equal size of the hemisphere over a receiver position, and representative rays can be drawn from the center of the hemisphere out through the center of each chunk of solid angle. (Figure 6) The length of each ray indicates the strength of the incident energy within each solid angle and its direction indicates from which approximate direction that energy arrived. Furthermore, the color of each ray indicates its approximate sound strength in decibels referenced into a color scale. Known as a soundrose diagram, this three-dimensional incident energy distribution can show the time interval incident energy where direction is displayed using rays to indicate both the lateralization at the surface and the area of the room last responsible for its final reception. (Figure 10) The use of ray and soundrose diagrams in acoustical research is not new [7], yet their application within the context of computer graphics visualization techniques warrants their inclusion in this work.

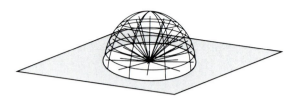

Figure 6: Sample Soundrose Construction

Visualization of the Overall Strength of Sound

The analysis of the overall strength of sound in a room can be approached in several ways. A certain amount of information can be determined simply using the geometric model of the space. More effectively, however, time interval flux or sound pressure levels, displayed at each surface in the environment using color can show global energy hot or cold spots. By displaying global sound pressure levels, global relative loudness levels can be estimated, and improper energy distributions can be recognized (Figure 11). Distinct acoustical aberrations which occur after the direct sound, such as low energy areas, echos or geometric concentrations, can be identified by visualizing the energy reaching the environment during short time intervals. Figures 12 to 23 are 12 frames each of 10 msec time interval, selected from an animation of the dynamic simulation of a sound energy impulse in the model hall. Unfortunately, the dynamic range with which the simulation began was so great that the low level resolution of the late acoustical energy is lost when the same color scale is used late in the simulation. For this reason, Figures 18 to 23 are displayed using a re-scaled color gradient.

Using the global methods described, areas of interest can then be investigated in detail. Echograms, which are plots of the energy (flux) or sound level versus time incident at a position, can be generated for chosen surfaces. From these graphs acoustic spikes or holes can be seen. The echograms can then be analyzed to help identify different types of echos or geometric focusing. Energy levels at particular time intervals can be chosen and the paths between the source and surfaces of the rays contributing to those levels can be shown. This process can not only identify the existence of a problem but also its probable geometric cause. (Figures 24 and 25)

Combined Visualization

Many of the visualization tools described can be simultaneously displayed. In this way, general trends in a room's distribution of clarity, spatial impression, and sound energy strength, in relation to both the reflective nature of the space and the time of propagation can be visualized. The combined visualization can take place on any number of dummy-heads made up of two surfaces which serve as abstractions of oversized ears. These ears can be sectioned to display their early to late ratio measurement of clarity in decibels. They can each have a protruding cone whose spread conveys a relative amount of lateral fraction and therefore the degree of perceived spatial impression. The relationship of the lateralization of received sound energy to the room's reflective properties can be visualized using soundrose diagrams superimposed on each ear surface. The length of a ray indicates its strength relative to other rays. A ray's color indicates its approximate sound strength in flux or decibels referenced into a color scale, and its direction indicates from which approximate direction that energy arrived. Overall sound strength received at each ear as well as at each surface in the environment if desired can be conveyed using the same color scale used to indicate the ray energy level in the soundrose diagrams.

One is able to evaluate and compare some of the important acoustical characteristics of each of the three environments by comparing only the combined visualizations of their acoustical

emit at a frequency of 1 kHz. Since a geometric approximation for diffraction was not implemented, only the absorption characteristics of surfaces and the air would be affected by a change in the frequency of the source.

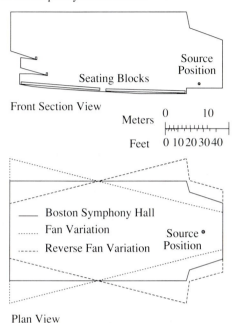

Front Section View

Meters 0   10

Feet 0 10 20 30 40

Plan View

Figure 2a (top): Boston Symphony Hall in Section
Figure 2b (bottom) Variations on Hall Design in Plan

The source was positioned along the center axis of each hall, exactly 10 feet from the front of the stage and 4 feet above the stage floor. The center direction of the source was directed at the center of the back wall of the first balcony. The source emission was weighted 65% in an isotropic spherical emission and 35% in a cosine weighted emission in the center direction. This distribution was chosen to simulate a semi-directional sound source.

Visualization of Clarity and Definition

The measure of early to late sound energy as expressed by the scalar measurement C_{80} serves as a good indicator of the clarity and definition of sound. This scalar measurement could be calculated for all receiver surfaces in an environment and displayed globally using a simple color scale. Then, each of the sample halls could be judged in terms of the absolute C_{80} levels at listener positions and by the variation in the C_{80} levels over many listener positions. If, however, one wants to easily see meaningful variations of the clarity level, and assimilate other acoustical information as well, an abstract icon can be cleverly used.

One way of producing such an icon would be to split an abstract receiver surface horizontally into a upper and lower section. The lower section would represent the energy level reaching the surface within the first 80 msec after the direct sound. The upper section would represent the energy level reaching the surface in the later time interval, spanning from 80 msec after the direct sound to infinity. Any energy level value could be chosen to be represented by the lower section of constant width. The upper section's width could then be sized as a fraction of that hypothetical level, so that the difference between the lower section in dBs and the upper section in dBs would equal the C_{80} value.

In the test environments, each of the ear-like surfaces on the dummy-heads serve as icons for the visualization. The lower section of each icon represents an early energy level of approximately 20 dB. (Figures 3 and 7)

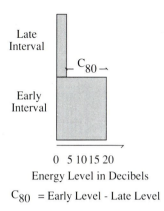

0 5 10 15 20
Energy Level in Decibels

C_{80} = Early Level - Late Level

Figure 3: Early-to-Late Ratio Icon - For the desired minimum C_{80} of 0 dB , the icon would have a top portion equal in size to the bottom section. The maximum value of 8 dB would correspond to a top portion equal to 3/5 of the bottom. Icons with top sections larger than the bottom sections or smaller that 3/5 of the bottom's width fall outside the preferred range of values.

Visualization of Spatial Impression

Similarly, lateral fraction, L_f, serves as a good scalar measurement of spatial impression which can be calculated for any number of surfaces in an environment and displayed globally using a simple color scale. The lateral fraction is the ratio of the early lateral reflected energy (over the first 80msec) to the total early energy including the direct energy. By the term lateral, it is meant to the degree it is received along the direction of the normal to the ear. The closer the early incident energy directions approach this normal direction, the greater the lateral fraction, and therefore, the greater the sense of spatial impression. In this case an icon can be generated to portray a relative amount of spatial impression at each receiver surface. A cone originating on the surface of each receiver and whose wide side is directed out in the normal direction can be used to represent the relative degree of spatial impression. To coincide with the intuition of the user, the icon can be manipulated so that the wider the cone angle, α, the greater the degree of perceived spatial impression. (Figures 4 and 8)

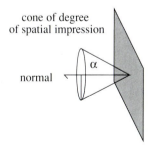

receiver surface

Figure 4: Spatial Impression Icon - The wider the cone angle, α, the greater the degree of perceived spatial impression.

Unfortunately, the cause of poor lateralization and thus deficient sound is not evident from the scalar value of lateral fraction. Lateralization depends on the complex reflective properties of the room, a combination of both geometry and surface attributes. Ray diagrams can allow the user to see the incident energy's relationship with the reflective properties of the room. There are two basic types of ray diagrams which are often used in the spatial design of a concert hall. Ray path diagrams show the paths followed by rays from the source to a

equation of lateral fraction includes only reflected energy and the denominator includes both the direct and reflected sound energy. The closer the incident energy direction approaches this normal direction, the greater its contribution to the lateral fraction, and therefore toward a sense of spatial impression. (Figure 1)

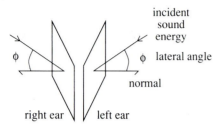

Figure 1: Definition of Lateralization

Overall Sound Strength

A third type of measurement characterizes the overall strength of sound. Unfortunately, the sensation of the strength of sound is based on a number of psychoacoustic factors. Not only is the perception of loudness not linear with the amount of sound energy received, the temporal nature of incident sound also affects its perception. However, as a simple approximation, a measurement of the overall energy at positions through time is useful in detecting possible sound strength problems.

Areas where there are anomalies in sound strength can be caused by a number of different situations. In a hall there may be positions in which the sound field is significantly weaker, either at a particular time or on average, than the desired normal level. These deficient spots can result from an inability to receive direct or reflected sound energy due to room geometry, or from surface or air absorption of sound energy during propagation. Within the normal design process these problems can be very difficult to predict on a global level (at all points in an environment).

In contrast to energy deficient areas, are those room positions of abnormally high energy on average or at particular instances of time. These acoustic phenomena result primarily from room geometry which directs energy toward specific areas. Most often these concentrations can be explained as the result of specular surface reflection. Some extreme examples of specular geometric concentration are whispering galleries, and dome focusing. In both of these situations, the walls in the rooms are shaped in manners which produce extremely consistent reflection from many positions all directed toward a singular area. Geometric situations in which specular focusing occurs can be very difficult to predict using contemporary design techniques, especially if the complexity of a room's shape is great.

A third defect which relates to the measurement of the overall strength of sound through time is acoustic echo. Echos are simply reflections that come after the direct sound and are strong enough to be heard as distinct. A common example of distant echo in a hall is the reflected sound heard by musicians on stage, coming from a highly specularly reflective back wall.

Visualization Techniques

The evaluation of the acoustical properties of a concert hall or auditorium is a difficult problem. But perhaps more difficult is the simultaneous assimilation of all of the information necessary to evaluate its acoustical nature. In addition to the three spatial parameters describing unique locations in space, one needs to be aware of the relative magnitudes and directions of the sound energy as well as its corresponding acoustical characteristics at different positions

through time. Furthermore, this information needs to be viewed in its relationship to the reflection properties of the enclosed space, and its dependence on both time and wavelength.

Efficient methods for representing these types of acoustical parameters in terms easily comprehended by the engineer/architect/designer have not yet been developed. Although analytical techniques for the simulation or measurement of the propagation of sound are available, the resulting information is lost using the crude measurements traditional in the practice today.

Computer graphics visualization methods offer some potential opportunities for the display and understanding of this multi-dimensional information. Standard three-dimensional perspective image generation methods with diffuse shading can portray the physical space. Color can be effectively utilized to provide relative scalar values of engineering parameters, but care must be taken to maintain the correct perception of the physical space. The display speed of current graphics workstations allows images to be dynamically updated fast enough to animate time-dependent phenomena. Lastly, abstract symbols and representations can be utilized to depict a wide variety of additional parameters. These icons can be sized large enough to be seen within the global context of the simulation, but small enough as to not affect one's perception of the global behavior.

Just displaying multi-dimensional information, however, is not necessarily going to give useful insight into a physical problem. The data presented must not overload the user's mind with overly specific and possibly insignificant information. It also must be displayed in ways which can be intuitively identified and easily understood.

The visualization techniques presented for displaying acoustical measurements serve as new examples of computer graphics visualization techniques. Their capability for simultaneously displaying multi-dimensional information can help in the understanding of the acoustics of a concert hall.

For comparison purposes, the acoustics of three particular hall designs are evaluated and compared. One model of a real hall was modeled and its design was varied to generate the data for the other two designs. The surfaces common between the models were assigned identical acoustical characteristics. Each test environment contained the same source description and relative position, and each contained a number of detailed listening devices known as "dummy-heads", positioned and oriented in identical positions with reference to the source. The acoustical characteristics of clarity and definition, spatial impression, and overall strength are depicted using icons and color. Although the simulation can be conducted using any particular wavelength of sound, the display of the frequency dependence of the simulation results is not addressed in the visualization examples following.

The primary model used in the simulation was a simplified version of Boston Symphony Hall. (Figure 2a) The environment consisted of approximately 400 surfaces which when meshed amounted to approximately 6000 polygons. The other two environments were based roughly on this model, with variations on the wall angles to produce a fan shaped and reverse fan shaped room when viewed in plan. (Figure 2b) The models remained identical in terms of ceiling and floor angles, but the stage size changed in accordance with the walls. The balconies in each of these rooms also conformed to its wall shape. The angle of slope of the balconies encircling the rooms was in each case equal to that shown in the hall section.

The acoustical attributes of the surfaces within each model were varied to approximate the different reflectance characteristics of different parts of the room. [14][9] The single source used in the tests of the simulation was chosen to simplify the problem. Wallace Sabine [17], considered the pioneer of modern acoustics, used ray theory around the turn of the 20th century in the formulation of his well known equation for the calculation of room reverberation time. In the late 1950's, Allred and Newhouse [1] first applied Monte Carlo Methods to calculate the mean-free paths of spaces by tracing rays on a computer. About a decade later, Krokstad, Strøm and Sørsdal [13] made the first attempt to use a computer to trace rays based on a simple geometric model to get an idea of the acoustical response of a hypothetical room. This was followed by Schroeder's digital simulation of simple reverberant spaces [19]. Haviland and Thanedar then extended earlier work with Monte Carlo methods in an attempt to obtain time histories of the pressure at a given point in a field [8]. Wayman and Vanyo used these and similar techniques applied to more complex environments [22]. Walsh [21] conducted similar research in the development of the Godot System.

Others have attempted to use another method similar to ray casting known as the image method to study the acoustical response of imaginary rooms. Interesting work has been done in this field, by Borish [3] and Edwards [6]. More recently, Sekiguchi, Kimura, Sugiyama have also been working on extending ray methods, using what is known as finite ray integration [18].

The ray method assumes that wave surfaces can be treated as rays normal to these surfaces and traveling in the direction of propagation in the medium. The behavior attributed to sound rays is similar to that of light rays in geometric optics, except for a few crucial differences. These differences stem from the sound ray's slower propagation speed, longer wavelength and higher rate of energy transfer to the surrounding environment. The most obvious distinction is the comparatively limited propagation speed of sound waves. Light propagates away from a source so quickly that the eye is unable to sense its temporal nature. The ear, on the other hand, is able to detect minute variations in sound pressure due to the longer time delays in a sound wave's propagation. Humans have the ability to perceive these variations even within small time scales of observation, on the order of 50 milliseconds.

Another important difference of sound waves when compared to those of light results from the relatively long wavelengths of sound. When the wavelengths of the sound rays are comparable to the boundary and irregularity dimensions of an environment, the behavior of sound rays is not easily compared to simple reflections or refractions in geometric optics. While the acoustical data generated for the visualization did not include the effects of diffraction, the simulation process could be modified to do so using a geometric theory of diffraction [11].

The last major difference between light and sound rays results from the tendency of sound to easily transfer its energy to matter with which it interacts. Little energy is lost by a light ray when it passes through unobstructed air. The theoretical sound ray on the other hand will see considerable attenuation, especially at high frequencies, since a ray's energy vibrates air molecules which in turn dissipates energy in the form of thermal exchange. A surface's acoustical reflectivity is also strongly affected by variations in air pressure caused by rays incident on its surface. For this reason the sound absorption characteristics of a surface depend on the the ray's angle of incidence in ways which are unlike those of light. All of these characteristics combine to make the behavior of sound more difficult to predict and comprehend than the behavior of light, and new visualization methods are required to represent its appropriate measurements.

The authors have used a modified specular and diffuse ray tracing algorithm combined with Monte Carlo techniques to simulate the time varying spatial distribution of sound.

Unfortunately, within the space limitations of this paper, it is not possible to provide the details of this simulation procedure. This material is currently being submitted for publication. The interested reader is referred to Stettner's thesis [20] and to the general acoustic's literature [5] and [12].

Characterization of Sound

Reverberation Time

For a long time, reverberation time and other early sound energy decay measurements were considered the primary objective parameters in the acoustical design of sound spaces.

Trying to characterize a hall's sound by using simple criteria, however, can be problematic. Recently, the inadequacy of using the reverberation quantity alone to predict the acoustics of a space has become widely realized [4] [10]. In response, a wide variety of relatively new acoustical measurements have been introduced. Three types of acoustical measurement now used characterize the clarity and definition, the spatial impression, and the overall strength of sound.

Clarity and Definition

The importance of early reflected sound energy to the intelligibility of speech sounds and to the clarity and definition of musical sounds is widely recognized [4]. If there is too much early reflected sound energy, the sounds of either music or speech will blend and lack definition. On the other hand if there is too little, the sound will be overwhelmed by the latter sound and clarity will be lost.

One of the most popular measurements of early to late sound energy was proposed by Reichhardt. [16] Reichhart's measure of clarity incorporated an early energy time of 80 msec, which he believed to be appropriate for music. He defined this measurement, C_{80}, as the log of the early arriving sound (from 0 msec to 80 msec after the direct sound) divided by the late sound energy arriving 80 msec and after the direct sound.

$$C_{80} = 10 \log \left(\int_0^{0.08} p^2(t)dt \bigg/ \int_{0.08}^{\infty} p^2(t)dt \right)$$

where p2(t) represents the medial value of sound pressure varying through time. C_{80} is expressed in decibels (dBs).

Spatial Impression

The measurement of spatial impression quantifies to what extent the listener senses being immersed in the sound as opposed to just receiving it and relates to the listener's sense of envelopment in the sound field and perceived broadening of the sound source. The subjective degree of spatial impression has been found to correlate with the ratio of lateral to frontal energy at a listener's position [15]. One useful measurement, found to be linear with the degree of spatial impression, is the lateral energy fraction, Lf, defined as the ratio of early lateral reflected energy (over the first 80msec) to the total early energy including the direct energy [2]. Expressed in the following equation:

$$L_f = \left(\sum_{t=5\,ms}^{80\,ms} r \cos\phi \bigg/ \sum_{t=0\,ms}^{80\,ms} r \right)$$

where ϕ is the angle between the reflection path and the axis through the listener's ears, r is the reflection energy, which is dependent on time, and t = 0 milliseconds is the time of the arrival of the direct sound energy. The numerator in the

Computer Graphics Visualization
For
Acoustic Simulation

Adam Stettner
Donald P. Greenberg

Program of Computer Graphics
Cornell University
Ithaca, NY 14853

Abstract

Computer simulations can be used to generate the spatial and temporal data describing the acoustical behavior of performance halls, but typically the analytical results are difficult to assimilate and compare. By using computer graphics to display the multi-dimensional data, substantially greater amounts of information than that conveyed by standard techniques can be communicated to the designer. This allows designs of different acoustical spaces to be tested, evaluated, and compared.

An example comparing the acoustical behavior of three different concert halls demonstrates these techniques and allows for the simultaneous assimilation of much of the information necessary to evaluate the acoustical nature of a space. The use of three-dimensional images, color, animation and abstract representation allows for the comprehension of the complex results of a scientific simulation. Specifically, the simultaneous display of particular icons familiar to the discipline enabled the simultaneous presentation of up to twelve parameters.

From a more general point of view, the procedures demonstrate how computer graphics can be utilized for the portrayal of multi-dimensional time dependent data. The visualization techniques are potentially useful for the display of three-dimensional vector fields in many scientific and design applications.

CR Categories and Subject Descriptors: I.3.0 [Computer Graphics]: General; J.2 [Computer Applications]: Physical Sciences and Engineering

Additional Keywords and Phrases: acoustics, simulation, scientific visualization, ray tracing, Monte Carlo.

Introduction

When architecture firms design major auditoriums and concert halls, they frequently build scale models and test them visually and acoustically. By coating the interiors of the models with reflective material and shining lasers from the stage positions, the sight and sound lines of the audience in a hall can be assessed. Acoustical qualities of the proposed space can be measured by conducting acoustical tests on the model using sources and receivers scaled in both frequency and size.

While these processes do give some insight into the acoustical behavior of the real hall, they are laborious, costly, and time consuming endeavors. It is more effective to use computer simulations combined with computer graphics visualization to test and evaluate the acoustical behavior in performance halls.

There are numerous advantages inherent in using computer simulation and visualization over the traditional approach of using scale modeling for acoustical analysis. With the increasing use of computers in the modeling and design of buildings, the geometric models needed to conduct the acoustical analysis will already exist, making additional simulations using the same database very convenient. Furthermore, the same computing environment used to design geometric spaces can be used to run acoustical analyses. Computer simulation of acoustical behavior would also be more flexible than physical scale modeling, since it would allow for changes to be easily made and then analyzed in a design. Lastly, computer simulation and visualization would make the acoustical nature of a space more easily and more thoroughly understood since the visualization allows for a global evaluation of many unique locations simultaneously through time.

The primary objective of this paper is to investigate techniques of displaying multi-dimensional data which are both comprehendible and useful to the user. The techniques will be specifically used to visualize acoustical measurements derived from the simulation data. Three model halls will be evaluated and compared.

Geometric Approximation of Sound Propagation

The relationship between Computer Graphics and acoustical design is more than the use of computers to model the physical environments and to display the results of the acoustic simulation. Sound propagation can be simulated with many techniques that are similar to those used to model illumination. These methods, in particular geometric ray tracing and reflection modeling, have been highly refined. By modifying these methods to take into account a few basic differences between light and sound, they can be well suited to acoustic simulation.

Sound can be described as wave motion within matter, but solving the three-dimensional wave equation for arbitrary geometrical environments is a difficult task. Formal analyses have been presented for some idealized shapes, such as a simple cube [12][5], but the application of wave theory to complexly shaped rooms is virtually impossible at this time because the boundary conditions to the wave equation cannot be formulated in a satisfactory way. The use of acoustical ray theory can

Fan Shape

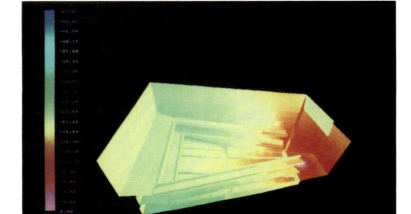

Box Shape

Reverse Fan

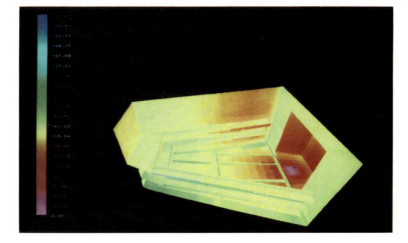

Figure 11: Time Summed Global SPL Over Entire Simulation - In the visualizations of the energy received by surfaces, the bottom color on the color scale represents the maximum incident sound pressure level and the colors as they approach blue are attenuations from this maximum level. A change between two adjacent basic hues, pink, red, yellow, green, aqua and dark blue, corresponds to a change of approximately 10 dB, which is an approximate change in perceived loudness of 2. The sound pressure levels corresponding to each surface energy summed over a time interval can be displayed as a color at each surface. When the energy incident on each surface in the environment is summed over the entire simulation, the fan design clearly has less energy reaching the back portions of the theater, producing a less uniform distribution of energy than the other designs.

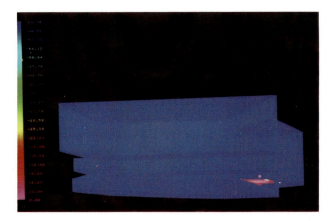

Figure 12: t = 0 - 10 msec

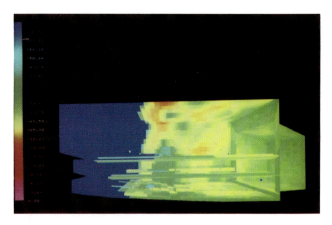

Figure 15: t = 90 - 100 msec

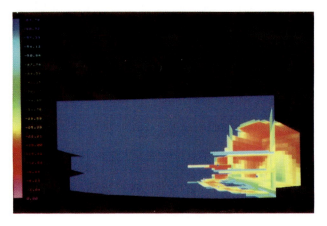

Figure 13: t = 30 - 40 msec

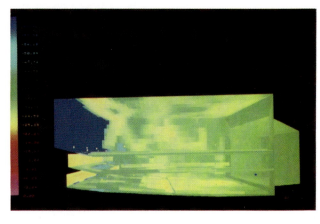

Figure 16: t = 120 - 130 msec

Figure 14: t = 60 - 70 msec

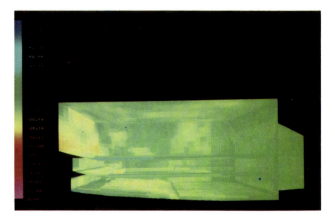

Figure 17: t = 150 - 160 msec

Figures 12 - 17 : Global Early Surface Sound Pressure Levels During Selected Time Intervals - Figure 12 is a side perspective view of the sound pressure levels on the surfaces of the box shaped model during the first 10 millisecond period after the beginning of the simulated impulse of energy. A diffuse lighting model is applied in Figure 12 to enable the viewer to see the environment. Figures 13 through 17 show a sequence of 10 millisecond time interval frames spaced 30 milliseconds apart, which demonstrate the propagation of the sound energy from the source to the surfaces of the environment. One can see the acoustical wave surface as an expanding sphere, then as many superimposed expanding spheres. There is also a distinct secondary wave approximately 20 milliseconds behind the primary wave due to the first reflection of sound from the stage. From these patterns, the distribution of the flux at the surfaces of the environment is discernable.

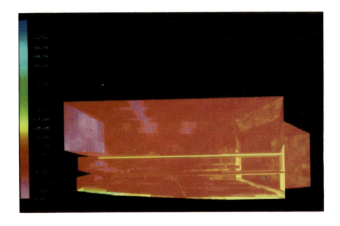

Figure 18: t = 180 - 190 msec

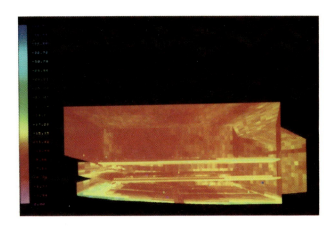

Figure 21: t = 240 - 250 msec

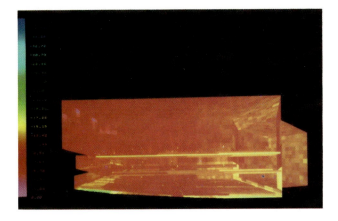

Figure 19: t = 200 - 210 msec

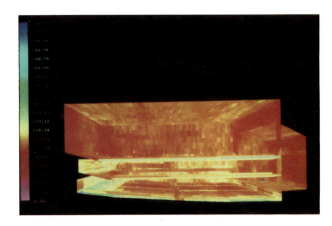

Figure 22: t = 260 - 270 msec

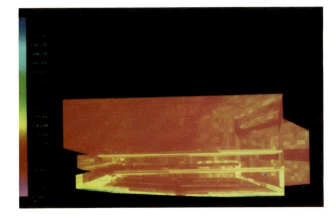

Figure 20: t = 220 - 230 msec

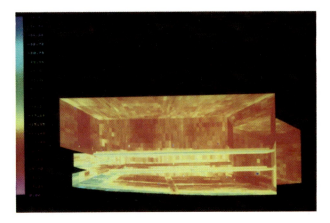

Figure 23: t = 280 - 290 msec

Figures 18 - 23: Global Late Surface Sound Pressure Levels During Selected Time Intervals - These figures are a continuation of 10 millisecond time interval frames in the simulated impulse propagation. Note that they are displayed using a re-scaled color gradient and a change in basic hue now corresponds to a change of approximately 7.5 dB or a 68 percent change in loudness. A number of possible acoustical problems are evident in this sequence. From an approximate time interval starting at 200 msec (Figure 19), to the end of the simulated impulse, there is a clearly little energy in the seating area below the first balcony. In this same area, there appears to be a geometric concentration of sound occurring in the time interval from 280 to 290 milliseconds as shown in figure 23. Another area of concern is the high energy areas on the front wall. Judging from the bright areas in figure 22 on the front wall of the stage, it appears that there might be some degree of echo disturbance on stage 260 to 270 milliseconds into the simulation.

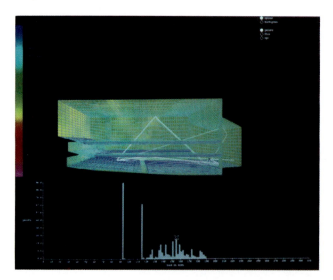

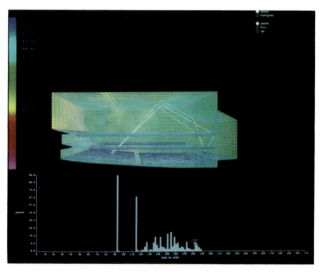

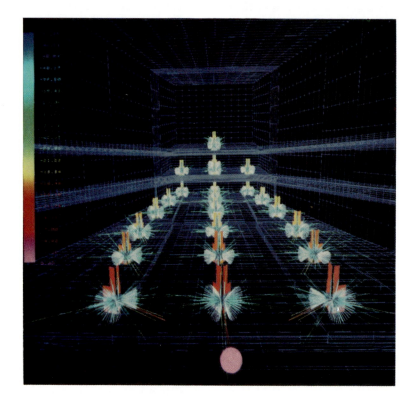

Figure 24 - 25 (top right and top left): Echograms of Receiver Surface and Contributing Ray Paths - These two figures show the 180 - 190 msec time interval surface sound pressure levels, as well as a two-dimensional time verse energy plot or echogram of a particular surface on a dummy-head in the model room. By choosing a spike of energy at any desired time interval or sub-interval, the ray paths responsible for that energy level can be displayed. The X-shaped cursor can be seen over a chosen time interval on each of the two figures, and the ray paths responsible for the energy level at that time interval are displayed in pink.

Figure 26 (bottom center): Combined C_{80} and L_f Icons, Soundrose and Sound Strength in Perspective Projection Summed Through Time - By combining the visualization methods discussed, one can comprehend nearly a dozen parameters important in acoustical evaluation, thus giving one the tools to simultaneously compare and evaluate the acoustical characteristics of each of the three environments.

Computer Graphics, Volume 23, Number 3, July 1989

Three Dimensional Terrain Modeling and Display for Environmental Assessment

Kazufumi Kaneda, Fujiwa Kato, Eihachiro Nakamae,
Hiroshima University
Saijo-cho, Higashi-hiroshima, 724 Japan

Tomoyuki Nishita,
Fukuyama University
Higashimura-cho
Fukuyama, 729-02 Japan

Hideo Tanaka, and Takao Noguchi
Tokyo Electric Power Co., Inc.
1-4-10 Irifune, Chuou-ku, Tokyo, 100 Japan

Abstract

A technique for compositing computer generated images of buildings and background images created from aerial photographs is described. The aerial photo data are mapped onto a terrain model based on cartographic data. The technique can be used to pre-evaluate visual impact of large scale construction by means of not only still images but also animations.

The technique can be briefly described as follows: 1) an accurate, three-dimensional terrain model is created based on cartographic data. 2) a hierarchy of aerial photo data at various resolutions is mapped onto the terrain model as a texture. 3) the height of trees is taken into account in regions near the viewpoint. 4) allowing intersections of terrain models with constructions facilitates geometric adjustments and shadowing.

CR Categories and Subject Descriptions: I.3.3 **[Computer Graphics]**: Picture/Image Generation; I.3.5 **[Computer Graphics]**: Computational Geometry and Object Modeling; I.3.7 **[Computer Graphics]**: Three-Dimensional Graphics and Realism
General Terms: Algorithms
Additional Key Words and Phrases: Contour Line, Terrain Model, Visual Environment, Environmental Assessment, Texture Mapping

1 Introduction

Pre-evaluation of visual impact of large construction projects, such as electric power plants, etc., has lately received a great deal of attention. Two methods have commonly been used; one is to paint the proposed building onto a landscape photograph, the other is to build a three dimensional scale model. The former method lacks objectivity as depending on an artist's skill, and the number of views generated is restricted because each view must be separately painted. Using a model case, the view point can be animated, but construction of the model is very time-consuming and expensive, camera angles may be restricted due to space limitations, and the resulting images are very

artificial looking.

In order to overcome these disadvantages, S. Uno et al. [15] developed a graphic system which overlays computer generated images onto a background photograph, E. A. Feibush et al. [4] proposed an anti-aliasing method for montages using digital filtering, and T. Porter et al. [13] presented a method which composites complex 3D images using an "α-channel".

In [9], some of the authors of the present paper proposed a montage method, in which a computer generated image of the proposed construction is overlaid onto a background photograph with fog and shadow effects. However, with this method the viewpoint is restricted by available background photos, and cannot be animated.

To address this problem, we here describe a new method, in which the construction is overlaid onto a background generated by mapping aerial photo data as a texture onto a 3D terrain model generated from cartographic data. In this way still images with nearly unrestricted viewpoints, as well as animations, may be generated.

The technique involves the following steps: 1) Input of contour lines from a topographical map. 2) Generation of a 3D terrain model from cartographic data. 3) Adjusting the color of digitized aerial photographs. 4) Mapping aerial photograph data as textures onto the terrain model. 5) Modification of model to take account of height of trees. 6) Overlaying computer graphic images of buildings etc. with their shadows onto the generated background.

A number of methods of generating 3D terrain models from contour lines have been described. They can be separated into two classes [12]: filling the area between contour lines with a triangular mesh [2], [1], and with a rectangular mesh [7], [5], [8]. In both cases, the main aim has been to generate views for flight simulators; i.e., to display mountains at some distance, from a considerable height. Because the viewpoint is at high altitude, the range of distance from the viewpoint to various points on the landscape is not very great. Therefore, patches of constant size, independent of distance from viewpoint, are generally satisfactory. A bird's-eye animation for Los Angeles basin was made by JPL [6], for example.

However, in environmental assessment images, the viewpoint will usually be very near the ground, i. e. at the level of the human eyes. In this case, small patch size results in very inefficient processing for regions distant from the viewpoint, while large patch size results in inadequate image quality in regions near the viewpoint (see Fig. 1).

©1989   ACM-0-89791-312-4/89/007/0207 $00.75

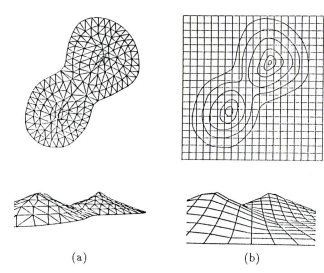

Figure 1: Terrain modeling. (a) Triangular mesh. (b) Rectangular mesh.

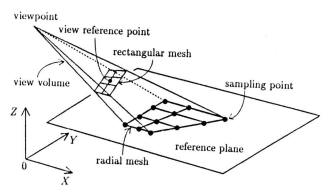

Figure 2: Generation of a radial mesh.

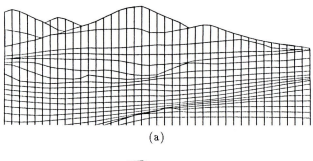

(a)

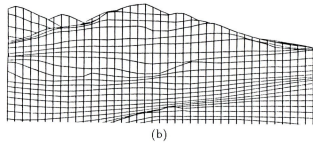

(b)

Figure 3: A terrain model. (a) Before subdivision in depth direction. (b) After subdivision in depth direction.

To overcome these problems, we use a radial mesh for the terrain model: the further from the viewpoint, the larger the patch size, resulting in a more even distribution of resolution over the landscape. This method also leads to high speed hidden surface removal because the rows of the mesh are generated in order of distance between these rows and the view point. However, the mesh must be recalculated when the viewpoint changes. A local processing method, described below, is used to increase the efficiency of generating the terrain model.

In addition, the height of trees and the shadows of large constructions cast onto the background in regions near the viewpoint are taken into account. The height of trees close to the viewpoint cannot be neglected, particularly when the viewpoint is close to the ground. For example, if a road passes through a wood, the road should be obscured by the trees for most viewpoints, although it is not obscured in the aerial photo. And the shadows cast onto the background by constructions are important for making realistic images especially when their location is close to the viewpoint.

In order to demonstrate the effectiveness of our method, we show some montages based on actual aerial photo data, with power substations, transmission towers, etc. overlaid.

2 Generation of Three Dimensional Terrain Model

2.1 Generation of Radial Mesh

A radial mesh, as shown in Fig. 2, can be easily generated as follows.

(1) A view volume (a square pyramid) is determined by the viewpoint, the view reference point, and the view angles. The base of the view volume is divided into a rectangular mesh whose density depends upon the desired display accuracy.

(2) The intersections of the lines which connect the viewpoint with each node in the rectangular mesh, and a

reference plane parallel to the xy-plane, are calculated. These points are called sampling points in the discussion below.

After perspective transformation, the sizes of patches of the terrain model are nearly constant in the horizontal direction, but in the vertical direction, the size depends upon the gradient of the terrain; the steeper the terrain, the larger the vertical size of the perspective-transformed patch (see Fig. 3 (a)).

To counter this problem, the radial mesh is recursively divided in the vertical direction until the vertical length of all patches satisfies the desired accuracy criterion. When the mesh is divided, a row of sampling points is inserted as shown in Fig. 4.

In this way, the mesh size on a screen becomes nearly constant and gives homogeneous topographic images as shown in Fig. 3 (b) where accuracy of the terrain model, especially in the region of the skyline, is improved.

Because the operation of this algorithm depends upon the location of the viewpoint, the terrain model must be regen-

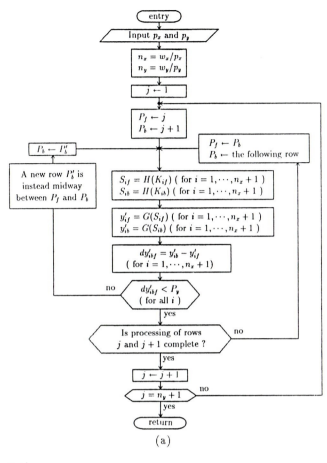

(a)

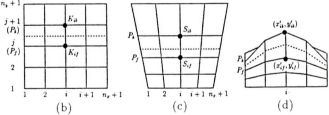

(b)   (c)   (d)

p_x, p_y : the horizontal and vertical resolutions in pixel units

n_x, n_y : the number of horizontal and vertical divisions

w_x, w_y : the width and height of the screen

j : the index of the row of the mesh being processed

P_f, P_b : the indices pointing to the rows preceding and following the new row

S_{if}, S_{ib} : the sampling points on the radical mesh corresponding to the intersections K_{if} and K_{ib} (see Fig. 4 (c))

K_{if}, K_{ib} : the intersections on rows P_f and P_b (see Fig. 4 (b))

$H(K)$: the operation to calculate the sampling points on the radical mesh corresponding to the intersection K on the rectangular mesh.

y'_{if}, y'_{ib} : y components of the screen coordinates of the sampling points S_{if} and S_{ib} (see Fig. 4 (d))

$G(S)$: the operation to calculate y component of the screen coordinate of the sampling point S

Figure 4: Method of subdividing a terrain model in the direction of depth. (a) Flow chart of subdividing a terrain model. (b) Rectangular mesh. (c) Radial mesh. (d) Perspective view.

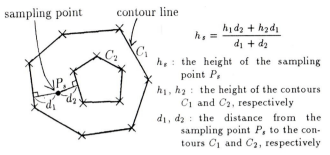

$$h_s = \frac{h_1 d_2 + h_2 d_1}{d_1 + d_2}$$

h_s : the height of the sampling point P_s

h_1, h_2 : the height of the contours C_1 and C_2, respectively

d_1, d_2 : the distance from the sampling point P_s to the contours C_1 and C_2, respectively

Figure 5: Calculation of the height of a sampling point.

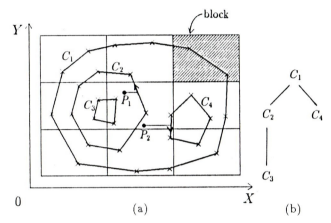

(a)   (b)

Figure 6: Calculation of height using a local method. (a) Contour segments are recorded for each block. (b) Hierarchy of contour inclusion.

erated every time the viewpoint is moved. However, through this disadvantageous process, hidden surface removal calculations reduce because of the property that the rows of the mesh are lined up in order of distance from the viewpoint. In the next section we will discuss a method for efficiently calculating a terrain model.

2.2 Calculation of Height Using Local Processing

The height of a sampling point is calculated by interpolating between the closest contour segments on either side (see Fig. 5). As a preprocessing step, the entire area is divided into a number of large blocks, and the contours running through each block are recorded as shown in Fig. 6 (a). For any sampling point (for instance, P_1 or P_2 in the figure), the nearest contour segment to its right within the same block is located (C_2 or C_4 in the figure). Then the contour is examined to see if it contains the sampling point. (Because all contours are defined in counter clockwise order, the sense of the angle determined by the sampling point and two ordered points of the contour indicates whether the point is contained in the contour.) The other contour is located based on a separately memorized hierarchy of contour inclusion, as shown in Fig. 6 (b). For P_1, the contour C_3 is immediately located, because it is the only contour directly contained by C_2. For P_2, the candidate contour pairs are either C_1 and C_2 or C_1 and C_4 because P_2 located at a col. C_2 is selected because it is closer to P_2 than C_4.

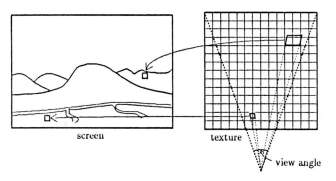

Figure 7: Problem caused by using a single texture resolution for mapping.

2.3 Utilizing Ridge Lines

The ridge line data must be used to display precise shapes of mountains because in most perspective view the ridge lines determine the appearance of the mountains.

A ridge line is given by the location and altitude of each sampling point on the line. The altitude at a mesh point between a ridge line and a contour is obtained by the same way as that described above except that the altitudes on the ridge line are interpolated.

3 Displaying the Terrain Model

3.1 Display at Nearly Constant Resolution Using Hierarchical Textures

The generated terrain model is displayed by mapping aerial photo data as a texture after perspective transformation and hidden surface removal. Only the texture of the central area has the image projected perpendicularly, especially in aerial photographs taken from relatively low altitude. Therefore, for mapping only the central area of aerial photos should be used. A mapping function from a terrain model to a texture element can be expressed as a function of the X and Y coordinates of the terrain model.

Images used for environmental assessment generally cover a broad range of depth, including regions very close, and quite far from the viewpoint. As shown in Fig. 7, if a single texture is used for the entire image, the resolution is wastefully high in distant regions, and inadequate in near regions.

In order to address this problem, a small scale aerial photo (A) covering the entire display area, and larger scale aerial photos (B, C, D) covering the area near the viewpoint are used (see Fig. 8). Textures at several resolutions are generated from these aerial photos on a hierarchical basis. For each region to be texture mapped, the corresponding texture whose perspective-transformed resolution is closest to that of the output device is selected. That is, high resolution textures generated from large scale aerial photos are employed for mapping regions close to the viewpoint. In the proposed method, high resolution textures are required only for the regions close to the viewpoint.

The colors of aerial photographs at different scales usually vary even for a single region, because of fog effect. To address this problem the technique of canceling the fog effect

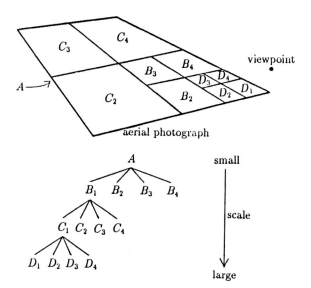

Figure 8: Hierarchy of textures at several scales.

Figure 9: Adjustment of the colors of each aerial photograph.

(refer to [9]) is applied to each aerial photograph. In Fig. 9, the colors of each photograph are adjusted to match that of the largest scale photo.

Digital ground plane generator [14] and mip mapping technique [16] are seemingly similar to the proposed method; however, their aims are quite different. Digital ground plane generator aims to display a boundless surface with a finite texture by using a technique of a nested hierarchy of stylized texture patterns. Mip mapping's aim is to minimize aliasing effects and to reduce the calculation time for overly high resolution textures. If the mip mapping were applied to mapping in this paper, high resolution texture (level D in Fig. 8) would have to cover the entire display area (A); i.e. a much greater amount of texture data is required.

3.2 Displaying Trees

In general, the height of trees is not reflected in contour lines on topographical maps. If the contour data are used without any alteration, regions which should be hidden by trees will be visible. For example, Fig. 10 (a) shows a scene

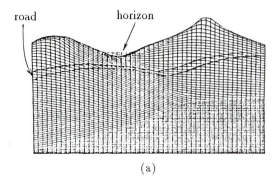

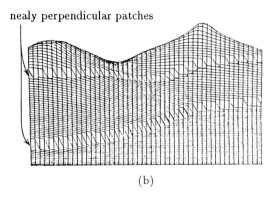

Figure 10: Taking into account of the height of trees. (a) Height of trees ignored. (b) Height of trees included.

in which a road and the horizon should be hidden by trees. The closer the camera position is to ground level, the more serious this problem becomes. We address this problem as follows.

(1) The height of trees is added to the height obtained from topographical contour maps. Referring to the aerial photo, the regions covered by trees, the color of the trees, and the average height of the trees, are specified. When a sampling point is located inside a region specified as tree covered, its color is compared to the tree color. If the color matches, the tree height for that region, modulated by a function, e.g. intensity of a texture color, is added to the contour height.

(2) Nearly perpendicular patches are generated at the boundary of tree covered regions. These patches have a very unnatural appearance, because of the enlargement in the vertical direction of the applied texture (see Fig. 10 (b)).

This problem is countered, as shown in Fig. 11, by rotating the boundary patches to lie horizontally, and mapping tree textures from near the boundary. However, the image still looks unnatural, particularly close to the viewpoint, because the mapped texture is not a side view of trees. The quality can be further improved by mapping some actual photographs of side views of trees instead of the aerial photo data in these regions.

In this way, the boundary between tree-covered and other regions is much more naturally displayed, and trees obscure roads, bases of towers, etc., as expected.

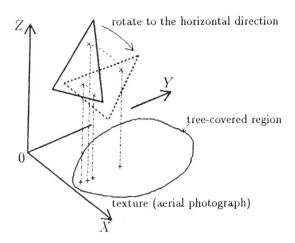

Figure 11: Mapping textures onto boundary patches of tree-covered regions.

3.3 Geometric Adjustment and Shadowing

Allowing intersection of the base of constructions with a complex shape terrain model usually facilitates their geometric adjustment. Bases which may intersect with the terrain model are specified in the input data in order to make shadowing easy.

Shadowing of constructions and terrain models is calculated by using shadow volumes [3]. Shadow volumes for constructions are calculated by using the light source and the contour edges of the convex polyhedra which form the constructions (refer to [11]). While for a terrain model its back faces should be used for making shadow volumes because these faces are fewer in number than front faces in environmental assessment views; the position of the sun is usually above the mountains. Therefore back faces are usually a minority.

4 Examples

Fig. 12 shows the effect of the terrain modeling techniques on the quality of generated images. Fig. 12 (a) shows several computer generated images, a power substation, several transmission towers, and a tank, compositing with a background image created from the aerial photo. In order to composite each image taking account of hidden surface removal, the 3D image composition method [10] was employed. No special processing described in section 3.2 for example has been done for trees in this image; roads and tower base are visible although they should be partially obscured by trees, so the image seems unnatural.

Fig. 12 (b) shows the effect of adding the tree height to the contour altitude; the image is improved a little. However, the boundaries of tree-covered regions look like cliffs because the resolution of the textures mapped onto these regions is very low and some triangular patches are clearly visible.

Fig. 12 (c) shows the effect of mapping actual side views of trees, as discussed in section 3.2, to boundaries of tree-covered regions. The resulting image looks relatively natural.

Figures 12 (a) and (b) were generated on a 500 × 363 display; the horizontal sampling pitch which indicates the

horizontal size of the mesh on the screen is 5.2 pixels. In Fig. 12 (c), the sampling pitch is set to 2 pixels, then the mountains are more accurately rendered.

Fig. 12 (d) is a recent photograph of the same region. Some differences from the computer generated montages are apparent and are due to the passage of time since the aerial photograph was taken.

In Fig. 13, we examine the relation between the resolution of the aerial photo data and the location of the viewpoint. Fig. 13 (a) was generated using aerial photographs with resolutions of 1/6000, 1/2000, and 1/1000, with the viewpoint 40 meters from the ground (see Fig. 8). In (b), a proposed switching station is overlaid onto the image of (a). In (c), only one aerial photo, at scale 1/6000, is used. Fig. (d) shows that relatively high quality montages can be generated, even with viewpoints at fairly low altitudes (7 meters), if aerial photos of high enough resolution are used. It is important for the ultimate resolution of the overlaid image to match that of the generated background. Mapped trees, rice straw racks and poles close to the viewpoint make the image more realistic. In (e), the same aerial photos as (a) are used, with the altitude of the viewpoint reduced to 1.4 meters. Fig. (f) is a recent photograph from almost the same viewpoint as that of (e), in which rice straw racks were omitted to compare with (f).

Fig. 14 shows the same landscape as Fig. 13, viewed from the opposite side. Notice the shadows cast on the ground by the base and towers of the switching station. The horizontal sampling pitch used for Figures 13 and 14 is 6.7 pixels and the display size, except for Fig. 13 (e), is 1000 × 666 pixels.

5   Conclusions

A new method for overlaying computer generated images onto background landscapes created by mapping aerial photos onto terrain models based on cartographic data has been described. This method exhibits the following advantages.

(1) The radial mesh results in approximately constant mesh density across the entire scene after perspective transformation.

(2) A hierarchy of aerial photo textures at various resolutions is used to assure approximately constant resolution of the texture maps after perspective transformation.

(4) Taking into account the height of trees, and mapping side views of trees at the boundaries of tree covered regions imparts a more natural appearance to the montage.

To demonstrate the usefulness of the method, several montages for environmental assessment of the construction of power substations have been generated.

Acknowledgment

The authors wish to thank Bonnie Sullivan for her assistance with the English manuscript. We would also like to thank the reviewers for their helpful comments.

References

[1] Agui, T., Miyata, K., and Nakajima, M. A Reconstructing Method of 3D Mountainous Shapes from Contours. *Trans. IEICE J69-D*, 12 (1986), 1905-1912, (in Japanese).

[2] Christiansen, N. H. and Sederberg, T. W. Conversion of Complex Contour Line Definitions into Polygonal Element Mosaics. *Computer Graphics 12*, 3 (1978), 187-192.

[3] Crow, F. C. Shadow Algorithms for Computer Graphics. *Computer Graphics 11*, 2 (1977), 242-247.

[4] Feibush, E. A., Leroy, M., and Cook, R. L. Synthetic Texturing Using Digital Filters. *Computer Graphics 14*, 3 (1980), 294-301.

[5] Gardner, G. Y. Simulation of Natural Scenes Using Textured Quadric Surfaces. *Computer Graphics 18*, 3 (1984), 11-19.

[6] Jet Propulsion Laboratory. Finale L. A. — The Movie. *SIGGRAPH '87 Film and Video Show* (1987).

[7] Marshall, R., Wilson, R., and Carlson, W. Procedure Models for Generating Three-Dimensional Terrain. *Computer Graphics 14*, 3 (1980), 154-162.

[8] Miller, G. S. P. The Definition and Rendering of Terrain Maps. *Computer Graphics 20*, 4 (1986), 39-48.

[9] Nakamae, E., Harada, K., Ishizaki, T., and Nishita, T. A Montage method: The Overlaying of the Computer Generated Images onto A Background Photograph. *Computer Graphics 20*, 4 (1986), 201-214.

[10] Nakamae, E., Ishizaki, T., Nishita, T., and Takita, S. Compositing 3D Images with Antialiasing and Various Shading Effects. *IEEE Computer Graphics & Applications 9*, 2 (1989), 21-29.

[11] Nishita, T., Okamura, I., and Nakamae, E. Shading Models for Point and Linear Sources. *ACM Transactions on Graphics 4*, 2 (1985), 124-146.

[12] Petrie, G. and Kennie, T. J. M. Terrain Modeling in Surveying and Civil engineering. *Computer Aided Design 19*, 4 (1987), 171-187.

[13] Porter, T. and Duff, T. Composing Digital Images. *Computer Graphics 18*, 3 (1984), 253-259.

[14] Rougelot, R. S. The General Electric Computed Color TV Display. Proceedings of the Second University of Illinois Conference on Computer Graphics. In *Pertinent Concepts in Computer Graphics. eds. Faiman, M. and Nievergelt, J.* University of Illinois Press (1969), 261-281.

[15] Uno, S. and Matsuka, H. A General Purpose Graphic System for Computer Aided Design. *Computer Graphics 13*, 2 (1979), 25-232.

[16] Williams, L. Pyramidal Parametrics. *Computer Graphics 17*, 3 (1983), 1-11.

Figure 12: Effect of the terrain modeling techniques. (a) Montage, height of trees ignored. (b) Montage, height of trees included. (c) Montage with side views of trees mapped onto boundary patches and increasing the horizontal sampling pitch. (d) Actual photograph of the site.

Figure 14: Changing the viewpoint.

Figure 13: Relationship between the resolution of the aerial photo data and the location of the viewpoint. (a) Background image created by mapping aerial photographs onto a terrain model. (b) Montage created using textures at several scales. (c) Montage created using only one texture resolution. (d) Viewpoint located relatively close to the ground. (e) Viewpoint located at the ground level. (f) Actual photograph of the site.

Computer Graphics, Volume 23, Number 3, July 1989

Good Vibrations:
Modal Dynamics for Graphics and Animation *

Alex Pentland and John Williams

Vision Sciences Group, E15-410
The Media Lab, M.I.T.
20 Ames St., Cambridge MA 02138

Abstract

Many of the problems of simulating and rendering complex systems of non-rigid objects can be minimized by describing the geometry and dynamics separately, using representations optimized for either one or the other, and then coupling these representations together. We describe a system which uses polynomial deformation mappings to couple a vibration-mode ("modal") representation of object dynamics together with volumetric models of object geometry. By use of such a hybrid representation we have been able to gain up to two orders of magnitude in efficiency, control temporal aliasing, and obtain simple, closed-form solutions to common (non-rigid) inverse dynamics problems. Further, this approach to dynamic simulation naturally lends itself to the emphasis and exaggeration techniques used in traditional animation.

1 INTRODUCTION

The idea of using computers to provide interactive simulation of non-rigid object dynamics has been a major goal of computer graphics, starting with Sketchpad [13], Thinglab [5], and the recent profusion of new computer graphics work on non-rigid dynamics [4,7,14]. Our project, which we have named Thingworld [10,11,12], was conceived as direct descendant of Sketchpad and Thinglab: our goal is to use interactive dynamic simulation of multibody situations to aid in physical design. In common with all previous attempts at achieving this goal, we have been confronted with the problem that the huge computational expense of calculating dynamic interactions prevents interactive simulation except for limited, toy situations. Furthermore, to be really useful to a designer, we must also be able to solve complex inverse dynamics problems, perform dynamic simulations for objects

*This research was made possible by National Science Foundation Grant No. IRI-87-19920 and by ARO Grant No. DAAL03-87-K-0005

defined by large spline surfaces or by constructive solid geometry, and render objects without undue temporal aliasing — all of which are quite difficult with standard techniques and representations.

In the Thingworld system we have been able to minimize each of these problems by describing the geometry and dynamics separately, using representations optimized for either one or the other, and then coupling these representations together using deformation mappings. In our system dynamic properties are described by *modal analysis*, a method of breaking non-rigid dynamics down into the sum of independent vibration modes. The advantage of the modal approach is that it breaks the dynamics problem into many small, independent problems. This allows us to achieve a level of control not possible with the massed equations normally used in dynamic simulation. As a consequence many common inverse dynamics problems can be solved in closed form, and many traditional animation techniques can be easily automated.

Because formulations for describing non-rigid motion have been based on point-wise representations of shape, the detection and characterization of collisions has always been a major fraction of the computational cost in multibody simulation systems. Further, analytic models of geometry (e.g., β-splines) cannot be used because there has been no way to relate analytically-specified shape to object dynamics. Because the Thingworld system describes non-rigid deformation in terms of whole-body deformation modes, we can relate object dynamics to object shape via global polynomial deformation mappings. This allows us to couple non-rigid object dynamics with analytic models of geometry (in our case superquadrics) so that we can more efficiently and accurately characterize the forces produced by collisions.

The plan of this paper is to first present short description of the modal method for representing and calculating non-rigid object dynamics. We will then show how the modal representation can be modified to produce great gains in efficiency, to reduce temporal aliasing, and to solve inverse dynamics problems. We will then describe how the method can be generalized to arbitrary geometric representations, thus allowing more efficient and accurate detection and characterization of object collisions. Finally, we will discuss how this system can be adapted to automatically produce many of the effects used in traditional animation.

215

2 MODAL DYNAMICS

2.1 Background: Finite Element Method

The finite element method (FEM) is a technique for simulating the dynamic behavior of an object. In the FEM the continuous variation of displacements throughout an object is replaced by a finite number of displacements at so-called nodal points. Displacements between nodal points are interpolated using a smooth function. Energy equations (or functionals) can then be derived in terms of the nodal unknowns and the resulting set of simultaneous equations can be iterated to solve for displacements as a function of impinging forces. In the dynamical case these equations may be written:

$$M\ddot{u} + D\dot{u} + Ku = f \qquad (1)$$

where $\mathbf{u}$ is a $3n$ x 1 vector of the (x, y, z) displacements of the n nodal points relative to the objects' center of mass, M, D and K are $3n$ by $3n$ matrices describing the mass, damping, and material stiffness between each point within the body, and $\mathbf{f}$ is a $3n$ x 1 vector describing the (x, y, z) components of the forces acting on the nodes. This equation can be interpreted as assigning a certain mass to each nodal point and a certain material stiffness between nodal points, with damping being accounted for by dashpots attached between the nodal points. The damping matrix D is often taken to be equal to sM for some scalar s; this is called mass damping.

To calculate the result of applying some force $\mathbf{f}$ to the object one discretizes the equations in time, picking an appropriately small time step, solves this equation for the new $\mathbf{u}$, and iterates until the system stabilizes. Direct (implicit) solution of the dynamic equations requires inversion the K matrix, and is thus computationally expensive. Consequently explicit Euler methods (which are less stable, but require no matrix inversion) are quite often applied.

Even the explicit Euler methods are quite expensive, because the matrices M, D, and K are quite large: for instance, the *simplest* 3-D parabolic element produces 60 x 60 matrices, corresponding to the 60 unknowns in the 20 nodal points (x_i, y_i, z_i) which specify the element shape. In most situations M, D, and K are very much larger than 60 x 60, so that typically hundreds or thousands of very large matrix multiplications are required for each second of simulated time. For more details see references [4,7,14,15].

2.2 Modal Analysis

Because M, D and K are normally positive definite symmetric, and M and D are assumed to be related by a scalar transformation, Equation 1 can be transformed into $3n$ independent differential equations by use of the *whitening transform*, which simultaneously diagonalizes M, D, and K. The whitening transform is the solution to the following eigenvalue problem:

$$\lambda\phi = M^{-1}K\phi \qquad (2)$$

where λ and ϕ are the eigenvalues and eigenvectors of $M^{-1}K$.

Using the transformation $u = \phi\bar{u}$ we can re-write Equation 1 as follows:

$$\phi^T M \phi \ddot{\bar{u}} + \phi^T D \phi \dot{\bar{u}} + \phi^T K \phi \bar{u} = \phi^T f \quad . \qquad (3)$$

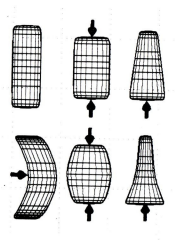

Figure 1: (a) A cylinder, (b) a linear deformation mode in response to compression, (c) a linear deformation mode in response to acceleration, (d) a quadratic mode in response to a bending force, (e) superposition of both linear and quadratic modes in response to compression, (f) superposition of both linear and quadratic modes in response to acceleration.

In this equation $\phi^T M \phi$, $\phi^T D \phi$, and $\phi^T K \phi$ are diagonal matrices, so that if we let $\bar{M} = \phi^T M \phi$, $\bar{D} = \phi^T D \phi$, $\bar{K} = \phi^T K \phi$, and $\bar{f} = \phi^T f$ then we can write Equation 3 as $3n$ independent equations:

$$\bar{M}_i \ddot{\bar{u}}_i + \bar{D}_i \dot{\bar{u}}_i + \bar{K}_i \bar{u}_i = \bar{f}_i \quad , \qquad (4)$$

where $\bar{M}_i$ is the ith diagonal element of $\bar{M}$, and so forth. Because the modal representation diagonalizes these matrices it may be viewed as *preconditioning* the mass and stiffness matrices, with the attendant advantages of better convergence and numerical accuracy.

What Equation 4 describes is the time course of one of the object's *vibration modes*, hence the name *modal analysis* [16]. The constant $\bar{M}_i$ is the generalized mass of mode i, that is, it describes the inertia of this vibration mode. Similarly, $\bar{D}_i$, and $\bar{K}_i$ describe the damping and spring stiffness associated with mode i, and $\bar{f}_i$ is the amount of force coupled with this vibration mode. The ith row of ϕ describes the *deformation* the object experiences as a consequence of the force $\bar{f}_i$, and the eigenvalue λ_i is proportional to the natural resonance frequency of that vibration mode.

Figure 1 illustrates the some of the first and second order modes of a cylinder. Figure 1(a) shows the cylinder at rest, (b) shows the cylinder experiencing a linear deformation in response to a compressive force, (c) shows the cylinder experiencing a linear shear deformation in response to an accelerating force, (d) shows a quadratic deformation in response to a centrally-applied (bending) force, and (e) and (f) show how both the linear and second order deformations can be superimposed to produce a more accurate simulation of the object's response to the compressive and accelerating forces shown in (b) and (c).

To obtain an accurate simulation of the dynamics of an object one simply uses linear superposition of these modes to determine how the object responds to a given force. Because Equation 4 can be solved in closed form, we have the result that for objects composed of linearly-deforming materials *the non-rigid behavior of the object in response to an impulse force can be solved in closed form for any time t.* The solution is discussed in Section 5.1. In environments with more complex forces, however, analytic solution becomes cumbersome and so numerical solution is preferred. Either explicit or implicit solution techniques may be used to calculate how each mode varies with time.

Non-linear materials may be modeled by summing the modes at the end of each time step to form the material *stress state* which can then be used to drive nonlinear plastic or viscous material behavior.

3 USING THE MODAL METHOD

Although the simple modal method offers some benefits in terms of efficiency and stability, its main advantage is that it allows us to control the computation in ways that are advantageous to various applications. In this section we detail some of the variations on the basic modal method that we have found to be particularly useful.

3.1 Increased Speed

Modes associated with high resonance frequencies normally have little effect on object shape. This is because, for a fixed excitation energy, the displacement amplitude for each mode is inversely proportional to the *square* of the mode's resonance frequency. Thus a relatively accurate and more efficient simulation of an object's dynamics can be accomplished by discarding the small-amplitude, high-frequency modes, and superimposing only the large-amplitude, low-frequency modes. We can determine which modes to discard by examining their associated eigenvalue, which is proportional to the resonance frequency.

The amount of error introduced by discarding high-frequency modes can be checked by occasionally substituting the displacements u produced by low-frequency modal analysis into the full equations. When significant error is found additional modes can be added. Exactly which modes to add can be determined by a principal components analysis of the error residuals.

One effect of discarding modes is, of course, to reduce the number of equations that must be considered within each time step. However, because the maximum allowable time step is inversely proportional to the highest resonance frequency in the system of equations, a more important effect of discarding high-frequency modes is that we can use much larger time steps. In typical situations we have found that the savings from fewer equations and larger times steps can reduce computation time by up to two orders of magnitude, while at the same time producing a reasonably accurate, realistic-looking animation.

3.1.1 Number of modes required

For the sake of increased efficiency, our approach has been to model only as many modes as are required. In a quick-and-dirty analysis — often sufficient during the initial phase of a design — only rigid-body or rigid-body plus linear strain modes may be used, resulting in large computational savings.

Later, more modes can be added to achieve any level of desired accuracy, although at greater cost.

We have found that most commonplace multi-body interactions can be adequately modeled by use of only rigid-body, linear, and quadratic strain modes, as is shown in Figures 1 and 2. Note that this is *not* true for bodies whose dimensions are quite disparate, however it is exactly these cases that can be adequately treated by either a one or two dimensional analysis, and thus are cases where the standard FEM is quite efficient.

3.1.2 Recomputing matrices and modes

Normally, in either the finite element or modal methods, the mass, damping, and stiffness matrices are not recomputed at each time step. The use of fixed M, D, and K (or, equivalently, fixed modes) is well-justified as long as the material displacements are small. The definition of "small," however, is quite different for different modes. Because the eigenvalue decomposition in Equation 2 performs a sort of principal-components analysis, it is the gross object shape (e.g., its low-order moments of inertia) determine the low-frequency modes, which as a consequence are quite stable. High-frequency modes are much less stable because they are determined by the fine features of the object's shape.

In the standard finite element formulation the action of each mode is distributed across the entire set of equations, so that one must recompute the mass and stiffness matrices as often as required by the very highest-frequency vibration modes. When these high-frequency modes are discarded the mass, damping, and stiffness matrices need to be recomputed much less frequently — a large computational savings. We have found, for instance, that in most animation sequences we can use a single, fixed set of low-frequency modes throughout the entire simulation.

3.1.3 An example

Figure 2 shows a example of computing non-rigid dynamic interaction: a ball colliding with a two-by-four. As can be seen, the interaction and resulting deformations look realistic despite the use of only first and second order modes. Perhaps the most impressive fact about this example, however, is the speed of computation: Using a Symbolics 3600 (with a speed of roughly one MIP), it requires only one CPU second to compute each second of simulated time!

3.2 Temporal Aliasing

One important side effect of discarding high-frequency modes is reduction in temporal aliasing artifacts. A dynamic simulation using the standard finite element method will produce very many small, high-temporal-frequency displacements. This is especially true for stiff materials. To avoid temporal aliasing artifacts these small displacements must be accurately tracked (requiring a small time step), and then averaged over time to produce each image. In modal analysis these high frequency displacements can be directly identified and discarded, thus reducing not only the number of time steps required, but also the need for time averaging in order to avoid temporal artifacts.

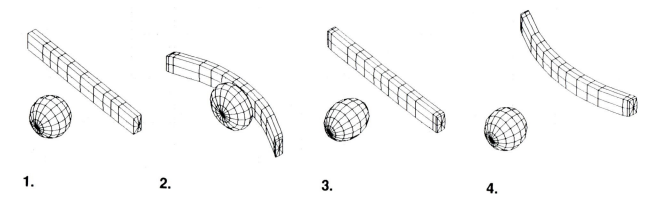

1. 2. 3. 4.

Figure 2: A ball colliding with a two-by-four

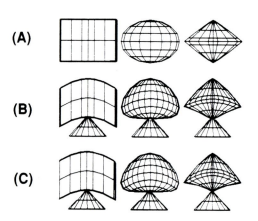

(A)

(B)

(C)

Figure 3: Low-order deformation modes are visually similar when objects have similar low-order moments of inertia.

3.3 Use of Approximate Modes

An object's low-order deformation modes can be thought of as the principal components of the object's repertoire of non-rigid behavior. These modes can be found by solving the eigenvalue problem of Equation 2, however for visualization purposes we have found that it is sufficient to use fixed, precomputed deformation modes that are parameterized only by the object's low order moments of inertia.

This is illustrated in Figure 3, which shows three objects colliding with a post after having been dropped from a few feet above the post. Figure 3(a) shows the original, undeformed objects. Figure 3(b) shows the collisions simulated using modes computed by solving Equation 2. In Figure 3(c) we have precomputed the modes of a rectangular solid with approximately the same moments as the object to be animated. These precomputed deformation modes were then used in place of the object's true modes in making the animation. Despite use of precomputed modes it can be seen that the collisions are visually very similar.

A more accurate variation on this theme is to use 20 nodal points (i.e., a simple 3-D parabolic element) to approximate the shape of the object to be animated. Equation 2 can

be solved relatively quickly for this number of nodal points, and the resulting modes will produce a reasonably accurate simulation. Such shortcuts to finding an object's modes can produce an important savings in interactive simulation systems such as Thingworld, where the user frequently changes each object's static geometry.

4 COMBINING DYNAMICS AND ANALYTIC GEOMETRY

One problem with standard non-rigid dynamical techniques is that they are based on use of a point-wise representation of geometry, thus forcing the representation of geometry and dynamics to be identical. As a consequence one cannot, for instance, specify details of geometry without incurring large costs in calculating dynamic behavior, nor can one directly animate objects defined by, for example, large spline patches or constructive solid geometry. The fact that the same representation must be used for both geometry and dynamics thus has a large impact upon the efficiency and accuracy of multibody simulations, where detailed specification of geometry is required to obtain accurate detection and characterization of collisions.

We have been able to combine separate representations of dynamic behavior and geometric form in order to avoid these problems. We have accomplished this by describing each mode by an appropriate polynomial function, and then using global deformation techniques [3] to establish the correspondence between dynamic state and geometric state. The result is an efficient scheme for simulating non-rigid dynamics that can be applied in a unified manner to objects whose geometry is defined using a wide range of techniques.

To accomplish this, we must first realize that modes may be classified by the complexity of the associated deformation, e.g., as 0th order (rigid body) modes, 1st order (linear deformation) modes, 2nd order (quadratic deformation) modes, and so forth, as was illustrated by Figure 1. Thus we can describe the deformation associated with each mode by use of polynomial deformation mappings of the appropriate degree. This is accomplished by performing a linear regression of a polynomial with m terms in appropriate powers of x, y, and z, against the n triples of x, y and z coefficients that compose ϕ_i, a $3n$ x 1 vector containing the elements of the

i^{th} row of ϕ:

$$\alpha = (\beta^T \beta)^{-1} \beta^T \phi_i \quad , \qquad (5)$$

where α is an m x 1 matrix of the coefficients of the desired deformation polynomial, β is an $3n$ x m matrix whose first column contains the elements of $\mathbf{u} = (x_1, y_1, z_1, x_2, y_2, z_2, ...)$, and whose remaining columns consist of the modified versions of $\mathbf{u}$ where the x, y, and/or z components have been raised to the various powers, e.g.,

$$\beta = \begin{pmatrix} x_1 & x_1^2 & x_1 & x_1 & ... \\ y_1 & y_1 & y_1^2 & y_1 & ... \\ z_1 & z_1 & z_1 & z_1^2 & ... \\ x_2 & x_2^2 & x_2 & x_2 & ... \\ y_2 & y_2 & y_2^2 & y_2 & ... \\ z_2 & z_2 & z_2 & z_2^2 & ... \\ \vdots & \vdots & \vdots & \vdots & \end{pmatrix} \quad . \qquad (6)$$

The question of which polynomial powers are the appropriate for a particular column of ϕ can be decided either by inspection (noting that the order of the deformation is related to the associated eigenvalue), or automatically by including all combinations of powers of x, y, and z (up to some limit), performing the regression, and then discarding coefficients with negligible magnitude.

The result is a polynomial model of the unit amplitude deformation associated with mode i. By simply scaling this polynomial deformation according to the mode's amplitude we can accurately copy the effects of this mode on the object's shape. By superimposing these deformations we obtain an accurate accounting of the object's non-rigid deformation.

4.1 Fast Collision Characterization

In complex, multi-body simulations the ability to efficiently detect and characterize collisions is extremely important. Unfortunately, the point-wise representations used by the standard FEM are quite poor at this task. When using a polygon representation, for instance, the computational complexity of collision detection is $O(nm)$ operations, where n is the number of polygons and m is the number of points to be considered after pruning via bounding box calculations [9].

In contrast, one can perform collision detection relatively efficiently when employing volumetric representations (e.g., superquadrics [2,6,10]) by making use of their inside-outside function. In our system the basic volumetric primitive is a superquadric, which is mapped from its canonical reference frame[1] to its three-space position by an affine transformation T. The normalized inside-outside function $D(x,y,z)$ for superquadrics is:

$$D(x,y,z) = \left[((x/a_1)^{2/\epsilon_1} + (y/a_2)^{2/\epsilon_1})^{\epsilon_1/\epsilon_2} + (z/a_3)^{2/\epsilon_2} \right]^{\epsilon_2} \qquad (7)$$

where the position (x, y, z) is relative to the object's canonical reference frame. The basic operation for collision detection, then, is to take points (x, y, z) sampled from the tested object's surface, apply T^{-1} to convert them to the canonical

---

[1]The canonical reference frame is when the object has zero rotation, and is centered at $(0, 0, 0)$

reference frame, and then substitute them into the inside-outside function. When the result is less than one the point is inside the surface, if greater then one the point is outside. Thus, the computational complexity is only $O(m)$, rather than $0(nm)$, where n and m are as before. As with other representations [9], to find the exact point in space-time at which contact between the two bodies occurred requires use of numerical minimization techniques, where both point position, T and Equation 7 are expressed as functions of time. In the Thingworld system we have found that the ability to perform fast collision detection using volumetric representations yields large computational savings.

4.2 Accuracy of Collision Characterization

A more subtle but perhaps equally important advantage of being able to use analytic representations in dynamic simulations is the ability to characterize the collision surface more quickly and precisely. For instance, one difficult problem that arises when using any discrete time technique is that colliding bodies often interpenetrate during a time step. The depth, area and shape of this penetration determines the repulsive force generated.

With point-wise (polygon) representations it is difficult to determine the interpenetration region, so that most systems ignore the contact area's shape and simply find the single point (normally a polygon vertex) that first contacted the surface. As a consequence the calculated force is often seriously in error. When using analytic representations of geometry, however, both surface normal and principal curvatures are readily available so that good closed form approximations to the depth, area and shape of the interpenetration region can be easily computed.

5 The Right Control Knobs

One of the most important aspects of any simulation or animation system is the ability to control the behavior of objects in a natural, intuitive, and convenient manner: in short, the system must have the right control knobs. In simulation systems such as Thingworld, one often needs to be able to solve simple inverse dynamics problems: For instance, to make something jump from here to there and land softly. In animation systems the same requirements arise, but in addition one needs to be able to produce pleasing but non-physically-realistic effects. In traditional animation some of the most important of these effects are called squash-and-stretch, anticipation, and exaggeration [8].

The control knobs for these sorts of things simply don't exist with standard approaches to dynamic simulation. Even simple inverse dynamics problems, for instance, require solving huge numerical minimization problems because all of dynamical equations are closely coupled together. Similarly, traditional animation effects such as squash-and-stretch can only be obtained by carefully jiggering material properties and external forces as a function of object position, velocity, and so forth.

The situation is quite different when using modal analysis, because closed-form solutions exist for each mode's behavior as a function of time, and because the various modal behaviors are independent of each other so that they may

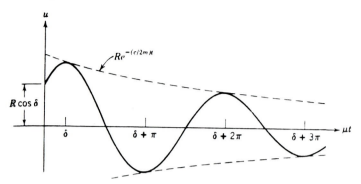

Figure 4: Damped vibration as a function of time.

be treated separately. Further, the low-order modes of an object seem to closely mimic many of the effects used in traditional animation.

5.1 Inverse Dynamics

The time behavior of each mode in response to an impinging force is given by Equation 4. The generic solution to this equation is

$$\bar{u}_i = Ae^{r_1 t} + Be^{r_2 t},$$
$$\text{for} \quad \bar{D}_i^2 - 4\bar{K}_i\bar{M}_i > 0, \quad r_1, r_2 < 0$$

$$\bar{u}_i = (A + Bt)e^{(\bar{D}_i/2\bar{M}_i)t},$$
$$\text{for} \quad \bar{D}_i^2 - 4\bar{K}_i\bar{M}_i = 0, \quad (8)$$

$$\bar{u}_i = e^{(\bar{D}_i/2\bar{M}_i)t}(A\cos\mu t + B\sin\mu t),$$
$$\text{for} \quad \mu = (4\bar{K}_i\bar{M}_i - \bar{D}_i^2)^{1/2}/2\bar{M}_i > 0$$

for the overdamped, critically damped, and underdamped cases, where

$$r_1, r_2 = \frac{-\bar{D}_i \pm \sqrt{\bar{D}_i^2 - 4\bar{K}_i\bar{M}_i}}{2\bar{M}_i} \quad (9)$$

and A and B depend on the initial conditions [1]. The third case, underdamped motion, occurs most commonly in mechanical systems and is referred to as "damped vibration." To see this we let $A = R\cos\delta$ and $B = R\sin\delta$ in Equation 8 to obtain

$$\bar{u}_i = Re^{-(\bar{K}_i/2\bar{M}_i)t}\cos(\mu t - \delta) \quad , \quad (10)$$

which is graphed in Figure 4.

Thus, once we know the amplitude and derivative of a mode at time zero, we can predict its behavior for all future times — or at least until an external force adds or subtracts energy from the mode. In particular, given initial conditions $\bar{u}_i(0) = \chi$, $\dot{\bar{u}}_i(0) = \dot{\chi}$, and underdamped free oscillation, then

$$\bar{u}_i(t) = \left(\chi^2 + (\frac{\dot{\chi}}{\mu} + \frac{\bar{D}_i\chi}{2\bar{M}_i\mu})^2\right)^{1/2} e^{\bar{K}_i t/2\bar{M}_i}\cos(\mu t - \delta) \quad (11)$$

where $\delta = \tan^{-1}[(\dot{\chi}/\chi + \bar{D}_i\chi/2\mu\bar{M}_i)/\chi]$. Using this relation we can achieve a desired object shape at some time t_1 by adjusting initial modal amplitude and velocity at time t_0. Similarly, we can specify the desired object shape at times t_0 and t_1, and then solve for the force required to achieve those

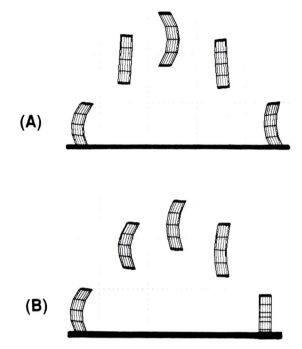

Figure 5: A time lapse illustration of a cylinder jumping and landing (a) with a hard thump, (b) softly. Time proceeds from left to right.

constraints. Thus, Equation 11 can provide us with closed-form solutions to many common inverse dynamics problems. For closed-form solutions under other initial conditions see reference [1].

5.1.1 Some Examples

Imagine that we want a cylindrical solid to jump from point A to point B, landing either softly or with a hard "thump". Further, imagine that we wish to control the cylinder by changing only the characteristics of it's "muscles," i.e., by controlling the displacement and spring constant associated with each deformation mode. The inverse dynamics problem, then, is to make sure that the cylinder has the correct amount of extension or compression at the point of landing so that it can achieve the desired type of landing.

The mathematics for calculating a trajectory that will take the cylinder from point A at time $t = t_0$ to point B is well known. That calculation will also give us the time $t = t_1$ at which landing will occur, and the force vector $f_{initial}$ needed to achieve the jump. If we idealize the geometry and time course of how the cylinder pushes against point A, then we can use standard kinematics to determine how much the cylinder must "crouch" and tense it's "muscles" (i.e., what initial modal displacements $\bar{u}_i(t_0)$ and spring constants $\bar{K}_i(t_0)$ are required) in order to produce the desired force vector.

Producing a jump by use of the spring energies stored in the various modes will leave each of the modes in some state $\bar{u}_i(t_0 + \epsilon) = \chi_i$, $\dot{\bar{u}}_i(t_0 + \epsilon) = \dot{\chi}_i$ as the cylinder leaves the surface. The inverse dynamics problem is then to set the spring constants $\bar{K}_i(t)$ (for $t_0 < t < t_1$) of the cylinder's

Figure 6: (a) Physical squash-and-stretch in a collision.

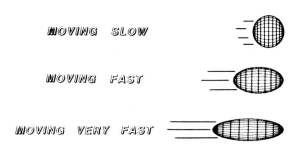

Figure 7: Stretching/squashing tied to velocity

"muscles" so that the natural oscillation of the cylinder exerts the desired motion-canceling force f_{final} on point B at the appointed instant in time.

To obtain f_{final} at $t = t_1$ we first determine what combination of modal amplitudes will exert the desired final force by computing

$$\bar{u}_i(t_1) = \bar{f}_i / \bar{K}_i(t_1) \qquad , \qquad (12)$$

where $\bar{f} = \phi^T f_{final}$, and the $\bar{K}_i(t_1)$ correspond to "tensing" the muscles for landing. We then solve Equation 11 with the given values of $t = t_1$, $\bar{M}_i$, $\bar{D}_i$, $\bar{u}_i(t_0) = \chi_i$, and $\dot{\bar{u}}_i(t_0) = \dot{\chi}_i$ in order to find a stiffness $\bar{K}_i(t)$, $t_0 < t < t_1$, such that $\bar{u}_i(t_1)$ has the desired value. [2] Thus Equation 11 provides a closed-form solution to such simple inverse dynamics problems — at least when we can idealize contact geometry, friction, etc. Examples of jumps computed in this manner are shown in Figure 5.

In most situations of interest, unfortunately, the particulars of geometry and friction are sufficiently complex and non-linear that there is no closed-form solution, so that one must still employ the sort of constrained minimization described in [17] to obtain a solution. However, as these examples illustrate, by using Equation 11 it appears that the problem can be reduced from several thousand free parameters to only a few dozen free parameters.

5.2 Control of Animation

The deformations caused by an object's low-order vibration modes correspond closely to the types of exaggeration and emphasis used in traditional animation. Thus, the amplitude of these low-order modes provides the control knobs needed for such animation.

A simple version of squash-and-stretch in collisions is well modeled by straightforward application of non-rigid dynamic simulation: things *do* squash and stretch during collisions, a shown in Figure 6. However, as applied in traditional animation, this notion goes well beyond simply obtaining physically-realistic deformations during a collision. It also occurs as a response to motion, to acceleration, and even in response to emotional states. By providing a "stretch/squash" control knob we can wire squashing-type

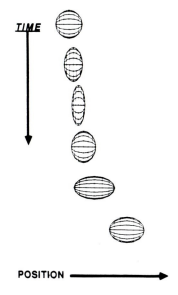

Figure 8: Stretching/squashing tied to speed minus acceleration; time proceeds from top to bottom.

deformations directly to other parameters, both physical and non-physical, in order to obtain interesting visual effects.

Examples of this are shown in Figures 7, 8 and 9, where we have wired the "stretch/squash" knob to various physical properties. Figure 7 shows three objects moving at different speeds. In this figure the amplitude of the stretching/squashing deformation is set equal the speed, so that as the object moves faster it becomes stretched out in the direction of motion.

Figure 8 shows a time series where the stretch/squash deformation is equal to the speed minus the acceleration, so that an accelerating object "piles up" in anticipation as the motion begins, and stretches out as the motion reaches steady state.

Finally, Figure 9 shows three mushrooms with both bending and stretching/squashing deformations tied to image x position: as a consequence the mushrooms "wilt" from left to right. The same deformations could be tied to emotional state, for instance, thus providing physical illustration of a character's state of depression or elation.

---

[2]The $\bar{K}_i(t_1)$ must of course be large enough that the modal displacements at $t = t_1$ (which are no larger than the displacements at $t = t_0$) generate sufficient energy.

Figure 9: Stretching/squashing to express emotional state.

6 SUMMARY

The idea of using computers to provide interactive simulation of non-rigid object dynamics has long been frustrated by the inability to efficiently calculate dynamic interactions, to solve inverse dynamics problems, to use geometry defined by splines or constructive solid geometry, and to avoid temporal aliasing problems. We have been able to minimize each of these problems by developing new, hybrid methods for representing and calculating object dynamics in which the object's geometry and dynamics are described by separate but yoked representations. The result is a system which is efficient at performing dynamic simulations, can be applied to a wide range of geometric models, and which is useful for implementing many of the techniques used in traditional animation.

REFERENCES

[1] Anderson, J. S., and Bratos-Anderson, M., (1987) Solving Problems in Vibrations, Longman Scientific and Technical Publ., Essex, England.

[2] Barr, A., (1981) Superquadrics and angle-preserving transformations, *IEEE Computer Graphics and Application, 1* 1-20

[3] Barr, A., (1984) Global and local deformations of solid primitives. Proceedings of SIGGRAPH '84, *Computer Graphics 18,* 3, 21-30

[4] Barzel, R., and Barr, A., (1988) A Modeling System Based On Dynamic Constraints, Proceedings of SIGGRAPH '88, *Computer Graphics,* Vol. 22, No. 4, pp. 179-188

[5] Borning, A., (1979), Thinglab – a constraint-oriented simulation laboratory. SSL-79-3, Xerox PARC, Palo Alto, CA.

[6] Gardiner, M. (1965) The superellipse: a curve that lies between the ellipse and the rectangle, *Scientific American,* September 1965.

[7] Issacs, P., and Cohen, M., (1987) Controlling Dynamic Simulation with Kinematic Constraints, Behavior Functions, and Inverse Dynamics, Proceedings of SIGGRAPH '87, *Computer Graphics,* Vol. 21, No. 4, pp 215-224.

[8] Lasseter, J., (1987) Principles of Traditional Animation Applied to 3D Computer Animation, Proceedings of SIGGRAPH '87, *Computer Graphics 21,* 4, 35-44

[9] Moore, M., and Wilhelms, J., (1988) Collision Detection and Response for Computer Animation, Proceedings of SIGGRAPH '88, *Computer Graphics 22,* 4, 289-298

[10] Pentland, A. (1986) Perceptual Organization and the Representation of Natural Form, *Artificial Intelligence Journal,* Vol. 28, No. 2, pp. 1-38.

[11] Pentland, A., (1987) Towards and Ideal 3-D CAD System, *SPIE conference on Machine Vision and the Man-Machine Interface,* Jan. 11-16, San Diego, CA.

[12] Pentland, A., and Williams, J. (1988) Virtual Construction, *Construction,* Vol. 3, No. 3, pp. 12-22

[13] Sutherland, I., (1963), Sketchpad: A Man-Machine Graphical Communications System, in Interactive Computer Graphics, in *1963 Spring Joint Computer Conference,* reprinted in H. Freeman, ed., IEEE Comp. Soc., 1980, pp. 1-19.

[14] Terzopoulos, D., Platt, J., Barr, A., and Fleischer, K., (1987) Elastically deformable models, Proceedings of SIGGRAPH '87, *Computer Graphics,* Vol. 21, No. 4, pp 205-214.

[15] Williams, J., Musto, G., and Hawking, G., (1987) The Theoretical Basis of the Discrete Element Method, *Numerical Methods in Engineering, Theory, and Application,* Rotterdam: Balkema Publishers

[16] Williams, J. and Musto, G. (1987) Modal Methods for the Analysis of Discrete Systems, *Computers and Geotechnics,* Vol. 4, pp 1-19.

[17] Witkin, A., and Kass, M. (1988) Space-Time Constraints, Proceedings of SIGGRAPH '88, *Computer Graphics 22,* 4, 159-168

Analytical Methods for Dynamic Simulation of Non-penetrating Rigid Bodies

David Baraff

Program of Computer Graphics
Cornell University
Ithaca, NY 14853

Abstract

A method for analytically calculating the forces between systems of rigid bodies in resting (non-colliding) contact is presented. The systems of bodies may either be in motion or static equilibrium and adjacent bodies may touch at multiple points. The analytic formulation of the forces between bodies in non-colliding contact can be modified to deal with colliding bodies. Accordingly, an improved method for analytically calculating the forces between systems of rigid bodies in colliding contact is also presented. Both methods can be applied to systems with arbitrary holonomic geometric constraints, such as linked figures. The analytical formulations used treat both holonomic and non-holonomic constraints in a consistent manner.

Categories and Subject Descriptors: I.3.5 [**Computer Graphics**]: Computational Geometry and Object Modeling; I.3.7 [**Computer Graphics**]: Three-Dimensional Graphics and Realism

Additional Key Words and Phrases: dynamics, constraints, simulation

1. Introduction

Recent work has focused on using the laws of Newtonian dynamics to simulate the motions of systems of rigid bodies. A realistic simulation of rigid bodies demands that no two bodies inter-penetrate. In order to enforce this constraint a simulator must first detect potential inter-penetration between two bodies and then act to prevent the two bodies from penetrating. However, in keeping with the laws of Newtonian dynamics, a realistic simulation should not prevent inter-penetration in an arbitrary manner. The simulator should calculate what forces would actually arise in nature to prevent bodies from inter-penetrating and then use these forces to derive the actual motion of the bodies. In order to calculate these forces an explicit formulation is necessary.

Traditional techniques from engineering and physics are not applicable to the problem of calculating forces between bodies in resting contact. These techniques assume that the systems of bodies being analyzed are in equilibrium. However, many of the simulations in computer graphics involve systems of bodies that are not in equilibrium. For example, the forces between the bricks in figure 1 cannot be calculated using traditional techniques.

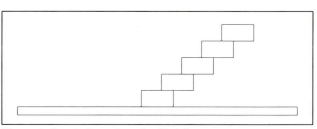

Figure 1. Overbalanced stack of bricks.

This paper focuses on the following specific problem: given a number of *non-colliding* rigid polyhedral bodies, calculate the forces that would naturally arise to prevent bodies from inter-penetrating. The bodies may also be constrained to satisfy certain geometrical relationships such as those present in articulated figures[2, 8]. An analytical solution to the problem is presented that uses linear programming techniques to formulate and heuristically solve a system of inequality and equality constraints on the forces. The system of constraints guarantees that the contact forces will prevent inter-penetration and satisfy the laws of Newtonian dynamics. The solution is generalized to yield an improved algorithm for calculating forces between colliding systems of rigid polyhedral bodies.

2. Previous Work

Analytical methods for calculating the forces between *colliding* rigid bodies have been presented by Moore and Wilhelms[13] and Hahn[7]. Both methods calculated the impulse between a single pair of bodies that collided at a single point. Moore and Wilhelms modeled simultaneous collisions as a slightly staggered series of single collisions and used non-analytical methods (below) to deal with bodies in resting contact. Hahn prevented bodies in resting contact from inter-penetrating by modeling their contact as a series of frequently occurring collisions. This model may be suitable for preventing inter-penetration in animation applications; however, it is not a valid analytical model of forces between bodies in resting contact.

"Penalty" methods that introduce restoring forces when objects inter-penetrate have also been presented. Terzopolous *et al.*[18] and Platt and Barr[16] produced highly realistic animations of rigid and deformable non-penetrating bodies. Inter-penetration was prevented in both papers by introducing arbitrary penalty forces that acted to separate penetrating bodies; a natural solution method, since dynamical correctness of these forces was not a focus of either paper. Moore and Wilhelms[13] introduced spring forces (a penalty method) to prevent bodies in resting contact from penetrating.

©1989   ACM-0-89791-312-4/89/007/0223 $00.75

2.1 Penalty Methods vs. Analytical Methods

Analytical methods offer several advantages over penalty methods. Penalty methods for rigid bodies are often computationally expensive, give only approximate results, and may require adjustments for different simulation conditions (figure 2).

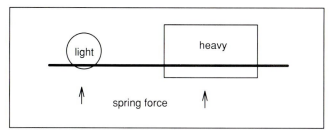

Figure 2. Differing amounts of inter-penetration from a penalty method.

These undesirable behaviors arise from the attempt to model infinite quantities (infinite rigidity of bodies, infinitely hard surfaces) with finite values. In particular, the differential equations that arise using penalty methods may be "stiff" and require an excessive number of time-steps during simulation to obtain accurate results. Additionally, the correctness of the simulation under penalty methods is very difficult to verify. In their defense, penalty methods for rigid bodies are simple to implement and are easily extendible to non-rigid bodies.

In contrast, analytical methods for rigid bodies give exact answers and produce differential equations that require far fewer time steps during simulation. The correctness of the simulation when using an analytical method is easily provable because analytical solutions are based directly on the laws of Newtonian dynamics. Analytical methods however are much more complex to derive and implement.

3. Simulation using Analytical Methods

Simulations of rigid bodies employing analytical methods should treat collision forces and resting contact forces differently. Analytically, collision forces are discontinuous impulsive forces in that they exist for a single instant of time and have the dimensions of mass times velocity (or equivalently force times time). Resting contact forces, or more simply, contact forces, are continuous over some non-zero interval of time and have the dimensions of mass times acceleration. The effects of collision forces are independent of non-impulsive forces such as contact forces or gravity. Impulsive forces cause discontinuities in a body's velocity; contact forces do not.

Our simulator iterates through time (time steps) by solving a first order system of coupled ordinary differential equations[1, 2]. Given the net force and torque on each body, the differential equations can be solved to yield the motion of the bodies. We adopt the usual method for solving the system of differential equations by using numerical integration procedures such as fourth order Runge-Kutta or Adams-Moulton[17] with adaptive time-step parameters. The integrator is given initial conditions in the form of the starting orientations, positions, and linear and angular velocities of all the bodies. As stated above, analytical methods introduce discontinuities in some of the velocities when collisions occur. It is unwise to blithely integrate over these collision times.[1]

Finding the time at which a collision occurs can be viewed as a root-finding problem. The collision time is found by using backtracking methods similar to those described by Moore and Wilhelms[13]. The collision time is bracketed by successively shorter time intervals until the colliding objects touch within a suitable tolerance.[2] Once the collision time has been calculated, the integrator is stopped (at the collision time) and collision forces are computed. Collision forces may be calculated using previous methods[7, 13] or by the improved collision method presented in section 8. The collision forces are used to compute the new velocities of the colliding bodies and then the integrator is restarted with new initial conditions. The new initial conditions are the positions and orientations at the time of the collision and the newly computed velocities. We call this series of steps *resolving* the collision. Since the computation of the new velocities (due to the collision forces) is independent of any contact forces, contact forces are not calculated until *after* collisions are resolved. Accordingly, the formulation of the resting contact problem implicitly assumes that no bodies in contact are colliding i.e. collisions have been resolved.

4. Modeling Contact

We will use the following terminology. Let two bodies A and B be in contact (colliding or resting) at some time t_0; A and B touch each other at some number of *contact points*. At time t_0, let p be the position of an arbitrary contact point in some world space. Define p_a and p_b as the positions of the two points of A and B that satisfy $p_a(t_0) = p = p_b(t_0)$ (figure 3).

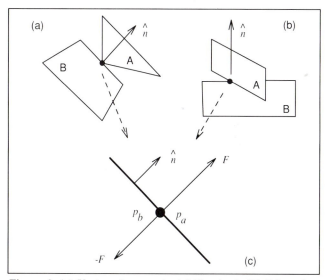

Figure 3. (a) Vertex-plane contact (side view). (b) Edge-edge contact. (c) Contact geometry.

p_a and p_b are functions of time; they track the motion of two specific points of A and B that coincide at time t_0. Both p_a and p_b vary according to the independent rigid body motions of A and B. The relative motion, $\dot{p}_a(t_0) - \dot{p}_b(t_0)$, indicates whether A and B are colliding, resting, or separating at point p at time t_0.

At each contact point there is a *contact force* $\vec{F}$, (possibly zero) between A and B and a unit surface normal $\hat{n}$. For vertex-plane contact, the body whose vertex is the contact point is identified as body A. $\hat{n}$ is defined as the outwards unit surface

[1]Numerical integrators assume that the functions they are integrating are continuous functions of time. If a function being integrated is discontinuous at some time t_0, the integrator must integrate up to t_0, stop, and then restart at t_0 with new initial conditions.

[2]We have found that using the relative displacements of inter-penetrating bodies to implement a *regula falsa* method results in much faster convergence than the simpler bisection method. Our tolerance was chosen empirically.

224

normal of B at p_b (figure 3a). For edge-edge contact, one body is identified as body A arbitrarily. $\hat{n}$ is defined as a unit vector mutually perpendicular to the two contacting edges and directed away from B (figure 3b). In the absence of friction, $\vec{F}$ is colinear with $\hat{n}$ for both vertex-plane and vertex-edge contacts. Thus, we may write $\vec{F} = f\hat{n}$ where f is the unknown magnitude of the contact force. From Newton's third law, if the force on A is $f\hat{n}$ then the force on B will be $-f\hat{n}$. Our goal is to calculate contact force magnitudes that prevent inter-penetration.

4.1 Degenerate Contact Points

For vertex-vertex contacts, one body is identified as body A arbitrarily; for vertex-edge contacts, the body whose vertex is a contact point is identified as body A. Physically, vertex-vertex contacts (figure 4a) and vertex-edge contacts are *indeterminate*: the surface normal $\hat{n}$ is not well defined and the direction of the contact force between A and B cannot be determined. Consequently, the physically correct behavior of A and B may be indeterminate during the interval in which degenerate contact points occur. In the absence of degenerate contact points, the physically correct behavior of A and B is unique.

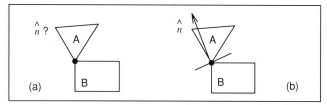

Figure 4. (a) Indeterminate vertex-vertex contact or vertex-edge contact (side view). (b) Removing indeterminacy by choosing $\hat{n}$.

Since the contact force direction is indeterminate, a direction for $\vec{F}$ must be chosen. To be consistent with our description of vertex-plane and edge-edge contacts we set $\hat{n}$ to be an arbitrary unit vector directed away from B.[3] We then write $\vec{F} = f\hat{n}$, with f an unknown magnitude. The choice of $\hat{n}$ at degenerate contact points implicitly determines a particular behavior for A and B. Usually, indeterminate configurations exist only instantaneously, so the choice of $\hat{n}$ for indeterminate configurations has little effect on the simulation.

However, if a configuration of bodies has degenerate contact points, calculating the correct contact force magnitudes is an NP-complete problem. This result follows directly from a theorem due to Palmer[15]. The problem remains NP-complete even after a direction for $\vec{F}$ is chosen. Solving NP-complete problems currently requires exponential time and is considered intractable. (See Palmer[15] and Garey and Johnson[3] for further discussion). The NP-completeness may be avoided by converting indeterminate contacts to determinate contacts. Our system does this by imagining that B has been locally extended in a plane normal to $\hat{n}$ as in figure 4b. This extension of B converts each indeterminate contact to the vertex-plane contact of figure 3a. Henceforth, indeterminate contact points are assumed to have been resolved in this manner.

4.2 Restricting Contact Points

Figure 5 shows regions of contact points between contacting bodies. In order to prevent inter-penetration, it is sufficient to consider relative motion at only the endpoints and vertices of the

---

[3]Our system chooses $\hat{n}$ by averaging nearby surface normals.

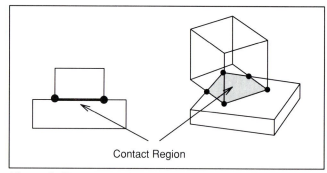

Contact Region

Figure 5. The contact force is assumed to be zero except at points marked with ●.

line segment and polygon contact regions shown. For polygonal contact regions, the motion produced by any distribution of contact forces over the entire contact region can be produced by equivalent forces acting on only the vertices of the contact region; the same is true for line segment contact regions[15]. Interior points of contact regions are not considered as contact points.

Thus, a configuration of bodies can be considered to have only finitely many contact points. Let n be the number of contact points; for $1 \leq i \leq n$, the known surface normal and unknown force magnitude at the ith contact point are written $\hat{n}_i$ and f_i. The unknown f_i's are grouped into a single vector of scalar unknowns, $\vec{f}$. For simplicity, we shall refer to f_i (the ith element of $\vec{f}$) as the contact force at point i, even though it is only the magnitude of the contact force. The actual force $\vec{F}_i$ at contact point i is given by $\vec{F}_i = f_i \hat{n}_i$.

5. Calculating Dynamically Correct Contact Forces

We can now place exact conditions on the contact forces we wish to calculate. A vector $\vec{f}$ of contact force magnitudes is *correct* if it satisfies the following conditions:

(1) The contact forces do not allow the bodies to inter-penetrate.

(2) The contact forces can "push" but not "pull".

(3) The contact forces occur only at contact points; once two bodies have separated at a contact point, there is no force between them at that contact point.

(4) Viewed as a function of time, contact forces are continuous.

Condition (4) is phrased somewhat informally, but the intuitive idea is that the force at a given contact point should vary smoothly over time (in the time interval between successive collisions). A correct vector of contact forces will produce motion that is dynamically correct. Note that more than one correct $\vec{f}$ may exist for a given configuration. Normally, the unique solution of forces for an "overdetermined" structure is found using the equations of compatibility; the assumption of absolute rigidity precludes the use of these equations[4]. However, all correct vectors $\vec{f}$ result in the same (dynamically correct) motion.

5.1 Non-penetration Constraints

To prevent inter-penetration it suffices to examine the relative motions of bodies at each contact point. At time t_0, let the ith contact point be at position p between bodies A and B and let the functions p_a and p_b be defined as in section 4. We would like to characterize the geometrical relationship between A and B in the neighborhood of p at some (future) time $t \geq t_0$. Define a *characteristic* function (of time) $\chi_i(t)$ that indicates at time t whether A

and B are: separate near p, touching near p, or inter-penetrating near p.[4] For vertex-plane contact a characteristic function may be written as

$$\chi_i(t) = \hat{n}(t) \cdot (p_a(t) - p_b(t)). \tag{1}$$

This function (locally) characterizes vertex-plane contacts: $\chi_i(t)$ is positive, zero, or negative according to whether $p_a(t)$ is outside, on, or inside B (figure 6). The same function may be used for edge-edge contacts: $\chi_i(t)$ is positive, zero, or negative according to whether the edge of A is outside, on, or inside B. In both cases, $\chi_i(t) < 0$ signals inter-penetration, and must be prevented.

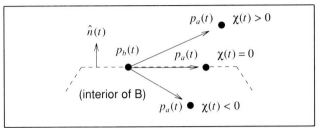

Figure 6. Characterization of three different positions of $p_a(t)$ relative to B at time t.

At time t_0, A and B touch ($p_a(t_0) = p_b(t_0)$); therefore

$$\chi_i(t_0) = \hat{n}(t_0) \cdot (p_a(t_0) - p_b(t_0)) = 0. \tag{2}$$

Since $\chi_i(t) < 0$ signals inter-penetration, $\vec{f}$ must guarantee that χ_i is a non-decreasing function at time t_0; equivalently, $\vec{f}$ must not allow the relative displacement in the $\hat{n}$ direction to decrease at time t_0.

Appendix A gives a derivation for $\dot{\chi}$ and $\ddot{\chi}$. $\dot{\chi}$ measures relative velocity in the $\hat{n}$ direction, while $\ddot{\chi}$ is a measure of relative acceleration. As such, the contact forces $\vec{f}$ at time t_0 determine $\ddot{\chi}(t_0)$; but $\dot{\chi}(t_0)$ is independent of the contact forces that exist at time t_0. From the simulator's viewpoint, χ (displacement) and $\dot{\chi}$ (relative velocity) are given at time t_0, while $\ddot{\chi}$ depends on the contact forces at time t_0.

What happens then if $\dot{\chi}_i(t_0) < 0$? This indicates that A and B are colliding (since $\chi_i(t_0)$ is decreasing). Since collisions are resolved before calculating contact forces, this will not occur. Conversely, if $\dot{\chi}_i(t_0) > 0$ then A and B are separating at contact point i, *regardless of the contact forces at time t_0*. Immediately after t_0, this contact point will not exist and thus there will be no contact force here by condition (3). Contact forces vary continuously by condition (4) so the contact force, f_i, must be zero at time t_0.[5] Thus, contact points with $\dot{\chi}_i(t_0) > 0$ may be ignored since the force at these points is zero and χ_i is increasing. We will assume that these contact points are discarded by some preprocessing step and ignore their existence hereafter.

The remaining case is:[6]

$$\dot{\chi}_i(t_0) = 0. \tag{3}$$

If $\vec{f}$ makes $\ddot{\chi}_i(t_0) < 0$, then p_a is accelerating into B and inter-penetration will immediately occur. Formally, if

---

[4]The use of a characteristic function serves several purposes. First, it makes possible simple correctness proofs for our methods. Second, it is extensible to contact between higher-order surfaces. Third, it allows a unified treatment of the different contact geometries.

[5]From calculus, if a continuous function $g(t)$ satisfies $g(t) = 0$ for $t > t_0$, then $g(t_0) = 0$.

[6]In practice, $\dot{\chi}_i(t_0)$ is compared to zero within an empirically determined tolerance value ε. This applies to all similar numerical comparisons in this paper.

$\chi_i(t_0) = \dot{\chi}_i(t_0) = 0$ and $\ddot{\chi}_i(t_0) < 0$ then χ_i is decreasing at time t_0, resulting in immediate inter-penetration. Thus, condition (1) may be written as

$$\ddot{\chi}_i(t_0) \geq 0, \tag{4}$$

corresponding to our intuition that $\vec{f}$ must not allow p_a to accelerate into B. Appendix A shows that the relative acceleration $\ddot{\chi}_i$ at time t_0 is a linear function of the contact force $\vec{f}$. To make this dependence clear, we will explicitly write $\ddot{\chi}_i$ as a function of $\vec{f}$, $\ddot{\chi}_i(\vec{f})$ with the implicit understanding that this occurs at time t_0. Condition (1) in the form

$$\ddot{\chi}_i(\vec{f}) \geq 0 \tag{5}$$

is now a constraint on $\vec{f}$. Figure 7 derives the constraints for a point mass resting on an inclined plane. (Refer to appendix A for a derivation of $\ddot{\chi}$ when body B is at rest).

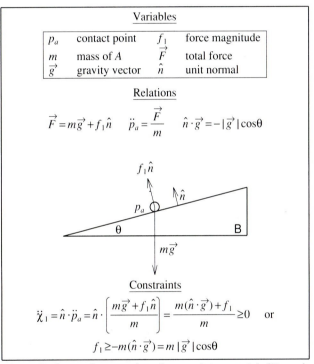

Figure 7. Constraint equations for a point mass A (with position p_a) resting on a fixed inclined plane B.

Figure 8 derives constraints for the contact forces between a block (body A) and a (fixed) floor (body B). Barzel and Barr[2] derive $\ddot{p}_a$; note that centripetal acceleration terms are absent from figure 8 since the block is at rest. Derivations for the other relations in figure 8 are found in Goldstein[5].

5.2 Matrix Formulations of Conditions (1) and (2)

From the preceding section, $\ddot{\chi}(\vec{f})$ is a linear function. Thus condition (1) may be written as a linear inequality

$$\ddot{\chi}_i(\vec{f}) = a_{i1}f_1 + a_{i2}f_2 + \cdots + a_{in}f_n - b_i \geq 0 \tag{6}$$

for $1 \leq i \leq n$. Condition (2), that contact forces only push, may be written as the inequality

$$f_i \geq 0 \tag{7}$$

for $1 \leq i \leq n$. Conditions (1) and (2) can be written more concisely using matrix notation: let A be the matrix of a_{ij}'s and $\vec{b}$ the

Variables

$p_{1,2}$	contact points	$\vec{r}_{1,2}$	body coordinates
$\vec{a}$	linear acceleration	$\vec{\alpha}$	angular acceleration
$f_{1,2}$	force magnitudes	$\vec{g}$	gravity vector
$\vec{F}$	total force	$\vec{\tau}$	total torque
m	mass	I	moment of inertia

Relations

$$\vec{F} = m\vec{g} + f_1\hat{n} + f_2\hat{n} \qquad \vec{\tau} = \vec{r}_1 \times f_1\hat{n} + \vec{r}_2 \times f_2\hat{n}$$

$$a = \frac{\vec{F}}{m} \qquad \vec{\alpha} = \frac{\vec{\tau}}{I} \qquad \ddot{p}_{1,2} = \vec{a} + \vec{\alpha} \times \vec{r}_{1,2} = \frac{\vec{F}}{m} + \frac{\vec{\tau}}{I} \times \vec{r}_{1,2}$$

Constraints

$$\ddot{\chi}_1 = \hat{n} \cdot \ddot{p}_1 = \hat{n} \cdot \left[\frac{m\vec{g} + f_1\hat{n} + f_2\hat{n}}{m} + \frac{\vec{r}_1 \times f_1\hat{n} + \vec{r}_2 \times f_2\hat{n}}{I} \times \vec{r}_1 \right] \geq 0$$

$$\ddot{\chi}_2 = \hat{n} \cdot \ddot{p}_2 = \hat{n} \cdot \left[\frac{m\vec{g} + f_1\hat{n} + f_2\hat{n}}{m} + \frac{\vec{r}_1 \times f_1\hat{n} + \vec{r}_2 \times f_2\hat{n}}{I} \times \vec{r}_2 \right] \geq 0$$

Figure 8. Constraint equations on the (unknown) contact force magnitudes $f_{1,2}$, for a block (A) supported by a fixed floor (B). The block is at rest.

vector of b_i's in equation (7). Then

$$A\vec{f} - \vec{b} = \begin{bmatrix} a_{11} & a_{12} & \cdots & a_{1n} \\ a_{21} & a_{22} & \cdots & a_{2n} \\ \vdots & \vdots & & \vdots \\ a_{n1} & a_{n2} & \cdots & a_{nn} \end{bmatrix} \begin{bmatrix} f_1 \\ f_2 \\ \vdots \\ f_n \end{bmatrix} - \begin{bmatrix} b_1 \\ b_2 \\ \vdots \\ b_n \end{bmatrix} = \begin{bmatrix} \ddot{\chi}_1(\vec{f}) \\ \ddot{\chi}_2(\vec{f}) \\ \vdots \\ \ddot{\chi}_n(\vec{f}) \end{bmatrix}. \quad (8)$$

Comparing the left- and right-hand sides componentwise,

$$\ddot{\chi}_i(\vec{f}) = (A\vec{f})_i - b_i, \quad (9)$$

so condition (1) can be expressed concisely as

$$A\vec{f} - \vec{b} \geq \vec{0} \quad (10)$$

or equivalently as

$$A\vec{f} \geq \vec{b}. \quad (11)$$

Condition (2) is stated as $\vec{f} \geq \vec{0}$.[7]

5.3 Linear Programming

Finding a vector $\vec{x}$ that satisfies $M\vec{x} \geq \vec{c}$ (where M is a matrix and $\vec{c}$ is a vector) and minimizes a linear function $z(\vec{x})$ is an example of the *linear programming* problem[10, 14]. In linear programming, the constraints between $M\vec{x}$ and $\vec{c}$ may mix "=" constraints with "≥" constraints. A general lower bound of the form $\vec{x} \geq \vec{0}$ is optional. Systems for which an $\vec{x}$ exists that satisfy all the constraints are *feasible systems* and each such $\vec{x}$ is

---
[7]For *n*-vectors $\vec{x}$ and $\vec{y}$, $\vec{x} \geq \vec{y}$ means $x_i \geq y_i$ for $1 \leq i \leq n$.

a *feasible solution*. Otherwise, the system is *infeasible*. Systems for which a feasible $\vec{x}$ exists that minimizes z are *bounded systems* and each such $\vec{x}$ is an *optimal solution*. Finding feasible (but not necessarily optimal) solutions is also a linear programming problem.

An $\vec{f}$ that satisfies conditions (1) and (2) can be expressed as a linear programming problem: *choose $\vec{f}$ subject to the constraints*

$$A\vec{f} \geq \vec{b} \quad \text{and} \quad \vec{f} \geq \vec{0}. \quad (12)$$

Linear programming is a polynomial time problem. A is typically sparse; thus linear programs involving A have expected $O(n)$ solution times if a sparsity exploiting linear programming package is used[12]. Appendix B discusses some numerical issues concerning the matrix A.

5.3 Formulating Conditions (3) and (4)

However, a feasible $\vec{f}$ with respect to equation (12) is not necessarily a correct $\vec{f}$. Intuitively, an $\vec{f}$ that satisfies conditions (1) and (2) may be an incorrect solution because it is "too strong". In figure 7, the only correct solution is $\vec{f} = (m|\vec{g}|\cos\theta)$. However, $\vec{f} = (2m|\vec{g}|\cos\theta)$ is a feasible solution (with respect to equation (12)) that prevents inter-penetration by incorrectly accelerating A away from B. Condition (3) will prevent this.

Recall that $\ddot{\chi}$ is a measure of relative acceleration. For the *i*th contact point, if

$$\ddot{\chi}_i(\vec{f}) > 0 \quad (13)$$

then χ_i is strictly increasing (since $\dot{\chi}_i = 0$ by assumption) and A and B are separating at this contact point. Call such a contact point a *vanishing* contact point and call all other contact points (where $\ddot{\chi}_i(\vec{f}) = 0$) *non-vanishing* contact points (figure 9).

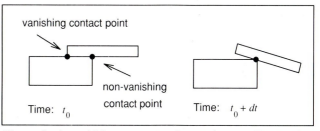

Figure 9. A vanishing contact point at time t_0. The bodies separate at the point immediately after time t_0.

From section 5.1, the contact force at a vanishing contact point is zero, by conditions (3) and (4). Condition (3) may be formulated as the statement

$$f_i\ddot{\chi}_i(\vec{f}) = 0 \quad (14)$$

because either contact point i is vanishing ($f_i = 0$ and $\ddot{\chi}_i(\vec{f}) > 0$) or non-vanishing ($\ddot{\chi}_i(\vec{f}) = 0$ and $f_i \geq 0$). Thus, the last constraint needed to guarantee correctness is equation (14), for $1 \leq i \leq n$. We can write all three constraints in the form

$$A\vec{f} \geq \vec{b}, \quad \vec{f} \geq \vec{0} \quad \text{and} \quad \sum_{i=1}^{n} f_i\ddot{\chi}_i(\vec{f}) = 0 \quad (15)$$

because $f_i \geq 0$ and $\ddot{\chi}_i(\vec{f}) \geq 0$ forces each term $f_i\ddot{\chi}_i(\vec{f})$ in the summation term of equation (15) to be non-negative, preventing cancellation. Since $\sum f_i\ddot{\chi}_i(\vec{f})$ is non-negative, any correct solution $\vec{f}$ minimizes this sum. Equation (15) can also be written as

$$A\vec{f} \geq \vec{b}, \quad \vec{f} \geq \vec{0} \quad \text{and} \quad \vec{f}^T A\vec{f} - \vec{f}^T\vec{b} = 0. \quad (16)$$

However, the term $\vec{f}^T A \vec{f}$ is *quadratic* in f_i; finding a correct $\vec{f}$ (a feasible solution to equation (16)) is an example of the *quadratic programming* problem. Quadratic programming, unlike linear programming, is an NP-hard problem in general[3]. For the (frictionless) contact model, A turns out to be positive semidefinite (PSD). Quadratic programs, when restricted to PSD matrices, can be theoretically solved in polynomial time[9], but no practical polynomial time algorithms are currently known[14]. Also, there is no reason to believe that A will remain PSD when friction is added to the model. For these reasons, we have not attempted to solve the problem of finding a correct $\vec{f}$ by direct methods. We have developed a successful heuristic algorithm for this problem. The algorithm, like any heuristic algorithm, can be made to fail on certain pathological examples.

6. Heuristic Solution Methods

A determinate configuration of bodies has only one physically correct motion; any correct $\vec{f}$ produces this motion. Thus, the correct set V of vanishing contact points for any configuration is unique. Once we know V, a correct $\vec{f}$ can be found using linear programming.

6.1 Calculating $\vec{f}$ given V

Suppose that we are given the (disjoint) index sets V and C:

$V = \{ j \mid$ contact point j is vanishing$\}$.

$C = \{ k \mid$ contact point j is not vanishing$\}$. (17)

For any correct solution $\vec{f}$, if $j \in V$ then $f_j = 0$, and if $k \in C$ then $\ddot{\chi}_k(\vec{f}) = 0$. Thus, given V, finding a correct $\vec{f}$ may be phrased as: *choose $\vec{f}$ subject to the constraints*

$$\forall j \in V \left\{ \begin{array}{l} f_j = 0 \\ \text{and} \\ \ddot{\chi}_j(\vec{f}) \geq 0 \end{array} \right\} \text{ and } \forall k \in C \left\{ \begin{array}{l} f_k \geq 0 \\ \text{and} \\ \ddot{\chi}_k(\vec{f}) = 0 \end{array} \right\}. \quad (18)$$

The constraints of this new system are all linear and conditions (1) and (2) are enforced. Condition (3) is also enforced since $f_i \ddot{\chi}_i(\vec{f}) = 0$ for $i \in V$ or $i \in C$.

The new system is formed from the original constraint $A\vec{f} \geq \vec{b}$. For each non-vanishing contact point, the "≥" constraint is changed to a "=" constraint since $\ddot{\chi}_k(\vec{f}) = 0$ is equivalent to $(A\vec{f})_k = b_k$. For each vanishing contact point, f_j is set to zero and the "≥" constraint is retained. Additionally, the jth column of A may be set to zero (since $f_j = 0$) to exploit increased sparsity in A. Figure 10 shows a quadratic constraint system for four contact points, and the linear system formed when $V = \{1,3\}$ and $C = \{2,4\}$.

However, we have no "oracle" that will provide us with the set V and we are currently unable to (efficiently) determine which contact points are vanishing. Finding V is easy for some configurations (figure 9), but not so for others. (As an example, try to determine the vanishing contact points of figure 1. Later frames from the simulation are given in figure 14). We can however take a guess as to which contact points are vanishing and then use the new linear system to test the guess. If the guess is correct, the new linear system will be feasible. Any feasible solution $\vec{f}$ found by a linear programming routine will be a correct solution. If the guess is incorrect, no $\vec{f}$ will satisfy the new system. The linear programming routine will report that the new system is infeasible, indicating the incorrectness of the guess. The obvious question is: how do we guess which contact points are vanishing and which are not?

Original System

$$\begin{bmatrix} a_{11} & a_{12} & a_{13} & a_{14} \\ a_{21} & a_{22} & a_{23} & a_{24} \\ a_{21} & a_{22} & a_{23} & a_{24} \\ a_{31} & a_{32} & a_{33} & a_{34} \end{bmatrix} \begin{bmatrix} f_1 \\ f_2 \\ f_3 \\ f_4 \end{bmatrix} \geq \begin{bmatrix} b_1 \\ b_2 \\ b_3 \\ b_4 \end{bmatrix} \text{ and}$$

$$f_i (A\vec{f} - b)_i = 0 \quad 1 \leq i \leq 4 \text{ (quadratic)}$$

New system

$$V = \{1,3\}, \quad C = \{2,4\}$$

$$\begin{bmatrix} 0 & a_{12} & 0 & a_{14} \\ 0 & a_{22} & 0 & a_{24} \\ 0 & a_{22} & 0 & a_{24} \\ 0 & a_{32} & 0 & a_{34} \end{bmatrix} \begin{bmatrix} f_1 \\ f_2 \\ f_3 \\ f_4 \end{bmatrix} \begin{array}{l} \geq \\ = \\ \geq \\ = \end{array} \begin{bmatrix} b_1 \\ b_2 \\ b_3 \\ b_4 \end{bmatrix} \text{ and } \begin{array}{l} f_1 = 0 \\ f_3 = 0 \end{array} \text{ (linear)}$$

Figure 10. Converting a quadratic system to a linear system, given V and C.

6.2 The Simplest Guess: $V = \varnothing$

To begin, note that a configuration that contains a vanishing contact point is, in a mathematical sense, *singular*. By this we mean to suggest that the existence of a vanishing contact point is a rare occurrence during a simulation.[8] A vanishing contact point occurs at a single instant of time t_0, when the contact point is in transition from existence to non-existence. Before t_0, the contact point is not vanishing, and after t_0 the contact point is non-existent and thus not considered. Thus vanishing contact points are only dealt with at an isolated instant of time t_0.

With this in mind, the obvious first guess is to set $V = \varnothing$, that is, guess that no contact points are vanishing. The linear system constructed from $V = \varnothing$ is: *choose $\vec{f}$ subject to the constraints*

$$A\vec{f} = \vec{b} \quad \text{and} \quad \vec{f} \geq \vec{0}. \quad (19)$$

Note that this problem cannot be solved using standard matrix techniques such as gaussian elimination, because of the inequality $\vec{f} \geq \vec{0}$, but must be solved as a linear programming problem. We have found that the guess $V = \varnothing$ is correct for the vast majority of cases.

6.3 Predicting a Non-Empty V

When a configuration with vanishing contact points is encountered, the initial guess $V = \varnothing$ results in an infeasible linear system. Our method of guessing V in this situation is to find an approximate solution $\vec{f}_a$ that satisfies the constraints

$$\ddot{\chi}_i(\vec{f}_a) \geq 0 \quad \text{and} \quad \vec{f}_a \geq \vec{0} \quad (20)$$

and use $\vec{f}_a$ to predict which contact points are vanishing.

Given an approximate solution $\vec{f}_a$, define the residual vector $\vec{r}$ as

$$A\vec{f}_a - \vec{b} = \begin{bmatrix} \ddot{\chi}_1(\vec{f}_a) \\ \ddot{\chi}_2(\vec{f}_a) \\ \cdot \\ \cdot \\ \ddot{\chi}_n(\vec{f}_a) \end{bmatrix} = \vec{r}. \quad (21)$$

If $\vec{f}_a$ is in fact a correct solution, then for all vanishing contact

---

[8] A more precise statement is that vanishing contact points occur with measure zero.

points j, $r_j = \ddot{\chi}_j(\vec{f_a}) > 0$ and for all non-vanishing contact points k, $r_k = \ddot{\chi}_k(\vec{f_a}) = 0$. The hope is that an incorrect, yet approximate solution $\vec{f_a}$ will indicate through its residual $\vec{r}$ which contact points are vanishing. Contact point i is guessed to be vanishing if and only if $r_i > 0$. The method of section 6.1 is then used to test the guess.

6.4 Finding Approximates

The current heuristic used for finding an approximate solution is: *choose* $\vec{f_a}$ *to minimize the objective function*

$$z(\vec{f_a}) = \sum_{i=1}^{n} f_{a_i} \qquad (22)$$

subject to the constraints

$$A\vec{f_a} \geq b \quad \text{and} \quad \vec{f_a} \geq 0. \qquad (23)$$

That is, we wish to find a minimum sum force solution that satisfies conditions (1) and (2). An optimal $\vec{f_a}$ can be found via linear programming since the objective function z is linear. Hopefully, an $\vec{f_a}$ that minimizes z will approximately minimize

$$\sum_{i=1}^{n} f_{a_i} \ddot{\chi}_i(\vec{f_a}) \qquad (24)$$

and thus be a good approximate to a correct solution. (Recall that a *perfect* minimizer of equation (24) is a correct solution).

The physical intuition behind this choice is that correct contact forces do no net work; therefore $\vec{f_a}$ should be chosen to do as little net work as possible. Hopefully, the minimum force solution $\vec{f_a}$ will do little net work. In practice we have found that the residuals formed using z are a good predictor of the vanishing contact points.

6.5 Dealing with Incorrect Predictions

The last question is what to do when there are vanishing contact points and $\vec{f_a}$ does not predict them correctly. One could of course test all the possible guesses, but for n contact points, there are 2^n different guesses, which would give an exponential algorithm. Our current implementation exploits the fact that configurations with vanishing contact points occur infrequently. When a correct solution $\vec{f}$ cannot be found, we use the approximate $\vec{f_a}$ obtained from the minimum sum force solution. Since $\vec{f_a}$ is not correct,

$$\sum_{i=1}^{n} f_{a_i} \ddot{\chi}_i(\vec{f_a}) > 0, \qquad (25)$$

and the contact force $\vec{f_a}$ adds energy to the system of bodies, producing incorrect results. The effect is mitigated by the fact that vanishing configurations are singular which means the incorrect $\vec{f_a}$ is applied for only a short time. Shortly after applying the incorrect $\vec{f_a}$ the simulator reaches a configuration where a correct $\vec{f}$ can be found. We have found that the short duration over which $\vec{f_a}$ is applied, coupled with the fact that $\vec{f_a}$ is usually a good approximate of a correct solution produces satisfactory results.

7. Additional Constraints

Holonomic constraints, which express equality constraints between bodies (e.g. articulated figures) can be added to the non-holonomic inter-penetration constraint in a consistent manner. Barzel and Barr[2] maintained holonomic constraints by introducing constraint forces that had to satisfy a linear system

$$A\vec{f} = b. \qquad (26)$$

This is consistent with our own formulation since linear programming allows equality constraints. Holonomic constraints are added to our system by imposing additional linear equality constraints on $\vec{f}$. Elements representing the holonomic constraint force are added to $\vec{f}$; these elements are not subject to condition (2), the non-negativity constraint. The entire system of constraints is solved as in section 6, except that the minimum sum force solution only takes into account the non-holonomic constraint forces. This is justified since the net work done by the holonomic forces is zero if the holonomic constraint equations are satisfied[5]. If no contact occurs, only holonomic constraints remain and the system of equations is the same as in Barzel and Barr[2]. We use the sparse linear programming package to solve this linear system in $O(n)$ time. Appendix B discusses some numerical issues involved with solving equation (26).

8. Simultaneous Collisions

The linear programming formulation for resting contact can be used to improve the performance of existing collision methods for certain configurations. There are two analytical methods for resolving collisions involving multiple contact points and/or bodies: impulses at contact points can be calculated and applied one at a time or the impulses can be calculated and applied simultaneously for all contact points. We call the former view the *propagation* model of collisions and the latter the *simultaneous* model of collisions; recent papers[7, 13] have used the propagation model for collisions. The two models are the same for collisions with a single contact point but may give give different results for some multiple contact point collisions. Figure 11 shows a collision between three equal mass billiard balls with no loss of kinetic energy.

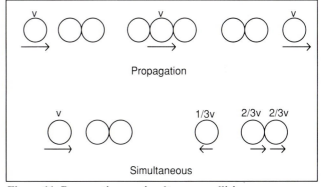

Figure 11. Propagation vs. simultaneous collisions.

The propagation model results in the right ball moving away from the motionless left and center balls. The simultaneous model results in the right and center balls moving with equal velocity away from the leftmost ball.

In other situations both models produce the same result, but the propagation model can require an excessive number of iterations to numerically converge. Figure 12 shows a ball of mass 9 colliding with a ball of mass 1, resting on an immovable floor. The collisions are totally inelastic; the propagation method iterates between calculating collision impulses between the two balls, and the smaller ball and the floor. After n iterations, the top ball will have $.9^n$ of its initial velocity v; a higher mass ratio would result in even slower convergence. In contrast, the simultaneous model would produce the limiting result (both balls at rest) in one iteration, regardless of the mass ratio.

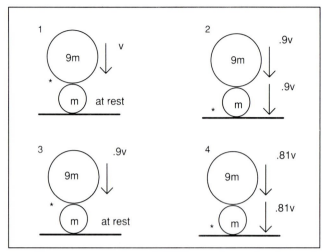

Figure 12. Convergence behavior of the propagation model. The * indicates where the collision impulse is being applied.

To calculate collision impulses for simultaneous collisions, we mimic the resting contact problem. At every contact point i, there is some impulse $J_i = j_i \hat{n}_i$ with $j_i \geq 0$ the unknown magnitude. The goal is to find a $\vec{j}$ that satisfies the laws of classical mechanics; given $\vec{j}$, the final linear and angular velocities of the bodies (the ultimate goal) can be calculated[11]. For contact point i, let v_i^- be the relative approach velocity in the $\hat{n}_i$ direction ($\dot{\chi}_i$ from section 5) and v_i^+ be the (unknown) relative recession velocity in the $\hat{n}_i$ direction. v_i^+ is a linear function of $\vec{j}$[11]. If $v_i^- > 0$, the bodies are separating.[9] Otherwise, the bodies are in resting contact ($v_i^- = 0$) or are colliding ($v_i^- < 0$).

The coefficient of restitution, ε, is defined for single contact collisions as

$$v_i^+ = -\varepsilon_i v_i^-. \tag{27}$$

The definition of ε does not readily extend to handle simultaneous collisions. The most that can be said is that if each $\varepsilon_i = 1$ then no kinetic energy is lost during the collision. We have chosen the following rules for simultaneous collisions. For each contact point in the collision, it is required that

$$v_i^+ \geq -\varepsilon_i v_i^- \tag{28}$$

i.e. the recession velocity must be at least as much as would occur for a single contact collision. The "$\geq$" is needed since body A might be pushed *away* from body B by some third body C (figure 13). Paralleling the resting contact problem, j_i is assumed to be zero if v_i^+ actually exceeds $-\varepsilon_i v_i^-$. A routine calculation shows that kinetic energy is conserved for multiple collisions when each $\varepsilon_i = 1$, and that for single contact point collisions, $v_i^+ = -\varepsilon_i v_i^-$ [5]. Since v_i^+ is a linear function of $\vec{j}$, the constraints can be written as

$$v_i^+(\vec{j}) + \varepsilon_i v_i^- \geq 0, \quad j_i \geq 0, \quad j_i(v_i^+(\vec{j}) + \varepsilon_i v_i^-) = 0 \tag{29}$$

for $1 \leq i \leq n$. This constraint system has the same form as the constraints of section 5, and the heuristic methods of section 6 can be used to solve for $\vec{j}$. Note that for the case of two bodies colliding at a single point without friction, the system reduces to one equation in one unknown.

[9]As in section 5.1, contact points with $v_i^- > 0$ are discarded, since the bodies are separating at these contact points. This may immediately result in another round of collision resolution, but the excessive iterative behavior of figure 12 should not occur.

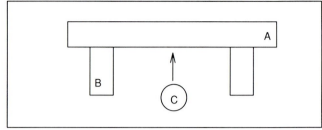

Figure 13. A is struck from below by C and pushed away from B. **The impulse between A and B should be zero.**

The simultaneous collision method can also enforce holonomic constraints. Holonomic constraints are maintained by imposing additional linear equality constraints of the form $v_i^+(\vec{j}) = v_i^-$. Components of $\vec{j}$ representing the holonomic constraint impulses are not subject to the non-negativity constraint. For the case of two linked figures colliding at a single point, our method is equivalent to Moore and Wilhelms' method[13] except that our system of equation is one third the size of Moore and Wilhelms'. The reduction in size of the system is a consequence of regarding $\vec{j}$ as the only unknown in the problem; the final linear and angular momenta are expressed in terms of $\vec{j}$.

9. Conclusion

We have presented an analytical method for finding forces between contacting polyhedral bodies, based on linear programming techniques. The solution algorithm currently used is heuristic. A generalization of the formulations presented yields an analytical method for finding simultaneous impulsive forces between colliding polyhedral bodies. Both methods allow holonomic geometric constraints to be maintained. A simulator has been constructed and a variety of simulations have been produced (figure 14). The major drawback of the current solution algorithm is the necessity of solving linear systems of inequalities. Linear programming software is considerably more complex than the software used to solve systems of linear equations; software for linear equations is also more readily available. Additionally, linear equations currently enjoy a much greater diversity of solution techniques than linear programming[6].

The other major concern is that the heuristic algorithm used will occasionally fail and an approximate (but incorrect) solution will be used. This adds energy to the simulation but does not result in any unsatisfactory visual effects. We have not pursued the issue of error due to incorporating incorrect solutions into the simulator because we believe that such work would be premature. The addition of friction to the model would be likely to render such work inapplicable. Also, numerical techniques currently under investigation may preclude the need for any heuristic algorithms at all.

Acknowledgements

This research was conducted under two NSF grants entitled "Interactive Input and Display Techniques" (#DCR8203979) and "Visualization for Scientific Computing" (#ASC8715478) and an AT&T Bell Laboratories PhD Fellowship. Simulation and displays were performed on equipment generously donated by Hewlett Packard Corporation and Digital Equipment Corporation. I thank Michael Cohen for preliminary discussions on this work, Jim Cremer for talking me out of some very wrong ideas, and Don Greenberg and Roy Hall for sound editorial advice and encouragement.

Appendix A

We derive expressions for $\dot{\chi}$ and $\ddot{\chi}$:

$$\chi(t) = \hat{n}(t) \cdot (p_a(t) - p_b(t)), \tag{30}$$

$$\dot{\chi}(t) = \dot{\hat{n}}(t) \cdot (p_a(t) - p_b(t)) + \hat{n}(t) \cdot (\dot{p}_a(t) - \dot{p}_b(t)) \tag{31}$$

and

$$\ddot{\chi}(t) = \ddot{\hat{n}}(t) \cdot (p_a(t) - p_b(t)) \tag{32}$$
$$+ 2\dot{\hat{n}}(t) \cdot (\dot{p}_a(t) - \dot{p}_b(t)) + \hat{n}(t) \cdot (\ddot{p}_a(t) - \ddot{p}_b(t)).$$

At time t_0, $p_a(t_0) = p_b(t_0)$ so

$$\dot{\chi}(t_0) = \hat{n}(t_0) \cdot (\dot{p}_a(t_0) - \dot{p}_b(t_0)) \tag{33}$$

and

$$\ddot{\chi}(t_0) = \hat{n}(t_0) \cdot (\ddot{p}_a(t_0) - \ddot{p}_b(t_0)) + 2\dot{\hat{n}}(t_0) \cdot (\dot{p}_a(t_0) - \dot{p}_b(t_0)). \tag{34}$$

Since $\hat{n}(t_0)$, $\dot{\hat{n}}(t_0)$, $\dot{p}_a(t_0)$, and $\dot{p}_b(t_0)$ are independent of $\vec{f}$ and $\ddot{p}_a(t_0)$ and $\ddot{p}_b(t_0)$ depend linearly on $\vec{f}$ [2, 5], $\ddot{\chi}(t_0)$ is a linear function of $\vec{f}$. For a vertex-plane contact with B fixed, $\hat{n} = \ddot{p}_b = 0$ and $\ddot{\chi}(t_0) = \hat{n}(t_0) \cdot \ddot{p}_a(t_0)$.

Appendix B

The purely non-holonomic constraint equation

$$A\vec{f} \geq \vec{b}, \quad \vec{f} \geq \vec{0} \quad \text{and} \quad \vec{f}^T A\vec{f} - \vec{f}^T \vec{b} = 0 \tag{35}$$

often involves a singular matrix A, yielding multiple solutions. A is singular if the physical structure is overdetermined (such as a chair with more than three legs resting on a floor). Barzel and Barr[2] note that the purely holonomic constraint equation

$$A\vec{f} = \vec{b} \tag{36}$$

is also often underconstrained or overconstrained.

Underconstrained systems in both cases are easily handled by linear programming methods. Overconstrained systems that are feasible (admit a solution) are also handled by linear programming methods. However, infeasible overconstrained systems require special attention. Note that the infeasibility arises from the holonomic constraint equations. We have encountered infeasible systems when using the techniques described by Barzel and Barr[2] to assemble models. We did not encounter infeasible constraints from assembled models with holonomic constraints.

Barzel and Barr deal with infeasible holonomic constraints by selecting the least-squares solution. They find the least-squares solution by using singular-value decomposition (SVD), but note that this does not exploit sparsity and is relatively slow. SVD methods, however, cannot be used when there are non-holonomic constraints that must be maintained. One possibility is to use linear programming to find a solution that minimizes the 1-norm (as opposed to the 2-norm) of the residual in equation (36): *choose $\vec{f}$ such that*

$$\| A\vec{f} - \vec{b} \|_1 \tag{37}$$

is minimized. (Equation (37) is a convex linear objective function, so the minimization is a linear programming problem). For purely holonomic systems, this approach might be faster than using an SVD method since sparsity can be exploited in linear programming methods. However, the complexity and relatively unrobust performance of linear programming methods (as compared with SVD methods) is such that the SVD method is probably preferable for purely holonomic systems.

References

1. Barzel, R. and Barr, A.H., "Dynamic constraints," *Topics in Physically Based Modeling*, course notes, vol. 16, SIG-GRAPH, 1987.

2. Barzel, R. and Barr, A.H., "A modeling system based on dynamic constraints," *Computer Graphics (Proc. SIG-GRAPH)*, vol. 22, pp. 179-188, 1988.

3. Garey, M.R. and Johnson, D.S., *Computers and Intractability*, Freeman, New York, 1979.

4. Gere, J.M. and Timoshenko, S.P., *Mechanics of Materials*, Wadsworth, Belmont, California, 1984.

5. Goldstein, H., *Classical Mechanics*, Addison-Wesley, Reading, Massachusets, 1983.

6. Golub, G. and Van Loan, C., *Matrix Computations*, John Hopkins University Press, Baltimore, 1983.

7. Hahn, J.K., "Realistic animation of rigid bodies," *Computer Graphics (Proc. SIGGRAPH)*, vol. 22, pp. 299-308, 1988.

8. Isaacs, P.M. and Cohen, M.F., "Controlling dynamic simulation with kinematic constraints," *Computer Graphics (Proc. SIGGRAPH)*, vol. 21, pp. 215-224, 1987.

9. Kozlov, M.K., Tarasov, S.P., and Hacijan, L.G., "Polynomial solvability of convex quadratic programming," *Soviet Mathematics Doklady*, vol. 20, no. 5, pp. 1108-1111, 1979.

10. Llewellyn, R.W., *Linear Programming*, Holt, Rinehart and Winston, 1964.

11. MacMillan, W.D., *Dynamics of Rigid Bodies*, Dover, New York, 1960.

12. Marsten, R.E., "The design of the XMP linear programming library," *ACM Transactions on Mathematical Software*, vol. 7, no. 4, pp. 481-497, 1981.

13. Moore, M. and Wilhelms, J., "Collision detection and response for computer animation," *Computer Graphics (Proc. SIGGRAPH)*, vol. 22, pp. 289-298, 1988.

14. Murty, K.G., *Linear Complementarity, Linear and Nonlinear Programming*, Heldermann Verlag, Berlin, 1988.

15. Palmer, R.S., *Computational Complexity of Motion and Stability of Polygons*, PhD Diss., Cornell University, January 1987.

16. Platt, J.C. and Barr, A.H., "Constraint methods for flexible models," *Computer Graphics (Proc. SIGGRAPH)*, vol. 22, pp. 279-288, 1988.

17. Shampine, L.F. and Gordon, M.K., *Computer Solution of Ordinary Differential Equations: The Initial Value Problem*, Freeman, 1975.

18. Terzopoulos, D., Platt, J.C., and Barr, A.H., "Elastically deformable models," *Computer Graphics (Proc. SIGGRAPH)*, vol. 21, pp. 205-214, 1987.

(a) Overbalanced stack of bricks.

(b) Dominoes.

(c) Destructive chain.

(d) Chain curling around a fixed pivot.

(e) Two blocks falling into a chain.

(f) Many blocks falling into a chain.

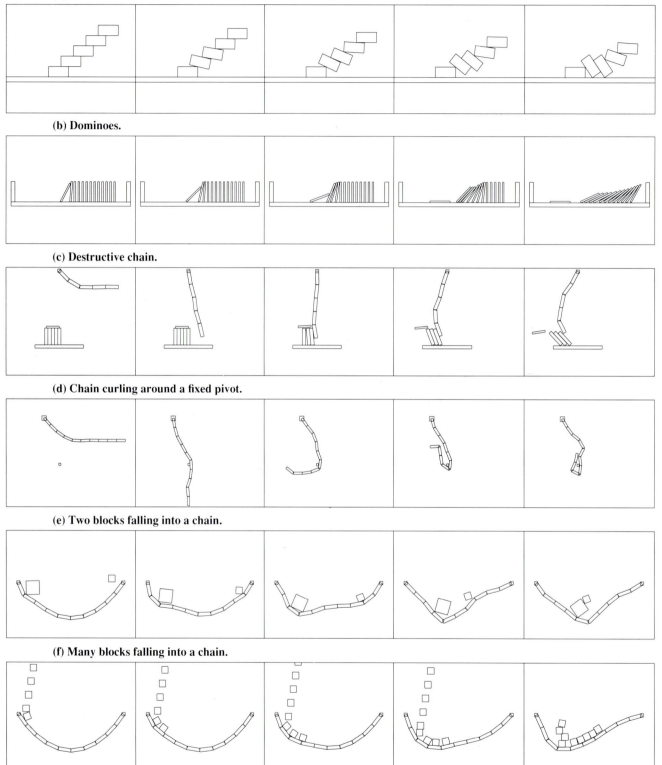

Figure 14. Assorted simulations (a-f).

Goal-Directed, Dynamic Animation of Human Walking

Armin Bruderlin
Thomas W. Calvert

School of Computing Science
Simon Fraser University
Burnaby, British Columbia, Canada V5A 1S6

ABSTRACT

This paper presents a hybrid approach to the animation of human locomotion which combines goal-directed and dynamic motion control. Knowledge about a locomotion cycle is incorporated into a hierarchical control process. The desired locomotion is conveniently specified at the top level as a task (e.g. walk at speed *v*), which is then decomposed by application of the concepts of *step symmetry* and *state-phase-timings*. As a result of this decomposition, the forces and torques that drive the dynamic model of the legs are determined by numerical approximation techniques. Rather than relying on a general dynamic model, the equations of motion of the legs are tailored to locomotion and analytically constrained to allow for only a specific range of movements. The dynamics of the legs produce a generic, natural locomotion pattern which is visually upgraded by some kinematic "cosmetics" derived from such principles as *virtual leg* and *determinants of gait*. A system has been implemented based on these principles and has shown that when a few parameters, such as velocity, step length and step frequency are specified, a wide variety of human walks can be generated in almost real-time.

CR Categories and Subject Descriptors: I.3.7: [Computer Graphics]: Three-Dimensional Graphics and Realism - Animation; G.1.7: [Numerical Analysis]: Ordinary Differential Equations.
Keywords: Animation, goal-directed animation, human figure animation, dynamics, kinematics, inverse kinematics.

1. INTRODUCTION

The specification and control of motion in human figure animation has always been a challenge, but two recent trends promise to relieve the tedious work of the animator. One involves high-level, goal-directed control, which reduces the amount of detail necessary to define a motion; the second involves applying dynamic analysis to the motion control process, leading to more realism in movements.

In traditional keyframing [13], the quality of a motion is usually directly proportional to the number of key positions specified. If the desired movements are complicated, the animator, rather than the system, does motion control. It has been recognized that if the

excessive amount of specification for character animation is to be reduced, higher level motion control is necessary [2, 7, 17]. At the lowest level, all movements are expressed by joint rotations over time, but these joint rotations must be coordinated within a limb, between limbs and are subject to the interaction of the whole figure with its environment. By incorporating knowledge or rules about these inter-relationships, tasks like grasping or jumping can be automated and presented to the user as parameterized goals. In such a goal-directed system, the global coordination of a motion is done by the computer. However, movements are still executed kinematically at the lowest level, and the impact of physical laws such as gravity or collisions on the motion process are ignored. To achieve realistic and natural movements, dynamic analysis must be applied as a motion control technique. By simulating the real world, objects move as they should move, according to physical laws. The drawback is that the animator has to specify motion in terms of forces and torques; this is neither intuitive nor easy, and it is complicated by the computationally expensive character of this approach. In the past, simulation of human figures concentrated on simple, elementary movements not involving coordination between several limbs (e.g. raising an arm or dropping an arm under the influence of gravity). By combining a goal-directed higher level control with dynamic simulation of motion, a system can be developed for economic and realistic animation of many co-ordinated human movements.

This paper introduces such a method for the purpose of animating human locomotion. To this end, we have implemented the KLAW (Keyframe-Less Animation of Walking) system to animate walking. Dynamic simulation provides the low-level control; a dynamic walking model, inspired by research in robotics [12] and biomechanics [4] produces a generic walking pattern from different sets of analytically constrained equations of motion which are applied as appropriate to the current state of the locomotion. Kinematic algorithms are applied to calculate all the body angles from the motion of the dynamic model. The dynamics, in turn, are regulated by a higher level control; the proper forces and torques which generate a desired locomotion are calculated as a result of a stepwise decomposition of a few walking parameters specified by the user. Thus, motion is specified conveniently and realistic animations are obtained based on the dynamic equations of motion without explicit specification of forces and torques.

The goal-oriented approach used in this paper builds on the work of Zeltzer [16], who developed a task-oriented system to animate human locomotion; although tasks like walking and jumping were implemented, the calculation of the joint angles were done kinematically and based on interpolation methods and clinical data. Thus it was not possible to easily realize variations in locomotion by changing step length or speed. The general

©1989   ACM-0-89791-312-4/89/007/0233 $00.75

approach to dynamic analysis which we have adopted is based on the work of Wilhelms [15], Armstrong [1] and others [3, 11]. Perhaps the most comprehensive approach is that of Wilhelms, who produced *Virya*, a dynamic system for the animation of human figures which also allows for kinematic and hybrid kinematic-dynamic motion specification. In the dynamic mode, however, forces and torques have to be input in order to achieve a motion. Badler *et al.* [2] have been developing kinematic techniques to animate human figures. They have proposed a higher level of control, where goals such as reaching for a certain position can be defined and the joint angles are found using inverse kinematic algorithms. They also investigated dynamic and kinematic animation of specific tasks (e.g. movement in a space vehicle). A system to animate legged figures was developed by Girard and Maciejewski [8]; dynamic control was applied to the body as a whole, and the legs were specified kinematically. The problem of constraining a foot to be on the ground during its support phase was formulated as an inverse kinematics problem and solved by means of a pseudoinverse jacobian.

2. THE KLAW SYSTEM

2.1 Overview

Legged locomotion describes an intricate activity where body translation results from rotational movements in the lower limbs; problems such as coordination between the legs, proper timing of the individual leg motions and balancing of the upper body have to be addressed. It is clear that humans and other animals, however, are able to walk effortlessly without conscious thought. This is because they are inherently goal-directed [17]. Rather than thinking in terms of forces and torques, humans walk with certain goals like speed or step length in mind — thus, a hierarchical control scheme is well suited to animate human locomotion. Figure 1 gives a structural outline of the KLAW system. The animator specifies a desired walk with up to 3 fundamental *locomotion parameters* which largely determine the pattern of motion and gait: forward velocity (*v*), step length (*sl*) and step frequency (*sf*). A major concern in constructing a goal-directed system has been the degree to which a task should be parameterized. The animator should have access to a simple, yet flexible set of movement commands that can generate a variety of instances of a task. In KLAW, therefore, in addition to the 3 locomotion parameters, up to 28 *locomotion attributes* [5] may also be specified which individualize the locomotion. The default values of these attributes may be modified by the animator. Examples are: lateral distance between the feet, toe clearance during swing, and maximum rotation and list of the pelvis. After parameter specification, the system computes and outputs the body angles as functions of time — these drive the animation of a human figure.

2.2 Levels of Control

Knowledge about a locomotion cycle occurs at three levels: the conceptual abstraction (high-level), the gait refinements (middle-level) and the physical abstraction (low-level). The conceptual level contains a few gait-specific rules or laws. These are utilized to transform the locomotion parameters into *step constraints* which are fed to the low-level control to "guide" the dynamic simulation of the legs. The middle-level control is responsible for the coordination of the motion and functionally operates much like a finite state machine as suggested by Zeltzer [16]. For instance, upon a "heel-strike" event, the state "single support" is changed to "double support". Hierarchically, the middle-level control manifests a stepwise reduction in the number of degrees of freedom along with a decrease in the levels of coordination (e.g. the single support state of a walk consists of a stance and a swing

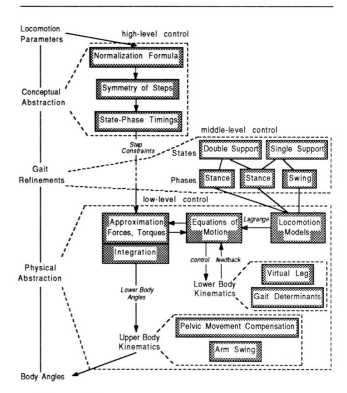

Figure 1: Schematic diagram of the control hierarchy in KLAW.

phase). The bottom level is represented by sets of specialized equations of motion; in fact, the phases are divided into subphases in which the equations are further constrained analytically. The low-level control uses the *step constraints* (which essentially are the durations and final leg angles for the stance and swing phases of a locomotion step) as conditions for a special kind of a boundary value problem. That is, the equations of motion are solved by approximating the forces and torques until the constraints are satisfied. For example, the simulation of the swing leg for the current step is repeated by varying the joint-torques until it swings forward in the exact time required and heel-strike occurs with the desired hip and knee angles. In practice, this process converges quite quickly.

2.3 Dynamic Model

A principal objective is to keep the dynamics simple, otherwise the internal calculation of the forces and torques becomes infeasible. As shown in figure 2, the swing leg is represented by two segments. The stance leg supports the upper body and is implemented as a length-changing telescopic segment which simulates knee flexion in the early part and plantar flexion of the ankle in the latter part of the stance phase (as explained later, for animation, a full leg with knee, ankle and metatarsal joints are superimposed). This approach is chosen since a linear force along the leg axis is much easier to control than additional torques at the leg joints.

The segment masses are assumed to be constant and the segments to be symmetrical. The latter implies that the principal axes of inertia are identical to the anatomical axes of rotation, and therefore the products of inertia are zero. Thus, the distribution of mass is solely defined by the moments of inertia which are calculated as described in appendix B. This simplification is justified for dynamic analysis in computer animation, since it has

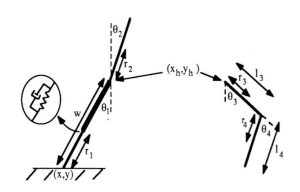

a) stance leg model with upper body   b) swing leg model
(inverted double pendulum with telescopic leg)   (double pendulum)

Figure 2: Dynamic models for the different phases in locomotion. θ_3 is negative in this configuration, all other angles are positive; see appendix B for anthropometric values.

no significant effect on the motion. The equations of motion are derived by the method of Lagrange [14] as shown in appendix A.1 and A.2. The ground constraint for the stance phase is implemented as an analytical constraint; assuming that the "dynamic foot" does not move during stance, the two degrees of freedom, x,y, are removed. In this way, there are a total of only 5 degrees of freedom $(w, \theta_1, \theta_2, \theta_3, \theta_4)$ and consequently 5 second order, nonlinear equations of motion. The equations are solved by an A-stable, standard numerical integration method [9] which has produced numerically stable results for this problem.

2.4 Control Principles

The execution of the different components in KLAW is based on four assumptions or principles:

1. The control hierarchy as illustrated in figure 1 is applied to each step of a walking sequence where a step is defined as the double plus the single support state (see also figure 3). While the high-level concepts are executed before the impending step, the low-level motion control takes place during the step. Thus, KLAW is able to adapt to changes in the locomotion parameters from step to step, i.e. accelerations and decelerations in the motion are possible with a granularity of one step.

2. Lower body dynamics and kinematics must be executed simultaneously. The dynamic simulation produces the generic locomotion pattern which is visually upgraded by kinematic measures. As explained in section 4, a human leg is superimposed onto the telescopic stance leg according to the *virtual leg* principle, and *gait determinants* like pelvic rotation or list get injected into the one-hip dynamic model. In a sense, the equations of motion guide the lower body kinematics, but the kinematic computations may, in turn, affect the dynamics. For instance, the simulation of the swing leg, where the foot is assumed to be locked, has to take into account the updated position of the heel as a result of the kinematic foot rotation, in order to achieve heel-strike properly at the end of a step. Similarly, the kinematic pelvic rotation can actually lower the hip during the swing phase, which might "force" the dynamic leg to increase its hip torque to avoid stubbing its toe. Though considerable kinematic "cosmetics" are applied, the dynamics are the very heart of the control for they guarantee natural looking rotational movements of the legs.

3. It is assumed that the upper body follows or depends on the lower body movements. Whereas the dynamic model accounts only for a natural forward and backward motion of the upper body (θ_2), the angles of the arms as well as the rotations in the shoulder and spine which compensate for pelvic movements are expressed as functions of the corresponding angles in the lower body. The arms, for example, swing forward with the opposite legs. Thus, these angles are calculated after the dynamic simulation.

4. The last assumption concerns the dynamic model discussed above: the simulations for the stance and swing phases are separated which greatly simplifies the control as well as the numerical integration process. The rationale is that the stance leg model constitutes the major propulsive element in bipedal locomotion. It supports the body and influences the swing leg by its hip motion. On the other hand, the swing leg has little or no effect on the stance leg and the upper body. Of course, this is not completely true in real human walking, but it can be justified by the fact that the mass of the leg is small compared to the total mass of the body (approx. 16 %). Hence, the swing leg does not change the inertia of the body significantly unless the motion during swing happens very suddenly, which is hardly the case for a moderate walk. Therefore, for each step, the simulation of the stance phase is executed first followed by the swing phase dynamics which incorporate the position of the hip (x_h, y_h) from the stance phase.

3. HIGH-LEVEL CONCEPTS

This section gives a discussion of the high-level control module whose task is to transform the 3 locomotion parameters v, sl and sf into the step constraints for the low-level control. At least one locomotion parameter (e.g. desired velocity) has to be input by the animator. If all 3 of the parameters are not specified, the system completes the parameters using a *normalization formula* (the parameters are also checked at this point to ensure that they are within anatomical limits defined by *locomotion attributes*, e.g. $sf_{max} = 182\,steps/min$). Once the locomotion parameters are accepted and specified, the step frequency and the *state-phase-timings* are applied to determine the durations of the stance and swing phases, and the step length is used with the *symmetry of steps* concept to compute the final conditions for each phase of the current step.

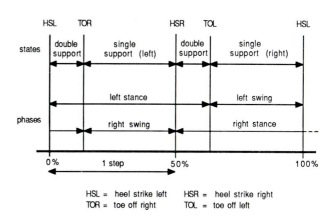

Figure 3: Locomotion cycle for bipedal walking.

Since rhythmic locomotion is just a series of recurring movements with the natural period of one stride (the locomotion cycle), it is sufficient to compute movements for one cycle. The human walking cycle has been thoroughly studied — see Inman [10], for example. For bipedal walking, a locomotion cycle consists of two steps. As long as a symmetric gait is assumed where the left and right leg perform the same movements, just shifted in time, the principal unit of locomotion can be reduced to one step (see figure 3). Walking is possible at a wide variety of combinations of sl and sf ($v = sl \cdot sf$). However, a person, when asked to walk at a particular velocity, is most likely to choose parameters which minimize energy expenditure. This observation is expressed in the experimentally derived equations [10], called *normalizing formulae*, which show a linear relationship between sl and sf, where sl and *body_height* are measured in m, and sf in *steps/min* :

$$\frac{sl}{sf \cdot body\_height} = 0.004 \qquad (1)$$

$$\Leftrightarrow sf^2 = \frac{v}{0.004 \cdot body\_height}, \quad \text{because of} \quad sl = \frac{v}{sf}.$$

The *body_height* normalizes the equation. It indirectly represents the length of the legs, which has an effect on the preferred step length. Based on equation (1), the locomotion parameters are now checked and supplemented if at least one is specified. For instance, if a velocity is defined, a "natural" step length and step frequency are calculated; in the case where a velocity and a step length are specified a more angular motion might result if the step length deviates significantly from the "natural" one (see also figure 10).

The step frequency is the input to the *state-phase-timings* calculation. A walking cycle consists of two steps (figure 3), each step having one double support state (ds) where both feet are on the ground and one single support state where one foot is off the ground. With respect to timing of the individual legs the following holds, assuming t to denote a duration:

$$t_{step} = t_{stance} - t_{ds} \quad \text{and} \quad t_{step} = t_{swing} + t_{ds}. \qquad (2)$$

Experimental data [10] suggest that in human walking there is an approximately linear relationship between the step frequency and the duration of the double support state as a percentage of a cycle, i.e. the duration of the double support state decreases with increasing step frequency. As t_{ds} vanishes, walking becomes running. Based on results from different experiments, t_{ds} can be described in terms of sf and t_{cycle} :

$$t_{ds} = (-0.16 \cdot sf + 29.08) \cdot t_{cycle} / 100.$$

Since sf is known as one of the locomotion parameters, and because of

$$t_{cycle} = 2 \cdot t_{step} = \frac{2}{sf},$$

t_{ds} can be determined, and consequently the values for t_{stance} and t_{swing} are obtained from equation (2). It should be noted that the length of the stance phase is greater than a step, i.e. $t_{stance} = t_{step} + t_{ds}$ (see figure 3). To simplify implementation and to satisfy the step-oriented control principle (assumption 1.), the stance phase of a leg is only simulated for the duration of a step and at heel strike, when the stance phase of the leading leg starts, the continuing stance phase of the hind leg is completed kinematically.

Step symmetry is based on a compass gait (figure 4), and means simply that at heel strike, provided that both legs are of the same

length, the angles of the legs measured from the vertical are identical. That is $\theta_1 = \theta_3$ at times t_1, t_2 and t_3. Further, θ_1 and θ_3 depend only on the step length sl. Most importantly, this remains true when the body is accelerating or decelerating, indicated in figure 4 by the increased step length at time t_3 (i.e. the body accelerated from t_2 to t_3).

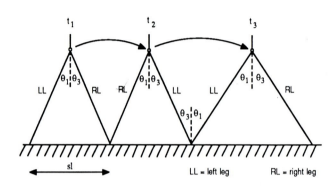

Figure 4: Symmetry of compass gait for different step lengths.

This principle is now adapted to the model in figure 5 to determine w, θ_1 and θ_3 at the end of a step (heel strike) utilizing the current step length sl. Although the actual step configuration at heel strike is no longer symmetric because of the introduction of a kinematic foot for the swing leg, the basic idea can still be applied. We just imagine the symmetric step situation when the foot is flat on the ground some time after impact (illustrated by the dashed line) and calculate "back in time". For this purpose, the step length sl is measured between $ankle_1$ and $ankle_2$. The effect of the foot at heel strike is that the absolute value of θ_3 is smaller than it would be without a foot (also, $\theta_3 < \theta_1$). In addition, the foot raises the position of the hip at impact, which has to be compensated by lengthening the telescopic stance leg beyond its initial length, i.e. $w > l_1$. The origin for the simulation of the stance leg stays fixed at $ankle_1$, which is at a distance l_9 above the ground.

For the following calculations, it is assumed that the ground is at zero height and θ_5 at impact is specified as one of the *locomotion attributes*. Given l_1, l_8, l_9, l_{11} and $\cos(\omega_8) = \frac{l_8}{l_{11}}$, the application of the cosine law yields

$$r^2 = l_1^2 + l_{11}^2 - 2 l_1 l_{11} \cos(\theta_5 + \omega_8), \quad \text{and}$$

$$\omega_3 = \cos^{-1}\left(\frac{l_1^2 + r^2 - l_{11}^2}{2 l_1 r}\right).$$

Since

$$ankle_1 = (x_a, y_a) = (x_{nh'} + l_8, l_9)$$

$$\text{where } x_{nh'} \text{ is } x_{nh} \text{ from previous step, and}$$

$$heel = (x_{nh}, y_{nh}) = (x_a + sl - l_8, 0)$$

$$hip = (x_h, y_h) = (x_a + \frac{sl}{2}, \sqrt{r^2 - (x_{nh} - x_h)^2}),$$

it follows that

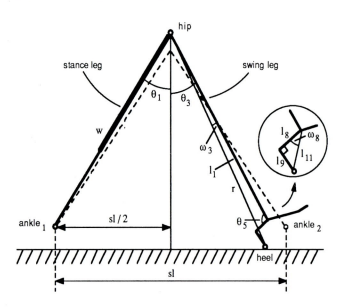

Figure 5: Dynamic model at heel strike: the swing leg is extended, a foot has been added kinematically, the upper body is ignored; θ_3 is assumed to be negative, all other angles are positive.

$$w = \sqrt{(y_h - y_a)^2 + (\frac{sl}{2})^2}$$

$$\theta_1 = \sin^{-1}\left(\frac{sl}{2w}\right)$$

$$\theta_3 = -\omega_3 - \sin^{-1}\left(\frac{x_{nh} - x_h}{r}\right). \tag{3}$$

These are the 3 final conditions for a locomotion step; together with the durations for the leg phases they form the *step constraints* that govern the execution of the low-level control and determine the motion by leading to the internal calculation of the applied forces and torques.

4. LOW-LEVEL CONTROL

The low-level control generates the actual motions by application of a mixture of dynamic and kinematic algorithms. The essence of this control is explained in this section and a full discussion can be found elsewhere [5]. The stance and swing phases of a locomotion cycle are examined separately. Although the dynamics are subject to the *step constraints* which force the execution of a particular step length and step frequency, they need to be guided to produce desired motions *during* a phase by applying rules about walking directly at this low level. For instance, regardless of the stiffness of the leg spring, the hip of the stance leg model must never be allowed to drop below its minimal value at heel strike in order to maintain some kind of a sinusoidal motion pattern; similarly, the swinging leg does not just swing forward to reach the final hip angle at impact, but the motion has to be timed appropriately throughout the swing to make it look real. For this purpose, additional restrictions are imposed in two ways: each phase is divided into a number of *subphases*, where the equations of motion are "fine-tuned" to further suit bipedal walking, and the trajectories of the applied forces and torques are expressed as specific functions of time. The dynamics account

not only for natural movements within a phase, but they also provide continuity across phases. For example, heel strike which occurs between the swing and the stance phase is treated as a collision, whereby the new initial conditions for the stance phase are calculated by the conservation of linear and angular momentum. Although the dynamically simulated motion appears natural in terms of timing and continuity, it does not show human characteristics. To humanize the movements, kinematic algorithms based on the principles of the *virtual leg* and the *determinants of gait* are integrated into the dynamic motion control process as shown below.

4.1 Calculation of Forces and Torques

The problem of finding the forces and torques to meet the desired constraints for each stance and swing phase is formally expressed as follows, assuming the matrix representation of the equations of motion as set out in appendix A:

$$A\ddot{q} = B(q, \dot{q}, F_{q_r}), \quad \text{subject to}$$
$$q(t_0) = \alpha, \quad q(t_e) = \beta \quad \text{and} \quad t_0 \le t \le t_e.$$

The generalized forces F_{q_r} are now the independent variables and the objective is to find the proper forces or torques such that, given the initial conditions $q(t_0)$, the system reaches the final conditions $q(t_e)$ in exactly time t_e. This is a classical *root-finding problem* where the roots F_{q_r} are approximated by numerical techniques.

As an example, consider the stance phase: the initial conditions come from the end of the preceding swing phase and the collision laws at heel strike. The final conditions are the hip angle θ_1 and the length of the leg w at time t_{step} as calculated from equations (3) and (2). The equations of motion are now iteratively integrated over the duration t_{step} by modifying the leg torque F_{θ_1} and the leg axis force F_w on each iteration until the final conditions are met.

The approximation of F_{q_r} is performed in two stages. First, the Bisection method computes a reasonable approximation which is then refined by the Secant method. This technique was employed because the Secant method converges fast, but needs a good first approximation [6]. A solution to F_{q_r} is usually obtained within a few iterations (between 6 and 10). Once the rhythmic phase of a locomotion sequence is reached, i.e. the forward velocity of the body as a whole is fairly constant, the algorithm converges even faster since the F_{q_r} profiles from one step are carried over to initialize the next.

4.2 Stance Phase

During stance the upper body is balanced by the torque F_{θ_2} the magnitude of which is determined by a simple spring and damping model. The leg torque F_{θ_1} is calculated by the approximation procedure described above to satisfy the hip angle θ_1 at the end of the step. Since experiments on human subjects utilizing electromyography and force plates [10] have shown that a significant torque at the hip occurs only just after heel strike and lasts for about 20 % of the cycle time, F_{θ_1} is applied as a step input torque which is turned off at $0.4 \cdot t_{step}$. The leg axis force F_w is approximated such that the telescopic leg w is extended to its desired value at the end of the step. The force profile of F_w is expressed as a spring and damper model of the form

$$F_w = k_w (l_1 + pa - w) - v_w \dot{w} , \qquad (4)$$

where k_w and v_w are spring and damping constants, respectively; l_1 is the unloaded length of the leg, w is the current leg length and $\dot{w}$ the velocity along the leg axis. A *position actuator, pa* (initially zero), actively controls the magnitude of the force; pa must be chosen such that the hip of the stance model prescribes a vertical sinusoidal curve typical in human walking [10]. The hip is therefore constantly monitored during stance: if it drops too low, pa is increased and if the leg extends too much, the value of pa is reduced. However, this method might cause the telescopic leg to become too long (particularly at a low walking speed where the leg does not shorten much after heel strike); if $w > l_1$ (which simulates a plantar flexion of the ankle) occurs too early in the stance phase an unnatural leg motion results. To prevent this, the stance leg is locked as soon as as it reaches a critical length which is either l_1 in the early part or the desired length as calculated by equation (3) towards the end of the stance phase. For this purpose the dynamics of the stance phase are divided into *subphases*: one in which the equations of motion apply as defined in appendix A.1 where the leg is represented by a telescopic inverted pendulum, and another phase in which the leg is defined as a rigid inverted pendulum, expressed by the following modifications to the matrix form of the equations:

$$a_{1,1} = 1, \quad b_1 = a_{1,3} = a_{3,1} = 0 \quad \text{and} \quad \dot{w} = 0 .$$

The subphases are coordinated by the middle-level finite state machine which basically switches between the different sets of equations of motion upon signaling of such events "leg too long". If the leg is locked because $w > l_1$, the lock is removed as soon as the event $\theta_1 > 0$ (leg passes through vertical) occurs, and an increase in pa extends the leg to the desired length at the end of the step.

The *virtual leg* principle describes the procedure which is applied to superimpose a human leg onto the telescopic stance leg (figure 6) at each time step during the simulation. Unfortunately, the number of possible configurations is infinite, i.e. a unique solution does not exist for the orientation of the segments from the hip (H) to the tip of the toe (T). This is a typical *inverse kinematics* problem, where the proximal (H) and distal (T) endpoints are given (H is known from the simulation, T is fixed during stance) and the task is to find the angles of the kinematic chain spanned between these endpoints. At least two of the four angles $(\theta_3, \ldots, \theta_6)$ must be known to fully specify a particular configuration. The information to calculate all leg angles is supplied by rules about the motion of the foot during the stance phase. These rules express a *normal* period just after heel-strike where the foot rotates around the heel until it is flat on the ground. The *normal* period ends when the ankle angle θ_5 reaches a limiting value, at which time the heel begins to come off the ground (*heel-off* period), i.e. the mid-foot rotates around M during this period with radius l_{12}. As soon as θ_6 reaches a limit, the *meta-off* period is entered where the whole foot rotates around T until the end of the stance phase (toe-off). Once θ_5 and θ_6 are known the hip and knee angles (θ_3, θ_4) are determined by simple trigonometric calculations.

The *determinants of gait* [10] mainly describe the movements of the pelvis during locomotion and play a major role in bestowing human appeal to the motion. Pelvic rotation (transverse plane), pelvic list (coronal plane) and a lateral displacement of the body — the body weaves slightly from side to side following the weight-bearing leg — have been implemented. By introducing a pelvis, the kinematics of the determinants basically add a second hip to the locomotion model and must therefore be applied after

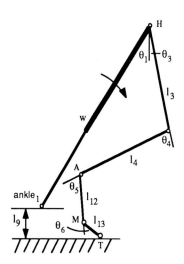

Figure 6: Superposition of a leg over the dynamic stance leg model. The proportions of the foot (l_{12}, l_{13}) are exaggerated.

the the stance phase simulation but before the simulation of the swing leg which uses the new position of this hip. The rotation (list) of the pelvis is a maximum (minimum) at heel-strike and a minimum (maximum) at mid-step, whereas the lateral displacement is a maximum shortly after toe-off and a minimum at heel-strike. These boundary values are specified as *locomotion attributes* and linear interpolation is applied to obtain all the intermediate angles. A linear interpolation is justified since the absolute displacements produced by the determinants are rather small.

4.3 Swing Phase

As with the stance phase, the simulation of the swing phase is broken up into subphases in order to achieve a natural movement of the leg. Three subphases are distinguished — they are illustrated in figure 7. During *swing1* (from t_0 to t_1) the ankle is constrained to move along the curve P until the toe is exactly under the knee. At the same time, the hip angle reaches a maximum, which is the desired value for heel strike as calculated by the symmetry of step concept. The *swing2* subphase lasts from t_1 to t_2 and is characterized by a rapid extension of the knee joint while the hip angle stays fairly constant. After the knee is fully extended at time t_2, a small moment at the hip forces the heel onto the ground during *swing3* to bring about heel-strike (at t_3). Whereas in the stance phase the subphases are triggered by events, the duration of each swing subphase is known *a priori*. Based on experimental data [4, 10], the end for *swing1* occurs at about 50 % of the time for the swing, which means that after half the swing time, the thigh of the swing leg has reached its desired orientation for heel strike. The end of *swing2*, marked by the straightening of the leg, takes place about 85 % into the swing, and the end of *swing3* coincides with the end for the swing phase. Because the time for the swing t_{swing} of the current step is known from the state-phase timing concept, the durations for the subphases can be readily determined. A foot is added kinematically to the model whereby the ankle and metatarsal angles are interpolated between their values at toe-off and heel-strike (the former are known from the kinematic *meta-off* period, the latter are specified as *locomotion attributes*).

During the *swing1* phase the hip torque F_{θ_3} is expressed as a

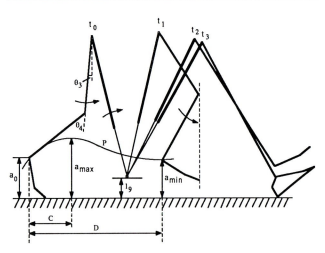

Figure 7: Illustration of swing phase; the kinematic foot proportions are exaggerated, the upper body is ignored.

decaying exponential function and numerically approximated such that the hip angle θ_3 reaches the desired value at time t_1. At the same time, the knee joint is locked for the dynamic simulation; at each time increment, the knee angle θ_4 is updated by forcing the ankle onto the curve P and the new value for θ_4 is fed back to the simulation process. This measure makes an explicit calculation of the knee torque unnecessary, and simplifies the integration procedure. The equations of motion are reduced as follows, assuming the matrix form of appendix A.2:

$$a_{2,2} = 1, \quad b_2 = a_{1,2} = a_{2,1} = 0 \quad \text{and} \quad \dot{\theta}_4 = 0. \tag{5}$$

The curve P is represented by a 4th order polynomial $y(x) = \sum_{i=0}^{4} A_i x^{4-i}$ where x and y are the coordinates of the ankle. The coefficients A_i are computed from the following 5 conditions:

$$
\begin{aligned}
y(0) &= a_0 \\
y(C) &= a_{max} \\
\dot{y}(C) &= 0 \\
y(D) &= a_{min} \\
\dot{y}(D) &= 0.
\end{aligned}
$$

The value for a_0 is computed at the end of the previous *meta-off* period. At a distance C, the ankle reaches the maximum height a_{max} during swing. Based on observations [4, 10], C amounts to about 30 % of the value for D. The latter, as well as a_{min}, are derived from the hip position (known from stance phase), hip angle (known from step symmetry) and the fact that the toe is directly under the knee at t_1. The value for a_{max} has been chosen somewhat arbitrarily, but in such a way that the faster the walk, the smaller a_{max}.

In the *swing2* phase the magnitude of the hip torque F_{θ_3} is calculated as a spring and damping model to hold the thigh in place, whereas the knee torque F_{θ_4}, whose profile is a decaying exponential function, is numerically approximated as to extend the leg at exactly time t_2. However, the foot might intersect with the ground while the knee is extending. This could result from small spring and damping constants, by an accentuated pelvic list

or a short step length. A recovery algorithm increases the hip torque temporarily just enough for the foot to clear the ground. This is achieved by repeating the simulation of the *swing2* phase with an incrementally increased position actuator similar to equation 4 until the foot clears the ground. Finally, in the *swing3* phase the leg is extended with the knee joint locked, which involves analytically constraining the equations of motion as in equation (5). A hip torque is applied, chosen by the numerical approximation process such that heel-strike occurs at time t_3 which is exactly t_{swing}.

5. RESULTS

It has been demonstrated that the KLAW system can produce a wide variety of quite realistic human walks upon specification of only a few parameters. Besides a desired body height, the mass of the body and a simulation time, the animator needs to specify at least one of the locomotion parameters to obtain a walking sequence. Since the algorithm is step-oriented, changes in the locomotion parameters over time can be accounted for with a granularity of one step. This allows for accelerations and decelerations in the locomotion, and even the extreme cases of starting and stopping are possible as shown in figure 8.

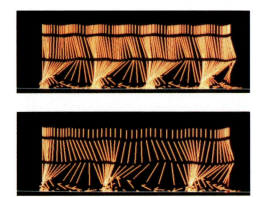

Figure 8: Motion of one leg for two complete walking sequences at different speeds; top: 2 *km/h*, 4 cycles, bottom: 5 *km/h*, 3 cycles.

The *locomotion attributes* are used to individualize a walk. For instance, by changing the amount of pelvic list as shown in figure 9, significant variations of a walk are generated even for the same locomotion parameters. Figure 10 illustrates the effects of different combinations of step length and step frequency for the same the walking velocity.

The system calculates a total of 56 angles for the 37 joints of the body model — 24 of these joints model the vertebrae in the spine — plus a position vector in space for each time step. Currently, these computations are performed not quite in real-time; for example, it took 37.3 sec of CPU time on a SUN3-50 computer with floating point processor to compute the motion of the 12 sec walk in figure 10, top. In practice, the *swing2* phase has been most expensive because of its recovery algorithm; although the duration of *swing2* is only about 35 % of the time for the swing, the simulation usually takes more time than for the *swing1* and *swing3* phases combined. It is clear that real-time animation can be achieved by using a faster processor and by customizing the numerical integration routines.

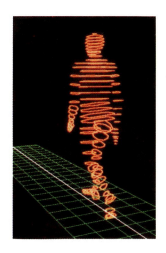

Figure 9: Illustration of pelvic list at toe-off.
Left: natural pelvic list, right: accentuated pelvic list.

6. CONCLUSIONS

A hybrid approach between goal-directed and dynamic motion control has been introduced to animate human walking. This meets two of the most important goals in human character animation — convenient specification and realistic motion production. The success of the approach demonstrates that it is feasible to build a knowledge base to guide the animation of a complex, co-ordinated human movement. It has been shown that the torques and forces which drive the dynamic simulation can be found automatically by iteratively approximating constraints defined by the knowledge base. We believe that the algorithm can be directly extended to other bipedal gaits and locomotion with more than two legs. Whereas running, for example, would require a modification of the dynamic model as well as the high-level concepts to account for the flight phase during which both legs are off the ground, additional legs are merely a coordination problem at the "state" level.

Since in practical terms, the dynamics could be regarded as an interpolation method between the key frames defined by some high level concepts (in this case, step symmetry and state-phase timings) we are currently investigating the possibility of building an entire animation system for articulated figures, where different classes of motions (locomotion, grasping, standing up, turning, etc.) are implemented as tasks which the animator can activate by a few motion parameters. The usefulness of such a system would greatly depend on the choice of parameters assigned to each task.

7. ACKNOWLEDGEMENTS

This work was supported in part by grants from the Social Sciences and Humanities Research Council of Canada and the Natural Sciences and Engineering Research Council of Canada. The authors acknowledge the contributions of Scott Selbie and Severin Gaudet.

APPENDICES

A. EQUATIONS OF MOTION

The equations of motion for the stance and swing phase below are based on figure 2 and were derived using the Lagrange method. The Lagrange equations for a system with n degrees of freedom can be written as

$$\frac{d}{dt}\left(\frac{\partial L}{\partial \dot{q}_r}\right) - \frac{\partial L}{\partial q_r} = F_{q_r}, \quad \text{where} \quad r = 1, 2, \ldots, n;$$

L = Lagrangian = $T - V$,
T = Kinetic Energy,
V = Potential Energy,
q_r = Generalized Coordinate
F_{q_r} = Generalized Force .

A.1 Stance Phase

For the stance phase, $n = 3$ and $q_r = [\, w, \theta_1, \theta_2 \,]^T$. F_{θ_1} and F_{θ_2} represent torques, F_w a force along the stance leg axis. Since the foot remains fixed on the ground during stance, i.e. $\ddot{x} = \ddot{y} = \dot{x} = \dot{y} = 0$, three equations of motion result. The meaning and values of anthropometric data are given in appendix B. In matrix form, $A\,\ddot{q} = B(q, \dot{q})$ where

A = inertia matrix ($n \times n$ matrix for n degrees of freedom)
q = solution vector
B = vector of transient terms (including the F_{θ_r}) ,

the equations are written as

$$\begin{bmatrix} m_2 & 0 & -m_2 r_2 \sin(\theta_2 - \theta_1) \\ 0 & I_1 + m_1 r_1^2 + m_2 w^2 & m_2 r_2 w \cos(\theta_2 - \theta_1) \\ a_{1,3} & a_{2,3} & I_2 + m_2 r_2^2 \end{bmatrix} \cdot \begin{bmatrix} \ddot{w} \\ \ddot{\theta}_1 \\ \ddot{\theta}_2 \end{bmatrix} =$$

$$\begin{bmatrix} F_w + m_2 w \dot{\theta}_1^2 + m_2 r_2 \dot{\theta}_2^2 \cos(\theta_2 - \theta_1) - m_2 g \cos\theta_1 \\ F_{\theta_1} - 2 m_2 w \dot{w} \dot{\theta}_1 + (m_1 r_1 + m_2 w) g \sin\theta_1 \\ \quad + m_2 r_2 w \dot{\theta}_2^2 \sin(\theta_2 - \theta_1) \\ F_{\theta_2} + m_2 g r_2 \sin\theta_2 - 2 m_2 r_2 \dot{w} \dot{\theta}_1 \cos(\theta_2 - \theta_1) \\ \quad - m_2 r_2 w \dot{\theta}_1^2 \sin(\theta_2 - \theta_1) \end{bmatrix}$$

A.2 Swing Phase

For the swing phase, $n = 2$ and $q_r = [\, \theta_3, \theta_4 \,]^T$. F_{θ_3} and F_{θ_4} represent torques. The translational motion of the hip of the swing leg does not impose additional degrees of freedom to the system, since this motion is determined by the stance phase model as follows:

$$x_h = x + w \sin\theta_1 \qquad\qquad y_h = y + w \cos\theta_1$$

$$\dot{x}_h = \dot{w} \sin\theta_1 + w \dot{\theta}_1 \cos\theta_1 \qquad \dot{y}_h = \dot{w} \cos\theta_1 - w \dot{\theta}_1 \sin\theta_1$$

$$\ddot{x}_h = \ddot{w} \sin\theta_1 + 2 \dot{w} \dot{\theta}_1 \cos\theta_1 \qquad \ddot{y}_h = \ddot{w} \cos\theta_1 - 2 \dot{w} \dot{\theta}_1 \sin\theta_1$$

$$\quad + w(\ddot{\theta}_1 \cos\theta_1 - \dot{\theta}_1^2 \sin\theta_1) \qquad - w(\ddot{\theta}_1 \sin\theta_1 + \dot{\theta}_1^2 \cos\theta_1),$$

where $\ddot{x} = \ddot{y} = \dot{x} = \dot{y} = 0$.

In matrix form, the two equations of motion are

$$
\begin{bmatrix}
I_3 + m_3\, r_3^2 + m_4\, l_3^2 & I_4 + m_4\, r_4^2 + m_4\, l_3\, r_4 \cos\theta_4 \\
\quad + I_4 + m_4\, r_4^2 + 2\, m_4\, l_3\, r_4 \cos\theta_4 & \\
a_{1,2} & I_4 + m_4\, r_4^2
\end{bmatrix}
\cdot
\begin{bmatrix}
\ddot{\theta}_3 \\
\ddot{\theta}_4
\end{bmatrix}
=
$$

$$
\begin{bmatrix}
F_{\theta_3} + (m_3\, r_3 + m_4\, l_3)\, (\ddot{x}_h \cos\theta_3 - \ddot{y}_h \sin\theta_3) \\
\quad + m_4\, r_4\, (\ddot{x}_h \cos(\theta_3 + \theta_4) - \ddot{y}_h \sin(\theta_3 + \theta_4)) \\
\quad + m_4\, l_3\, r_4\, \dot{\theta}_4\, (2\, \dot{\theta}_3 + \dot{\theta}_4)\, \sin\theta_4 \\
\quad - m_3\, g\, r_3 \sin\theta_3 - m_4\, g\, (l_3 \sin\theta_3 + r_4 \sin(\theta_3 + \theta_4)) \\
F_{\theta_4} + m_4\, r_4\, (\ddot{x}_h \cos(\theta_3 + \theta_4) - \ddot{y}_h \sin(\theta_3 + \theta_4)) \\
\quad - m_4\, l_3\, r_4\, \dot{\theta}_3^2 \sin\theta_4 - m_4\, g\, r_4 \sin(\theta_3 + \theta_4)
\end{bmatrix}
$$

B. ANTHROPOMETRIC DATA

Table B-1 lists the *relative* (lengths are fractions of body height, masses are fractions of body mass) anthropometric data of the segments used by the dynamics and lower body kinematics. l_i denote lengths, m_i masses, r_i distances to centers of mass and γ_i radii of gyration. It should be noted, that except for r_1, which is measured from the distal end, the centers of mass are given from the proximal end of a segment. The radii of gyration are specified with respect to the center of mass:

segment	i	l_i	m_i	r_i	γ_i
pelvis	0	0.10059	-	-	-
leg	1	$l_3 + l_4$	$m_3 + m_4$	0.553	0.326
upper body	2	0.47	0.678	0.5	0.496
thigh	3	0.23669	0.1	0.433	0.323
shank	4	0.24556	0.061	0.606	0.416
mid foot	5	0.0858	-	-	-
toe	6	0.04734	-	-	-
hind foot	8	0.02959	-	-	-
ankle-footbase*	9	0.03846	-	-	-
heel-ankle*	11	0.04853	-	-	-
ankle-1st metatarsal*	12	0.08901	-	-	-
1st metatarsal-toe tip*	13	0.0496	-	-	-

Table B-1: Anthropometric values of lower body segments
(the * indicates a distance rather than a segment length).

The *absolute* anthropometric data, including the moments of inertia I_i, are calculated by the system once the values for body height and body mass are specified. As an example, if the total body height is to be $1.8\,m$ and the body mass $80\,kg$, the following values result for the thigh:

$$
\begin{aligned}
m_{3_{abs}} &= 8\,kg, \\
l_{3_{abs}} &= 0.426\,m \\
r_{3_{abs}} &= r_3 \cdot l_{3_{abs}} = 0.184\,m, \\
\gamma_{3_{abs}} &= \gamma_3 \cdot l_{3_{abs}} = 0.138\,m, \\
I_3 &= m_{3_{abs}} \cdot (l_{3_{abs}} \cdot \gamma_{3_{abs}})^2 = 0.0276\,kg\,m^2.
\end{aligned}
$$

REFERENCES

1. William W. Armstrong, Mark Green. The Dynamics of Articulated Rigid Bodies for Purposes of Animation. Graphics Interface '85, Proceedings, 1985, pp. 407-415.

2. Norman I. Badler, Kamran H. Manoocherhri, Graham Walters. "Articulated Figure Positioning by Multiple Constraints". *IEEE Computer Graphics and Applications 7*, 6 (June 1987), 28-38.

3. Ronen Barzel, Alan H. Barr. A Modeling System Based On Dynamic Constraints. SIGGRAPH '88, Proceedings, August, 1988, pp. 179-188.

4. Royce Beckett, Kurng Chang. "An Evaluation of the Kinematics of Gait by Minimum Energy". *J. Biomechanics 1* (1968), 147-159.

5. Armin Bruderlin. Goal-Directed, Dynamic Animation of Bipedal Locomotion. Master Th., School of Computing Science, Simon Fraser University, 1988.

6. Richard L. Burden. *Numerical Analysis.* Prindle, Weber & Schmidt, 1985.

7. Thomas W. Calvert. The Challenge of Human Figure Animation. Graphics Interface '88, Proceedings, 1988, pp. 203-210.

8. Michael Girard, Anthony A. Maciejewski. Computational Modeling for the Computer Animation of Legged Figures. ACM SIGGRAPH '85, Proceedings, July, 1985, pp. 263-270.

9. Alan C. Hindmarsh. "LSODE and LSODI, Two New Initial Value Ordinary Differential Equation Solvers". *ACM-SIGNUM Newsletter 15*, 4 (1980), 10-11.

10. Verne T. Inman, Henry J. Ralston, Frank Todd. *Human Walking.* Williams & Wilkins, Baltimore, 1981.

11. Paul M. Isaacs, Michael F. Cohen. "Controlling Dynamic Simulation with Kinematic Constraints, Behavior Functions and Inverse Dynamics". *Computer Graphics 21*, 4 (July 1987), 215-224.

12. Marc H. Raibert. "Legged Robots". *Communications of the ACM 29*, 6 (1986), 499-514.

13. David Sturman. Interactive Keyframe Animation of 3-D Articulated Models. Graphics Interface '86, Tutorial on Computer Animation, 1986.

14. Dare A. Wells. *Theory and Problems of Lagrangian Dynamics.* McGraw-Hill, New York, 1967.

15. Jane Wilhelms. Virya- A Motion Control Editor for Kinematic and Dynamic Aniamtion. Graphics Interface '86, Proceedings, 1986, pp. 141-146.

16. David Zeltzer. "Motor Control Techniques for Figure Animation". *IEEE Computer Graphics and Applications 2*, 9 (1982), 53-59.

17. David Zeltzer. Knowledge-Based Animation. ACM SIGGRAPH/SIGART, Workshop on Motion, 1983, pp. 187-192.

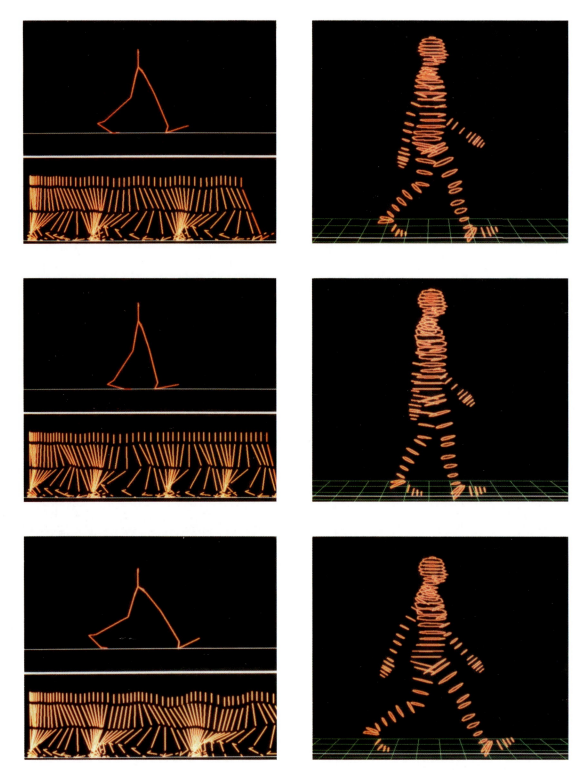

Figure 10: Heel-strike for 3 walking sequences at $v = 5 \ km/h$.
Top: natural walk, only v was specified, $sl = 0.77 \ m$ and $sf = 107.5 \ steps/min$ were chosen by the system.
Middle: short step walk, v and $sl = 0.50 \ m$ were specified, $sf = 166.7 \ steps/min$ was chosen by the system.
Bottom: long step walk, v and $sl = 1.05 \ m$ were specified, $sf = 79.4 \ steps/min$ was chosen by the system.

Computer Graphics, Volume 23, Number 3, July 1989

Layered Construction for Deformable Animated Characters

John E. Chadwick
David R. Haumann
Richard E. Parent

The Ohio Supercomputer Graphics Project
The Advanced Computing Center for the Arts and Design
The Department of Computer and Information Science
The Ohio State University

Abstract

A methodology is proposed for creating and animating computer generated characters which combines recent research advances in robotics, physically based modeling and geometric modeling. The control points of geometric modeling deformations are constrained by an underlying articulated robotics skeleton. These deformations are tailored by the animator and act as a muscle layer to provide automatic squash and stretch behavior of the surface geometry. A hierarchy of composite deformations provides the animator with a multi-layered approach to defining both local and global transition of the character's shape. The muscle deformations determine the resulting geometric surface of the character. This approach provides independent representation of articulation from surface geometry, supports higher level motion control based on various computational models, as well as a consistent, uniform character representation which can be tuned and tweaked by the animator to meet very precise expressive qualities. A prototype system (Critter) currently under development demonstrates research results towards layered construction of deformable animated characters.

CR Categories and Subject Descriptors: 1.3.7 [Computer Graphics]: Graphics and Realism: Animation; 1.3.5 [Computer Graphics]: Computational Geometry and Object Modeling. Additional Key Words and Phrases: free form deformations, robotic manipulators, kinematics, dynamics, character animation.

1. Introduction

Rendering quality has improved to the point that images with very high levels of photo-realism and full of textural detail may readily be achieved. The development of special purpose graphics engines and massively parallel hardware suggest extremely complex rendering will soon be economically feasible for computer character animation production. The largest obstacle facing the realization of computer character animation is the motion specification itself. An anatomically precise geometric model must also move with an equal degree of realism or we do not accept the illusion. Current commercial animation software literally mimics the key frame methodology of traditional animation. Some successful animated films have been realized with these animation systems; however, much of the burden of specifying the motion of the character form is placed on the animator. The current research efforts of the authors focus on providing a more efficient and effective animation environment designed specifically for constructing and animating characters. We are investigating techniques to exploit the power of computational models so as to provide the animator with fine tuned local control as well as the ability to orchestrate complexity with higher level control.

1.1. Traditional Animation

Animation in a general sense could be defined as "things changing over time". If we are to address the problem of character animation, then this definition is not adequate. The problem of character animation can best be described by the title of the animation bible: "The Illusion of Life", written by Thomas and Johnston [1]. The focus is not on the problem of completing a given motion task, but more importantly on how this motion task is performed by the character. All the elements involved in an animated character must cooperate in a very synchronized harmony. This does not necessarily require realistic behavior, but behavior that is believable, full of an expressive quality which captures the personality of the character. The principles of animation as developed in the Disney heydays are very colorfully presented in [1]. Lasseter provides solid working examples of how these principles have been applied to track based key frame animation [2]. The track based key frame animation approach [3][4] provides a general solution to the animation problem; however, the ability to produce quality animation is principally the burden of the animator. Getting an animation to "jump into life" is the craft of the animator, yet to literally model the methodology of traditional drawn animation grossly underestimates the computational power potentially available by the medium. If we can formalize some of the concepts which underlie the principles of traditional animation such as Squash and Stretch, Exaggeration, Follow Through and Overlapping Action, then we may provide the animator with more intuitively parameterized models while more effectively exploiting the available computational resources.

1.2. Geometric Deformations

The animation of deformable characters requires geometric models of soft tissue which change over time. Lundin and Van Bearle and others have applied surface patch descriptions to model smooth character form [5]. Recently Forsey and Bartels describe a method for hierarchical B-spline refinement which allows for multiple levels of control ranging from broad high level surface description to low level fine tuning control in regions of intricate detail [6]. Barr introduced geometric modeling deformations which provide abstract data manipulation operators creating a useful sculpting metaphor [7]. Sederberg and Parry introduced the concept of Free Form Deformations (FFDs) based on hyperpatch solids [8]. FFDs provide the flexibility of general free form spline control coupled with the sculptural flexibility of deformations. For purposes of animation, a key advantage to abstracting deformation control from that of the actual surface description is that the transition of form is no longer dependent on the specifics of the surface itself. FFDs provide the foundation for deformations implemented by the authors.

1.3. Simulation Models

A new area of computer graphics research focuses on the simulation of the physical properties of object models. The motion and shape deformation of the objects can be simulated through applied physics [9]. Barr, Terzopoulos, Platt, Fleischer, and Haumann have applied discrete macro molecular abstractions of the substance properties of the object to model flexible elastic behavior [10][11]. The discrete molecular components of the object can be viewed as point masses interconnected by springs with stiffness and damping attributes based upon the physical properties of the object. Hahn, and Moore and Wilhelms have coupled rigid body dynamics with collision detection and reactive forces to provide realistic animation of objects tumbling and colliding through space [12][13]. Terzopoulos and Fleischer have extended their model to include rigid and flexible components as well as inelastic behavior [14][15]. The finite element lattice used by Terzopoulos et al for flexible models is analogous to the hyperpatch control lattice [10]. Here the spline concept has been extended to include physical properties from whence splines originally sprung :) . Physically based models have proven extremely successful at animating "inanimate" or "not consciously moving" objects. Miller has provided striking results based on a physical model for simulating the self motivated motion dynamics of snakes and worms [16]. The field of biomechanics has been concerned for some time with modeling the physical properties of body tissues as it relates to the areas of artificial implants [39] and the healing of surgical wounds [40], to name just a few. The main difficulties in modeling the dynamics of soft body parts are the structural inhomogineity and the inelastic, time-dependent behaviors of the regions involved. For example, skin, fatty tissue, muscle, and skeleton all exhibit different physical properties complicated by the presence of migratory fluids (blood and lymph) as well as actively contracting muscles. Thus accurate physical simulations of these combined structures requires complex, viscoelastic, anisotropic models such as those presented by Fung [41]. All these simulation methods offer great potential for character animation; however, harnessing this computational power remains largely a problem of animator control. Barr, Barzel, Kass, Platt and Witkin have addressed the control issue by providing user specified constraints, which are then resolved through coupling physical models with constraint satisfaction methods based on various optimization criteria [17][18][19][20].

The ability to control articulated figures is a long standing problem addressed by the robotics community. Robotics research has been applied to the problems of computer animation. Girard and Maciejewski introduced inverse kinematics to the figure animation community by providing computational models for legged locomotion [21][22]. Badler et al. have also employed inverse kinematics towards figure animation, as well as a system for specifying figure positioning based on constraint satisfaction [23]. The dynamic simulation of articulated hierarchies has also been applied to computer animation by Armstrong

and Green, and Wilhelms [24][25]. With dynamics we achieve greater physical realism, but the ability to control the desired applied forces to meet specific motion requirements remains an open problem. Animator applied forces such as joint torques seem far less intuitive than direct kinematic specification of joint angles. Isaacs and Cohen applied inverse dynamics, also popular within the robotics community, as a mechanism for integrating kinematic and dynamic control [26]. Often in character animation, however the dynamics are secondary to conveying the emotions of the character.

Due to the complexity of articulated figure motion , a level of control which is higher than the manual specification of every individual moving parameter is needed. Zeltzer addresses the problem of articulated figure control by using a higher level "director" control approach [27]. Animator specified goal directed behavior is resolved through decoupling the goals into task level routines provided by a robust motion library. For the animator, behavioral models are a naturally intuitive means of high level control. In addition behavioral models may algorithmically suggest to the viewer conscious decision making processes on the part of the animated characters. Amkraut and Reynolds have provided models for bird flocking behavior [28][29]. Flocking behavior provides a good example of higher level control orchestrating complexity. From the character animation perspective director level control is often desirable but not sufficient, because it does not allow the animator precise control over the fine details of motion. What is needed is an intermediate "actor" level of control which allows the animator to control, perhaps even act out the gestural details of a character's movement. The layered approach to characters presented in this paper is designed to support motion generated by simulation models while also providing precise control of the transition of the character's form.

2. Layered Construction

In his 87 Siggraph paper [2] Lasseter stresses that the advantage offered by computer animation is one of working the animation in layers. The ability to isolate parameters is essential to fine tuning motion via local control. The ability to additively build an animation in layers provides an effective means for creating complex motion. We would like to extend this notion to motion specified through simulation by building the character in layers and specifying the relationship between the layers through parametric constraints. A layer can be defined as a conceptual simulation model which maps higher level parametric input into lower level outputs. The animator specifies various constraint relationships between the layers and can control the global motion from a high level. The animator defines the layers of the character by specifying parameters and conditions of the constraints. This describes how the character moves and not the specifics of the explicit motion. By providing layers of the character related through parametric constraints, low level motion can be automated through higher level control.

This layered philosophy and the notion that the computer becomes manager of the interacting relationships of the various parametric layers is central to the design of the Critter system developed by the authors. The ability to define attributes as constraints provides a methodology where more emphasis is placed on constructing the character so that less emphasis is needed in actually scripting an animation. Parametric constraints provide the animator with control of gestural detail, while providing consistent, automatic motion control based on layered constraints. This layering philosophy has been adopted both in construction and animation for computer generated characters.

Previous research efforts have also attempted to model animated characters through a layered construction approach. Burtnik and Wein presented a 2-D approach to bending a digitized drawing about an underlying articulated figure using constrained deformations [30]. Parent presented a 3-D approach to bending geometric surfaces about articulated forms for purposes of character animation [31]. Tony De Peltrie was an exciting example where a digitized character geometry was applied to an underlying articulated skeleton. The Thalmanns have created a human factory system designed to animate synthetic actors [32]. Dick Lundin and Susan VanBearle provided animated dancers by algorithmically weaving a surface patch skin on top of an underlying articulated skeleton as well as integrating dynamics to model free fitting clothing [5]. John Donkin's Dinosaur provides another example where a digitized surface geometry skin is fit to an underlying articulated skeleton [33]. These methods were designed to meet specific film production demands. They primarily focus on a three layered approach (motion specification, articulated skeleton, geometric skin) and are tailored to special purpose models. The current approach of the authors provides a more general solution by using a four layered construction approach. The approach described in this paper not only fits a geometric skin to an articulated skeleton, but also captures the fluid squash and stretch behavior of the surface geometry by providing volumetric muscle bulging, dynamic fatty tissue response, and creasing at the joint. The Critter system is designed to provide a flexible interface to the animator for constructing and animating deformable characters.

The authors' philosophy supports a four layered approach from high to low levels as follows:

1. Motion specification
   (referred to as the behavior layer in the critter system)
2. Motion Foundation, articulated armature
   (critter skeleton layer)
3. Shape transition, squash and stretch
   (critter muscle and fatty tissue layer)
4. Surface description, surface appearance and geometry
   (critter skin, clothing and fur layer)

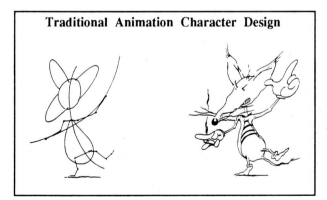

Traditional Animation Character Design

Figure 1.

The layered construction approach adopted by the Critter system is similar to the construction methods described for traditional drawn characters (Figure 1). The stick figure drawing is analogous to the robotics armature or skeleton. The drawn blobby volumetric shapes used to flesh out the character form are analogous to muscle and fatty tissue and help provide consistent fluid squash and stretch transitions in shape. The detailed character sketch is representational of the visible surface geometric "skin". The key advantage to the layered computer methodology is that once the layered character is constructed, only the underlying skeleton need be scripted for an animation; consistent

yet expressive shape dynamics are generated automatically. Various character layers can be used as templates for other similar character forms, thereby providing a robust library of extendable character parts.

The skeleton (second) layer is an underlying articulated hierarchy which provides the foundation for controlling the motion of the character. The muscle layer is then added on top of and attached to the skeleton hierarchy. The foundation for the muscles are represented by freeform deformations. The control points of the deformations are constrained by the positioning (joint angles) and forces (joint torques) applied to and by the underlying skeleton. These deformations then act to glue and deform the actual geometric skin to the underlying skeleton. The skin layer represents the actual visible surface geometry to be rendered. The current implementation supports polygonal skin data based on the existing modeling and rendering environment at ACCAD. The application of FFDs as a foundation for muscle and fatty tissue deformations provides for general extension to potential surface patch, algebraic, or volumetric skin. Each skin object is attached relative to a link in the skeletal hierarchy. This attachment defines the local coordinate space of the skin component. The skin object may then be attached to any number of deformations. Rigid "skin" objects may be connected directly to the skeleton with zero connecting muscles. This allows the system graceful degradation to a basic object hierarchy. Figure 2 provides an example where no muscle layer was provided. A skeleton database (Critter skin) of several bones was attached to a simplified articulated skeleton to provide a reasonable number of controllable joints.

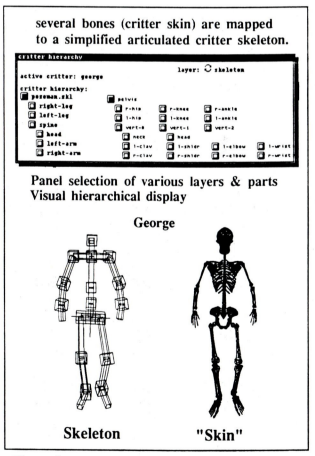

several bones (critter skin) are mapped to a simplified articulated critter skeleton.

Panel selection of various layers & parts Visual hierarchical display

George

Skeleton   **"Skin"**

Figure 2.

The behavior (first) layer which represents the actual motion specification need only be applied to the skeleton parameters. A general purpose attribute based behavioral foundation was provided so that the animation system could be easily extended to include various computational motion models. The foundation for behavior provides a pose vector which contains the character position, orientation and joint angles for each frame. Additional structures are provided to house velocities, accelerations, joint torques, and user specified gesture attributes. To date, the interactive and animation behavior models within the Critter system are based on forward and inverse kinematics with additional procedural modeling capabilities. The muscle and skin layers can be automatically generated based on a given skeletal state.

3. Skeleton Layer

A description is provided of the skeleton layer to clarify the interaction of the articulation hierarchy to the deformations which are built on top of and constrained by the skeleton. The skeleton acts as the character foundation, providing the articulation hierarchy from which additional layers are built and constrained.

The skeleton data includes:
1. Tree structured hierarchy of robotic manipulators
2. Robotic joint-link parameters (Denevit & Hartenberg)
3. Joint angle constraints and physical attributes (max, min, zero, stiffness, mass properties)

The basic joint hierarchy has been extended to a hierarchy of manipulators. A manipulator is basically a sequential chain of interconnected joints and links. Each manipulator may contain any number of child manipulator parts. A child manipulator may be connected to any joint within its parent manipulator chain so that none of the generality of a basic joint hierarchy is lost. The manipulator extension lends itself readily to robotic kinematic and dynamic motion models, in particular inverse kinematics. Denevit & Hartenberg parameters (figure 3) are implemented as the basic joint construct, where:

$$\text{Joint}_i = [\ a_i,\ \alpha_i,\ d_i,\ \theta_i\ ]$$

a_i and α_i represent the link parameters where α_i is the twist angle between links and a_i represents the link length. θ_i and d_i represent the joint parameters where θ_i is the joint angle and d_i the offset length along the axis of joint rotation. A more detailed description of the D & H parameters can be found in the robotics literature [34][35][36]. These joint primitives provide only sin-

gle degree of freedom joint motion. If θ_i is varied over time as a parameter then the joint is rotational. If d_i is varied over time as a parameter then the joint is translational. Primitive robotic joints can be combined at common origin ($a_i = d_i = 0$) with perpendicular joint axis ($\alpha_i = 90^o$) to create universal (2-rotary axis) and ball (3-rotary axis) joints.

Minimum and maximum joint angle constraints provide the animator with the capability to restrict the range of joint motion. The zero angle and stiffness at the joint provide the animator with control over the relative bending at each joint within a manipulator when automated by inverse kinematic control. Mass properties: mass, center of mass, and inertia tensor (distribution of mass) parameters are also provided; however, current behavior models and interactive figure control do not as yet exploit the robotic dynamic models for articulated figures. A more detailed description of the Critter skeleton may be found in [37].

4. Muscle and Fatty Tissue Layer

The constrained deformation layer is central to Critter construction. The deformation acts as the connecting relationship for mapping the geometric skin data to the underlying articulated skeleton foundation, while capturing the flexible fluid quality of squash and stretch behavior. To automate the squash and stretch behavior, the animator specifies muscle and fatty tissue attributes by defining constraint relationships with the underlying skeletal parameter state. The foundation for the muscle and fat deformations is based on Free Form Deformations (FFDs) [8]. Composite tricubic bezier based hyperpatches (or parametric solids) are used as the basis for the FFD as muscle deformation abstractions. The current implementation of muscle and fatty tissue structures represents each muscle primitive as a pair of adjoining FFDs (Figure 4). In an attempt to provide muscle abstractions which deform the skin surface a prototype set of functional deformation operators are provided. Muscles are represented by a pair of FFDs. This provides 7 planes of control points orthogonal to the adjoining joint link axis: four planes for each FFD (cubic bezier) with one plane shared as the adjoining connection between deformations. The two control planes at either end of the muscle deformation (adjoining planes) function principally to preserve continuity across connected muscles. Continuity can also be preserved between a muscle and a non-existing (null muscle) by assuming the null muscle remains undeformed. The remaining three planes (mid planes) function to model the abstract muscle behavior resulting from kinematic or dy-

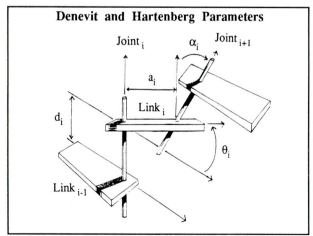

Denevit and Hartenberg Parameters

Figure 3.

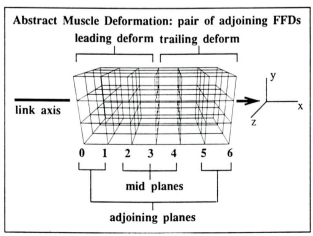

Abstract Muscle Deformation: pair of adjoining FFDs

Figure 4.

namic attributes of the skeletal state. Each operator or muscle type provides a set of parameters for defining the relationship of the control points of the FFDs with the kinematic and dynamic skeletal parameters.

Free form deformations can best be described as a cubical volume in which geometric objects are submersed. If we think of this cube as a chunk of jello which can be bent, shaped, or contorted, then the objects within the volume are distorted accordingly. The basis of the FFD is a trivariate hyperpatch or parametric solid. A set of control points form a three dimensional lattice within the cube. These control points are used by the blending functions to map parametric weights to positions in space. For each vertex comprising the objects embedded within the cube, the three parametric weights can be determined, which when substituted into the blending functions for the undeformed cube, produce the position of that vertex in the undeformed object. By manipulating the control points which form the lattice, the cube solid is deformed. The resulting vertex positions of the deformed object are computed by using the deformed lattice control points in the hyperpatch blending functions and then sampling at the parametric weights associated with the original undeformed vertices.

Current deformations are based on kinematic, dynamic, or sculpted constraints. To provide automatic squash and stretch behavior of the character, muscle deformations are modeled to provide bulging and bending of the character geometry based on the kinematic state of the articulated skeleton. To increase the expressiveness of the character the dynamics of the passively deformable body parts such as flesh and underlying soft tissue are modeled to provide automatic follow through and overlapping action. Exaggeration can be produced by adding sculpted deformations which give the animator explicit control over the shape transition of the character form.

4.1. Kinematic Deformation

By providing muscle deformations which are constrained by the kinematic skeletal state, automatic, consistent squash and stretch behavior can be achieved. While in reality our muscles control the skeletal joint motion, from an animation perspective we inversely would like the skeletal joint motion to automatically create the resulting muscle flexion required to meet the specified motion. The kinesiology literature suggests the following mechanical properties of joint and muscle action [38]:

Elasticity- When tension is applied to a muscle, a passive elongation results accompanied by a reduction of the cross sectional area of the muscle. A weight attached to a relaxed muscle causes an elongation (E) which is directly proportional to the original muscle length (L) and to the pulling force (F) and a constant (k) which varies for each body, and inversely proportional to the cross sectional area (A).

$$E = \frac{F * L * k}{A}$$

Contractility- is the ability of the muscle to shorten by nervous stimuli. The contraction of the muscle is an active process, as opposed to the passive elastic elongation. The muscle tension represents the force, while the change in length during contraction represents the distance covered by the application of this force, whose product is the visible work accomplished. A constant relationship exists between the natural length of the muscle, the variable length of the contracted muscle, and the degree of rotation at the joint. For each unit of shortening (S) there is a constant rotation angle (θ).

$$S = \theta * k$$

The basic property of contraction can be applied to algorithmic models such that the kinematic joint angles act as controlling parameters for abstract muscle behavior. Flexor and extensor muscle deformation models function to provide the visible result of muscle contraction. The algorithm for resolving the resulting control points of a flexor - extensor for each frame follows:

1. The overall shortening of the muscle = joint angle * displacement ratio. This shortening is propagated across each control plane of the muscle by the square of the ratio of length up to control plane / total muscle length.

2. The implied shortening is countered by scaling up and out along the local y & z coordinates. If all muscle boundaries are active, then this scaling will be distributed equally in all directions for each of the 3 midplanes (see Figure 4). If one boundary side is not active, then the scale factored is doubled along the active boundary opposing the not active side. Fixed boundaries can be used to shape the deformation, as in the biceps example (Figure 5.), or to maintain null continuity, in particular, areas in which the deformation intersects a skin component object. The radius ratio determines the relative scale factors of the two exterior mid planes (2 & 4). The center mid plane (3) is resolved by line plane intersection to maintain continuity across the contracted surface.

3. The adjoining planes of the flexor - extensor are maintained to assure continuity with actively connected muscles, or remain undeformed with the exception of shortening along the link axis (x).

In addition to kinematic muscle contraction, tendon deformations model the bending at the joint. This is designed to cover very short regions of the character where a single geometric skin crosses over a joint, covering part of two or more skeletal links to account for underlying bone tissue. The control points of the tendon FFDs are resolved for each frame based on the following algorithm:

1. Determine the bisection angle of the joint. If the angle exceeds the threshold angle, then bisect the threshold angle; else bisect the joint angle. For a hinge joint bisection angle = angle / 2. For joints with more than one degree of freedom we need to know the resulting axis of rotation. Quaternions provide a convenient means of resolving the single axis, and angle about the axis resulting from multiple rotations about several axes. Using this axis & and angle we can now resolve the bisection angle.

2. Rotate mid planes by bisection angle about their local z axes. We rotate planes 2 & 3 by the bisection angle, and plane 4 by -bisection angle. (When the trailing deform is rotated about the joint by the joint angle plane 4 will have proper bisection alignment)

3. Project mid planes 2 & 4 onto boundary cube of deform. Scale control points to avoid intersections with interior region of deform. (This scaling is motivated by underlying bone structure forcing the skin and muscle to stretch, not penetrate deform interior)

4. Slide planes 0 & 1 away from plane 2; slide planes 5 & 6 away from plane 4. Find closest point to adjoining planes. Use this point as reference to maintain distance from adjoining plane to midplane.

5. Rotate trailing deform by joint angle at joint.

6. Use line plane intersection for line segments connecting each control point pair from midplanes 2 & 4, intersected with bisection plane or midplane 3 (plane at joint). Modify control points of joint plane 3 at intersection to maintain C1 continuity.

7. If threshold is exceeded, rotate joint plane by additional angle (bisection of (joint angle - threshold angle))

8. Use line plane intersection to maintain continuity for outside control points only (crease now forms for interior points)

9. Working out from midplanes (2 & 4) towards adjoining planes (1, 2, 5, 6) check for intersection with bisection plane at joint (3). If intersection occurs within bounded plane (0 < t < 1 for parametric line segments) then set control points which cross bisection plane 3 to intersection point. Use parametric weight t to scale control plane out to maintain volume from squash.

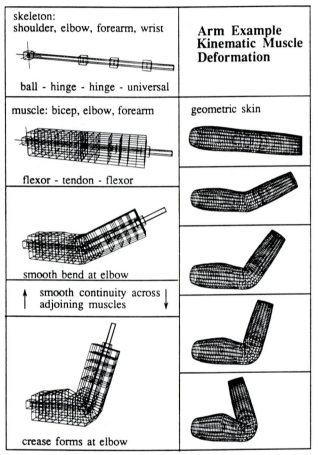

Figure 5.

4.2. Dynamic Deformation

From the point of view of computer generated character animation, we wish to capture the dynamic properties of soft body structures, but without incurring the costs of a complete physical model. Of the physical properties that the simulation must handle, one of the most desirable effects is that of large deformations (in homage to Tex Avery!). In addition, viscous effects must be modeled in order to realistically simulate the damped oscillations of soft parts which result from the character's motion. Finally, the model must allow for spatial variations of the physical properties so as to model the different structures within the character. Fortunately, for these purposes, a complete physical model is unnecessary because, given the space-time scales of interest, many of the effects due to the variation in structures are visually insignificant, or can be greatly simplified. The model of deformable body parts presented here was developed specifically to capture these nonlin-

ear, viscoelastic and anisotropic properties, yet includes spatial simplifications which help reduce the computational cost. Our technique maps the control points of the FFD to point masses in a similarly shaped force lattice. Dynamic simulation is performed on the mass particles and the resulting motion is mapped back onto the FFD control points thus determining the resulting object deformations.

The physical model we employ is a three-dimensional extension to one developed using the behavioral test-bed described in [11]. The model consists of a three-dimensional grid of point mass elements (3 degrees of freedom) connected by viscously damped Hookean springs. The spatial simplifications of the dynamics models results from the one to one mapping maintained between the point masses and the control points of the FFDs. To capture shear strain behavior, spring elements are connected diagonally between mass elements on adjacent planes. Thus, if one were to isolate one "cube" from the grid, it would appear as having one point mass at each of the eight corners, with each mass being directly connected by spring elements to the remaining seven (see Figure 6). Intuitively, the springs aligned with the major axes serve to maintain the linear dimensions of the body, while the cross springs help maintain the angular relationships between the grid planes.

The dynamics are simulated by marching along at discrete sub-frame time steps. At each step, the spring forces are calculated and applied to the point masses, which respond by accelerating in the direction of the net force applied. Using a 2nd order runge-kutta scheme with adaptive stepsize, the equations of motion are integrated to determine the subsequent position and velocity of each point mass. In order to transfer the motion of the animated character to the physical model, we allow certain chosen mass points to be rigidly fixed to the character skeleton, while the remaining mass points are free to dynamically respond. In effect, these fixed points represent the rigid structure of the internal skeleton of the character. As the character moves, changes in the positions of the attached points result in spring displacements which force the remaining mass points into motion.

Dynamics is applied as a post processing step after the articulated skeletal motion has been completed. The steps are as follows:

1. The entire motion of the character as specified through high level control is precomputed.

2. Once computed, the position information for each control point for each FFD at each frame in the animation is known. Certain points of each FFD are designated as non dynamic (fixed to move along these pre-computed "paths").

3. The corresponding physical models are constructed. The motion paths of the non-dynamic control points are used as scripts to drive the corresponding point masses within the dynamics model. The remaining points are free to move as a result of forces generated with the force lattice.

4. Once the dynamic simulation is completed the positions of the free point masses are mapped back onto the positions of the corresponding "dynamic" control points of the FFD. This determines the dynamically deformed shapes of the objects affected by the FFD.

5. Continuity is maintained across internal regions of the shared midplane, and with adjoining or null deformations.

The selection of the physical constants is performed upon the basis of the visual appeal of the resulting motion. The user controls the spring constants, damping coefficients, and the mass properties of each element individually or of the model as a whole. We do not attempt to make these parameters correspond to actual measured values, relying instead upon the animators tastes, which can fall anywhere within the real-surreal spectrum.

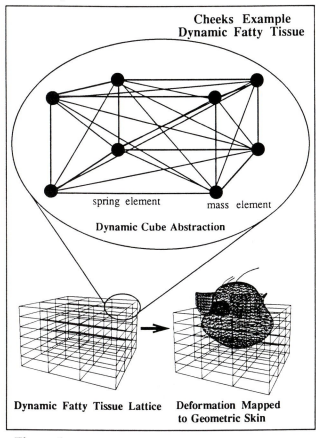

**Cheeks Example
Dynamic Fatty Tissue**

spring element   mass element

Dynamic Cube Abstraction

**Dynamic Fatty Tissue Lattice   Deformation Mapped
to Geometric Skin**

Figure 6.

4.3. Sculpted Deformation

A fundamental design objective of the authors was to provide a general system for constructing and animating computer generated characters. Sculpted deformations provide the most general, but also the most labor intensive deformation primitive supported by the Critter system. Sculpted deformations are principally key framed deformations. The animator sculpts the deformations by moving individual control points of the 3-D lattice defining the FFDs, or through translation, scale or rotation of control point planes or selected control point groupings of the FFDs. These key deformations are then bound to a key attribute. If the application of deformation is to imply muscle reaction, then the key attribute may be constrained by the controlling skeletal joint angle. Several key deformations may be stored as extremes relative to various joint angle positions. The resulting deformation for any given skeletal state is then determined by applying cubic spline interpolation for each corresponding control point of the FFDs. The parametric weight of the interpolation is based on the relation of the current joint angle to the surrounding key angle attributes associated with each key deformation. Sculpted muscles can be used if other muscle models do not adequately provide the shape transition desired, or to add definition to other muscle models.

Sculpted deformations may also be used to provide deformations representational of emotional contortions. Gestural quali-

ties may be sculpted to provide visual exaggeration. Classic cartoon examples of gestural deformation are pride ("V") and sorrow (slumped). The ability to drive a sculpted deformation by an attribute exterior to the skeletal parameters frees the animator to control the parametric blending of various key deformations by any behavior parameter. This removes the automatic nature of the deformation, requiring that animator to now control the level of deformation from the scripted behavior. This was added as an exception to the rule of only specifying skeletal attributes via behavior for added flexibility and generality. For example, breathing can effectively be modeled by oscillating the driving parameter of a sculpted deformation algorithmically.

4.4. Continuity

Maintaining smooth continuity is integral to the function of muscle deformations. The ability to build complex musculature in layers depends readily on the ability of these composite muscle deformations to maintain smooth C1 continuity where desired. For bezier curves this requires a colinear relationship of the three corresponding control points from each midplane. Initial implementations discussed in [37] provided this colinear condition by placing the central midplane control point at the line of intersection of the neighboring midplane control points based on a line - plane intersection calculation. This worked. However it was extremely limited in controlling the shape of the bend, and provided little capability for the animator to control the implied underlying bone tissue. Least square line fitting was implemented to provide the model for securing continuity across adjoining deformations. Rather than an all or nothing line fit, a best fit strategy is employed based on the chi-square merit function. Animator specified weights for each control point can be used to sculpt the resulting continuous boundary regions.

Least square line fitting:

$$p(u) = p(u; a,b) = a + bu$$

Chi-square merit function:

$$\chi^2(a,b) = \sum_{i=1}^{N} ((p_i - a - bu_i) / \sigma_i)^2$$

σ_i represents the uncertainty associated with each p_i assuming the u_i's are known. We want to minimize the merit function to determine a and b, by setting the partial derivatives with respect to a and b to zero:

$$\delta\chi^2/\delta a = -2 \sum_{i=1}^{N} ((p_i - a - bu_i) / \sigma_i^2) = 0$$

$$\delta\chi^2/\delta b = -2 \sum_{i=1}^{N} ((u_i (p_i - a - bu_i)) / \sigma_i^2) = 0$$

We can now solve for the best fit line given two equations and two unknowns (a & b). Let $w_i = 1 / \sigma_i^2$ were w_i represents the respective relative weight of contribution for the associated p_i. We now consider these weights as an intuitive means of controlling the shape of the resolved continuous curve as opposed to a measure of uncertainty. The animator provides weights for each control point of the deformations to sculpt the resolved continuous form.

Overlapping continuity is resolved by providing "null" continuity across borders which affect overlapping regions. Null continuity simply implies that the first two control points remain fixed so that the border region maintains unchanged with respect to its first derivative.

5. System Overview

Figure 7 provides a diagram of the information flow within the current Critter system implementation and how it relates to the animator interface. The construction of Critters is tightly coupled with the interactive animation process. The animator can tune and tweak the character while scripting an animation.

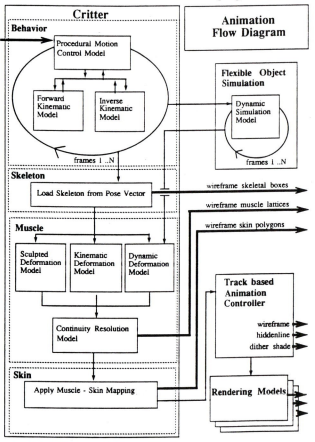

Figure 7.

The system allows the animator to construct motion studies which aid in the intuitive understanding of the character parameter space. Given an established Critter, the behavior attributes are processed initially for each frame. This creates a skeletal pose vector for each frame. If dynamic muscles are present then this precomputed behavior is fed to the dynamic simulation process which then computes the dynamics for the complete sequence of frames. Kinematic and sculpted deformations as well as the deformation to skin mappings are computed on the fly, so that direct access to any frame can be provided in pseudo real time (with the exception of muscle- skin mapping which is on the order of a second running on a sun4/110 workstation). The animator may interactively select viewing of skeleton, muscle or skin layers within the Critter system, or pipe this information into Chalk, a track based animation system developed by John Donkin. The integration with Chalk provides animators with the ability to integrate Critter motion with track based motion and

supports various display capability (B&W dithered shading, and hiddenline, as well as a link to various rendering algorithms developed by Scott Dyer).

5. Results

Bragger Bones, a character designed by Don Stredney provided the first attempt at a full character representation (Figures 8, 9, 10 & 11). Initial studies concentrated on the character's limbs and head. Kinematic deformations were placed on the arms and legs and dynamic deformations were placed on the cheek region of the head. Flexor deformations were used to model the biceps, forearms, thighs and calves, while tendon deformations were used to model the elbows and knees. Figure 9 presents every 5th frame from an animation test. The biceps contraction was exaggerated by a factor of 1.5. The bending at the elbows was thresholded to form a crease at an angle of 40 degrees., while the bending at the knees was thresholded at 30 degrees. Default continuity weighting was used for all deformations. Adjoining continuity was maintained between biceps, elbow and forearm deformations, as well as between thigh, knee and calf deformations. Null continuity was maintained at the top of the dynamic cheek deformation so that a smooth surface resulted between the dynamic cheeks and the rigid top of the head.

6. Summary

The Critter system developed at ACCAD provides multi-layered construction and animation of deformable characters. The deformation layer can be constructed by layering several local and global deformations which are constrained by the underlying articulated skeleton. By placing more emphasis on constructing a more elaborate character model, less emphasis is placed on the parameter specification required to script an animation. Squash and Stretch, Follow through and Overlapping Action as well as Exaggeration become more automatic, and consistent. The methodology presented provides a more automatic environment for the animator to meet desired animation specifications. Through computational models which formalize the principles of animation a more intuitive parameterization for the animator is provided. This approach does not attempt to replace animators by algorithmic models, but intends instead to provide them with a more powerful medium for artistic creativity.

Figure 8. Bragger Bones

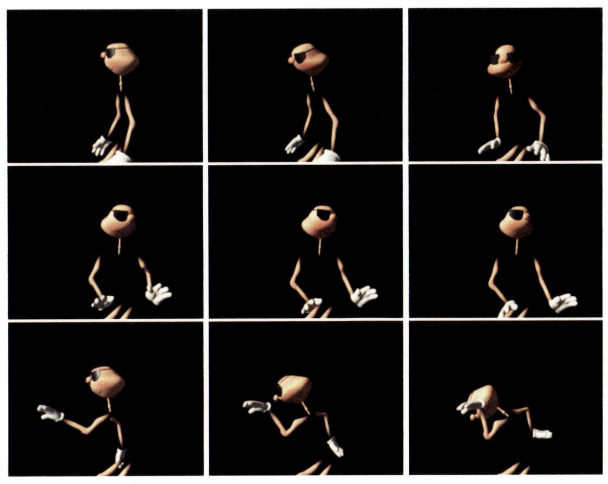

Figure 9. Bragger Animation Test: Kinematic and Dynamic Deformations.
(Every 5th frame, left to right, top to bottom)

Figure 10. Dynamic Cheek Deformation
(top right frame from above)

Figure 11. Kinematic Arm Deformations
(bottom right frame from above)

251

7. Acknowledgments

Don Stredney designed the initial prototype critters, and provided valuable background assistance in anatomy and kinesiology, as well as providing the hand drawn illustrations for this paper. Michael Girard provided valuable insight into related robotics issues. John Donkin provided the chalk - critter interface, with system support from John Fujii, who was invaluable in getting the illustrations for this document. The rendering software was developed by Scott Dyer. The illustrations and video examples were produced using apE utilities provided by the Ohio Supercomputer Graphics Group. And a special thanks to C.G. for the pasteups and everything. Thanks to Chuck Csuri and Tom Linehan for the environment and opportunity at AC-CAD, and to the Ohio Supercomputer Center. This work was supported in part by a grant from Cray Research.

8. References

[1.] Thomas & Johnston, "Disney Animation: The Illusion of Life", Abbeville Press, New York, '84.

[2.] Lasseter, John, "Principles of Traditional Animation Applied to 3D Computer Animation", Computer Graphics, Vol. 21, No. 4, '87.

[3.] Gomez, Julian, "Twixt: A 3-D Animation System", Proceedings of Eurographics 84, '84.

[4.] Sturman, David, "Interactive Keyframe Animation of 3-D Articulated Models", Proc. Graph. Interface, '84.

[5.] Van Bearle, "A Case Study of Flexible Figure Animation", 3-D Character Animation by Computer Course Notes, Siggraph '87.

[6.] Forsey & Bartels, "Hierarchical B-Spline Refinement", Computer Graphics, Vol. 22, No. 4, '88.

[7.] Barr, Alan, "Global and Local Deformations of Solid Primitives", Computer Graphics, Vol. 18, No. 3, July, '84.

[8.] Sederberg & Parry, "Free Form Deformations of Solid Geometric Models", Computer Graphics, Vol. 20, No. 4, '86.

[9.] Barr, Alan, "Dynamic Constraints", State of the Art in Image Synthesis Course Notes, Siggraph, '86.

[10.] Terzopoulos, Platt, Barr, and Fleischer, "Elastically Deformable Models", Computer Graphics, Vol. 21, No. 4, July, '87.

[11.] Haumann & Parent, "The Behavioral Testbed: Obtaining Complex Behavior from Simple Rules", The Visual Computer, Special Issue on Mechanics, Control and Animation, Vol. 4, No. 6, Dec., '88.

[12.] Hahn, James, "Realistic Animation of Rigid Bodies", Computer Graphics, Vol. 22, No. 4, '88.

[13.] Moore and Wilhelms, "Collision Detection and Response for Computer Animation", Computer Graphics, Vol. 22, No. 4, '88.

[14.] Terzopoulos and Fleischer, "Modeling Inelastic Deformation: Viscoelasticity, Plasticity, Fracture", Computer Graphics, Vol. 22, No. 4, August'88.

[15.] Terzopoulos and Witkin, "Physically Based Models with Rigid and Deformable Components", IEEE CG&A, November, '88.

[16.] Miller, Gavin, "The Motion Dynamics of Snakes and Worms", Computer Graphics, Vol. 22, No. 4, '88.

[17.] Witkin, Fleischer, & Barr, "Energy Constraints on parameterized Models", Computer Graphics, Vol. 21, No. 4, '87.

[18.] Barzel & Barr, "A Modeling System Based on Dynamic Constraints", Computer Graphics, Vol. 22, No. 4, '88.

[19.] Witkin and Kass "Spacetime Constraints", Computer Graphics, Vol. 22, No. 4, '88.

[20.] Platt and Barr, "Constraint Methods for Flexible Objects", Computer Graphics, Vol. 22, No. 4, '88.

[21.] Girard & Maciejewski, "Computational Modeling for Computer Animation of Legged Figures", Computer Graphics, Vol. 19, No. 3, '85.

[22.] Girard, Michael, "Interactive Design of 3-D Computer Animated Legged Animal Motion", Chapel Hill Interactive Computer Graphics Interface Workshop, '86.

[23.] Badler, Manoochehri, Walters, "Articulated Figure Positioning by Multiple Constraints", IEEE CG&A, June, '87

[24.] Armstrong & Green, "The Dynamics of Articulated Rigid Bodies for purposes of Animation", Proc. Graphics Interface 85, '85.

[25.] Wilhelms, Jane, "Using Dynamic Analysis for Realistic Animation of Articulated Bodies", IEEE CG&A, June, '87.

[26.] Isaacs and Cohen, "Controlling Dynamic Simulation with Kinematic Constraints, Behavioral Functions and Inverse Dynamics", Computer Graphics, Vol. 21, No. 4, July, '87.

[27.] Zeltzer, David, "Representation and Control of Three dimensional Computer Animated Figures", Ph.D.. Dissertation, The Ohio State University, '84.

[28.] Amkraut, Susan, "Flock: A Behavioral Model for Computer Animation", M.A. Thesis, The Ohio State University, '89.

[29.] Reynolds, Craig, "Flocks, herds and Schools; A Distributed Behavioral Model", Computer Graphics, '87.

[30.] Burtnyk & Wein, "Interactive Skeleton Techniques for Enhancing Motion Dynamics in Key Frame Animation", CACM, Vol. 19., No. 10, Oct. '76.

[31.] Parent, Richard, "A System for Generating 3-Dimensional Data for Computer Graphics", Ph.D. Dissertation, The Ohio State University, '77.

[32.] Magnenat-Thalmann & Thalmann, "The Direction of Synthetic Actors in the Film Rendezvous a Montreal", IEEE CG&A, Dec., '87.

[33.] Donkin, John, personal communication '88.

[34.] Denavit & Hartenberg, "A Kinematic Notation for Lower-Pair Mechanisms Based on Matrices", J Appl Mech, Vol. 23, '55.

[35.] Whitney, "The Mathematics of Coordinated Control of Prosthetic Arms and Manipulators", Journal of Dynamic systems, Measurement, and Control, Dec., '72.

[36.] Klein, Huang, "Review of Pseudoinverse Control for Use with Kinematically Redundant Manipulators", IEEE Transactions on Systems, Man, and Cybernetics, Vol SMC-132, No. 3, March/April '83.

[37.] Chadwick and Parent, "Critter Construction: Developing Characters for Computer Animation', Proceedings Pixim, '88.

[38.] Steindler, Arthur, "Kinesiology of the Human Body", Charles C. Thomas Publisher, Springfield Illinois, '55.

[39.] Burstein, A., Frankel, V., "The Viscoelastic Properties of Some Biological Materials", Materials in Biomedical Engineering Vol. 146, Article 1, p. 158-165, Annals of the New York Academy of Sciences, January 1968.

[40.] Schneider D., et al.,"In Vitro Biaxial Stress-Strain Response of Human Skin", Arch Otolaryngol Vol 110, p. 329-333, May 1984

[41.] Fung, Y. C., Biomechanics: Mechanical Properties of Living Tissues, Springer-Verlag, New York, 1981.

[42.] Lundin, R. Ruminations of a Model Maker IEEE Computer Graphics and Applications 7(5):3-5 May 1987

[43.] Waters, K. A Muscle Model for Animating Three-Dimensional Facial Expression Computer Graphics 21(4):17-24 (Siggraph Proceedings) July 1987

[44.] Weil, J. The Synthesis of Cloth Objects Computer Graphics 20(4):49-54 (Siggraph Proceedings) August 1986

Hypertexture

Ken Perlin
Courant Institute of the Mathematical Sciences
New York University

Eric M. Hoffert [†]
AT&T Pixel Machines

ABSTRACT

We model phenomena intermediate between shape and texture by using space-filling applicative functions to modulate density. The model is essentially an extension of procedural solid texture synthesis, but evaluated throughout a volumetric region instead of only at surfaces.

We have been able to obtain visually realistic representations of such shape+texture (*hypertexture*) phenomena as hair, fur, fire, glass, fluid flow and erosion effects. We show how this is done, first by describing a set of base level functions to provide basic texture and control capability, then by combining these to synthesize various phenomena.

Hypertexture exists within an intermediate region between object and not-object. We introduce a notion of *generalized boolean shape operators* to combine shapes having such a region.

Rendering is accomplished by *ray marching* from the eye point through the volume to accumulate opacity along each ray. We have implemented our hypertexture rendering algorithms on a traditional serial computer, a distributed network of computers and a coarse-grain MIMD computer. Extensions to the rendering technique incorporating refraction and reflection effects are discussed.

CR Categories and Subject Descriptors: C.1.2 [**Processor Architectures**]: Multiprocessors - *parallel processors*; I.3.3 [**Computer Graphics**]: Picture/Image Generation - *display algorithms - viewing algorithms*; I.3.5 [**Computer Graphics**]: Computational Geometry and Object Modeling - *curve, surface, solid and object representations*; I.3.7 [**Computer Graphics**]: Three Dimensional Graphics and Realism - *animation - visible line/surface algorithms*;

©1989   ACM-0-89791-312-4/89/007/0253 $00.75

General Terms: volume modeling, noise, turbulence, translucency, opacity, volume rendering, parallel rendering, distributed rendering

Additional Key Words and Phrases: hypertexture, generalized boolean, density modulation function (DMF), ray marching, furrier synthesis

1. Introduction

In computer graphics objects are traditionally modeled as sets having infinitesimally thin boundary surfaces. Often a computed or digitized texture or displacement is then mapped onto the surface for enhanced realism. However, there are limitations in treating object boundaries merely as surfaces.

Many objects, such as fur or woven materials, have a complex definition which is at best awkward, and at worst impossible, to describe by a surface model. For other objects, such as eroded materials or fluids, a highly complex boundary is actually an artifact of a process that is often more readily described volumetrically. Still other objects, such as flame, clouds, or smoke, don't actually have a well defined boundary surface at all.

We have found that the appearance of many such objects can be described directly by some applicative function, evaluated over a sampling of some region of R^3. Within this framework we are intuitively working with a solid block of material; visual characteristics of objects can be finely tuned by inserting numerical controls into their defining functional descriptions [3]. In that sense this work extends the procedural texture generation work of [5]. As in [5], we make use of a single controllable stochastic *noise* function together with a toolkit of shaping functions and programming constructs.

We render hypertexture by combining ideas from volume rendering ([1],[7],[8],[10],[16]) with some new extensions particularly suited to this model.

---

† Current address: Apple Computer, Cupertino, CA

1.1 Overview

In this paper, we first discuss the modeling issues of hypertexture. Instead of modeling objects as connected surfaces, we model objects as distributions of density. We describe a mechanism to generate simple base-shape density distributions. These base-shapes have a hard region where they are completely solid, and a soft region where they are indeterminate. Whenever we are in the soft region, we can apply a toolkit of shaping functions, allowing the flexibility to create and manipulate volumetric form. An analogy is to think of this region as malleable, where the user can push in, pull out, twist or otherwise deform simulated matter in a controllable manner. We also develop a CSG style scheme to combine shapes using the operators union, intersection, difference and complement.

When the foundation of modeling has been described we show how hypertexture is rendered. The renderer needs to evaluate many density samples throughout the volume since the model can become highly detailed and may contain a high degree of depth complexity. The rendering stage of the process allows a user to control the color and opacity of the object at every point in R^3 via the use of color maps. Since hypertexture rendering is relatively expensive ($O(n^3)$ with respect to image resolution), we have implemented both distributed and parallel renderers.

2. Modeling Hypertexture

In order to describe hypertexture, we need to introduce the concepts of:

- an *Object Density Function* $D(\mathbf{x})$ with range $[0,1]$ which describes the density of a 3D shape for all points $\mathbf{x}$ throughout R^3. The *soft region* of an object consists of all $\mathbf{x}$ such that $0 < D(\mathbf{x}) < 1$.

- a *Density Modulation Function* (DMF) f_i, which is used to modulate an object's density within its soft region. Each DMF is used to control some aspect of an object's spatial characteristics; a collection of DMFs comprises a volume modeling toolkit.

Hypertexture is created by successive application of DMFs f_i to an object's $D(\mathbf{x})$:

$$H(D(\mathbf{x}), \mathbf{x}) = f_n(\ldots f_2(f_1(f_0(D(\mathbf{x})))))$$

The DMF f_i can be of three types: position-dependent, position-independent and geometry-dependent. Position-dependent DMFs are $f(\mathbf{x})$, position-independent are $f(k)$ where k is a scalar and geometry-dependent DMFs may depend on variables other than $\mathbf{x}$ such as density gradient in the vicinity of $\mathbf{x}$.

2.1 Soft Objects

Formally, a soft object is a density function $D(\mathbf{x})$ over R^3, where D is 1.0 inside the object, 0.0 outside the object, and $0.0 < D < 1.0$ in a region of nonzero thickness in between. As an example, consider the sphere centered at $\mathbf{c}$ of radius r and softness s. This can be defined by the density function:

$$
\begin{aligned}
D_{[\mathbf{c},r,s]}&(\mathbf{x}): \\
r_1^2 &:= (r-s/2)^2 \\
r_0^2 &:= (r+s/2)^2 \\
r_x^2 &:= (x_x-c_x)^2 + (x_y-c_y)^2 + (x_z-c_z)^2 \\
D &:= \textit{if } r_x^2 \leq r_1^2 \textit{ then } 1.0 \textit{ else} \\
&\quad \textit{if } r_x^2 \geq r_0^2 \textit{ then } 0.0 \textit{ else } (r_0^2-r_x^2)/(r_0^2-r_1^2)
\end{aligned}
$$

where r_0 is the the outer ($D=0$) boundary, r_1 is the inner ($D=1$) boundary and r_x is the radius of the sphere at the point $\mathbf{x}$.

2.2 Generalized Booleans

We extend the boolean operations of set union, set complement, set intersection and set difference[†] to soft objects A and B through their density functions $a(\mathbf{x})$ and $b(\mathbf{x})$:

- **intersection**: $A \cap B \equiv a(\mathbf{x})b(\mathbf{x})$

- **complement**: $\bar{A} \equiv 1.0 - a(\mathbf{x})$

- **difference**: $A - B = A \cap \bar{B} \equiv a(\mathbf{x}) - a(\mathbf{x})b(\mathbf{x})$

- **union**: $A \cup B = \overline{\bar{A} \cap \bar{B}} \equiv a(\mathbf{x}) + b(\mathbf{x}) - a(\mathbf{x})b(\mathbf{x})$.

As with traditional boolean shape operators, we can construct expressions of arbitrary complexity to represent combinations of different primitive shapes. By using boolean algebra, soft objects can be added or subtracted with smooth and controllable fillets at the regions where they join. Note that the size of the region where objects join can be controlled by modifying the width of each object's soft region. It should be noted that these operations don't actually form a complete boolean algebra (since from the above definitions $A \cap A \neq A$ and $A \cap \bar{A} \neq \Phi$) but do allow for standard set operations.

2.3 Base Density Modulation Functions

Here are the base level DMFs that higher-order DMFs are

---

† There is a rough analogy here to the principles of fuzzy set theory [18]. We choose algebraic sum and algebraic product for union and intersection, respectively [19], instead of the fuzzy set theoretic *min* and *max* operators [18], because the former preserve continuity. This is needed to maintain smoothness of fillets at the regions where objects join. It would be interesting also to try the *min* and *max* operators.

built upon.

bias

We use bias to either push up or pull down an object's density. A function that controls mean, $bias_b$ is a power curve defined over the unit interval such that $bias_b(0)=0$, $bias_b(1/2)=b$, and $bias_b(1)=1$. By increasing or decreasing b, we can thus bias the values in an object's soft region up or down. $Bias_{0.5}$ is the identity function over $[0,1]$.

Bias can be defined by the power function:

$$t^{\frac{ln(b)}{ln(0.5)}}$$

gain

We use gain to make an object's density gradient either flatter or steeper. A function that controls variance, $gain_g$ is defined over the unit interval such that: $gain_g(0)=0$, $gain_g(1/4)=(1-g)/2$, $gain_g(1/2)=1/2$, $gain_g(3/4)=(1+g)/2$, and $gain_g(1)=1$. By increasing or decreasing g, we can thus increase or decrease the rate at which the midrange of a object's soft region goes from 0.0 to 1.0. $Gain_{0.5}$ is the identity function over $[0,1]$.

Gain can be defined as a spline of two bias curves:

$$if\ t < 0.5\ then\ bias_{1-g}(2t)\ /\ 2$$
$$else\ 1 - bias_{1-g}(2-2t)\ /\ 2$$

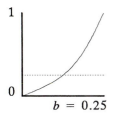 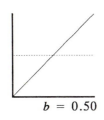 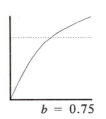

$b = 0.25$ $b = 0.50$ $b = 0.75$

Different *bias* curves

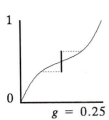 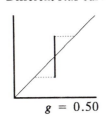 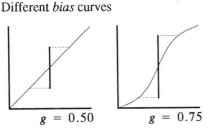

$g = 0.25$ $g = 0.50$ $g = 0.75$

Different *gain* curves

noise

An approximation to white noise band-limited to a single octave, *noise* [5] allows us to introduce randomness into the digital signal without sacrificing either continuity or control over spatial frequency.

We implement *noise* as a summation of pseudorandom spline knots, one for each point on the integer lattice of R^3. The knot $\Omega_{i,j,k}$ at lattice point (i,j,k) consists of a pseudorandom linear gradient $\Gamma_{i,j,k}$ weighted in each dimension by a smooth drop off function $\omega(t)$[†]:

$$\Omega_{i,j,k}(u,v,w) = \omega(u)\omega(v)\omega(w)\ (\Gamma_{i,j,k} \bullet (u,v,w))$$

where "$\bullet$" denotes vector inner product. We choose for $\omega(t)$ the cubic weighting function:

$$if\ |t|<1\ then\ 2|t|^3-3|t|^2+1\ else\ 0$$

giving the spline a support of 2 in each dimension, so that in practice for any given point in R^3 we only need to take the sum of the 2^3 nearest spline knots. Thus our *noise* implementation is defined at point (x,y,z) by:

$$\sum_{i=\lfloor x \rfloor}^{\lfloor x \rfloor +1} \sum_{j=\lfloor y \rfloor}^{\lfloor y \rfloor +1} \sum_{k=\lfloor z \rfloor}^{\lfloor z \rfloor +1} \Omega_{i,j,k}(x-i,y-j,z-k)$$

where "$\lfloor\ \rfloor$" denotes the floor function.

For speed, we implement the pseudo-random gradient by hashing (i,j,k) to create an index into a precomputed gradient table $\mathbf{G}$:

$$\Gamma_{i,j,k} = \mathbf{G}[\phi(i+\phi(j+\phi(k)))]$$

where:

• $\phi(i) = P[i_{mod\ n}]$, where P is a precomputed array containing a pseudorandom permutation of the first n integers,

• $\mathbf{G}$ is a precomputed array of n pseudorandom vectors uniformly distributed on the unit sphere,

• n is the length of the P and $\mathbf{G}$ arrays (in practice, we find $n=256$ to be a reasonable value).

To ensure that each element $\mathbf{v}$ of $\mathbf{G}$ is uniformly distributed on the unit sphere, we employ a three step Monte Carlo

† It would have been somewhat faster and simpler to use a constant Γ (which is essentially a wavelet model), but we have found that this produces visible artifacts at the lattice points, where gradient becomes zero.

technique:

> (1) generate each coordinate of **v**, choosing
>   uniformly from the interval [−1,+1]
> (2) if |**v**|>1.0 then goto (1)
> (3) normalize the length of **v**

It is important to use the three-fold table lookup of "$\phi(i+\phi(j+\phi(k)))$" above for hashing the three integer lattice coordinates (i,j,k), so that neighboring lattice points will not have correlated indices into the gradient table **G** (which would otherwise be visible as unsightly patterns).

turbulence

Because of its great general utility in building higher level DMFs, we also include the *turbulence* function of [5] as a base function, defined by:

$$\sum_i abs\left(\frac{1}{2^i}\,noise\,(2^i\,\mathbf{x})\right)$$

Note that this is not a true turbulence model, but merely a method of simulating the appearance of turbulent activity.

arithmetic base functions

The set of base functions is rounded out by basic mathematical routines such as the *abs* and *sine* functions, together with arithmetic and control flow operations.

2.4 Higher Level Functions (Hypertextures)

In this section, we describe how to create and combine DMFs to generate hypertextural phenomena. In most of our examples, the shape defined by the object density function of the hypertexture is very simple, such as a cube, sphere or torus. The DMFs shape the soft region of these objects; color and alpha maps determine the mapping of density to color and transparency.

Basic Noise

Figure **noisy sphere** shows a sphere with noise of frequency **f** and amplitude **1/f** used to scale the radius:

$$D(\mathbf{x}) = sphere\left(\mathbf{x}\left(1+\frac{1}{f}\,noise\,(f\mathbf{x})\right)\right)$$

The frequency controls the number of bumps on the surface; the amplitude controls their height.

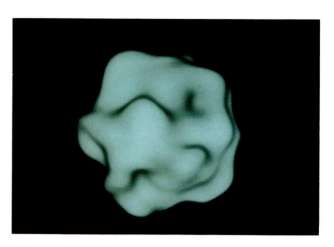

noisy sphere

Varying Frequency

Figure **high-frequency noisy sphere** shows the same sphere with noise of twice the frequency and half the amplitude. This creates smaller but similarly shaped perturbations of the surface.

Varying Amplitude

Figure **high-amplitude noisy sphere** is the same as above but with amplitude increased, so that the noise modulation dominates the shape.

Combining Frequencies

Figure **fractal sphere** shows the same sphere again, with noise of many different frequencies summed together:

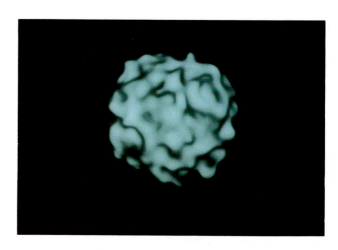

high-frequency noisy sphere

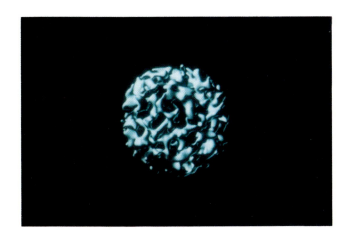

high-amplitude noisy sphere

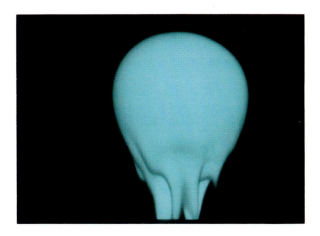

dripping sphere

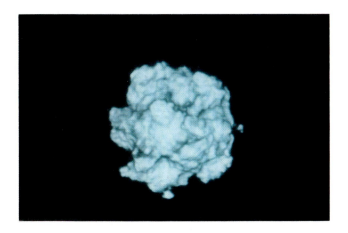

fractal sphere

blue glass

$$D(\mathbf{x}) = sphere(\mathbf{x}\,(1 + \sum_i \frac{1}{2^i f} noise(2^i f \mathbf{x})))$$

The base frequency here is f; at each step of the summation, amplitude is inversely proportional to frequency. Now the shape takes on a characteristic $\frac{1}{f}$ fractal appearance.

Shaped noise

Figure **dripping sphere** illustrates what happens when we use noise to modulate only the y component of $\mathbf{x}$ in order to simulate the appearance of dripping material.

Transparency

Figure **blue glass** illustrates the notion of refractive hypertexture. In this case, rays are bent following Snell's law [20] whenever the refractive index encountered by the renderer at a sample is different from its value at the previous sample. We add an extra channel to the renderer's color table to modulate refractive index as a function of density. In this example we apply it to one of the noisy spheres seen earlier.

Erosion

Figure **eroded cube** is an example of an erosion model. We use generalized booleans to generate this composite shape by applying the **intersection** operator to combine a fractal sphere with a cube. The turbulence function is also used here, to create color variations through the hypertexture as in [5].

Fire

Figure **fire ball** was created by the density function:

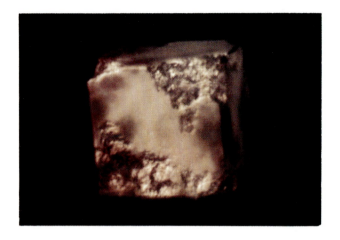

eroded cube

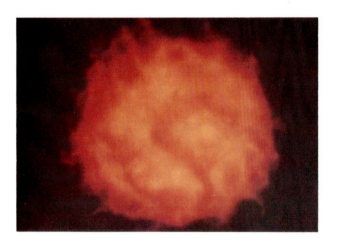

fire ball

$$D(\mathbf{x}) = sphere(\mathbf{x}\,(1 + turbulence(\mathbf{x})))$$

The color map is structured in this case so that low densities map to red, higher densities to yellow. This is a direct extension to three dimensions of the flame model used to create the **Solar Corona** of [5].

We now describe an example of hypertexture in greater detail, to give a sense of how these algorithms are developed.

Hair and Fur

We create furlike hypertexture in stages. First we start with a soft object defined by $D(\mathbf{x})$. The fur will exist in the object's soft region, each filament growing out from the inner boundary (where $D = 1.0$) towards the outer boundary (where $D = 0.0$).

We first project each point $\mathbf{x}$ in the soft region perpendicularly down to the inner solid boundary surface using the

geometry-dependent function **project**. At the surface we compute *noise* of high frequency *freq*, and use it to modulate the object density $D(\mathbf{x})$, as follows:

$$s := noise(freq * \mathbf{project}(\mathbf{x}))$$
$$f := gain_{0.9}(bias_{0.3}(s)) * D(\mathbf{x})$$

Figure **furry donut** shows this algorithm applied to a donut shaped object. The *bias* and *gain* adjustments are used to shape the noise profile into a relatively hard boundary (*gain* adjustment) with more empty space than hair (*bias* adjustment). The hairs will all be of the same length, equal to the width of the object's soft region. The projection function can be computed analytically here, since the object's geometry is well understood. This is an example of a geometry-dependent DMF.

To make the fur curly as in figure **tribble** we use *noise* to displace $\mathbf{x}$ before projecting. We use a vector valued function **noise** for this, instead of the usual scalar *noise*

furry donut

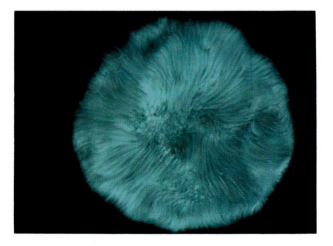

tribble

function, so that the displacement will occur in an arbitrary direction. This creates a sort of three dimensional ripple glass effect, as though straight hair were being seen through a distorted space:

$$d := D(\mathbf{x})$$
$$\mathbf{x}' := \mathbf{x} + gain_{0.8}(1 - d) * curliness * \mathbf{noise}(\mathbf{x})$$
$$s := noise(freq * \mathbf{project}(\mathbf{x}'))$$
$$f := gain_{0.9}(bias_{0.3}(s)) * d$$

There are several things to note in the above algorithm. The scalar variable *curliness* controls the magnitude of the curl. We use the expression $gain_{0.8}(1 - d)$ to shape the curl, so that the hairs are initially straight where they grow out of the root (where $D = 1.0$), and gradually curl up as they reach the outer boundary (where $D = 0.0$). The vector valued **noise** function is built from *noise* as:

$$\mathbf{noise} = \left[noise(\mathbf{x}-\sigma), noise(\mathbf{x}), noise(\mathbf{x}+\sigma) \right]$$

where the offset vector σ is made large enough so that the three calls to *noise* are guaranteed to return uncorrelated values (since each call will encounter an entirely different set of pseudorandom knots).

Note how in all of the above we create a relatively simple algorithmic mechanism with a small number of scalar variables that control aspects of perceptual interest (filament length, fineness, curliness, etc). As in [5], these are essentially knobs that a user of a hypertexture system can adjust at a high level to synthesize a particular variety of fur, without necessarily knowing the details of furrier synthesis.

3. Rendering Hypertexture

Implementation of hypertexture rendering is only practical using volume rendering techniques, since hypertextural objects often have no well defined surfaces. Since volume rendering techniques have time complexity $O(n^3)$ with respect to resolution, they are typically slow. Fortunately the DMF evaluation is independent at each sample point, so hypertexture is particularly suitable for parallel or distributed implementations. We have found that designing and rendering hypertexture can be done on a serial von Neumann machine, but is *much* more enjoyable when computed in parallel. This section focuses on the hypertexture rendering algorithm and its different implementations.

3.1 Ray Marching Algorithm

In this section, we describe the *ray marching* algorithm [1] to generate images of hypertexture. As in traditional ray casting, the ray marcher casts a ray into model space for every pixel. We first clip each ray to a parallelpiped that bounds the hypertexture volume, using the optimal

bounding test of [13]. If the ray does not intersect the parallelpiped, we move to the next pixel for processing. If the ray does intersect the parallelpiped, the ray parameters μ_0 and μ_1, representing respectively the entry and exit points of the parallelpiped, are computed. Ray marching begins at the ray parameter value μ_0, and proceeds at a fixed increment $\Delta\mu$. We sample the model along the ray at points:

$$\mathbf{x} = \mathbf{x}_{\mu_0} + k \, \Delta\mathbf{x}_\mu$$

where

$$k = 0, 1, 2, \dots \text{ such that } \mu_0 + k \, \Delta\mu \le \mu_1$$

and $\Delta\mathbf{x}_\mu$ is the displacement along the ray, in model space, at each increment.

Aliasing of hypertexture is a potential problem. In practice we have achieved excellent results by manually tuning each hypertexture to be frequency clamped [17] as a function of ray-marching step size. For example, in the turbulence function described above, we stop the iteration when the period of the noise function is as small as the size of $\Delta\mathbf{x}_\mu$. The fact that an empirical approach works so well is encouraging but is clearly not definitive[†].

At each point along the ray, we first evaluate a DMF $f(\mathbf{x})$. If $0 < f(\mathbf{x}) < 1$, then we evaluate the field gradient ∇f, normalize it, and use it as a normal vector for diffuse and/or specular shading, as well as for any refraction and reflection computations. To compute ∇f it is sufficient to evaluate f at two points perpendicularly off the ray in mutually perpendicular directions $\Delta\mathbf{x}_v$ and $\Delta\mathbf{x}_\omega$. Since we have already computed the result of f at our previous sample $\mathbf{x}-\Delta\mathbf{x}_\mu$, we can then approximate the gradient of f with respect to (μ, v, ω) by the finite difference vector:

$$\left[f(\mathbf{x})-f(\mathbf{x}-\Delta\mathbf{x}_\mu), f(\mathbf{x}+\Delta\mathbf{x}_v)-f(\mathbf{x}), f(\mathbf{x}+\Delta\mathbf{x}_\omega)-f(\mathbf{x}) \right]$$

To convert this gradient vector in (μ, v, ω) space into a gradient vector in (x, y, z) space, we multiply by the transformation matrix:

$$\begin{bmatrix} \Delta\mathbf{x}_\mu \\ \Delta\mathbf{x}_v \\ \Delta\mathbf{x}_\omega \end{bmatrix}$$

---

† A more systematic approach to antialiasing hypertexture is still a subject of research. We conjecture that it will involve discovering perceptually equivalent tradeoffs between different base functions (so that, for example, increasing gain at small scales, which increases gradient will automatically force the properly reduced amplitude).

The ray basis vectors $\Delta \mathbf{x}_\mu$, $\Delta \mathbf{x}_v$, and $\Delta \mathbf{x}_\omega$ can be precomputed once per ray. For an orthogonal view, they only need be computed once for the entire image.

Note that the expense of ray marching triples within an object's soft region, since computing ∇f requires us to evaluate f three times instead of just once per sample.

We must also accumulate opacity for visibility determination. A method similar to that of [7] is employed along the ray, so that at the kth step:

$$t := \alpha_k(1-\alpha)$$
$$color := color + t * color_k$$
$$\alpha := \alpha + t$$

where $color_k$ and α_k are sample color and opacity, respectively. To ensure resolution independence, we make opacity a function of both density and step-size:

$$\alpha_k := 1-(1-density)^{c \ * \ step-size}$$

where c is a normalizing constant. Color is the product of the shading value and the user specified color. The color mapping can be as simple or as complex as desired; step functions or splines may be appropriate. This same approach to color mapping was taken in [5]. Color maps are typically used to identify or isolate particular features in a scalar field [10]. Here again the local gradient ∇f is used to estimate the local normal vector. The use of opacity allows us to see amorphous or very fine volumetric features with a great deal of clarity.

The above differs from the method of [7], since we proceed in a front to back order (as we move along the ray from its entry point towards its exit point) as opposed to back to front order. If the accumulated opacity reaches unity, the evaluation along a ray stops before we exit the volume. This avoids unnecessary computation for regions that are entirely obscured.

Since in practice we have been able to tune our hypertextures empirically to be frequency clamped [17], do have not needed to use supersampling. We note though that stochastic ray marching might be employed as an extension of our algorithm, implemented by firing jittered rays with jittered step phases within each pixel. Similarly, motion blur might be achieved by sampling rays over time [21]. Other improvement might be made by utilizing recent work on optimization of ray marching [12].

Running Time

An $n \times n$ image requires $O(n^3)$ sample evaluations, so running time rises dramatically with increased resolution. Since increasing resolution by a factor of 4×4 increases

running time by 64, we usually do our quick "is it even there?" tests at a resolution of 32×32, which take a few seconds, our rough tests at 128×128, which take a few minutes, and our final runs at 512×512, which take a few hours if run serially. As a rule of thumb, we see how many seconds a run takes at 32×32 to estimate how many serial hours it will be at 512×512. Final runs would take anywhere from 3 to 15 hours, depending on hypertexture complexity, on a single Sun 4-260 workstation. To improve this performance, we have taken the two following approaches to parallelizing the algorithm.

Parallel Rendering

The ray marcher was implemented in C on an AT&T Pixel Machine [14], an MIMD coarse-grain computer with general purpose floating-point processors, having relatively little memory per processor. In our implementation each of 64 processors uses an identical hypertexture program to compute a different interleaved subset of the final screen image, an arrangement that tends to optimize load balancing among processors.

Our memory requirements are particularly small because hypertexture is highly procedural. The only significant data space required is for color maps, alpha map and the noise function lookup tables. The sum of these is less than 5 Kbytes. Thus we are able to maintain a complete copy of the database at each processor.

Since hypertexture can be evaluated independently at each pixel, and because each processor maintains its own database, this implementation has the following characteristics:

- it executes independently and asynchronously at each node
- no interprocessor communication is required
- the cost associated with parallelizing the algorithm is negligible

We have found that increasing the number of processors produces a linear (optimal) decrease in execution time. Therefore in principle hypertexture could be generated interactively, since with enough processors, the time to render an image would be bounded only by the time to render the slowest pixel (in our experience, a fraction of a second at most).

Distributed Rendering

In addition to implementing the ray-marcher on a parallel computer, we also implemented the distributed ray-marching computation over a local-area network of Unix workstations on a shared Network File System. Each workstation runs the identical program, compiled for its particular processor, to compute different pixels of the same image. In practice we have observed a linear speedup over the single processor serial version of the algorithm, using the dozen or so workstations in our lab.

4. Summary, Conclusions and Future

We have described a new modeling technique which modulates shape by applying procedural texture to a continuous volumetric region. The method contrasts with previous techniques in that we manipulate matter throughout R^3, instead of only at surfaces. This approach allows us to create the appearance of complex, real-world phenomena that would be difficult or impossible to generate with previous methods. The computational model is $O(n^3)$ but optimally parallelizable, achieving linear decreases in execution time with increases in the number of processors.

Clearly the model as described is highly empirical, leaving unanswered the disturbing question of why such simple techniques produce such visually convincing results. Prior work [22] has led us to believe that there is a sound perceptual basis for this, and that in general procedural textures can be organized into a human perceptual taxonomy. We plan in future work to extend this taxonomy to the description of hypertexture.

Our newest research concentrates on applying hypertexture to empirical shape data such as cranio-facial structures and teapots. By performing preprocessing passes through volumetric shape images, we are currently implementing cast shadows and extending geometry-dependent functions such as the **project** operator of fur hypertexture to empirical shapes at $O(n^3)$ cost. We also plan to incorporate more sophisticated shading models, in particular the anisotropic shading of Kajiya [23].

5. Acknowledgements

The authors greatly appreciate the insightful comments of Don Mitchell, Jim Conant, Dave Weimer, Jim Demmel, and Mark Perlin. The reviewers' comments were invaluable. In particular Ken would like to honor the request of one reviewer by offering a most humble apology for inflicting the term "furrier synthesis" on an unsuspecting scientific populace.

References

[1] Tuy, H. and Tuy, L. Direct 2-D Display of 3-D Objects, *IEEE Computer Graphics and Applications 4*, 10 (October 1984), pp. 29-33.

[2] Lorensen, W. Marching Cubes: A High Resolution 3D Surface Construction Algorithm, In *Computer Graphics 21*, 4 (July 1987), pp. 163-169.

[3] Perlin, K. Functionally Based Modeling. *SIGGRAPH Course Notes* (August 1988).

[4] Frieder, G., Gordon, D. and Reynolds, R. A. Back-to-Front Display of Voxel-Based Objects, *IEEE Computer Graphics and Applications*, (January 1985), pp. 52-60.

[5] Perlin, K. An Image Synthesizer, In *Computer Graphics 19*, 3 (July 1985).

[6] Kaufman, Arie. Efficient Algorithms for 3D Scan-Conversion of Parametric Curves, Surfaces and Volumes, In *Computer Graphics 21*, 4 (July 1987).

[7] Levoy, Marc. Volume Rendering: Display of Surface from Volume Data, *IEEE Computer Graphics and Applications* (May 1988), pp. 29-36.

[8] Drebin, R., Carpenter, L. and Hanrahan, P. Volume Rendering, In *Computer Graphics 22*, 4 (August 1988).

[9] Sabella, Paolo. A Rendering Algorithm for Visualizing 3D Scalar Fields, In *Computer Graphics 22*, 4 (August 1988).

[10] Upson, C. and Keeler, M. V-BUFFER: Visible Volume Rendering, In *Computer Graphics 22*, 4 (August 1988).

[11] Kaufman, A. and Bakalash, R. A 3D Cellular Frame Buffer, *Proceedings of EUROGRAPHICS 1985* (September 1985), Nice, France, pp. 215-220.

[12] Amanatides, J. and Woo, A., A Fast Voxel Traversal Algorithm for Ray Tracing, *Proceedings of EUROGRAPHICS 1987* (Amsterdam, Holland), pp. 3-10.

[13] Toth, D. L., On Ray Tracing Parametric Surfaces, In *Computer Graphics 19*, 3 (August 1985).

[14] Potmesil, M. and Hoffert, E., The Pixel Machine: A Parallel Image Computer, In *Computer Graphics 23*, 3 (August 1989).

[15] Blinn, J., A Generalization of Algebraic Surface Drawing, "*ACM Transactions on Graphics 1*," pp 235., 1982.

[16] Kajiya, J., Herzen, B., "Ray Tracing Volume Densities," In *Computer Graphics 18*, 3 (August 1984).

[17] Norton, A. Clamping: A Method of Antialiasing Textured Surfaces by Bandwidth Limiting in Object Space. In *Computer Graphics 16*, 3 (August 1982).

[18] Zadeh, L. A., *Fuzzy Sets and Applications (selected papers)*, John Wiley and Sons, New York, 1987.

[19] Zimmerman, H. J., *Fuzzy Set Theory - and Its Applications*, Kluwer-Nijhoff, Hingham, 1985, pp. 30-36.

[20] Menzel, D. H., ed., *Fundamental Formulas of Physics, vol. 2*, Dover, New York, 1960, pp. 370-371.

[21] Cook, R., Distributed Ray Tracing, In *Computer Graphics 18*, 3 (August 1984).

[22] Perlin, K., *Synthesizing Realistic Textures by the Composition of Perceptually Motivated Functions* [Ph.D. Dissertation], New York University, (Feb. 1986).

[23] Kajiya, J., Anisotropic Reflection Models. In *Computer Graphics 19*, 3 (August 1985).

Algorithms for Solid Noise Synthesis

J. P. Lewis

Computer Graphics Laboratory
New York Institute of Technology

ABSTRACT

A solid noise is a function that defines a random value at each point in space. Solid noises have immediate and powerful applications in surface texturing, stochastic modeling, and the animation of natural phenomena.

Existing solid noise synthesis algorithms are surveyed and two new algorithms are presented. The first uses Wiener interpolation to interpolate random values on a discrete lattice. The second is an efficient sparse convolution algorithm. Both algorithms are developed for *model-directed synthesis*, in which sampling and construction of the noise occur only at points where the noise value is required, rather than over a regularly sampled region of space. The paper attempts to present the rationale for the selection of these particular algorithms.

The new algorithms have advantages of efficiency, improved control over the noise power spectrum, and the absence of artifacts. The convolution algorithm additionally allows quality to be traded for efficiency without introducing obvious deterministic effects. The algorithms are particularly suitable for applications where high-quality solid noises are required. Several sample applications in stochastic modeling and solid texturing are shown.
CR Categories and Subject Descriptors: I.3.3 [**Computer Graphics**]: Picture/Image Generation; I.3.7 [**Computer Graphics**]: Three-Dimensional Graphics and Realism – *color, shading, shadowing, and texture.*
General Terms: Algorithms, Graphics.
Additional Key Words and Phrases: Solid noise, texture, stochastic modeling, simulation of natural phenomena, texture synthesis, fractals.

1 INTRODUCTION

A solid noise is a random-valued function $f : R^3 \rightarrow R$. "Noise" is used to denote a random function with some known statistical properties. Solid noises are a subset of the concept of *solid textures* introduced in computer graphics by Perlin [17,18] and Peachy [16]).

Solid noises have been used for texturing three-dimensional objects by assigning the color at a visible point on the surface as a function of the noise value at that point in space. In this role, solid textures have several advantages over conventional texture mapping:

- Surfaces with Gaussian curvature can be textured homogeneously, without distortions such as poles that occur in texture mapping.

- The spatial nature of the noise correlation makes possible certain effects which would be difficult with texture mapping, for example, the "carved out of" effect [18] which uses the fact that noise features (e.g. veins in simulated rock) can cross overhangs in the object (Fig. 7).

Solid noises also have many potential applications in describing complex/irregular forms or movement; a few possibilities are shown in Section 5 of this paper.

2 SOLID NOISE ALGORITHMS

In all applications, it is desirable that a solid noise algorithm be controllable and free of artifacts. Consistent with recent work [18,9,11], the noise power spectrum is considered as a reasonably powerful and intuitive framework for developing control over the noise.

When the noise is used for surface texturing, efficiency is a major consideration, since the three-dimensional variants of even simple computations such as linear interpolation are fairly expensive when the computation is required at each pixel. It is desirable that the noise synthesis algorithm allow quality to be traded for efficiency where appropriate, e.g. for previewing or for background objects which do not need a high-quality noise. For most applications it is probably preferable to trade some control for efficiency rather than adopting an efficient method that has intrinsic artifacts.

For animation applications the solid noise should also be bandlimited. Although the aliasing of an improperly sampled noise function will often not be objectionable in a still picture (due to the same principle evident in stochastic sampling [5] - objectionable Moire patterns result from the structured sampling of a structured signal), the same aliased noise used in an animation will typically produce characteristic "shimmering" or "bubbling" aliasing effects.

While a large variety of particular three-dimensional random-valued functions are conceivable, most can be decomposed into a basic noise source and some functional or procedural transformation of this noise. As argued by Perlin [18], the noise source should be a controllable "primitive" that allows the user to define various ad hoc solid noise functions in terms of this noise primitive.

This paper presents two algorithms for the synthesis of high-quality solid noises with control of the noise power spectrum and (optionally) distribution functions. Considerations that lead to the selection of these particular algorithms are also described.

©1989   ACM-0-89791-312-4/89/007/0263 $00.75

```
#define RANTABLEN /* something prime */
float Rantab[RANTABLEN];
int Indx[ILEN],Indy[ILEN],Indz[ILEN];

float hash3(float x,y,z)
{
    int i = HASH( Indx[LOWBITS(x)], Indy[LOWBITS(y)], Indz[LOWBITS(z)] );
    return( Rantab[i % RANTABLEN] );
}
```

Fig. 1: Pseudocode for the lattice white noise function.

2.1 MODEL-DIRECTED SYNTHESIS

Although the linear filtering algorithms for obtaining noises having desired power spectra are well understood [13], these algorithms are not ideally suited to the requirements of computer graphic modeling and rendering. In particular, in place of the regular and ordered sampling that is fundamental to digital signal processing we require a *model-directed synthesis*, in which the noise function is constructed only at particular points determined by the object model, and in an order that may depend on the model or the viewpoint. In a texturing application, these points are the points on the object's surface that project without occlusion to pixels in a perspective projection of the object. Similarly, in a modeling application the noise may be constructed at a limited and irregular set of points, e.g., the vertices of a polygonal model.

Digital filters assume regular sampling and spatial or temporal ordering (causality) of the input signal and consequently cannot meaningfully operate at isolated points in space. The direct application of a digital filtering approach for solid noise synthesis would thus result in a solid region of filtered noise enclosing the points of interest. This is very costly in terms of storage, since the storage size of a solid noise varies with the cube of the resolution. The direct FFT or digital filter synthesis of a medium- or high-resolution solid noise is usually impractical in this respect. Also it would seem inefficient to construct the noise over a solid region when it is only needed at isolated points, though this may depend on the number of points required and on the respective algorithms. A third drawback of digital filtering approaches is that since the noise is sampled it needs to be interpolated from the sampling lattice to the locations of interest.

Model-directed synthesis can be achieved by constructing the input noise signal as needed at synthesis time, and by employing an acausal and metaphorically continuous rather than sampled filtering approach. Since the spatial ordering of the synthesis is unknown, particular regions may be visited multiple times. The input noise construction must be *internally consistent* (in the terminology of [8]): independent constructions of a particular point must produce the same value. While model-directed synthesis approaches are suited for many computer graphics problems, it is evident that they cannot easily use the coherence provided by regular sampling and consequently will be more costly than standard filtering approaches for constructing regularly sampled noises.

2.2 LATTICE WHITE NOISE

A consistent uncorrelated ("white") noise can be generated using a hash-like pseudo-random function of the mantissa bits of the location coordinates x, y, z. One such function was described in [4]. A variation of this function uses the low-order bits of each coordinate (scaled suitably) to index a corresponding randomly permuted 'indirection table' of indices into a second table of uncorrelated random values with the desired probability density. The three resulting indexes are hashed to form an index into the prime-length random value table (Fig. 1).

The HASH3 function generates an uncorrelated periodic noise, with the period determined by the number of coordinate bits which are retained. The function takes on new values only on the lattice defined by the low bits of the coordinate mantissas, thus "lattice noise". For most purposes it will be necessary to interpolate or filter the noise values on the lattice to obtain a continuous and correlated solid noise.

2.3 PERLIN ALGORITHM

Perlin [17,18] outlined a model-directed solid noise algorithm based on interpolating a location hashing function such as HASH3. The resulting noise is employed as a spectral basis function, with a desired noise $\hat{\eta}$ being approximated by a weighted sum of basis noises η_k at different scales:

$$\hat{\eta}(\boldsymbol{\rho}) = \sum a_k \eta_k(k\boldsymbol{\rho}) \qquad (1)$$

The characteristics of the resulting noise are determined by the selected interpolation approach. The cubic polynomial interpolation suggested in [18] has certain disadvantages. Interpolation in several dimensions using the separable tensor product of a one-dimensional interpolation scheme results in preferred directions along the coordinate system axes; this artifact can only be avoided by using an intrinsically multi-dimensional interpolation approach. Cubic polynomial interpolation in three dimensions is also quite expensive. The direct tensor product scheme for cubic spline interpolation requires a support of $4^3 = 64$ points as well as $16(x) + 4(y) + 1(z) = 21$ spline evaluations [2]. The interpolation must be repeated for each basis function in the spectral summation (1).

One popular implementation of Perlin's approach employs Hermite interpolation, using the lattice noise to define gradients at the (eight) nearest-neighbor points on the lattice [10]. These values are separably interpolated using a cosine-like function. While this approach is considerably more efficient than a cubic spline interpolation, it has stronger directional artifacts (Fig. 2). Another drawback is that the noise value and second-derivative are both zero at the lattice points. The directional trends and regularly spaced zeros are visible (e.g. see Fig. 3), though it may be possible to disguise them through application of the summation (1).

In order to be approximately orthogonal, candidate spectral basis functions should be zero beyond a particular range of frequencies ("bandpass"). Approaches which use standard (meaning non-oscillatory, energy minimizing, spline-like) interpolation methods to interpolate an uncorrelated noise lattice produce a low-pass rather than a band-pass random function, however, since they do not remove or attenuate the low frequency portion of the original noise power spectrum (which has equal expected power at all frequencies) (Fig. 4.) This can be seen in part by considering the zero frequency: interpolation will not remove the mean. From a signal-processing viewpoint, standard interpolation methods have

Fig. 4: Computed amplitude spectrum (zero frequency at left) of a long one-dimensional section of the noise shown in Fig. 2. The spectrum is not bandpass.

the effect of attenuating high frequencies [19] (also see problem 26 in [3]).

One misinterpretation of the summation (1) is that, by analogy with Fourier summation, a bandpass noise might be produced using a lowpass noise primitive by subtracting a more bandlimited noise from a given noise, in the hope of removing the low-frequency portion of the spectrum. Power spectra of mutually uncorrelated noises cannot be meaningfully subtracted however: $S(\eta_1 - \eta_2) = S(\eta_1) - 2C(\eta_1, \eta_2) + S(\eta_2)$ where $C(\eta_1, \eta_2) = 0$ is the covariance between the noises. Eq. (1) is a spectral summation but not a Fourier summation.

The high-frequency (amplitude) spectrum of the Perlin basis noise using cubic interpolation falls off as λ^{-4} since the amplitude spectral envelope of a C_n function is λ^{-n-2} [3]. This also is not ideally bandlimited. We conclude that polynomially interpolated noise does not provide an ideal spectral basis.

The various disadvantages of polynomial interpolation for a spectral synthesis approach are avoided in the Wiener interpolation algorithm presented in section 3 below.

2.4 GARDNER AND PEACHY ALGORITHMS

Gardner [9] developed a naturalistic texturing function based on a modified Fourier series. This approach is unusual in its use of a conceptually *deterministic* function to simulate irregular texture.[1] The function appears as a product of two one-dimensional series in x and y (as described it is two-dimensional but an equivalent three-dimensional function can be formulated). A *separable* function $f(u, v) = f_u(u)f_v(v)$ has strong directional artifacts that make it unsuitable for simulating a naturalistic texture even if the component functions f_u, f_v are characteristic sections of the desired texture. Gardner overcame this 'checkerboard effect' by coupling the phases of each term in the u-series to v, and conversely. The resulting texture is not separable and is sufficiently complex that it mimics a random texture when applied carefully.

The spectrum of the Gardner function has not been analyzed but is not (as might be supposed) directly defined by the Fourier series coefficients. This can be seen by considering the kth term of the u-series evaluated along a diagonal profile with u and v varying:

$$f_k(u) = a_k \sin(\omega_k u + I \sin(\omega_{k-1} v))$$

This is a form of frequency modulation. From [1]

$$\sin(\theta + I \sin \beta) =$$

$$J_0(I) \sin \theta + \sum_{k=1}^{\infty} J_k(I) \left\{ \sin(\theta + k\beta) + (-1)^k \sin(\theta - k\beta) \right\}$$

so although the Gardner texturing function has a line spectrum, it is more complex than suggested by its Fourier series resemblance (also it is evident that it is not strictly bandlimited).

Peachy [16] proposed solid function generation by the composition (e.g. sum or product) of several lower-dimensional functions. If the functions are random the result is a solid noise. As in the Gardner algorithm, the composition function can be designed to eliminate separability but the absence of an intrinsically three-dimensional correlation structure may be visually evident.

3 WIENER INTERPOLATION ALGORITHM

Wiener interpolation differs from other interpolation approaches in that it is based on the expected correlation of the interpolated function. Since the autocorrelation or autocovariance function is equivalent information to the power spectrum, Wiener interpolation is particularly suited for noise synthesis where control of the noise correlation and spectrum is required. Control of the noise spectrum is intrinsic to Wiener interpolation, so problems with band-limiting and the expensive spectral summation (1) are avoided.

Wiener interpolation has many other potential applications in computer graphics (e.g., as the basis for an improved stochastic subdivision method [11], or possibly as an approach to resampling stochastically sampled images for display). Some additional characteristics and advantages of Wiener interpolation are:

- The data can be arbitrarily spaced.

- The algorithm applies without modification to multi-dimensional data.

- Wiener interpolation of discrete data is simple, requiring only the solution of a linear equation.

- In an estimation application the algorithm provides an error or confidence level associated with each point on the interpolated surface.

- The algorithm is optimal by a particular criterion (see below) which may or may not be relevant.

- The interpolation can be made local or global to the extent desired. This is achieved by adjusting the covariance function so that points beyond a desired distance have a negligible correlation.

- The interpolation can be as smooth as desired, for example, an analytic covariance function will result in an analytic interpolated curve or surface.

- The interpolation need not be "smooth", for example, the correlation can be negative at certain distances, oscillatory, or (in several dimensions) have directional preferences.

(The last three properties result from the direct spectral control provided by Wiener interpolation.)

There are a number of formulations and variations of Wiener interpolation [20,7]. A simple probabilistic formulation suitable for solid noise interpolation will be used here. The description requires two concepts from probability:

- The correlation of two random variables is the expectation of their product, $\mathbf{E}[xy]$. The autocorrelation or autocovariance function of a random process (noise) is the correlation of pairs of points from the process:

$$C(t_1, t_2) = \mathbf{E}[\eta(t_1)\eta(t_2)]$$

For homogeneous noise, this expectation is a function only of the distance between the two points: $C(t, t + \tau) =$

---

[1]While the computer implementation of any random process is necessarily deterministic, there is a practical as well as a conceptual difference, in that the period of an n-term Fourier series is $2n$ samples whereas the period of a simulated random process is usually considerably larger, as determined by the period of the pseudo-random number function.

$C(\tau) = \mathbf{E}[\eta(t)\eta(t + \tau)]$. The variance is the value of the autocovariance function at zero. (Auto)covariance refers to the correlation of a process whose mean is removed and (usually) whose variance is normalized to be one.

- Expectation behaves as a linear operator, so any factor or term which is known can be moved "outside" the expectation. For example, assuming a and b are known,

$$\mathbf{E}\{a\eta + b\} = a\mathbf{E}[\eta] + b$$

Also, the order of differentiation and expectation can be interchanged, etc.

Wiener interpolation estimates the value $\hat{\eta}$ of the process η at a particular location as a weighted sum of the values η_j observed at some number of other locations:

$$\hat{\eta} = \sum a_j \eta_j \qquad (2)$$

The weights a_j are chosen to minimize the expected squared difference or error between the estimate and the value of the "real" process at the same location:

$$\mathbf{E}\left\{(\eta - \hat{\eta})^2\right\} \qquad (3)$$

The reference to the "real" process in (3) seems troublesome because the real process may be unknowable at the particular location, but since it is the *expected* error which is minimized, this reference disappears in the solution.

Wiener interpolation is optimal among linear interpolation schemes in that it minimizes the expected squared error (3). When the data have jointly Gaussian probability distributions (and thus are indistinguishable from a realization of a Gaussian stochastic process), Wiener interpolation is also optimal among nonlinear interpolation schemes.

3.1 DERIVATION

By the *orthogonality principle* [21,14], the squared error of a linear estimator is minimum when the error is orthogonal in expectation to all of the known data, with "orthogonal" meaning that the expectation of the product of the data and the error is zero:

$$\mathbf{E}\{(\eta - \hat{\eta})\eta_k\} = 0 \quad \text{for all} \quad k$$

Substituting $\hat{\eta}$ from (2),

$$\mathbf{E}\left\{(\eta - \sum a_j \eta_j)\eta_k\right\} = 0 \qquad (4)$$

$$\mathbf{E}\left\{\eta\eta_k - \sum a_j \eta_j \eta_k\right\} = 0$$

The expectation of $\eta\eta_k$ is the correlation $C(t - t_k)$, and likewise for $\eta_j \eta_k$, so:

$$C(t - t_k) = \sum a_j C(t_j - t_k)$$

or

$$\mathbf{Ca} = \mathbf{c} \qquad (5)$$

This equation can be solved for the coefficients a_j. The coefficients depend on the positions of the data η_j through the covariance function, but not on the actual data values; the values appear in the interpolation (2) though. Also, (5) does not directly involve the dimensionality of the data. The only difference for multidimensional data is that the covariance is a function of several arguments: $\mathbf{E}[pq] = C(x_p - x_q, y_p - y_q, z_p - z_q, \ldots)$.

3.2 COST

From (5) and (2), the coefficients a_j are $\mathbf{a} = \mathbf{C}^{-1}\mathbf{c}$, and the estimate is $\hat{\eta} = \eta^t \mathbf{C}^{-1}\mathbf{c}$. The vector $\mathbf{c}$ changes from point to point, but $\eta^t \mathbf{C}^{-1}$ is constant for given data, so the interpolation cost is a dot product

$$\hat{\eta} = <\eta^t \mathbf{C}^{-1}, \mathbf{c}> \qquad (6)$$

of two vectors whose size is the number of data points.

3.3 EVALUATION

The spectral definition possible in Wiener interpolation is proportional to the number of data points considered in the interpolation. For simple spectra requiring a small neighborhood of points (e.g. 3^3 or 4^3 points), the computation (6) appears to be considerably more efficient than polynomial spline interpolation. A fair degree of spectral control can be achieved if larger neighborhoods are used, for example, oscillatory (bandpass) noises are possible. The expensive spectral summation (1) is also avoided

The disadvantage of this algorithm is intrinsic to the approach of *interpolating* an uncorrelated noise lattice: the three-dimensional covariance function, centered at a noise lattice point, should strictly be zero when sampled at any other lattice point, since these points are not correlated. For an isotropic covariance, this requires that $C_1(\tau) = 0$ at distances $\tau = \delta\sqrt{i^2 + j^2 + k^2}$ for all lattice offsets $i + j + k >= 1$ (δ is the lattice spacing). The covariance structure is thus artificially constrained. If the specified covariance does not satisfy this constraint, the interpolation error (confidence measure) will be non-zero and the realized covariance will be somewhat different than that specified.

4 SPARSE CONVOLUTION ALGORITHM

A second algorithm avoids the covariance function constraints of the noise lattice interpolation approach but retains the direct spectral control of the Wiener interpolation approach. In addition, it has the advantage of conceptual simplicity.

In this algorithm a three-dimensional noise is synthesized by the convolution of a three-dimensional kernel $h(\boldsymbol{\rho})$ with a Poisson noise process γ

$$\eta(\boldsymbol{\rho}) = \int_{R^3} \gamma(\boldsymbol{\sigma})h(\boldsymbol{\rho} - \boldsymbol{\sigma})d\boldsymbol{\sigma} \qquad (7)$$

The Poisson process consists of impulses of uncorrelated intensity distributed at uncorrelated locations in space:

$$\gamma(\boldsymbol{\rho}) = \sum a_k \delta(\boldsymbol{\rho} - \boldsymbol{\rho}_k)$$

($\boldsymbol{\rho}_k$ is the location of the kth impulse). This is a 'sparse' form of white noise, hence "sparse convolution".

The power spectrum S_y at the output of a linear time-invariant filter (expressible as a convolution) is related to the input spectrum S_x by [21]

$$S_y(\omega) = S_x(\omega)|H(j\omega)|^2$$

where H is the Fourier transform of the filter impulse response or kernel h. Since γ is uncorrelated its transform is a constant, so the spectrum of a noise synthesized by sparse convolution is simply the (deterministic) spectrum of the kernel, scaled by a constant.

4.1 EFFICIENCY

Sparse convolution has several advantages for digital computation. Because of the impulsive nature of the noise, the convolution integral (7) reduces to a summation over the impulses:

$$\eta(\boldsymbol{\rho}) = \sum a_k h(\boldsymbol{\rho} - \boldsymbol{\rho}_k) \qquad (8)$$

Thus, the synthesis is reduced naturally to a computationally realizable form without requiring sampling (and subsequent interpolation) of the noise.

The quality of the noise can be varied as required for the application by varying the density of the Poisson noise. This is an important property, since e.g. background objects or interactive previewing applications may not require full quality noise. A density of less than one impulse per kernel volume produces a "lumpy" noise with little spectral definition. Typical applications require a density of several impulses per kernel volume, and noises produced with a density of 10 or more points per kernel are usually not distinguishable from those produced by convolving with a uniformly sampled (non-sparse) white noise, though the sparse convolution is considerably more efficient.

For an isotropic noise the kernel h is also isotropic and (assuming it is non-zero over a finite radius) can be approximately evaluated by a one-dimensional table lookup. In this case the summation (8) can be restricted to only those impulses γ_k within the kernel radius of the location ρ. The problem then is to identify these points efficiently, in particular, without requiring examination of all points and an expensive distance computation requiring a square-root.

This can be accomplished with an appropriate construction of the Poisson process γ. A simple construction is to define a large but finite sampling lattice over the noise domain and approximate the Poisson process by choosing N Poisson-distributed impulses in each voxel. The voxels can then be numbered, and the voxel number serves as a random number generator seed for generating the impulses within that voxel. The lattice spacing and kernel radius are conveniently set to one (with space scaled accordingly). Then the impulses lying within a unit radius of a particular location ρ are those in the voxel containing ρ and in the adjacent voxels. The summation (8) is modified accordingly. Square roots are entirely removed by using the squared distance $|\rho - \rho_k|^2$ to index a prewarped kernel table $\hat{h}(\tau) = h(\sqrt{\tau})$.

The author's implementation of sparse convolution uses standard tricks such as fixed-point computation. In addition, the noise impulses ρ_k are stored in a cache array as they are computed, and are reused if the next location falls within the same voxel. With these optimizations, the algorithm using one impulse per voxel is slightly slower than the previously described Hermite implementation of Perlin's algorithm, but does not have visible artifacts and provides some control over the spectrum.

The upper-left panel in Fig. 5 shows a planar section of a sample texture generated with the sparse convolution algorithm using a smooth cosine kernel $1/2 + 1/2\cos(\pi\tau)$, $|\tau| < 1$. The texture does not reveal the synthesis coordinate system or display other artifacts.

5 APPLICATIONS

A solid noise algorithm is most useful as a primitive in a language that allows one to easily define functional or procedural transformations of the noise. An important characteristic of this language is that it should allow functions to be *dynamically defined* at modeling/rendering/animation time – the "user" should have the freedom to define an ad hoc function in the model, rather than requiring the original programmer of the graphics system to anticipate and implement libraries of special-purpose functions. This requires either an interpreted language or user-compiled functions that are dynamically linked with the graphics system. An interpreted language was described in [18], while the shade-trees approach [6] appears to use compiled functions that are dynamically linked to an interpreted expression evaluator.

In the language approach adopted by the author, a small and portable public-domain Lisp language interpreter was adapted to

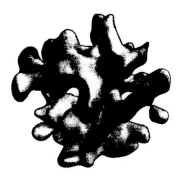

Fig. 8: Porous object model defined by the iso-density surface of a solid noise.

allow compiled C language functions to be dynamically linked and called from Lisp. This approach avoids the definition and implementation of a new special-purpose language, and permits functions to be implemented in either Lisp or C or some combination of these. Typically a function is developed in Lisp, and if needed the inner loops are reimplemented in C and dynamically "glued" together with Lisp.

Stepping back from the full power of procedural manipulation of the noise, we note that the special case of a functional transformation is useful from an analysis-resynthesis viewpoint, since a desired probability density (a commonly measured random texture characteristic) can be obtained by functional transformation [12].

5.1 SOLID TEXTURE

Although spectral synthesis adequately simulates most homogeneous random textures, many textures have some structural features that cannot be simulated using this approach. Such textures can often be simulated using a procedural transform of a homogeneous texture. An example is the marble texture described in [18]. Another example of a procedural transform is the solid wood texture shown in (Figs. 6, 7). The structure of concentric rings parallel to the tree trunk is produced using a periodic or (preferably) quasi-periodic function $xtab$ of the radial distance from the z axis. This function describes the color variation across a radial section of a typical ring. Natural irregularity is introduced by perturbing the radial distance by a solid noise:

$$wood(\rho) = xtab[\sqrt{\rho.x^2 + \rho.y^2} + \eta(\rho)]$$

(where $\rho.x$ denotes the x-component of ρ). Various refinements are possible, for example, the radial distance can be replaced by a random monotonic function of this distance, thereby creating radial regions of densely or sparsely separated rings to simulate periods of slow or fast growth. Fig. 6 shows planar sections of several solid wood simulations, where the perturbation noise η and the ring cross section function $xtab$ are altered to simulate different woods. Fig. 7 shows a figure model with a solid wood texture. This surface/texture combination would be difficult to achieve using texture mapping.

5.2 STOCHASTIC MODELING

An interesting stochastic modeling approach utilizing solid noise is to define objects as the equal-density surface of a solid noise. The overall shape of the object can be controlled by multiplying

Fig. 12: Trajectories of a number of particles forced by a vector solid noise.

the noise by an analytic density function that tapers to zero outside of the desired object shape. This approach can produce porous and highly irregular shapes such as the coral-like form in Fig. 8.

5.3 STOCHASTIC DEFORMATION

This is a powerful stochastic modeling technique which uses a vector-valued solid noise (vector field) $v : R^3 \rightarrow R^3$ to perturb an existing object model. Three independent scalar solid noises form the components of the vector field. Stochastic deformation is particularly efficient for polygonal boundary-represented models, since only the vertices are perturbed.

Stochastic deformation can be used to simulate the individuality of natural objects by slightly deforming a prototype object model (Figs. 9, 11). The noise can be varied to produce either realistic or caricatural individuality.

Large-amplitude or iterated deformation can produce self-intersecting or twisted forms which do not resemble the original object (Fig. 10). A deformation can be animated by offsetting the object location by a continuously changing vector before perturbing, effectively moving the object through the noise.

5.4 CORRELATED FLOW

Solid noises may be employed as a correlated random environmental factor for many physically motivated simulations. For example, a solid noise can be used as a force field to produce turbulent trajectories or flow. Fig. 12 shows the trajectories of a number of particles obeying a simple dynamics equation $\ddot{\rho} = \eta(\rho)$. The resulting collection of trajectories displays bifurcations and resembles animal fur and other natural structures. Fig. 13 is a frame from a brief animation in which the trajectories are animated by the previously mentioned technique of moving the model through the noise. The trajectories are rendered to produce the effect of an "organic fireball".

6 CONCLUSION

In addition to their demonstrated use in solid texturing, solid noises have direct applications in stochastic modeling. In both modeling and texturing it is desirable that the solid noise synthesis be controllable, efficient, and free of artifacts. Spectral synthesis provides a framework for assessing the control and quality of various synthesis approaches. Existing solid noise algorithms were surveyed from this viewpoint.

Two new algorithms were described and evaluated. Both algorithms provide improved spectral control and efficiency. The sparse convolution algorithm is attractive in that it allows a trade-off between quality and efficiency as required by the application, without introducing gross artifacts. Several solid texturing and stochastic modeling examples visually illustrate the control and quality achievable with this algorithm.

Symbols

$S(\lambda)$	power spectrum
$C(\tau)$	autocovariance function
h	filter kernel
γ	uncorrelated noise
η	correlated synthesized noise
ρ, σ	locations in space
λ, ω	frequency, angular frequency

Acknowledgements

The figure model in Fig. 7 was developed by Dick Lundin and Susan VanBaerle. The head model used in Fig. 9 was developed by Fred Parke [15] with additions by Rebecca Allen, Steve Di-Paola and Robert McDermott. Thanks to Paul Heckbert and Lance Williams for discussions.

References

[1] Abramowitz, M. and Stegun, I., *Handbook of Mathematical Functions*. Dover, New York, 1965.

[2] Bohm, W., Farin, G. and Kahmann, J., A Survey of Curve and Surface Methods in CAGD. *Computer Aided Geometric Design 1*, 1 (1984), 1-60.

[3] Bracewell, R., *The Fourier Transform and Its Applications*. McGraw-Hill, New York, 1965.

[4] Carpenter, L., Computer Rendering of Fractal Curves and Surfaces. Supplement to Proceedings of SIGGRAPH '80 (Seattle, July 1980). In *Computer Graphics 14*, 3 (July 1980), 180.

[5] Cook, R., Stochastic Sampling in Computer Graphics. *ACM Transactions on Graphics 5*, 1 (January 1986), 51-72.

[6] Cook, R., Shade Trees. Proceedings of SIGGRAPH '84 (Minneapolis, July 23-27 1984). In *Computer Graphics 18*, 3 (July 1984), 223-231.

[7] Deutsch, R., *Estimation Theory*. Prentice-Hall, New Jersey, 1965.

[8] Fournier, A., Fussell, D., and Carpenter, L., Computer Rendering of Stochastic Models. *Communications ACM 25*, 6 (June 1982), 371-384.

[9] Gardner, G., Simulation of Natural Scenes Using Textured Quadric Surfaces. Proceedings of SIGGRAPH '84 (Minneapolis, July 23-27 1984). In *Computer Graphics 18*, 3 (July 1984), 11-20.

[10] Heckbert, P., *Personal communication*.

[11] Lewis, J.P., Generalized Stochastic Subdivision. *ACM Transactions on Graphics 6*, 3 (July 1987), 167-190.

[12] Lewis, J.P., Methods for Stochastic Spectral Synthesis. In *Proceedings of Graphics Interface 86* (Vancouver, May 1986), 173-179.

[13] Oppenheim, A. and Schafer, R., *Digital Signal Processing*. Prentice Hall, Englewood Cliffs, N.J., 1975.

[14] Papoulis, A., *Probability, Random Variables, and Stochastic Processes*. McGraw-Hill, New York, 1965.

[15] Parke, F., Parameterized Models for Facial Animation. *IEEE Computer Graphics and Applications 2*, 9 (Nov. 1982), 61-68.

[16] Peachy, D., Solid Texturing of Complex Surfaces. Proceedings of SIGGRAPH '85 (San Francisco, July 22-26 1985). In *Computer Graphics 19*, 3 (July 1985), 279-286.

[17] Perlin, K., A Unified Texture/Reflectance Model. In SIGGRAPH '84 *Advanced Image Synthesis* course notes (Minneapolis, July 1984).

[18] Perlin, K., An Image Synthesizer. Proceedings of SIGGRAPH '85 (San Francisco, July 22-26 1985). In *Computer Graphics 19*, 3 (July 1985), 287-296.

[19] Schafer, R. and Rabiner, L., A Digital Signal Processing Approach to Interpolation. *Proc. IEEE 61*, 6 (June 1973), 692-702.

[20] Wiener, N., *Extrapolation, Interpolation, and Smoothing of Stationary Time Series*. Wiley, New York, 1949.

[21] Yaglom, A., *An Introduction to the Theory of Stationary Random Functions*. Dover, New York, 1973.

Fig. 2: Planar section of a solid noise synthesized by Hermite interpolation of a lattice of uncorrelated values. The noise shows directional artifacts and is zero at the lattice points.

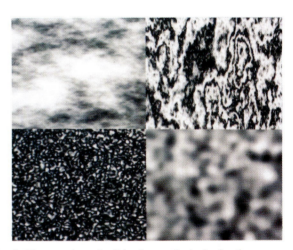

Fig. 5: Planar sections of solid noises synthesized using the sparse convolution algorithm.

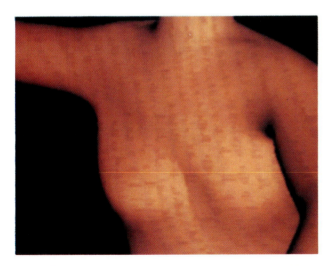

Fig. 3: Three-dimensional figure textured with a procedural solid wood texture which uses the solid noise shown in Fig. 2 as a primitive. Noise artifacts resulting from the regularly spaced zeros of this noise primitive are visible (compare with Fig. 7).

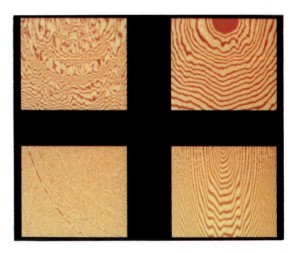

Fig. 6: Sections of solid wood textures synthesized by procedural transformation of suitable homogeneous textures.

Fig. 7: Solid wood texture applied to a figure model.

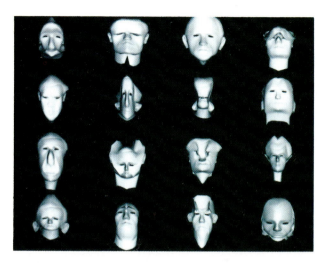

Fig. 9: Individual head models generated by displacing the vertices of a prototype polygonal head model with a vector solid noise.

Fig. 10: A shape created by distorting a polygonal sphere by a vector solid noise.

Fig. 11: Shrubbery created by stochastic deformation.

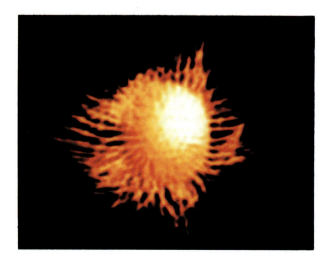

Fig. 13: An object rendered from trajectories as in Fig. 12.

Fig. 14: Cloud studies using solid noises in a rendering algorithm similar to that in [9].

RENDERING FUR WITH THREE DIMENSIONAL TEXTURES

James T. Kajiya
Timothy L. Kay
California Institute of Technology
Pasadena, Ca. 91125

Abstract. We present a method for rendering scenes with fine detail via an object called a *texel*, a rendering primitive inspired by volume densities mixed with anisotropic lighting models. This technique solves a long outstanding problem in image synthesis: the rendering of furry surfaces.

Introduction

Rendering scenes with very high complexity and a wide range of detail has long been an important goal for image synthesis. One idea is to introduce a hierarchy of scale, and at each level of scale have a corresponding level of detail in a hierarchy of geometric models (Crow 1982). Thus very complex small objects may have a hierarchy of progressively simplified geometric representations.

However, for very fine detail, a significant problem has so far prevented the inclusion of furry sufaces into synthetic images. The conventional approach gives rise to a severe, intractable aliasing problem. We feel that this aliasing problem arises because geometry is used to define surfaces at an inappropriate scale. An alternative approach is to treat fine geometry as texture rather than geometry. We explore that approach here.

This paper presents a new type of texture map, called a *texel*, inspired by the volume density (Blinn 1982). A texel is a 3-dimensional texture map in which both a surface frame—normal, tangent, and binormal— and the parameters of a lighting model are distributed freely throughout a volume. A texel is not tied to the geometry of any particular surface. Indeed, it is intended to represent a highly complex collection of surfaces contained within a defined volume. Because of this the rendering time of a texel is independent of the geometric complexity of the surfaces that it extracts. In fact, with texels, one can dispense with the usual notion of geometric surface models altogether. That is, it is possible to render texels directly, foregoing referents to any defined surface geometry.

We will use the idea of texels to represent fuzzy surfaces and present an algorithm for rendering such surfaces.

Review of High Complexity Rendering

Many attempts to model scenes with very high complexity have been made. One method is to attack the problem by brute force computing. A very early effort by Csuri, et al.(1979) generated images of smoke and fur with thousands of polygons. More recently, Weil(1986) rendered cloth with thousands of Lambert cylinders. Unfortunately, at a fairly large scale, microscopic geometric surfaces give rise to severe aliasing artifacts that overload traditional antialiasing methods. These images tend to look brittle: that is, hairs tend to look like spines.

The brute force method fails because the desired detail should be rendered through textures and lighting models rather than through geometry. What is desired is *the painter's illusion*, a suggestion that there is detail in the scene far beyond the resolution of the image. When one examines a painting closely the painter's illusion falls apart: zooming in on a finely detailed object in a painting reveals only meaningless blotches of color.

The most successful effort to render high complexity scenes are those based on particle systems (Reeves 1983, Reeves and Blau 1985). We believe their success is due in part to the fact that particle systems embody the idea of rendering without geometry. Along the path of the particle system, a lighting model and a frame are used to render pixels directly rather than through a notion of detailed microgeometry. In some sense, this paper represents the extension of particle systems to ray tracing. As the reader will readily discern, even though our rendering algorithm is radically different, particle systems and texels are complementary, e.g. particle systems could be used to generate texel models. Indeed, this paper can be modified to render particle systems in a manner that is independent of the number of particles rendered.

Gavin Miller in (Miller 1988) advanced a solution that uses a combination of geometry and a sophisticated lighting model much in the spirit of this paper to make images of furry animals. However, like particle systems, the complexity of the geometric part of his algorithm is dependent on the number of hairs.

The idea of texels is inspired by Blinn's idea for rendering volume densities (Blinn 1982). Blinn presented an algorithm to calculate the appearance of a large collection of microscopic spherical particles uniformly distributed in a plane. This enabled him to synthesize images of clouds and dust and the rings of Saturn. Because Blinn was interested in directionally homogeneous atmospheres, he analytically integrated his equations to yield a simple lighting model.

In Kajiya and Von Herzen (1984), Blinn's equations were solved for nonhomogeneous media by direct computation. It was essentially a volume rendering technique for ray tracing. Because our work is based on that earlier effort, we now briefly discuss the relevant equations from Kajiya and Von Herzen (1984).

As a beam of light travels through a volume of spherical particles, it is scattered and attenuated. The attenuation is dependent on the local density of the volume along the ray. The scattering is dependent on the density of the particles scattering the light and the albedo of each particle. The amount of scattering varies in different directions due to the particle partially occluding scattering in certain directions. This scattered light then is attenuated and rescattered by other particles.

©1989   ACM-0-89791-312-4/89/007/0271 $00.75

This model ignores diffraction around scattering particles.

In ray tracing, we follow light rays from the eye backwards toward the light sources (figure 1). The progressive attenuation along the ray due to occluding particles is computed for each point along a ray emanating from the eye. At each point on the ray through the volume, we measure the amount of light that scatters into the direction toward the eye. This light is then integrated to yield the total light reaching the eye. In this work we use Blinn's low albedo single scattering approximation. That is, we assume that any contribution from multiple scattering is negligible. We assume that the light is scattered just once from the light source to the eye. The accuracy of this assumption is relatively good for low albedo particles and suffers as the albedo increases (Blinn 1982, Rushmeier and Torrance 1987).

Figure 1 shows a schematic of the situation. A volume containing particles with density $\rho(x, y, z)$ at each point is penetrated by a ray. The light reaching the eye is computed along the ray R. At each point $P = (x(t), y(t), z(t))$ of the ray at distance t, the illumination I_i for each light source is multiplied by a *phase factor* $p(\cos\theta)$ that indicates how much of the light is scattered from the light source to the ray. The brightness is then weighted by the density ρ of the particles at this point. The attenuation between point P and A due to the medium is given by an integral of the density along the ray. The equations are:

$$T = e^{-\tau \int_{t_{near}}^{t_{far}} \rho(x(s), y(s), z(s))\, ds} \tag{1}$$

and

$$B = \int_{t_{near}}^{t_{far}} e^{-\tau \int_{t_{near}}^{t} \rho(x(u), y(u), z(u))\, du}$$
$$\times \left[\sum_i I_i(x(t), y(t), z(t)) p(\cos\theta) \right] \tag{2}$$
$$\times \rho(x(t), y(t), z(t))\, dt$$

Equation 1 calculates the transparency T of the density ρ. It says that that each small distance ds along a ray multiplicatively accumulates the transmission coefficient by $e^{-\tau \rho ds}$. The coefficient τ converts the density of the particles into an attenuation coefficient. The quantities t_{near}, t_{far} are the near and far distances of the density that contribute to the calculation.

Equation 2 calculates the brightness B by integrating the brightness of each piece dt along the ray $(x(t), y(t), z(t))$ according to three factors. The *first factor* introduces the attenuation of the medium along the ray into the surface. Bright particles buried deep within a density are occluded by many particles, thus the accumulated transmission coefficient is low and the particle will not contribute much light to the pixel. Note that this factor is calculated as in equation 1. The *second factor* multiplies the illumination I_i for each light source i reaching the particle (which is given as a transmission as in equation 1), times the lighting model for each single particle, this is given by the phase factor $p(\cos\theta)$. This phase factor is a function of the angle θ between the light direction and the eye direction. It represents the amount of occlusion of the scattered light and is much like the phase of the moon. The *third factor* weights the brightness by the density of particles at a given point. A few bright particles will contribute less light than a large number of dimmer particles.

Calculating the illumination component I_i can be done in many ways. Blinn (1982) assumed a homogeneous field and calculated the transparency of the medium from point P to point C_i for each light source i (figure 1). Kajiya and Von Herzen (1984) assumed an infinite distance (viz. collimated) light source and precalculated the intensities for each point in the volume by marching along a parallel wavefront. Rushmeier and Torrance (1987) solve a system of linear equations to yield I_i.

Following Blinn(1982), many workers have expanded on the volume density theme: Voss(1983), Max(1983), Kajiya and Von Herzen(1984), Max(1986b, 1986c), Rushmeier and Torrance(1987), and Nishita, Miyawaki and Nakamae(1987). These algorithms extended Blinn's original work to rendering densities with nonuniform distribution, to high

albedo solutions, and to more general geometries. Rushmeier and Torrance(1987) represents the most sophisticated effort to date, calculating a physically accurate distribution of light for true multiple scattering—albeit with isotropic scattering models.

The recent popularity of scientific visualization has engendered much recent activity in volume rendering, e.g. Sabella(1988), Upson and Keeler (1988), Drebin, Carpenter, and Hanrahan(1988). The technique outlined in this paper has direct application to the volume rendering of vector fields. In particular, one result of this work has particular relevance to volume rendering: the importance of shadows. In the results section, we have rendered an identical texel with and without shadows. As the pair of torii in figures 10 and 11 show, rendering without taking into account shadows creates a situation that is so unphysical that the data cannot be properly interpreted by our visual system.

We also point out that the technique presented in this paper fits well into the ray tracing/distributed ray tracing/rendering equation framework. That is, texels can be mixed with the wide variety of primitives already amenable to ray tracing. It is not clear whether texels can be made compatible with the radiosity approach to image synthesis.

Texels

In Kajiya and Von Herzen(1984) it was suggested that volume densities were potentially capable of rendering many complex objects beyond particles of dust and smoke: this would include phenomena such as hair and furry surfaces. We began this work attempting to generalize volume density rendering along these lines. During the course of the investigation, we found that the idea of using volume densities to model surfaces is not entirely appropriate. Although the idea of distributing lighting models instead of spherical particles within the volume density is the right idea, we have found that one cannot not simply replace particle lighting models with surface lighting models. The physics of scattering from surfaces is so different from that of particles that new equations governing the rendering process must be derived.

To generalize volume densities we now introduce texels. In practical terms, a texel is a three dimensional array of parameters approximating visual properties of a collection of microsurfaces. If texels are to be used to replace geometry—such as trees on the side of a mountain—then the microsurfaces of leaves and branches will be stored into the volume array. At each point in space, several items must be stored. First is the density of microsurfaces. That at certain points, space is empty; at others, there is a dense array of leaves. A second item distributed throughout space is a lighting model. In a texel, each leaf is not stored as a polygon. Instead the collection of leaves is represented by a scattering function that models how light is scattered from the aggregate collection of surfaces contained within a volume cell. This scattering function is represented by a pair of quantities, the first is a *frame*, that is a representative orientation of a microsurface within the cell, and a *reflectance function*.

Texels may be generated many different ways. We have not investigated techniques for generating texels for many interesting cases. For example, the geometry for the trees could be sampled into three–dimensional arrays using some sort three–dimensional scan–conversion technique. We have not done this, however. For representing fur, the generation of texels is straightforward and is presented in a section below.

Texels are intended to simulate a volume cell that contains bits of surfaces, not spherical particles. Thus the first component of a texel is a *scalar density* ρ which represents not relative volume, but an approximation to *relative projected area* of the microsurfaces contained within a volume cell. The second component of a texel is a field of *frames B*, that is the local orientation of the microsurface within a volume cell. The third component is a field of *lighting models* Ψ, which determine how light scatters from this bit of surface.

Definition. A *texel* is a triple $\rho, \mathbf{B}, \psi$ consisting of a scalar density $\rho(x, y, z)$, a frame bundle $\mathbf{B} = [\mathbf{n}(x, y, z), \mathbf{t}(x, y, z), \mathbf{b}(x, y, z)]$, and a

field of bidirectional light reflection functions

$$\Psi(x, y, z, \theta, \phi, \psi).$$

The scalar density ρ measures how much of the projected unit area of a volume cell is covered by microsurfaces. It should properly be a higher tensor quantity that takes into account the viewing vector, but we adopt the approximation that this quantity is an isotropic quantity and hence a scalar.

The frame bundle **B** indicates the local orientation of the surfaces within the texel. It is a field of coordinate basis vectors n, t, b that are called the *normal, tangent,* and *binormal* fields, resp.

The bidirectional light reflection function Ψ indicates the type of surface contained therein. It is possible to combine B and Ψ into a single anisotropic lighting model field, but we have separated them because, often, either component may be taken to be constant throughout the volume while the other varies.

Texels appear to be a natural extension of a volume density. Because in a volume density the spheres are physically and materially isotropic, the frame and reflectance fields are homogeneous. Thus they do not need to be distributed throughout a density but can be established as single quantities. Texels simply generalize this a bit.

Rendering Texels

How can one modify volume densities to model hair? A naive approach would be to simply reinterpret the density ρ to reflect the densities of the hair at each volume cell; and to modify the lighting model at each point to correspond to scattering from a cylinder instead of a sphere. Unfortunately this direct approach, while correct in spirit, has flaws.

For an insight into understanding why volume densities are not appropriate for rendering microsurfaces, consider the rendering of a single plane surface via a volume density (figure 2). Assume that the surface is stored into a volume density so that it bisects the cube. The optical depth of the surface is so high that it simulates an opaque surface. Let the phase factor of the particle lighting model be say a Lambertian surface lighting model in equations 1 and 2. Let us not use equations 1 and 2 to calculate both the transparency and the brightness of the surface.

For the transparency calculation, even though the optical depth parameter τ is set very high, the line integral of the density in the exponent will be vanishingly small. This is because the surface is infinitely thin, so the line integral will pierce the surface at only a single point. This yeilds an integral of 0.

A similar problem occurs in the brightness calculation. The brightness integrand yields a finite value whose contribution to the integral along the ray will be zero, since it is nonzero only for a single point.

Thus the transparency and brightness for this surface will both be zero—an invisible surface! Obviously, volume rendering needs to be modified somewhat to be able to render surfaces. The problem is that the relative *volume* of microsurfaces does not determine brightness and opacity for surfaces as it does for point particle densities. A single surface with zero volume can be completely opaque and can reflect 100% of its incident light. Yet its relative volume will be zero. Thus, what is called for is something like a density which is given by Dirac delta functions. This, along with a more general lighting model, is the essence of the texel idea.

Texels are rendered in a manner which is similar to that for volume densities, suitably generalized. Again, the equations model the situation schematized in figure 1. The texel containing surfaces with projected area density $\rho(x, y, z)$ at each point is penetrated by a ray. The light reaching the eye is computed along the ray R. At each point $P = (x(t), y(t), z(t))$ of the ray at distance t, the illumination I_i for each light source is multiplied by the bidirectional reflectance function Ψ that indicates how much light is scattered from the light source to the

ray. The brightness is then weighted by the projected area density at this point. The attenuation between point P and A due to the medium is given by an sum of the density along the ray.

The equations for a texel illumination are

$$T = e^{-\tau \sum_{s=\text{tnear}}^{\text{tfar}} \rho(x(s), y(s), z(s))} \tag{3}$$

and

$$B = \sum_{t=\text{tnear}}^{\text{tfar}} e^{-\tau \sum_{u=\text{tnear}}^{t} \rho(x(u), y(u), z(u))}$$
$$\times \left[\sum_i I_i(x(t), y(t), z(t)) \Psi(x(t), y(t), z(t), \theta, \phi, \rho) \right] \tag{4}$$
$$\times \rho(x(t), y(t), z(t))$$

Equations 3 and 4 are similar to equations 1 and 2. Equation 3 is just equation 1 with the line integral replaced by a sum. We write the sum because integrating Dirac delta functions on microsurfaces sums the contribution at each microsurface.

In equation 4, the relationship to equation 2 is also evident. The integral has again been replaced by a sum. The attenuation along the ray segment AP in figure 1 is represented by the first term in the product. The second term models the scattering of light from the microsurface. As in equation 1 there is a term for each light source. The illumination I_i reaching the microsurface is multiplied by the bidirectional light reflection function Ψ of the microsurface. Finally, the projected area density scales the reflected light in the third term.

The transmission equation 3 for texels is a formal *sum* instead of an integral. This formal sum is taken over each of the surfaces in the density along the ray. If this sum is infinite, then the transmission coefficient is zero, indicating that the density is totally opaque. The brightness equation 4 is also a formal sum instead of an integral. This is because, at each surface intersecting a ray, we are adding the brightness contribution of the surface at that point.

It would appear that equation 4 would always yield an infinite quantity, but recall that the terms of the formal sum will be zero where there are no surfaces and behind any surface the optical depth will be high and will attenuate all contributions to zero. Thus the sums are finite.

Calculation of the incident intensities I_i are computed by using equation 1 recursively. That is, a ray is shot from the point P to each light source i (figure 1). The transmission coefficient is calculated from equation 1. The intensity I_i is simply the brightness of the light source attenuated by the transmission coefficient along the segment PC_i.

The algorithm just outlined would be impossibly expensive if the sums were to be evaluated by adding terms corresponding to every point along the original ray. The algorithm presented in the next section approximates these sums by a Monte Carlo treatment that computes expected values of random samples along the ray, in the spirit of distributed ray tracing (Cook, et al. 1984).

Texel Rendering Algorithm

The texel rendering algorithm computes the above sums by approximating them with with expected values of random samples along the ray. To find the intensity of light emanating backwards from a given ray, the intersection of the ray and each texel boundary is calculated. The distances along the ray of these intersections then forms an interval from t_{near} to t_{far} along the ray, shown as point A and D of figure 1. To compute the sum, we use the technique known as *stratified sampling*. We divide up the ray into a series of segments (delineated by tick marks along the ray in figure 1). In each segment a random point is chosen to calculate the scattering term, e.g. point P. The illumination I_i is calculated by recursively shooting a ray toward each light source as discussed

in the previous section. Finally the sum over segments are calculated to approximate the quantities in equations 3 and 4.

1. Intersect a ray with the all texel boundaries to find t_{near}, t_{far} for each texel. Sort all intersections from front to back and match with distance. Let $T_{near} = \min t_{near}$ where the minimum is over all segments. Similarly $T_{far} = \max t_{far}$.

2. Divide up the ray from T_{near} to T_{far} into ray segments S_i of length L, where $\frac{1}{L}$ is a reference length parameter, the number of samples per unit distance in world coordinates set by the user. (The last segment may be shorter than L).

3. Set transparency to unity.

4. FOR each segment.

   4.1 Shoot shadow rays from the sample toward every light source to calculate the amount of light reaching this point.

   4.2 Calculate brightness from lighting model and illumination intensity and multiply by transparency to give overall brightness contribution to the pixel `pixel = pixel + trans * lightModel`.

   4.3 Multiply transparency by $e^{\tau \rho}$, the transmission coefficient of the segment.

5. At the end segment, calculate brightness as above but normalize by fractional length of the segment.

Step 5 in the algorithm above is required to avoid bias in the Monte Carlo calculation. If the final segment were to be treated as a full length section then the averages would be thrown off. This has an effect of making the edges of the volume appear slightly more opaque than they should be.

This section presents an algorithm for rendering a single texel. However, to make pictures of fuzzy objects, four steps must be carried out. These are the creation of the texels, the mapping of texels into world space, the intersection of rays with texels, and the computation of the lighting model.

Generating Texels for Hair

We will now direct our attention to methods for generating texels that represent patches of hair. The general problem involves long flowing hair. Particle systems could be used to trace the trajectories of the individual hairs through a three–dimensional array. The particle would leave an "anti–aliased" trail of density that would be summed in with previous densities.

A texel representing hair may be simplified by storing only the density ρ and the frame B at each point. The bidirectional reflectance function Ψ is constant for each hair and common to all hairs (if the hair does not change color). Thus it is not necessary to store it throughout the volume. For the lighting model derivation we treat an individual hair as an infinitely thin cylindrical surface. Thus, the only element of the frame that is necessary is the tangent vector along the hair. The rest of the frame B, normal and binormal, do not enter into the lighting calculations and were omitted. Thus a particle system generating hair would not only leave a track of density but also store a tangent vector representing the direction of the velocity of the particle.

The teddy bear model presented in this paper uses a single texel replicated over the bear's skin. The contents of the texel were generated using a much simplified version of the particle system approach. All hairs on the teddy bear are straight lines that point in the same direction, perpendicular to the scalp (in texel space). This implies that the hairs will lie along an axis of the three–dimensional array used to store the texel. Thus the tangent vectors are all the same in that they all perpendicular to the scalp. Thus they were also excluded from volume structure.

The bear's fur texel was stored as a 40x40x10 array. The contents of the array were designed based on several criteria:

1. The "hairs" are distributed as a Poisson disk.

2. The Poisson disk is created with a torus topology, so the single texel can tile the entire bears surface without showing seams.

3. Animal fur often comes in two layers, an "overcoat," and an "undercoat." The undercoat is a dense cover of short fur, while the overcoat is a sparser distribution of long hair. We have found this to be an important feature for avoiding a brushlike appearance.

A "modeling" program allowed us to search the parameter space and presented us with top and side projections of the texel. Using purely aesthetic (and largely arbitrary) judgement, the texel used in figures 15 and 16 was created.

Mapping Texel To World Space

By placing texels over the surface of the bear, we created a bear whose fur flows smoothly over its entire body, while at the same time shows local randomness. However, a texel represented as a three-dimensional array, is shaped as a rectangular solid, at least in texel space. The texels must be mapped onto the shape of the bear in a continuous way to avoid gaps.

The teddy bear was modeled using a new technique called generative models. Each body part (head, body, ear, arm, leg, and nose) was constructed by designing a parametric mapping Φ from a rectangle U (parameterized by u and v) into world space R^3. If we were to render the bear as polygons (as we do in the case of the bear's nose), we would chop the rectangle into a mesh of $n \times m$ small squares. Each square would be mapped vertex by vertex through Φ into world space. The resulting objects (bilinear patches) would then be rendered (usually by further approximating each patch as two triangles). Figure 3 demonstrates this approach. For the sake of simplicity, all figures will present just two dimensions when possible. The extension to three dimensions is obvious.

The texel cubes are mapped into world space in exactly the same way. The parameterized rectangle is chopped into $n \times m$ small squares. Each square is mapped into world space and is identified with the base of a texel (figure 4). (In the case of the teddy bear, a single texel was replicated over the entire surface of the bear.)

The mapping Φ defined by the generative modeling specifies what happens only to the base of each texel. The texel's third dimension (height) must also be mapped into world space. This mapping specifies if the fur on the bear stands straight out or if it lies down. The extension of Φ to the third texel dimension need only be defined for the corners of the texel. Once the corners of the texels are mapped, they are no longer necessarily boxes. Additionally, the gaps between adjacent texels disappear (figure 5). The linear nature of the texel interpolation described in a following sections assures that the hairs within a texel will flow in the same general direction as the corners.

A modeling program was created that allowed the designers to manipulate the orientation of the corners of the texels. The program starts with the corners of each texel sticking straight out (i.e., the corners of each texel correspond with the surface normals of the scalp). The corners are then perturbed by global Fourier maps.

Intersecting Rays With Texels

A texel is shaped as a rectangular solid in texel space. The mapping of the texel into world space as described above changes each of the six faces of the rectangular solid into a bilinear patch. The intersection of a ray with a texel is accomplished by intersecting the ray with the six faces of the texel in world space.

Intersecting Rays with Bilinear Patches

Each edge of a bilinear patch, as well as all "horizontal" and "vertical" cross sections on the patch are straight lines. All other cross sections of a bilinear patch are quadratics. Therefore, it seems reasonable that the ray–patch intersection calculation should involve solving the quadratic equation.

A ray is defined by the equation $R = at + b$ with $0 \leq t$. The 3-vectors a and b specify the origin and direction cosines of the ray. A bilinear patch is of the form $P = Auv + Bu + Cv + D$ with $0 \leq u \leq 1$ and $0 \leq v \leq 1$ where $A, B, C,$ and D are also triples.

The intersection of the ray R with the patch P occurs when $R = P$. Expanding into components yields three equations of the form,

$$A_1 uv + B_1 u + C_1 v + D_1 t + E_1 = 0, \qquad (5a)$$

$$A_2 uv + B_2 u + C_2 v + D_2 t + E_2 = 0, \qquad (5b)$$

and

$$A_3 uv + B_3 u + C_3 v + D_3 t + E_3 = 0. \qquad (5c)$$

These equations should be reordered so that the first is the one with the largest D coefficient. This will assure that, in the case of a patch aligned with an axis, the denominators in the equations that follow will be reasonable (thereby avoiding floating point overflows).

The first equation is solved for t, yielding

$$t = -\frac{A_x uv + B_x u + C_x v + E_x}{D_x}, \qquad (6)$$

which can be substituted into the remaining two equations to remove references to t, resulting in two equations of the form

$$F_2 uv + G_2 u + H_2 v + I_2 = 0 \qquad (7a)$$

and

$$F_3 uv + G_3 u + H_3 v + I_3 = 0. \qquad (7b)$$

These two equations can be multiplied by F_3 and F_2 respectively, and the uv term can be eliminated, giving a linear equation relating u and v. Solving for u and backsubstituting into equation (7a) or (7b) results in a quadratic equation in v. Once v is determined, u quickly follows, as does t.

When solving the quadratic equation (of the form $ax^2 + bx + c = 0$), there is a possibility that the coefficient on the square term (a) may be very small. This could occur, for example, when the four points of the bilinear patch are coplanar. Since we are looking only for values of $0 \leq u \leq 1$, we can compute if a is too small using the equation

$$b + sgn(b)\sqrt{b^2 - 4ac} < 2a. \qquad (8)$$

If the equation fails to hold, then the root would be out of the range $-1 \leq u \leq 1$, and need not be computed. This and similar tests will help avoid floating point overflows.

Mapping Ray–Texel Intersections to Texel Space

Once the intersections of the ray with the texel have been computed, they must be mapped into texel space. Then the texel properties (such as density and tangent vector) can be found by trilinear interpolation from the texel arrays.

To compute the mapping, all the intersections are sorted. Ideally, they will come in pairs, the first of the pair ("near") representing the ray entering the texel, and the second ("far") representing the ray leaving the texel. The intersections yield pairs of the form $(f_{\text{near}}, u_{\text{near}}, v_{\text{near}}, t_{\text{near}})$ and $(f_{\text{far}}, u_{\text{far}}, v_{\text{far}}, t_{\text{far}})$, where f is the index of the face intersected, (u, v) is the patch coordinate for the intersection in face f, and t is the distance along the ray for the intersection.

Each intersection is mapped back to the texel in texel space, resulting in points of the form $(x_{\text{near}}, y_{\text{near}}, z_{\text{near}}, t_{\text{near}})$ and $(x_{\text{far}}, y_{\text{far}}, z_{\text{far}}, t_{\text{far}})$, where (x, y, z) is the coordinate withing the unit texel of the intersection. The t values remain unchanged.

The (x, y, z) coordinates of an intersection in texel space will fall in the unit cube. At least one of the components will actually be either 0 or 1, except when an intersection happens for $t < 0$. In this case, the (x, y, z) coordinates of the intersection must be adjusted by interpolation to match the point on the ray where $t = 0$.

To render the scene, the shader must know the value of the texel at many points along the ray. Because the t parameter is invariant under the texel–space–to–world–space mapping, we can use it as the interpolant to compute the texel space coordinate for any value of t. The three components are

$$\frac{t - t_{\text{near}}}{t_{\text{far}} - t_{\text{near}}}(x_{\text{far}} - x_{\text{near}}) + x_{\text{near}}, \qquad (9a)$$

$$\frac{t - t_{\text{near}}}{t_{\text{far}} - t_{\text{near}}}(y_{\text{far}} - y_{\text{near}}) + y_{\text{near}}, \qquad (9b)$$

and

$$\frac{t - t_{\text{near}}}{t_{\text{far}} - t_{\text{near}}}(z_{\text{far}} - z_{\text{near}}) + z_{\text{near}}. \qquad (9c)$$

Lighting model for hair

There are two components forming the lighting model for a single hair, the diffuse and specular. The diffuse component is derived essentially from the Lambert shading model applied to a very small cylinder. The specular component is an ad hoc model similar to the Phong light reflection model that has been modified for cylindrical surfaces.

A more rigorous approach to defining a lighting model would be something along the lines of Kajiya (1985), of Cabral, Max, and Springmeyer (1987), or of Krueger (1988). These papers propose algorithms to convert the the surface microgeometry to be represented in the volume directly to lighting models. We have found, however, that the exact form of the details of the lighting model not to be particularly critical to the quality of the images. Examination of the images show that our ad hoc approach is adequate.

The geometry for deriving the hair lighting model is shown in figure 6. An individual hair is a line segment specified by a position x_0 and a tangent vector t. The light vector l points from x_0 to the light source. The eye vector e indicates the direction of the scattered light toward the eye. All of these vectors are assumed to be of unit length. The projection l' of l onto the plane perpendicular to t forms the second basis vector. The third basis vector b is chosen to be perpendicular to both the previous basis vectors.

The diffuse component

The diffuse component of the hair reflection model is obtained by integrating a Lambert surface model along the circumference of the half cylinder facing the light source. As shown in figure 7, we integrate over the half circle visible from the light source. The back of the surface is not illuminated. The orthonormal basis formed from the three vectors t, l', b are easily calculated. The first basis vector is t, which is perpendicular to the texel base. The second vector l' is the projection of the light vector l onto plane P containing all the normals to the cylinder. The vector l' is given by

$$l' = \frac{l - (t \cdot l)t}{\|l - (t \cdot l)t\|}. \qquad (10)$$

It is easy to see that b, orthogonal to t and l' is calculated as

$$b = l \times t. \qquad (11)$$

These three vectors are shown in figure 6.

The total amount of light scattered per unit length of cylinder is integrated over the semicircle from shadow terminator to shadow terminator (figure 7). Let us parameterize the position along the cylinder by θ where θ ranges between 0 and π radians. As a function of θ the normal vector n to the cylinder is

$$n = b(\cos\theta) + l'(\sin\theta). \qquad (12)$$

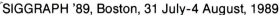

The Lambert model gives the intensity of reflected light as $\Psi(\theta) = (k_d)l \cdot n$, where k_d is the diffuse reflection coefficient. Thus to find the total amount of light per unit length we integrate along the circumference of the half cylinder. The line integral element ds along the cylinder is given in terms of θ by $r\,d\theta$, so

$$
\begin{aligned}
\Psi_{diffuse} &= k_d \int_0^\pi l \cdot n\, r\, d\theta \\
&= k_d\, r \int_0^\pi l \cdot \left(b(\cos\theta) + l'(\sin\theta)\right)\, d\theta \\
&= k_d\, r\, l \cdot l' \int_0^\pi \sin\theta\, d\theta \\
&= (K_d)l \cdot l'
\end{aligned}
\tag{13}
$$

where K_d absorbs all the quantities independent of l and l'. Substituting the definition of l' into the definition yields a particularly simple expression for the diffuse component:

$$
\begin{aligned}
\Psi_{diffuse} &= K_d\, l \cdot \frac{l - (t \cdot l)t}{\|l - (t \cdot l)t\|} \\
&= K_d\, \frac{1 - (t \cdot l)^2}{\sqrt{1 - (t \cdot l)^2}} \\
&= K_d\, \sin(t, l).
\end{aligned}
\tag{14}
$$

Thus the diffuse lighting component is proportional to the sine between the light and tangent vectors. Thus if the tangent of the hair is pointing straight at the light, the hair is dark. This is readily observed in real hair.

The specular component

Calculating the highlights on a hair requires some term capturing specularity. We could have derived a specular term in a similar manner starting from the ad hoc Phong specular model. However, the process is more difficult and the resulting model quite complex. We chose instead to invent an ad hoc specular model in the same spirit as the Phong model modified to approximate some diffraction around the hair. The model is motivated by figure 8.

Any light striking the hair is specularly reflected at a mirror angle along the tangent. Since the normals on the cylinders point in all directions perpendicular to the tangent, the reflected light should be independent of the azimuthal component of the eye vector. Thus the reflected light forms the cone whose angle at the apex is equal to the angle of incidence as shown in figure 8. The actual highlight intensity is given as

$$
\Psi_{specular} = k_s \cos^P(e, e')
\tag{15}
$$

where k_s is some specular reflection coefficient, e is the vector pointing to the eye, and e' is the specular reflection vector contained in the cone closest to the eye vector, and p is the Phong exponent specifying the sharpness of the highlight. The highlight is thus a maximum when the eye vector is contained in the reflected cone and falls off with a Phong dependence.

To calculate this model we note that the only quantities entering into the calculation are the angle of incidence and the angle of reflection with respect to the tangent vector, θ and θ'. The intensity is given by

$$
\begin{aligned}
\Psi_{specular} &= k_s \cos^P \theta - \theta' \\
&= k_s (\cos\theta\, \cos\theta' + \sin\theta\, \sin\theta')^P \\
&= k_s (t \cdot l\; t \cdot e + \sin(t, l) \sin(t, e))^P
\end{aligned}
\tag{16}
$$

These quantities are easily calculated from the original vectors.

Results

Figure 9 shows a single texel of hair. Discounting the base plane, no geometric model has been used to create this image. Figure 10 shows a closer view of the rightmost edge of figure 9. Note that the painter's illusion breaks down on the close up view. We should switch from the texel representation to actual geometry when viewing the model at this resolution.

Figures 11, 12, 13 and 14 show a number test images displaying torii covered by texels, modeling brushlike fur. These show what happens when the corners of the texels are not deformed by Φ.

Figures 11 and 12 are identical except that figure 11 was rendered with the shadows turned off, so that every cell is always illuminated. It is evident that self shadowing of the texel is one of the principal cues for realism.

Figures 15 and 16 show two versions of a teddy bear. The underlying geometric model is identical for each bear. Different Fourier coefficients were used for defining each local texel deformation. Fewer, larger texels appear in figure 15. The processor time for each of these images was substantially the same. These images have a resolution of 1280 by 1024 pixels. No antialiasing was done.

Precise measurements of the CPU time are somewhat problematic, as each image was rendered concurrently on a network of large IBM mainframes. We used a total of twelve 3090 processors and four 3081 processors. On average, we obtained approximately 30%–50% of each processor. Total wall clock time was about 2 hours.

Further Work

The question of how to turn geometry into texture has not yet been solved. This paper represents only a start on the problem. An automatic way of generating texel densities from complex geometric models is currently unknown to us. We speculate that the theory known as *geometric measure theory* may provide the key mathematical insights into this problem.

Applying texels to other complex scenes is also left open: consider the problem of rendering a forest covering a mountainside in the distance. Instead of having thousands of polygons, each tree and bush could be modeled as an appropriate texel. When the texels themselves become very small, one can merge several into a larger texel, somehow adding densities and merging lighting functions.

We have not modeled long hair, or curly hair; only fur. This is an interesting modeling task especially when one decides to include the dynamical behavior of long hair in an animation. We believe that the methods presented in this paper will adequately render long hair once the modeling problems are solved.

References

Blinn J.F. and Newell M.E. (1976) "Texture and Reflection in Computer Generated Images" Comm. ACM 19,10, 542-547.

Blinn J.F. (1977) "Models of Light Reflection for Computer Synthesized Pictures" Computer Graphics 11,2, 192-198.

Blinn J.F. (1978) "Simulation of Wrinkled Surfaces" Computer Graphics 12,3, 286-292

Blinn J.F. (1982) "Light Reflection Functions for Simulation of Clouds and Dusty Surfaces" Computer Graphics 16,3, 21-29.

Cabral B., Max N. and Springmeyer R. (1987) "Bidirectional Reflectance Functions from Surface Bump Maps" Computer Graphics 21,4, 273-282.

Catmull E.E. (1974) *A Subdivision Algorithm for Computer Display of Curved Surfaces*, Ph.D., U. of Utah.

Cook R.L., Porter T. and Carpenter L. (1984) "Distributed Ray Tracing" Computer Graphics 18,3, 137-146.

Cook R.L. (1984) "Shade Trees" Computer Graphics 18,3, 223-232.

Crow F.C. (1982) "A More Flexible Image Generation Environment", Computer Graphics 16,3, 9-18.

Csuri C., Hakathorn R., Parent R., Carlson W. and Howard M. (1979) "Towards an interactive high visual complexity animation system" Computer Graphics 13,2, 289-299.

Drebin R.A., Carpenter L., and Hanrahan P. (1988) "Volume Rendering", Computer Graphics 22,4, 65-74

Kajiya J.T. and Von Herzen B. (1984) "Ray Tracing Volume Densities" Computer Graphics 18,3, 165-174.

Kajiya J.T. (1985) "Anisotropic Reflection Models" Computer Graphics 19,3, 15-22.

Krueger W. (1988) "Intensity Fluctuations and Natural Texturing" Computer Graphics 22,4, 213-220.

Miller G.S.P. (1988) "The Motion Dynamics of Snakes and Worms" Computer Graphics 22,4, 169-178.

Max N.L. (1986a) "Light Diffusion through Clouds and Haze" Computer Vision, Graphics and Image Processing 33, 280-292.

Max N.L. (1986b) "Atmospheric Illumination and Shadows" Computer Graphics 20,4, 117-124.

Max N.L. (1986c) "Shadows for Bump Mapped Surfaces" in *Advanced Computer Graphics*, Springer V., 145-156.

Nishita T., Okamura I. and Nakamae E. (1985) "Shading Models for Point and Linear Sources" ACM Trans. on Graphics 4,2, 124-146.

Nishita T., Miyawaki Y. and Nakamae E. (1987) "A Shading Model for Atmospheric Scattering Considering Luminous Intensity Distribution of Light Sources" Computer Graphics 21,4, 303-310.

Ohira T. (1983) "A Shading Model for Anisotropic Reflection" Tech. Rep. Inst. El. and Comm. Eng of Japan (in Japanese) 82,235, 47-54.

Peachey D.R (1985) "Solid Texturing of Complex Surfaces" Computer Graphics 19,3, 279-286.

Perlin K. (1985) "An Image Synthesizer" Computer Graphics 19,3, 287-296.

Reeves W.T. (1983) "Particle Systems—A Technique for Modeling a Class of Fuzzy Objects" Computer Graphics 17,3, 359-376.

Reeves. W.T. and Blau R. (1985) "Approximate and Probabilistic Algorithms for Shading and Rendering Structured Particle Systems" Computer Graphics 19,3, 313-322.

Rushmeier H.E. and Torrance K.E. (1987) "The Zonal Method for Calculating Light Intensities in the Presence of a Participating Medium" Computer Graphics 21,4, 293-302.

Sabella P. (1988) "A Rendering Algorithm for Visualizing 3D Scalar Fields", Computer Graphics 22,4, 51-58.

Takagi J., Yokoi S. and Tsuroka S. (1983) "Comment on the Anisotropic Reflection Model" Bull. of SIG. Graphics and CAD, Inf. Proc. Soc. of Japan. (in Japanese) 11,1, 1-9.

Upson C., Keeler M. (1988) "VBUFFER: Visible Volume Rendering", Computer Graphics 22,4, 59-64.

Acknowledgments

Thanks to Al Barr for technical discussions, and to Hewlett Packard Corporation for their donation of the HP9000 Model 350SRX workstations to the Caltech Computer Science Graphics Lab.

Our appreciation to John Snyder for modeling and remodeling (and reremodeling) the bear.

We wish to express our thanks to IBM and Alan Norton of IBM T.J. Watson Research Center at Yorktown Heights their financial support and gracious donation of a considerable amount of 3090 time.

We also thank the reviewers whose many comments have been invaluable in improving our exposition.

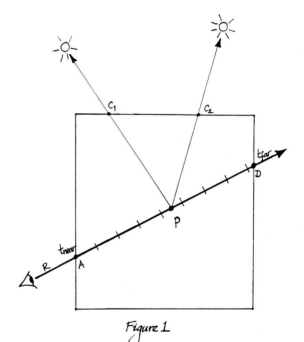

Figure 1

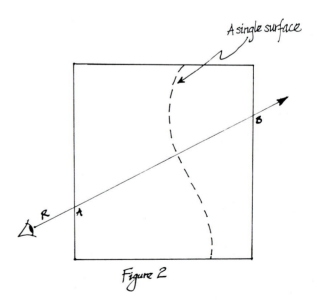

Figure 2

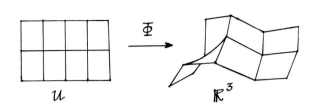

Figure 3

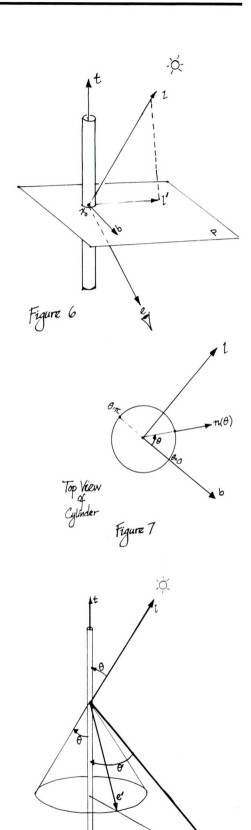

Figure 6

Figure 7

Top View
of
Cylinder

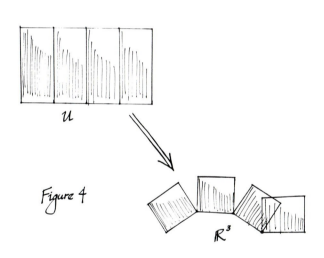

Figure 4

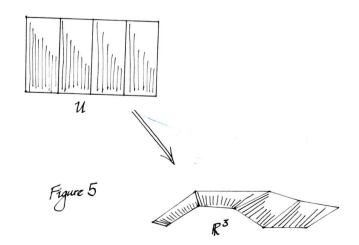

Figure 5

Figure 8

Figure 9

Figure 10

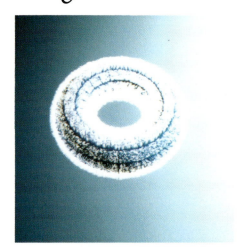

Figure 11

Figure 12

Figure 13

Figure 14

Figure 15

Figure 16

Computer Graphics, Volume 23, Number 3, July 1989

Antialiased Ray Tracing by
Adaptive Progressive Refinement

James Painter and Kenneth Sloan
University of Washington

ABSTRACT

We describe an antialiasing system for ray tracing based on adaptive progressive refinement. The goals of the system are to produce high quality antialiased images at a modest average sample rate, and to refine the image progressively so that the image is available in a usable form early and is refined gradually toward the final result.

The method proceeds by adaptive stochastic sampling of the image plane, evaluation of the samples by ray tracing, and image reconstruction from the samples. Adaptive control of the sample generation process is driven by three basic goals: coverage of the image, location of features, and confidence in the values at a distinguished "pixel level" of resolution.

A three-stage process of interpolation, filtering, and resampling is used to reconstruct a regular grid of display pixels. This reconstruction can be either batch or incremental.

CR Categories and Subject Descriptors: I.3.3 [Computer Graphics]: Picture/Image Generation – Display algorithms
Additional Keywords and Phrases: Adaptive Sampling, Antialiasing, Filtering, Progressive Refinement, Ray Tracing.

Department of Computer Science, FR-35 Seattle WA 98195 U.S.A.

This work was supported in part by the National Science Foundation under grant numbers DCR - 8505713, CCR - 8612543, and IRI - 8081932.

1. Introduction

Raster graphics is inherently a sampling process. A rendering program is given a scene description and should produce a "realistic" approximation of it for display. The scene description and the physical model of lighting embodied in the rendering program define an image function giving a color at each point in a continuous domain representing the screen plane. The rendering program's output is a discrete array of *pixel* values representing colors at points on a discrete regular grid representing the screen. Because rendering is a sampling process, it is prone to aliasing artifacts where the frequency spectrum of the image function is not band limited before sampling.

Ray casting methods of rendering have become popular in the last several years. Their benefits include conceptual simplicity and the ability to model complex lighting effects such as shadows, transparency, and reflections. One of the major disadvantages has been their susceptibility to aliasing artifacts. These methods are prone to aliasing because they sample the image function only at discrete points in its domain. Aliasing can be reduced, however, if the sampling pattern is generated by a stochastic process which is uncorrelated with the image function. These randomly placed samples can be filtered and resampled at the screen resolution for display.

Ray tracing is a very slow process, particularly when antialiasing algorithms are used. Should a mistake be made in constructing the model for rendering, hours of cpu time may be lost before the error is realized. Typically, low resolution images are created first for previewing and then discarded. A ray tracing algorithm which produces a usable image relatively quickly and refines it gradually to the final image would alleviate this problem.

This paper describes a new method for antialiased ray tracing which proceeds by adaptive subdivision of the image plane.

2. Prior Work

Several researchers [2], [7] have explored the idea of progressive refinement in image generation. The main difference in this work is the rendering method. Our method is based on ray tracing rather than z-buffer [2], or radiosity [7] algorithms. Our own earlier work [3] relates progressive refinement in image transmission to the rendering problem.

Previous researchers in the area of antialiased raytracing have been concerned with three subproblems: selection of efficient sampling patterns, methods to adaptively control the sample rate, and filters for image reconstruction.

2.1 Sampling Pattern Selection

Stochastic sampling methods for image synthesis have been reported in [9], [8], [11], and [15]. The qualities desired in a stochastic sampling pattern are that it minimize visible aliasing artifacts, minimize visible noise, and be efficiently evaluated. The spectral characteristics of the noise are also important: the human visual system is more sensitive to narrow-band noise than broadband noise and to low frequency noise rather than high frequency noise. The noise properties of a sampling pattern can be evaluated by examining the *Power Spectral Density* of the sampling pattern applied to a constant image function.

Two families of sampling patterns have been examined in the literature: Jittered sampling divides the domain to be sampled into a regular lattice of rectangular cells. A sample is distributed uniformly into each lattice cell. Jittered sampling ensures that the sampling pattern avoids large gaps. Poisson Disk distributions sample over the domain uniformly but with the added constraint that no two samples may be closer than a specified minimum distance. Poisson disk sampling ensures that the sampling pattern avoids excessive clumping. The Poisson disk distribution has been used as a model for the distribution of photoreceptors in primates [19].

The relative merits of jittered sampling and Poisson disk sampling have been discussed in [11], [8], and [15]. Jittered sampling is favored by Cook because the samples can be produced efficiently. Mitchell favors the spectral properties of Poisson disk distributions because they minimize low frequency noise introduced in the sampling processes. He gives an algorithm for efficiently approximating a Poisson disk distribution at a fixed sample rate. A variant of jittered sampling, hierarchical sampling, has been used effectively with a variable sample rate.

2.2 Adaptive Sampling Rate

Computer-generated images do not exhibit uniform local image variation. Edges between objects are areas of high contrast (or variance), while large, uniform objects and backgrounds yield regions which have little local variation. *Adaptive sampling* adjusts the sample rate locally to concentrate samples where they are needed most: at edges and other regions of high contrast. This can substantially reduce the number of samples required to achieve the desired image accuracy.

Adaptive sampling requires an *error estimator* and a *stopping condition*. The error estimator indicates how closely the sample values represent the local mean of the image function, or alternatively, the local noise level present in the sampled image. The stopping condition is a threshold on the error estimator used to determine when enough samples have been taken.

Lee, Redner and Uselton [13] present an error estimator based on local image variance. Their sampling approach is based on area sampling of each pixel, evaluating the output image as an expected value of the input image sampled over an area. Under the assumption that the image function has a normal distribution locally (a questionable assumption), they develop a confidence interval test which gives the probability that the *variance of the sample mean* is below a specified tolerance. Sampling continues until the desired probability is reached.

Traditionally, stopping conditions for simulation experiments are based on a confidence interval of the *mean estimator* itself rather than its variance [5]. The error estimator given in [13] does not directly specify a desired confidence interval of the mean but instead, of its variance. Since the mean is the parameter we are

interested in estimating, it would be more appropriate to apply the confidence interval analysis to it directly.

Dippé and Wold [11] propose a different error estimate based on the root mean square signal to noise ratio (RMS SNR) of the stochastically sampled and reconstructed image function. They show that the RMS SNR is proportional to the square root of the sample rate. The constant of proportionality depends on the image function and the reconstruction filter but is independent of sample rate. The RMS SNR is approximately the absolute value of the difference between the stochastically sampled and filtered function and the perfectly filtered function. This allows an estimate of the rate of change of the RMS SNR as a function of the square root of the sample rate to be estimated from the sampled and filtered image at two different sample rates.

Mitchell [15] suggests that variance is not an appropriate measure of perceived image variation, because the human visual system does not exhibit linear response properties to rapid changes in intensity. Instead, he proposes that *contrast* is a better measure.

Adaptive sample rate control places an additional burden on the sample generation scheme. Since it is not known in advance how many samples are to be taken, every prefix of an ordered set of samples should be well distributed over the sample area. Algorithms which produce samples in a raster scan order are unsuitable. The hierarchical sampling method given in [12] is a suitable method for generating jittered sampling patterns. Dippé suggested that Poisson Disk samples can be created in a uniform order by coupling the minimum distance constraint to the local sample rate. As more samples are needed in a given area, the minimum distance is decreased. Mitchell avoids the problem by using a very limited form of adaptation with only two different sample rates

Mitchell [15] uses a two level technique to accomplish a limited form of sample rate adaptation. The image is first sampled at a moderate sampling rate. Areas of high contrast are sampled at a higher rate. Contrast is measured over a neighborhood of approximately 8 samples. This avoids the problems of previous methods which required many samples per pixel just to determine the image variation over a single sampling region. It is liable, however, to completely miss small objects which fall between the samples in the initial, rather coarse, sampling.

2.3 Image Reconstruction

Once the input image function has been sampled at a set of stochastic sample points, it must be filtered prior to resampling for display. Filtering accomplishes two purposes. First, the image function should be filtered to limit its high frequency content to avoid aliasing when it is resampled for display. Second, the filter can be used to attenuate noise introduced in the stochastic sampling process.

The properties of a filter depend on its width and its shape. Practical filters have a finite width, that is, they are non-zero except on a finite region. Commonly used filter shapes include box filters, triangular filters, raised cosine filters and Gaussian filters. The choice of filter width and shape depends on the desired attenuation of frequencies above $N_{1/2}$ (the Nyquist limit), and the tolerance for attenuation of frequencies below $N_{1/2}$. In addition, the computational costs must be considered. Extremely wide filters are expensive to compute by direct convolution.

A varying sample rate compounds the problem of applying a filter. The number of samples under the filter kernel will vary depending on the local sample rate. If direct convolution is used, areas with more samples appear brighter than areas with fewer samples. Dippé suggested that the filter should be normalized: the sum of the weighted sample values should be divided by the sum of the filter weights. A normalized filter improves matters but does not eliminate the problem. Some consideration must be made for the size of the region each sample represents. Otherwise, image values in areas of dense sampling will dominate nearby areas which are sparsely sampled. Ideally, we would like to weight each sample point by the volume contained under the filter function over the area the sample represents. The hierarchical sampling method associates a cell with each sample. This cell provides a natural region for use in weighting the sample.

Mitchell attacks the problem with a multi-stage filter. The sampled image function is filtered multiple times with filters of wider and wider support, resulting in lower and lower cutoff frequencies. The narrow filters in the early stages average densely sampled regions into single samples covering a larger region. Subsequent stages average these larger regions into pixel sized samples for display. Mitchell used four stages of box filters with three different widths. While a single box filter does not provide adequate high frequency attenuation, repeated box filtering does, approaching a Gaussian filter in the limit.

3. System Description

Our method is composed of three stages: sample generation, sample evaluation and image reconstruction (resampling).

3.1 Sample Generation

The purpose of the sample generator is to choose points in the spatial domain of the image where the image function is to be evaluated. Information from prior samples is used to decide which areas of the image have the greatest need for additional samples. In addition, the sample generator determines when to stop sampling. It should also order the samples to allow for progressive refinement of the rendered image.

Early methods [13], [12] treat the sample generation problem independently at each pixel. Each pixel is sampled until a stopping condition is meet. Samples taken for one pixel are not used for other pixels. One of the major problems with this approach is that a fairly high minimum sample rate (typically 8 samples per pixel) is required simply to determine that a pixel is uninteresting and need not be sampled further.

Later work [15] lowers the average sample rate, in part by sharing samples between pixels. This lowers the minimum sample rate required to evaluate the stopping condition. [15] uses a very simple, two level stopping condition. The image is first sampled at a coarse sample rate. Selected areas are sampled at a finer rate as needed. It is our belief that a further reduction in the sample rate will be realized if the sample rate is allowed to vary over a wider range of values.

Our sample generator is based on *hierarchical integration*, a sampling method described by Kajiya in [12]. Kajiya applied hierarchical integration independently to each pixel. We apply the technique to refine the entire image plane.

3.1.1 Data Structures

In our implementation, as in [12], the sample generator maintains a k-D tree [1] containing all the samples taken. The k-D tree is a binary tree which partitions the two dimensional image plane by alternately splitting in x and y. On even levels, the domain is split along a line parallel to the x axis. On odd levels, the domain is split along lines parallel to the y axis.

The leaf nodes in the tree store the raw sample values and positions. An internal node of the tree stores an estimate of the mean value of the image function over the region covered by that node, an estimate of the variance of this mean estimate (*internal variance*), and the number of samples in the subtree rooted at this node. All nodes also store an external measure of variance. The *external variance* is computed from the mean estimates of the node and all of its neighbors at the same level in the tree.

3.1.2 Refinement Rules

When a new sample is needed, a path from the root to a leaf is followed leading to the region with the greatest need for further refinement. At each (binary) branch in the k-D tree, a decision is made as to which subnode to refine. The decision is based on the variance estimates (both internal and external) of the node, the area of the node, the number of samples already contained in the node and the level of the node in the tree.

We distinguish a level of the tree, called the *pixel* level which is the level of the tree corresponding to pixels in the anticipated reconstruction. The goal of the refinement process is to produce the best answers at the pixel level. This leads to different strategies above and below the pixel level.

At coarse levels, above the pixel level, we are driven by the progressive refinement goals: *Coverage* —refine large regions before smaller ones and *Feature Location* —refine "edge" cells before non "edge" cells.

A heuristic is required to rank the pixel level nodes according to refinement priority. We use the product of external variance and area as a priority measure. The area term enforces the coverage goal while the external variance enforces the feature location goal. Nodes at the pixel level, or leaves above the pixel level, are assigned a priority by direct computation. Internal nodes above the pixel level are assigned a priority value which is the maximum of the two child priority values. Thus, a path can be followed from the root to the highest priority pixel by always branching toward the subnode with higher priority (ties are broken randomly.)

At finer levels, below the pixel level, our only goal is to increase our confidence in the mean of the pixel level node above. To do this, we use the principles of stratified sampling [13]. If two subnodes have mean estimates of μ_1 and μ_2 and mean estimate variances of σ_1 and σ_2 and are of equal area, the mean of the parent node can be estimated as $\mu = (\mu_1 + \mu_2)/2$ with variance of the mean estimate given by $\sigma = (\sigma_1 + \sigma_2)/4$. This mean estimate is often better and never worse than that given by the mean of all the sample values. If we want to improve the mean estimate of the parent node, the best choice is to refine the subnode with the highest mean variance. This is the only refinement principle used in hierarchical sampling [12] since it only operates below the pixel level.

3.1.3 Stopping Condition

The stopping condition is based on a confidence interval test. A desired confidence level and confidence interval is selected. For example, we require that 99% of the time ($\alpha = .01$, the confidence level) the mean estimate at each pixel will be within $1/255$ (the confidence interval) of the correct value. We can take into account the nonlinear response characteristics of human visual perception by allowing the confidence interval to vary with the mean estimate value. For example, we might specify that small mean estimates require a smaller confidence interval than large mean estimates.

The confidence interval for a given confidence level can be computed from the variance of the mean estimate and the number of samples taken, [5]. If the desired confidence level is $1 - \alpha$, the confidence interval is given by $t_{\alpha/2}\sigma$ where $t_{\alpha/2}$ is taken from the student-t distribution with $n - 1$ degress of freedom, n is the number of samples contributing to the mean estimate, and σ is the variance of the mean estimate.

When the sample count within a pixel node is small, the mean estimate variance can approximated from the external variance.

A subtree rooted at a pixel level node is "closed off" when the confidence interval at the desired confidence level becomes at least as small as the desired confidence interval. Once closed off, no more samples will be taken within the subtree. An internal node above the pixel level is closed off when both of its offspring are closed.

The confidence interval test is not the only stopping condition. A *coverage* condition is imposed to ensure that small objects are not missed completely. We require that all nodes are refined at least to the pixel level to ensure that no objects larger than one pixel are missed. Note however that no direct limit on the number of samples within a pixel is required. An upper bound on number of samples per pixel can be determined from the confidence interval and confidence level requirements.

3.2 Sample evaluation

The purpose of the sample evaluator is to evaluate the image function at a single point in the image plane. In this implementation, the image function is evaluated by a ray tracing algorithm [18]. The sample evaluator used here is part of **Renaissance**, a modelling and rendering system developed at the University of Washington [14].

3.3 Reconstruction

The purpose of the reconstruction process is to resample the image function on a regular grid for display. This can be considered as a three step process: First, an interpolation scheme is used to interpolate color values between the samples generated by the sample generator. Next, the resulting image function is convolved with a low-pass filter to reduce aliasing and to attenuate high frequency noise introduced in the original sampling process. Finally, the filtered image function is point sampled at the center of each pixel of the display. In practice, the last two steps are combined so that the filtered image function need only be evaluated at the center of each display pixel.

3.3.1 Piecewise Constant Interpolation

We first consider a very simple interpolant: piecewise constant. While the interpolant is not particularly well behaved (it's not continuous) it makes the filter convolution computationally efficient.

The k-D tree data structure generated during sampling provides a basis for our interpolation scheme. The data structure partitions the plane into rectangular cells aligned with the coordinate axes, each containing exactly one sample point. An obvious interpolant, albeit not a continuous one, is to assign the value of the sample to the entire cell in which it is contained. This gives a piecewise constant image function defined everywhere in the image plane.

The piecewise constant form of the interpolated image function can be exploited to simplify filtering. Convolution of a filter with a constant function reduces to integration of the filter function.

$$i(u, v) * f(u, v)$$
$$= \int_{-\infty}^{\infty} \int_{-\infty}^{\infty} i(u', v')f(u - u', v - v')\, du'\, dv'$$
$$= C \iint_{R} f(u - u', v - v')\, du'\, dv'$$

where $i(u, v)$ is constant with value C over the region R and zero elsewhere.

To find the contribution one of the sampling cells makes on a display pixel, we need only integrate the filter function over the sample cell and multiply it by the value in the cell. The filtered image value at a pixel is evaluated by summing the contributions from all the sample cells which overlap the domain of the filter function centered at the pixel.

$$I(x, y) = \sum_{s \in S} C(s) \iint_{R \cap s} f(u - u', v - v')\, du'\, dv' \qquad (3.1)$$

where
I is the value to be assigned to pixel (x, y),
S is the set of sample cells that overlap the filter support, and
R is the filter support centered at pixel (x, y).

For polynomial filters, the integral can be evaluated analytically. When analytic integration is intractable, the filter can integrated approximately and stored in a *summed area table* as described in [10]. The summed area table stores the pre-integrated filter function. Integrals of the filter function over sample cells can be evaluated by querying the filter summed area table at the corners of the sample cell. The idea of storing the *filter* function in a summed area table has been explored in font filtering, [16].

A bivariate filter function $f(u, v)$ is separable if it can be decomposed into the product of two univariate filters, $f_1(u)f_2(v)$. Most filters used in computer graphics are separable. A separable filter kernel can be stored more compactly as two 1-D summed area tables rather than one 2-D summed area table. The space required is $O(N)$ rather than $O(N^2)$ where N is the number of discrete intervals used to approximate the filter.

The example images shown in the figures were reconstructed using a Lanczos windowed sinc filter [4] over a 7x7 pixel filter support. The filter was discretized and stored as a 1-D summed area table with 4096 entries.

3.3.2 Higher Degree Interpolants

The method described above uses a particularly simple interpolant to simplify convolution with the filter function. We are currently considering reconstruction methods using higher quality interpolants.

First, the sample points can be used to triangulate the image plane using a Delaunay triangulation, [17]. A triangle based interpolation scheme can be used to interpolate a surface through the sample values. The simplest interpolation scheme is piecewise planar: interpolate within each triangle in the plane formed by the three triangle vertices. This scheme produces an image function which is C^0, but not C^1. C^1 triangle based interpolation is also possible [6].

Next, the interpolated image function must be convolved with the filter function and evaluated at the pixel centers. When the filter function and the image function are both piecewise polynomial, this convolution can be performed analytically. When analytic convolution is not tractable, a discrete approximation may be used. However, the usual summed area table requires rectangular regions. We are currently exploring appropriate data structures for discrete convolution over triangular patches.

3.3.3 Progressive Reconstruction

One of the the goals of this work is to have the rendered image available in a usable form very early in the rendering process and to progress incrementally toward the final result. We have seen that the sample generator meets this goal. In this section we consider the impact of the progressive refinement goal on reconstruction algorithms.

When the time required for reconstruction is much smaller than the sample generation and evaluation time, the image can be reconstructed from scratch from the available samples each time an update is desired. Hence, a fast batch method may be adequate for viewing intermediate results. A slower, higher quality reconstruction method can be used for the final image.

An alternative is an incremental reconstruction scheme. Each time a new sample is taken, the pixels affected by the sample are updated.

The reconstruction method described in section 3.3.1 is batch oriented. The value of a each pixel is determined only after all the samples which affect it are known. With a little effort, the computation can be reordered to allow an incremental algorithm. When a sample cell is created, a single term from the sum in equation 3.1 can be evaluated. This term can be added to a running sum for the pixel. This must be done for every pixel affected by the sample cells, those whose filter supports overlap the sample cell. When a sample cell is subdivided, its contribution must be subtracted from the pixels it affects and the contribution of its new subcells added in.

The reconstruction methods described in section 3.3.2 can also be evaluated incrementally by the use of an incremental Delaunay triangulation algorithm. Each time a triangular tile is included or removed, its contribution to each pixel affected is evaluated and added or subtracted respectively.

4. Performance

Two test images are shown in Figures 2 and 3 to illustrate the performance of the system. The tables below give performance statistics for the system when evaluating the two test images. The cpu time is divided into three categories: sample generation, sample evaluation, and reconstruction. Note that sample evalutation time dominates. The cost of evaluating samples via ray tracing is high enough that the time spent generating sample points and filtering the samples for reconstruction is relatively unimportant. Note that as the resolution increases the average sample rate decreases. This is accounted for by the fact that with increasing resolution, the ratio of "edge" pixels to "internal" pixels in general decreases. Images involving fractal based textures may not show this behavior.

Figures 4 and 5 show the number of rays required at each pixel as an intensity image. The intensity image is scaled from full black at 0 samples per pixel to full white at 20 samples per pixel. Any pixels above 20 samples per pixel are painted red. The histograms of the number of samples show that nearly all pixels require fewer than 10 samples per pixel.

Comparisons with data reported in [13] show a significant reduction in the sample rate required. It is difficult to compare our performance figures with [15] since he did not report comparable statistics.

5. Conclusions

We have presented a rendering system which produces high quality antialiased images with relatively low average sample densities. A single adaptive sampling mechanism can be used to achieve several, sometimes conflicting, goals. This method generalizes hierarchical integration [12]. At coarse levels of resolution, we concentrate on producing a low-quality sketch of the final image. The emphasis is on *detecting* objects and features (such as edges.) Subsequent samples are aimed at refining these features. Finally, we concentrate on improving the accuracy of averages over "pixel-sized" pieces of the image.

The quality of images reconstructed from these samples is roughly the same everywhere in the image. The amount of work done can be controlled interactively ("that looks good enough") or by a pre-set specification of the image quality.

A two parameter family of reconstruction algorithms for scattered samples has been presented. The methods consist of three phases: interpolation, filtering and resampling. The interpolation scheme and reconstruction filter may be selected to choose a particular reconstruction method from this family.

6. Acknowledgements

Dan O'Donnell provided the lamp model. Gemini Lasswell provided the solid texture function for the teapot. Thanks to the UW Grail group for providing a rich supply of ideas and a software base to build on.

References

1. Bentley, Jon L. and Friedman, J.J. Data Structures for range searching. *ACM Comp. Surv. 11*, 4 (1979), 397–409.

2. Bergman, Larry, Fuchs, Henry, Grant, Eric and Spach, Susan Image Rendering by Adaptive Refinement. *Computer Graphics 20*, 4 (Aug., 1986), 29–37, Proceedings of SIGGRAPH '86 (Dallas, Texas, August 18-22, 1986).

3. Blanford, Ronald P., Painter, James S. and Sloan, Kenneth R. Adaptive Sampling, Transmission, and Rendering of Images. *SPIE Proceedings 1077* (Jan., 1989), SPIE Conference on Human Vision, Visual Processing, and Digital Display.

4. Blinn, James F. Return of the Jaggy. *IEEE Computer Graphics and Applications 9*, 2 (Mar., 1989), 82–89.

5. Burr, Irving W. *Applied Statistical Methods.* Academic Press, New York, NY, 1974.

6. Cendes, Zoltan J. and Wong, Steven H. C^1 Quadratic Interpolation Over Arbitrary Point Sets. *IEEE Computer Graphics and Applications 7*, 11 (Nov., 1987), 8–16.

7. Cohen, Michael F., Chen, Shenchang E., Wallace, John R. and Greenberg, Donald P. A Progressive Refinement Approach to Fast Radiosity Image Generation. *Computer Graphics 22*, 4 (Aug., 1988), 75–82, Proceedings of SIGGRAPH '88 (Atlanta, Georgia, August 1-5, 1988).

8. Cook, Robert L. Stochastic Sampling in Computer Graphics. *ACM Transactions on Graphics 5*, 1 (Jan., 1986), 51–72.

9. Cook, Robert L., Porter, Thomas and Carpenter, Loren Distributed Ray Tracing. *Computer Graphics 18*, 3 (July, 1984), 137–146, Proceedings of SIGGRAPH '84 (Minneapolis, Minnesota, July 23-27, 1984).

10. Crow, Franklin C. Summed-Area Tables for Texture Mapping. *Computer Graphics 18*, 3 (July, 1984), 207–212, Proceedings of SIGGRAPH '84, (Minneapolis, Minnesota, July 23-27, 1984).

11. Dippé, Mark A.Z. and Wold, E.H. Antialiasing through Stochastic Sampling. *Computer Graphics 19*, 3 (July, 1985), 69–78, Proceedings of SIGGRAPH '85, (San Francisco, California, July 22-26, 1985).

12. Kajiya, James T. The Rendering Equation. *Computer Graphics 20*, 4 (Aug., 1986), 143–150, Proceedings of SIGGRAPH '86, (Dallas, Texas, August 18-22, 1986).

13. Lee, Mark E., Redner, Richard A. and Uselton, Samuel P. Statistically Optimized Sampling for Distributed Ray Tracing. *Computer Graphics 19*, 3 (July, 1985), 61–67, Proceedings of SIGGRAPH '85 (in San Francisco, CA, July 22-26, 1985).

14. Lounsbery, J. Michael The Renaissance Modeling System. Dept. of Computer Science, Univ. of Washington, Tech. Rep. #89-01-05, Jan., 1989.

15. Mitchell, Don P. Generating Antialiased Images at Low Sampling Densities. *Computer Graphics 21*, 4 (July, 1987), 65–69, Proceedings of SIGGRAPH '87 (Anaheim, CA, July 27-31, 1987).

16. Naiman, Avi and Fournier, Alain Rectangular Convolution for Fast Filtering of Characters. *Computer Graphics 21*, 4 (July, 1987), 233–242, Proceedings of SIGGRAPH '87, (Anaheim, CA, July 27-31, 1987).

17. Preparata, Franco P. and Shamos, Michael I. *Computational Geometry: An Introduction.* Springer-Verlag, New York–Heidelberg–Berlin, 1985.

18. Whitted, Turner J. An Improved Illumination Model for Shaded Display. *Communications of the ACM 23*, 6 (June, 1980), 343–349.

19. Yellott, James I. Jr. Spectral Consequences of Photoreceptor Sampling in the Rhesus Retina. *Science 221* (July, 1983), 392–385.

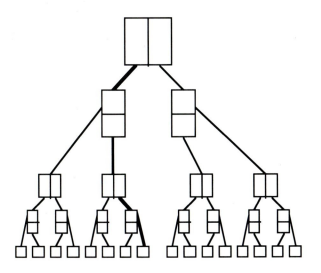

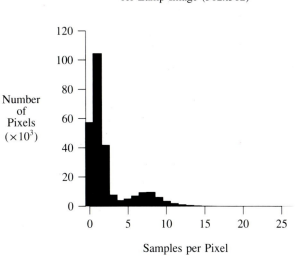

Samples per Pixel Histogram
for Lamp Image (512x512)

Figure 1. The k-D subdivision of the image plane. The bold path leads to the next node to be subdivided.

Algorithm Performance: Lamp Image

Resolution	Cpu time (seconds)			Rays per Pixel
	Generate	Evaluate	Reconstruct	
64	250.5	2900	286.1	5.002930
128	753.9	9800	906.6	3.905520
256	2117.9	33900	2883.7	3.012775
512	7075.3	103620	9505.7	1.880589

Algorithm Performance: Teapot Image

Resolution	Cpu time (seconds)			Rays per Pixel
	Generate	Evaluate	Reconstruct	
64	125.1	710	169.2	2.607670
128	456.8	2680	605.6	2.347838
256	1777.9	9594	2276.7	2.139068
512	6466.6	34217	8629.7	1.970165

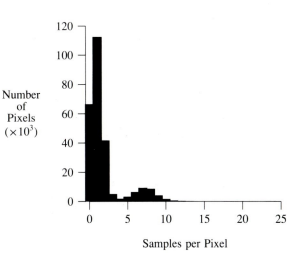

Samples per Pixel Histogram
for Teapot Image (512x512)

Figure 2. A lamp image generated from a CSG model with approximately 13 primitives, rendered at 768x768.

Figure 4. The number of samples per pixel generated for the lamp image, shown as a gray-scale image ranging from 0 = black to 20 = white. Values greater than 20 are shown in red; the maximum value is 24.

Figure 3. A teapot image generated from a boundary representation model with approximately 28 bi-cubic patches subdivided to produce approximately 3600 triangles, rendered at 768x768, using a procedural texture model.

Figure 5. The number of samples per pixel generated for the teapot image, shown as a gray-scale image ranging from 0 = black to 20 = white. Values greater than 20 are shown in red; the maximum value is 26.

Ray Tracing Deterministic 3-D Fractals

John C. Hart*, Daniel J. Sandin*, Louis H. Kauffman†

*Electronic Visualization Laboratory
†Dept. of Mathematics, Statistics and Computer Science

University of Illinois at Chicago

Abstract

As shown in 1982, Julia sets of quadratic functions as well as many other deterministic fractals exist in spaces of higher dimensionality than the complex plane. Originally a boundary-tracking algorithm was used to view these structures but required a large amount of storage space to operate. By ray tracing these objects, the storage facilities of a graphics workstation frame buffer are sufficient. A short discussion of a specific set of 3-D deterministic fractals precedes a full description of a ray-tracing algorithm applied to these objects. A comparison with the boundary-tracking method and applications to other 3-D deterministic fractals are also included.

CR Categories and Subject Descriptors:
I.3.7 [Computer Graphics]: Three Dimensional Graphics and Realism — Color, shading, shadowing and texture.

General Terms: Algorithms, Theory.

Additional Keywords and Phrases: fractal, quaternions, distance estimate, ray tracing, surface determination.

1 Introduction

Computer graphics has greatly aided the investigation of the dynamics of iterative functions. Stan-

©1989   ACM-0-89791-312-4/89/007/0289 $00.75

dard 2-D frame buffer techniques have provided sufficient visual information about the structures since most of the research has concentrated on the dynamics of complex variables. However, recent investigations into higher-dimensional dynamical systems [14,15,3,5,17] have shown the need for 3-D visualization tools that will give researchers a better understanding of these objects.

One such method is ray tracing, but this method is prohibitively slow unless an efficient ray-surface intersection computation is used. While these functions are available for Euclidean surfaces, they do not exist (yet) for fractal ones. However, using an unusual construction called the unbounding volume, made possible by a recent advance in the study of dynamics, swift ray tracing of these deterministic fractal objects is possible.

Prior to the description of the algorithm, a specific family of 3-D deterministic fractals, quaternion Julia sets, is outlined. The generation algorithm is then developed using this family as example. Rendering procedures specific to fractal surfaces are then discussed. Finally, the algorithm is compared with its predecessor [14] and applications to other families of 3-D deterministic fractal objects are shown.

2 Dynamics in the Quaternions

The dynamics of quadratic functions have been observed mainly in the complex plane. However, as shown first in 1982 [14], they exist in the 4-D space of the quaternions as well. A discussion of the special properties of Julia sets in the quaternions, for which the ray-tracing algorithm was developed to visualize, is preceded by an introduction to dynamics and quaternion algebra.

2.1 Dynamics of Quadratic Functions

The examples used in this paper are derived from the quadratic function

$$f_\mu(z) = z^2 + \mu, \tag{1}$$

where z is the iterated variable and μ is a constant parameter of the equation.

The dynamics of a function f are expressed as the n-fold application of function f to an initial value z. The result is denoted as $f^n(z)$ and should not be confused with simply raising the result of $f(z)$ to the nth power.

The resulting value $f^n(z)$ is used to classify the initial point z depending on its attraction to infinity. Two sets may be constructed under this classification. The filled-in Julia set $\mathcal{K}_\mu$ and the Mandelbrot set $\mathcal{M}$.

Definition 1 $\mathcal{K}_\mu = \{z : \lim_{n \to \infty} f_\mu^n(z) \not\to \infty\}$

Definition 2
$$\mathcal{M} = \{\mu : \lim_{n \to \infty} f_\mu^n(z_c) \not\to \infty, f_\mu'(z_c) = 0\}$$

Note that z_c is the critical point of the function. There is only one critical point of eq. (1) and it is always 0. Several critical points are common for polynomials of degree 3 or greater.

The interesting property that Julia and Mandelbrot sets share is that they are both fractal [12] possessing detail at every level of magnification.

2.2 The Quaternions

The values z and μ are commonly defined as real or complex. However, these values may be defined in any algebraic system closed under addition and multiplication. One such system, the quaternions [7], possesses the additional benefit of having four dimensions.

Definition 3 *A quaternion value q is a four-tuple consisting of one real part and three imaginaries*

$$q = q_1 + q_i \mathbf{i} + q_j \mathbf{j} + q_k \mathbf{k}$$

where $\mathbf{i}, \mathbf{j}, \mathbf{k}$ are imaginary units,

$$\mathbf{i}^2 = \mathbf{j}^2 = \mathbf{k}^2 = -1. \tag{2}$$

Algebraic operations can be defined in the quaternions by treating the quaternion values as polynomials of three variables $\mathbf{i}, \mathbf{j}, \mathbf{k}$. For example, the coefficients of the sum of two quaternion values may be found by adding their corresponding coefficients.

Quaternion multiplication is also similar to polynomial multiplication but with the special cases

$$\mathbf{ij} = \mathbf{k}; \; \mathbf{jk} = \mathbf{i}; \; \mathbf{ki} = \mathbf{j}, \tag{3}$$

and

$$\mathbf{ji} = -\mathbf{k}; \; \mathbf{kj} = -\mathbf{i}; \; \mathbf{ik} = -\mathbf{j}, \tag{4}$$

revealing an unfortunate side effect of the quaternions: noncommutative multiplication.

2.3 Julia Sets in the Quaternions

By using the rules of quaternion algebra, eq. (1) can be iterated in the quaternions and Julia sets may be computed. Since the complex plane is a subset of the quaternions, the same complex Julia sets exist in the quaternions but often have extensions outside the complex plane. In fact, if μ has an imaginary component, then the extensions are nontrivial, containing more information than their complex subsets.

A subset of these extensions can be visualized in 3-D by examining the intersection of the 4-space with a 3-space such as that spanned by $1, \mathbf{i}, \mathbf{j}$ at $0\mathbf{k}$. It should be mentioned that the Julia sets of eq. (1) in the 3-space spanned by $\mathbf{i}, \mathbf{j}, \mathbf{k}$ at 0 are always concentric spheres centered at the origin [8].

An interesting property about quaternion Julia sets is that given two complex Julia sets differing only by a rotation about the origin, their supersets in 3-D may have completely different shapes. The rotation of the Julia set in the complex plane is computed by incorporating the homeomorphism

$$g_\theta(z) = e^{i\theta} z \tag{5}$$

into the iterated function such that

$$f_{\mu,\theta}(z) = g_\theta(f_\mu(g_\theta^{-1}(z))) \tag{6}$$

which suffices to rotate the positive real axis into the positive imaginary axis and so forth in a counterclockwise manner about the origin in the complex plane. The resulting Julia set is merely rotated in the complex plane but appears quite differently in the quaternions since its intersection with the imaginary 3-space is changed. See [15,8] for details.

3 Ray Tracing 3-D Julia Sets

Ray tracing is one of the more realistic methods of rendering objects. Easily accounting for hidden surfaces and self-shadowing, it also provides a method for displaying reflection, transparency and refraction. Mathematical objects may be ray traced by detecting

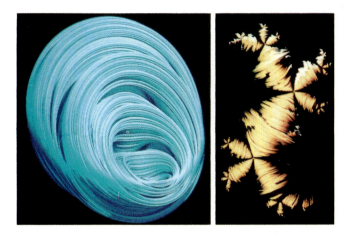

Figure 1: A quaternion Julia set before and after a quarter turn in the complex plane.

their boundaries during a ray-casting step and rendering the surfaces by allowing the ray to be deflected off to a light source.

A naive method to ray trace a quaternion Julia set is to sample each point at a given resolution along each ray. This is not an entirely ridiculous method since it is the basis of some volumetric rendering algorithms [10]. However, it is not practical when applied to fractal objects since each point's classification may rely on a large number of function iterations. With the use of a new ray-tracing mechanism, the amount of sample points per ray is greatly reduced.

3.1 Unbounding Volumes

One method of increasing the speed of ray tracing is the use of *bounding volumes*. A bounding volume, usually a sphere or ellipsoid, envelopes several surfaces such that if a ray does not intersect the bounding volume it does not intersect the surfaces contained in it.

Bounding volumes are quite useful in hastening ray tracing of stochastically-defined fractal surfaces [9,4]. Unfortunately their application to deterministic fractals has not been as successful. However, with the discovery of the distance estimate, we can increase the speed of ray tracing deterministic fractals using *unbounding volumes*.

Unbounding volumes are defined as volumes that do *not* contain any part of the object. Thus, given any point outside the object, the ideal bounding volume is the largest volume that does not intersect the object centered at the point. If this volume is a sphere then its radius is the distance to the object. Given a point and a deterministic fractal object, its exact distance cannot be computed efficiently but it can be

estimated in time proportional to the time it takes to determine if the point is external to the object.

The lower bound of the distance from a point external to the deterministic fractal set is given as

$$d(z) = \frac{\sinh G(z)}{2e^{G(z)}|G'(z)|} \log G(z), \qquad (7)$$

where $G(z)$ is the electrostatic potential at point z and $G'(z)$ is the gradient of this potential. For the quadratic family, the approximation

$$d(z) = \frac{|f^n(z)|}{2|f'^n(z)|} \log f^n(z) \qquad (8)$$

is sufficiently accurate [13,6]. See [17] for the computation of $f'(z)$.

By using a distance estimate we can define an unbounding volume of a deterministic fractal set as a sphere that is guaranteed not to intersect[1] nor contain the set in question. Since the distance estimate may be much smaller than the distance along the ray to the object, several repeated distance calculations must be made as the ray is traversed from eye to surface.

3.2 Ray Traversal

Given the set of unbounding spheres completely surrounding an object, a ray is traversed from the eye through the projection plane to the object, testing and incrementing at each point along the ray. By incrementing by the radius of the unbounding sphere, we leap along the ray until we approach the surface.

As the current point on the ray approaches the surface, the unbounding spheres get smaller and smaller. To hasten convergence, a small number ϵ is defined as the minimum ray increment. This increment should be set to give the best depth resolution with respect to the resolution of the projection plane.

The ray traversal equation may be stated inductively given the eye position r_0 and a point in the projection plane $p_{x,y}$ as

$$r_{n+1} = r_n + m \max d(r_n), \epsilon. \qquad (9)$$

where m is a unit slope vector of the ray

$$m = \frac{p_{x,y} - r_0}{|p_{x,y} - r_0|}. \qquad (10)$$

---

[1]With the exception of a single point.

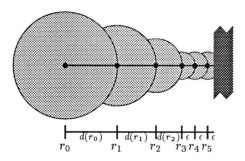

Figure 2: Ray traversal using unbounding spheres.

3.3 Thin Objects

Often the extensions of $\mathcal{K}$ into 3-D are very thin, such as when $\mathcal{K}$ is a dendrite. This creates the possibility that incrementing by ϵ may traverse the ray completely through the object.

This problem has also had manifestations in the 2-D study of these images such as the complex Mandelbrot set. To show that the "islands" off the main continent of $\mathcal{M}$ are connected to it, the Mandelbrot set may be defined computationally as

$$\mathcal{M}_\epsilon = \{z : d(z) < \epsilon\} \tag{11}$$

where $d()$ is the distance estimate as defined in eq. (7). The result is the "hairy" Mandelbrot set [13] revealing its dendritic structures[2].

A similar technique is used to ray trace dendritic sheets in 3-D. By terminating ray traversal when the distance is less than the minimum ray increment, thickness is added to the object while maintaining its structure and detail.

3.4 Avoiding Bad Distance Estimates

When the approximation to eq. (7) is used, it is inaccurate when z is far from the set. This can result in exaggerated distance estimates which could possibly push the ray far into the interior of the object.

To avoid these bad estimates a single bounding volume may be used to contain the fractal set if it can be bounded. Another alternative is to set a maximum distance to increment along the ray.

4 Rendering Fractal Surfaces

The deterministic family of fractals has provided computer graphics with the most complicated borders.

---
[2]Note that these hairs may be seen very clearly as the set $\mathcal{M}_\epsilon - \mathcal{M}$.

The surfaces defined by these borders in 3-D, although quite chaotic, often reveal the structure of the object. A proper rendering of a fractal surface should reveal its order while hinting at its chaos.

Since the surface of a fractal is infinitely convoluted, its normal can only be approximated. The approximated normal signifies the structure of the surface while at finer resolutions the light is scattered in all directions. Thus the surfaces should be diffusely shaded using the Lambertian model.

Also, to achieve the most information from each view, it is often better to use axle light instead of ambient light. By defining a point light source at the eyepoint, every viewable point on the object will receive light and thus even heavily-shadowed sections of the object will reveal information about themselves.

4.1 Normal Approximation

One reason fractal lines, such as the border of $\mathcal{K}$, are so interesting is that they are nondifferentiable. The slope at any point is undefined because closer examination shows that the point has different surroundings. Hence, when expanded to surfaces, 3-D fractal surfaces are nondifferentiable and thus have no exact normal defined.

In order to realistically render these surfaces a shading model must be used which requires the definition of a surface normal. Normals may be approximated by examining a point's relationship with its surroundings. Two approximations have been found to work quite well: Z-buffer neighbors, previously discussed in [14], and the gradient.

4.1.1 Z-buffer Neighbors

As shown in [14], the surface normal of a fractal surface may be approximated as the cross product of two vectors embedded in the surface. Given a buffer of visible z-values Z we can define three points

$$X = \{\epsilon, 0, Z_{x+\epsilon,y} - Z_{x,y}\} \tag{12}$$
$$Y = \{0, \epsilon, Z_{x,y+\epsilon} - Z_{x,y}\} \tag{13}$$
$$O = \{0, 0, Z_{x,y} - Z_{x,y}\} \tag{14}$$

where ϵ is the width of an element in the z-buffer. The surface normal may then be approximated as the normal of the plane defined by these three points.

4.1.2 Gradient Computation

The previous method is a useful normal determination tool if a Z-buffer is maintained during rendering. Ray tracing does not require a Z-buffer so a normal approximation method using a single point in 3-space would be more useful.

This can be accomplished by computing the gradient of a point on the surface. The gradient may be computed in a 3-D density map as

$$
\begin{aligned}
N_x &= D_{x+\epsilon,y,z} - D_{x-\epsilon,y,z} \\
N_y &= D_{x,y+\epsilon,z} - D_{x,y-\epsilon,z} \\
N_z &= D_{x,y,z+\epsilon} - D_{x,y,z-\epsilon}
\end{aligned}
\tag{15}
$$

where $D_{x,y,z}$ is the density at the point x, y, z.

The density function of a deterministic fractal is defined on its exterior and can be any continuous function based loosely on the distance to the set. Two useful functions are the potential $G()$ and the estimated distance $d()$. The latter should be used when possible since it is more closely associated with the actual distance although the former works when a distance estimate is not defined.

Other gradient functions may be defined based on the number of samples taken. The 6-point gradient may be augmented by adding samples from points sharing edges producing an 18-point gradient. By including points sharing corners, a 26-point gradient results.

4.2 Clarity

Since these objects are fractal, they should reveal more detail when closely inspected. However, if the minimum ray increment ϵ is constant, the surfaces will not reveal a finer structure when examined. A variable-resolution system is required such that closer sections of the object are defined at higher resolutions as suggested in [2].

One method of increasing the depth resolution is to set ϵ to a function of distance from the eye. The clarity function $\Gamma_{\alpha,\delta}$ is defined

$$
\Gamma(d) = \alpha d^{\delta}
\tag{16}
$$

given d, the Euclidean distance from the eye to the current location on the ray,

$$
d = |r_n - r_0|.
\tag{17}
$$

The parameter δ is a depth-cueing exponent and α is an empirical proportion defining the depth resolution of the object.

Three effects are defined by varying the depth-cueing exponent. When the clarity function is constant, inverse depth cueing occurs giving the appearance that farther objects have more detail. This may seem useless but is quite adequate when viewing entire fractal objects from a distance. Linear clarity

δ	$\Gamma()$	Effect
0	Constant	Inverse clarity
1	Linear	Even clarity
2	Quadratic	Exaggerated depth

Table 1: Depth-cueing exponents and their effects on renderings

gives an even clarity appearance with close objects appearing as detailed as far. Quadratic depth cueing gives an exaggerated depth cue, blurring distant surfaces.

The α parameter is tuned to balance the equilibrium of order and chaos. Setting α too small will produce a very noisy surface whereas a large α will wash out detail. When defining α a good starting point is to set it to an order of magnitude smaller than the pixel width.

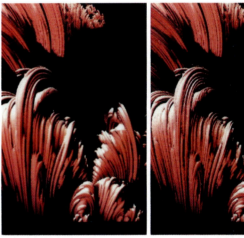

Figure 3: The same Quaternion Julia set rendered twice to show the difference between constant and linear clarity.

Thus, by setting

$$
\epsilon = \Gamma_{\alpha,\delta}(|r_n - r_0|)
\tag{18}
$$

a variable-resolution rendering system is constructed allowing small details of the surfaces to be investigated without overcomputing the other visible surfaces. The increment ϵ may also be used in the gradient computation as the distance along the axes to sample nearby densities.

5 Application to Other Deterministic Fractals

The quaternions are convenient to observe 3-D dynamics since all three dimensions may be spanned by a single variable. Other 3-D spaces may be constructed using multiple real or complex variables. Complex Julia sets form a 3-D object when they are stacked [14,12]. The cubic connectedness locus is a four-dimensional object when its two parameters are complex [5,17]. Also, Iterated Function Systems may be three-dimensional if they are specified with affine transformations of three real variables [1].

5.1 Julia Set Stacks

A Julia set stack may be specified in 3-D as a slice (i.e. zeroset) of the four dimensional space $C \times C$ defined by the two complex variables z and c from eq. 1. By looking at the z-planes and varying some single-dimension function of c to define the third dimension, the Julia sets may be stacked to form a 3-D object.

There currently is no proven distance underestimate for this set although some images may be generated using empirical formulas based on the Mandelbrot set distance estimate.

Figure 4: Stack of Julia sets for $\text{Im}(c) = 0$.

5.2 The Cubic Connectedness Locus

The cubic connectedness locus $\mathcal{C}$ is specified by the cubic function

$$f_{a,b}(z) = z^3 - 3a^2 z + b, \qquad (19)$$

where z is a complex variable and a, b are complex parameters. The parameter a is squared in the equation because the two critical points of the equation are $\pm a$.

Since a and b are both complex, a *double* complex plane is constructed that houses the four-dimensional cubic connectedness locus. The locus in this case consists of two components, $\mathcal{C}^+$ and $\mathcal{C}^-$, based on the status of the appropriate critical point.

Definition 4 $\mathcal{C}^+ = \{a, b : \lim_{n \to \infty} f_{a,b}^n(a) \not\to \infty\}$

Definition 5 $\mathcal{C}^- = \{a, b : \lim_{n \to \infty} f_{a,b}^n(-a) \not\to \infty\}$

A picture of this set may be found in [17], presumably created using the technique outlined in [14].

At the moment, a distance estimate does not exist for this set either. However, the cubic connectedness locus has been proven to be connected [5] suggesting that potential measurement and therefore distance estimation may be possible.

5.3 3-D Iterated Function Systems

The most useful forms of deterministic fractals are Iterated Function Systems or IFS's. An IFS can be created to simulate almost any form using the Collage Theorem [1]. Then, given only the resulting set of iterative equations, the form can be reconstructed.

Recently, deterministic IFS Julia and Mandelbrot set functions have been discovered and their exteriors have been categorized according to escape iterations not unlike their quadratic counterparts [1,19]. This suggests that perhaps potential and distance measurements can be made on these sets as well.

6 Comparison with Boundary Tracking

The ray-tracing algorithm's predecessor, Boundary Tracking [14], generates 3-D Julia sets by first locating a starting point on the boundary of the object and then recursively detecting its neighbors until the entire boundary is scanned. To converge, this algorithm must constantly verify that neighboring points have not been previously tested, which requires the efficient storage of all previously generated points. Thus, the Boundary Tracking algorithm runs in object-space and therefore object-time[3].

The main advantage of Boundary Tracking is that objects are only generated once and may be repositioned as often as desired, requiring only re-rendering. Using the ray-tracing technique, repositioning of the object requires re-generation of the viewable sections of the object as well as re-rendering. However, since the image-time ray-tracing algorithm generates these objects more efficiently than the object-time Boundary Tracking algorithm, it is the best choice for parameter-space animations such as varying μ in eq. (1), θ in eq. (5) or the k axis component of the viewable subspace of the quaternions.

---

[3]See [20] for a discussion of image-space vs. object-space and image-time vs. object-time.

The main disadvantage of Boundary Tracking is that it requires storage of every point in the object. This amount of storage can approach cubic proportions since the number of points defining a surface is $O(r^D)$, the resolution r of the surface raised to its fractal dimension D [12]. The ray tracing technique, using image-space, requires exactly $r^2 + O(1)$ space[4], the storage resources of a graphics workstation frame buffer.

Another problem with Boundary Tracking is constant resolution. However, a variable-resolution Boundary Tracking algorithm was developed to create [16] by generating certain sections of the set already known to be closely examined in the fly-by at higher resolutions. Although Boundary Tracking saves computing time by generating the object only once, the ray-tracing algorithm is the better choice for fly-bys since its dynamic resolution allows a more realistic inspection of the surface.

Finally, ray tracing allows certain special effects such as reflections and refractions. The former produces the interesting effect of revealing only macroscopic images of its environment; the subtle details are lost in the convoluted interreflections of the fractal surface. Refraction as well as simple transparency should be avoided until a reliable internal distance estimate is developed to prevent minimum increments in the interior of the sets.

7 Conclusion

The research on this project began as a method of visualizing quaternion Julia sets in 3-D using the resources of a common computer graphics workstation. The first attempt relied on the Inverse Iteration method of generating Julia sets [11,18] which operated in image-space and object-time but produced less than satisfactory results due to inherent problems of the process itself magnified by the addition of an extra dimension [8]. The ray-tracing solution, being forward iterative, does not experience the problems of the Inverse Iteration method while still requiring only image-space.

7.1 Parallel Implementation

The current implementation of the algorithm runs on an AT&T Pixel Machine with 64 parallel processors each running at about 10 MFLOPS. The architecture

of the Pixel Machine, each processor connected only to its portion of the frame buffer, dictates that image-space, image-time algorithms will run at the most optimal level.

The ray-tracing code is replicated into 64 equivalent programs running simultaneously as if in a race, each generating and rendering its $\frac{1}{64}$th of the image. Of course, the first operation of each program is to find out which pixel with respect to the entire frame buffer it is working on.

Currently, full screen images (1280 × 1024) take about an hour to generate. When positioning the object, lower image resolutions are used to create a more interactive environment. Also, reducing the depth resolution will increase the speed of the algorithm.

7.2 Acknowledgments

The authors wish to thank Alan Norton and Charlie Gunn for their communications, AT&T for its major grant to the Electronic Visualization Laboratory which supported this research, Maggie Rawlings for her artistic advice with the illustrations, and Tom DeFanti and Maxine Brown for their assistance with the manuscript. This research would not have been possible without the efforts of the faculty, staff and students of the Electronic Visualization Laboratory.

References

[1] Barnsley, M. F. *Fractals Everywhere*. Academic Press, New York, 1988.

[2] Barr, A. H. Ray tracing deformed surfaces. *Computer Graphics 20*, 4 (1986), 287–296.

[3] Blanchard, P. Disconnected Julia sets. *Chaotic Dynamics and Fractals* (1986), 181–201.

[4] Bouville, C. Bounding ellipsoids for ray-fractal intersection. *Computer Graphics 19*, 3 (1985), 45–51.

[5] Branner, B., and Hubbard, J. H. The iteration of cubic polynomials, Part I: The global topology of the parameter space. *Acta Mathematica 160*, 3 (1988), 143–206.

[6] Fisher, Y. *The Science of Fractal Images*. Springer-Verlag, New York, 1988, ch. Exploring the Mandelbrot Set, pp. 287–296.

[7] Hamilton, W. R. *Elements of Quaternions*, 3rd ed. Vol. 1–2, Chelsea Publishing Company, New York, 1969.

---

[4]If the gradient normal approximation method is used, a Z-buffer is not required. The only other considerable amount of memory used is a small array the size of the maximum allowable iteration count used to optimize the computation of the distance estimate [17].

[8] Hart, J. C. *Image Space Algorithms for Visualizing Quaternion Julia Sets.* Master's thesis, University of Illinois at Chicago, 1989.

[9] Kajiya, J. T. New techniques for ray tracing procedurally defined objects. *ACM Transactions on Graphics 2*, 3 (1983), 161–181.

[10] Levoy, M. Display of surfaces from volume data. *IEEE Computer Graphics and Applications 8*, 3 (1988), 29–37.

[11] Mandelbrot, B. B. Fractal aspects of the iteration of $z \rightarrow \lambda z(1 - z)$ for complex λ and z. *Annals New York Academy of Sciences 357* (1980), 249–259.

[12] Mandelbrot, B. B. *The Fractal Geometry of Nature*, 2nd ed. Freeman, San Francisco, 1982.

[13] Milnor, J. *Computers in Geometry and Topology.* Marcel Dekker, Inc., 1989, ch. Self-similarity and hairiness in the Mandelbrot set, pp. 211–257.

[14] Norton, V. A. Generation and rendering of geometric fractals in 3-D. *Computer Graphics 16*, 3 (1982), 61–67.

[15] Norton, V. A. Julia sets in the quaternions. To appear in *Computers and Graphics.*

[16] Norton, V. A., and Melton, E. A close encounter in the fourth dimension. *SIGGRAPH Video Review 39* (1988), 30.

[17] Peitgen, H. *The Science of Fractal Images.* Springer-Verlag, New York, 1988, ch. Fantastic Deterministic Fractals, pp. 169–218.

[18] Peitgen, H., and Richter, P. H. *The Beauty of Fractals.* Springer-Verlag, New York, 1986.

[19] Prusinkiewicz, P., and Sandness, G. Koch curve as attractors and repellers. *IEEE Computer Graphics and Applications 8*, 6 (1988), 26–40.

[20] Sutherland, I., Sproul, R., and Schumacker, R. A characterization of ten hidden-surface algorithms. *Computing Surveys 6*, 1 (1974), 1–55.

Figure 5: A dendritic quaternion Julia set, set in a sea whose waves are periodic functions of the distance estimate.

Figure 6: Close up of the surface of the quaternion Julia set shown in fig. 3.

Figure 7: Close up of an interesting section of the Julia set for $\theta = 110°$

Guaranteed Ray Intersections with Implicit Surfaces

Devendra Kalra
Alan H. Barr
Computer Science Department
California Institute of Technology
Pasadena, California 91125

Abstract

In this paper, we present a robust and mathematically sound ray-intersection algorithm for implicit surfaces. The algorithm is guaranteed to numerically find the nearest intersection of the surface with a ray, and is guaranteed not to miss fine features of the surface. It does not require fine tuning or human choice of interactive parameters. Instead, it requires two upper bounds: "L" that limits the net rate of change of the implicit surface function $f(x, y, z)$ and "G" that limits the rate of change of the gradient. We refer to an implicit surface with these rate limits as an "LG-implicit surface."

Existing schemes to intersect a ray with an implicit surface have typically been guaranteed to work only for a limited set of implicit functions, such as quadric surfaces or polynomials, or else have been ad-hoc and have not been guaranteed to work. Our technique significantly extends the ability to intersect rays with implicit surfaces in a guaranteed fashion.

CR Categories and Subject Descriptors: I.3.3 (Picture/Image Generation) – display algorirthms; I.3.5 (Computational Geometry and Object Modeling) – Curve, surface, solid and object representations, Geometric algorithms, languages and systems; I.3.7 (Three-Dimensional Graphics and Realism) – Color, shading, shadowing and texture, Visible line / surface algorithms;

Keywords: Implicit Surfaces, Ray Tracing, Rendering, Sampling, Subdivision, Lipschitz Constant.

1 Introduction

The task of intersecting rays with implicit surfaces (see Figure 1) is an important part of the theory and application of ray casting and ray tracing. Implicit functions can be used to represent some useful and interesting surfaces. They also have a nice composition property in that they can be combined in geometrically useful and concise ways to generate new implicit functions. Examples of these are the algebraic surfaces introduced by Blinn [BLINN 82] and extensions (Figure 16 and 20).

The reader might be surprised to find that it is impossible to create an algorithm (based solely on the evaluation of the implicit function at points in space) which is guaranteed to correctly intersect a ray with an *arbitrary* implicit surface. For any algorithm that could be constructed, there exist troublesome functions f(x,y,z) for which important parts of the surfaces are missed. Figure 2 illustrates this problem. In this example, we would need information about the existence of a spike in between the sample points, which is not available from the values of the function obtained at the sample points.

Thus, to guarantee ray intersections with implicit surfaces, some sort of auxiliary information is needed. In our case, we have chosen this auxiliary information to be the L and G rate limits.

©1989   ACM-0-89791-312-4/89/007/0297 $00.75

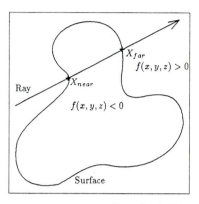

Figure 1: An implicit surface is defined by $f(x, y, z) = 0$. $f(x, y, z)$ is negative inside the surface, positive outside the surface and zero on the surface. The ray intersects the surface at X_{near} and X_{far}.

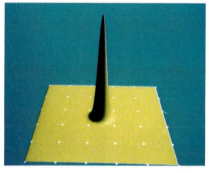

Figure 2: A spike function demonstrates some of the difficulties of sampling without sufficient information about the function being sampled. The above surface at each of the samples has zero curvature; the samples do not indicate the presence of a spike since the spike falls between the sampling points.

1.1 A Need For "Guaranteed" Algorithms

Some readers might question the utility of developing an apparently complex algorithm using the mathematical machinery of L and G bounds. They could also question the need to directly render complex modeling primitives, instead of converting into more easily renderable objects such as polygons. Finally, they might question the utility of implicit functions at all. They could believe that there would be no need for surface types beyond bicubic patches, quadric surfaces, and polygons for their modeling needs.

The answer to the first question is straightforward. Given the L and G numeric rate constants, our algorithm actually is quite simple and easy to implement. The amount of code for the algorithm is relatively small and is easily put into a standard ray tracing program.

More importantly, however, the algorithm *guarantees* that we will find all of the correct ray intersections in the entire image. If we were to first convert the implicit model into polygons, we would have to produce a "guaranteed" polygonal tesselation of the surface. This is a non-trivial task for general implicit surfaces, and could depend on the camera view angles and viewing parameters of the scene. (Our technique can be adapted to produce guaranteed polygonalizations, but we feel direct rendering is easier).

Even in directly rendering a geometric primitive, rather than its polygonal tesselation, a "guaranteed" technique, which does not require any corrective interaction or fine tuning of parameters by a human being, is most valuable. This is especially attractive to people making computer animation. In fact, we frequently use computer animation as a means to verify the accuracy of our rendering algorithms. Imagine running long scripts to make a movie and then finding that frame number 129 has pixel dropouts because the frame uses a particular camera angle and parameters for the rendering algorithm that worked for other frames but do not work for this frame. The recourse is to find the right set of parameters for this frame and restart the animation until we notice other anomalies. With a guaranteed "direct" method, one is assured of the correctness of the whole sequence, without re-rendering frames.

Even in making still-frames, much time is spent modeling a scene. With an algorithm that guarantees the correctness of the rendering, there is less to worry about, as changes are made to other object parameters of the scene.

The utility of having a wider variety of surface types can be seen in Figures 16 and 20. The polygonal or patch representation for these objects would be more difficult to specify and would require more data than implicit techniques.

Finally, developing a "direct" guaranteed algorithm that works every time without any searches through a parameter space was an exhilarating research experience for us.

1.2 Previous Methods To Render Implicit Surfaces

An implicit surface S is defined by a function $S : f(\mathbf{x}) = 0$. The function is negative inside the surface and positive outside (Figure 1).

Polynomial Implicit Functions

The efforts to render implicit surfaces have been two-fold. The first approach has been to limit types of implicit functions. [HANRAHAN 83] limited the implicit functions to be polynomial functions of spatial variables. Using some results presented in [USPENSKY 48] and [COLLINS and AKRITAS] and a theorem due to Descartes, this method gurarantees the nearest intersection of a ray with a polynomially defined implicit surface. [MIDDLEDITCH et al 85] have also used polynomially defined surfaces to generate some kinds of blend surfaces.

Polygonizing Implicit Surfaces

The second approach has tried to render more general implicit surfaces by polygonizing implicit surfaces.

There is a basic difficulty with using a naive polygonization of a surface. With a view independent polygonization algorithm, we could either end up rendering too many polygons when the object covers very small number of pixels on the screen or rendering too few polygons when the objects covers a large area on the screen. [VON HERZEN 87] has attempted to deal with view dependent polygonization. On the other hand, ray casting automatically samples an object at a level that depends on the object's coverage of the screen.

It is also more natural and easier to model some objects in one modeling domain than another. The pictures in this paper have been modeled in a sculptor's paradigm of adding a little clay here or removing a little clay there. This can be done most naturally with blended implicit functions.

However, some researchers have polygonized implicit surfaces with varying success. The schemes that try to polygonize implicit surfaces compute the value of $f(\mathbf{x})$ defining the surface for points P_i on a grid. These methods consider segments at whose two endpoints $f(\mathbf{x})$ has opposite signs. Then the intersection of S with this segment is approximated by various methods such as linear interpolation. These "intersections" along the edges of the rectangular boxes forming the sampling lattice are then connected according to some heuristics to form polygons. These polygons are then rendered. See [WYVILL 87[1]], [WYVILL 87[2]], and [BLOOMENTHAL 87].

Forming polygons out of approximate intersections along the box edges is heuristic and leaves ambiguities in many cases when more

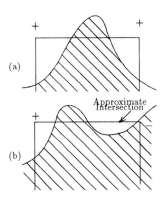

Figure 3: Possible problems with a naive Implicit Surface Polygonizing Algorithm; (a) small features are liable to missed because both sample points are outside the surface, (b) incorrect intersections may be computed because of strange behaviour of the function near the sample points.

than one possibility exists. A second more important problem with the above algorithm is that they are based only on the values of the implicit function at certain points. As noted before, this means that features finer than the sampling grid will be either completely ignored (Figure 3(a)) or the approximate intersections formed will be grossly incorrect (Figure 3(b)). There is not enough information in the function values even to provide an estimate of the size of the sampling grid.

In section two, we describe our mathematical approach. In section 3, we describe an overview of the algorithms, while in section 4 we describe the algorithms in more detail. In sections 5 and 6, we describe our results and conclusions, and provide supplemental mathematical information in the appendices.

2 Our Approach: Creating LG-Surfaces

We present an algorithm that

a) Guarantees that the smallest features of the surface are sampled.

b) Obtains the nearest intersection of a ray from the origin of the ray with the implicit surface S represented by the implicit function $f(\mathbf{x})$.

We do not generate polygons, but obtain guaranteed numerical intersections of rays with the implicit surface.

2.1 Mathematical Preliminaries:

We first present some mathematical definitions and preliminaries:

Definition of Implicit Surface:

A general implicit surface S is defined by (See Figure 1)

$$f(x, y, z) = 0$$

or, in vector notation,

$$f(\mathbf{x}) = 0$$

Ray Definition

We define a ray via:

$$\mathbf{x} = \boldsymbol{\alpha} t + \boldsymbol{\beta}, \quad t \geq 0,$$

where vector $\boldsymbol{\alpha}$ is a unit vector ray direction and vector $\boldsymbol{\beta}$ is the origin of the ray corrsponding to $t = 0$.

Definition of $F(t)$

Given a function $f(\mathbf{x}) = 0$ of spatial variables $\mathbf{x} = (x, y, z)$, we substitute

$$\mathbf{x} = \boldsymbol{\alpha} t + \boldsymbol{\beta}$$

into $f(\mathbf{x})$ to define

$$F(t) = f(\boldsymbol{\alpha} t + \boldsymbol{\beta}) \qquad (1)$$

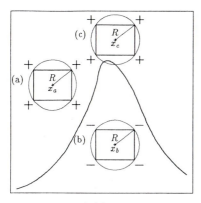

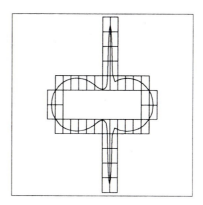

Figure 4: Given a point x_0, $r = f(x_0)/\mathcal{L}$ is the radius of the sphere S around x_0 such that $f(x)$ does not change sign in S. $\mathcal{L}$ is the Lipschitz constant in equation 3 in the region of S. Spheres (a) and (b) are guaranteed not to intersect the surface since Lipschitz radii $r_a = f(x_a)/\mathcal{L}_a < R$ and $r_b = f(x_b)/\mathcal{L}_b < R$. However, $r_c > R$ and S_c may intersect the surface.

Figure 5: The straddling boxes of a surface as found by part A, Space Pruning step of the algorithm. The figure shows a two-dimensional slice through the three dimensional collection of boxes.

Definition of $g(t)$

We now define a new function

$$
\begin{aligned}
g(t) &= \frac{dF}{dt} \\
&= \boldsymbol{\alpha} \cdot \nabla f(\mathbf{x})|_{\alpha t + \beta}
\end{aligned}
\tag{2}
$$

Note that $g(t)$ is the directional derivative of $f(\mathbf{x})$ along the ray direction $\boldsymbol{\alpha}$ ('g' relating to "gradient").

Definition Of Lipschitz Constant $\mathcal{L}$

A (positive) real number $\mathcal{L}$ is called a *Lipschitz constant* on a function $f(\mathbf{x})$ in a region $\mathcal{R}$, if given any two points $\mathbf{x}_1$ and $\mathbf{x}_2$ in $\mathcal{R}$, the following condition holds:

$$
\|f(\mathbf{x}_1) - f(\mathbf{x}_2)\| < \mathcal{L} \|\mathbf{x}_1 - \mathbf{x}_2\|
\tag{3}
$$

where $\|.\|$ is a vector norm.

If the constant $\mathcal{L}$ exists, a *lipschitz condition* is said to exist on the function $f(\mathbf{x})$ in the region $\mathcal{R}$. (See Figure 4.)

We also note that other schemes based on Lipschitz Constants have been used for accurate sampling of parametric surfaces by [VON HERZEN 87], [VON HERZEN 88] and [VON HERZEN 89].

2.2 LG-surface Description

We define an LG surface to be an implicit function $f(x, y, z)$ which has bounds on the net rate of change of the function and its directional derivative (that we call L and G). Mathematically, these bounds are the *Lipschitz constants* as defined above; Lipschitz constants have other useful applications in applied mathematics and numerical analysis (see [GEAR 71] and [LIN AND SEGEL74]).

Definition of LG-surfaces

Let **L** be the Lipschitz constant for the function $f(\mathbf{x})$ in a three-dimensional region $\mathcal{R}$ and **G** be the Lipschitz constant for the corresponding function $g(t)$ in a closed interval $\mathcal{T} = [t_1, t_2]$, ie.,

$$
\|f(\mathbf{x}_a) - f(\mathbf{x}_b)\| \le L \|\mathbf{x}_a - \mathbf{x}_b\|
\tag{4}
$$

$$
\|g(t_a) - g(t_b)\| \le G \|t_a - t_b\|.
\tag{5}
$$

for any $x_a, x_b \in \mathcal{R}$ and any $t_a, t_b \in \mathcal{T}$.

An implicit surface S represented by an implicit function $f(\mathbf{x}) = 0$ is an **LG-implicit surface**, if the Lipschitz constants **L** and **G** as defined above exist and are computable.

2.3 How To Compute L's and G's

It can be seen from equation (3) that a Lipschitz constant is a measure of the maximum rate of change of a function in a region over which the function is defined. This can be seen by dividing equation 3 by $\|\mathbf{x}_1 - \mathbf{x}_2\|$, taking the limit as $\mathbf{x}_1 \to \mathbf{x}_2$ and using the definition of derivative.

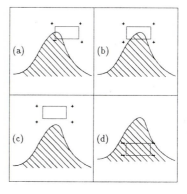

Figure 6: What is straddling? The box vertices straddle the surface if at least one of the vertices of the box is inside and at least one of the vertices is outside the surface (case (a)). Cases (b), (c) and (d) are all non-straddling.

Computing L:

Given a three dimensional rectangular region $\mathcal{R}$, we shall call the Lipschitz constant for $f(\mathbf{x})$ for $\mathcal{R}$ to be L. L is equal to or greater than the maximum rate of change of $f(\mathbf{x})$ in $\mathcal{R}$. That is

$$
L \ge \max_{\mathcal{R}} \left| \nabla f(\mathbf{x}) \right|
\tag{6}
$$

Computing G:

Given a one dimensional closed interval $\mathcal{T} = [t_1, t_2]$, we call the Lipschitz constant for $g(t)$ in $\mathcal{T}$ to be G. T is equal to or greater than the maximum rate of change of $g(t)$ in $\mathcal{T}$. That is

$$
G \ge \max_{\mathcal{T}} \left| \frac{dg}{dt} \right|
\tag{7}
$$

The algorithm works faster for smaller values of L and G.

3 Rendering LG-surfaces

We render LG-surfaces by casting rays and obtaining intersections of the ray with the surface using two algorithms, A and B.

Algorithm A) Space Pruning

Algorithm A is an efficiency measure. Even if algorithm A is not used, the ray intersection method in algorithm B is guaranteed to work.

This algorithm prunes away large parts of space that are guaranteed not to contain any part of the LG-surface as in Figure 5. We obtain a volume $\mathcal{V}$, composed of non-overlapping rectangular boxes, that contains the whole surface. The vertices of each of the boxes in $\mathcal{V}$ straddle the surface (figure 6). This initial pruning reduces the space in which we have to search for intersections of rays with the surface.

Algorithm B) Ray Intersection

In algorithm B, the volume $\mathcal{V}$ in space generated in the algorithm A is used to intersect a ray with the surface. The rectangular boxes composing $\mathcal{V}$ are intersected with a ray in order of appearance along the ray. In any box, if one or more intersection exists, the nearest intersection is determined and we are done with this ray. The algorithm guarantees that if an intersection in the box exists, the intersection is found. Further, if more than one intersection exists, the nearest one is computed (nearest to the origin $t = 0$ of the ray $\alpha t + \beta$).

We now discuss each algorithm in more detail.

3.1 Part A: Pruning Away Empty Regions Of Space

The vertices of a rectangular box are said to *straddle* an implicit surface if at least one of the vertices lie inside the surface and at least one of the vertices lie outside. In Figure 6, part (a) shows a straddling box. We do not consider the box vertices in part (b) to be straddling even though the box itself contains a part of the surface. Boxes (c) and (d) are obviously non-straddling. The sign of $f(\mathbf{x})$, the inside-outside function for the surface tells if the point $\mathbf{x}$ is inside or outside the surface.

Algorithm A (Space Pruning) of the algorithm is shown in pseudo code in Figure 7 and in pictures in Figure 8. In this algorithm, we start with a bounding box that surrounds the surface of interest (Figure 8, step 1). This bounding box is subdivided (Figure 8, step 2) to some level n and sub-boxes guaranteed not to contain any portions of the surface are thrown away ((Figure 8, step 6 Box B_1). Only boxes that straddle the surface are kept (Figure 8, step 4 Box B_4). By keeping the boxes that only straddle the surface, each box is guaranteed to contain a part of the surface and we get a collection of boxes that lie close to the surface.

Given a sub-box B, how do we decide if it is to be accepted and not pruned away?

If B straddles the surface, it certainly contains a part of the surface and it is kept (Figure 8, step 4 box B_4).

If B does not straddle the surface, it still might contain a portion of the surface (Figure 8, step 4 box B_3). The L Lipschitz constant tells us if B does not contain any part of the surface: Let $\mathbf{x}_0$ be the center of B, and d be half the length of the principal diagonal of B. Since the maximum rate of change with respect to distance of $f(\mathbf{x})$ is L and the maximum distance of any point in B from $\mathbf{x}_0$ is d, the maximum change in the value of $f(\mathbf{x})$ in B from $f(\mathbf{x}_0)$ is Ld. Hence if

$$|f(\mathbf{x}_0)| > Ld \tag{8}$$

then $f(\mathbf{x})$ is guaranteed to stay the same sign that it has at $\mathbf{x}_0$ and never assume a value of zero in B and hence B can be thrown away (fig 7, steps 5 and 6, box B_1).

If B does not satisfy condition in equation (8), it is subdivided into eight sub-boxes and each of the sub-boxes is checked again to check that it satisfies either the straddling condition or equation (8). In Figure 8, step 7, B_3 is subdivided and upon subdivision we find some sub-boxes that straddle the surface. For box B_2, none of the sub-boxes straddle the surface and the subdivision is stopped after condition (8) is satisfied.

Figure 5 shows a surface and its straddling box forming $\mathcal{V}$ as found by our algorithm.

This initial subdivision in algorithm A is not an essential requirement for the algorithm. It is guaranteed to work even if the initial subdivision level $n = 0$, i.e., no initial subdivision of the bounding box is performed. The level of initial subdivision does effect the performance of the ray-intersection.

Subdivision Termination

Is it guaranteed that the subdivision algorithm terminates?

If any of the vertices of a box lies exactly on the surface, condition (8) will never be satisfied. Even if we compute the smallest possible L, we can meet the condition $|f(\mathbf{x}_0)| = Ld$ rather than the inequality. Hence, we have to stop subdivision at some level if it does not stop in the natural course of the algorithm. Since we compute the intersections numerically, stopping the intersection when the box size becomes smaller than the tolerance of the numerical method is a natural condition to use. Experimentally, in all the pictures we have computed

Step	1.	Compute a bounding box B for surface
	2.	Subdivide B to a level n
	3.	For each sub-box b
	4	Accept b if b straddles surface
		else
	5.	Compute L for b
	6.	If $|f(\mathbf{x}_0)| > Ld$
	7.	Reject b
		else
	8.	Subdivide b into eight sub-boxes
	9.	For each sub-box of b,
	10.	Repeat the above

Figure 7: Algorithm A prunes away parts of space guaranteed not to contain any portion of the surface. The algorithm is shown in pictures in Figure 8. The steps in this figure and in Figure 8 correspond.

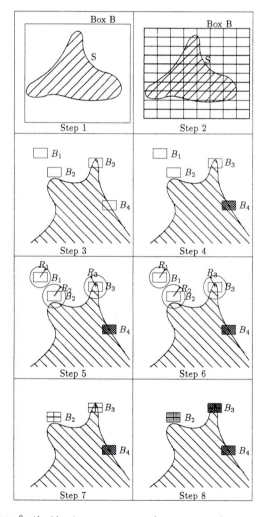

Figure 8: Algorithm A prunes away parts of space guaranteed not to contain any portion of an LG-surface. Cross hatched boxes are added to $\mathcal{V}$, lightly shaded boxes are thrown away. The pseudocode for the algorithm is given in Figure 7. The steps in this figure and in Figure 7 correspond.

so far, such a terminating condition has never taken place. The straddling condition occurred before the box reached the numerical precision limit.

3.2 Part B: Intersection of a Ray with an LG-surface

This part of the algorithm is designed to guarantee finding the intersection of a ray with an LG-surface nearest to the origin of the ray.

In algorithm A, we have formed a set of boxes that comprise a volume $\mathcal{V}$ and the vertices of each of the boxes in $\mathcal{V}$ straddle the surface. The volume $\mathcal{V}$ completely encloses the surface of interest. Hence all intersections lie in $\mathcal{V}$. $\mathcal{V}$ is composed of non-overlapping boxes. The ray intersection problem is now broken down into a simpler problem:

a) Find the box in $\mathcal{V}$ nearest to the origin of the ray.

b) Compute any ray intersections in this box; if none exist, consider the next box in order.

The problem of finding the nearest box is described later in section 4. Here we consider the following problem.

Problem Statement

Intersection of a ray with the surface in a straddling box: Given a ray and a box B whose vertices straddle the surface, either ensure that there is no intersection of the ray with the surface in B or find the nearest intersection.

Preliminaries

We wish to compute intersections along the ray $\alpha t + \beta$. Hence, we are interested in the behavior of $f(\mathbf{x})$ along the ray. As defined in equation 1, $F(t)$ represents the behavior of $f(\mathbf{x})$ along the ray and

$$g(t) = \frac{dF}{dt}.$$

An intersection is given by values of t such that

$$F(t) = 0.$$

The reliability of our ray intersection algorithm depends on our ability to determine if $g(t)$ becomes zero in an interval. The following two cases describe two important situations, one in which there is exactly one ray-surface intersection in an interval, and second in which there is none.

1. If $F(t_1)$ and $F(t_2)$ are of opposite signs at two points t_1 and t_2 along the ray, $t_1 < t_2$, there is at least one intersection between t_1 and t_2. Further, if $g(t) = dF/dt$ does not become zero between t_1 and t_2, there is exactly one intersection between the ray and the surface in the interval from t_1 to t_2 (see below[1]).

2. If $F(t_1)$ and $F(t_2)$ have the same sign at t_1 and t_2 along the ray, $t_1 < t_2$ and $g(t) = df/dt$ does not become zero between t_1 and t_2, there is no intersection between the ray and the surface in the interval from t_1 to t_2.

Given that G is the Lipschitz constant for $g(t)$ in an interval $[t_1, t_2]$ and

$$t_m = (t_1 + t_2)/2 \qquad d = (t_2 - t_1)/2,$$

if

$$|g(t_m)| > Gd \qquad (9)$$

in $[t_1, t_2]$, then $g(t)$ nevers becomes zero in the interval. (G is equal or more than the maximum rate of change of $g(t)$ and d is the maximum distance along the ray from t_m.) Gd is the maximum possible change in $g(t)$ from $g(t_m)$.

```
1.   Intersect ray αt + β with box B in t₁ and t₂, t₂ > t₁
2.   Compute G with respect to midpoint tₘ = t₂ + t₁/2
     Let half distance d = (t₂ − tₘ)/2
3.   if |g(tₘ)| > Gd
4.       if F(t₁) and F(t₂) are of opposite signs
5.           there is exactly one intersection:
                 compute intersection via newton
                 iteration or regula falsi
         else
6.           there is no intersection in the
                 interval [t₁, t₂]
     else
7.       ||g(tₘ)|| < Gd
8.           subdivide into two subintervals [t₁, tₘ]
             and [tₘ, t₂]
9.           and repeat steps 2 to 8 on each subinterval
             until tₘ − t₁ < ε or t₂ − tₘ < ε
```

Figure 9: Algorithm to intersect a ray with an LG-surface. Given a box B, determine if there is no intersection in B or else compute the nearest intersection. ϵ is the tolerance of the numerical method used to compute the intersection.

B) Ray Intersection Algorithm

The ray intersection algorithm is delineated in Figure 9.

We will use the above observations to design our ray intersection algorithm. We are looking for the interval $[t_1, t_2]$ nearest to the origin of the ray with exactly one intersection. Given a box B, we will make decisions about closest intersections of the surface S and the segment of the ray in the box.

Let the ray intersect box B in points P_1 and P_2 corresponding to the ray parameter values t_1 and t_2. Let t_m be the midpoint of the segment between t_1 and t_2,

$$t_m = \frac{t_2 + t_1}{2}, \qquad d = (t_2 - t_1)/2.$$

How to Find a Ray intersection

1. If $F(t_1)$ and $F(t_2)$ are of opposite signs and $||g(t_m)|| > Gd$, there is exactly one intersection between t_1 and t_2. The intersection is computed numerically using a newton iteration and regula falsi method.

2. If $F(t_1)$ and $F(t_2)$ have the same sign and $||g(t_m)|| > Gd$, there is no intersection between t_1 and t_2. The next box B along the ray is considered. If there are no more boxes along the ray, the ray does not hit the surface.

If equation 9 is not satisfied in $[t_1, t_2]$, the interval is sudivided into two sub-intervals at t_m and the two subintervals $[t_1, t_m]$ and $[t_m, t_2]$ tested in order.

Interval Subdivision Termination

The termination condition of the interval subdivision algorithm needs equation 9 to be satisfied. Since both G and d are positive, if $g(t)$ becomes exactly zero along the ray, this condition is never satisfied and the algorithm will not terminate naturally. This situation occurs at the *silhouette edges* of the surface[2]. At a point P_s on the silhouette edge, the gradient of $f(\mathbf{x})$ is perpendicular to the ray and hence the directional derivative $g(t)$ is zero. Hence at P_s condition (9) will never be satisfied.

To avoid an infinite subdivision, one has to stop when $|t_2 - t_1|$ becomes less than the precision of the numerical method used to compute the intersections, typically of the order of 10^{-8}. The surface will be smooth within the same error tolerance. The above considerations also imply that the algorithm spends more time near the silhouette edges. This is shown in Figure 12.

3.3 Note about the Algorithm

Note that the Space Pruning algorithm has to be done only once for each surface. The same volume $\mathcal{V}$ can be used repeatedly to make multiple pictures of that surface. Hence if we wish to make many

---

[1] If a continuous function f(t) attains two consecutive zero values at t_1 and t_2, by the mean value theorem, there exists at least one point between t_1 and t_2 where $df/dt = 0$.

[2] A point P_s on a surface $S : f(\mathbf{x}) = 0$ is said to be on a silhouette edge with respect to a view point P_v, if the ray originating from P_v and passing through P_s is tangent to S.

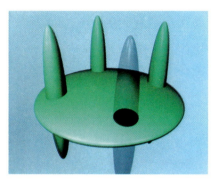

Figure 10: The procedure of creating the blended solid of Figure 11. The transparent ellipsoid is a negative function. All other ellipsoids are positive ellipsoids. Each ellipsoid has a different "blending factor".

Figure 11: A blended solid made out of four positive ellipsoids and one negative solid. The whole solid is defined by one composite implicit function.

images of the same surface as say, in a movie, we should spend a little more extra computation in the Space Pruning algorithm by using a finer initial subdivision (since finer boxes save computation in the ray-intersection algorithm).

4 Implementation Details of the LG-Surface Ray Intersection Algorithm

In this section we describe some details of our implementation of the algorithm and the kind of surfaces that we have considered so far for implementation. We are building a library of L's and G's for various functions that will be useful to implement more surfaces.

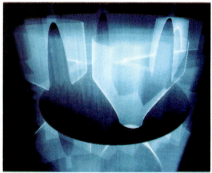

Figure 12: Pseudo color picture of Figure 11 showing that the ray-intersection algorithm spends more time at the silhouette edges. Brighter regions consumed more time.

4.1 Implementing A New Surface

To add a new surface to be rendered by our algorithm, the following functions have to be defined for the surface:

```
double inside_outside(x, y, z)
double x, y, z;
```
   inside_outside() returns the value of the implicit inside-outside function $f(\mathbf{x})$ of the surface. $f(\mathbf{x})$ is negative for points inside the surface and positive for points outside.

```
double lipschitz_constant(box_min, box_max)
double box_min[3], box_max[3];
```
   lipschitz_constant() returns the value of a Lipschitz Constant for the surface in the box bounded by two vertices box_max and box_min. Note that the value returned need not be the best estimate of the Lipschitz Constant. In fact, even a global Lipschitz Constant may be returned everytime. However, the algorithm is computationally more efficient for tighter estimates of Lipschitz Constants. The correctness of the algorithm remains unchanged irrespective of the tightness of the estimate of the Lipschitz constant.

```
double grad_lipschitz_constant(ray, t1, t2)
raytype ray;
double t1, t2;
```
   grad_lipschitz_constant() returns the value of a Lipschitz Constant G, the directional derivative of $f(\mathbf{x})$ along the ray, between the ray parameters t1 and t2. Again, we do not need the tightest value of G, although tight bounds will save computation.

4.2 Computing A Bounding Box

To start the algorithm, a bounding box of the surface is required. How a bounding box is computed, of course, depends on the type of surface being considered. It should be, however, noted that the algorithm will work on any given bounding box. The algorithm will just render **all** the portions of the surface in the given box. In addition, a conservative estimate of the bounding box, too large a bounding box, penalizes mostly the first algorithm. Since a major portion of the bounding box that is guraranteed not to contain any part of the surface is pruned away in the first algorithm, the ray intersection in the second algorithm does not lose in computational efficiency much even with a large initial bounding box.

4.3 Surfaces Considered So Far

Admittedly, computing L's and G's for a general function $f(\mathbf{x})$ might require some mathematical prowess. We have computed L's and G's for some special surfaces to test our algorithm and have computed a series of images. As explained in the future work section, we are enlarging the library of available surfaces. This will be available in a forthcoming Caltech Technical Report.
   The first example is an ellipsoid for which

$$f(x, y, z) = ax^2 + by^2 + cz^2 - 1,$$

For a rectangular region $\mathcal{R}$ bounded by $(x_{min}, y_{min}, z_{min})$ and $(x_{max}, y_{max}, z_{max})$, L is given by,

$$L_{\mathcal{R}} = 2\sqrt{a^2|x|_{max}^2 + b^2|y|_{max}^2 + c^2|z|_{max}^2} \qquad (10)$$

G for an ellipsoid is independent of where it is computed along a ray $(x, y, z) = \alpha t + \beta$ and is given by

$$G = 2(a\alpha_x^2 + b\alpha_y^2 + c\alpha_z^2) \qquad (11)$$

To make more interesting surfaces, we have considered *generalized algebraic surfaces* as presented by Blinn in [BLINN 82]. We have extended them to non-spherical inside-outside functions.

Generalized Algebraic Surfaces

We briefly discuss the concept of Blinn's generalized algebraic surfaces.
   Given a scalar function $f(x, y, z)$, he defines a new function,

$$e(x, y, z) = Be^{Af(x,y,z)},$$

where A and B are constants.

Figure 13: A surface perhaps reminiscent of biological or anatomical structures.

He then defines a sum function,

$$P(x, y, z) = \sum_{i=1}^{n} B_i e^{A_i f_i(x,y,z)}$$

The function $P(x, y, z)$ is a "blended" version of the individual functions $f_i(x, y, z)$. The exponentiation causes the blending to be gradual. The parameters A_i control the smoothness and parameters B_i control the relative contribution of the participating functions f_i. Note that B_i's could be negative enabling one to "carve" out material from another solid. An example with positive and negative B_i's is shown in Figure 11.

L, G's for generalized algebraic surfaces

We have computed L's and G's for blended surfaces comprised of ellipsoids, superquadrics and some other implicit surfaces. These results are given in appendices A.2.1 and A.2.2 and in [KALRA and BARR 89]. These results can be used to compute any of the pictures in this paper.

4.4   Organizing Sub-boxes In An Octree

The boxes generated in the Space Pruning algorithm and used in the ray intersection algorithm are arranged in an octree. Although octrees have been used by various people such as [GLASSNER 84], our octrees differ in some respects. Each of the node in our octree corresponds to a rectangular box. The children of a node are sub-boxes that straddle the surface.

Our octrees are not fully populated. Since the boxes that comprise the volume $\mathcal{V}$ generated in the first algorithm tend to be near the surface (because of the straddling condition), a large portion of the bounding box of the surface does not contain any sub-boxes in $\mathcal{V}$. Hence, although each of the nodes in our octree may potentially contain eight sub-nodes, most nodes will have fewer.

We also adjust the box of each node to tightly bound the boxes of its children nodes. Since we keep only straddling boxes out of the eight possible boxes of a node, many nodes have fewer than eight children and the box for a node shrinks in a lot of cases. See Figure 14. In the figure the dotted boxes show the boxes before shrinking and the solid boxes after shrinking. This shrinking is propagated all the way to the root of the octree. During ray-intersection, the smaller boxes result in many more trivial rejects and we do not have to uselessly examine the children of many nodes.

The octree organization of boxes presents a convenient way to find the box nearest to the origin along a ray. If the ray does not intersect the bounding box of any node N, the sub-tree rooted at N does not need to be considered. If the ray does hit the node box, the ray is intersected with each of its possible eight children, the boxes that are hit are arranged in a heap sorted by the near intersection of the ray with the box, and the boxes in the heap are tried in order.

5   Results

We have used the algorithm presented in this paper to compute a series of pictures shown in this paper. Figures 11 to 20 were all computed using our algorithm. Compare Figures 2 and 15. Our algorithm takes

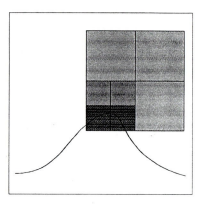

Figure 14: Shrinking of Parent Nodes. The bounding box of a parent is shrunk to the union of the boxes of its children nodes. The shrinking is propagated all the way to the root. The figure shows two levels of subdivision. The darkest shaded box represents the box to which the bounding boxes of both parent nodes are shrunk.

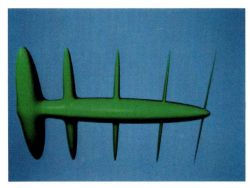

Figure 15: A row of spikes of decreasing thickness. The algorithm has no problem finding the smallest features.

care of the problem of missing fine features in Figure 2. The spikes in the picture change from thick to thin and the algorithm has no problem finding the finest of them without any fine tuning. The spikes in Figure 15 may be as fine as desired and the algorithm will find them. As advertized, we have found that the algorithm produces accurate intersections for all surfaces for which we can compute L's and G's.

We can use the algorithm presented in this paper even for functions that have not yet been analyzed. Since the L's and G's required need not be the smallest possible, we can use conservative global numbers and still make images of surfaces represented by these functions. We would have to spend extra computational effort because of large L's and G's. This approach, however, is an "indirect approach" and might

Figure 16: A golf ball composed of a positive sphere and smaller negative spheres.

Figure 17: This implicit surface is generated by subtracting two spheres from a sphere. Note the thin bridge and the hole. Such fine features would be missed by most ad-hoc algorithms.

Figure 18: Another surface generated by combinations of positive and negative implicit functions.

Figure 19: A fish generated by combinations of superquadratics and ellipsoids.

Figure 20: A wiffle ball is created from a large solid sphere from which we subtract 25 ellipsoids and one smaller sphere.

require some fine tuning in the event that we choose too low estimates for L's and G's and thus obtain errors in the images.

6 Conclusions

In this paper we have presented a method to produce guaranteed intersections with a broad class of Implicit Surfaces. The most important feature of this algorithm is that it is a robust "direct" method. The method does not require any fine tuning or human choice of interactive parameters. The picture of a surface within the bounding box provided for the surface is guaranteed to be numerically correct. Further, if L and G's can be computed locally for regions rather than globally, the algorithm adapts the computational effort required over different regions of the surface automatically.

Essentially, our algorithm is based on fundamental mathematical properties of functions and is correct by construction. With the algorithm presented in this paper, we have reduced the problem of ray tracing difficult implicit surfaces to the problem of finding L's and G's for the function representing the surface.

7 Future Work

Our algorithm presents an opportunity to use implicit surfaces as a useful tool for computer modeling. Our future work is directed in two directions.

First, we are working towards creating or identifying a collection of useful implicit functions and computing the Lipschitz constants L and G, for these functions. We have already had some success in computing the desired Lipschitz constants for deformations, like twists, bends and tapers (See [BARR 84] for details of deformations).

Second, we are looking at applications of implicit surfaces where our algorithm can be used with advantage to render the surfaces. The picture in Figure 13 has inspired us to look at biological applications. We are considering modeling bones and other anatomical structures using blended surfaces as used in this paper. Another application is to use energy-based constraint methods ([TERZOPOULOS et al] and [PLATT and BARR]) to fit blended surfaces to digital data such as generated in tomography.

Another possible application is in adaptive anti-aliasing. Given a box, our algorithm can find if there is any surface in the box. Given that rays passing through the corners of a pixel miss the surface, an extension of this algorithm can be used to determine if there are any portions of the surface in the interior of the pixel and to possibly cause subdivision.

We have also been considering computational improvements to the algorithm. Computing a single number L for a rectangular box B actually gives us the radius of the circumscribing sphere S of the box as shown in Figure 4. Since we use only the box, the region in the sphere S outside B is wasted. Using three Lipschitz constants L_1, L_2 and L_3, one for each of the three coordinate directions in place of a single L will make the algorithm more efficient. This is in some ways similar to methods in [VON HERZEN 89] and [VON HERZEN 88].

8 Acknowledgements

We would like to thank Steve Gabriel for his helpful comments and also to Harold Zatz. Thanks also are due to our sponsors for this work, Apple Computer, AT&T, Hewlett Packard, IBM, and the National Science Foundation.

A Computing L and G

A.1 Lipschitz Constants For Sum Of Functions

Given a set of functions $f_1(\mathbf{x})$, $f_2(\mathbf{x})$, ..., $f_n(\mathbf{x})$, with Lipschitz constants $L_1, L_2, ..., L_n$ respectively in a region $\mathcal{R}$, define the sum function F_s as

$$F_s = \sum_{i=1}^{n} f_i(\mathbf{x}).$$

Then the Lipschitz constant L_s of $F_s(\mathbf{x})$ in $\mathcal{R}$ satisfies the relation,

$$L_s \le \sum_{i=1}^{n} L_i$$

A.2 Computing L and G for generalized algebraic surfaces

A.2.1 Case 1: Ellipsoidal Blending Functions

An ellipsoidal blending function is defined as

$$f(x,y,z) = Be^{-Ar(x,y,z)} \qquad (12)$$

where

$$r(x,y,z) = a^2 x^2 + b^2 y^2 + c^2 z^2 \qquad (13)$$

We sketch out the derivation of computing L and G here. For details see the Caltech CS Technical Report [KALRA and BARR 89].

Computing L in a region $\mathcal{R}$

The L lipschitz constant is computed by computing the gradient of $f(x,y,z)$ in equation 12, taking its magnitude and maximizing it over a rectangular region.

For a rectangular region $\mathcal{R}$ bounded by $(x_{min}, y_{min}, z_{min})$ and $(x_{max}, y_{max}, z_{max})$, L is given by,

$$L_{\mathcal{R}} = 2ABR_{max}e^{-Ar_{min}} \qquad (14)$$

where

$$R = \sqrt{a^4 x^2 + b^4 y^2 + c^4 z^2}.$$

Note that R_{max} and r_{min} occur at the maximum and minimum distances respectively of any point in $\mathcal{R}$ from the origin. Note that, if the region $\mathcal{R}$ straddles any of the coordinate planes, r does NOT take its minimum value at $(x_{min}, y_{min}, z_{min})$ which is one of the vertices of $\mathcal{R}$.

Computing G in an interval $\mathcal{T} = [t_1, t_2]$

The G lipschitz constant is computed by substituting $(x,y,z) = \alpha t + \beta$ in equation 12 to obtain $F(t)$, differentiating to obtain $g(t) = dF/dt$ and maximizing dg/dt over the interval $[t_1, t_2]$.

Define

$$h(t) = -2ABe^{-Ar}\left(k_1 - A\left(k_1 t + k_2\right)^2\right)$$

where

$$k_1 = a^2\alpha_x^2 + b^2\alpha_y^2 + c^2\alpha_z^2$$
$$k_2 = a^2\alpha_x\beta_x + b^2\alpha_y\beta_y + c^2\alpha_z\beta_z$$

Thus

$$G = \max_{t \in \mathcal{T}} h(t)$$

But $h(t)$ can have a maximum value only at the endpoints t_1 or t_2, or else at a stationary point of $h(t)$,

$$t_3 = \frac{-\sqrt{3k_1/2A} - k_2}{k_1}$$

$$t_4 = \frac{-k_2}{k_1}$$

$$t_5 = \frac{\sqrt{3k_1/2A} - k_2}{k_1}$$

See Figure 21.
Thus

$$G = \max_{t_i \in \mathcal{T}} h(t_i)$$

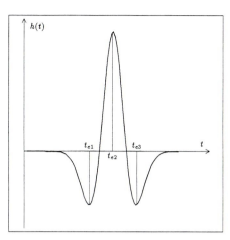

Figure 21: Plot of $h(t) = dg(t)/dt$ along a ray. To compute G, pick the maximum value of $h(t)$ in any interval (t_1, t_2).

A.2.2 Case 2: Superquadratic Blending Functions

An superquadric blending function is defined as

$$f(x,y,z) = Be^{-Ar(x,y,z)} \qquad (15)$$

where

$$r(x,y,z) = (x^n + y^n)^{\frac{m}{n}} + z^m \qquad (16)$$

The mathematics for L and G gets somewhat involved and we shall sketch out the derivation steps. Please see [KALRA and BARR 89] for full expressions and details.

Method to Compute L in a region $\mathcal{R}$

Differentiate $f(x,y,z)$ with respect x, y and z respectively and maximize the partial derivatives over a rectangular region $\mathcal{R}$ bounded by $(x_{min}, y_{min}, z_{min})$ and $(x_{max}, y_{max}, z_{max})$ to get L_1, L_2 and L_3 respectively.

$$L_1 = max\left(mABe^{-Ar}\left[(x^n + y^n)^{\frac{m}{n}-1}x^{n-1}\right]\right)$$

$$L_2 = max\left(mABe^{-Ar}\left[(x^n + y^n)^{\frac{m}{n}-1}y^{n-1}\right]\right)$$

$$L_3 = max\left(mABe^{-Ar}z^{m-1}\right)$$

We then use

$$L = \sqrt{L_1^2 + L_2^2 + L_3^2}.$$

Method to Compute G in an Interval $[t_1, t_2]$

To compute G, substitute

$$(x,y,z) = (\alpha t + \beta)$$

in f(x,y,z). Differentiate to get g(t). Differentiate again and maximize over an interval $[t_1, t_2]$.

We found the use of a symbolic manipulation package such as [SMP] very useful in substituting for common sub-expressions etc. during the derivation of L's and G's.

Again, for more details see the Caltech CS Technical Report [KALRA and BARR 89].

A.3 Lipschitz Constants For Deformations

Let $h(x,y,z)$ be an inside/outside function. Let $\mathbf{D}(x,y,z)$ be a deformation function. The deformation function $\mathbf{D}(\mathbf{x})$ maps a 3-d point to another 3-d point. Examples are taper, twist, and bend [BARR 84].

The inside-outside function of the surface generated by deforming $h(x,y,z)$ by the deformation $\mathbf{D}$ is given by

$$f(x,y,z) = h(\mathbf{D}^{-1}(\mathbf{x}))$$

Computing L in a region $\mathcal{R}$

A Lipschitz constant L for a region V is computed as

$$L \geq \max_{x \in V} \left\| \frac{\partial f}{\partial x_i} \right\|.$$

where $\|\cdot\|$ represents a vector norm.

Computing G in an interval $[t_1, t_2]$

Define

$$g(t) = \frac{d}{dt} f(\alpha t + \beta).$$

for a ray $x = \alpha t + \beta$.

Then G for an interval $\mathcal{T}$ along the ray is computed as

$$G \geq \max_{t \in \mathcal{T}} \left| \frac{dg(t)}{dt} \right|.$$

The detailed derivation and expressions for L and G may be found in [KALRA and BARR 89].

References

[BARR 81] Alan H. Barr, *Superquadrics and Angle-Preserving Transformations*, IEEE Computer Graphics and Applications, Jan '81.

[BARR 84] Alan H. Barr, *Global And Local Deformations of Solid Primitives*, Computer Graphics, July '84.

[BLINN 82] James F. Blinn, *A generalization of Algebraic Surface Drawing*, ACM Transactions on Graphics, Vol. 1, No. 3, July 1982, pp 235-256.

[BLOOMENTHAL 85] Jules Blomenthal, *Modeling the Mighty Maple*, Computer Graphics, Vol 19, No. 3, July 1985.

[BLOOMENTHAL 87] Jules Blomenthal, *Polygonization of Implicit Surfaces*, Course Notes on "The Modeling of Natural Phenomena", Siggraph 1987.

[COLLINS AND AKRITAS 76] Collins, G.E. and Akritas, A. G., *Polynomial real root isolation using Descartes' rule of signs*, Proc. 1976 ACM Symposium on Symbolic and Algebraic Computation.

[GEAR 71] Gear, C. William, *Numerical Initial Value Problems in Ordinary Differential Equations*, Prentice-Hall, Englewood Cliffs, NJ, 1971.

[GLASSNER 84] Space Subdivision for Fast Ray Tracing, *Andrew S. Glassner*, IEEE Computer Graphics and Applications, October '84.

[HANRAHAN 83] Pat Hanrahan, *Ray Tracing Algebraic Surfaces*, Computer Graphics, July '83.

[KALRA and BARR 89] Devendra Kalra and Alan H. Barr, *Guaranteed Intersections with Implicit surfaces*, Caltech Computer Science Tech Report.

[LIN AND SEGEL 74] Mathematics Applied To Deterministic Problems In The Natural Sciences, *C. C. Lin and L. A. Segel*, Macmillan Publishing Co., Inc., New York.

[LORENSEN AND CLINE 87] Marching Cubes: A high resolution 3d surface construction algorithm, *William E. Lorensen and Harvey E. Cline*, Computer Graphics, July 1987.

[MIDDLEDITCH et al 85] Alan E. Middleditch and Kenneth H. Sears, *Blend Surfaces for Set theoretic volume Modeling Systems*, Computer Graphics, Vol. 19, No. 3, July 1985, pp. 161-170.

[PLATT and BARR] John Platt and Alan Barr, *Constraint Methods for Flexible Models*, Computer Graphics, Aug 88.

[SMP] Steven Wolfram et al., *SMP: A symbol manipulation Package*, California Institute of Technology, 1981.

[TERZOPOULOS et al] Demetri Terzopoulos, John Platt, Al Barr, Kurt Fleischer, *Elastically Deformable Models*, Computer Graphics, July 87.

[USPENSKY 48] Uspensky, J. V., *Theory of Equations*, McGraw-Hill, 1948.

[VON HERZEN 84] Brian P. Von Herzen, *Sampling Deformed, Intersecting Surfaces with Quadtrees*, Master's Thesis, Caltech, 1984.

[VON HERZEN 88] Brian Von Herzen, *Applications of Surface Networks to Sampling Problems in Computer Graphics*, Caltech Ph D Thesis.

[VON HERZEN 89] Brian Von Herzen, Alan H, Barr, Harold R. Zatz, *Collision Determination for Parametric Surfaces*, Caltech CS Technical Report.

[WYVILL 86] Space Division for Ray Tracing in CSG, *Geoff Wyvill, Tosiyasu L. Kunii and Yasuto Shirai*, IEEE Computer Graphics and Applications, April '86.

[WYVILL 87[1]] Solid Texturing of Soft Objects, *Geoff Wyvill, Brian Wyvill, Craig Pheeters*, IEEE Computer Graphics and Applications, December '87.

[WYVILL 87[2]] Animating Soft Objects, *Geoff Wyvill, Craig Pheeters, Brian Wyvill*, The Visual Computer, (1986)2.

Parameterized Ray Tracing

Carlo H. Séquin and Eliot K. Smyrl[†]

Computer Science Division
Electrical Engineering and Computer Sciences
University of California, Berkeley, CA 94720

ABSTRACT

The construction and refinement of a computer graphics scene is unacceptably slow when using ray tracing. We introduce a new technique to speed up the generation of successive ray traced images when the geometry of the scene remains constant and only the light source intensities and the surface properties need to be adjusted. When the scene is first ray traced, an expression parameterized in the color of all lights and the surface property coefficients of all objects is calculated and stored for each pixel. Redisplaying a scene with a new set of lights and colors then consists of substituting values for the corresponding parameters and re-evaluating the expressions for the pixels. This parameter updating and redisplay takes only a few seconds, as compared to the many minutes or hours required to ray trace the entire scene again, but it uses much more memory and disk space. With suitable expression sharing, however, these storage needs can be reduced to an acceptable level.

CR Categories and Subject Descriptions:
I.3.3 [*Computer Graphics*]: Picture/Image Generation - *Display algorithms*
I.3.7 [*Computer Graphics*]: Three-Dimensional Graphics and Realism - *Color, shading, shadowing, and texture*

General Terms: Algorithms, Graphics

Additional Key Words and Phrases: Ray Tracing, Rendering, Parameterization, Surface Properties, Runlength Encoding, Subexpression Elimination, Hashing

---

[†] Current Address: Pixar, San Rafael, CA

---

1. INTRODUCTION

The production of a computer graphics scene normally proceeds in stages: first, the various objects are created, then the scene is assembled, a proper view point is chosen, and finally the artist adjusts the colors and surface properties of the various objects and the lighting of the scene. Realistic and sophisticated scenes with shadows, reflections, and other lighting phenomena are often rendered with ray tracing methods [Whitted80], which are, however, computationally very demanding. Thus the re-rendering of a scene after every minor adjustment is time consuming and tedious.

Furthermore, shading equations used in ray tracing often contain many coefficients that interact in complex ways. It is difficult even for experienced users to determine values that will produce the desired results when redisplaying after every small coefficient change takes such a long time.

In these examples, the adjustment of the surface properties and light intensities leaves the scene geometry unchanged; thus a ray going through a particular pixel will always hit the same object. *Parameterized Ray Tracing* is a method to re-render a ray traced scene which avoids retracing the path of the various rays after some adjustments to surface properties, colors, or lighting. This method calculates and stores a parameterized expression for each pixel as the scene is ray traced with a variant of an ordinary ray tracing program. These expressions explicitly contain all potential contributions from the various surfaces hit by the ray and by its reflected and refracted secondary and higher order components. The parameters in these expressions are the colors and intensities of the various ambient and directional light sources and the coefficients defining the surface properties of the various objects. Updating the surfaces and lights in a scene then consists of substituting values for these parameters and recalculating the expressions for the pixels in the display.

The most straightforward implementation of the parameterized ray tracing concept is fairly simple, but it is slow and uses excessive amounts of memory. By incorporating several refinements, it is possible to reduce the time necessary to ray trace a scene and to redisplay successive images, as well as to reduce the amount of memory required to hold the expressions. The process of updating and redisplaying then takes only a few seconds, a significant improvement over the many minutes or hours required to ray trace the entire scene again. This allows rapid production of an image by an artist and also makes the effects of changes in surface properties much more obvious and intuitive. This technique could even be used to provide a tutorial tool to demonstrate the visual effects of the many coefficients typically associated with the description of realistic physical surfaces.

The next section reviews the shading equation used for building up the parameterized expressions for each pixel. Subsequently we present the development of our renderer from the

SIGGRAPH '89, Boston, 31 July-4 August, 1989

above basic concept to a practical implementation with reasonable memory requirements and performance; we also show how the display times and memory needs decrease with subsequent stages of development and refinement.

2. SHADING EQUATION

Figure 1 shows schematically the ray associated with one pixel leaving the eye and striking a surface A, which is both reflective and transparent. Thus a secondary ray is reflected, represented by the solid line, and another one, represented by the dashed line, is transmitted through the surface. The reflected ray strikes the surface of a solid object B, which is also reflective. The subsequent reflected ray then strikes another surface C, again reflective and transparent. The transmitted ray finally strikes the dark object D which is neither reflective nor transparent. The reflected ray hits one of the "background walls" which also terminates the ray. In order to derive an expression for the resulting pixel color seen by the eye, the contributions of these various components of the ray tree must be determined and properly summed.

Our parameterized ray tracer was implemented as a variation of the already-existing ray tracer UgRay [Marsh87], developed as part of the Berkeley UniGrafix environment, and the latter program's paradigms for surface color, reflectance, and lighting were automatically adopted. For this ray tracer, the color visible on a surface is computed with the equation:

$$I = \qquad \text{(resulting intensity)} \qquad (1)$$

$$i_a k_d c \qquad \text{(ambient illumination term)}$$
$$+ \sum_{lights} i_l k_d c (\hat{n} \cdot \hat{l}) \qquad \text{(diffuse illumination term)}$$
$$+ \sum_{lights} i_l k_s (\hat{n} \cdot \hat{h})^p (m c + (1-m)) \qquad \text{(specular illumination term)}$$
$$+ I_s k_s (m c + (1-m)) \qquad \text{(contribution of reflected ray)}$$
$$+ I_t k_t c \qquad \text{(contribution of transmitted ray)}$$

In this equation:
I = the red, green, and blue intensities of the color returned.
The unchanging geometry coefficients are:
$\hat{n}$ = unit vector normal to surface at the intersection point,
$\hat{l}$ = unit vector pointing toward one of the light sources,
$\hat{r}$ = unit vector in direction of ray,
$\hat{h}$ = unit vector half-way between $\hat{r}$ and $\hat{l}$.
The light source parameters that can be varied are:
i_a = intensity of ambient light,
i_l = intensity of light arriving from a light source.
The surface properties that can be varied are:
c = color of the surface at the point of intersection,
k_d = coefficient of diffuse reflection,
k_s = coefficient of specular reflection,
k_t = coefficient of transmission,
p = constant specifying specular highlight sharpness,
m = metalness of the surface.
The colors of secondary rays from other surfaces are:
I_s = color returned by a specularly reflected ray,
I_t = color returned by a transmitted ray.

This equation, similar to the shading equation in [Whitted80], is used to build the expressions for all pixels in the image. It must be evaluated separately for the red, green, and blue components of the intensity I using the appropriate R, G, or B components of the parameters i_a, i_l, and c as well as the secondary intensity contributions I_s and I_t.

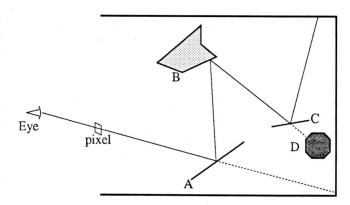

Figure 1: The Ray Tree for One Pixel

The reflected and transmitted ray intensities, I_s and I_t, are the components I returned from some other surface. They may therefore change during an update and affect the value of the expression and the color of the pixel. These terms induce a tree structure on the evaluation of the resulting color of a pixel with subtrees that represent the values of reflected and transmitted higher order components. To evaluate an expression tree, these subexpressions are successively evaluated and "passed up the tree" to higher-level expressions. Finally the highest level expression at the root of the tree is evaluated and the actual pixel color is determined.

Each node in this tree corresponds to one surface interaction and is represented by one expression of the form of Eqn.(1). Figure 2 shows the tree representing the scene in Figure 1. The nodes at A, B, and C represent interactions with the corresponding reflective or transparent surfaces. Interaction with surface D creates a leaf-node, since it is neither reflective nor transparent. "Background" represents ray tree components that leave the explicitly defined scene and are assigned a background color.

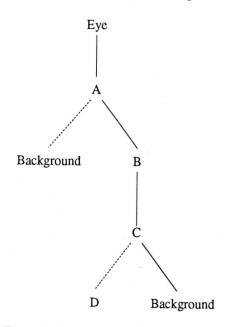

Figure 2: The Expression Tree for Figure 1.

The various surface properties used in Eqn.(1), c, k_d, k_s, k_t, p, and m, may be viewed collectively as a *surface property vector*. All nodes at any level in the expression tree that refer to the same surface have the *same* surface property vector, independent

308

of viewing angle or surface orientation. Thus a surface property vector need be stored only once for each surface, not once for every ray that strikes the surface. Expression nodes thus contain only a reference to the appropriate surface property vector rather than a complete copy of the vector.

3. PRELIMINARY DEMONSTRATION

Table 1 shows the problem posed by standard ray tracing: the time necessary to generate successive images becomes unacceptable as scene resolution and complexity increase.

For Scene A (see plate A), ray tracing was performed on an HP 9000 Model 350SRX workstation with a Motorola 68020 processor, a floating-point coprocessor and 6 Megabytes of main memory. This scene contains some fractal mountains in the background and a few regular, reflective geometric objects in the foreground. It is illuminated with ambient light and with one directional light source; no shadow calculations have been performed. This scene contains 1080 faces and requires 775 kilobytes of memory for scene storage at any resolution. The runtimes for standard ray tracing shown in Table 1 were obtained with UgRay, using uniform spatial subdivision [Fujimoto86] to give good performance on complicated scenes. For a high-resolution image, the ray tracing time may exceed an hour, so any kind of interactive updating is clearly impossible.

Scene B (see plate B) drives home the magnitude of the problem. This scene combines many transparent and reflective objects, shadows, fog, ambient light, and three directional light sources, and was also rendered with anti-aliasing by adaptive oversampling [Whitted80]. It has 3576 faces and requires 7.89 Megabytes of scene storage memory. The rendering time given here is for a VAX 8650 with a floating-point coprocessor and 64 Megabytes of memory. The HP machine was not able to render this picture because it did not have enough memory and spent an excessive amount of time in paging. Even with a significantly more powerful computer, the time required to generate one image obviously precludes any realistic attempt to generate a series of images in order to fine-tune surface properties.

With this problem in mind, we first implemented a straightforward preliminary version of the basic concept of parameterized ray tracing. In this initial implementation, the only parameter varied was **c**, the surface color. This allowed the intensity expression (1) to be collapsed into the much simpler form

$$I = \mathbf{c}\,\gamma + \kappa + \mathbf{I}_s\,(\sigma_c\mathbf{c} + \sigma) + \mathbf{I}_t\,\tau_c\,\mathbf{c} \qquad (2)$$

where

$$\gamma = \mathbf{i}_a\,k_d + \sum_{lights}\mathbf{i}_l\,k_d\,(\hat{n}\cdot\hat{l}) + \sum_{lights}\mathbf{i}_l\,k_s\,(\hat{n}\cdot\hat{h})^p\,m$$

$$\kappa = \sum_{lights}\mathbf{i}_l\,k_s\,(\hat{n}\cdot\hat{h})^p\,(1-m)$$

$$\sigma_c = k_s\,m$$

$$\sigma = k_s\,(1-m)$$

$$\tau_c = k_t$$

and where γ and κ are vectors of three elements: one for each of R, G, and B. γ, κ, σ_c, σ, and τ_c are calculated *once* for each expression, so there are nine values for each expression that can be precomputed during ray tracing to reduce expression storage requirements and to make update evaluation faster. An expression node comprises these values, together with pointers to at most two subexpressions and a pointer to the surface property vector which in this case consists of only the surface color **c**.

Standard Ray tracing	
SCENE A 1080 faces	0.8 Mb
100×100 pixels	34 sec
250×250 pixels	207 sec
500×500 pixels	833 sec
1280×1024 pixels	5219 sec
SCENE B 3576 faces	8 Mb
1024×768 pixels	73140 sec

Table 1: Memory and CPU Requirements for Ray Tracing

Image updating and evaluation then proceeds by evaluating the entire tree for each pixel in a post-order traversal. Each node is evaluated using equation (2) with the node's stored values, its subtrees, and the surface color it references. Successive contributions are passed up the tree until a final pixel color can be calculated and displayed.

Parameterized Ray Tracing		
	Redisplay	Memory Use
SCENE A 1080 faces		
100×100 pixels	2 sec	1.3 Mb
250×250 pixels	9 sec	7.3 Mb
500×500 pixels	? sec	>20 Mb

Table 2: Preliminary Parameterized Ray Tracing

The results from this restricted implementation, given in Table 2, clearly demonstrated that the basic concept worked: update times for small images were typically reduced by about an order of magnitude. However, it became clear that a larger speed-up was necessary to make parameterized ray tracing practical for interactive scene refinement. Furthermore, medium-resolution images required more memory than the HP workstation could handle. Thus unless steps were taken to reduce memory requirements, only the most trivial scenes would be tractable even on midsize computers with several tens of Megabytes of memory.

4. ALGORITHM REFINEMENT

The primary goals through the development process were to reduce memory requirements and the time necessary for redisplaying an image. This was accomplished primarily by reducing the number of expression nodes, which clearly reduces the amount of data that must be stored, but also speeds up the update and redisplay of the image since fewer expression nodes need to be evaluated. Further speed improvements are achieved if the data structure gets small enough so that it fits entirely into main memory, reducing the large paging overhead.

This section presents and discusses various enhancements added to the basic concept in order to achieve the above two goals. For didactic reasons, we present these enhancements in the chronological order in which we implemented them, although some early developments were later superseded. The corresponding performance improvements will be compared in Section 5.

309

4.1. Sharing Expression Trees

Many of the developments took advantage of various forms of image coherence. Objects and faces on objects in a typical scene often cover many adjacent pixels, and thus, over some horizontal and vertical extent, pixels may be of identical color. It is then natural that all these pixels should share the same expression tree. In smooth shaded faces, adjacent pixels may often be very similar but not quite identical, so some quantitative decision must be made as to when pixels are similar enough so that they can share an expression tree.

The computed total color value of a pixel, however, is not a sound basis for comparison; the resulting color may be an accidental coincidence of quite different combinations of various parameter values. In general this similarity would not persist when the parameters are changed.

The comparison therefore requires a complete match of the entire expression trees. To determine whether two pixels are similar enough to share an expression tree, all geometric coefficients associated with each expression node in one tree are compared to the corresponding coefficients in the other tree. For this comparison, the range of the geometric dot products [0,1] is uniformly divided into $1/\varepsilon$ regions of size ε, and any two coefficients that lie in the same region are defined to be equivalent.

4.2. Runlength Encoding

The first improvement to the preliminary implementation was the addition of simple runlength encoding, taking advantage of the horizontal coherence of objects. The tree of the newest ray traced pixel is compared to the tree of the previous pixel on the current scan line. If it is similar enough, the new expression tree is discarded and the length of the current pixel run is increased by one. In the end, each run is represented by one expression tree, a starting x-value, and its length in number of pixels. This is similar to the span buffers found in [Whitted82] but has been extended to include all the rendering information needed for ray tracing.

Scanlines are now represented by a list of runs, rather than an array of pixel trees. Evaluation proceeds as before, except that only a single tree is evaluated for an entire run, and all the associated pixels are displayed together.

4.3. Selective Expression Updating

If the user adjusts one surface's color or other properties, it is unnecessary to reevaluate every expression in the image. To speed up reevaluation of many expression trees, the last computed value of the corresponding subtree is stored at each node of the tree, and a flag in each surface property vector indicates whether there was a change made to this surface. This flag is set during an update for all those surface property vectors that have been changed by the user. Before a node is evaluated, the flag on its associated surface property vector is checked; the node is reevaluated only if it has actually changed, otherwise, the "old" value is passed up the tree. However, if any expression node changes, all nodes above it must be reevaluated, even if the flags on their associated surface property vectors are not set. For example, consider a scene with a blue plate reflected in a shiny pink ball; if the blue surface is changed, all pixels on the shiny pink surface containing the blue reflection must also change, even though the node representing the shiny pink surface does not have its flag set.

Although every expression node is still examined, actual calculation is now done only for nodes that need it. This enables much faster image update when only a limited area of the image is changed. For example, consider an image containing one small silver ball and other non-silver objects. If the silver is made shinier then only the expression trees containing the ball, or

reflected or transmitted rays that hit the ball, need to be reevaluated. All other pixels are simply redrawn with their old values. The cost of redisplay after a change of some parameters now depends on the number of nodes affected by the change.

4.4. 2-D Runlength Encoding

In addition to horizontal coherence, objects usually have some vertical coherence, which can be exploited by a variation on runlength encoding, dubbed *2-D runlength encoding*. In addition to comparing the new pixel to the previous pixel on the current line, the pixel is compared with the three nearest pixels on the previous scan line. Thus two-dimensional areas and entire polygons can in principle be represented by a single expression tree. This further reduces the number of expressions. Scan lines still consist of runs, but now runs on different scan lines may point to the same expression tree.

4.5. Subexpression Sharing with Hashing

So far, only pixels that were physically contiguous were able to share expression trees. However, a particular surface may be seen through several holes, and the background color often shows up in many separate discontiguous areas. The key to reducing the number of expressions for such a scene is to use a good scheme to find all such similar areas and permit them to share a single expression tree. Some kind of hashing scheme comes readily to mind for this purpose. We have used such an approach, and generalized it to permit sharing not only of entire expression trees, but of subtrees as well.

In an average scene, many expression subtrees may be similar, even if the upper levels of the tree are different. For example, two differently-colored reflective walls may reflect the same floor polygon. Thus the subtree representing the ray contribution from the floor polygon can be shared between the two expression trees. This idea is very similar to the concept of common subexpression elimination found in many optimizing compilers [Tremblay85, Aho86].

Our hashing scheme determines when subtrees might be equivalent and should be compared in detail. After the expression tree for a new pixel has been constructed, its nodes are entered into one of several hash tables in a bottom-up manner. If a node to be entered is similar enough to some node already in the table, the new node and its subtrees may be discarded and replaced by a reference to the already-existing node and its subtrees. In this way equivalent subtrees of all sizes throughout the image may be compared and redundant copies eliminated. The determination of node similarity is performed by comparing the entire subtrees rooted at those nodes. This is done in the same way as the comparison of complete expression trees (Section 4.1).

As mentioned above, a temporary coincidence may allow nodes with different surface property vectors to appear the same, but this may change whenever any surface properties are altered. Because each node only represents one surface, nodes may be distinguished immediately if they refer to different surface property vectors. Therefore, nodes with different vectors need not be compared further. A separate hash table is created for each surface property vector, containing all the nodes that use this vector. The result is a greater separation of nodes and thus greater hashing efficiency.

The hash function for expression nodes is based *only* on geometric coefficients: light source directions, ray directions, and normal vectors; these are the only properties that cannot change during an update process. This separates nodes that may temporarily appear similar but will respond differently to coefficient changes. The geometric coefficients are represented in the expression nodes by the dot product terms in equation (1).

After much experimentation, we chose the Weinberger hash function *hashpjw* given in [Aho86], which performs bit operations to fold individual bytes of a string into an integer result, and returns this result modulo a prime number equal to the hash table size. We construct the result by successively folding in the bytes of the geometric coefficients truncated down to an ε-region boundary (Section 4.1). This function gives a very even distribution of nodes over the hash table, and all nodes within the same ε-region will hash to the same location.

In our implementation, collisions are resolved by chaining. When a node is classified into a particular chain by the index returned from the hash function, it is compared to the other nodes in the chain. If it is equivalent to another node in the sense described above, the new node is discarded, and a reference is created to the equivalent node. Since new entries are added at the front of the chains in the hash tables, new nodes will be compared to the most recent entries. This exploits the coherence in the picture to minimize the number of comparisons that need to be made.

Hashing supersedes simple 1-D or 2-D runlength encoding. Each node is now compared to nodes anywhere in the scene that hash to the same table location, not just to nodes from adjacent pixels. However, the scanline ordering of the data structure is preserved, with each scanline comprising runs of identical pixels as before. As a result, a given expression tree is still referenced by whole pixel runs, but these runs may now be scattered throughout the image.

4.6. Production of Intermediate File

The parameterized ray tracing process consists of two distinct phases. The first phase is the generation of expression trees as the scene is ray traced, and the second phase is the interactive process of successively changing parameters and redisplaying the image. These two phases were separated into two programs linked by an intermediate file that is generated by the first program and read by the second one. The file contains all the surface property vectors, the light source information, expression nodes, and scanline information in a binary encoded form.

This intermediate file was not only convenient during development, allowing the different programs to be developed separately, but also gives the user more flexibility in scene generation. An image once produced can be kept in such an intermediate file, and the user may then come back to the image whenever and as often as desired to change different parameters.

4.7. One-Time-Only Expression Updating

As noted above, expression trees may be associated with more than one pixel run, and since runs are examined in scanline order, a tree may be encountered and thus evaluated more than once. Since subtrees are shared throughout the scene, any node or subtree may also be evaluated more than once. To avoid redundant evaluations, a serial number was attached to successive image updates, and a corresponding field in each expression node is set to the number of the current update. If a node is encountered more than once during a single update, this number field will reveal this, and the previously computed value stored at this node will be used.

4.8. Generalization of Parameters

The above optimizations and refinements improved the performance and reduced the memory requirements significantly. Thus we could afford to lift the preliminary restriction that only the surface color **c** could be varied, and allowed all of the surface properties and light source intensities to change. This required a more general form of storing the expression nodes, both in memory and in the intermediate file format, since equation (2) no longer applies. The only numbers stored directly with the expressions are now the dot product terms in equation (1), two for each

light source. All surface properties are now kept explicitly in the surface property vectors, and light source intensities are kept in similar "light source intensity vectors".

4.9. Addition of More Advanced Features

The parameterization was extended further to handle various more complex features available in UgRay such as antialiasing, fog, attenuation of rays in solids, and local light sources. A concurrent change in the coefficient storage format from floating-point to fixed-point saved more memory. Although UgRay does not currently handle spline surfaces, our method can easily accommodate curved surfaces and other features commonly found in ray tracing programs.

We also attempted to further speed up the algorithm by optimizing the data structure and node evaluations for cases where the user wants to vary only a limited set of parameters. However, even with a reduced set of parameters the shading equation (1) requires significant computation for each node evaluation, and we obtained little speed improvement in most cases. Since this version of the program actually required more memory, this "optimization" was abandoned.

5. PERFORMANCE AND STORAGE IMPROVEMENTS

Table 3 shows the improvements made by the successive refinements described in Section 4 for the example of a 500×500 pixel rendering of Scene A. Note that minimum and maximum redisplay times are given because selective expression updating (Section 4.3) allows redisplay time to vary with the number of nodes affected by a change.

	Ray trace time (sec)	Redisplay time (sec)	Memory usage (Mb)
Standard (UgRay)	833	833	0.8
Preliminary version	> 200,000	?	> 20.0
Runlength encoding	934	10	2.5
Selective updating	949	3 to 7	2.8
2-D runlength encoding	936	3 to 6	1.6
Hashing	904	2 to 5	0.9
Full parameterization	917	5 to 8	1.2
Final implementation	910	5 to 8	1.2

**Table 3: Development Summary
Scene A with 500×500 resolution**

Overall, ray tracing time has increased by only about 10% over the time used by the standard ray tracer, UgRay. Redisplay time, on the other hand, has been reduced by a factor of 100 to 170. This performance improvement has been bought by an increase in memory usage; but note that of the 1.2 Mb required, 0.8 is used by the ray tracer for scene storage. The parameterization overhead on memory is only 50%. Disk storage for the intermediate file has concurrently increased by a factor of 5 over that of an ordinary UgRay image file.

Ray tracing	Ray trace time (sec)	Redisplay time (sec)	Memory usage (Mb)
Standard	4904	4904	8
Parameterized	5640	30 to 81	28

Table 4: Scene B with 512×512 resolution

The gearbox scene statistics in Table 4 are for the VAX 8650 again. Parameterized ray tracing has reduced the average redisplay time for this difficult image from over an hour to a time on the order of one minute, which is just acceptable for interactive refinement.

6. DISCUSSION AND CONCLUSIONS

With all the discussed refinements included, parameterized ray tracing achieves a speed improvement for redisplay by factors ranging from 50 to 175 for a scene composed of polyhedral objects. The additional overhead in initial ray tracing time to generate the various expression trees is only about 10% to 15%. This performance improvement for scene updates comes at the cost of increased storage requirements. The main memory requirements increase by about a factor of 3, while the intermediate file that holds all the expression trees can be 10 to 15 times larger than the corresponding UgRay image file. In view of the continued rapid improvements in memory and disk technology, these increased storage demands seem acceptable.

However, for any given machine, we can always construct a scene that is so complex that it will no longer fit into the available main memory. This will result in significant paging overhead and lead to a dramatic performance drop. Unfortunately the current data structure shows little locality in its accesses since the node expressions can be shared between arbitrary pixels. An open research issue is to look for data structures that have more locality in their accesses and that might promise more gradual performance degradation when they exceed the available memory. In an environment with limited memory, it might even be worthwhile to restrict subtree sharing in favor of better disk management.

Currently every expression is examined at each update, but only those that need to be changed are reevaluated. Is there a way to avoid even examining nodes that do not need to be changed? Conceptually, a network of pointers is required that links a changing parameter to everything that can be affected. Our current tree structure provides connections only in the opposite direction, and requires every node to check all possible sources of a change. The enhanced structure would need to add pointers from every surface property vector and light intensity vector to all nodes that use them, and also pointers from all nodes to their parents. Then the nodes affected by a parameter change could be found directly and reevaluated, and this change could be propagated up the expression trees. We estimate that such a data structure would increase memory needs by about 20%, while reducing redisplay time by as much as 90% in some cases. This work is currently in progress.

Parameterization techniques similar to those we have explored are applicable to other rendering algorithms, and in fact to many algorithms in which an investment of time to precompute a structured representation of invariants can significantly speed up later computation. For example, the concept of pixel parameterization was inspired by older rendering techniques that explicitly return all visible polygons found during hidden-surface elimination [Hamlin77, Sequin85]. These polygons can be similarly linked to parameterized surface property vectors, permitting color changes without the need for redoing the hidden-surface calculations.

Radiosity algorithms use other techniques to take advantage of a fixed scene geometry. After calculating the form-factor matrices once, light source intensities and object colors can be changed rapidly by simply changing the patch brightnesses and then re-solving the matrices [Cohen85].

Parameterized ray tracing has proven useful not only for scene development and refinement, but also to provide an "interactive tutorial" for the many somewhat counter-intuitive surface property coefficients found in our shading formula. Novice users often experience great difficulties in obtaining exactly the parameter values they want for a particular surface. Parameterized ray tracing allows them to "twiddle" the various coefficients individually or together and discover their effects on the appearance of a surface. Overall, the response of a few initial users to our prototype of a parameterized ray tracer has been quite positive.

Acknowledgements

This work was supported by a National Science Foundation Graduate Fellowship, and is part of the research done in the context of the CISE Institutional Infrastructure Program: "Massive Information Storage, Management, and Use" at U.C. Berkeley. It was also supported by a grant from Tektronix, Inc.

References

AHO, ALFRED V., RAVI SETHI, AND JEFFREY D. ULLMAN, *Compilers: Principles, Techniques, and Tools,* Addison-Wesley, Reading, Mass., 1986.

COHEN, MICHAEL F. AND DONALD P. GREENBERG, "The Hemi-Cube: a Radiosity Solution for Complex Environments," Proceedings of SIGGRAPH '85 (San Francisco, California, July 22-26). In *Computer Graphics 19*, 3, pp. 31-40, July 1985.

FUJIMOTO, AKIRA, TAKAYUKI TANAKA, AND KANSEI IWATA, "ARTS: Accelerated Ray-Tracing System," *IEEE Computer Graphics and Applications*, pp. 16-26, Apr. 1986.

HAMLIN, GRIFFITH AND C. WILLIAM GEAR, "Raster-Scan Hidden Surface Algorithm Techniques," *Computer Graphics*, vol. 11, no. 2, pp. 264-271, Summer 1977.

MARSH, DONALD M., "UgRay: An Efficient Ray-Tracing Renderer for UniGrafix," Tech. Report UCB/CSD 87/360, U.C. Berkeley, May 1987.

SEQUIN, CARLO H. AND PAUL R. WENSLEY, "Visible Feature Return at Object Resolution," *Computer Graphics and Appl.,* vol. 5, no. 5, pp. 37-50, May 1985.

TREMBLAY, JEAN-PAUL AND PAUL G. SORENSON, *The Theory and Practice of Compiler Writing,* pp. 620-631, McGraw-Hill, New York, 1985.

WHITTED, TURNER, "An Improved Illumination Model for Shaded Display," *CACM*, vol. 23, no. 6, pp. 343-349, June 1980.

WHITTED, TURNER AND DAVID M. WEIMER, "A Software Testbed for the Development of 3D Raster Graphics," *ACM Transactions on Graphics*, vol. 1, no. 1, pp. 43-58, January 1982.

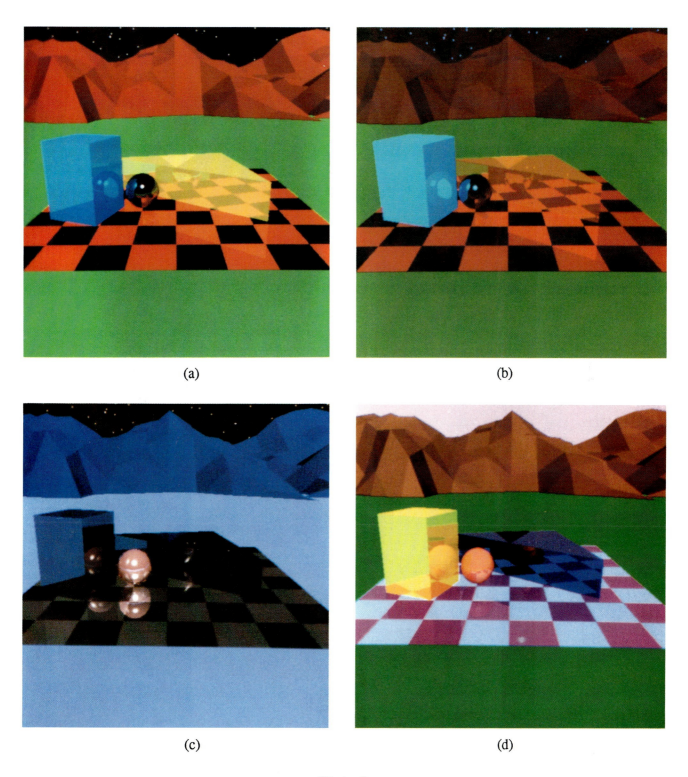

(a)

(b)

(c)

(d)

Plate A

This scene has been ray traced only once. All changes shown are the result of varying various surface property or light source vectors and reevaluating the pixel expression trees. Plate A is a simple test scene composed of three geometrical objects placed on a checkerboard in front of a fractal mountain range. In (a) the blue cube, the yellow prism, and the red tiles are lightly reflective. In (b) the light has changed to blue, which is clearly visible in the highlight on the shiny ball. In (c) the colors of the mountains and the plain have changed, and the two polyhedra and the entire checkerboard have been made highly reflective with an underlying grayish-silvery color. The ball has changed to a glossy pink. In (d) the colors of all objects including the sky have been changed. The reflectivity of the ball and the checkerboard have been reduced.

(a)

(b)

(c)

(d)

Plate B

This scene has also been ray traced only once. All changes shown are the result of varying various surface property vectors and reevaluating the pixel expression trees. Plate B is a more complicated test scene consisting of a gear assembly in a transparent display case with a few spare parts lying around. In (a) the box is made of regular glass held together by bronze clips. In (b) the tiles have turned red and the gears now have green faces with copper teeth. In (c) the glass has been replaced by less transparent pink plastic plates held together with silver clamps. Furthermore, the gear teeth have been given a chalk-white color. In (d) we use the regular glass again. All the gears and clips are silver, but take on a golden sheen because of the yellow sky.

A RAY TRACING ALGORITHM FOR PROGRESSIVE RADIOSITY

John R. Wallace, Kells A. Elmquist, Eric A. Haines
3D/EYE, Inc.
Ithaca, NY.

ABSTRACT

A new method for computing form-factors within a progressive radiosity approach is presented. Previously, the progressive radiosity approach has depended on the use of the hemi-cube algorithm to determine form-factors. However, sampling problems inherent in the hemi-cube algorithm limit its usefulness for complex images. A more robust approach is described in which ray tracing is used to perform the numerical integration of the form-factor equation. The approach is tailored to provide good, approximate results for a low number of rays, while still providing a smooth continuum of increasing accuracy for higher numbers of rays. Quantitative comparisons between analytically derived form-factors and ray traced form-factors are presented.

CR Categories and Subject Descriptors: I.3.3 [**Computer Graphics**]: Picture/Image Generation - Display algorithms. I.3.7 [**Computer Graphics**]: Three-Dimensional Graphics and Realism

General Terms: Algorithms

Additional Key Words and Phrases: radiosity, ray tracing, progressive refinement, distributed ray tracing, global illumination.

INTRODUCTION

The synthesis of realistic images requires the evaluation of a shading model which simulates the propagation of light within an environment. To obtain images quickly, local shading models are often used in which shading is computed based only on direct illumination by the light sources. Realistic shading, however, requires the use of a global illumination model, in which secondary illumination provided by light reflected from other surfaces and the shadowing of one surface by another are taken into account.

In recent years much work has been applied to methods for evaluating the Lambertian diffuse illumination model. For Lambertian diffuse reflection, the intensity of light reflected by a surface is given by:

$$I_{out} = \rho \int_{2\pi} I_{in}(\Theta)\cos\theta \; d\omega \qquad (1)$$

where

I_{out} = intensity of reflected light
ρ = diffuse reflectivity
θ = angle between surface normal and incoming direction Θ
$I_{in}(\Theta)$ = intensity of light arriving from direction Θ

For local illumination models, the evaluation of this equation is straightforward, since the incoming light, I_{in}, arrives only from the light sources. However, for a global illumination model the problem is more difficult, since incoming light may arrive via secondary reflection from any surface visible to the point to be shaded. Evaluation is recursive, since the light arriving from other surfaces depends in turn on light arriving at those surfaces.

Several approaches to solving this problem have been developed. One direction has been to extend conventional ray tracing using a monte carlo solution of the integral equation [7][8][20][13][19][17]. Radiosity methods derived from the field of radiative heat transfer have also been applied successfully [10][4][16][5]. The radiosity method has the attractive characteristic of providing a view-independent solution. Hence, once the solution has been performed, a hardware renderer can be used to display the scene from changing viewpoints at interactive rates.

Despite the advantage of view independence the radiosity method was, until recently, considered impractical for scenes of high complexity. Both the time and storage costs of the algorithm were $O(n^2)$ (where n is the number of surfaces). However, the performance of the radiosity method has been greatly improved through the use of a progressive refinement strategy that provides good images early in the solution process [6].

©1989   ACM-0-89791-312-4/89/007/0315 $00.75

In the progressive radiosity algorithm, illumination is computed one step at a time. At each step, the reflected or emitted illumination provided by a single surface is distributed to all the other surfaces. The determination of where the illumination falls in the scene is accomplished using the *hemi-cube* algorithm, in which the scene is scan converted from the point of view of the surface providing illumination. In effect, light is shot out from the source in a predefined uniform set of directions to land where it may in the environment. Although the overall progressive radiosity approach provides an important improvement over previous radiosity methods for graphics, the use of the hemi-cube to determine illumination suffers inherently from aliasing and undersampling, particularly as the scene complexity increases.

In this paper a new progressive radiosity algorithm is described in which ray tracing is used to determine the distribution of illumination from each primary or secondary source. The process of determining illumination can then be turned around; instead of shooting light out from the source in the uniform directions determined by the hemi-cube pixels, the new algorithm samples the illumination source from the point of view of each of the other surfaces in the environment. Illumination is determined at exactly those points for which shading is desired, and problems of inadequate sampling and aliasing are reduced.

In addition to improving illumination sampling, ray tracing provides new directions for broadening the scope and increasing the efficiency of radiosity. Examples include:

- non-physical light sources (e.g., point lights, unattenuated lights)

- shadow testing against exact geometries

- ability to turn shadows on or off on a surface by surface basis

- continuous shading of curved surfaces modeled by independent polygonal facets

- shadows due to semi-transparent surfaces (filters)

Several of these features are illustrated in the results section.

The new algorithm was developed as part of a software package providing photorealism extensions to Hewlett-Packard's Starbase graphics interface. The development of this package demanded that all the primitives, attributes and other 3D graphics functionality provided by Starbase, a typical graphics interface, be supported for radiosity.

The next section of this paper reviews the basic progressive radiosity algorithm and the inherent problems arising from the use of the hemi-cube in a progressive algorithm. The third section provides a solution to these problems in the form of a ray tracing algorithm for evaluating form-factors, the central step of the new progressive radiosity approach. Results are presented in the fourth section.

PROGRESSIVE RADIOSITY

The radiosity approach computes diffuse global illumination by solving a system of equations expressing the dependence of the energy leaving each surface on that arriving from every other surface. The energy leaving a surface is given by:

$$B_i A_i = E_i A_i + \rho_i \sum_{j=1}^{n} B_j A_j F_{ji} \qquad (2)$$

where

B_i = radiosity of surface i (energy per unit area)
A_i = area of surface i
E_i = emitted energy per unit area
ρ_i = reflectivity of surface i
B_j = radiosity of surface j
A_j = area of surface j
F_{ji} = form-factor from surface j to surface i

The *form-factor*, F_{ji}, gives the fraction of energy leaving surface j that arrives at a second surface i.

An equation of this form exists for every surface in the scene. The resulting system of simultaneous equations can be solved using iterative techniques to determine the surface radiosities. A final shading calculation then uses these surface radiosities to determine the radiosity at the vertices of smaller polygonal *elements* into which the surfaces have been subdivided. Following the radiosity solution, Gouraud interpolation based on the element vertex radiosities can be used to render smoothly shaded images.

Unfortunately, forming the matrix prior to the solution requires determining and saving the form-factor between each surface and every other surface, a process that is $O(n^2)$ both in time and memory (where n is the number of surfaces). The progressive radiosity approach overcomes this difficulty by solving the radiosity equations in a series of steps. The solution proceeds as follows:

do until converged
    Select surface with greatest reflected and/or
        emitted energy
    Compute form-factors from that surface to all
        surface elements in environment
    Based on form-factors, add contribution from source
        surface to radiosity of each element

The form-factors from the source surface to the receiving elements are computed using the *hemi-cube* algorithm [4], in which all elements are projected, scan converted and z-buffered onto the five faces of a hemi-cube positioned at the source surface. In the early steps, the source surfaces chosen will be the light emitters since other surfaces will have as yet received very little illumination. Subsequent steps will select secondary sources, starting with those surfaces that received the most light directly from the light sources, and so on.

Since each solution step updates the radiosity of all surfaces, the increasingly accurate result can be displayed following each step. An estimated ambient term derived from the known energy yet to be distributed can be added to improve the image. Useful images can thus be produced very early in the solution process. There are, however, inherent problems in using a hemi-cube placed at the source surface to determine form-factors. These problems will be discussed in the next section, following a brief discussion of some related approaches.

SHOOTING ALGORITHMS

In the progressive radiosity algorithm, the hemi-cube can be pictured as "shooting" light out from the source surface on which it is placed. The pixels of the hemi-cube determine a uniform point sampling of the environment as seen from the source. The form-factor from the source to a receiving surface, and thus the energy it receives, depends on the summed effect of any sample points that "landed" on the surface.

The usual strategy for determining shading in computer graphics is to follow the path of light from the eye into the scene, thus avoiding the consideration of light that doesn't reach the eye. Ray tracing and its derivatives distributed ray tracing and path tracing are classic examples of this approach. However, such methods do not have information about where in the scene to look for important sources of light, other than the light emitters themselves. Hence, for a diffuse surface, much sampling may be expended on directions from which little energy turns out to arrive.

By starting at the emitters and at each step sending into the environment the light from the source of greatest reflected or emitted energy, the progressive radiosity algorithm continually has information about where energy arrives from. Attention can thus be focused on the most important sources of illumination. Even very small secondary sources that happen to reflect a great deal of light will be detected, a very difficult case when working entirely from the eye, as pointed out by Ward [19].

Several shading methods previous to progressive radiosity have noted the possible advantages of working from the point of view of the source. In an early experiment by Appel shading was determined by shooting random rays from the light source into the scene, with the density of hits on a surface representing the shading value [1]. This approach was abandoned because of the large number of rays required to get smooth results.

Arvo [2] describes an algorithm for determining the secondary illumination of diffuse surfaces by light reflected or refracted by specular surfaces. Rays are shot from a point light source, refracted and reflected by specular surfaces, until they finally land on a diffuse surface. The diffusely reflected portion of the ray's energy is recorded on an *illumination map* for the surface, that is, a grid mapped parametrically to the surface. The incoming energy is gathered to the vertices of the grid, which then provide diffuse shading values during a conventional ray tracing rendering of the scene. Arvo points out that "illumination rays must be many times as dense as the grid points" [2]. Otherwise, the shading produced is statistically uneven.

Chattopadhyay [3] also describes a shading algorithm in which ray tracing from the primary light sources is used to determine the direct illumination of diffuse surfaces, which are then treated as secondary light sources for a radiosity solution. The final image is determined by conventional ray tracing.

Limitations of the Hemi-cube

As noted by both Appel and Arvo, the foremost difficulty with the shooting approach is uneven and inadequate sampling. For the hemi-cube, a surface that is large in the image may, when viewed from the light, be small enough to fall between the hemi-cube pixels. Such a surface will receive no illumination (figure 1). In addition, since the hemi-cube is a uniform sampling method, it will produce aliasing. The shading of a fine grid of small polygons will show a distinct plaid pattern if the polygons are small enough to alias on the hemi-cube (figure 2.) Increasing the resolution of the hemi-cube to reduce these effects becomes expensive and, in any case, can never guarantee adequate sampling for all polygons.

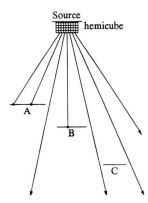

Figure 1. Determining form-factors from a source to receiving surfaces A, B and C using a hemi-cube placed at the source. Surface C incorrectly receives no illumination.

A second difficulty with the use of the hemi-cube for progressive radiosity is that sources are normally surfaces with area. Performing a single hemi-cube at a source surface is equivalent to reducing that source to a point. To approximate an area source, hemi-cubes must be performed at several points on the surface. However, the number of points necessary for a good approximation depends on how close the source is to the surface it illuminates. Using the hemi-cube, the number of points representing the source area will be the same for all receiving surfaces, since all surfaces are projected onto each hemi-cube.

Finally, a hemi-cube placed on a source can only determine form-factors to receiving surfaces with finite areas (the elements), not to point receivers (i.e., differential surface areas). Thus the radiosities at the element vertices, which are used to actually render the final image, cannot be determined directly. The radiosity at each vertex must be determined by

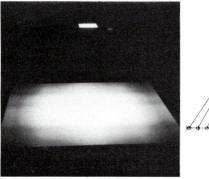 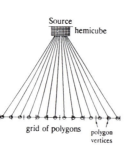

Figure 2. a) Aliasing due to uniform sampling imposed by the hemi-cube. A surface subdivided into 11 by 13 elements is illuminated by a light source. b) The regular hemi-cube sampling pattern interacts with the regular receiving grid to generate aliasing.

averaging the radiosity of the elements surrounding it. This introduces an additional level of imprecision and is a particular problem when shading curved surfaces approximated by independent polygonal facets. Continuity of shading across such surfaces is normally ensured by calculating shading directly at the facet vertices using the true surface normal, as in Gouraud shading [11].

AN IMPROVED PROGRESSIVE RADIOSITY SOLUTION

Clearly, the benefits of following light from the emitters provided by progressive radiosity are worth preserving. Fortunately, the problems described in the previous section are not fundamental to the progressive algorithm. They originate from the fact that form-factors are determined by viewing the scene from the source to see what surfaces are visible in a uniform set of directions.

What is ignored by this approach is that the points at which shading must ultimately be determined are the element vertices. It is the shading at these vertices that will be used when images of the environment are finally rendered. All of the problems just described may be eliminated by determining the illumination of these vertices directly.

The new approach to progressive radiosity proceeds as follows. As before, at each solution step the surface with the most reflected and/or emitted energy to contribute to the environment is treated as the source surface. Instead of performing a hemi-cube at this source, each element vertex in the scene is then visited and a form-factor is computed from the source surface to the vertex by shooting rays from the vertex to sample points on the source.

This eliminates the sampling problems inherent in the hemi-cube approach, since illumination is guaranteed to be computed at every vertex (figure 3). Since the form-factors are computed independently at each vertex, each form-factor may be computed to any desired accuracy. The number of sample points on the source may vary from one vertex to the next, thus allowing area sources to be approximated as accurately as desired. Furthermore, the true surface normal at the vertex may be used, thus solving the problem of continuous

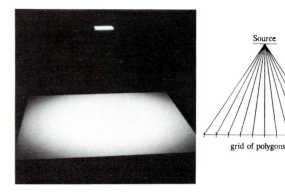

Figure 3. a) Aliasing does not occur when illumination is computed directly at the vertices of the elements, as shown schematically in b).

shading of independent surface facets.

The use of ray tracing to point sample source-to-vertex form-factors is the key development in the new algorithm.

A Ray Tracing Algorithm For Computing Form-Factors

Ray tracing has already been used as a method for determining form-factors [14][15]. In each of these works, form factors between a surface and one or more other surfaces are determined by tracing rays outwards from the surface in directions distributed over the entire hemisphere above the surface. No knowledge about the energy arriving from other surfaces is available at the time form-factors are computed. Thus, there is no opportunity for concentrating sampling effort on surfaces that will have the most effect on the illumination of the point.

In progressive radiosity, the problem to be solved at each solution step is more restricted, since the surface with the most energy to emit or reflect into the environment is known. For each element vertex in the scene it is only necessary to determine the form-factor from the single source surface to the vertex (more rigorously, a differential area located at the vertex).

In what follows, a technique for numerically integrating the form-factor equation using ray tracing is derived. The development of this technique was driven by the constraint that it provide good, approximate results for a low number of rays, while allowing increasingly accurate results for higher numbers of rays.

The derivation begins with the equation for the form-factor from differential area dA_1 to a differential area dA_2 (figure 4a) [18]:

$$dF_{dA_1-dA_2} = \frac{\cos\theta_1 \cos\theta_2}{\pi r^2} \, dA_2 \qquad (3)$$

where

θ_1 = angle between normal at dA_1 and direction to dA_2
θ_2 = angle between normal at dA_2 and direction to dA_1
r = distance between the areas

For the form-factor to a finite area A_2 equation 3 must be integrated over the finite area:

$$F_{dA_1-A_2} = \int_{A_2} \frac{\cos\theta_1 \cos\theta_2}{\pi r^2} dA_2 \qquad (4)$$

This integral can be solved analytically for simple configurations, but in general it must be evaluated numerically.

Numerical integration may be accomplished in a straightforward manner by approximating the integral as the sum of form-factors computed for smaller regions of area ΔA_2 (figure 4b):

$$F_{dA_1-A_2} = \sum_{i=1}^{n} \frac{\cos\theta_{1i} \cos\theta_{2i}}{\pi r_i^2} \Delta A_2 \qquad (5)$$

However, equation 5 breaks down if ΔA_2 is large relative to the distance; as r becomes less than one, ΔA_2 must shrink correspondingly, or the result grows without bound.

To limit the subdivision of the source and thus the cost of computing form-factors while avoiding the difficulty of equation 5, the delta areas are treated explicitly as finite areas. An equation for the form-factor from finite delta areas can be obtained by approximating each delta area by a simple finite geometry for which an analytical solution is available.

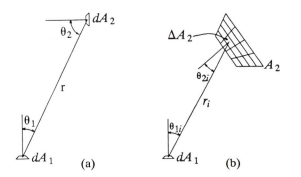

Figure 4. a) Form-factor from differential area 1 to differential area 2. b) Numerical integration of form-factor from differential area 1 to finite area 2.

Analytical solutions for a variety of configurations can be found in the literature [18][12]. Because of its simplicity, a disk has been chosen as the finite area upon which to base the approximation. The form-factor from a differential area dA_1 to a directly opposing receiving disk of area A_2 and radius a is given by:

$$F_{dA_1-A_2} = a^2 / (r^2 + a^2) \qquad (6)$$

Using the reciprocity principle,

$$dA_1 F_{dA_1-A_2} = A_2 dF_{A_2-dA_1} \qquad (7)$$

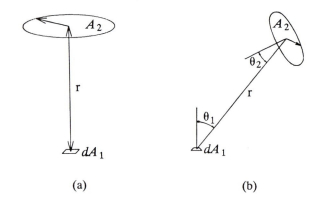

Figure 5. a) Configuration for form-factor between disk and differential area facing each other on parallel planes. b) Configuration for approximate form-factor between arbitrarily oriented disk and differential area.

the form-factor from a disk source to a differential area receiver (figure 5a) can be obtained:

$$dF_{A_2-dA_1} = dA_1 / (\pi r^2 + A_2) \qquad (8)$$

This relationship can be generalized by making some approximations. The effect of different orientations of the source and receiving areas can be approximated by including the cosines of the angles between the normal at each surface and the direction between the source and the receiver (figure 5b).

$$dF_{A_2-dA_1} = dA_1 \cos\theta_1 \cos\theta_2 / (\pi r^2 + A_2) \qquad (9)$$

A further approximation is to assume that the area is disk shaped. The accuracy of this approximation depends, of course, on the area's actual shape. A study of the effects of these approximations is presented in the results section.

To evaluate the form-factor from a general source to a vertex, the source is divided into delta areas. The form-factor due to each delta area is computed using equation 9. Occlusion is tested by shooting a single ray from the receiving vertex to the center of the delta area on the source. This ray is a simple shadow ray, in other words, it provides only a yes or no answer to the question of whether anything is intersected. In further discussion, this will be referred to as sampling the source, and rays will be said to be shot from the vertex to sample points on the source. If sample points are distributed uniformly on the source then the total form-factor is simply the sum of the form-factors computed for each sample point i:

$$dF_{A_2-dA_1} = dA_1 \frac{1}{n} \sum_{i=1}^{n} \delta_i \frac{\cos\theta_{1i} \cos\theta_{2i}}{\pi r_i^2 + A_2/n} \qquad (10)$$

where

n = number of sample points on source
δ_i = 1 if sample point is visible to vertex, 0 if occluded

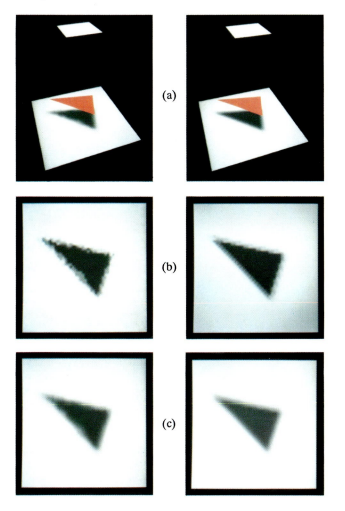

Figure 6. Comparison of uniform versus jittered sampling for low number of sample points. Uniform sampling is shown in the right hand images, jittered in the left. Rays were shot to four points on the source. a) View of emitter illuminating plane consisting of 50 by 50 grid of elements. b) Note large scale noise for jittered sampling on left. Uniform sampling on right shows aliasing at shadow boundary. c) Result of filtering the vertex radiosities using a box filter of the nearest vertex neighbors.

This equation has a number of desirable characteristics. The presence of the area in the denominator prevents the result from growing without bound for small r. This allows approximate form-factors to be computed using large delta areas, and hence, a low number of sample points. Thus, a fast, approximate radiosity solution can be obtained using a very small number of rays (as few as one ray per vertex per source). The accuracy of the result increases as the number of sample points is increased. This can be seen by observing that as n grows larger the term A_2/n tends towards zero and each term of the summation approaches the equation for a form-factor from a differential area to a differential area (equation 3). Thus, a smooth continuum of results is available depending on the amount work one is willing to do.

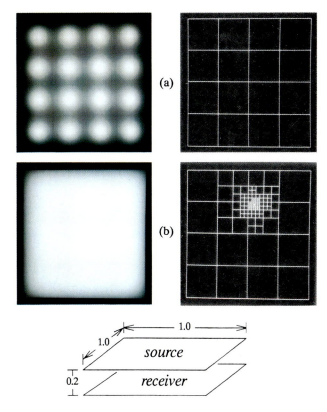

Figure 7. a) Artifacts due to inadequate sampling of large, close source. The receiving polygon consists of 30 by 30 elements. The source subdivision is shown on the right. b) Result of adaptively subdividing the source. Source subdivision for a typical element vertex (location shown by small circle) is shown on the right.

According to equation 2, the radiosity of a surface i due to energy received from a single source j is

$$B_iA_i = \rho_iB_jA_jF_{ji} \tag{11}$$

By substituting equation 10 into this equation, the equation for the radiosity at vertex 1 due to illumination by source 2 is obtained:

$$B_1 = \rho_1B_2A_2\frac{1}{n}\sum_{i=1}^{n}\delta_i \frac{\cos\theta_{1i}\ \cos\theta_{2i}}{\pi r_i^2 + A_2/n} \tag{12}$$

Note that the differential area in equation 10 has canceled out.

At each step of the progressive solution the contribution made by the current source to the radiosity of each element vertex in the environment is computed using equation 12.

Sample Point Distribution

There are a number of ways to choose the points on the source to which rays are shot. The simplest is to generate a single set of sample points spaced at even intervals on the

source. However, the use of a constant, uniform distribution of sample points on the source can produce form-factor aliasing, which is particularly noticeable at shadow edges. If the surface mesh is fine enough, for a small number of sample points overlapping sharp-edged shadows may appear where only one soft-edged shadow is expected (figure 6).

The problem of aliasing can be addressed in several ways. Some improvement may be gained by simply filtering the vertex radiosities using a weighted average of neighboring vertex radiosities, as shown in figure 6c. However, this can only be done if the vertex connectivities are known.

One approach to eliminating aliasing is to jitter the location of the sample points on the source. This converts the aliasing to noise [8][9] and is a powerful antialiasing approach if the number of samples is high enough. However, stochastic methods in image synthesis generally take advantage of the fact that noise at the pixel level is not interpreted by the eye as structure in the image. In the radiosity method shading is evaluated at the vertices of a surface mesh in object space, not at individual pixels. In the image these vertices may be separated by tens of pixels, with intervening pixels shaded by interpolation. Statistical irregularities that might be acceptable for neighboring pixels become artifacts at this scale. This is particularly true when the number of samples is very small. An example of this result is shown in figure 6.

In general, obtaining accurate form-factors in difficult cases requires increasing the sampling rate, that is, the number of sample points on the source. Since the form-factor from a source to a vertex is computed independently of all other vertices, the number of sample points used to represent the source can be varied from vertex to vertex as necessary. One possibility is to simply recompute the form-factor for a given vertex-source pair using successively greater numbers of uniformly distributed sample points, until the difference between the resulting form-factors drops below a certain criterion. Thus, at vertices lying on shadow boundaries many rays may be shot to achieve an accurate form-factor, while vertices completely inside or outside the shadow will require a much smaller number. This technique was used for the shading of the office in figure 10.

When a large number of sample points are required, however, the use of a uniform distribution can be extremely wasteful. Figure 7 illustrates a particularly difficult case, a large source very close to the receiving surface. When a uniform distribution of 16 samples is used, the results are clearly inadequate. Increasing this number will expend unnecessary effort in shooting rays from each vertex to points that make little difference. The solution is to subdivide the source adaptively for each receiving vertex, as shown in figure 7b. For each receiving vertex, the source was initially subdivided uniformly into 16 delta areas. The form-factors and the amount of energy received from each delta area were determined by shooting a ray to the center of the area. Each delta area was then subdivided recursively until the amount of energy received fell below a user specified criterion. Note that when the source is subdivided into unequal areas, the summation in equation 12 must become the area weighted average of the form-factors due to each of the delta areas.

The images in the following results section were all computed using uniformly spaced sample points. Filtering of the vertex radiosities was also used where connectivity information was available.

RESULTS

Form factors obtained using ray tracing from a vertex to an area source are compared to analytical results for several configurations in figures 8 and 9. The analytical formulas were obtained from Howell [12]. These results illustrate several characteristics of point sampling using equation 10.

The results are quite close for a square source. Accuracy decreases as the source becomes more oblong (figure 8). The results also become less accurate as the source and vertex move off axis from one another (figure 9). However, since the magnitude of the form-factors decreases at the same time, relative error is greatest at angles where incoming energy will make the smallest contribution. In each case, increasing the number of sample points brings the approximate result closer to the correct result.

In figure 10 an office scene has been rendered for three successive points in the solution process. The image in figure 10a was generated by an initial step in which direct illumination due to light sources was computed without shadow testing, an easy modification to the ray sampling algorithm that provides a fast initial image. Figure 10b was rendered after nine solution steps and consists of direct illumination by the light sources with shadow testing. Figure 10c was rendered after 21 solution steps and took 12 minutes on a Hewlett-Packard 9000 Series Model 835 turboSRX workstation (all subsequent statistics are for this machine). The office model contains 903 polygons, nine area light sources and 22,775 element vertices.

In figure 11 a quadratic spline surface trimmed with several cubic spline trimming curves is illuminated by an area light source. The resulting shading is smooth, even though the elements used to approximate the spline surface are small. (The spline surface is subdivided into 28 by 42 elements.) Such surfaces would require the use of a very high hemi-cube resolution to avoid aliasing. The scene contains 6086 element vertices. It was computed for 10 steps and took 3 minutes. Five sample points per source were used.

The use of ray tracing allows the geometry used for shadow testing to be different from that used to represent objects for shading and rendering. For example, in figure 12 a lattice constructed of spheres and cylinders is illuminated by an area light source. The spheres and cylinders are divided into polygonal elements for shading and display. However, for shadow testing during the form-factor computation, the ray tracer intersects the original, true surface geometries. The ability to use different geometric representations for shadow testing and for shading and rendering provides an important source of efficiency for radiosity, since representing complex shading can require subdividing surfaces into a very large number of small elements. By ray tracing against the original geometries surfaces can be represented by as many elements as desired without increasing the cost of each shadow test. The model consists of 64 spheres and 108 cylinders. The

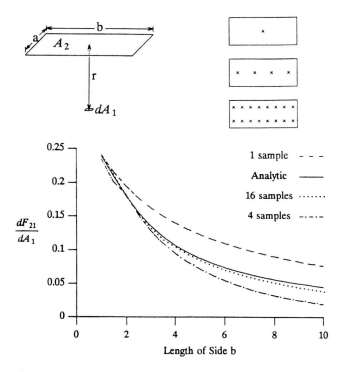

Figure 8. Variation of accuracy with source geometry. The configuration is shown at upper left. The length of side b was varied, while the other parameters were kept constant at a = 1.0 and r = 1.0. The distribution of samples on the source for 1, 4 and 16 points is shown at top right.

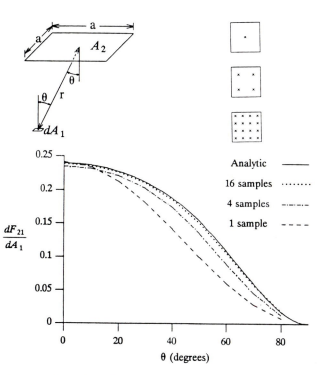

Figure 9. Variation of accuracy with source-receiver orientation. The source and receiver lie in parallel planes. Angle θ was varied, while a and r were kept constant at 1.0. The distribution of samples points on the source is shown at top right.

scene contains 33,314 element vertices and was computed for ten solution steps in 5 minutes. Five sample points per source were used.

In figure 13 a set of planetary gears is illuminated by an area light on the ceiling and a point spotlight from the left. Radiosity is generally associated with area light sources. However, other, non-physical, light sources are a common feature of emerging graphics standards like PHIGS+. The point spotlight is handled during the solution by tracing a single ray from the vertices to the light for shadow testing. The amount of energy per unit area received at each vertex is determined using the lighting equation defined by the Star-

base graphics interface for this type of source. Other non-physical light sources have been integrated in the same way, including lights at infinity and unattenuated point lights. The model consists of 38 cylinders, 8 toruses and 1906 polygons. The scene contains 28,402 element vertices. The solution was run for ten steps and took 14 minutes. Five sample points per source were used (except for the point light).

Figure 14 contains a view looking down the nave of Chartres cathedral. The radiosity solution was performed on only two bays of the model. The complete nave was then simulated by copying and translating the shaded bays three more times. All the curved surfaces in this model are represented by indepen-

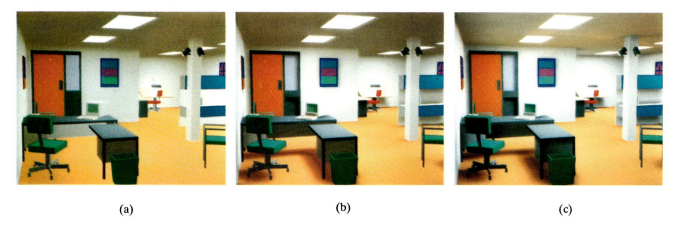

(a)   (b)   (c)

Figure 10. An office after a) one, b) nine and c) 21 solution steps.

Figure 11. A quadratic spline trimmed using cubic spline curves.

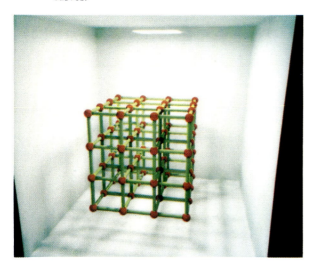

Figure 12. A lattice constructed of spheres and cylinders.

Figure 13. A set of planetary gears illuminated by a point spot light on the left and and an area light on the ceiling.

dent polygonal facets and are shaded using true surface normals at the vertices. The original two bays contain 9916 polygons total and 74,806 element vertices. There are 30 light sources (the stained glass windows were each treated as a single area light source, with the stained glass added during rendering). The solution was run for 60 steps and took 59 minutes. One sample point per source was used. Approximately 1.1 million rays were shot.

CONCLUSIONS AND FUTURE DIRECTIONS

A method of computing form-factors using ray tracing has been presented. This method is particularly useful in the context of a progressive radiosity approach, where form-factors are calculated with respect to only one source at each step of the solution. The use of ray tracing ensures adequate sampling by allowing illumination to be computed directly at the element vertices. By tracing rays from the vertices to uniformly distributed points representing finite delta areas on the source, smooth shading can be achieved for a very small number of rays. The independent computation of form-factors at each vertex allows the illumination of each vertex to be computed as accurately as desired.

Ray tracing is a flexible and powerful point sampling tool that opens up a number of new directions for radiosity. In particular, future work should investigate the possibilities provided by the independent computation of each source-to-vertex form-factor. For example, for a given vertex, shadow testing could be foregone if the maximum amount of energy that the vertex could receive from the source was below a certain level. This would eliminate work that is currently expended on surfaces that are very far away from a source. Pursuing this strategy even further, the number of element vertices on a surface could be varied depending on the

Figure 14. The nave of Chartres Cathedral.

potential amount of energy to be received from the current source.

The use of ray tracing to determine form-factors in a radiosity approach simplifies the integration of radiosity with standard 3D graphics interfaces. Features common to these interfaces, such as non-physical light sources and facet modeling of curved surfaces can easily be handled. When fully integrated with such an interface, the progressive strategy can be extended so that images rendered at interactive rates using a hardware shader can then smoothly progress to the realism provided by the full radiosity solution.

ACKNOWLEDGMENTS

Particular thanks go to Michael Cohen for contributions to both the development of the algorithm and the writing of this paper. Samir Hanna, Don Greenberg and Dave Larson also provided helpful readings of early drafts. The team that developed the radiosity and ray tracing software included Louise Watson and Dan Loewus, as well as the authors, at 3D/EYE, Inc. and Ken Martin, Dave Larson, Kent Montgomery and Joan Bushek at Hewlett-Packard. Modeling credits go to John Lin for Chartres cathedral, Adam Stettner for the office and Paul Booth for the gears. All models except the spline and the lattice where produced using Hewlett-Packard ME Series 30. All images were photographed by Lee Melen.

REFERENCES

1. Appel, Arthur, "Some Techniques for Shading Machine Renderings of Solids," Proceedings of the Spring Joint Computer Conference 32, 1968, pp. 37-49.

2. Arvo, James, "Backwards Ray Tracing," Developments in Ray Tracing, SIGGRAPH Course Notes, Vol. 12, 1986.

3. Chattopadhyay, Subdeb, and Akira Fujimoto, "Bi-Directional Ray Tracing," *Computer Graphics 1987: Proceedings of CG International '87*, Springer-Verlag, Tokyo, 1987.

4. Cohen, Michael F. and Donald P. Greenberg, "A Radiosity Solution for Complex Environments," *Computer Graphics (SIGGRAPH '85 Proceedings) 19*, 3 (July 1985), pp. 31-40.

5. Cohen, Michael F., Donald P. Greenberg, David S. Immel, Philip J. Brock, "An Efficient Radiosity Approach for Realistic Image Synthesis," *IEEE Computer Graphics and Applications 6*, 2 (Jan. 1986), pp. 26-35.

6. Cohen, Michael F., Shenchang Eric Chen, John R. Wallace, Donald P. Greenberg, "A Progressive Refinement Approach to Fast Radiosity Image Generation," *"Computer Graphics (SIGGRAPH '88 Proceedings) 22*, 3 (August 1988), pp. 75-84.

7. Cook, Robert L., Thomas Porter and Loren Carpenter, "Distributed Ray Tracing," *Computer Graphics (SIGGRAPH '84 Proceedings) 18*, 3 (July 1984), pp. 137-145.

8. Cook, Robert L., "Stochastic Sampling in Computer Graphics," *ACM Transactions on Graphics 5*, 3 (January 1986), pp. 51-72.

9. Dippe, Mark A. Z., Erling Henry Wold, "Antialiasing Through Stochastic Sampling", *Computer Graphics (SIGGRAPH '85 Proceedings) 19*, 3, pp. 69-78.

10. Goral, Cindy M., Kenneth E. Torrance, Donald P. Greenberg, Bennet Battaile, "Modeling the Interaction of Light Between Diffuse Surfaces," *Computer Graphics (SIGGRAPH '84 Proceedings) 18*, 3 (July 1984), pp. 213-222.

11. Gouraud, Henri, "Continuous Shading of Curved Surfaces," *IEEE Transactions on Computers 20*, 6 (June 1971), pp. 623-629.

12. Howell, John R., *A Catalog of Radiation Configuration Factors*, McGraw-Hill, New York, 1982.

13. Kajiya, James T., "The Rendering Equation," *Computer Graphics (SIGGRAPH '86 Proceedings) 20*, 4 (August 1986), pp. 143-150.

14. Malley, Thomas J. V., "A Shading Method for Computer Generated Images," Master's Thesis, The University of Utah, 1988.

15. Maxwell, Gregory M., Michael J. Bailey, and Victor W. Goldschmidt, "Calculations of the Radiation Configuration Factor Using Ray Casting," *Computer-Aided Design 18*, 7 (September 1986), pp. 371-379.

16. Nishita, Tomoyuki and Eihachiro Nakamae, "Continuous Tone Representation o6 Three-Dimensional Objects Taking Account of Shadows and Interreflection," *Computer Graphics (SIGGRAPH '85 Proceedings) 19*, 3 (July 1985), pp. 22-30.

17. Rushmier, Holly E., "Realistic Image Synthesis for Scenes With Radiatively Participating Media," Doctoral Thesis, Cornell University, 1988.

18. Siegel, Robert and John R. Howell, *Thermal Radiation Heat Transfer*, Hemisphere Publishing Corp., Washington DC, 1981.

19. Ward, Gregory J., Francis M. Rubinstein, Robert D. Clear, "A Ray Tracing Solution for Diffuse Interreflection,"*Computer Graphics (SIGGRAPH '88 Proceedings) 22*, 3 (August 1988), pp. 85-92.

20. Whitted, Turner, "An Improved Illumination Model for Shaded Display," *Communications of the ACM 32*, 6 (June 1980), pp. 343-349.

Improving Radiosity Solutions
Through the Use of Analytically Determined
Form-Factors

Daniel R. Baum, Holly E. Rushmeier[+] and James M. Winget

Silicon Graphics Computer Systems
2011 N. Shoreline Blvd.
Mountain View, CA 94039-7311

[+]**George W. Woodruff School of Mechanical Engineering**
Georgia Institute of Technology
Atlanta, GA 30332-0405

Abstract

Current radiosity methods rely on the calculation of geometric factors, known as form-factors, which describe energy exchange between pairs of surfaces in the environment. The most computationally efficient method for form-factor generation is a numerical technique known as the hemi-cube algorithm. Use of the hemi-cube is based on assumptions about the geometry of the surfaces involved. First, this paper examines the types of errors and visual artifacts that result when these assumptions are violated. Second, the paper shows that these errors occur more frequently in progressive refinement radiosity than in the originally proposed full matrix radiosity solution. Next, a new analytical technique for determining form-factors that is immune to the errors of the hemi-cube algorithm is introduced. Finally, a hybrid progressive refinement method that invokes the new technique to correctly compute form-factors when hemi-cube assumptions are violated is presented.

CR Categories and Subject Descriptors: I.3.3 [Computer Graphics]: Picture/Image Generation — display algorithms, viewing algorithms; I.3.7 [Computer Graphics]: Three-Dimensional Graphics and Realism — color, shading, shadowing, and texturing.

General Terms: Algorithms.

Additional Key Words and Phrases: analytical form-factor, global illumination, progressive refinement, radiosity, Z-buffer.

1. Introduction

Generating realistic computer images requires accurate modelling of visible light. The radiosity method has proven to be a useful approach for computer graphics illumination calculations. For efficiency, radiosity methods rely on a numerical algorithm known as the hemi-cube algorithm [4] to compute form-factors. This paper examines the sources of error in the hemi-cube algorithm and develops a new technique to analytically determine form-factors and eliminate these errors.

The radiosity method, borrowed from thermal engineering [15] and introduced to computer graphics by Goral et al. [10] and Nishita and Nakamae [13], models light interreflections between diffuse surfaces. In the original, full matrix radiosity method, the environment to be rendered is discretized into small surfaces. Geometric factors,

known as form-factors, which describe the energy exchange between surfaces are calculated for each pair of discrete surfaces. The form-factors are then used to generate a set of simultaneous equations defining the interrelationships between surfaces in the environment. Given the emitted intensities of light sources, the simultaneous equations are solved to yield the intensity of light leaving each small surface. Once the intensities have been calculated, the environment can be viewed from any direction without performing additional illumination calculations.

The primary advantage of the radiosity method is that, unlike ray-tracing, the solution is view independent. Precomputed light intensities from the radiosity method can be used for interactively directed tours of synthetic environments. Because of its view independence, the full matrix method has been implemented in several image synthesis testbeds [9][18].

In the radiosity method, much of the computational burden is in the determination of the form-factors. In an environment of N surfaces, N^2 form-factors must be determined. Originally, in Goral's presentation, form-factors were calculated by numerical integration of contour integrals [16]. This approach, however, did not allow for hidden surfaces. In Nishita and Nakamae's approach, again using numerical integration, hidden surfaces were detected by performing visibility tests between pairs of vertices. Cohen replaced these techniques with the hemi-cube algorithm which efficiently determines form-factors in the presence of hidden surfaces by combining Nusselt's analogy from heat transfer with the Z-buffer algorithm from computer graphics [4].

Even when the hemi-cube algorithm is used, a disadvantage of the full matrix radiosity method is the large computation and storage requirement prior to image generation. Cohen et al. [6] developed a revised method that greatly reduced the time to first image and overall storage costs by applying progressive refinement [3] to the radiosity method. In progressive refinement radiosity, the process of finding all form-factors and then solving a set of equations is replaced by a process that sequentially computes the incremental effect on all surfaces of the light emitted and/or reflected from each surface. Generally, a small number of light sources and bright surfaces determine most of the global illumination in an environment. By processing these first, the progressive method quickly iterates to a good estimate of the global illumination. The disadvantage of a long wait to first image is converted to the advantage of quickly obtaining an estimate of the global illumination of the environment. Furthermore, since form-factors are computed on-the-fly for each iteration, storage costs are reduced from $O(N^2)$ to $O(N)$.

For efficiency, the progressive refinement approach utilizes the hemi-cube algorithm to compute form-factors. The hemi-cube algorithm is based on various assumptions about environmental

©1989   ACM-0-89791-312-4/89/007/0325 $00.75

geometry. When these assumptions are violated, the hemi-cube algorithm produces inaccurate form-factors, which in turn produce visual artifacts in the image. The structure of the progressive refinement method causes the hemi-cube assumptions to be violated more frequently and to a greater extent than in the full matrix method. As a result, not only are the visual artifacts more pronounced, but the method generally will not converge to the same solution as the more exact full matrix method.

This paper presents a new approach for calculating form-factors, employing a hybrid combination of analytical and numerical techniques. The analytical technique does not rely on the geometric assumptions underlying the hemi-cube algorithm. Thus, by employing the new analytical technique when the hemi-cube assumptions are violated, inaccuracies of form-factors and subsequent visual artifacts can be reduced and often eliminated.

The next section reviews the formulations of the full matrix and progressive radiosity techniques. Section 3 explains the assumptions underlying the hemi-cube algorithm and examines the inaccuracies that result when these assumptions are violated. In Section 4, the impact of the hemi-cube form-factor errors on both the full matrix and progressive radiosity solutions is investigated. Additionally, Section 4 explains why, in general, the progressive refinement method and the full matrix method do not produce equivalent solutions. In Section 5, an analytical technique for computing form-factors is formulated that is independent of the geometric assumptions required for the hemi-cube. Section 5 also integrates the new technique into a hybrid progressive refinement method. The implementation and results of the new algorithm are presented in Section 6.

2. Full Matrix And Progressive Refinement Radiosity Algorithms

In this section, a brief review of the full matrix and progressive refinement radiosity methods is presented in preparation for later error analysis.

2A. Full Matrix Radiosity

In the full matrix (FM) radiosity method, the light intensity leaving each surface in the environment is found by solving the following matrix equation:

$$
\begin{bmatrix}
1-\rho_1 F_{11} & -\rho_1 F_{12} & \cdots & -\rho_1 F_{1N} \\
-\rho_2 F_{21} & 1-\rho_2 F_{22} & \cdots & -\rho_2 F_{2N} \\
\vdots & \vdots & \cdots & \vdots \\
-\rho_N F_{N1} & -\rho_N F_{N2} & \cdots & 1-\rho_N F_{NN}
\end{bmatrix}
\begin{bmatrix}
I_1 \\ I_2 \\ \vdots \\ I_N
\end{bmatrix}
=
\begin{bmatrix}
I_{E1} \\ I_{E2} \\ \vdots \\ I_{EN}
\end{bmatrix}
\quad (1)
$$

where: ρ_i = reflectivity of surface i

I_i = intensity of surface i (for diffuse surfaces = radiosity of surface i $/\pi$)

I_{Ei} = the emitted intensity of surface i

N = the number of surfaces in the environment

The form-factor, F_{ij}, equals the fraction of energy leaving surface i that arrives at surface j and is given by:

$$
F_{ij} = \frac{1}{A_i} \int_{A_i} \int_{A_j} \frac{\cos\theta_i \cos\theta_j \; HID \; dA_j dA_i}{\pi r_{ij}^2} \quad (2)
$$

where: θ_i, θ_j, and r_{ij} are shown in Fig. 1

HID is equal to 1 if dA_i is visible to dA_j and is equal to 0 otherwise.

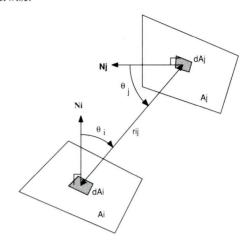

Figure 1. Form-factor Geometry

Implicit in Eq. (1) is the assumption that the intensity across each surface is constant. Equation (2) can be viewed as the average over area Ai of the integral over Aj.

Solving Eq. (1) for a coarse discretization of the environment yields a good global estimate of illumination, but does not give the detail required for a realistic image. Details are obtained without increasing the size of the matrix in Eq. (1) by using a substructuring method developed by Cohen et al. [5], based on a hierarchy of surfaces [14]. Each surface is divided into relatively large subsurfaces or *patches*. Each patch is further divided into subsurfaces, termed *elements*. Form-factors are found from each element to each patch. Patch-to-patch form-factors are then calculated using:

$$
F_{ij} = \frac{1}{A_i} \sum_{e \in E_i} A_e \; F_{ej} \quad (3)
$$

where: E_i is the set of elements in patch i

F_{ij} = the form factor from patch i to patch j

F_{ej} = the form factor from element e to patch j

A_e, A_i = the areas of element e and patch i, respectively

Using these patch-to-patch form-factors, the intensity of each patch is found by solving Eq. (1). The intensity of each element is then calculated using back substitution:

$$
I_e = \rho_e \begin{bmatrix} F_{e1} & F_{e2} & \cdots & F_{eN} \end{bmatrix}
\begin{bmatrix} I_1 \\ I_2 \\ \vdots \\ I_N \end{bmatrix} \quad (4)
$$

where the I_N are the intensities of the N patches in the environment.

2B. Progressive Refinement Radiosity

Progressive refinement (PR) radiosity can be viewed as the radiosity equivalent of backward ray tracing [2] or two-way ray tracing [18]. Intensities in the environment are incremented by *shooting* energy out from surfaces for which estimates of intensity have already been found. The incremented intensities are found from the following equation:

$$\begin{bmatrix} \Delta I_1 \\ \Delta I_2 \\ \vdots \\ \Delta I_N \end{bmatrix} = I_i \begin{bmatrix} \rho_1 F_{1i} \\ \rho_2 F_{2i} \\ \vdots \\ \rho_N F_{Ni} \end{bmatrix} \qquad (5)$$

where: I_i = the intensity of a surface i for which an intensity estimate has already been made

ΔI_e = the increment in the estimated intensity for element e.

As in the FM solution, a low cost, detailed solution is needed. Again, patch/element substructuring is employed. Intensity I_i on the right hand side of Eq. (5) is *shot* from the relatively large patches. Incremental intensities on the left hand side are calculated for the smaller elements.

3. Calculation Of Form-Factors Using The Hemi-Cube Algorithm

In this section the formulation and assumptions of the hemi-cube algorithm are reviewed. Then, for each assumption, the errors associated with its violation are discussed.

3A. The Hemi-Cube Algorithm

Both the FM and PR radiosity methods require form-factors F_{ij} between every pair of surfaces. The first step in simplifying the integral for F_{ij} in Eq. (2) requires two geometric assumptions: first, the proximity assumption, *that the distance between surfaces A_i and A_j is great compared to the effective diameter of A_j*; second, the visibility assumption, *that the visibility of surface i from dA_j does not change*. The form-factor may then be approximated as:

$$F_{ij} \cong \int_{A_j} \frac{\cos \theta_i \cos \theta_j \; HID \; dA_j}{\pi r_{ij}^2} \qquad (6)$$

In the hemi-cube (HC) algorithm, form-factors are found by placing a HC over the center of surface i, as shown in Fig. 2. Each side of the HC is discretized into *hemi-cube pixels*. The form-factors from the center of surface i to each of these pixels are precomputed and are termed *delta form-factors*. All surfaces are projected onto each face of the HC using the Z-buffer algorithm to determine visibility.

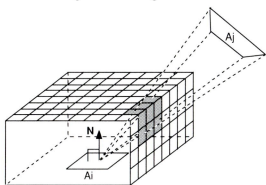

Figure 2. The Hemi-cube

In the limiting case of an infinite resolution HC, the integral over A_j in Eq. (6) may be replaced with a summation over the associated HC pixels. In practice, only finite resolution HCs are possible. The third major assumption, the resolution or aliasing

assumption, is *that the true projection of each visible surface onto the HC be accuractely accounted for using a finite resolution HC*. This assumption and the equivalence of form-factors implied by Nusselt's analogy [15], allows the form-factor F_{ij} to be approximated by:

$$F_{ij} \cong \sum_{q \in Q_{ij}} \Delta F_q \qquad (7)$$

where: Q_{ij} is the set of HC pixels through which surface j is visible to the center of surface i.

ΔF_q is the delta form-factor associated with pixel q.

The HC algorithm is efficient for finding the form-factors F_{ij} from surface i to all other surfaces j (i.e. a matrix row). However, in the PR method, the form-factors F_{ji} from all surfaces j to a surface i are needed (i.e. a matrix column). In this case, the HC algorithm can be used to find F_{ij}, followed by application of the reciprocity relationship to yield:

$$F_{ji} = \frac{A_i}{A_j} F_{ij} \qquad (8)$$

Note that the accuracy of F_{ji} depends strongly on the accuracy of F_{ij}, A_i, and A_j.

3B. Errors Created By The Violation Of The Proximity Assumption

The proximity assumption is violated whenever surfaces are adjacent to one another. Consider two perpendicular surfaces, S_1 and S_2, of dissimilar size as shown in Fig. 3. The analytical values of the form-factors between these surfaces are $F_{21} = .247$ and $F_{12} = .0494$. The limiting values of these form-factors calculated with an infinite resolution hemi-cube are equal to the analytical values of the form-factors calculated from the centers of the surfaces: $F_{d21} = .238$ and $F_{d12} = .00857$. The approximation F_{d21} is relatively good, since the area of S_2, is much smaller than the area of S_1. In general, except for points near the boundary of S_2 and S_1, the distance from S_2 to any particular point on S_1 is nearly the same for all points on S_2. The approximation F_{d12} is quite poor, however. The distance from the center of S_1 to points in S_2 is quite different than the distance from the edges of S_1 to points on S_2. Since form-factor dependence on distance is non-linear, the effects of changing distance do not cancel out, and the result is a poor estimate of the form-factor.

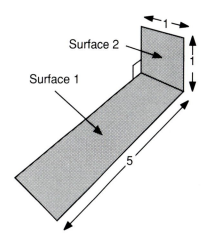

Figure 3. Two perpendicular surfaces of dissimilar size

Errors in form-factors are not limited to surfaces oriented at right angles to one another. In Fig. 4a we consider nine geometries: three possible HC pixel locations in combination with three possible element normal orientations. In Fig. 4b, the relative errors between true form-factors and form-factors calculated with the HC algorithm are plotted versus normalized distance for each geometry. Normalized distance is the distance between the patch center and the element center, divided by the patch diameter. For example, an element with a normal that is parallel to the patch normal, and that projects onto a pixel on the corner of the hemi-cube, the relative error in the form-factor is greater than 100% for normalized distances less than 0.3, and comes within 2.5% only for normalized distances greater than 1. For all of the geometries, the form-factors produced with the HC algorithm converge to the true values as the distance is increased. It is also true, however, that relative errors approach infinity as the normalized distance approaches zero. In the worst case, the two surfaces must be separated by at least five patch diameters (assuming a square patch) for the relative error to drop below 2.5 percent.

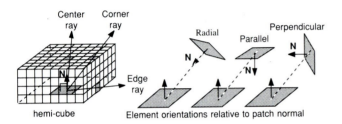

Figure 4a. Geometric orientations used to generate Figure 4b

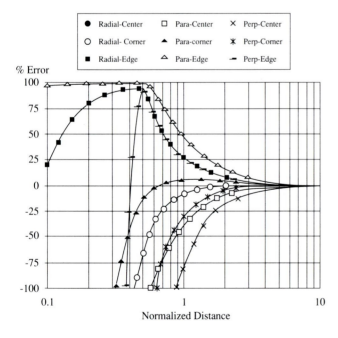

Figure 4b Relative errors between HC computed form-factors and true values (note Radial-Center is equivalent to Para.-Center)

3C. Errors Created By The Violation Of The Visibility Assumption

The visibility assumption requires that the variable HID stay constant across surface i for any given HC pixel j. Because HID is a discontinuous function (either 0 or 1), the single point evaluation is a possible source of significant error. In Fig. 5, the center of surface 1 has a complete view of surface 2, while intervening surface 3 obscures much of surface 1 from surface 2. In this case, the HC algorithm will overestimate F_{12} by using F_{d12} calculated from the center of surface 1.

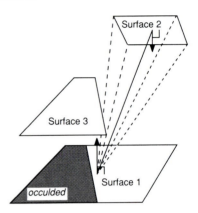

Figure 5. Geometry where form-factor from center of surface 1 to surface 2 is a poor estimate of F_{12} because of intervening surface 3

3D. Errors Created By The Violation Of The Aliasing Assumption

The aliasing assumption, that surfaces project *exactly* onto whole numbers of HC pixels, results in a problem very similar to that encountered in image display [8]. Consider the geometry shown in Fig. 6. An accurate value of the form-factor requires the true projected area of the surface onto the HC. Because of the finite resolution of the HC pixels however, the projected area and resultant form-factor may be either over or under estimated.

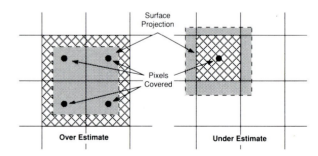

Figure 6. HC aliasing can cause over/underestimate of projected surface area

In many cases, HC aliasing results in intensity errors that are not visually detectable. However, HC aliasing can cause significant errors and disturbing visual artifacts when calculating form-factors to or from light sources. HC aliasing can be reduced by increasing the HC resolution or by using multiple HC samples and filtering the results (thus increasing the computational expense of finding form-factors).

4. Impact Of Hemi-Cube Form-Factor Error On Radiosity Solutions

In this section, the impact of errors arising from the violation of the proximity, visibility, and aliasing assumptions will be considered for both the FM and PR methods.

4A. Impact Of Errors In Full Matrix Radiosity

Using patch/element substructuring and invoking the HC algorithm from smaller elements, the FM method effectively numerically integrates the outer integral of Eq. (2).

In FM, the HC is located at the center of a small element and utilized to determine form-factors from the small element to larger patches. Therefore, violation of the proximity assumption is generally infrequent. This is demonstrated in Fig. 7. In the figures, S_1 is a light source, and S_2 is a white reflecting surface. Figure 7a shows the correct solution, i.e. when I_2 is equal to $F_{21}I_1$. Figure 7b shows the solution when the FM method is used with the approximation that I_2 equals I_1F_{d21}. As seen in the figures, the intensity of S_2 as computed by the FM method is quite close to the correct solution.

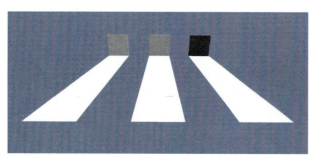

Figure 7a,b,c. Flat shaded renderings of geometry described in Fig. 3. Using true intensity values $I_1 = 1.0$, $I_2 = 0.247$ (left), using FM solution $I_1 = 1.0$, $I_2 = 0.238$ (center), and using PR solution $I_1 = 1.0$, $I_2 = 5(0.00857) = 0.0429$ (right).

Recall the situation in which the visibility assumption is violated as depicted in Fig 5. The probability of a violation decreases as the size of surface 1 decreases. Again, because the FM method utilizes the HC from a small element, visibility errors are less likely to occur.

Finally, consider the effects of aliasing error. In FM radiosity, for a given HC resolution, HC aliasing effects occur as a light source is made smaller [7]. As the light source size decreases, the number of HC pixels covered by the projection of the light onto the HCs of neighboring elements may vary substantially. This variation in computed projected area typically appears as a plaid pattern in the image.

4B. Impact Of Errors In Progressive Refinement Radiosity

By placing the HC at patches rather than elements, the PR method implicitly assumes that the outer integral of Eq. (2) is constant, rather than numerically integrating it as in the FM approach. For this reason, when patch/element substructuring is used, the PR method will not converge to the same solution as the FM method.

Since the PR method uses the HC to find form-factors from the patch to the smaller elements, the proximity assumption is frequently violated. Figure 7c shows the solution of the two perpendicular surfaces with the approximate form-factors obtained from a PR

approach. Light is shot out from the source S_1 and the intensity of S_2 is given as $I_1F_{d12}A_1/A_2$. Clearly, the PR approach grossly underestimates intensity in this case. The global effects of this type of error are demonstrated in Figs. 8 and 9, both images of a cubical room containing a sphere resting on a pillar. Fig. 8 was generated using the FM method, Fig. 9 with the PR method. Note the areas where surfaces are in close proximity: the common edges between walls and the joining of the pillar with the floor. In Fig. 9 these areas are too dark in the PR method due to violation of the proximity assumption.

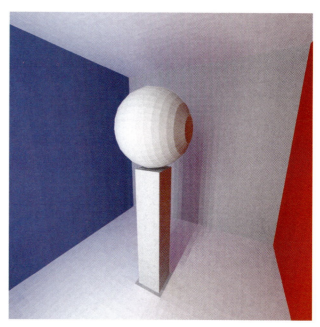

Figure 8. Flat shaded image of cubical room generated with FM method

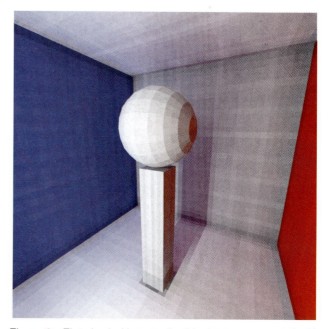

Figure 9. Flat shaded image of cubical room generated with original PR method.

Visibility errors are more frequent in PR than in FM because form-factors are determined from relatively large patches. This effect

was noted in the original PR approach, and the recommended solution was to subdivide the shooting patch. The following criteria were given: subdivide a shooting patch if 1) there is a large intensity gradient across the patch and/or 2) if any element-to-patch form-factors exceed unity.

These criteria are necessary but not sufficient. Criterion 1 fails to improve the most critical form-factors — those from light sources. Figure 4 shows that element-to-patch form-factors computed with the HC can erroneously exceed unity when the element is extremely close to the patch. Thus, criterion 2 only corrects the size of the shooting patch when other surfaces lie very close to the patch.

In PR, HC aliasing is most apparent when shooting from a light source. For a given HC resolution, aliasing effects will appear and worsen as surfaces are subdivided into smaller elements. Fig. 9 shows the plaiding effect which can occur when computing form-factors from the light source.

5. Calculation Of Accurate Form-Factors

The inaccuracies due to violation of HC assumptions can be reduced or eliminated by recognizing that the HC serves two distinct functions: first, visibility determination between surfaces, second, form-factor calculation at the HC pixel level. For pairs of surfaces which do not violate the HC assumptions discussed in the previous section, the HC algorithm can be used for both visibility and form-factor calculation. When computing form-factors involving surfaces which are too close relative to their size, or for form-factors involving light sources, the HC should be used only for visibility determination. For these special cases, the form-factors should be determined by an alternate more accurate method. In this paper, the form-factors for close surfaces and the form-factors involving light sources are determined using an analytical formula.

A general approach to the generation of efficient algorithms is the appropriate application of specialized analytical simplifications prior to invocation of more general numerical methods. Many analytical solutions for form-factors have been determined for specific geometries [12]. However, for environments containing surfaces of arbitrary size and orientation a more general approach is needed. Some general analytical simplifications of the form-factor integral which are useful in numerical calculations have been outlined by Walton [17]. The most common simplification is application of Stoke's theorem to reduce the form-factor double area integral to a double contour integral. As mentioned earlier, Goral used the contour integral form to calculate form-factors.

In this paper, we propose an algorithm in which the outer integral in Eq. (2) will be integrated numerically while the inner integral will be evaluated analytically. By applying Stoke's theorem, the inner area integral can be reduced to a contour integral. For an arbitrarily oriented planar polygon, this contour integral can be evaluated pointwise for a differential surface area dA_j in closed form as:

$$F_{dA_j A_i} = \frac{1}{2\pi} \sum_{g \in G_i} N_j \cdot \Gamma_g \qquad (9)$$

where: G_i is the set of edges in surface i

N_j is the surface normal for the differential surface j

Γ_g is a vector with magnitude equal to the angle gamma (in radians) illustrated in Fig. 10, and direction given by the cross product of the vectors R_g and R_{g+1} as illustrated in Fig. 10.

A detailed derivation of Eq. (9) can be found in [11].

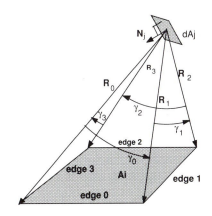

Figure 10.   Geometry for evaluating analytical form-factor

Next we describe a procedure for combining Eq. (9) with the HC algorithm within the framework of the PR method. To minimize computational expense we employ a hybrid combination of the HC and analytical calculations. The hybrid method processes HC pixels in the standard fashion until detecting a violation of the geometric assumptions. For those selected pixels analytic evaluation is used. The new procedure uses the same patch/element substructuring as the previous radiosity methods. We first describe the application of this new approach to simple convex environments, then to more complex environments with hidden surfaces.

5A. Application To Convex Environments

In a convex environment all surfaces are in full view of one another. Variations of intensity across individual surfaces are continuous since there are no shadows. The procedure has two stages: first, the highly radiative surfaces are processed, then the remaining surfaces are considered. Usually the highly radiative surfaces correspond to light sources. To facilitate the description of the new method, light sources are used in place of highly radiative surfaces.

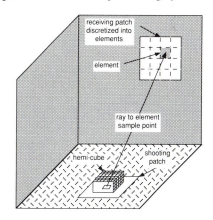

Figure 11.   Using the HC to identify element sample points

Initially, the energy is shot from each light L. All elements in the environment are projected onto a HC positioned over the center of L. As shown in Fig. 11, each HC pixel corresponds to a sample point on a visible element. Each sample used in determining the form-factor F_{eL} is weighted by the area of the pixel projected onto the element, ΔA_{ep}, divided by the total visible element area. The increment of intensity for each element e is equal to the element-to-light form-factor, F_{eL}, times the light intensity, I_L. The form-factors F_{eL} are found by:

Initialize: For all elements e{

$$F_{eL} = 0$$

}

Process: Project all elements onto HC centered over L

For each HC pixel p and associated sample point on element e{

$$F_{eL} \mathrel{+}= F_{eL}^{analytical} \ \Delta A_{ep}$$

}

Normalize: For all elements e{

$$F_{eL} \mathrel{/}= \sum \Delta A_{ep}$$

}

where: $F_{eL}^{analytical}$ is computed using Eq. (9)

ΔA_{ep} is the element area associated with pixel p.

Note that using this procedure:

1.) The accuracy of F_{eL} is independent of the point chosen on the light source with respect to geometrical errors.

2.) Here ΔA_{ep} plays the role of dA_j in Eq. (9), thus the assumption that the area from which the form-factor is calculated is small is satisfied by calculating from these small, sub-element sized areas.

3.) F_{eL} is a weighted average of samples, rather than a sum depending on sample count. Because the magnitude of F_{eL} does not depend directly on the number of HC pixels onto which element e projects, HC aliasing effects will begin to occur only when some elements entirely miss being projected onto the HC, rather than when the projection of elements cover a relatively small number of pixels. To minimize sensitivity to aliasing, we apply this analytical approach to find all form-factors from elements to light sources, regardless of whether the elements and light source are in close proximity.

In the second stage, the remaining surfaces are processed. Since these surfaces have a smaller effect on the overall illumination, the analytical approach is only required for surfaces found in close proximity. For *far* surfaces the patch-to-element form-factor is computed using the original HC algorithm followed by the application of reciprocity to yield the desired element-to-patch form-factor. Given an upper bound on the acceptable form-factor error, the criterion for whether two surfaces are close to each other can be determined using information from Fig. 4. With this criterion the procedure for non-light source patch is:

Initialize: For all elements e{

$$F_{ei}^{A} = F_{ie}^{N} = 0$$

}

Process: Project all elements onto HC centered over patch i

For each HC pixel p and associated sample point on element e{

IF ($D_{ep} < D_{min}$)

$$F_{ei}^{A} \mathrel{+}= F_{ei}^{analytical} \ \Delta A_{ep}$$

ELSE

$$F_{ie}^{N} \mathrel{+}= \Delta F_{p}$$

}

Normalize: For all elements e whose form-factors were computed analytically{

$$F_{ei}^{A} \mathrel{/}= \sum \Delta A_{ep}$$

}

For all elements{

$$F_{ei} = F_{ei}^{A} + \left(\frac{A_i}{A_e} \right) F_{ie}^{N}$$

}

where: F_{ei}^{A} is the analytically computed portion of F_{ei}

F_{ie}^{N} is the numerically computed portion of F_{ei}

D_{ep} is the distance from the origin of the HC on patch i to sample point p on element e

D_{min} is the minimum distance derived from Fig. 4 such that the HC form-factor satisfy acceptable error bounds

ΔF_p is the delta form-factor associated with pixel p from Eq. (7)

Using the analytical formula together with the closeness criterion substantially increases accuracy at a small computational expense.

5B. Application To A Non-Convex Environment

In a non-convex environment, not all surfaces have an unobstructed view of one another. While the HC is useful for determining visibility of an element from one particular point on a shooting patch, it provides no information on whether the element has unobstructed view of the entire shooting patch. Using either reciprocity alone to find F_{ji} (as in the original PR method) or using the analytical formula described above assumes a full view of the shooting patch and gives an incorrect result when part of the shooting patch is occluded.

To avoid violation of the visibility assumption, each shooting patch must be subdivided until its components are either fully visible to or fully hidden from each element in the environment. We propose two methods for detecting when such subdivision is necessary. First, visibility errors in using the procedure described in Section 5A can be detected in a non-convex environment by forming the following sum after finding all the element-to-patch form-factors to patch i:

$$TOTAL\_F = \sum_{e} \frac{A_e}{A_i} F_{ei} \qquad (10)$$

The value of TOTAL_F in Eq. (10) is the approximation of the sum of F_{ie} for all elements e in the environment. For the interior of a closed region, this sum should be unity. If the sum is greater than 1.0, some form-factors have been over estimated because of partially hidden surfaces. If the sum exceeds unity by a small amount (e.g. less than a few percent), the form-factors are approximately correct. In this instance, to avoid shooting out more energy from patch i than it actually has, the form-factors F_{ei} should be normalized by:

$$F_{ei} \mathrel{/}= TOTAL\_F \qquad (11)$$

If the sum exceeds 1.0 by a significant amount then visibility errors exist for one or more surfaces in the environment. In this instance, the shooting patch needs to be subdivided, and the procedure recursively applied to each *sub-patch*.

A precise estimate of visibility is particularly crucial when shooting from light sources. The above procedure generates an average visibility error estimate over the entire environment. Errors in form-factors from lights, even for a relatively small number of elements, can produce undesirable artifacts. To avoid such errors, we

employ the following more stringent procedure when shooting from light sources:

Initialize:	Subdivide the shooting patch into four sub-patches $\Delta V = 0$
Process:	For each sub-patch s {
	$\quad N_{se} =$ [number of HC pixels covered by
	$\qquad$ element e]
	}
	For each element e in the environment {
	$\quad \Delta V_e = \max N_{se} - \min N_{se}$
	$\quad$ IF ($\Delta V_e > tol_e$)
	$\qquad \Delta V += \Delta V_e$
	}
Check:	IF ($\Delta V > tol$) {
	$\quad$ Subdivide each sub-patch and apply this
	$\quad$ procedure recursively
	}
where:	tol_e and tol are preset tolerances that are used for all light sources

This light source subdivision criteria is much more effective than the criteria put forth in the original PR method (as outlined in Section 4B). In particular, a light source does not typically develop an intensity gradient, so the original criterion based on these gradients never produces light source subdivision. Additionally, the second criterion, an element-to-patch form-factor exceeding unity, will produce subdivision only if a visible element lies very close to the light source.

6. Results

The algorithm introduced in this paper is implemented in C on the Silicon Graphics Iris 4D series of superworkstation running the Unix™ operating system. We took advantage of various features of the superworkstation architecture to accelerate the performance of our testbed implementation. All projection/visibility/item-buffer computations for the HC are performed in hardware using the Geometry Pipeline™ and hardware Z-buffer [1]. Once the item-buffers for each face of the HC are generated by the raster system, they are read back to host memory and processed by the host processor(s).

Comparisons of three different radiosity algorithms against a reference solution were performed. The environment chosen was a sphere resting on a pillar in a cubical room. A FM solution where the test environment was discretized into 328 patches and 8176 elements was used as the reference solution. The same surface discretization was used in all test runs. The methods compared to the reference solution were the original PR method, the new hybrid PR method that computes form-factors analytically when surfaces are close, and a version of the new method that always determines form-factors analytically. All three variants of the progressive refinement method used identical HC resolutions: 400 by 400 when shooting from the light source and 200 by 200 elsewhere.

To help validate the accuracy of the algorithms, provide an objective error measure, and supplement visual image comparison, a numerical error estimate was developed. The error estimate is based on the L_2 norm of the piecewise constant **rgb** field over non-emitting surfaces. The relative error measure compared to a reference solution is defined as:

$$\text{Error} = \frac{\left| \mathbf{I}^{Ref} - \mathbf{I}^{Compare} \right|_2}{\left| \mathbf{I}^{Ref} \right|_2} \qquad (12)$$

where the Lp norm of an **rgb** field **I** is defined by:

$$| \mathbf{I} |_p = \sqrt[p]{\sum_{e \in E_n} \sum_{c \in \text{rgb}} (I_{ec})^p A_e} \qquad (13)$$

and E_n is the set of non-emitting elements with areas A_e.

Intermediate and final element intensities for each variant of the PR method were recorded. These intensities were compared with the reference solution using the error measure above. Test results are summarized in Fig. 12. It should be noted that the *ambient term* as originally proposed by Cohen [6] was not used. The term, a heuristic approximation of the ambient illumination, was defined for display purposes only. Since it is not part of the actual solution, it was removed to more clearly portray the accuracy of the different algorithms.

The original progressive algorithm converged to within 19% of the reference solution. Comparing the resultant image, Fig. 9, with that of the reference solution, Fig. 8, reveals rather large differences.

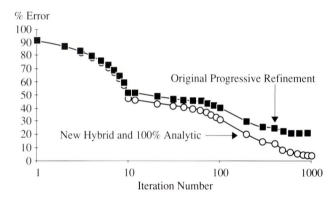

Figure 12. Relative error by iteration for original and new hybrid PR methods

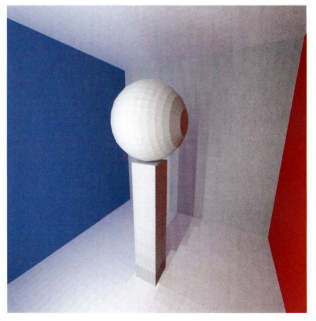

Figure 13. Flat shaded image of cubical room using the new hybrid PR method

As shown in Fig. 12, the new hybrid PR method converged to within 4% of the reference FM solution. Additionally, the difference in the relative errors between the 100% analytic and the hybrid was less than 0.01% at every iteration thus validating the closeness criterion. For the test environment, the hybrid method processed 62% of the HC pixels analytically. Converging to virtually the same solution, the hybrid method took 47.5 minutes compared to 70.9 minutes for the 100% analytical variant. A visual comparison between the reference solution (Fig. 8) and the solution of the new hybrid method (Fig. 13) shows that visual differences are almost imperceptible.

To further demonstrate the viability of the new techniques, the hybrid method was run on a more complex environment. The modelled environment is the Barcelona Pavilion designed by Mies van der Rohe in 1929. The model consists of 2,676 patches and 10,041 elements; it includes numerous light sources of varying size

Figure 14. View of main room in Barcelona Pavilion

Figure 15. View from utility room in Barcelona Pavilion

and a high level of geometric detail. Although the number of elements has increased only slightly, the number of patches is almost an order of magnitude larger. For this reason it was impractical to compute the $O(N^2)$ storage FM solution; in contrast, the various $O(N)$ PR methods were viable. The results of the new hybrid PR method are shown in two scenes from a walk-thru of the pavilion in Figs. 14 and 15. In the images, note the shadow detail, diffuse interreflections, and the lack of HC aliasing artifacts (plaiding)

7. Conclusion

This paper detailed the three assumptions underlying the numerical HC algorithm: proximity, visibility, and aliasing. When any of these assumptions are violated, the HC algorithm produces inaccurate form-factors causing visual artifacts in the resultant images. Although both the FM and PR methods as originally proposed rely on the HC algorithm to determine form-factors, it was shown both theoretically and empirically that the PR approach is much more likely to violate the HC assumptions. As a result, the PR method will generally not converge to the same solution as the more accurate FM method.

A new analytical technique to compute form-factors that is immune to the errors of the HC algorithm was introduced. Finally, a hybrid PR method that combines the new analytical technique with the original HC algorithm was presented. The hybrid method computes form-factors analytically when violations of the HC assumptions are detected and computes form-factors numerically otherwise.

8. Acknowledgements

We gratefully acknowledge the support of the entire Silicon Graphics team. In particular, Efi Fogel cofounded the radiosity project and wrote much of the testbed software. Dave Ligon modeled the Barcelona Pavillion. Tom Davis provided valuable input on the derivation of Eq. 9., and Rolf Van Widenfelt wrote visualization software. Val Jermoluk and Bill Staab expedited required equipment for this collaborative research effort. Paul Haeberli and Mark Compton prepared all color images in this paper for accurate reproduction by creating digital color separations using image processing tools that come standard with SGI's IRIX™ operating system.

Finally, we thank George Walton of the National Bureau of Standards for providing useful information about existing computer programs for computing form-factors.

9. Reference

1. Akeley, Kurt, Tom Jermoluk, "High Performance Polygon Rendering," *Computer Graphics(SIGGRAPH '88 Proceedings)*, Vol.22, No.4, August 1988, pp.239-246.

2. Arvo, James, "Backward Ray Tracing," *Developments in Ray Tracing(SIGGRAPH '86 Course Notes)*, Vol.12, August 1986.

3. Bergman, Larry, Henry Fuchs, Eric Grant, Susan Spach, "Image Rendering by Adaptive Refinement," *Computer Graphics (SIGGRAPH '86 Proceedings)*, Vol.20, No.4, August 1986, pp.29-38.

4. Cohen, Michael F., Donald P. Greenberg, "The Hemi-Cube: A Radiosity Solution for Complex Environments," *Computer Graphics(SIGGRAPH '85 Proceedings)*, Vol.19, No.3, July 1985, pp.31-40.

5. Cohen, Michael F., Donald P. Greenberg, David S. Immel, Philip J. Brock, "An Efficient Radiosity Approach for Realistic Image Synthesis," *IEEE Computer Graphics and Applications*, Vol.6, No.2, March 1986, pp.26-35.

6. Cohen, Michael F., Shenchang Eric Chen, John R. Wallace, Donald P. Greenberg, "A Progressive Refinement Approach to Fast Radiosity Image Generation," *Computer Graphics (SIGGRAPH '88 Proceedings)*, Vol.22, No.4, August 1988, pp.75-84.

7. Cohen, Michael F., "A Consumer's and Developer's Guide to Radiosity," *A Consumer`s and Developer's Guide to Image Synthesis(SIGGRAPH '88 Course Notes)*, 1988.

8. Crow, Franklin C., "The Aliasing Problem in Computer-Generated Shaded Images," *Communications of the ACM*, Vol.20, No.11, November 1977, pp.799-805.

9. Domancich, Micheline. "Graphics Research: A Rambling Tour of French Research Labs Finds Them Hard at Work," *Computer Graphics World* (July 1988) pp. 113-114.

10. Goral, Cindy M., Kenneth E. Torrance, Donald P. Greenberg, Bennett Battaile, "Modeling the Interaction of Light Between Diffuse Surfaces," *Computer Graphics(SIGGRAPH '84 Proceedings)*, Vol.18, No.3, July 1984, pp.213-222.

11. Hottel, Hoyt C., Adel F. Sarofim, *Radiative Transfer*, McGraw-Hill, New York, NY, 1967.

12. Howell, J. R., *A Catalog of Radiation Configuration Factors*, McGraw-Hill, New York, 1982.

13. Nishita, Tomoyuki, Eihachiro Nakamae, "Continuous Tone Representations of Three Dimensional Objects Taking Account of Shadows and Interreflection," *Computer Graphics (SIGGRAPH '85 Proceedings)*, Vol.19, No.3, July 1985, pp.23-30.

14. Samet, Hanan, Robert E. Webber, "Hierarchical Data Structures and Algorithms for Computer Graphics, Part II: Applications," *IEEE Computer Graphics and Applications*, Vol.8, No.4, July 1988, pp.59-75.

15. Siegel, Robert, John R. Howell, *Thermal Radiation Heat Transfer*, Hemisphere Publishing Corp., Washington DC, 1981.

16. Sparrow, E. M., "A New and Simpler Formulation for Radiative Angle Factors," *Transactions of the ASME, Journal of Heat Transfer*, Vol.85, No.2, 1963, pp.81-88.

17. Walton, George. N., "Algorithms for Calculating Radiation View Factors Between Plane Convex Polygons with Obstructions," *Fundamentals and Applications of Radiation Heat Transfer (24th National Heat Transfer Conference and Exhibition)*, HTD-Vol.72, August, 1987, pp.45-52.

18. Zhu, Yining, Qunsheng Peng, Youdong Liang, "PERIS: A Programming Environment for Realistic Image Synthesis," *Computers and Graphics*, Vol.12, No.3/4, 1988, pp.299-308.

A General Two-Pass Method Integrating Specular and Diffuse Reflection.

François Sillion, Claude Puech

Laboratoire d'Informatique de l'Ecole Normale Supérieure
U.R.A. 1327, CNRS

Abstract

We analyse some recent approaches to the global illumination problem by introducing the corresponding *reflection operators*, and we demonstrate the advantages of a two-pass method. A generalization of the system introduced by Wallace *et al.* at Siggraph '87 to integrate diffuse as well as specular effects is presented. It is based on the calculation of *extended form-factors*, which allows arbitrary geometries to be used in the scene description, as well as refraction effects. We also present a new sampling method for the calculation of form-factors, which is an alternative to the *hemi-cube* technique introduced by Cohen and Greenberg for radiosity calculations. This method is particularly well suited to the extended form-factors calculation. The problem of interactive display of the picture being created is also addressed by using hardware-assisted projections and image composition to recreate a complete specular view of the scene.

CR Categories and Subject Descriptors: 1.3.3 [Computer Graphics]: Picture/Image Generation - Display Algorithms. 1.3.7 [Computer Graphics]: Three-Dimensional Graphics and Realism.
    Additional Key Words and Phrases: radiosity, interreflection, two-pass method, extended form factors, z-buffer, progressive refinement, global illumination, ray tracing.

1 Introduction

The problem of light interreflection has been one of the main issues for realistic image synthesis during the last few years. It is now widely known that local lighting models are not sufficient to com-

LIENS : 45, rue d'Ulm. 75230 Paris Cedex 05. FRANCE.
Tel : (33) (1) 43 29 12 25 ext. 32-16. Fax : (33) (1) 46 34 05 31.
e-mail : sillion@frulm63.bitnet, puech@frulm63.bitnet.

©1989   ACM-0-89791-312-4/89/007/0335 $00.75

pute an accurate distribution of light within an environment [13] [1] [5]. The multiple reflections of light on the objects in the scene account for a large part of the total distribution of light, and a global solution must therefore be computed, for the intensity of light at some point may depend on the intensity at any other point. The first global models, ray tracing and radiosity, made strong assumptions about the reflection process, namely that it is either purely specular or purely diffuse.

During the last three years, some advanced models have been introduced that allow arbitrary reflection modes to be used. We review these models briefly in section 2, and show how to describe them using a common formulation, similar to the one introduced by Kajiya with the *rendering equation* [11]. This leads to a new computational system (section 3) extending the work of Wallace *et al.* [16]. It is a general two-pass system that permits the inclusion of refraction among the effects modeled, and removes the previous restriction that all specular surfaces must be planar mirrors. We then present a sampling method using adaptive subdivision (section 4) particularly suited to our two-pass method, and show that it is an interesting alternative to the classical hemi-cube technique [3] in the diffuse radiosity case as well. Finally, we show in section 5 how to produce pictures integrating a complete specular behavior at interactive rates, using multiple hardware z-buffers.

2 A reformulation of previous models using the *rendering equation*

At the Siggraph '86 conference, Kajiya introduced an equation describing the transfer of light between surfaces in an environment [11]. We shall here reformulate some recent models within this framework, and introduce different kinds of reflection operators, corresponding to the assumptions made by these models.

2.1 The equation

Kajiya's rendering equation is the following :

$$I(x, x') = g(x, x')[\varepsilon(x, x') + \int_S \rho(x, x', x'')I(x', x'')dx''].$$

(We use here the exact formulation of Kajiya's paper, and we shall not discuss this formulation. The reader is invited to refer to [11] for further details and a discussion of its validity). Let us just recall what the different terms of this equation mean :
    The domain S, over which the integral is calculated, is the union of the surfaces of all objects composing the scene. $I(x, x')$ is the transport intensity from point x' to point x, $g(x, x')$ is a visibility function between x and x', which value is 0 if x and x' cannot see

each other, and $\frac{1}{d(x,x')^2}$ otherwise. $\varepsilon(x,x')$ is the transport emittance from x' in the direction of x. $\rho(x,x',x'')$ is a bi-directional reflectance function at point x', with respect to the directions of x and x''.

2.2 The global reflection operator

As Kajiya states it in his paper, one can define a reflection operator $\mathcal{R}$ as an integral operator which describes the effects of the reflection on all surfaces on a given light distribution, and express the rendering equation as :

$$I = g\,\varepsilon + \mathcal{R}I$$

(please note that the visibility term is integrated in the reflection operator. This means that the reflected light appears only at points that can see the reflector). The rendering equation can then be formally inverted to give an expression which makes apparent the contributions of the successively scattered terms.

$$I = \sum_{n=0}^{\infty} \mathcal{R}^n g\,\varepsilon$$

2.3 Direct solution using Monte-Carlo integration

Stochastic sampling, as introduced in the computer graphics field by Cook *et al.* [4], gives a way to actually evaluate the reflection integral, which was further investigated by Kajiya, in the same paper where he coined the rendering equation. This is an elegant solution because it solves the entire equation, for all directions converging to the viewpoint, but it involves sampling a huge number of directions, if complex reflective behaviors are to be modeled. Furthermore, the solution is dependent on the light sources in the scene. The problem is to find a general law for the choice of the samples, solving the tradeoff between accurate sampling and computation time. The method introduced by Ward *et al.* [17] at Siggraph '88 can be used to reduce the number of samples at each stage, as it concentrates on specular, rapidly-varying effects, calculating the slowly-varying "ambient" effects less often.

2.4 Radiosity-based solution

At the same '86 conference, Immel *et al.* [10] presented another general solution of a similar equation, based on the previous radiosity method. The basic idea of radiosity is to discretize the space of variables in the transfer equations, thus transforming the integral equation into a system of linear equations. This involves computing the matrix elements of the reflection operator. The solution of the linear system is inherently a global solution, and the good points of radiosity are that the geometric dependency of the matrix elements needs not to be recomputed if only lighting conditions are changed, and that the solution is independent from the viewpoint, as it gives an intensity value for each discretized sample.

In the classical radiosity method [8],[3], the discretization is performed by defining an intensity value (radiosity) for each of a number of surface patches. It is then assumed that the directional distribution of the emitted light is lambertian (diffuse).

The method of Immel *et al.* is more general, because it removes the restriction that surfaces must be lambertian reflectors. This is done by taking as a discrete unit a couple (patch, direction), with a finite number of patches, and a finite number of directions. The matrix coefficients of operator $\mathcal{R}$ are calculated during the solution process, using the visibility information provided by the usual hemicube [3, see also section 4.1 for a definition of the hemi-cube].

Immel's solution is thus a complete solution, like Kajiya's path

tracing, but it involves computing and solving a gigantic linear system of equations. Even if the matrix is very sparse, the CPU power needed makes it unpractical for application purposes. Therefore, some hybrid solutions have been proposed, which attempt to capitalize on ray tracing or radiosity strengths.

2.5 Shao's progressively refined form-factors

At Siggraph '88, Shao *et al.* [15] presented a method allowing rendering of specular effects, while maintaining a relatively low CPU cost. Their method is a simplification of Immel's one where, instead of keeping track of the energy emitted by each patch for each direction, one only considers the energy emitted from a patch to another patch (thus grouping together all corresponding directions). Recall that for the diffuse radiosity this reduces further to one energy value per patch, since the distribution of this energy among the other patches is entirely specified by Lambert's law (plus the visibility information from the hemi-cubes). Shao's idea is to use the geometrical information provided by the hemi-cube as energy transfer information. The percentage of energy leaving a given patch, say i, for another patch j is estimated by considering the geometrical relationships between patch i and all other patches in the scene, which allows a directional analysis of the impinging light on i. In other words, one determines where the incoming light comes from, in order to decide whether it is reflected toward patch j or not. Shao's use of the terminology "form factor" is somewhat misleading, although the definition matches the one for the usual form factors, since it depends on the current distribution of light in the scene, and not only on geometrical aspects. Another way to express this idea is to introduce the reflection operator modeled by such form factors. It is easy to see that each step of Shao's iterative procedure computes a "current" light distribution I_k, such that

$$I_k = g\,\varepsilon + \mathcal{R}_k I_k \qquad \Leftrightarrow \qquad I_k = \sum_{n=0}^{\infty} \mathcal{R}_k^n g\,\varepsilon$$

by performing a radiosity solution with a current reflection operator $\mathcal{R}_k$. The initial operator $\mathcal{R}_0$ is a diffuse (Lambertian) operator, which corresponds to the usual diffuse form factors. The form factors are re-computed at each stage, producing a new reflection operator based on the current light distribution, and the whole process is started again. The crucial point in the method is the derivation of $\mathcal{R}_k$ (the improved form factors at step k), from a given light distribution I_{k-1}.

The convergence of the process towards the correct distribution of light is established using a subtle argument in Shao's paper, and can be intuitively guessed (but not proved) since each step basically adds to the description of the light leaving a given patch the light reflected from the directions where "new" light has arrived. Thus specular propagation of light is simulated, and the contribution of each step is decreasing as the process runs.

One important thing to note is that, even if I_k successfully converges towards the correct distribution, this is not the case for $\mathcal{R}_k$. The final operator $\mathcal{R}_\infty$ is different from the global reflection operator $\mathcal{R}$, as it models only light transfers that actually occur under the given lighting conditions. In other words, the effets of $\mathcal{R}_\infty$ and of $\mathcal{R}$ on the limit distribution I_∞ are the same. This implies that the form factors must be re-computed when lighting conditions change, in contrast to conventional radiosity.

Although this method, like Immel's one, produces directional information about the light leaving each patch, the authors had to add a final ray tracing pass in order to accurately render the rapid changes in the specular effects across the surfaces, as seen from the eye. However, this method is not inherently a two-pass method like the ones studied later in this paper (see discussion in section 3.3).

2.6 Two-pass methods

First introduced by Wallace *et al.* [16] in a specific case, the two-pass approach is based on a distinction of reflection modes. The essence of the approach is to have a radiosity program calculate the diffuse part of light, and a ray tracing program calculate the specular part. Unfortunately, one cannot completely separate the computation of the diffuse and the specular components for the light, because the light itself is not diffuse nor specular; these qualifications apply in fact only to the reflection modes of the light. In other words, some quantity of light can be specularly reflected by a surface S_1, then diffusely reflected by a surface S_2, and so on...(figure 1).

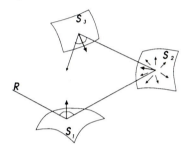

Figure 1: Light traveling along the path R becomes successively "specular" (from S_1 to S_2), "diffuse" (from S_2 to S_3), and "specular" again (after S_3).

3 The extended two-pass method

We present a two-pass method, referred to as the *extended two-pass method* in the sequel, which allows all types of reflection modes to be simulated, removes the restriction in [16] that specular surfaces must be planar mirrors, and includes refraction among the set of lighting effects modeled.

3.1 The basic equations

In our method, we separate light reflection into two modes :

- A diffuse reflection : some part of the incident light is re-emitted according to Lambert's law.

- A specular (directional) reflection (and refraction) : some other part is re-emitted around the directions associated with the incident direction by Snell's laws.

In other words, we express the reflectance function as a sum :

$$\rho(x, x', x'') = \rho^d(x') + \rho^s(x, x', x'')$$

ρ^d is the diffuse reflection coefficient at point x', and ρ^s is the specular (anisotropic) reflection function, which depends on the positions of points x and x'' relative to point x'. For fixed points x and x', this specular function, as a function of x'', exhibits a peak around the mirrored image of point x by the surface at point x' (and another peak around the refracted direction). The exact form of this function needs not to be specified at this point.

Furthermore, we shall assume that all self-emission of light in the scene is purely diffuse (i.e. $\varepsilon(x, x') \equiv \varepsilon(x')$).

Under these assumptions, we can, by replacing ρ by its full expression, rewrite Kajiya's rendering equation as :

$$I(x, x') = g(x, x')\beta(x') + \mathcal{T}I(x, x')$$

where β depends only on x' :

$$\beta(x') = \varepsilon(x') + \rho^d(x') \int_S I(x', x'')dx''$$

and $\mathcal{T}$, the *specular reflection–refraction operator*, is such that :

$$\mathcal{T}I(x, x') = g(x, x') \int_S \rho^s(x, x', x'')I(x', x'')dx''$$

$\mathcal{T}$ is a linear operator, transforming the light distribution I into the distribution obtained by allowing one specular reflection and refraction on all surfaces in the scene (figure 2). The new equation states the relationship between the directional (I) and isotropic (β) distributions, and it can be formally inverted to yield :

$$I = [1 - \mathcal{T}]^{-1}g\beta \quad = \quad [\sum_{k=0}^{\infty} \mathcal{T}^k]g\beta \quad = \quad \mathcal{S} \cdot g\,\beta \qquad (1)$$

where $\mathcal{S} = \sum_{k=0}^{\infty} \mathcal{T}^k$, the *global specular operator* represents the

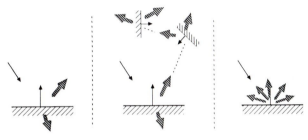

| (a) Operator $\mathcal{T}$ | (b) Operator $\mathcal{S}$ | (c) Operator $\mathcal{D}$ |

Figure 2: Effects of the operators $\mathcal{T}$ (specular reflection–refraction), $\mathcal{S}$ (global specular reflection–refraction) and $\mathcal{D}$ (diffuse reflection) on a single light ray.

effect of all possible specular reflections on distribution I. We can be sure that the infinite sum converges, as the eigenvalues of $\mathcal{T}$ have a module strictly less than one. Indeed, the energy balance within the enclosure states that the total reflected intensity is less than the incident intensity, the difference being absorbed by the various materials.

The distribution β may be expressed in the same manner as :

$$\beta = \varepsilon + \mathcal{D} \cdot I. \qquad (2)$$

where $\mathcal{D}$ is the *diffuse reflection operator*, defined by :

$$\mathcal{D}I(x') = \rho^d(x') \int_S I(x', x'')dx''.$$

The operator $\mathcal{D}$ represents the effect of a single diffuse reflection (on all surfaces), on distribution I. It is the operator used in the conventional radiosity method.

Finally, replacing I by its value given by equation (1) in equation (2), we find an equation on the isotropic distribution β.

$$\boxed{\beta = \varepsilon + \mathcal{D} \cdot \mathcal{S} \cdot g\beta.} \qquad (3)$$

3.2 How to use these equations

We shall now discuss how the above formulation of the rendering equation leads to a calculation algorithm. Until now, we only dealt with integral equations. By dividing the environment into patches of finite size, we can turn these integrals into summations over the patches. Let us assume for now a purely specular behavior, which means that the function ρ^s actually equals zero everywhere but in the exact reflected and refracted directions. This assumption is not really necessary here, we merely use it for sake of clarity, as it permits the use of a conventional ray-tracing algorithm.

The two passes of the algorithm will first estimate the isotropic distribution β, and then derive the complete distribution I, for the directions reaching the eye. It is important to see that none of these two passes can be omitted. The result of first pass is a distribution of light where each patch acts as a diffuse illuminator, even if the amount of energy emitted depends on the specular interactions within the environment (see figure 13, and comments in section 6). It should be stressed here that the discretization of the objects into patches is necessary only for the radiosity-like calculation, and not for the ray-tracing calculation. We can thus use a simpler, more compact representation of objects, to be used in all the ray-tracing part of the process.

First pass : diffuse light.

Equation 3 gives us a way to calculate the "isotropic" distribution of light β. In fact, this is a radiosity equation, like the one introduced by Goral *et al.*, with the diffuse reflection operator being replaced by the product $\mathcal{D} \cdot \mathcal{S}$. The usual radiosity method solves this equation by computing geometrical form-factors, which represent the relationships between all patches in the scene. These form-factors are used to build the matrix of the diffuse reflection operator, and this matrix is then numerically inverted. This suggests that a radiosity method, in which only the form-factor calculation needs to be modified, will give us the distribution β. More precisely, the notion of form-factor will be extended to include specular effects.

The extended form-factors have a slightly different meaning, compared to the usual ones :

F_{ij} is the proportion of the energy leaving surface element i and reaching surface element j, **after any number of specular reflections or refractions.**

Wallace *et al.* also use some extended form factors, but they only allow one reflection on planar mirrors. Our extended form factors are more general because they allow an arbitrary number of specular interactions, with patches of any geometry. The calculation of these extended form-factors can be derived just by closer examination of the equation. We want to model the action of the operator $\mathcal{D} \cdot \mathcal{S}$, which is equivalent to determining where the light received by some point – or surface element – comes from, after having been operated on by this operator. The operator $\mathcal{D}$ means that we must consider all the surface elements visible from that point, as in a classical form factor computation, and the operator $\mathcal{S}$ that, for each of these elements, we have to study a tree of reflected and refracted rays. The process is summarized in figure 3.

We can use these extended factors in a classical radiosity process : we form the matrix relating the distributions ε and β by multiplying the form-factors by the diffuse reflectance values for

each wavelength band [8] , and we invert the matrix using an iterative Gauss-Seidel algorithm [9] (the actual matrix to be built and inverted is in fact the matrix of the operator $[1 - \mathcal{D}\mathcal{S}g]$, as $\beta = [1 - \mathcal{D}\mathcal{S}g]^{-1} \varepsilon$. It is worth noting here that the diffuse reflection coefficients can be changed very easily, as in the classical radiosity process, since they have no impact on the extended form-factors. Conversely, the specular coefficients are used in the computation of the extended form-factors, and thus can not be changed without re-calculating these factors.

Second pass : directional distribution

The directional distribution of light, I, must be computed for all directions of space converging to the observation point. We calculate this distribution with equation (1) derived above. The distribution β has been calculated by the extended radiosity process, so that we just have to evaluate the effects of applying operator $\mathcal{S}$ to it. Let us recall that $\mathcal{S}$ represents the effect of any number of specular reflections–refractions. In order to compute I for all directions reaching the eye, it is sufficient to use a classical ray-tracing algorithm from the eye position, with only the following modifications :

- No shadow rays are needed, which makes the process faster than conventional ray-tracing. Also the computation time is not dependent on the number of light sources.

- The "shading model" is trivial. It is simply the value of the distribution β calculated at the given point.

The general case for specular reflection

We modeled the global specular reflection operator as a *ray-tracing operator* because of the pure specular behavior assumption. It is possible to use a more complicated reflectance function, as long as there is a way to compute the effect of the operator $\mathcal{S}$. A distributed ray-tracing algorithm [4] could be used for this purpose, both in the computation of the extended form-factors, and in the second pass. Wallace's method, which uses z-buffer computations and simulates distributed ray tracing, could be used as well. It is important to note, however, that the same computational method should be used in the extended form factor computation (first pass), and in the final rendering (second pass), if true light transfer simulation is wanted. Otherwise we can obtain images with a very realistic rendering, including non-mirror specular reflectance functions, but with an incomplete "diffuse" solution, if pure ray tracing was used in the first pass.

3.3 Discussion

The two-pass approach is certainly a good compromise between image fidelity and CPU cost, as it uses the respective strength of ray tracing and radiosity to compute the different components of light. Although it involves the computation of extended form factors, which requires more CPU than the computation of diffuse form factors, this method has a number of advantages against Shao *et al.*'s method :

- It is independent of light distribution. If the extended form factors are stored in a file, a new picture can be generated with new lighting conditions, at the only expense of the radiosity solution and the second pass (see last section of this paper for a method to display the final images more quickly).

- There is no need to store the hemi-cubes for the specular patches.

```
For each surface element i {
    For each direction in space d {
        Trace a ray in direction d.
        Distribute the elementary form-factor of the
        direction among the objects in the ray-tracing tree.
    }
}
```

Figure 3: Calculation of the extended form-factors.

- Specular patches do not have to be finely subdivided. A problem that appears when studying the reflection of light on a specular surface is that directions of interest vary rapidly on the surface (fig. 4). Therefore, all specular patches should be finely subdivided in order for Shao *et al.*'s method to produce accurate results.

Figure 4: Precision in specular reflection.

On the other hand, Wallace's "image method" (though restricted to plane mirrors) and our ray tracing technique, allow specular patches to be treated as a whole, without further substructuring.

This lack of precision for specular reflection is precisely the reason that makes Shao *et al.* use a ray-traced second pass, and one can wonder if the precision of specular transfers is not as important during the first pass than during the second. Actually, it would make more sense to either use Shao's method as one pass, with finely subdivided specular patches (but then there will be a huge number of hemi-cubes to store), or a complete two-pass method like the one presented here.

However, Shao's method could prove very useful for simple environments, if a complex reflectance function is to be used.

4 An alternative to the *hemi-cube* sampling technique.

A new sampling method using adaptive subdivision is introduced for the calculation of form-factors, which is an alternative to the hemi-cube technique [3]. The use of an adaptive subdivision scheme proves especially useful when extended form-factors are to be computed, as it reduces the number of rays to be shot, but our statistics show that the approach is efficient even for the diffuse case, especially for high sampling resolutions. We shall first explain the method in the diffuse case, and then show how it can be used for extended form factors.

4.1 Adaptive sampling of the half-space

In a radiosity program, the form-factor calculation requires a sampling of the solid angle visible from a given surface element. We should therefore analyse a whole half-space above the tangent plane at this point, in order to account for all possible transfers of light. Cohen and Greenberg suggested to replace the sampling hemisphere by a hemi-cube of unit size, and to project the environment on its faces [3]. The faces are subdivided in "pixels" and a fast classical algorithm (z-buffer) is used to solve the visibility problems (figure 5). A surface element is thereby associated with each pixel, and the corresponding component of the form-factor (which has been pre-calculated) is added to the form-factor between the two elements. We present here a different method, where we project the environment only once, on a plane parallel to the tangent plane at the given point. We then choose to consider only a restricted area on this plane, thus neglecting all the portion of the half-space that projects itself out of the selected area. This approximation is

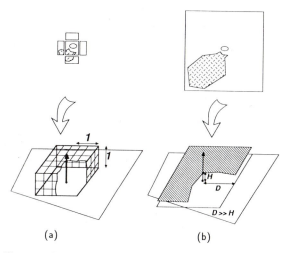

(a)   (b)

Figure 5: By using a single projection, the five images of the hemi-cube become a unique, very deformed image.

made possible by the angular dependency of the form-factor : in the calculation of the form-factor, one must integrate a numerical function depending on the cosine of the angle between the direction of sight and the surface normal. The contribution of directions that are nearly tangential to the surface considered is thus much smaller than the one of almost perpendicular directions. More precisely, the energy diffused through the differential cone shown on figure 6 is given by : $\triangle P = P_0 \sin 2\theta d\theta$ [8] (P_0 is the total radiated power).

We can estimate an upper bound for the energy fraction that is neglected when we analyse the energy being diffusely emitted through a square area of size $2D$, centered in a projection plane at a distance H from the emitting surface (with $H \ll D$, see figure 6). Actually, the "lost" energy is less than the energy radiated in the directions with $\theta \in [\frac{\pi}{2} - \varepsilon, \frac{\pi}{2}]$, if $\tan \varepsilon = \frac{H}{D}$. The neglected energy fraction is such that :

$$\frac{\triangle P}{P_0} < \sin 2\varepsilon \cdot \varepsilon$$

ε is small compared to one, so that we can write $\tan \varepsilon \approx \varepsilon$ and $\sin 2\varepsilon \approx 2\varepsilon$. Finally we get

$$\frac{\triangle P}{P_0} \approx 2\varepsilon^2 \approx 2(\frac{H}{D})^2$$

If, for example, we decide that an error of 1% is acceptable, we calculate the value of the ratio $\frac{D}{H}$: $\frac{D}{H} \approx \varepsilon^{-1} \approx \sqrt{\frac{2P_0}{\triangle P}} \approx 14$. (We used this value in our implementation of the radiosity method). The above estimation relies on a lambertian distribution for the emitted light, but this condition is met even for the extended form factors, since light distribution β is lambertian.

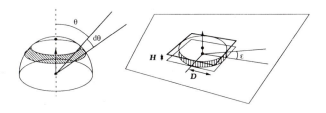

Figure 6: The differential solid angle is $d\omega = 2\pi \sin \theta d\theta$.

We now have to analyse the projection of the scene on our "screen". Due to the perspective distortion induced by the projection, it seems unreasonable to sample uniformly the inside of the square. This would lead to oversampling the external regions, in order to obtain a sufficient resolution at the center. We divide the screen in variable-size "proxels" (*projection elements*), each proxel contributing for about the same amount to the form-factor.

The elementary form-factor associated from the origin with a rectangular area, bounded by x_1, x_2, y_1, y_2 (see figure 7) is given by [8][3] :

$$\triangle F_{x_1,x_2,y_1,y_2} = \int_{x_1}^{x_2} \int_{y_1}^{y_2} \frac{H^2}{(x^2 + y^2 + H^2)^2} dx dy.$$

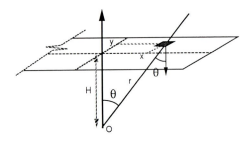

Figure 7: Geometry for the calculation of the elementary form-factors.

We want to find a sequence of integers $(x_i)_{i=0\ldots N}$, N being a fixed resolution, such that $x_0 = 0$, $x_N = D$, and

$$\forall i,j \quad \triangle F_{x_i,x_{i+1},x_j,x_{j+1}} \approx \frac{1}{N^2}.$$

Practically, due to the radial symmetry of the integrand, the above requirement is impossible to meet. We chose the values so that all $\triangle F$ along the axes have approximately the same value, by numerically estimating the integral (see figure 8).

We obtain a partition of the plane in rectangular regions, by a number of axis-parallel lines. The location of these lines (the $(x_i)_{i=0\ldots N}$) needs only to be calculated once, for a given resolution. They are stored in a file, and will be used as proxel coordinates. For each patch in the scene, we want to analyse the projection of the environment on this rectangular grid, and associate another patch to each proxel.

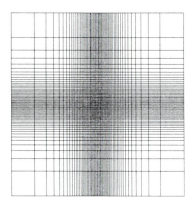

Figure 8: Subdivision of the screen in "proxels". We want to obtain regions with equal contributions to the form-factor.

In order to capitalize on the spatial coherence of the projection, we use an adaptive subdivision scheme to analyse the image on the screen, as introduced by Warnock [18].

The principle of this algorithm is to analyse the projected image in a rectangular region of the plane, or window. If the content of the window is "simple enough", or in other words, if the visibility problem is solved, the algorithm stops. In all other cases, the window is subdivided, and the process applied to the sub-windows.

Once the contents of a window have been identified as corresponding to a given surface element, we should add to the form-factor of this element the contribution of the window. The contribution of the different proxels, which are not all equal, are pre-calculated and stored in a table, but still, as a window could (and should) contain many proxels, we do not want to sum all the proxel contributions within the window. We therefore store in the table, in place of the (i, j) proxel contribution, the sum of the contributions of all proxels $(p, q)_{p \leq i, q \leq j}$, following an idea used for example by Crow [6] to store textures. In this way, the contribution of any window can be estimated in constant time, with only one addition and two subtractions : if the integrals are stored in a bi-dimensional array T, we have :

$$\triangle F_{x_i,x_j,y_k,y_l} = T[j,l] - T[j,k] - T[i,l] + T[i,j].$$

4.2 Generation of the extended form factors

The above algorithm is able to associate an elementary form factor to any rectangular region of the projection plane, corresponding to diffuse emission towards this window. While for traditional radiosity the regions are simply patch visibility regions, this is no longer true for the extended form factors, since we want to follow the light along specular reflections. Actually, when Warnock's algorithm detects a window, and an associated patch, rays are shot at the corners of the window, and the ray trees are compared. A subdivision criterion is tested, which basically states that the first few levels of the tree should be the same. If this is not the case, the window is subdivided and new rays are shot. We see that the algorithm is only modified by a post-process to be executed for each Warnock window. Once a window is subdivided enough so that the ray-tracing trees at the corners match, the elementary form factor associated with the window is distributed among the objects in the tree. In order to avoid shooting the same rays several times during the subdivision, a storage algorithm has been developed, that only requires $2N$ storage locations, where N^2 is the number of proxels [7].

4.3 Comparison to the hemi-cube method

An analysis of running times has been performed with the two algorithms, for different sampling resolutions (figure 9). Times were obtained on a Bull DPX-5000 minicomputer, and represent the time needed to compute a whole set of diffuse form factors, for the scene shown on figure 15. The resolutions of the hemi-cube and the proxel plane can be compared because they correspond to the same sampling cell size at the center of the plane. However, both programs were software implementations. There is little doubt that a hardware-assisted hemi-cube, as suggested in [16], would be much faster.

We see that the two methods are comparable in time consumption, but that the hemi-cube times seem to increase more rapidly with the resolution. This is predictable, since a depth test must be performed at each pixel, while the subdivision in Warnock's algorithm depends mainly on the projected image. Asymptotically, for a given scene, the time needed by our algorithm is bounded by a linear growth, as the subdivision occurs only on "edges" in the

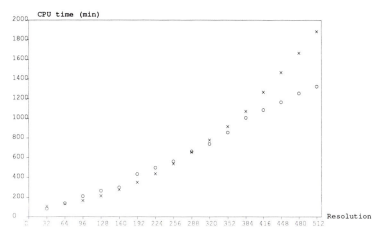

Figure 9: Comparison of running times (1152 patches). A resolution of N means a $N \times N$ grid. (o) stand for our unique projection method, and ($\times$) for the hemi-cube program.

image plane. Therefore, in the diffuse case, it can be interesting to use our method for large resolutions (which provide more accurate form factors).

When extended form factors are to be computed, for the extended two-pass method, our algorithm allows a strong decrease in the number of rays to be shot, and should therefore be preferred to the hemi-cube.

5 One step further towards interactivity

Cohen *et al.* [2] presented at Siggraph '88 a reformulation of the radiosity solution which allows the display of intermediate images, that gracefully converge towards the correct solution. This is a significant advance in the process of making realistic rendering practical for designers, because it makes the interaction loop shorter between the human and the machine. It is important to notice that the first pass of our extended two-pass method can be adapted in the same way. Our experiments show that for a "typical" scene such as the room shown on figure 15, progressively refined images integrating specular reflections and refractions of "diffuse" light are generated at a speed which is only 20 % less than that of Cohen *et al.*'s method (see table 1 and comments).

The problem remains, however, to interactively display a complete solution, including the eye-related specular effects (action of the operator $\mathcal{S}$). We present a method, based on hardware-assisted z-buffer and image composition, which solves this problem for planar mirrors. This method is not meant to replace the second pass completely, as it is limited to such mirrors, but instead the goal is to quickly display a picture incorporating some important specular effects. It should be stressed that the solution process as expressed by Cohen *et al.* is still independent of the viewpoint, so that a person sitting in front of a workstation is able to move through the scene while the solution progresses. We show how to accelerate the rendering of mirror effects when viewing conditions are allowed to change.

5.1 Quick generation of a picture with mirrors

If a particular patch is a planar mirror, one can view the intensity coming from a point on the patch towards the eye as a composition of the (diffuse) radiosity of the patch, and of the intensity arriving from the reflected direction. If a picture has been computed, with the viewpoint transferred to its reflected position relative to the

mirror, one can easily retrieve this reflected intensity (figure 10).

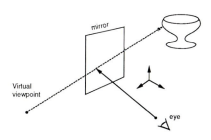

Figure 10: Calculation of a reflected image.

Care must be taken of a few points while computing the reflected image :

- Reflection on the mirror changes the orientation of the coordinate system.

- An additional clipping plane (the mirror itself) should be considered.

On most modern graphics workstation such as the Hewlett-Packard 835-SRX used in our implementation, an off-screen portion of the frame buffer can be used to compute the reflected image. Displaying the complete picture then only involves masking (to extract the portion of the picture where the mirror is seen) and a frame buffer to frame buffer copy of a block of pixels. Thus the extra time required to display the final picture, including first reflection on planar mirrors, is about the number of mirrors times the time needed for a z-buffered projection. For a simple scene like the one shown in figure 14, the display time is roughly doubled, which allows interaction with the picture (the complete display must be done each time the radiosity values are updated by the solution process).

5.2 Moving the viewpoint

When the viewpoint is to be moved "continuously", and for complex scenes, even a factor two in the display time is too much. On the other hand the precision required for displayed images is less, because each frame is displayed only for a very short time. To reduce the time spent for each picture, we actually store a reflected picture bigger than the size of the mirror. If the viewpoint is far enough from the mirror for the perspective to be almost parallel, the projected image for a new viewpoint can be approximated by a sub-image of this current reflected image. The additional z-buffer calculation can thus be performed less often, say for example each third or fourth picture.

Figure 11 explains how the "old" reflected image is used to create a new mirror reflection, when the view point moves in a plane perpendicular to the mirror (on figure 11 the mirror is "vertical" and the viewpoint moves in a horizontal plane). Index 1 denotes the "old" viewing situation, and index 2 the new one, for which the picture must be calculated. The idea is to use the portion of the old image (segment) indicated by the thick line. Lengths L_1 and L_2 are easily calculated given the viewpoints and the mirror, and represent the widths of the mirror images (they can be expressed in pixels). The main problem here is to choose a "distance" parameter (called h in the figure) that will be used to correlate the two views. Small values of h would result in a negligible difference between the pictures, while large values would destroy all coherence between them.

Noting that

$$\frac{u}{v} = 1 + \frac{L_1}{h \tan \beta_1} \qquad \text{and} \qquad L_1 + u = L_2 + v \ ,$$

we use a fixed h value, and calculate u and v accordingly. These values represent the displacement of the reflected picture in the image plane. Generalization is straightforward, and we see that an approximate reflected picture can be generated with very little computation.

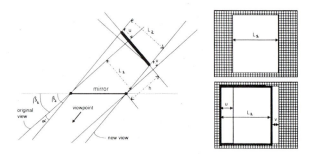

Figure 11: Estimating the translation in image plane.

6 Results

A transparent sphere

Figure 12 shows different renderings of a simple test scene, composed of a transparent sphere illuminated by three colored spotlights. The effect of treating refraction during the first pass is particularly visible.

Why two passes ?

Figure 13 shows different treatments of the same scene, calculated under the same lighting conditions. It is apparent that the inclusion of specular effects is critical to the realism of the image (Illumination of the table and of the back of the vase for example).

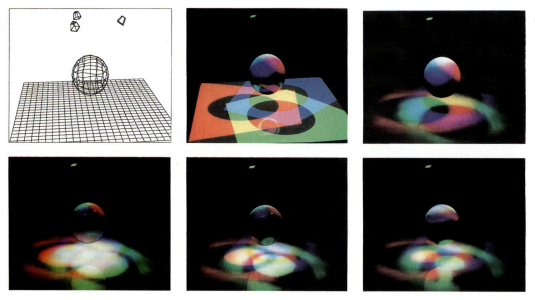

Figure 12: Top to bottom, left to right : (1) Scene geometry. (2) Ray-traced picture. (3) Conventional Radiosity. (4) Refraction index 1.025. (5) Refraction index 1.1. (6) Refraction index 2.0.

Note that the complex colored shadows on the floor are rendered by ray-tracing, but the shadow boundaries are too sharp. Furthermore the light traveling from each spotlight, through the sphere, and reaching the ground is ignored. The general aspect of the radiosity picture is good, with penumbrae effects, but some lighting effects are still ignored. The output of our general system is presented for three different values of the refracting index of the sphere. The realism of these pictures is due in a large part to the light refracted by the sphere on the plane. We can see that, as the refraction index increases, the illuminated area in the geometrical shadow of the sphere first shrinks, and then grows and becomes more diffuse. This is due to the modification of the light's path through the sphere with the refraction index. Similarly, we see that this illuminated area takes the color of the corresponding spotlight when it is concentrated enough. This area is actually illuminated by the three spotlights, but receives more light through the sphere, because of the concentration of rays.

Figure 13: (a) Diffuse solution. (b) Diffuse first pass, with a ray-traced second pass. (c) Complete two-pass solution.

Figure 14: (a) Virtual image. (b) Approximation for translated viewpoint. (c) Virtual image, for translated viewpoint.

Mirror simulation

Figure 14 shows different views from the room shown on figure 15, obtained with the composition method explained in section 5. The first picture (a) was produced by computing the reflected image from a virtual viewpoint. The second picture (b) illustrates the use of a simple translation in the relected image plane, when the viewpoint is moved to the right. Note that the light on the lower table becomes visible in the mirror. The third image (c) uses a virtual viewpoint again, but with the new viewing conditions, for comparison with the approximation in (b). We can see that the image of the light on the lower table is correctly placed by the approximation, while the light closer to the mirror was moved too far to the right. This is an illustration of the "correlation distance" h, which means that only objects within a certain distance range from the mirror will be correctly rendered.

Figure 15: The room used for the mirror simulation of figure 14

Computation times

Calculation of a complete row of form factors (seconds).

	Number of patches	Normal form factors	Extended form factors
room (fig. 15)	1152	12.18	14.41
sphere (fig. 12)	802	3.60	16.2

Second pass (1280 × 1024 pixels, in minutes).

	Second pass	Conventional ray tracing
room	108	196
sphere	76	148

Table 1: Computation times (Bull DPX 5000).

Some computation times are given in table 1. They indicate the average time spent calculating a row of form factors, for two test scenes. This parameter was chosen because it gives the radiosity refresh rate in the progressive refinement program. However our implementation is distributed over a network of workstations, and this refresh time is actually divided by the number of processors. The extended form-factors are of course more expensive to compute, but for environments containing few specular patches, we see that the ratio remains very reasonable. The ray tracing times listed show that the second pass is appreciably faster than a complete conventional ray tracing, because no shadow rays are traced.

7 Conclusions

A reformulation of previous global interreflection algorithms within the framework of the *rendering equation* has been presented. This formulation uses *reflection operators* to describe the interaction of light with the objects, and allows a more precise comparison of different algorithms. This presentation shows the power of a two-pass approach, as compared to Shao *et al.*'s progressive refinement method.

Our general two-pass method extends the work of Wallace *et al.*, by allowing multiple specular reflections and refractions, and by removing the previous restriction to planar mirrors. This generalization is very important for promoting a broader use of such light simulation methods.

A new sampling method for the calculation of form factors has been presented here; it is an alternative to the hemi-cube technique. The method capitalizes on the coherence shown by an environment's view, taken from a random patch. Analysis shows that the method is comparable to the hemi-cube technique for classical radiosity, and may be even better as the resolution is increased. However, it proves especially interesting when ray-tracing is used in the calculation of extended form-factors, because it provides a way to reduce the number of rays being traced.

Finally, the mirror simulation described allows the construction of an interactive system that effectively simulates simple specular surfaces. This method should be used together with the progressive refinement technique of Cohen *et al.*, and could for example be the basis of an architectural simulation software.

Future work on interactive display of complete pictures will include efficient ways to cope with rotations of the view direction, without having to project the whole scene for each view. A preprocessing could for example associate to "each" direction the set of objects which can be seen from a given mirror in that direction.

Some further directions deserve investigation: first, no account is taken of the possible interaction of light with the propagation medium. The zonal method, presented by Rushmeier and Torrance [14], could probably be integrated with the system, for it is based on a radiosity approach. Some other approximations on the reflectance functions should also be tried out, together with the associated form-factor computation algorithms. As mentioned above, a distributed ray-tracing algorithm could be readily used in order to take into account a more sophisticated reflectance function. But better algorithms could certainly be used in place of this brute force method.

The adaptation of the method to parallel or distributed computers also deserves attention, for the main part of the computation time is devoted to geometric calculations that are largely independent of one another.

Figure 16: A test scene for the two-pass method. Hevea tree database courtesy of AMAP.

Acknowledgements

Particular thanks go to Olivier Devillers, who helped clarify the ideas presented here, and wrote the ray-tracing code used in the program. We would also like to thank Michael Cohen for his very helpful comments on an early version of this paper.

References

[1] James F. Blinn. Models of light reflection for computer synthesized pictures. *Computer Graphics*, 11:192–198, 1977. Proceedings SIGGRAPH 1977.

[2] Michael F. Cohen, Shenchang Eric Chen, John R. Wallace, and Donald P. Greenberg. A progressive refinement approach to fast radiosity image generation. *Computer Graphics*, 22(4):75–84, August 1988. Proceedings SIGGRAPH 1988 in Atlanta.

[3] Michael F. Cohen and Donald P. Greenberg. The hemi-cube : A radiosity solution for complex environments. *Computer Graphics*, 19(3):31–40, July 1985. Proceedings SIGGRAPH 1985 in San Fransisco.

[4] Robert L. Cook, Thomas Porter, and Loren Carpenter. Distributed ray tracing. *Computer Graphics*, 18:137–147, July 1984. Proceedings SIGGRAPH 1984 in Minneapolis.

[5] Robert L. Cook and Kenneth E. Torrance. A reflectance model for computer graphics. *ACM Transactions on Graphics*, 1:7–24, 1982.

[6] Franklin C. Crow. Summed-area tables for texture mapping. *Computer Graphics*, 18:207–212, July 1984. Proceedings SIGGRAPH 1984 in Minneapolis.

[7] Olivier Devillers, Claude Puech, and François Sillion. *CIL : un modèle d'illumination intégrant les réflexions diffuse et spéculaire*. Technical Report 87-12, Laboratoire d'Informatique de l'ENS, 45 rue d'Ulm, 75230 Paris Cedex 05, France, October 1987.

[8] Cindy M. Goral, Kenneth E. Torrance, Donald P. Greenberg, and Bennett Battaile. Modeling the interaction of light between diffuse surfaces. *Computer Graphics*, 18(3):213–222, July 1984. Proceedings SIGGRAPH 1984 in Minneapolis.

[9] Robert W. Hornbeck. *Numerical Methods*. Quantum Publishers, 1975.

[10] David S. Immel, Michael F. Cohen, and Donald P. Greenberg. A radiosity method for non-diffuse environments. *Computer Graphics*, 20(4):133–142, August 1986. Proceedings SIGGRAPH 1986 in Dallas.

[11] James T. Kajiya. The rendering equation. *Computer Graphics*, 20(4):143–150, August 1986. Proceedings SIGGRAPH 1986 in Dallas.

[12] T. Nishita and E. Nakamae. Continuous tone representation of three-dimensional objects taking account of shadows and interreflection. *Computer Graphics*, 19(3):23–30, July 1985. Proceedings SIGGRAPH 1985 in San Francisco.

[13] Bui-Tuong Phong. *Illumination for Computer Generated Images*. PhD thesis, University of Utah, 1973.

[14] Holly E. Rushmeier and Kenneth E. Torrance. The zonal method for calculating light intensities in the presence of a participating medium. *Computer Graphics*, 21(4):293–302, July 1987. Proceedings SIGGRAPH 1987 in Anaheim.

[15] Min-Zhi Shao, Qun-Sheng Peng, and You-Dong Liang. A new radiosity approach by procedural refinements for realistic image synthesis. *Computer Graphics*, 22(4):93–101, August 1988. Proceedings SIGGRAPH 1988 in Atlanta.

[16] François Sillion. *Simulation de l'éclairage pour la synthèse d'images : Réalisme et Interactivité*. PhD thesis, Université Paris XI, June 1989. (available from LIENS).

[17] John R. Wallace, Michael F. Cohen, and Donald P. Greenberg. A two-pass solution to the rendering equation : a synthesis of ray-tracing and radiosity methods. *Computer Graphics*, 21(4):311–320, July 1987. Proceedings SIGGRAPH 1987 in Anaheim.

[18] Gregory J. Ward, Francis M. Rubinstein, and Robert D. Clear. A ray tracing solution for diffuse interreflection. *Computer Graphics*, 22(4):85–92, August 1988. Proceedings SIGGRAPH 1988 in Atlanta.

[19] John E. Warnock. *A Hidden-Surface Algorithm for Computer Generated Halftone Pictures*. Technical Report 4-15, University of Utah Computer Science Dept., June 1969. NTIS AD 753 671.

Incremental Computation of Planar Maps

Michel Gangnet   Jean-Claude Hervé   Thierry Pudet   Jean-Manuel Van Thong

Digital Equipment Corporation
Paris Research Laboratory
Rueil–Malmaison, France

Abstract

A *planar map* is a figure formed by a set of intersecting lines and curves. Such an object captures both the geometrical and the topological information implicitly defined by the data. In the context of 2D drawing, it provides a new interaction paradigm, *map sketching*, for editing graphic shapes.

To build a planar map, one must compute curve intersections and deduce from them the map they define. The computed topology must be consistent with the underlying geometry. Robustness of geometric computations is a key issue in this process. We present a robust solution to Bézier curve intersection that uses exact forward differencing and bounded rational arithmetic. Then, we describe data structure and algorithms to support incremental insertion of Bézier curves in a planar map. A prototype illustration tool using this method is also discussed.

CR Categories and Subject Descriptors: I.3.5 [Computer Graphics]: Computational Geometry and Object Modeling – Curve, surface, solid, and object representations; Geometric algorithms, languages, and systems; I.3.6 [Computer Graphics]: Methodology and Techniques – Interaction techniques; G.1.1 [Numerical Analysis]: Interpolation – Spline and piecewise polynomial interpolation; J.5 [Arts and Humanities]: Arts, fine and performing.

Additional Keywords and Phrases: Bézier curves, forward differences, curve intersection, planar maps, map sketching.

©1989   ACM-0-89791-312-4/89/007/0345 $00.75

1 Introduction

There is growing interest in the robustness of geometric computations [10,6,13]. Different graphics algorithms have different sensitivity to numerical errors. In some cases numerical errors are acceptable. In others, one can find ways around them. However, exact computation is sometimes mandatory. The following examples demonstrate the range of effects.

When scan–converting 3D polygons, rounding errors on face equations will not prevent the z–buffer method from rendering a scene. The few erroneous pixels may not even be visible. This is a case where numerical errors are innocuous. A second example is a function performing point location in a polygon with a parity test, using floating point arithmetic. If the result returned by this function is used for identification of the polygon and, say, modification of its color, then it is acceptable for the function to return an empty result when a reliable answer cannot be computed. Hence, in some 2D drawing programs, the user must click well inside a polygon to select it (which is better than selecting the wrong polygon). As a third example consider a program implementing an algorithm which presumes infinite precision. The Bentley–Ottmann algorithm [3,20] for reporting intersections of a set of non vertical line segments relies on the fact that two segments may intersect iff there exists a position of the vertical sweep–line where they are consecutive. If the implementation produces an error when inserting a new segment in the sweep–line then some intersections may be missed. In this case, it is imperative to provide an exact answer.

Methods involving topological decisions based on geometric computations are generally difficult to implement. We describe a robust solution to an intersection problem which arises in the context of a 2D drawing application. A set of lines and curves like in Fig. 1 dissects the plane into vertices, edges and faces. This type of geometric object is known in graph theory as a map of a planar multigraph [24], hence the name *planar map* we use below, and in computational geometry as an *arrangement* in the plane [7]. Data structures describing embeddings of planar graphs in the plane can be traced back to Baumgart's winged-edge data structure and have been studied by numerous researchers [20,12,9]. It is standard practice to distinguish between the geometry, the position of the vertices, geometric definition of the edges and the topology, the incidence and adjacency of the vertices, edges, and faces.

The problem addressed here is building a data structure to support *incremental insertion* of new curves in a planar map, dynamically computing new intersections and updating the data structure. In this case, topological information has to be deduced from geometrical information. When two curves intersect at a new vertex, the ordering of the four edges around the vertex provides topological information used to follow the contour of a face incident to the vertex. If floating point arithmetic is used, it has been shown that the computed slopes can give the wrong order [10,18]. This is similar to the Bentley–Ottmann algorithm example above.

Our first implementation [19] used the Bentley–Ottmann algorithm and rational arithmetic to compute the planar map formed by a set of line segments, [11] is the description of a 2D illustration tool based on this first software. The method was not incremental and the map had to be recomputed each time a new segment was added. In [5], Greene and Yao solve the intersection problem for line segments by working directly in the discrete plane. In [8], Edelsbrunner et al. study arrangements of Jordan curves in the plane from a theoretical point of view.

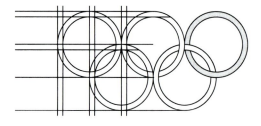

Figure 1: A planar map.

In the next section, the utility of planar maps for 2D drawing is briefly discussed. Section 3 details curve intersection. First, Bézier curves are interpolated by polylines using forward differencing. Then, the intersection between two interpolating polylines is computed with rational arithmetic, we show how it is possible to limit the number of bits in this process and how to control the quality of the interpolation. Section 4 describes the map data structure and the two main algorithms used in the planar map construction process: incremental insertion of a curve and point location in a map. The map topology is computed from the geometry of the polylines. Since exact arithmetic is used in this process, the map topology, although it may be different from the topology defined by the true curves, is always consistent with the geometry of the interpolating polylines.

2 Map Sketching

Our interest in planar maps is motivated by practical concerns: with traditional graphic arts media (pencil, eraser, ink,

etc.), it is common practice to build shapes by drawing lines and curves, erase some pieces thereof, and color or ink the areas they delimit (see [1] and Fig. 2).

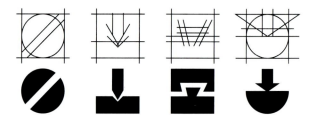

Figure 2: Graphic design by space division
(B. Munari *in* [1]).

The design of logos and monograms, floor plan sketching by architects, cartoon cells drawing and inking are examples where this technique is used. In typical drawing software there is no way to mimic this method. If Fig. 3a is drawn by the user of a drawing application as four lines, it is impossible for him to color the rectangle (as in Fig. 3b) since no such rectangle exists. If the drawing were computed as a planar map, this dual interpretation would be possible.

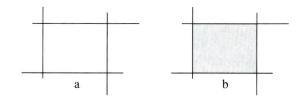

a   b

Figure 3: Four lines and a rectangle.

In [2], we have proposed two extensions to the 2D graphics drawing paradigm: a) objects are multicolor, multicontour shapes (i.e., planar maps), b) they are constructed by iteration of three basic steps: drawing, erasing, and coloring. We call this technique *map sketching* and have implemented it in prototype illustration software used to draw the figures in this paper. Fig. 4 illustrates map sketching. Strokes drawn by the user are incrementally added to the map describing the drawing. Two additional operations are allowed on a map: edge erasing and face coloring. These steps can be iterated in any order. Map sketching closely parallels the traditional pencil and eraser method and is more natural and more efficient for constructing certain classes of drawings. User interface design issues in map based illustration software are discussed in [2].

Figure 4: Map sketching.

3 Bézier Curve Interpolation and Intersection

3.1 Overview

Curves to be inserted in a map are first converted to Bézier form [21,4]. The incremental insertion algorithm (Sec. 4) has two requirements. First, intersection points must be ordered without error along a curve by their parameter values, including the case of self-intersection. Second, if two or more curves intersect at one point, they must be ordered without error around the point. To meet these requirements, we use the following strategy:

1. The control points of the Bézier curves have integer coordinates on a grid large enough for 2D graphics applications. Grid size is discussed in Sec. 3.4.

2. The curve is replaced with an interpolating *polyline*. We compute an *exact* interpolation of the curve by exact forward differencing (FD). It is necessary that enough bits are available to perform FD without a loss of precision (Sec. 3.2). Rather than storing polylines in the data structure, they are computed as needed.

3. Computing the intersection of two exact polylines causes an explosion in the number of bits. Thus, we round the points of an exact polyline to the grid. This reduces the intersection of two *rounded polylines* to the intersection of line segments whose endpoints have integer coordinates. Ordering two intersection points along the same line segment and ordering two intersecting line segments around their intersection point is done with rational arithmetic. Note that the intersection points *are*

not rounded since this could modify the map topology.

4. Finally, it is natural with the map sketching technique to use an existing intersection point as a new curve endpoint. We will show how to achieve this without increasing the bit length of the arithmetic (Sec. 3.4).

The map deduced from the intersection process is the one defined by the rounded polylines. No other rounding occurs. The map topology, although it may be different from the topology defined by the true curves, is always consistent with the geometry of the rounded polylines.

3.2 Interpolation Method

Wang [25,23] gives the following result. If the de Casteljau subdivision algorithm (midpoint case) is applied down to depth k to a polynomial Bézier curve of degree $d \geq 2$ with control points V_r, where:

$$k = \left\lceil \log_4 \frac{d(d-1)}{8} \frac{D}{\epsilon} \right\rceil, \qquad (1)$$

then, all the chords (straight line segments) joining the endpoints of the 2^k control polygons which are the leaves of the subdivision tree are closer to the curve than the threshold ϵ. In (1), $D = \max_{0 \leq r \leq d-2} \|V_{r+2} - 2V_{r+1} + V_r\|$ and $\|v\| = \max(|x_v|, |y_v|)$ for a vector v. D can be called the *diagonal* of the curve. Since reference [25] is not available to us, an independent proof of this result is given in appendix A, together with a bound on the chord length.

Consider the chord endpoints $E_i, 0 \leq i \leq 2^k$. They form a polyline E. It is faster to use ordinary FD [16] than subdivision to compute E. Since *a priori* subdivision computes the complete tree to depth k, FD with fixed step size 2^{-k} will generate the same polyline, provided that exact computations are done in both cases. We now show that the number of bits needed to perform exact FD is bounded. Suppose that the control points of the curve have coordinates coded into b bits. Then, computing the subdivision tree down to depth k requires at most $b + kd$ bits for the coordinates of the E_i. In the FD loop, the only values involved in the ith iteration are the forward differences $\Delta^j E_i$, $0 \le j \le d$. Since we know from subdivision that, for all i, the computation of $E_i = \Delta^0 E_i$ requires at most $b + kd$ bits, $\Delta^j E_i$ requires at most $b + kd + j$ bits. Thus, exact FD with step size 2^{-k} can be performed on the curve if $b + (k + 1)d$ bits are available.

To limit the total number of bits needed when updating a planar map, the intersection algorithm uses *rounded* polylines. FD computes the exact coordinates of the E_i which are then rounded to b bits.

3.3 Intersection Algorithm

Bézier curve intersection is studied by Sederberg and Parry [23]. In two of the algorithms they consider, rejection of non-intersecting pieces of two curves is done by bounding box comparison. FD is not convenient for successive midpoint evaluations of a curve. To take advantage of bounding boxes, a preprocessing step breaks the rounded polylines into monotonic pieces. For such a piece, the box of any subpiece is given by its endpoints coordinates. This method is also used by Koparkar and Mudur [14] with another curve evaluation method. During the planar map construction process, a new curve is intersected with a subset of the curves already inserted in the map. The preprocessing of the new curve finds the monotonic pieces, saving data to be used in later computations. The new curve is then immediately inserted in the map.

Preprocessing. Let C be the new curve. a) use FD to compute the exact polyline E and the rounded polyline P of C, b) store P in an array, to be discarded after the insertion of C, c) find the monotonic pieces of P, d) at the end of a monotonic piece, save the permanent data associated with it, that is, its first and last indices (i_f, i_l), its bounding box, its quadrant, and the FD context at i_f (i.e., $\Delta^j E_{i_f}$, for all j). All these steps can be performed in one single FD loop.

Intersection. It is enough to consider the intersection of a monotonic piece of P, with indices (i_f, i_l), with a monotonic piece of an existing curve G, with indices (j_f, j_l), whose bounding boxes overlap. First, compute Q, the rounded polyline of G, between j_f and j_l using the FD context at j_f which has been saved when preprocessing G, and store the result into an array. Then, search the intersecting chords using binary subdivision on the respective arrays (the box of any subset of points considered in this subdivision is given by its two endpoints and the quadrant information). In the map sketch-

ing application, the existing curve G may be partially erased. In this case only the monotonic pieces containing a non-erased part of G are intersected with C.

Two special cases must be handled: rounded chords with a null length, and partially overlapping polylines (i.e., non transverse intersections). After preprocessing, a new curve is intersected with itself to detect multiple points and self-overlapping. Naturally, line segments are not subdivided since they are ready for intersection. It is worthwhile to cache partially or totally generated curves. Two cases are frequent: a) the same monotonic piece of G intersects different pieces of C, b) successive new curves intersect the same existing curve.

3.4 Topology Consistency

This section describes how a consistent topology is obtained from the geometrical data given by the intersection process. For illustration software, the input can be rounded to an integer grid if the grid size is large enough and if the scaling factors are limited accordingly. A typical case is to output the results on a $24'' \times 24''$ page at 300 dpi. Then, input control points may be defined on twice as large an area, to permit clipped curves. We must also choose a maximum zoom factor: a reasonable value is 8. Since the rounded chords must have even coordinates (see below), the input is scaled up by a factor of two. The control points coordinates are thus coded on $b = 18$ bits. Setting $\epsilon = 1$ in equation (1) gives $k = 10$ for a degree 4 curve with the maximum diagonal, which is twice the grid size. Thus, 62 bits are needed for the exact FD of this curve, this goes up to 102 bits for a degree 7 curve with the same diagonal. The much more usual case of a cubic with a $4''$ diagonal is 45 bits.

If chord intersection is performed on the exact polylines the number of bits grows very rapidly. When two chords AB and CD intersect at I, the coordinates of I and the values of the two parameters u and v such that $AI = uAB$ and $CI = vCD$ must be computed exactly. All of these can be expressed as rational numbers; for example, $u = (AC \times CD) \div (AB \times CD)$ where $\times$ is the cross product. With endpoints coded on $b + kd$ bits, this is $2(b + kd) + 3$ bits for the numerator and the denominator of the rationals. Since different intersections along the same chord are ordered by comparing their rational parameter values, the final number of bits is $4(b + kd) + 6$. For the first curve in the example above, this is 238 bits. The situation is worse if we want to use an existing intersection as the endpoint of a new curve. Setting $b = 238$ in the above computations gives 1118 bits. As noted by Forrest and Newell [10], the major drawback in the rational arithmetic approach is the blow-up in the number of bits.

To limit this number, the chord endpoints of the exact polylines are rounded to even integer values. Chord intersection is done on the rounded chords and the intersection points are exactly represented as rational numbers. To use an exist-

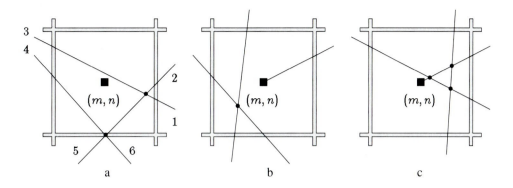

Figure 5: Vertex (m, n) and chord ordering.

ing intersection point as the endpoint of a new curve without increasing the bit length, we consider the semi-open rectangles $R_{m,n} = [m - 1, m + 1) \times [n - 1, n + 1)$, where m and n are even. Since the vertical and horizontal lines limiting the rectangles have odd coordinates, there are no rounded chords collinear with these lines. So, it is always possible, if two or more chords intersect inside $R_{m,n}$, to order them along the boundary of $R_{m,n}$ by using either the coordinates of their intersections with the lines limiting the rectangle or their slopes if they leave $R_{m,n}$ at exactly the same point (Fig. 5a). We define the center of $R_{m,n}$ as the *vertex* of the intersection points lying inside $R_{m,n}$. This associates intersection points with vertices but does not round their coordinates. To use a chord intersection point as the endpoint of a new curve, we do not use the point itself but the coordinates of the associated vertex (Fig. 5b). Therefore, small faces lying inside a single rectangle will not be represented in the map data structure (Fig. 5c).

On a curve, an intersection point is represented as a *parameter value* $p = (i, u)$ where i is the chord index on the polyline and u a rational number giving the exact position of the point on the chord. Since all chords have now rounded endpoints, ordering two intersection points along one curve requires at most $4b + 6$ bits. We need also to order the intersections of the chords with the lines limiting the rectangles $R_{m,n}$. These are Bézier curves of degree 1, thus the stated bound is valid. In the common case where only one intersection point is associated with a vertex, the slopes are used to order the chords, requiring at most $2b + 3$ bits. In addition, the method must support the erasing of curve pieces limited by intersection points. It is therefore necessary to keep the initial data defining the curve and to mark as erased or non-erased the corresponding pieces. As noted above, the intersection algorithm uses this information to return only actual intersections. A curve is removed from the map data structure iff it has been totally erased.

The method has two limitations. First, intersection is performed on the rounded polylines. Thus, there are situations (e.g., tangencies) where intersections between the true curves are ignored. Likewise, polylines may intersect even if true curves do not (e.g., two concentric circles with very close radii interpolated by regular polygons whose sides intersect pairwise). Second, the topology of a map computed in this way is not invariant under general affine transforms. Thus, the map has to be recomputed from the original data whenever it is rotated or scaled. The first limitation is inherent in any linear interpolation process. However, for 2D graphics applications, it is always possible to prevent any visible effects by choosing an appropriate grid size. The second limitation can only be solved by using exact arithmetic on real numbers or symbolic computation on algebraic curves, which are currently too slow for interactive applications. Without recomputing the map, it is possible to perform integer translation (i.e., dragging) and scaling by a power of 2 (i.e., zooming), if we remain inside the grid.

In this section, we have shown that a robust method for the computation of planar maps with linearly interpolated Bézier curves requires at most $b + (k + 1)d$ bits for the FD step and $4b + 6$ bits for the intersection and sorting steps. Our implementation uses a variable length integer arithmetic package coded in assembly language. In practice, the average size of the numbers involved in the process is much smaller than the above bounds. The only operation we must perform on rational numbers is comparison, which is two integer multiplications and a test. The value of b is a parameter of the program, allowing the grid size to be adapted to the resolution of the display.

4 Data Structure and Algorithms

After describing the planar map data structure, we detail below the two main algorithms. Curve insertion uses point location in a map to find the face containing the first endpoint of a curve. However, since point location is equivalent to the insertion of a dummy line segment, curve insertion will come first.

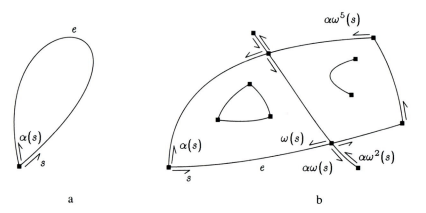

Figure 6: Map topology.

4.1 Planar Map Description

A map contains two different sets of data. The first one describes the geometry of the curves and their intersections, and the second contains the topological data. In what follows, the word curve should be understood as the rounded polyline associated with the curve.

Geometry. When inserted, a curve is cut into *arcs* by the other curves. An arc is described by its endpoints on the curve. Each *point* (i.e., an intersection or a curve endpoint) is known by its parameter value $p = (i, u)$ on the curve, as in Sec. 3.4. An intersection yields two points, one on each curve. As parameters are totally ordered along a curve, an arc is noted below as a parameter interval $[p_1, p_2]$. Arcs are marked as either erased or non-erased.

Topology. The mapping defined in Sec. 3.4 associates with each point a unique vertex. To support arc overlap, we attach to an arc an *edge* connecting its vertices. Arcs lying entirely in one rectangle R_{mn} are not considered. Overlapping arcs share the same edge. The geometry of an edge is the geometry of one of the arcs it *supports*. Different edges can connect the same pair of vertices. The ordering of the edges around a vertex is the chord ordering defined by the rectangles R_{mn}.

To access the faces of a planar map, it is convenient to consider an edge as two directed edges, called *sides*. If an edge e is a loop incident to the vertex v, then the clockwise (cw) and counterclockwise (ccw) orientations along e define the two sides associated with e (Fig. 6a). Two mappings are defined on the sides of a map: $\alpha(s)$ is the side next to s in the ccw order around the vertex incident to s, and $\omega(s)$ is the other side of the edge [17]. We note the ordering of the sides around a vertex, α-*order*. To follow the boundary containing a side s, the compound mapping $\alpha\omega$ is applied repeatedly until back in s (Fig. 6b). The result is a face boundary

called a *contour*. Contours with a ccw orientation are *outer* contours, others are *inner* contours. Adding a virtual inner contour located at infinity, there is exactly one inner contour for each face of a map.

The edges may form several connected components which are partially ordered by inclusion in the plane. This partial ordering is described by an *inclusion tree* whose nodes are the contours. The root is the virtual inner contour at infinity. The leaves are either inner contours with no connected component included or outer contours with an empty interior. This tree is stored in the data structure and used by the curve insertion and point location algorithms.

4.2 Curve Insertion

We say that an arc is *visible* in a face if this arc is supported by an edge of which at least one side is in a contour bounding the face. Curve insertion uses the method described in Sec. 3 to compute the intersections between a new curve C and all the arcs visible in the faces where C is lying (Fig. 7). Along C, p is the current parameter value and $next(p)$ the parameter value of the next intersection point, $p < next(p)$.

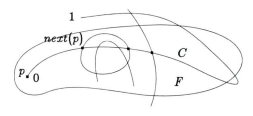

Figure 7: Curve insertion (first iteration).

Step 1. Using point location (Sec. 4.3), find the face F containing the first point of C. Set parameter p to 0.

Step 2. If F has already been processed, jump to step 3. Otherwise, compute the intersections between arc $[p, 1]$ and all the arcs visible in F. Cut the arc $[p, 1]$ and the intersected arcs of F at each intersection point and create the corresponding vertices and sides. At the end of this step, there are no more intersections between p and $next(p)$, and the α-order around the vertices along C has been updated.

Step 3. If there is no overlapping, create an edge between the vertices associated with p and $next(p)$, link it with the arc $[p, next(p)]$ in the data structure, and update the inclusion tree accordingly (see appendix B). Otherwise, the edge already exists, link it with the arc $[p, next(p)]$.

Step 4. If $next(p) = 1$ then stop. Otherwise, let s be the side of arc $[next(p), next(next(p))]$ associated with $next(p)$. Since the α-order around the two corresponding points is known, s is known. Set F to the face incident to $\alpha(s)$, and p to $next(p)$. Repeat step 2.

An arc is visible in at most two faces but an existing curve G can be visited several times. However, the intersection between the arc $[p, 1]$ of C and G is done only once: the first time an arc of G becomes visible in the current face F. The intersection points located outside F are stored for further use.

4.3 Point Location

Given a query point with integer coordinates, the point location algorithm returns either a face, an edge, or a vertex. In map sketching, all selections are done through this algorithm (e.g., coloring a face or selecting an existing intersection as the endpoint of a new curve). A first method is to intersect a line segment S with all curves. S is defined by the query point M, with parameter 0, and a point outside the bounding box of the map, with parameter 1. If no intersection is found, M is inside the infinite face. Else, retain the curve G whose intersection is closest to M. This intersection is known by its parameter values p on S and q on G. The parameter q gives the arc of G containing the intersection. If $p = 0$, then M is exactly on the edge supporting this arc. Otherwise, M is inside one of the two faces incident to the edge. The side which sees M to its right gives the answer (a side defines a unique orientation on a curve).

This method does not take advantage of the partition of the plane defined by the faces of the map. To reduce the average number of visited curves, the following algorithm uses face adjacency (Fig. 8). This algorithm is similar to the curve insertion algorithm, but it uses curve intersection instead of arc intersection. We say that a curve is *visible* in a face if one of its arcs is visible in the face.

Step 1. Set F to the infinite face and S to $[0, 1]$. S is the line segment defined above.

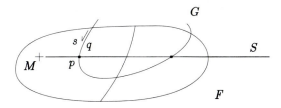

Figure 8: Point location.

Step 2. If F has no outer contours then return F. Otherwise, intersect S with the curves visible in the outer contours of F (if two or more curves are overlapping, it is enough to consider one of them). If there is no intersection, return F. Otherwise, let e be the edge which gives the smallest parameter p on S, and s the side of e which sees M to its right . If s is part of an outer contour, return F. Otherwise, set S to $[0, p]$ and set F to the face incident to s.

Step 3. Intersect S with the curves visible in the inner contour of F. If there is no intersection, call recursively step 2. Otherwise, let e be the edge which gives the smallest parameter p on S, and s the side of e which sees M to its right, s is necessarily part of an inner contour. Set F to the face incident to this contour and S to $[0, p]$. Repeat step 3.

As curve insertion does, point location may visit a curve several times, but only one intersection with S is performed. The geometric tests are performed on rational numbers, they are thus exact. Indications on the complexity of both algorithms are given by the horizon theorem for Jordan curves included in [8]. However, this last result cannot be applied in a straightforward way as the number of intersections between two polylines may be greater than the number of intersections between the true curves, and the polylines may be partially overlapping.

5 Conclusion

A method has been presented which allows for incremental construction of planar maps. Robustness of the computation and consistency between geometry and topology are achieved through linear interpolation of Bézier curves and exact intersection of the rounded resulting polylines. Our main goal was to produce fast and reliable code to be used in the context of 2D drawing.

Though it has some limitations, the method described in this paper gives a powerful tool for constructing illustrations. The planar map data structure allows also for automated compound operations, such as the ones described by Fig. 9 and 10. Fig. 11 and 12 show illustrations produced with the map sketching technique.

Figure 9: Cleaning a face removes its dangling edges.

Figure 10: Cookie–cutter.

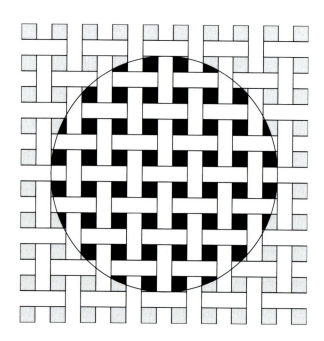

Figure 11: Wickerwork.

Figure 12: CHI'88 logo.

Acknowledgements

We would like to thank Dominique Michelucci for his contribution to the initial work on planar maps done at Ecole des Mines de Saint-Etienne. We thank Leo Guibas and Lyle Ramshaw for helpful discussions. We are grateful to Patrick Baudelaire for his encouragement during the project.

A A priori Subdivision

A polynomial Bézier curve of degree d is defined by:

$$V(t) = \sum_{r=0}^{d} V_r B_r^d(t), \quad 0 \le t \le 1,$$

where the V_r are the $d+1$ control points that form the control polygon of $V(t)$, and $B_r^d(t) = \begin{pmatrix} d \\ r \end{pmatrix} t^r (1-t)^{d-r}$ is the rth Bernstein polynomial of degree d [21,4].

If v is a vector in the Euclidean plane, we note $\|v\|$ the quantity $\max(|x_v|, |y_v|)$. For $d \ge 2$, the *diagonal D* and the *length L* of the control polygon of $V(t)$ are defined as:

$$D = \max_{0 \le r \le d-2} \|V_{r+2} - 2V_{r+1} + V_r\|,$$
$$L = \max_{0 \le r \le d-1} \|V_{r+1} - V_r\|.$$

D is considered by Wang [25,23] as a subdivision criterion.

Computing the first and second derivatives of $V(t)$ and using the properties of the Bernstein polynomials gives, for all t in $[0, 1]$:

$$\|V^{(2)}(t)\| \le d(d-1)\, D, \qquad (2)$$
$$\|V^{(1)}(t)\| \le d\, L. \qquad (3)$$

To find the number of subdivisions, we use a chord interpolation theorem [22] which states that: if $f(t)$ is a real valued function of class C^∞ on $[a, b]$, then, for all t in $[a, b]$:

$$|f(t) - c(t)| \leq \frac{(b-a)^2}{8} \max_{a \leq t \leq b} \left| f^{(2)}(t) \right|, \qquad (4)$$

where $c(t)$ is the chord (straight line segment) between $(a, f(a))$ and $(b, f(b))$. This result is used by Lane [15] in the context of curve rendering.

Let σ, $0 < \sigma \leq 1$, be a step size on the interval $[0, 1]$ and n the integer such that $n\sigma = 1$. This defines n intervals $I_i = [i\sigma, (i+1)\sigma]$, and n chords $C_i(t)$ with endpoints $E_i = V(i\sigma)$ and $E_{i+1} = V((i+1)\sigma)$. Let ϵ be a given threshold measuring the maximum allowed deviation between the curve and the chords C_i. We want to ensure that:

$$\|V(t) - C_i(t)\| \leq \epsilon \qquad (5)$$

holds for all i, $0 \leq i < n$, and all t in I_i.

Applying (4) to the coordinates of $V(t)$ on the interval I_i and using the bound (2), it is straightforward to see that any $\sigma \leq 1$ such that:

$$0 < \sigma^2 \leq \frac{8\epsilon}{d(d-1)D} \qquad (6)$$

will satisfy (5).

Let k be the smallest integer such that $\sigma = 2^{-k}$ satisfies (6), then:

$$k = \left\lceil \log_4 \frac{d(d-1)}{8} \frac{D}{\epsilon} \right\rceil \qquad (7)$$

Equation (7) is cited in [23] as a result derived by Wang.

We can now bound the length of the chords given by *a priori* subdivision of depth k. The mean value theorem applied to $V(t)$ on interval I_i gives:

$$\|E_{i+1} - E_i\| \leq \sigma \max_{t \in I_i} \|V^{(1)}(t)\|.$$

The maximum of $\|V^{(1)}(t)\|$ over I_i is less than or equal to its maximum over $[0, 1]$. Using (3), one gets:

$$\|E_{i+1} - E_i\| \leq \sigma \, dL.$$

The bound on σ from (6) gives for all i, $0 \leq i < 2^k$:

$$\|E_{i+1} - E_i\| \leq \sqrt{\frac{8d}{d-1}} \frac{L}{\sqrt{D}} \sqrt{\epsilon}.$$

B Updating the Inclusion Tree

The degree d of a vertex v is the number of sides incident to v, v is a *dangling vertex* if $d(v) = 1$. If both sides of an edge are in the same contour, it is a *dangling edge*, otherwise it is a *border edge*. A dangling edge is *connecting* if it has no dangling vertex, *terminal* if it has exactly one dangling vertex, and *isolated* if it has two dangling vertices. A loop incident to a vertex v with $d(v) = 2$ is an *isolated border edge*.

An edge falls into one of the following types:

1. a terminal edge with both sides in an inner contour,

2. a connecting edge with both sides in an inner contour,

3. a border edge with both sides in two distinct inner contours,

4. a border edge with one side in an inner contour and the other side in an outer contour,

5. an isolated edge,

6. a terminal edge with both sides in an outer contour,

7. a connecting edge with both sides in an outer contour,

8. an isolated border edge.

When inserting a curve, new edges may be added to the map. Adding an edge implies creating its sides, vertices, and updating the α-order around the latter. The updated contours are thus available through the mapping $\alpha\omega$. The inclusion tree is updated *after* each new edge addition, it is therefore possible to find the type of a new edge by counting its dangling vertices and checking the updated contours. The inclusion tree is then updated by performing the following actions, indexed by edge type:

2. merge: inner & outer $\rightarrow$ inner

3. split: inner $\rightarrow$ inner & inner

4. split: outer $\rightarrow$ outer & inner

5. create: outer

7. merge: outer & outer $\rightarrow$ outer

8. create: outer & inner

For example, if an edge of type 2 is added to a map, one inner contour and one outer contour are merged to give a single inner contour.

When erasing a curve or an arc, old edges may be removed from the map. The inclusion tree is updated *before* each old edge removal, using the same tests as above. When the type of the edge has been found, the inclusion tree is updated by performing the following actions, indexed by edge type:

2. split: inner $\rightarrow$ inner & outer

3. merge: inner & inner $\rightarrow$ inner

4. merge: outer & inner $\rightarrow$ outer

5. delete: outer

7. split: outer $\rightarrow$ outer & outer

8. delete: outer & inner

Adding or removing an edge of type 1 or 6 (i.e., terminal edges) does not modify the inclusion tree.

References

[1] D. Baroni. *Art Graphique Design.* Editions du Chêne, Paris, 1987.

[2] P. Baudelaire and M. Gangnet. *Planar Maps: an Interaction Paradigm for Graphic Design.* In *CHI'89 Proceedings*, Addison-Wesley, 1989.

[3] J.L. Bentley and T.A. Ottmann. Algorithms for Reporting and Counting Geometric Intersections. *IEEE Trans. on Comput.*, 28(9), 1979.

[4] T.D. DeRose and B.A. Barsky. Geometric Continuity for Catmull-Rom Splines. *ACM Transactions on Graphics*, 7(1), 1988.

[5] D.H. Greene and F.F. Yao. Finite–Resolution Computational Geometry. In *Proc. 27th IEEE Symp. on Found. Comp. Sci.*, Toronto, 1986.

[6] D. Dobkin and D. Silver. Recipes for Geometry and Numerical Analysis. In *Proceedings of the Fourth Annual ACM Symposium on Computational Geometry*, ACM Press, New York, 1988.

[7] H. Edelsbrunner. *Algorithms in Combinatorial Geometry.* Springer-Verlag, New York, 1987.

[8] H. Edelsbrunner, L. Guibas, J. Pach, R. Pollack, R. Seidel, and M. Sharir. *Calculating Arrangements of Segments, Circles, or Other Curves in the Plane.* 1988. Submitted for publication.

[9] H. Edelsbrunner and L.J. Guibas. *Topologically Sweeping an Arrangement.* Research Report #9, Digital Equipment Systems Research Center, Palo Alto, 1986.

[10] A. R. Forrest. Geometric Computing Environments: Some Tentative Thoughts. In *Theoretical Foundations of Computer Graphics and CAD*, Springer-Verlag, 1988.

[11] M. Gangnet and J.C. Hervé. D2: un éditeur graphique interactif. In *Actes des Journées SM90*, Eyrolles, Paris, 1985.

[12] L. Guibas and J. Stolfi. Primitives for the Manipulation of General Subdivisions and the Computation of Voronoi Diagrams. *ACM Transactions on Graphics*, 4(2), 1985.

[13] C.M. Hoffmann, J.E. Hopcroft, and M.S. Karasick. Towards Implementing Robust Geometric Computations. In *Proceedings of the Fourth Annual ACM Symposium on Computational Geometry*, ACM Press, New York, 1988.

[14] P.A. Koparkar and S.P. Mudur. A new class of algorithms for the processing of parametric curves. *Computer-Aided Design*, Vol. 15, 1983.

[15] J.F. Lane. *Curve and Surface Display Techniques.* Tutorial, ACM SIGGRAPH'81, 1981.

[16] S.L. Lien, M. Shantz, and V. Pratt. Adaptive Forward Differencing for Rendering Curves and Surfaces. *ACM Computer Graphics*, Vol. 21(4):111–118, 1987.

[17] P. Lienhardt. Extensions of the Notion of Map and Subdivision of a Three–Dimensional Space. In *STACS'88*, Lecture Notes in Computer Science 294, 1988.

[18] D. Michelucci. *Thèse.* Ecole Nationale Supérieure des Mines de Saint-Etienne, Saint-Etienne, 1987.

[19] D. Michelucci and M. Gangnet. Saisie de plans à partir de tracés à main-levée. In *Actes de MICAD 84*, Hermès, Paris, 1984.

[20] F.P. Preparata and M.I. Shamos. *Computational Geometry: an Introduction.* Springer-Verlag, New York, 1985.

[21] L. Ramshaw. *Blossoming: A Connect-the-Dots Approach to Splines.* Research Report #19, Digital Equipment Systems Research Center, Palo Alto, 1987.

[22] M. H. Schultz. *Spline Analysis.* Prentice Hall, 1973.

[23] T.W. Sederberg and S.R. Parry. Comparison of three curve intersection algorithms. *Computer-Aided Design*, Vol. 18, 1986.

[24] W.T. Tutte. *Graph Theory.* Addison-Wesley, 1984.

[25] G. Wang. The Subdivision Method for Finding the Intersection between two Bézier Curves or Surfaces. *Zhejiang University Journal*, 1984. Cited in reference [23].

A Characterization of Ten Rasterization Techniques

Nader Gharachorloo
Satish Gupta
IBM Thomas J. Watson Research Center
Yorktown Heights, NY 10598

Robert F. Sproull
Ivan E. Sutherland
Sutherland, Sproull, and Associates, Inc.
4516 Henry Street, Pittsburgh, PA 15213

Abstract

With widespread use of raster scan displays and the ever-increasing desire for faster interactivity, higher image complexity, and higher resolution in displayed images, several techniques have been proposed for rasterizing primitive graphical objects. This paper characterizes the performance of these techniques and shows how they evolve for more complex images on higher resolution displays. This characterization will not only show the strengths and deficiencies of existing rasterization techniques, but will also reveal new architectures for future raster graphics systems.

Introduction

The raster-scan display is now the most popular computer output device because of the rapid decrease in the cost of semiconductor memories and the low cost of raster-scan CRTs. Such displays are now used in a wide range of applications, from home computers to engineering design to flight simulation.

Raster-scan displays are most commonly driven by a frame buffer, a memory that stores the color value for every picture element on the screen and refreshes the display continuously. The process of generating these picture element values from a geometric description of the image is known as rasterization. The principal strength of the frame buffer is that it can show an arbitrary image on the display with an arbitrary number of primitive objects, subject only to the limit of spatial and intensity resolution of the display device. The weakness of a frame buffer is that a great many bits must be changed to change the picture. Because of their large size, frame buffers are usually implemented using the highest density, and hence the slowest, memory chips. The difficulty of accessing pixel data rapidly in such frame-buffer memories can be overcome by several different techniques. This paper will characterize ten such techniques.

These techniques will be characterized along three aspects of the display user's desires: interactivity, image complexity, and resolution. *Interactivity* is determined by how rapidly the im-

age is updated and hence how rapidly the user can interact with his application. *Image complexity* is characterized by the number of the primitive objects (shaded triangles, vectors, characters) displayed. *Resolution* refers strictly to the number of pixels on the display device and will provide a measure of how these techniques are likely to evolve as resolution increases. Examining the full spectrum of rasterization techniques will help predict the evolution of future graphics architectures.

Background

Figure 1 shows a typical rasterization system based on the frame buffer. The host computer generates graphical primitives, the rasterization processor converts these primitives into pixel values and stores them in the frame buffer, which is accessed continuously to refresh the screen. Any rasterization system must be able to receive graphical primitives, rasterize these primitives, and continuously refresh the raster display. Given that all rasterization systems must satisfy these common input and output requirements, the only fundamental difference among rendering systems is the frame-buffer memory organization and the rasterization processor to match it.

Before examining the details of different rasterization techniques, it is necessary to have an understanding of the primitives being rasterized, the sources of parallelism in the rendering problem, and the organization of the rasterization processor.

Rasterization Primitives

We have chosen three primitives for characterization: Gouraud-shaded three-dimensional triangles, two-dimensional vectors, and characters. With the advent of windowing systems, it is desirable that the same rasterization system be capable of efficiently rendering all three types of primitives on the same screen. Higher-level curve and surface primitives can be broken down into these basic primitives, i.e. polylines and triangular meshes.

Three-dimensional triangles are represented by three vertices, each of which is described by x,y,z screen coordinates and an r,g,b color triplet. The triangle is rasterized by linearly interpolating the depth and color values for each pixel inside the triangle and conditionally updating the frame buffer and the z-buffer values only if the triangle is visible [25]. Most systems use 8 or 24 bits per pixel for storing color values and 16 or more bits per pixel for storing depth information.

Given P triangles of average pixel area A, a total of $P \times A$ pixels must be accessed to render the scene. Assuming the

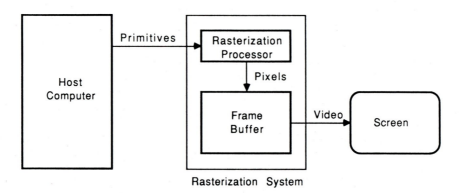

Figure 1. Prototypical frame buffer system.

scene covers a screen of N pixels and that each triangles are overlaid in D layers everywhere, we have [33]:

$$P \times A = N \times D$$

where D is the depth complexity. The average height or width of a triangle is proportional to

$$Average\_width = Average\_height = \sqrt{A} = \sqrt{ND/P}$$

For performance comparisons, the average values are good approximations to the actual area and height distributions.

The average depth complexity, D, is dependent upon the type of scene being rendered: tesselated or non-tesselated. Consider rendering a scene composed of several spheres, each of which is rendered with 100 triangles. Tesselating the sphere into smaller triangles (say 1000) will increase the number of triangles while reducing the area of each triangle. In this case, D remains constant, while P increases and A decreases. Zooming out will have a similar effect. On the other hand, adding more spheres to the scene will increase the depth complexity, but will not change the average area of each triangle in the scene. This is a non-tesselated scene, where P and D change without affecting A. Typical scenes mix tesselated and non-tesselated characteristics and the response time is bounded by the response time for these two extremes.

Two-dimensional vectors are represented by a pair of x,y endpoints. Vectors are rasterized by drawing a digitized line between the endpoints [5]. The performance of the various rasterization techniques is sensitive to the angular distribution of the vectors. We consider two types of angular vector distributions: uniform and the 25/25/50 distribution. For some applications, all angles are equally likely and the angular distribution is uniform. For applications that do not allow rotation (such as electrical circuit design), we will assume that 25% of the vectors are horizontal, 25% are vertical, and the remaining 50% have an equal probability over all angles with a slight preference for 45 degrees, which we will ignore. We will assume that there are V vectors with an average length of L pixels.

For characters, we will assume that they tesselate the whole screen, and hence the area of each character is N/C, where C is the number of characters on the screen.

Parallelism in Rasterization

To meet the requirements of interactive systems that demand response in less than a second, or even less than a tenth of a

second, rasterization must use parallel processing. Different kinds of parallelism can be exploited, such as:

Pixel Level: Parallelism within a pixel to access and interpolate up to six parameters in parallel: x,y,z,r,g,b.

Primitive Level: Parallelism within a triangle to access several pixels along a horizontal span or in a rectangular region.

Multiple Primitive Level: Parallelism obtained by rasterizing several primitives at once.

Frame Level: Parallelism within a frame to process several sub-frames or full frames at once.

Effective exploitation of parallelism requires tradeoffs due to overhead computations associated with parallelizing any problem. Optimal solutions minimize the parallelization overhead and maximize the speedup. We assume that the overhead processing can be overlapped with the parallel rasterization and hence make no attempt to compare overhead costs. In some cases, the overhead due to parallelism may exceed the speedup.

Rasterization Processors

For low-performance applications, a general-purpose processor can be used for rasterization. Somewhat greater performance can be achieved with "graphics processors" which have specialized instructions for rasterization [3, 23]. These processors usually require several instruction cycles to compute the value of each pixel to be stored, thus limiting the update rate. Equally limiting is the update rate of the frame-buffer memory designs used with these processors. If only a single pixel can be written in a memory cycle, performance is low. Clearing the million pixels on a 1024 × 1024 screen will take 1/4 second, assuming each memory cycle requires 250 ns. Although the speed of the frame-buffer memory can be increased by using Static RAM memory chips, these are more expensive and bulkier than conventional Video RAMs.

A first step in parallel rasterization is to design a special processor that computes one pixel value in every clock cycle. Wide data paths are used to access the parameters of the geometry primitive (x,y,z,r,g,b) in parallel, rather than sequentially as required in a conventional microprocessor. To achieve even greater performance, pixel values for several pixels in the same graphics primitive are computed in parallel.

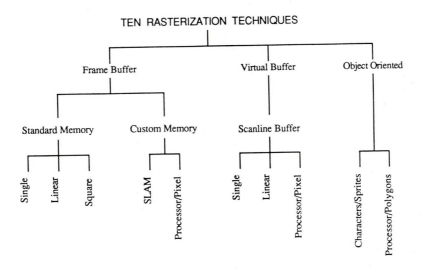

Figure 2. Ten rasterization techniques.

High-performance rasterization requires special rasterization processors and special frame-buffer organizations. The memory is designed to access more than one pixel in a single cycle, and the processor uses parallelism to compute pixel values fast enough to keep the frame-buffer memory busy. These structures use primitive-level parallelism.

The response time increases linearly with the number of primitives (P, V, or C). The rasterization time for each primitive is the sum of two pieces: the constant setup time for the primitive rasterization loop and the iteration time for the rasterization loop, which is proportional to the size of the primitive. If setup and iteration are overlapped, the total time is the maximum of the setup and the iteration time. Systems with fast setup hardware do best on small size primitives, while systems with fast iteration hardware do best on larger primitives. Although scenes are composed of both small and large primitives, the rasterization of an average primitive is typically dominated by the iteration time. Henceforth, we will characterize only the average iteration time and assume the setup time is performed in parallel or is negligible.

Taxonomy

Figure 2 shows a taxonomy of ten rasterization techniques surveyed in this paper. The three primary branches categorize the techniques based on their underlying pixel memory model:

Frame-buffer techniques that allocate a memory location for every pixel in the frame and rasterize all primitives into this random-access memory.

Virtual-buffer or partial-buffer techniques that rasterize primitives into a small portion of the screen memory and reuse this virtual portion repeatedly to construct the full frame.

Object-oriented techniques that refresh the display directly from computations on each primitive and therefore may operate without a frame buffer.

Frame-Buffer Techniques

The frame buffer is a two-ported memory: the refresh port is used to read the pixel values in serial order for displaying the raster image and the update port is used by the rasterization processor to change the picture at arbitrary locations on the screen. Before the introduction of Video RAM chips [24], single-ported dynamic RAM chips were used to implement frame buffers. In these frame buffers the refresh port consumed a significant fraction of the frame-buffer bandwidth. The Video RAM augments the dynamic RAM with an on-chip shift register that can be loaded in a single memory cycle and can be shifted out asynchronously to refresh the CRT, freeing the random-access port for use by the rasterization processor. High-performance systems often contain two frame buffers, where one is used to display the current frame while the other is used to render the next frame.

Today, most frame buffers are implemented using 256 Kilobit and 1 Megabit Video RAM chips [39]. The 256K Video RAM is organized as a 64K × 4 RAM with 4 bits available in parallel both at the random and the serial ports. These chips have random-acess cycle times of $Tcyc$ (typically 250 nsec), with faster "Page mode" access to locations in the same page (256 bit bank for 64K × 4 RAMs), namely Tpm (typically 125 nsec). For read-modify-write cycles, we will assume a cycle time of $Trmw$ (typically 375 nsec). The serial port has a cycle time of $Tser$ (typically 40 nsec).

As memory chips become more dense, high-performance rasterizers become more difficult to design because the memory bandwidth does not increase as fast as the memory capacity. For example, switching from 64K × 4 Video RAMs to 256K × 4 Video RAMs results in a factor of four reduction in maximum available memory bandwidth for equivalent memory capacity. Techniques that obtain high performance by operating many memory chips in parallel are less effective for fewer memory chips. To counteract this problem, designers turn to more exotic memory organizations or to special-purpose memory chips that do some of the rasterization processing on-chip.

The frame-buffer techniques described in this section differ in the number of pixels that are accessed in each cycle and in the geometric configuration of the pixels in each access. The single-pixel organization accesses a single pixel in each cycle. The linear array organization accesses a few pixels that lie together on the same horizontal scan line. The square array organization accesses in one cycle a small square of pixels. In each of these structures, only a modest number of pixels are accessed in parallel (up to about 100) and the rasterization processor or processors are distinct from the memory.

Achieving greater performance requires specially-designed memory chips that integrate the memory and rasterization processors. The scan-line access memory (SLAM) accesses all pixels on a single scan-line in one cycle, while the Pixel-Planes design accesses every pixel in the frame buffer in one cycle.

Single Pixel Access

The single-pixel technique organizes the frame buffer to access one pixel in each memory cycle. Although normal updates will require full memory cycles, if successive updates lie on the same scanline, page-mode cycles can be used to increase rasterization speed.

For three-dimensional primitives, we assume that the frame buffer is augmented by a z-buffer that provides one depth value each memory cycle. For the rasterization of three-dimensional primitives, we need to read, compare, and write the depth value for every pixel in the primitive. Using the read-modify-write memory cycle, a pixel can be updated in time $Trmw$. When the scan conversion is done in raster order, faster page-mode cycles can be used. An even faster technique that uses VRAMs to implement the z-buffer is shown in Figure 3. The depth value stored in the z-buffer is read from the serial port, compared, and written back into the update port in page mode such that the average pixel update time is reduced to $Tpm[40]$. Note that the pixel value write is overlapped with z-buffer write.

Linear Array Access

A linear-array frame buffer is organized so that each cycle accesses W pixels that lie along a continuous part of a horizontal scanline of the image. Successive sets of W pixels are called words; boundaries between words occur after every multiple of W pixels in the scanline. Access is normally to a particular word, though it is possible to access W pixels starting at any arbitrary pixel location by using different parts of two consecutive words. Such arbitrary access requires providing different memory chips with one or the other of two consecutive addresses [4, 31, 32]. Although pixel-aligned access can provide a performance advantage over word-aligned arrays, computing two memory addresses can lead to a longer memory cycle, and hence can offset the gain in performance.

The linear array is potentially capable of a W-fold speedup over the single-pixel structure. However, this maximum speedup can be achieved only if the primitives being rasterized are parallelizable such that W horizontal pixels can be updated in every memory cycle. Since this may not be the case, the speedup must be discounted by an efficiency factor, which is a function of both W and the average number of horizontal pixels (span) in the primitive being rasterized. Figures 4a and

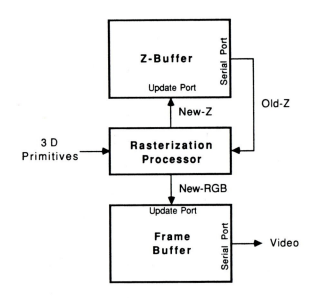

Figure 3. Fast Z-buffer.

4b plot the speedup $Slint$, for the word and pixel aligned linear array organizations for typical character and triangle span sizes (8 and 32) against different word sizes. For the word aligned case, the point of diminishing returns is at word sizes that are greater than twice the average span size, and for pixel aligned case it is achieved when the word size is greater than the average span size. If the spans are sufficiently big relative to the word size, then the speedup is independent of the word aligned or pixel aligned memory organization.

For vectors, the speedup provided by the linear array memory organization depends on the angular distribution of the vectors. Figures 4c and 4d show the vector speedup $Slinv$ for different word sizes. Figure 4c shows vector speedup for a 25/25/50 distribution of vectors. This distribution exhibits a rapid increase in vector drawing speed with larger word sizes due to the speedup of horizontal and nearly horizontal vectors. For uniformly distributed vectors, shown in Figure 4d, the performance increase with increasing word size is less dramatic.

To realize the maximum speedup of vectors in the linear array organization requires that a full horizontal run be generated in every memory cycle. An algorithm for generating lines by run-length has been described by Bresenham [6, 7]. For a pixel-aligned linear array with $W = 16$, the speedup for uniformly distributed vectors would be 2.3 and would increase to 5.3 for the 25/25/50 distribution because of the greater fraction of horizontal vectors.

Square Array Access

Based on the belief that graphical objects are no more likely to be short and wide than tall and thin, several frame buffers have been built to access a square array of $M \times M$ pixels in each memory cycle [9, 27, 32, 36]. Such an organization can take advantage of two-dimensional locality in the scan conversion of primitives. As an example, a character 8 pixels wide and 12 pixels high could be stored in two memory cycles in an 8×8 organization, but would require 12 memory cycles in a linear array. The techniques used for providing pixel aligned

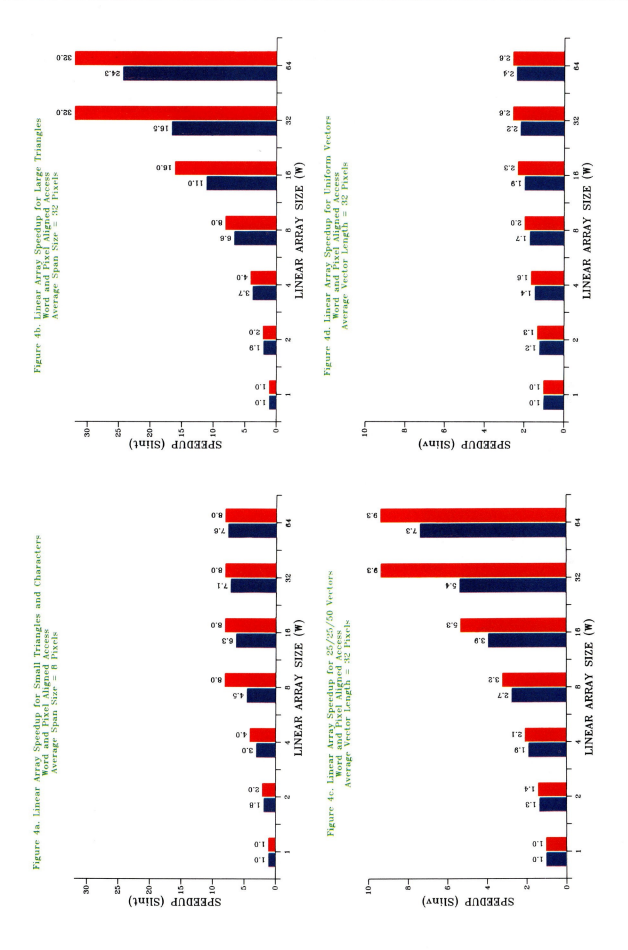

Figure 4a. Linear Array Speedup for Small Triangles and Characters
Word and Pixel Aligned Access
Average Span Size = 8 Pixels

Figure 4b. Linear Array Speedup for Large Triangles
Word and Pixel Aligned Access
Average Span Size = 32 Pixels

Figure 4c. Linear Array Speedup for 25/25/50 Vectors
Word and Pixel Aligned Access
Average Vector Length = 32 Pixels

Figure 4d. Linear Array Speedup for Uniform Vectors
Word and Pixel Aligned Access
Average Vector Length = 32 Pixels

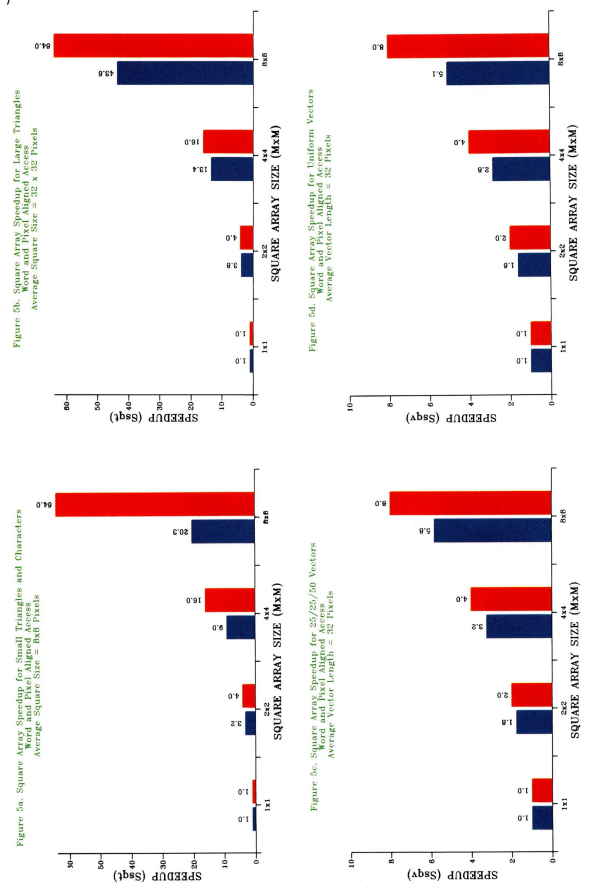

Figure 5a. Square Array Speedup for Small Triangles and Characters
Word and Pixel Aligned Access
Average Square Size = 8x8 Pixels

Figure 5b. Square Array Speedup for Large Triangles
Word and Pixel Aligned Access
Average Square Size = 32 x 32 Pixels

Figure 5c. Square Array Speedup for 25/25/50 Vectors
Word and Pixel Aligned Access
Average Vector Length = 32 Pixels

Figure 5d. Square Array Speedup for Uniform Vectors
Word and Pixel Aligned Access
Average Vector Length = 32 Pixels

addressing for linear arrays can be extended to square arrays [32].

As for the linear organization, the potential performance of the square organization must be reduced by an efficiency factor, which is a function of the size of the square, M, and the average area of the primitives being rasterized. Figures 5a and 5b show the possible speedup $Ssqt$, i.e., the average number of pixels that can be written in each memory cycle, for different word sizes ($M \times M$) for typical character and triangle sizes (8 and 32). Notice that pixel alignment has a higher payoff as the square size approaches the size of the primitives.

The square organization achieves speedup for vectors of any orientation, while the linear organization is able to achieve parallelism only for horizontal vectors. The overall speedup ($Ssqv$) achieved is shown in Figures 5c and 5d. A 4×4 pixel-aligned square array will increase vector-generation speed by a factor of four for any distribution of vector orientations. In an $M \times M$ array, vector generation can be done either by generating M pixels sequentially in the time required by one memory cycle, or by using an algorithm that chooses from a set of predefined $M \times M$ strokes [18, 30].

Scan Line Access

The Scan Line Access Memory (SLAM) architecture is the extreme case of a linear array where the array size is equal to the width of the screen, and a scanline of pixel processors work in parallel to update the memory [11]. SLAM implements on one chip a modified Video RAM and pixel processors that can update horizontal spans of any size in each memory cycle. SLAM is a memory chip architecture that can be used as a component to implement single, linear, or square frame-buffer accesses. Since each individual memory chip accesses only a few bits of every pixel, this memory design cannot be easily extended to 3D z-buffer algorithms.

The performance of SLAM is like that of the linear array with $W = \sqrt{N}$. Since SLAM can write an arbitrary horizontal span of a triangle in a single cycle, $Slint = \sqrt{A}$, the width of a triangle. For vectors, SLAM's speedup is $Slinv$, like that for the linear array but somewhat better because of the larger value of W. Performance on characters is limited by the rate with which font data can be delivered to the SLAM and whether more than one character can be written in a single cycle. We have chosen to characterize SLAM's character performance equal to that of the linear array.

Full Frame Access

At the extreme in parallel access, a frame buffer that can access all N pixels on the screen in a single cycle can write any object in a single cycle. Such a structure generally requires N pixel processors as well. Parameters describing a graphics primitive are broadcast to all processors, and each processor computes a pixel value to store in its associated pixel, or decides that the primitive does not affect its pixel, and leaves the current value unchanged.

This technique is implemented in Pixel-Planes [12]. A triangle is described by three plane equations $F_i(x,y) = A_i x + B_i y + C_i = 0$. The plane equation coefficients, A, B, C are broadcast bit serially to bit-serial pixel processors that evaluate the F_i to determine which pixels lie inside the polygon. Each pixel location has sufficient bits to store depth and color values. The interior pixels then evaluate $Z(x,y) = A_z x + B_z y + C_z$ and compare the value to the stored value to determine which pixels are visible. Finally, the red, green, and blue intensities are calculated in three passes by evaluating three equations of the form $R(x,y) = A_r x + B_r y + C_r$. For a triangle, a total of about 300 bits are broadcast serially to the pixel processors. The number of bits is proportional to log N and can hence be considered a constant. The response time is independent of screen resolution, but depends on the number of triangles on the screen and the speed of serial broadcast.

Virtual-Buffer Techniques

Virtual buffer techniques rasterize primitives into a band buffer and use the band buffer repeatedly to construct the whole image a piece at a time. The primary motivation for a virtual buffer memory is to exchange the large and slow frame buffer memory for a smaller and faster virtual buffer memory to increase performance. The virtual buffer organization for a 1024×1024 screen ranges anywhere from a 1024×1 scanline buffer, or 1024×16 band buffer, or 32×32 square virtual buffer. Larger virtual buffers such as a 1024×512 half-frame buffer or a 512×512 quarter-frame buffer have been implemented primarily to save memory rather than to increase performance. Virtual buffers have been used to prepare raster images for laser printers [35].

Virtual buffers may be used in two distinct ways: in a sweep algorithm or as a pixel cache. Sweep algorithms make one pass over the entire image, assigning the virtual buffer to successive portions of the image in turn. For each assignment, the virtual buffer is cleared, primitives are rasterized into it, and the virtual buffer is then output, either in real time to a display or laser printer, or in near real time to a full-frame buffer. Alternatively, a virtual buffer can be used as a pixel cache, a fast window on a conventional frame buffer [2]. In the course of rasterizing a scene, the contents of the virtual buffer may be exchanged with those in the frame buffer many times.

The strategies for sorting primitives into bands for rasterization are strongly influenced by the size of the virtual buffer. To best realize the advantages of virtual buffer techniques, the primitives must be structured so that all primitives corresponding to each virtual buffer can be rasterized together. For large virtual buffers (i.e. 1024×512) it is acceptable to make two passes over the primitives, where in the first pass all primitives are clipped to the top half of the screen and in the second pass they are clipped to the bottom half. For smaller virtual buffers, multipass strategies fail because of the large transformation and clipping overhead. A common technique is to sort primitives according to the topmost line on which the primitive is activated. A Watkins-style [37] active edge list algorithm is then implemented, where new primitives are activated by insertion and rasterized primitives are deactivated by deletion. Alternatively, an active polygon ring [16] can generate all the horizontal spans for the current line in the virtual buffer before proceeding to spans in the next line. The smaller the virtual buffer, the larger the overhead of dealing with leftover primitive information that must be saved for the next buffer. A full discussion of sorting strategies and overhead is beyond the scope of this paper. Our characterizations

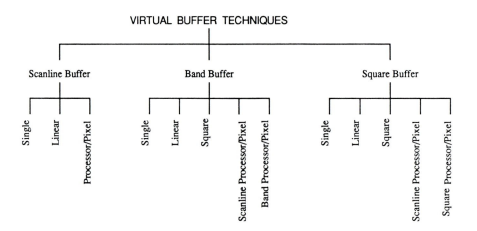

Figure 6. Taxonomy of Virtual Buffers.

of performance assume that these activities are overlapped with rasterization, and are therefore ignored.

As the examples suggest, there are three possible virtual buffer organizations: scan line virtual buffers, multiple scan line virtual buffers, and square virtual buffers. Figure 6 shows the taxonomy for all possible virtual buffer techniques. This paper will characterize only the scanline virtual buffer technique.

Scan Line Virtual Buffer

The scanline virtual buffer uses a single scan line buffer for rasterization. For every scanline on the display, the rasterization processor updates the contents of the current scanline, while the previous scanline is either being directly shifted out to the screen or into an intermediate frame buffer as shown in Figure 7. If the screen is being updated directly, then the next scanline must be shifted in while the current scanline is being updated. The virtual buffer technique is best utilized when the time taken to update a scanline is comparable to or greater than the time taken to shift the scanline in or out. It is better used in a sweep algorithm than as a pixel cache.

Transfer of the virtual buffer contents to the frame buffer does not cause any memory bottlenecks because the frame buffer can be updated serially (possibly through the video port) and requires only one access per pixel to the frame buffer. Multiple memory accesses caused by overlapping objects (D times for triangles) are handled within the virtual buffer, and only the final image is sent to the frame buffer. The z values are never needed for the whole image and hence exist only in the virtual buffer.

As in the case of frame buffers, a scanline virtual buffer can be updated either as a single pixel at a time [20], in a horizontal word with W pixels [35], or using a processor for every pixel of the scan line [16]. The response time for single and W pixel updates is the same as for frame buffers, improved only by the faster memory cycle of the virtual buffer Tvb. Using fast static memories, these could potentially lead to a two- to ten-fold performance improvement over the frame buffer.

Super Buffer

The Super Buffer [15, 16] takes advantage of VLSI chip technology by constructing a linear systolic array of pixel processors to rasterize horizontal span primitives into an on-chip virtual scan line buffer. A complementary active polygon ring generates all the horizontal span primitives for each scan line from polygon descriptions. The highly pipelined structure and the systolic communication of the rasterization processors allow the system to be clocked as fast as 40 nsec. The Super Buffer has sufficient processing power to rasterize the image in real time so that the frame buffer can be avoided. However, without a frame buffer, any virtual-buffer architecture will have a limit on the complexity of the image it can display. In the case of the Super Buffer, the limit is that the number of spans per scanline cannot exceed the number of pixels in a

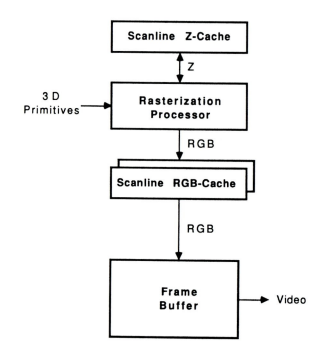

Figure 7. Scan Line Virtual Buffer.

scanline. The use of a frame buffer allows the system to degrade gracefully with increasing image complexity.

Object-Oriented Techniques

Object-oriented techniques refresh the display directly from processors that compute in real time how to display each primitive and therefore operate without any pixel memory. Object-oriented techniques can be broken down into two categories: techniques that deal only with non-overlapping objects, and techniques that resolve object overlap according to a preassigned priority or by performing depth comparisons.

Character/Sprite Displays

The most common object-oriented display is the character display, where the screen is split into a fixed number of non-overlapping character boxes. The display is generated from a list of characters sorted in raster order. For each character in the list, the corresponding image is read from a character lookup table to generate a video signal in real time [21].

By making the character definitions loadable, arbitrary geometric shapes such as lines and polygons can be shown. For each character box, the vectors and polygons must first be clipped against the box and then rasterized to the pixel resolution of the box. If a similar box exists in the lookup table, then that character is referenced, otherwise a new character must be loaded into the lookup table. The size of the character lookup table limits the complexity of images that can be displayed. The response time for displaying such images is limited by the coding of the images into loadable character definitions rather than by the update of the display list. Note that as the size of the lookup table approaches the size of the corresponding frame buffer, arbitrarily complex images can be displayed.

By allowing the character boxes to have arbitrary size, to appear anywhere on the screen, and to overlap, geometric images can be generated more easily. Such character boxes are often called *sprites* and are commonly used in video games. These systems are typically limited to two to eight sprites and use logic to select the pixels from the frontmost nonempty sprite for display on the screen.

Processor per Polygon

Maximum parallelism can be extracted from the scene by assigning a processor to every polygon. As the image is being rasterized, each of the P processors incrementally computes and reports its color and depth at that pixel. For pixels outside the polygon, the processor reports the maximum depth. The pixel with the minimum depth will have its color displayed on the screen. The minimum depth can be found by using a comparator tree of size $P \log P$ [14, 38] .

The number of required polygon processors can be reduced significantly by assigning a processor to only those polygons that are active on a given scanline [10]. Scanlines are computed by pipelining a pixel stream through the processors and overwriting pixel values that are deeper than the interpolated depth for the local polygon. This avoids the need for a separate comparator tree. Furthermore, by using a frame buffer as a frame store device and recirculating the pixel stream through the processors, the system can virtually rasterize scenes of any complexity with a fixed number of polygon processors.

The response time for triangles is independent of the number of triangles and is $NTppoly$ where $Tppoly$ is the clock rate for the polygon processor, assuming there are enough processors to accommodate all triangles on the most complex scan line. If Tpp is less than or equal to the pixel clock, the display can be refreshed directly, otherwise the image must be stored in a frame buffer. Vectors are converted to polygons and then rendered.

Frame Parallelism

All of the rasterization techniques we have surveyed may be configured to use frame parallelism, that is, to rasterize with separate parallel processor/memory configurations separate subparts of the frame [13, 22, 28, 29]. A video signal is generated by scanning out pixel values from the subframes in an appropriate order. The effectiveness of this approach is reduced because objects may not be distributed uniformly over the screen and some overhead will be incurred by objects that cross subframe boundaries and must be examined by more than one subframe. However, frame parallelism overcomes a key problem with heavy use of primitive parallelism, namely that the number of pixels accessed in one memory cycle may vastly exceed the number of pixels in a single primitive, thus wasting memory bandwith and rasterization processor power. At the extreme, full-frame access of a million pixels is largely wasted to rasterize a 100-pixel triangle.

The Pixel-planes 5 architecture [13] is an example of a square virtual buffer that uses frame parallelism. Pixels in the virtual buffer are accessed using the processor per pixel technique, using logic-enhanced memory chips similar to those in the earlier Pixel-Planes systems. The buffer is 128x128 pixels in size, and because most polygons will fit within a given 128x128 region of the screen, the virtual buffer can provide a performance similar to the earlier processor per pixel frame buffer systems. The full systems contains a number of such virtual buffers, operating on separate streams of polygon input data. The screen is divided into a number of 128x128 regions, and the virtual buffers are dynamically allocated to these regions in such a way that the virtual buffers process equal numbers of polygons, and loading is balanced.

Performance Characterization

Our taxonomy has shown ten different techniques that will rasterize a given set of primitives to yield identical images. From the user's point of view, the key parameter that differentiates the techniques is response time. Although other system parameters such as cost, size, power, available technology, and design effort cannot be ignored, we believe response time serves well as a common metric for making first-order comparisons among different techniques. There are many implementation factors that influence the response time of any system, but our main interest is to know the theoretical performance limit that a given technique can achieve under comparable operating conditions.

Figure 8 presents expressions for response times for each of the ten different techniques. The expressions are given in terms of a small set of parameters that characterize the image being rasterized. They allow us to understand how the per-

	Tesselated Triangles	Non-Tesselated Triangles	Vectors	Characters
Frame Buffer Techniques				
Single Pixel	$NDTpm$	$PATpm$	$VLTcyc$	$NTpm$
Linear Array (W)	$\dfrac{NDTcyc}{Slint}$	$\dfrac{PATcyc}{Slint}$	$\dfrac{VLTcyc}{Slinv}$	$\dfrac{NTcyc}{Slint}$
Square Array ($M \times M$)	$\dfrac{NDTcyc}{Ssqt}$	$\dfrac{PATcyc}{Ssqt}$	$\dfrac{VLTcyc}{Ssqv}$	$\dfrac{NTcyc}{Ssqt}$
SLAM	$\sqrt{NDP}\ Tcyc$	$P\sqrt{A}\ Tcyc$	$\dfrac{VLTcyc}{Slinv}$	-
Pixel-Planes	$300PTpp$	$300PTpp$	$300VTpp$	-
Scan Line Virtual Buffer Techniques				
Single Pixel	$NDTvb$	$PATvb$	$VLTvb$	$NTvb$
Linear Array (W)	$\dfrac{NDTvb}{Slint}$	$\dfrac{PATvb}{Slint}$	$\dfrac{VLTvb}{Slinv}$	$\dfrac{NTvb}{Slint}$
Super Buffer	$\sqrt{NDP}\ Tsb$	$P\sqrt{A}\ Tsb$	$\dfrac{VLTsb}{Slinv}$	-
Object-Oriented Techniques				
Character Display	-	-	-	$CTcyc$
Processor/Polygon	$NTppoly$	$NTppoly$	$VTppoly$	-

Notations

$Tcyc$ = Frame buffer cycle time
Tpm = Frame buffer page mode cycle time
Tpp = Pixel-Planes clock speed
Tvb = Virtual buffer cycle time
Tsb = Super buffer clock speed
$Tppoly$ = Processor/polygon clock speed
$Slint$ = Speedup for Triangles with Linear Access
$Slinv$ = Speedup for Vectors with Linear Access
$Ssqt$ = Speedup for Triangles with Square Access
$Ssqv$ = Speedup for Vectors with Square Access

N = Number of pixel on screen
D = Average depth complexity of 3D images
P = Number of 3D triangles
A = Average pixel area of triangles
V = Number of vectors in image
L = Average pixel length of vectors
C = Number of characters in image
W = Word Size for Linear Access
M = Word Size for Square Access

Figure 8. Response time for the ten rasterization techniques.

formance of the techniques changes when the parameters are changed. They help determine how the response will change when the number of primitives increases, the average size of triangles changes, the technology parameters such as memory cycle times decrease, or the screen resolution increases. The reader is cautioned that these expressions are approximate, and ignore a great many important factors in actual implementations. Our characterization is intended to illustrate gross performance effects, and does not precisely evaluate any of the techniques.

Three-Dimensional Triangles

We list two expressions for response times for triangle primitives: the tesselated case, in which P and A may change but D remains constant, so $N \times D$ pixels are updated; and the non-tesselated case, in which A remains constant but P and D may change, so $P \times A$ pixels are updated. In both cases, $P \times A = N \times D$. For single-pixel access, the response time is the number of pixels updated, multiplied by the cycle time for each pixel. The response time for the linear and square frame buffer organizations is similar to the single pixel case except

	Single	*Linear Word aligned*	*Linear Pixel aligned*	*Square Word aligned*	*Square Pixel aligned*
FB Access	*1x1*	*16x1*	*16x1*	*4x4*	*4x4*
FRAME BUFFER					
Tcyc	*250 nsec*	*250 nsec*	*250 nsec*	*250 nsec*	*250 nsec*
Polygons/sec					
Large (32x32)	*4K*	*43K*	*62K*	*52K*	*62K*
Small (8x8)	*62K*	*390K*	*500K*	*562K*	*1,000K*
Vectors/sec					
Uniform (32)	*125K*	*245K*	*290K*	*350K*	*500K*
25/25/50 (32)	*125K*	*490K*	*662K*	*405K*	*500K*
VIRTUAL BUFFER					
Tvb	*100 nsec*	*100 nsec*	*100 nsec*	*100 nsec*	*100 nsec*
Polygons/sec					
Large (32x32)	*10K*	*110K*	*155K*	*130K*	*155K*
Small (8x8)	*155K*	*975K*	*1,250K*	*1,405K*	*2,500K*
Vectors/sec					
Uniform (32)	*312K*	*612K*	*720K*	*875K*	*1,250K*
25/25/50 (32)	*312K*	*1,225K*	*1,665K*	*1,012K*	*1,250K*

Figure 9. Peak Performance for Single, Linear, and Square Memory Organizations.

that a speedup factor of *Slint* or *Ssqt* is applied. SLAM performance is the same as that of the linear array, with $Slint = Average\_width = \sqrt{A}$. Pixel-Planes broadcasts about 300 bits to render each triangle and hence has a response time of $300PTpp$ independent of the size of the triangles. The response time for virtual buffer single, linear, and Super Buffer organizations is given by substituting the virtual buffer access time for the corresponding frame buffer cases. The processor per polygon has a fixed response time of *NTppoly* , which is independent of the area and number of polygons in the scene. If *Tppoly* is less than or equal to the pixel clock then the display can be refreshed directly in real time, otherwise the image needs to be buffered in a frame store.

Vectors

The analysis for vectors is similar to that for non-tesselated triangles, but the number of pixels updated is the product of *V* , the number of vectors displayed, and *L* , the vector length. Since the vector response time is linearly proportional to vector length, as opposed to quadratic sensitivity of polygon response to polygon height or width, we have chosen to characterize non-tesselated vectors only. However, the vector response time is strongly sensitive to the angular distribution of vectors, which is reflected in the speedup factors *Slin* for the techniques that can update more than one pixel along a scanline and *Ssq* for the techniques that update rectangular arrays of pixels.

Characters

We assume that characters tesselate the entire screen and thus require that all *N* pixels be updated for a new page of text. The difference between the architectures is primarily the different memory update speeds and the speedup factors *Slint* and *Ssqt*, which depend on the size of the memory word and the size of the characters.

Observations

Given so many techniques to choose from, how does one decide which one to use? The exact decision for a system designer is invariably based on the intended application, and the cost and performance requirements. This characterization of the various possible techniques can be used only as a guideline for system design. Three key observations emerge from this characterization:

> Updating pixels in parallel is an effective means of increasing the performance of rasterization. However, parallelism beyond the average size of the primitives is inefficient.

For all the techniques and primitives, the response time is always directly proportional to the memory cycle time. The faster response time of virtual buffer techniques is due purely to the fact that they use smaller and faster memory parts than their frame-buffer counterparts, which results in a performance gain of 2-10 times.

Lastly, an increase in screen resolution, i.e. from $N_1 = 512 \times 512$ to $N_2 = 1024 \times 1024$ will slow down the vector response time by a factor of $\sqrt{N_2/N_1} = 2$, whereas the triangle response time drops by a factor of $N_2/N_1 = 4$. SLAM and Super Buffer are exceptions because their performance is not sensitive to triangle width, so their performance degrades by a factor of $\sqrt{N_2/N_1} = 2$.

Case Study

To understand the performance limits of different techniques, we have tabulated the performance for single, linear, and square access frame buffers in Figure 9. For the parallel access cases, we have chosen to access 16 pixels in parallel as a 16×1 linear array or as a 4×4 square. Using the polygon and vector speedup factors from Figures 4 and 5, and the performance equations in Figure 8, we can predict the maximum theoretical performance for each of these cases. Observe that switching from single pixel access to parallel pixel access increases the performance by a factor of 2 to 16. However, within the different parallel techniques, the performance does not vary by more than a factor of 2.5.

The performance numbers are directly influenced by memory cycle times. Virtual buffer techniques may use fast memory cycle times in the 25-100 nsec range, which will directly increase the performance by factors of 2.5-10 over their corresponding frame buffer counterparts.

It is interesting to compare the predicted peak performance with the actual performance of some commercial graphics systems. The Silicon Graphics 4D GT Graphics Workstation is rated at 400K short vectors/sec and 100K-120K 100-pixel polygons/sec [1]. It has a screen resolution of 1280x1024, using 5×4 word-aligned square frame buffer organization, $Tcyc = 250nsec$ for vectors, and $Trmw = 500nsec$ for polygons. The table predicts a peak vector performance of 350K-405K vectors/sec. After correcting for the longer memory cycle, the table predicts a peak polygon performance of 26K large polygons/sec and 280K small polygons/sec which translates to about 180K 100-pixel polygons/sec. A closer look at the machine architecture reveals that it is not strictly a 5×4 square organization, but more like 5 independent sets of 1×4 image processors. If we assume that each column receives one span out of every five then the architecture behaves more like a single 1×20 linear array, and the table predicts a peak performance of 195K small polygons/sec, or about 125K 100-pixel polygons/sec.

Another interesting case is the HP 320 SRX, which is rated at 300K vectors/sec and 16K large polygons/sec [17, 34] It has a screen resolution of 1280×1024, 4×4 word-aligned square organization for vectors ($Tcyc = 360nsec$), that is switched to a 1×1 single-pixel access into a linear virtual buffer (pixel cache) for polygons ($Tvb = 60nsec$). Correcting for the cycle times, the table predicts 240K-300K vectors/sec and a peak polygon performance of 260K small and 17K large polygons/sec.

The Future of Rasterization

Users of graphics systems will continue to require higher levels of performance and function in the future. Semiconductor technologies will continue to make this feasible. New and better rasterization techniques will be required to provide for the needs of future systems. The characterization of the current techniques provide a framework to develop future techniques.

To achieve higher rendering performance, it is necessary to overcome the frame buffer bandwidth bottleneck. Semiconductor technology will soon enable us to design video memory chips with 4 megabit densities and logic chips with over one million transistors. At such high circuit densities, interchip communication bandwidth becomes the primary bottleneck, forcing designers to integrate the rasterization processor and frame buffer memory onto the same chip. One may choose to enhance the video memory with rasterization logic, which is the message carried by SLAM and Pixel Planes, or enhance the rasterization processor with fast local memory, which is the message of virtual buffer techniques. Higher circuit densities, combined with integrating the rasterization processor and frame buffer memory will lead to lower size and cost. A 512×512 frame buffer with 8 bits/pixel will occupy only half of a 4 megabit VRAM chip. The other half could be used to implement the rasterization processor. The result will be a high performance single chip rasterization system. Still greater performance can be achieved by operating several such chips in parallel, partitioning the frame buffer into several planes or spatially into rectangles or bands.

Rendering algorithms will continue to use larger numbers of bits per pixel to provide higher levels of functionality. Graphics systems have already made a transition from 1 bit/pixel to 8 and 24 bits/pixel to provide color and smooth shading. Double buffering doubles the number of bits per pixel to obtain smooth animation. Z-buffers require an additional 16-32 bits per pixel, resulting in a total of up to 100 bits/pixel. The trend of using larger number of bits per pixel to provide higher functionality will continue and force graphics systems to provide multiple sets of buffers totalling to 100 - 1000 bits per pixel. The extra memory could be used to provide realtime video capture, anti-aliasing, transparency, texture mapping, image compositing, direct CSG rendering, and shadows. On the other hand, providing such a large number of bits per pixel with physical memory may become prohibitively expensive. Virtual buffer techniques have demonstrated that a fast small physical memory can be reused to execute algorithms requiring a large number of bits per pixel.

Our characterization suggests that designers are going to face stiff problems getting another factor of 4-10 in rasterization performance. Bulk memory speeds will not grow by this factor. Improving the speed of rasterization techniques surveyed here requires integrating on one chip logic and small fast memories, a capability not well supported by today's ASIC design and fabrication techniques. Nevertheless, we should expect to see more designs using "pixel caches" or virtual buffers for the same reason caches are used on all high performance computers: small memories have fast response.

Another general approach to achieving high performance is to divide the screen spatially into multiple non-overlapping sub-frame buffers or multiple overlapping frame buffers and rasterize the primitives into each buffer independently in parallel. While the cost of these approaches rises at least linearly with performance, the engineering is straightforward. We can see these structures emerging as an important part of high performance systems [13].

It is very likely that the rasterization systems of the future will not be based on any one single technique, but will use a creative combination of the best features of known techniques to obtain even higher levels of performance.

Acknowledgements

We would like to thank John Eyles and Henry Fuchs for contributing to the section on Pixel Planes.

Bibliography

1. K. Akeley and T. Jermoluk. High Performance Polygon Rendering. *Proceedings of SIGGRAPH*, 22(4):239-246, August 1988.

2. B. Apgar, B. Bersack, and A. Mammen. A Display System for the Stellar Graphics Supercomputer Model GS1000. *Proceedings of SIGGRAPH*, 22(4):255-268, August 1988.

3. Mike Asai, Graham Short, Tom Preston, Richard Simpson, Derek Roskell, and Karl Guttag. The TI34010 Graphics System Processor. *Computer Graphics and Applications*, 6(10):24-39, October 1986.

4. A. Bechtolsheim and F. Baskett. High-Performance Raster Graphics for Microcomputer Systems. *Computer Graphics*, 14(3):43-47, July 1980.

5. J.E. Bresenham. Algorithm for computer control of a digital plotter. *IBM Systems Journal*, 4(1):25-30, July 1965.

6. J.E. Bresenham. Raster Line Run Length Slice Algorithm, IBM System Communication Division, TR 29.0180, Research Triangle Park, North Carolina. January 1978.

7. J.E. Bresenham. Incremental Line Compaction. *The Computer Journal*, 25(1):116-120, 1982.

8. J.H. Clark. The Geometry Engine: A VLSI Geometry System for Graphics. *Computer Graphics*, 16(3):127-133, July 1982.

9. J.H. Clark and M.R. Hannah. Distributed Processing in a High-Performance Smart Image Memory. *LAMBDA (Now VLSI Design)*, (4th. Quarter):40-45, 1980.

10. M. Deering, S. Winner, B. Schediwy, C. Duffy, and N. Hunt. The Triangle Processor and Normal Vector Shader: A VLSI System for High Performance Graphics. *Proceedings of SIGGRAPH*, 22(4):21-30, August 1988.

11. S. Demetrescu. High Speed Image Rasterization Using Scan Line Access Memories. *Proc. 1985 Chapel Hill Conference on VLSI*, pages 221-243, Computer Science Press, 1985.

12. H. Fuchs and J. Poulton. Pixel Planes: A VLSI-Oriented Design for a Raster Graphics Engine. *VLSI Design*, 2(3):20-28, 3rd. Quarter 1981.

13. H. Fuchs, J. Poulton, J. Eyles, T. Greer, J. Goldfeather, D. Ellsworth, S. Molnar, G. Turk, B. Tebbs, and L. Israel. A Heterogeneous Multiprocessor Graphics System Using Processor-Enhanced Memories. *Proceedings of SIGGRAPH*, 1989.

14. D. Fussell and B.D. Rathi. A VLSI-Oriented Architecture for Real-Time Raster Display of Shaded Polygons. *Proc. of Graphics Interface*, pages 373-380, 1982.

15. N. Gharachorloo, S. Gupta, E. Hokenek, P. Balasubramanian, B. Bogholtz, C. Mathieu, and C. Zoulas. Subnanosecond Pixel Rendering with Million Transistor Chips. *Proceedings of SIGGRAPH*, 22(4):41-49, August 1988.

16. N. Gharachorloo and C. Pottle. SUPER BUFFER: A Systolic VLSI Graphics Engine for Real Time Raster Image Generation. *Proc. 1985 Chapel Hill Conference on VLSI*, pages 285-305, Computer Science Press, 1985.

17. A. Goris, B. Fredrickson, and H. Baeverstad. A Configurable Pixel Cache for Fast Image Generation. *IEEE CG&A*, pages 24-32, 1987.

18. S. Gupta. Architectures and Algorithms for Parallel Updates of Raster Scan Displays, Computer Science Department, Carnegie-Mellon University, CMU-CS-82-111, Pittsburgh, PA. December 1981.

19. S. Gupta, R.F. Sproull, and I.E. Sutherland. A VLSI Architecture for Updating Raster Scan Display. *Computer Graphics*, 15(3):71-78, July 1981.

20. J.H. Jackson. Dynamic Scan-converted Images with a Frame Buffer Display Device. *Proceedings of SIGGRAPH*, page 163, 1980.

21. B.W. Jordan, Jr. and R.C. Barrett. A Cell Organized Raster Display for Line Drawings. *Comm. of the ACM*, 17(2):676, Febraury 1974.

22. M. Kaplan and D. Greenberg. Parallel Processing techniques for Hidden Surface Removal. *Proceedings of SIGGRAPH*, page 300, August 1979.

23. L. Kohn and S.W. Fu. A 1,000,000 Transistor Microprocessor. *ISSCC*, pages 54-55, February 1989.

24. R. Matick, D.T. Ling, S. Gupta, and F.H. Dill. All Points Addressable Raster Display Memory. *IBM Journal of Res. and Dev.*, 28(4):379-382, July 1984.

25. W.M. Newmann and R.F. Sproull. Principles of Interactive Computer Graphics. *McGraw Hill*, 1973.

26. H. Niimi, Y. Imai, M. Murakami, S. Tomita, and H. Hagiwara. A Parallel Processor System for Three Dimensional Color Graphics. *Proceedings of SIGGRAPH*, page 67, July 1984.

27. I. Page. Disarray: A 16 x 16 RasterOp processor. *Eurographics 83*, pages 367-377, Amsterdam: North Holland, 1983.

28. F.I. Parke. Simulation and Expected Performance Analysis of Multiple Processor Z-Buffer Systems. *Siggraph*, pages 48-56, 1980.

29. R. Schumacker. A New Visual System Architecture. *Proc. of Second Interservice/Industry Training Equipment Conf.*, page 1, November 1982.

30. R.F. Sproull. Using Program Transformations to Derive Line-Drawing Algorithms. *ACM Transactions on Graphics*, 1(4):259-273, 1982.

31. R.F. Sproull. Frame Buffer Display Architectures. *Annual Review of Computer Science*, 1:19-46, Annual Reviews Inc., 1986.

32. R.F. Sproull, I.E. Sutherland, A. Thompson, and S. Gupta. The 8 by 8 Display. *ACM Transactions on Graphics*, 2(1):32-56, January 1983.

33. I.E. Sutherland, R.F. Sproull, and R.A. Schumacker. A Characterization of Ten Hidden-Surface Algorithms. *Computing Surveys*, 6(1):1, March 1974.

34. R.W. Swanson and L.J. Thayer. A Fast Shaded-Polygon Renderer. *Proceedings of SIGGRAPH*, pages 95-102, 1986.

35. C.P. Thacker, E.M. McCreight, B.W. Lampson, R.F. Sproull, and D.R. Boggs. Alto: A Personal Computer". *Computer Structures: Readings and Examples*, McGraw Hill, 1981.

36. A.M. Walsby. Fast colour raster graphics using an array processor. *Eurographics 80*, pages 303-313, Amsterdam: North Holland, 1980.

37. G.S. Watkins. A Real Time Visible Surface Algorithm, University of Utah, UTEC-CSC-70-101, June 1970.

38. R. Weinberg. Parallel Processing Image Synthesis and Anti-Aliasing. *Proceedings of SIGGRAPH*, pages 147-154, July 1982.

39. M.C. Whitton. Memory Design for Raster Graphics Displays. *Computer Graphics and Applications*, 4(3):48-65, March 1984.

40. Paul Winser. 3D Graphics for Consumer Applications- How Realistic Does it Have to Be?. *Eurographics*, 1988.

SEPARABLE IMAGE WARPING
WITH SPATIAL LOOKUP TABLES

George Wolberg
Terrance E. Boult

Department of Computer Science
Columbia University
New York, NY 10027
[wolberg | tboult]@cs.columbia.edu

ABSTRACT

Image warping refers to the 2-D resampling of a source image onto a target image. In the general case, this requires costly 2-D filtering operations. Simplifications are possible when the warp can be expressed as a cascade of orthogonal 1-D transformations. In these cases, separable transformations have been introduced to realize large performance gains. The central ideas in this area were formulated in the 2-pass algorithm by Catmull and Smith. Although that method applies over an important class of transformations, there are intrinsic problems which limit its usefulness.

The goal of this work is to extend the 2-pass approach to handle arbitrary spatial mapping functions. We address the difficulties intrinsic to 2-pass scanline algorithms: bottlenecking, foldovers, and the lack of closed-form inverse solutions. These problems are shown to be resolved in a general, efficient, separable technique, with graceful degradation for transformations of increasing complexity.

CR Categories and Subject Descriptors: I.3.3 [Computer Graphics]: Picture/Image Generation; I.4.3 [Image Processing]: Enhancement — Geometric correction, filtering.
Additional keywords and Phrases: 2-pass, scanline algorithm, warping, bottleneck, foldover, antialiasing.

1. INTRODUCTION

Image warping is a geometric transformation that redefines the spatial relationship between points in an image. This area has received considerable attention due to its practical importance in remote sensing, medical imaging, computer vision, and computer graphics. Typical applications include distortion compensation of imaging sensors, decalibration for image registration, geometrical normalization for image analysis and display, map projection, and texture mapping for image synthesis.

Image warping has benefited dramatically from developments in separable geometric transformation algorithms. Also known as scanline algorithms, these methods reduce a 2-D resampling problem into a sequence of 1-D scanline resampling operations. Machines based on these techniques produce limited real-time video effects for the television industry.

The central ideas to scanline algorithms are presented in the seminal paper by Catmull and Smith [1]. They describe a 2-pass technique that decomposes the 2-D resampling problem into two orthogonal 1-D resampling stages. This is the basis for almost all of the other separable work. Nevertheless their approach suffers from problems known as "bottleneck" and "foldover" — difficulties which can result in visual artifacts and costly memory requirements.

This work was supported in part by NSF grant CDR-84-21402, NSF grant IRI8800370, and DARPA grant N00039-84-C-1065.

This paper introduces a novel scanline algorithm which properly addresses these limitations. This extends the benefits of separable transformations to efficiently process arbitrary spatial mappings — geometric transformations that, until now, required costly 2-D resampling operations.

Section 2 of this paper introduces separable geometric transformation algorithms with special emphasis on the Catmull-Smith algorithm. Section 3 describes the novel scanline warping algorithm. Examples are presented in section 4. Finally, section 5 discusses conclusions and future work.

2. BACKGROUND

Separable geometric transformation algorithms, also known as *scanline algorithms*, spatially transform 2-D images by decomposing the mapping into a sequence of orthogonal 1-D transformations. The primary motivation for scanline algorithms is efficiency. Traditionally, geometric transformations have been formulated as either forward or inverse mappings operating entirely in 2-D. While either forward or inverse mappings can be used to realize *arbitrary* mapping functions, they are costly. Separable algorithms present an alternate technique that, for a small decrease in accuracy, yield significant computational savings.

2.1. DEFINITIONS

A *spatial transformation* defines a geometric relationship between each point in the input and output images. The general mapping function can be given in two forms: either relating the output coordinate system to that of the input, or vice versa. Respectively, they can be expressed as

$$[x, y] = [X(u,v), Y(u,v)], \qquad (1)$$

or

$$[u, v] = [U(x,y), V(x,y)] \qquad (2)$$

where $[u,v]$ refers to the input image coordinates corresponding to output pixel $[x,y]$, and X, Y, U and V uniquely specify the spatial transformation. Since X and Y map input onto output, they are referred to as the forward maps, while U and V are known as the inverse maps.

2.1.1. Forward Mapping

The *forward mapping* consists of interpolating each input pixel into the output image at positions determined by the X and Y mapping functions. Each input pixel is passed through the spatial transformation where it is assigned new output coordinate values. Since this is a mapping from pairs of integers to pairs of reals, filtering is required to generate the output image.

The real-valued output positions assigned by X and Y present complications. For discrete images, pixels are taken to be finite elements defined to lie on a (discrete) integer lattice. Implementing the spatial transformation as a point-to-point mapping can give rise to two types of problems: holes and overlaps. The shortcomings of point-to-point mappings are avoided using a four-corner mapping paradigm which considers input pixels as square patches assumed to be transformed into quadrilaterals in the output image. Because the projection of an input pixel is free to lie anywhere in the output image, the projections often straddle several output pixels, or lie embedded in one. An *accumulator array* is required to properly integrate all input pixel fragments that contribute to each output pixel. Partial contributions are handled by scaling the input intensity by the relative area of the output pixel that it covers.

There are two main problems in the forward mapping process. First, costly intersection tests are needed to derive the area coverage. Second, additional filtering is necessary to ensure that a single input value is correctly handled when undergoing magnification. For a complete review see [5, 11].

2.1.2. Inverse Mapping

The *inverse mapping* operates in screen order, projecting each output coordinate into the input image via U and V. The value of the data sample at that point is copied onto the output pixel. Again, filtering is necessary to combat aliasing artifacts. The principal advantages of this method are that no accumulator array is necessary and output pixels which lie outside a clipping window need not be evaluated. This method is useful when the screen is to be written sequentially, U and V are readily available, and the input image can be stored entirely in memory.

Inverse mappings are more commonly used to perform spatial transformations. By operating in scanline order at the output, square output pixels are back-projected onto arbitrary quadrilaterals in the input. The quadrilaterals, also known as *preimages*, may cover many input pixels. Each preimage must be sampled and convolved with a low-pass filter to compute an intensity at the output. In general, the input image is not accessed in scanline order. Efficient approaches to sampling and convolution have received much attention in the recent literature [3, 4, 5, 6, 11].

2.1.3. Separable Mapping

Separable mapping decomposes the forward mapping function into a series of 1-D transforms. This offers several advantages. First, the resampling problem is made simpler since reconstruction, area sampling, and filtering can now be done entirely in 1-D. Second, efficient data access and substantial savings in I/O time can be realized because the input image can be read in row/column order and the output image produced in scanline order. Third, the approach is amenable to stream-processing techniques such as pipelining, and facilitates the design of hardware to operate at real-time video rates.

It is important to elaborate on our use of the term separable. In signal processing literature, a filter T is said to be separable if $T(u,v) = F(u)G(v)$. We extend this definition by defining T to be separable if $T(u,v) = F(u) \circ G(v)$. This simply replaces multiplication with the composition operator in combining both 1-D functions. The definition we offer for separablity in this paper is consistent with standard implementation practices. For instance, the 2-D Fourier Transform, separable in the classic sense, is generally implemented by a 2-pass algorithm. The first pass applies a 1-D Fourier Transform to each row, and the second applies a 1-D Fourier Transform along each column of the intermediate result.

Multi-pass scanline algorithms that operate in this sequential row-column manner are referred to as separable in this paper. The underlying theme is that processing is decomposed into a series of 1-D stages that each operate along orthogonal axes. For example, image rotation has been shown to be decomposable into a 2-pass

scale/shear succession [1], a 4-pass scale/shear sequence [10], and a 3-pass shear transformation [7, 9].

2.2. CATMULL-SMITH ALGORITHM

The most general presentation of the 2-pass technique appears in the seminal work described by Catmull and Smith in [1]. That paper tackles the problem of mapping a 2-D image onto a 3-D surface and then projecting the result onto the 2-D screen for viewing. They show that in some cases a 2-D resampling problem can be replaced with two orthogonal 1-D resampling stages.

2.2.1. First Pass

In the first pass, each horizontal scanline (row) is resampled according to spatial transformation $F(u)$, generating an intermediate image I in scanline order. All pixels in I have the same x-coordinates that they will assume in the final output; only their y-coordinates now remain to be computed. Since each scanline will generally have a different transformation, function $F(u)$ will usually differ from row to row. Consequently, F can be considered to be a function of both u and v. Obviously, $F(u,v)$ is identical to $X(u,v)$. We rewrite $F(u,v)$ as $F_v(u)$ to denote that F is applied to horizontal scanlines, each having constant v. Therefore, the first pass is expressed as

$$[x, v] = [F_v(u), v] = [X(u,v), v]. \qquad (3)$$

This relation maps each $[u,v]$ point onto I, an intermediate image in the $[x,v]$ plane.

2.2.2. Second Pass

In the second pass, each vertical scanline (column) in I is resampled according to spatial transformation $G(v)$, generating the final image in scanline order. The second pass is more complicated than the first pass since the expression for G assumes we can get $[u,v]$ from $[x,v]$ so that we can access $Y(u,v)$. This requires us to solve the equation $X(u,v) - \tilde{x} = 0$ for u to obtain $u = H_x(v)$ for vertical scanline (column) $\tilde{x}$. Function H, known as the *auxiliary function*, represents the u-coordinates of the inverse projection of $\tilde{x}$, the column we wish to resample. Thus, for every column in I, we compute $H_x(v)$ and use it together with the available v-coordinates to index into mapping function Y. The second pass is therefore expressed as

$$[x, y] = [x, G_x(v)] \qquad (4)$$

where $G_x(v)$ refers to the evaluation of $G(x,v)$ along vertical scanlines with constant x. It is given by

$$G_x(v) = Y(H_x(v), v) \qquad (5)$$

The relation in Eq. (4) maps all points in I from the $[x,v]$ plane onto the $[x,y]$ plane, defining the final image.

2.2.3. Bottleneck Problem

After completing the first pass, it is sometimes possible for the intermediate image to collapse into a narrow area. If this area is much less than that of the final image, then there is insufficient data left to accurately generate the final image. This phenomenon, referred to as the *bottleneck problem* in [1], is the result of a many-to-one mapping in the first pass followed by a one-to-many mapping in the second pass. An example is the rotation of an image by 90°. Each row will collapse onto a point, resulting in an intermediate image consisting of a diagonal line. Obviously, no inverse function can resolve the intensities for the second pass.

In both [1] and [8], it is suggested that a solution to this problem lies in considering all the possible orders in which a separable algorithm can be implemented. Four variations, collectively referred to as V, are possible to generate the intermediate image:

1) Transform u first.

2) Transform v first.

3) Transpose the input image and transform u first.

4) Transpose the input image and transform v first.

In each case, the area of the intermediate image can be calculated. They suggest implementing the transformation with the variation that yields the largest intermediate area. For instance, an 87° rotation is best implemented by first rotating the image by 90° via image transposition and then applying a −3° rotation using the 2-pass technique. They purport that the above heuristic has not been known to fail, however no proof of its correctness is given.

We now give three difficulties with their solution to the bottleneck problem. The most critical problem is that the area of the intermediate image is a global measure which may fail to highlight compression variations in local areas. Although the heuristic seems to be satisfactory for the transformations considered in their original paper, it is inadequate for arbitrary mappings — the mappings considered here. For example, consider warping an image into a circular region with each row becoming a radial line, i.e., $(x, y) \rightarrow (r, \theta)$. This demonstrates a simple example in which different areas of the output map are best computed from different variations of V; no single transform from V could correctly process the entire image.

The second problem is that the heuristic does not properly consider aliasing artifacts. In particular, maximizing the intermediate area may require excessive compression in the second pass. For example, in Fig. 8 of [8] variations (1) and (2) were used to map a regular grid onto a sphere. Although variation (2) maximized the area of the intermediate image, it actually caused more severe aliasing. This non-intuitive result is due to error properties of cascading 1-D filters to approximate a 2-D filter (see section 3.5.)

The third difficulty arises when the closed-form approximation to the intermediate area does not exist. While this does not prove troublesome in simpler domains, the evaluation of the intermediate areas for complex spatial mappings requires as much or more work as computing the first passes for each variation in V.

2.2.4. Foldover Problem

The 2-pass algorithm is particularly well-suited for mapping images onto surfaces with closed-form solutions to auxiliary function H. The process is more complicated for surfaces of higher order, e.g., bilinear, biquadratic, and bicubic patches, which may be self-occluding. This makes F or G become multi-valued at points where the image folds upon itself, a problem known as *foldover*.

Foldover can occur in either of the two passes. A partial solution for *single* folds in G is to compute output pixels in back-to-front order, overwriting the hidden layers. Generating the image in this manner becomes more complicated for surfaces with more than one fold. In the general case, this becomes a hidden surface problem.

The only reasonable solution has been to severely limit the amount of foldover, (e.g., up to three folds for cubic surfaces) and to use additional framebuffers to store the folded layers. This solution is inefficient inasmuch as an entire framebuffer must be utilized even if only a small folded area is involved.

2.2.5. Computing Auxiliary Function H

Closed-form solutions do not exist for H unless the patch has no folds. When folds occur, a solution $u = H_x(0)$ is found for the first horizontal scanline. Since surface patches are assumed to be smooth, a Newton-Raphson iteration method can be used to solve for $H_x(1)$ using the solution from $H_x(0)$ as a starting value. The need to evaluate H can be avoided altogether if we make use of earlier computations. In particular, we have H use the u-coordinates associated with the preimage of a pixel in the intermediate image. Thus, by introducing an auxiliary framebuffer to store these u's while we are in the first pass, H becomes available by trivial lookup table access.

2.3. DISCUSSION

The 2-pass algorithm has been shown to apply to a wide class of transformations of general interest. These mappings include the perspective projection of rectangles, bivariate patches, and superquadrics. Smith has discussed them in detail in [8]. In that paper, he emphasizes the mathematical consequence of decomposing mapping functions X and Y into a sequence of F followed by G. Smith distinguishes X and Y as the *parallel warp*, and F and G as the *serial warp*, where *warp* refers to resampling. Serial warps offer dramatic computational reductions with only minor degradation. Nevertheless, they are plagued by several complications: the bottleneck problem, foldovers, and computing auxiliary function H.

3. DESCRIPTION OF ALGORITHM

In this section we describe an algorithm that addresses the difficulties that are particular to 2-pass methods. The result is a separable approach that is general, accurate, and efficient, with graceful degradation for transformations of arbitrary complexity.

3.1. OVERVIEW

The goal of this work is to realize an arbitrary warp with a separable algorithm. The proposed technique is an extension of the Catmull-Smith approach where attention has been directed toward solutions to the bottleneck and foldover problems, as well as removing the need for closed-form inverses. Conceptually, the algorithm consists of four stages: intensity resampling, coordinate resampling, distortion measurement, and compositing. Figure 3.1 shows the interaction of the stages. Note that bold arrows represent the flow of images through a stage, and thin arrows denote those images which act upon the input. The subscripts x and y are appended to images which have been resampled in the horizontal and vertical directions, respectively.

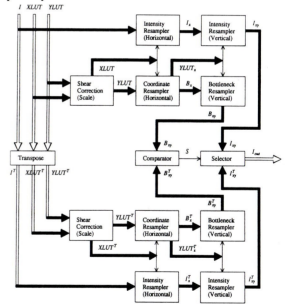

Figure 3.1: Block diagram of the algorithm.

The intensity resampler applies a 2-pass algorithm to the input image. Since the result may suffer bottleneck problems, the identical process is repeated with the transpose of the image. This accounts for the vertical symmetry of Fig. 3.1. Pixels which suffer excessive bottlenecking in the natural processing can be recovered in the transposed processing. In our implementation, we realize transposition as a 90° clockwise rotation so as to avoid the need to reorder pixels left to right.

The coordinate resampler computes spatial information necessary for the intensity resampler. It warps the spatial lookup table $Y(u,v)$ so that the second pass of the intensity resampler can access it without the need for an inverse function.

Local measures of shearing, perspective distortion, and bottlenecking are computed to indicate the amount of information lost at each point. This information, together with the transposed and non-transposed results of the intensity resampler, are passed to the compositor. The final output image is generated by the compositor which samples those pixels from the two resampled images such that information loss is minimized in the final output.

3.2. SPATIAL LOOKUP TABLES

Scanline algorithms generally express the coordinate transformation in terms of forward mapping functions X and Y. Sampling X and Y over all input points yields two new real-valued images, $XLUT$ and $YLUT$, specifying the point-to-point mapping from each pixel in the input image onto the output images. This paper refers to $XLUT$ and $YLUT$ as *spatial lookup tables* since they can be viewed as 2-D tables which express a spatial transformation.

In addition to $XLUT$ and $YLUT$ we also provide a mechanism for the user to specify $ZLUT$ which associates a z-coordinate value with each pixel. This allows warping of planar textures onto non-planar surfaces, and is useful in dealing with foldovers. Our goal, however, is not to solve the general 3-D viewing problem. The z-coordinates are assumed to be from a particular point of view which the user determines before supplying $ZLUT$ to the system.

The motivation for introducing spatial lookup tables is generality. Our goal is to find a serial warp equivalent to any given parallel warp. Thus, we find it impossible to retain the mathematical elegance of closed-form expressions for the mapping functions F, G, and the auxiliary function, H. Therefore, assuming the forward mapping functions, X and Y, have closed-form expressions seems overly restrictive. Instead, we assume that the parallel warp is defined by the samples that comprise our spatial lookup tables. This provides a general means of specifying arbitrary mapping functions.

For each pixel (u,v) in input image I, spatial lookup tables $XLUT$, $YLUT$, and $ZLUT$ are indexed at location (u,v) to determine the corresponding (x,y,z) position of the input point after warping. This new position is orthographically projected onto the output image. Therefore, (x,y) is taken to be the position in the output image. (Of course, a perspective projection may be included as part of the warp.) The z-coordinate will only be used to resolve foldovers. This straightforward indexing applies only if the dimensions of I, $XLUT$, $YLUT$, and $ZLUT$ are all identical. If this is not the case, then the smaller images are upsampled (magnified) to match the largest dimensions.

3.3. INTENSITY RESAMPLING

This section discusses how spatial lookup tables are used to resample intensity images. The 1-D intensity resampling algorithm is well-suited for hardware implementation and compatible with spatial lookup tables. It is the basis of the 2-pass intensity resampling stage depicted in the first row of Fig. 3.1.

3.3.1. 1-D Intensity Resampler

The central benefit of separable algorithms is the reduction in complexity allowed by 1-D resampling algorithms which provide efficient solutions for the image reconstruction and antialiasing components of resampling. Fant presents a detailed description of such a 1-D algorithm that is well-suited to hardware implementation and compatible with spatial lookup tables [4]. It is the principal 1-D resampling method used in separable transformations, including that of the work presented here.

The process treats the input and output as streams of pixels that are consumed and generated at rates determined by the spatial mapping. The input is assumed to be mapped onto the output along a single direction, i.e., with no folds. As each input pixel arrives, it is weighted by its partial contribution to the current output pixel and integrated into a single element accumulator. For input pixels that spread out over many output pixels, image reconstruction is currently implemented with linear interpolation.

3.3.2. Example

Consider the 1-D arrays shown in Fig. 3.2. The first row is taken from $XLUT$, the second from $YLUT$, and the third from input intensity image I. The next two arrays show $YLUT$ and I resampled according to $XLUT$.

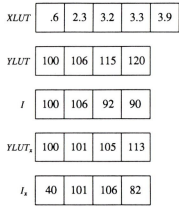

$XLUT$	.6	2.3	3.2	3.3	3.9

$YLUT$	100	106	115	120

I	100	106	92	90

$YLUT_x$	100	101	105	113

I_x	40	101	106	82

Figure 3.2: Resampling example.

The computation of the resampled intensity values is given below.

$$I_x[0] = \mathbf{100}\,(.4) = 40$$
$$I_x[1] = [\mathbf{100}\,(1-.4+1.7) + \mathbf{106}\,(.4+1.7)]\,(1) = 101$$
$$I_x[2] = [\mathbf{100}\,(1-1.4+1.7) + \mathbf{106}\,(1.4+1.7)]\,(.3) + \mathbf{106}\,(.7) = 106$$
$$I_x[3] = [\mathbf{106}\,(1-.7+.9) + \mathbf{92}\,(.7+.9)]\,(.2) + \mathbf{92}\,(.1) + \mathbf{90}\,(.6) = 82$$

The algorithm demonstrates both image reconstruction and antialiasing. When we are not positioned at pixel boundaries in the input stream, linear interpolation is used to reconstruct the discrete input. If more than one input element contributes to an output pixel, the weighted results are integrated into an accumulator to achieve antialiasing. The intersection tests needed for weighting are, of course, one-dimensional.

3.3.3. 2-Pass Intensity Resampling

The 1-D intensity resampler is applied to the image in two passes, each along orthogonal directions. The first pass resamples horizontal scanlines, warping pixels along a row in the intermediate image. Its purpose is to deposit them into the proper columns for vertical resampling. At that point, the second pass is applied to all columns in the intermediate image, generating the output image.

In Fig. 3.1, input image I is shown warped according to $XLUT$ to generate intermediate image I_x. In order to apply the second pass, $YLUT$ is warped alongside I, yielding $YLUT_x$. This resampled spatial lookup table is applied to I_x in the second pass as a collection of 1-D vertical warps. The result is output image I_{xy}.

The intensity resampling stage must handle multiple output values to be defined in case of foldovers. This is an important implementation detail which has impact on the memory requirements of the algorithm. We defer discussion of this aspect of the intensity resampler until section 3.6, where foldovers are discussed in more detail.

3.4. COORDINATE RESAMPLING

$YLUT_x$ is computed in the coordinate resampling stage depicted in the second row of the block diagram in Fig. 3.1. The ability to resample $YLUT$ for use in the second pass has important consequences: it circumvents the need for a closed-form inverse of the first pass. As briefly pointed out in [1], that inverse provides exactly the same information that was available as the first pass was computed, i.e., the u-coordinate associated with a pixel in the intermediate image. Thus, instead of computing the inverse to index into $YLUT$, we simply warp $YLUT$ into $YLUT_x$ allowing direct access in the second pass.

3.4.1. Coordinate Resampler

The coordinate resampler is similar to the intensity resampler. It differs only in the notable absence of antialiasing filtering — the output coordinate values in $YLUT_x$ are computed by point sampling $YLUT$. Interpolation is used to compute values when no input data is supplied at the resampling locations. However, unlike the intensity resampler, the coordinate resampler does not weigh the result with its area coverage nor does the resampler average it with the coordinate values of other contributions to that pixel. This serves to secure the accuracy of edge coordinates, even when the edge occupies only a partial output pixel.

3.4.2. Example

The following example is offered to demonstrate the coordinate resampling algorithm. Consider the arrays shown before in Fig. 3.2. $YLUT_x$ in the example is the output of the coordinate resampling as computed below. Notice that the output consists of point samples taken at pixel boundaries in the output stream. They are not influenced by any other entries deposited into their respective output pixels. The computations are given below.

$$YLUT_x[0] = 100\,(1-0+1.7)+106\,(0+1.7) = 100$$

$$YLUT_x[1] = 100\,(1-.4+1.7)+106\,(.4+1.7) = 101$$

$$YLUT_x[2] = 100\,(1-1.4+1.7)+106\,(1.4+1.7) = 105$$

$$YLUT_x[3] = 106\,(1-.7+.9)+115\,(.7+.9) = 113$$

As mentioned before, the user can define $ZLUT$ which associates a z-coordinate with each pixel. While it does not appear in the system block diagram of Fig. 3.1, we also apply this resampling to $ZLUT$ in exactly the same manner as it was applied to $YLUT$.

3.5. DISTORTIONS AND ERRORS

In forward mapping, input pixels are taken to be squares that map onto arbitrary quadrilaterals in the output image. Although separable mappings greatly simplify resampling by treating pixels as points along scanlines, the measurement of distortion must necessarily revert to 2-D to consider the deviation of each input pixel as it projects onto the output.

As is standard, we treat the mapping of a square onto a general quadrilateral as a combination of translation, scaling, shearing, rotation, and perspective transformations. Inasmuch as separable kernels exist for realizing translations and scale changes, these transformations do not suffer degradation in scanline algorithms and are not considered further. Shear, perspective and rotations, however, offer significant challenges to the 2-pass approach. In particular, excessive shear and perspective contribute to aliasing problems while rotations account for the bottleneck problem.

We first examine the errors introduced by separable filtering. We then address the three sources of geometric distortion for 2-pass scanline algorithms: shear, perspective, and rotation.

3.5.1. Filtering Errors

One of the sources of error for scanline algorithms comes from the use of cascaded orthogonal 1-D filtering. Let us ignore rotation for a moment, and assume we process the image left-to-right and top-to-bottom. Then one can easily show that scanline algorithms will, in the first pass, filter a pixel based only on the horizontal coverage of its top segment. In the second pass, they will filter based only on the vertical coverage of the left-hand segment of the input pixel. As a result, a warped pixel generating a triangular section in an output pixel is always approximated by a rectangle (Fig. 3.3). Note this can be either an overestimate or underestimate, and the error depends on the direction of processing. This problem is not unique to our approach. It is shared by all scanline algorithms known to us.

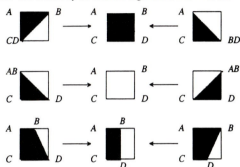

Figure 3.3: Examples of filtering errors.

3.5.2. Shear

Figure 3.4 depicts a set of spatial lookup tables which demonstrate horizontal shear. For simplicity, the example includes no scaling or rotation. The figure also shows the result obtained after applying the tables to an image of constant intensity (100). The horizontal shear is apparent in the form of jagged edges between adjacent rows.

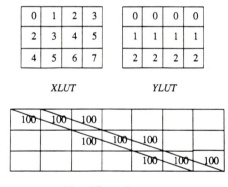

Aliased Output Image

Figure 3.4: Horizontal shear: Spatial LUTs and output image.

Scanline algorithms are particularly sensitive to this form of distortion because proper filtering is applied only *along* scanlines — filtering issues *across* scanlines are not considered. Consequently, horizontal (vertical) shear is a manifestation of aliasing along the vertical (horizontal) direction, i.e., between horizontal (vertical) scanlines. The prefiltering stage described below must be introduced to suppress these artifacts *before* the regular 2-pass algorithm is applied.

This problem is a symptom of undersampled spatial lookup tables, and the only real solution lies in increasing the resolution of the tables by sampling the continuous mapping functions more densely. If the continuous mapping functions are no longer available to us, then new values are computed from the sparse samples by interpolation. (In this paper, linear interpolation is assumed to be adequate.)

We now consider the effect of increasing the spatial resolution of *XLUT* and *YLUT*. The resulting image in Fig. 3.5 is shown to be antialiased, and clearly superior to its counterpart in Fig. 3.4. The values of 37 and 87 reflect the partial coverage of the input slivers at the output. Note that with additional upsampling, these values converge to 25 and 75, respectively. Adjacent rows are now constrained to lie within 1/2 pixel of each other. The error constraint can be specified by the user and the spatial resolution for the lookup tables can be determined automatically. This offers us a convenient mechanism in which to control error tolerance and address the space/accuracy tradeoff. For the examples herein, both horizontal and vertical shear are restricted to one pixel.

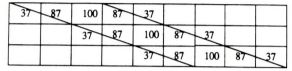

Figure 3.5: Corrected output image.

By now the reader may be wondering if the shear problems might be alleviated, as was suggested in [1], by considering a different order of processing. While the problem may be slightly ameliorated by changing processing direction, the real problem lies in undersampling the lookup tables. They are specifying an output configuration (with many long thin slivers) which, because of filtering errors, cannot be accurately realized by separable processing in any order.

3.5.3. Perspective

Like shear, perspective distortions may also cause problems by warping a rectangle into a triangular patch which results in significant filtering errors. In fact, if one only considers the warp determined by any three corners of an input pixel, one cannot distinguish shear from perspective projection. The latter requires knowledge of all four corners. The problem generated by perspective warping can also be solved by the same mechanism as for shears: resampling the spatial lookup tables to ensure that no long thin slivers are generated. However, unlike shear, perspective also effects the bottleneck problem because, for some orders of processing, the first pass may be contractive while the second pass is expansive. This perspective bottlenecking is handled by the same mechanism as for rotations, as described below.

3.5.4. Rotation

In addition to jagginess due to shear and perspective, distortions are also introduced by rotation. Rotational components in the spatial transformation are the *major* source of bottleneck problems. Although all rotation angles contribute to this problem, we consider those beyond 45° to be inadequately resampled by a 2-pass algorithm. This threshold is chosen because 0° and 90° rotations can be performed exactly. If other exact image rotations were available, then the worst case error could be reduced to half the maximum separation of the angles. Local areas whose rotational components exceed 45° are recovered from the transposed results, where they obviously undergo a rotation less than 45°.

3.5.5. Distortion Measures

Consider scanning two scanlines jointly, labeling an adjacent pair of pixels in the first row as *A*, *B*, and the associated pair in the second row as *C*, and *D*. Let (x_A, y_A), (x_B, y_B), (x_C, y_C), and (x_D, y_D) be their respective output coordinates as specified by the spatial lookup tables. These points define an output quadrilateral onto which the square input pixel is mapped. From these four points it is possible to determine the horizontal and vertical scale factors necessary to combat aliasing due to shear and perspective distortions, and also

determine if extensive bottlenecking is present. For convenience, we define

$$\Delta x_{ij} = |x_i - x_j|; \quad \Delta y_{ij} = |y_i - y_j|; \quad s_{ij} = \Delta y_{ij} / \Delta x_{ij}.$$

Pseudo-code for the procedure is given below.

```
bottleneck = 0                          /* Initially no bottleneck */
IF( Δy_AB ≤ Δx_AB ){                     /* AB remains horizontal */
      vfctr = max ( Δx_AC, Δx_BD )       /* measure horizontal shear */
} ELSE IF( s_AB ≤ s_AC ){                /* AC remains vertical */
      hfctr = max ( Δy_AB, Δy_CD )       /* measure vertical shear */
} ELSE bottleneck = 1                    /* Bottleneck occurs */
```

If *AB* has not rotated from the horizontal by more than 45°, then its error due to bottlenecking is considered acceptable, and we say that it remains "horizontal." Only the vertical aliasing distortions due to horizontal shearing and/or perspective need to be considered in this case. The vertical scale factor, *vfctr*, for *XLUT* and *YLUT* is given by $vfctr = MAX(\Delta x_{AC}, \Delta x_{BD})$. Briefly, this measures the maximum deviation in the horizontal direction for a unit step in the vertical direction. To ensure an alignment error of at most ε, the image must be rescaled vertically by a factor of $vfctr/\varepsilon$. Examples of quadrilaterals that satisfy this case are illustrated in Fig. 3.6.

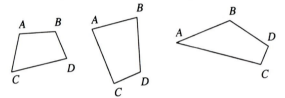

Figure 3.6: Warps where *AB* remains horizontal.

If *AB* is rotated by more than 45°, then we say that it has become "vertical" and two possibilities exist: vertical shearing/perspective or rotation. In order to consider vertical shear/perspective, the magnitude of the slope of *AC* is measured in relation to that of *AB*. If $s_{AB} \le s_{AC}$, then *AC* is considered to remain vertical and the pixel is tested for vertical shear/perspective. (In order to enhance computational efficiency and to avoid divide-by-zero errors, the test condition is actually posed in terms of multiplication only.) If the test condition is satisfied, the horizontal scale factor, *hfctr*, for the spatial lookup tables is expressed as $hfctr = MAX(\Delta y_{AB}, \Delta y_{CD})$. Briefly stated, this measures the the maximum deviation in the vertical direction for a unit step in the horizontal direction. Again, alignment error can be limited to ε by rescaling the image horizontally by a factor of $hfctr/\varepsilon$. Examples of this condition are shown in Fig. 3.7.

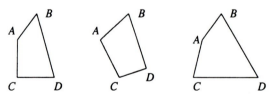

Figure 3.7: *AB* has rotated while *AC* remains vertical. Vertical shear.

If, however, angle *BAC* is also found to be rotated, (i.e., neither of the above tests are satisfied) then the entire quadrilateral *ABCD* is considered to be bottlenecked because it has rotated and/or undergone a perspective distortion. The *bottleneck* flag is set to one to denote the presence of the bottleneck problem at this pixel and, as described below, its contributions will be taken from the transposed result. This case is depicted in Fig. 3.8.

The code fragment listed above is applied to each input pixel. Currently, the maximum values of $hfctr/\varepsilon$ and $vfctr/\varepsilon$ are used to scale the spatial lookup tables before they enter the 2-pass resampling stage. In this manner, the output of this stage is guaranteed to be free

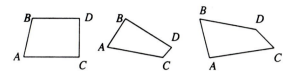

Figure 3.8: Both *AB* and *AC* have rotated. Bottleneck problem.

of aliasing due to undersampled spatial lookup tables. In the future, we will examine using this as a local measure to adaptively resample the tables.

3.5.6. Bottleneck Distortion

The bottleneck problem was described earlier as a many-to-one mapping followed by a one-to-many mapping. The extent to which the bottleneck problem becomes manifest is intimately related to the order in which the orthogonal 1-D transformations are applied. The four possible orders in which a 2-D separable transformation can be implemented are listed in section 2.2.3. Of the four alternatives, we shall only consider variations (1) and (3). Although variations (2) and (4) may have impact on the extent of aliasing in the output image (see Fig. 8 of [8]), their roles may be obviated by upsampling the spatial lookup tables before they enter the 2-pass resampling stage.

A solution to the bottleneck problem thereby requires us to consider the effects which occur as an image is separably resampled with and without a preliminary image transposition stage. Unlike the Catmull-Smith algorithm which selects only one variation for the entire image, we are operating in a more general domain which may require either of the two variations over arbitrary regions of the image. This leads us to develop a local measure of bottleneck distortion which is used to determine which variation is most suitable at each output pixel. Thus alongside each resampled intensity image, another image of identical dimensions is computed to maintain estimates of the local bottleneck distortion.

A 2-pass method is introduced to compute bottleneck distortion estimates at each point. As above, the *bottleneck* flag is determined for each input pixel. If no bottlenecking is present, then the area coverage of that input pixel is integrated into bottleneck image B_x. If, however, the *bottleneck* flag is set to one, then that pixel makes no contribution to B_x. The bottleneck image thus reflects the fraction of each pixel in the intermediate image *not* subject to bottleneck distortion in the first pass. The computations are simple, and serve a secondary function in that the entries correspond exactly to the weights needed for antialiasing in the intensity resampling stage. Thus we are getting a local distortion measure at virtually no additional cost.

The second pass resamples intermediate image B_x in the same manner as the intensity resampler, thus spreading the distortion estimates to their correct location in the final image. The result is a double-precision bottleneck-distortion image B_{xy}, with values inversely proportional to the bottleneck artifacts. The distortion computation process is repeated for the transpose of the image and spatial lookup tables, generating image B_{xy}^T.

Since the range of values in the bottleneck image are known to lie between 0 and 1, it is possible to quantize the range into N intervals for storage in a lower precision image with $\log_2 N$ bits per pixel. This space/accuracy tradeoff will be assessed in future work. We point out that the measure of area is not exact. It is subject to exactly the same errors as intensity filtering.

3.6. FOLDOVER PROBLEM

Up to this point, we have been discussing our warping algorithm as though both passes resulted in only a single value for each point. Unfortunately, this is often not the case — a warped scanline can fold back upon itself.

In [1] it was proposed that multiple framebuffers be used to store each level of the fold. While this solution may be viable for low-order warps, as considered in [1] and [8], it may prove to be too costly for arbitrary warps where the number of potential folds may be large. Furthermore, it is often the case that the folded area may represent a small fraction of the output image. Thus, using one frame buffer per fold would be prohibitively expensive, and we seek a solution which degrades more gracefully.

If we are to allow an image to fold upon itself, we must have some means of determining which of the folds are to be displayed. The simplest mechanism, and probably the most useful, is to assume that the user will supply not only *XLUT* and *YLUT*, but also *ZLUT* to specify the output z-coordinates for each input pixel. In the first pass *ZLUT* will be processed in exactly the same way as *YLUT*, so the second pass of the intensity resampler can have access to the z-coordinates.

Given *ZLUT* we are now faced with the problem of keeping track of the information from the folding. A naive solution might be to use a z-buffer in computing the intermediate and final image. Unfortunately, while z-buffering will work for the output of the second pass, it cannot work for the first pass because some mappings fold-over on themselves in the first pass only to have some of the "hidden" part exposed by the second pass of the warp. Thus, we must find an efficient means of incorporating all the data, including the foldovers, in the intermediate image.

3.6.1. Representing Foldovers

Our solution is to maintain multiple columns for each column in the intermediate image. The extra columns, or layers, of space are allocated to hold information from foldovers on an as-needed basis. The advantage of this approach is that if a small area of the image undergoes folding, only a small amount of extra information is required. When the warp has folds, the intermediate image has a multi-layered structure, like that in Fig. 3.9.

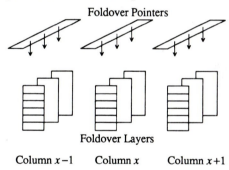

Figure 3.9: Data structure for folded warps.

While this representation is superior to multiple frame buffers, it may still be inefficient unless we allow each layer in the intermediate image to store data from many different folds (assuming that some of them have terminated and new ones were created). Thus, we reuse each foldover layer whenever possible

In addition to the actual data stored in extra layers, we also maintain a number of extra pieces of information (described below), such as various pointers to the layers, and auxiliary information about the last entry in each layer.

3.6.2. Tracking Foldovers

It is not sufficient to simply store all the necessary information in some structure for later processing. Given that folds do occur, there is the problem of how to filter the intermediate image. Since filtering requires all the information from one foldover layer to be accessed coherently, it is necessary to track each layer across many rows of the image. For efficiency, we desire to do this tracking using a purely local match from one row to the next. The real difficulty in the matching is when fold layers are created, terminated, or bifurcated. We note that any "matching" must be a heuristic, since without strong assumptions about the warps, there is *no* procedure to match folds from one row to another. (The approach in [1] assumes that the Newton-Raphson algorithm can follow the zeros of the auxiliary function H correctly, which is true only for simple auxiliary functions with limited bifurcations.)

Our heuristic solution to the matching problem uses three types of information: direction of travel when processing the layer (left or right in the row), ordering of folds within a column, and the original u-coordinate associated with each pixel in the intermediate image.

First, we constrain layers to match only those layers where the points are processed in the same order. For instance, matching between two leftward layers is allowed, but matching between leftward and rightward layers is not allowed.

Secondly, we assume the layers within a single column are partially ordered. Within each column, every folded pixel in the current row is assigned a unique number based on the order in which it was added to the foldover lists. The partial order would allow matching pixels 12345 with 1?23??4 (where the symbol ? indicates a match with a null element), but would not allow matching of 12345 with 1?43??2.

Finally, we use the u-coordinate associated with each pixel to define a distance measure between points which satisfies the above constraints. The match is done using a divide-and-conquer technique. Briefly, we first find the best match among all points, i.e., minimum distance. We then subdivide the remaining potential matches to the left and to the right of the best match, thus yielding two smaller subsets on which we reapply the algorithm. For hardware implementation, dynamic programming may be more suitable. This is a common solution for related string matching problems.

Consider a column which previously had foldover layers labeled 123456, with orientation *RLRLRL*, and original u-coordinates of 10,17,25,30,80,95. If two of these layers disappeared leaving four layers, say *abcd*, with orientation *RLRL* and original u-coordinates of 16,20,78,101, then we would do the matching finding *abcd* matching 1256 respectively.

3.6.3. Storing Information from Foldovers

Once the matches are determined, we must rearrange the data so that the intensity resampler can access it in a spatially coherent manner. To facilitate this, each column in the intermediate image has a block of pointers that specify the order of the foldover layers. When the matching algorithm results in a shift in order, a different set of pointers is defined, and the valid range of the previous set is recorded. The advantage of this explicit reordering of pointers is that it allows for efficient access to the folds while processing.

We describe the process from the point of view of a single column in the intermediate image, and note that all columns are processed identically. The first encountered entry for a row goes into the base layer. For each new entry into this column, the fill pointer is advanced (using the block of pointers), and the entry is added at the bottom of the next fold layer. After we compute the "best" match we move incorrectly stored data, reorder the layers and define a new block of pointers.

Let us continue the example from the end of the last section, where 123456 was matched to 1256. After the matching, we would then move the data, incorrectly stored in columns 3 and 4 into the appropriate location in 5 and 6. Finally we would reorder the columns and adjust the pointer blocks to reflect the new order 125634. The columns previously labeled 34 would be marked as terminated, and considered spares to be used in later rows if a new fold layer begins.

3.6.4. Intensity Resampling with Foldovers

A final aspect of the foldover problem is how it affects the 2-D intensity resampling process. The discussion above demonstrates that all the intensity values for a given column are collected in such a way that each fold layer is a separate contiguous array of spatially coherent values. Thus, the contribution of each pixel in a fold layer is obtained by standard 1-D filtering of that array.

From the coordinate resampler, we obtain $ZLUT_{xy}$, and thus, merging the foldovers is equivalent to determining which filtered pixels are visible. Given the above information, we implement a simple z-buffer algorithm, which integrates the points in front-to-back order with partial coverage calculations for antialiasing. When the accumulated area coverage exceeds 1, the integration terminates. Note that this z-buffer requires *only* a 1-D accumulator, which can be reused for each column. The result is a single intensity image combining the information from all visible folds.

3.7. COMPOSITOR

The compositor generates the final output image by selecting the most suitable pixels from I_{xy} and I_{xy}^T as determined by the bottleneck images B_{xy} and B_{xy}^T. A block diagram of the compositor is shown in center row of Fig. 3.1.

Bottleneck images B_{xy} and B_{xy}^T are passed through a comparator to generate bitmap image S. Also known as a *vector mask*, S is initialized according to the following rule.

$$S[x,y] = (B_{xy}[x,y] \leq B_{xy}^T[x,y])$$

Images S, I_{xy}, and I_{xy}^T are sent to the selector where I_{out} is assembled. For each position in I_{out}, the vector mask S is indexed to determine whether the pixel value should be sampled from I_{xy} or I_{xy}^T.

4. EXAMPLES

This section illustrates some examples of the algorithm. The top row of Fig. 4.1 shows two images that will be used as source images for numerous examples. We refer to these images as the checkerboard and as Madonna. The bottom row of that figure shows the final result of warping the checkerboard and Madonna into a 360° circle. This transformation takes each row of the source image and maps it into a radial line. This corresponds directly to a mapping from the Cartesian coordinate system to the polar coordinate system, i.e., $(x, y) \rightarrow (r, \theta)$.

Figure 4.2 illustrates the output of the intensity resampler for the non-transposed and transposed processing. I_{xy} appears in the upper-left quadrant, and I_{xy}^T is shown in the upper-right. The lower-right quadrant shows S, the vector mask image. S selects points from I_{xy} (white) and I_{xy}^T (black) to generate the final output image I_{out}. Gray points in S denote equal bottleneck computations from both sources. Ties are arbitrarily resolved in favor of I_{xy}^T. In the bottom-left quadrant of Fig. 4.2, the two spatial lookup tables $XLUT$ and $YLUT$ that defined the circular warp, are displayed as intensity images, with y increasing top-to-bottom, and x increasing left-to-right. Bright intensity values in the images of $XLUT$ and $YLUT$ denote high coordinate values. Note that if the input were to remain undistorted $XLUT$ and $YLUT$ would be ramps. The deviation from the ramp configuration depicts the amount of deformation which the input image undergoes.

Figure 4.3 demonstrates the effect of undersampling the spatial lookup tables. The checkerboard is again warped into a circle. However, $XLUT$ and $YLUT$ were supplied at lower resolution. The jagginess in the results are now more pronounced.

Figure 4.4 illustrates an example of foldovers. The lower-left quadrant shows $XLUT$ and $YLUT$. A foldover occurs because $XLUT$ is not monotonically increasing from left to right. In the upper-right quadrant, the output image is composed by simply selecting the closest pixels. Note that dim pixels appear at the edge of the fold as it crosses the image. This subtlety is more apparent along the fold upon the cheek. The intensity drop is due to the antialiasing filtering that correctly weighted the pixels with their area coverage along the edge. This can be resolved by integrating partially visible pixels in front-to-back order. As soon as the sum of area coverage exceeds 1, no more integration is necessary. Fortunately, the bottleneck image can be used to directly supply the area coverage data. The improved result appears in the lower-right quadrant.

Figure 4.5 shows the result of bending horizontal rows. As we scan across the rows in left-to-right order, the row becomes increasingly vertical. This is another example in which the traditional 2-pass method would clearly fail since a wide range of rotation angles are represented. The remaining figures show additional warps. In the "89" figure, a Monet painting was warped into a semi-donut that was used as a primitive in assembling the image.

5. CONCLUSIONS AND FUTURE WORK

This paper describes a separable algorithm for realizing arbitrary warps which are specified by spatial lookup tables. It greatly extends the class of warps which can take advantage of separable techniques. As a result, it is possible to design real-time hardware built around off-the-shelf 1-D resamplers.

Our approach is based on the solution of the three main difficulties of the Catmull-Smith approach: bottlenecking, foldovers, and the need for a closed-form inverse. In addition, we addressed some of the errors caused by filtering, especially those caused by insufficient resolution in the sampling of the mapping function. Through careful attention to efficiency and graceful degradation, we developed a method that is no more costly than the Catmull-Smith algorithm when bottlenecking and foldovers are not present. However when these problems do surface, they are resolved at a cost proportional to their manifestation. Since the underlying data structures continue to facilitate pipelining, this method offers a promising hardware solution to the implementation of arbitrary spatial mapping functions.

The limitations of the work can be separated into two classes: inherent limitations, and those to be addressed by future work. The primary inherent limitation is that which is imposed by the separable nature of the filtering — the combination of two 1-D filtering operations is not as flexible as true 2-D filtering. A secondary inherent limitation is that, as a forward mapping, the entire input image and spatial map must be used even if much of it will be clipped out of the final image. Future work should allow the clipping to be done as part of the first pass coordinate resampling.

One of the limitations to be overcome by future work is that of incorporating local adaptive sampling in response to the local measure of shear. The difficulties to be overcome include data representation (the shape of the intermediate image might be far from rectangular), and proper reconstruction filtering for the spatial lookup tables.

A second avenue for future research is a detailed study of the error properties of the approach, and how they are affected by choice of reconstruction filter, processing order, and sampling density. We know that certain perspective distortions can be ameliorated by processing in different orders, and we hope that a local measure incorporating both bottleneck distortion and perspective distortion can be developed.

Further work remains to be done in extending this method to 3-D for warping volumetric data in medical imaging, e.g., CAT scans. Other applications include scientific visualization, whereby parameters may be mapped onto different warping functions. Visual music would then be possible by using filtered sound to perturb the spatial lookup tables. This would prove to be a valuable extension to existing visualization tools. Since warping is a process common to many disciplines, there are likely to be many applications which can exploit the results of this work.

6. REFERENCES

[1] Catmull, E. and A.R. Smith, "3-D Transformations of Images in Scanline Order," *Computer Graphics*, (SIGGRAPH '80 Proceedings), vol. 14, no. 3, pp. 279-285, July 1980.

[2] Cook, R.L., "Stochastic Sampling in Computer Graphics," *ACM Trans. on Graphics*, vol. 5, no. 1, pp. 51-72, January 1986.

[3] Dippe, M.A.Z and E.H. Wold, "Antialiasing Through Stochastic Sampling," *Computer Graphics*, (SIGGRAPH '85 Proceedings), vol. 19, no. 3, pp. 69-78, July 1985.

[4] Fant, K.M., "A Nonaliasing, Real-Time Spatial Transform Technique," *IEEE Computer Graphics and Applications*, vol. 6, no. 1, pp. 71-80, January 1986.

[5] Heckbert, P., "Survey of Texture Mapping," *IEEE Computer Graphics and Applications*, vol. 6, no. 11, pp. 56-67, November 1986.

[6] Mitchell, D., "Generating Antialiased Images at Low Sampling Densities," *Computer Graphics*, (SIGGRAPH '87 Proceedings), vol. 21, no. 4, pp. 65-72, July 1987.

[7] Paeth, A.W., "A Fast Algorithm for General Raster Rotation," *Graphics Interface '86*, pp. 77-81, May 1986.

[8] Smith, A.R., "Planar 2-Pass Texture Mapping and Warping," *Computer Graphics*, (SIGGRAPH '87 Proceedings), vol. 21, no. 4, pp. 263-272, July 1987.

[9] Tanaka, A., M. Kameyama, S. Kazama, and O. Watanabe, "A Rotation Method for Raster Image Using Skew Transformation," *Proc. IEEE Conference on Computer Vision and Pattern Recognition*, pp. 272-277, June 1986.

[10] Weiman, C.F.R., "Continuous Anti-Aliased Rotation and Zoom of Raster Images," *Computer Graphics*, (SIGGRAPH '80 Proceedings), vol. 14, no. 3, pp. 286-293, July 1980.

[11] Wolberg, G., "Geometric Transformation Techniques for Digital Images: A Survey," Columbia University Computer Science Tech. Report CUCS-390-88, December 1988. To appear as a monograph by IEEE Computer Society Press.

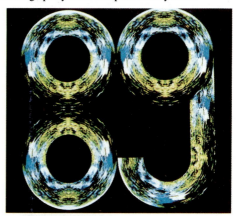

Figure 4.7

Figure 4.1: 360° warp.

Figure 4.4: Foldover.

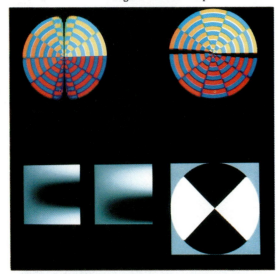

Figure 4.2: Intermediate results of 360° warp.

Figure 4.5: Bending.

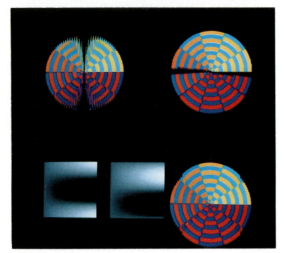

Figure 4.3: Artifacts due to undersampled spatial lookup tables.

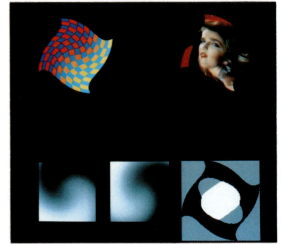

Figure 4.6: Vortex.

Madonna reprinted with permission of Warner Bros. Records.

An Efficient Algorithm For Hidden Surface Removal

Ketan Mulmuley

The University of Chicago

1 Abstract

We give an efficient, randomized hidden surface removal algorithm, with the best time complexity so far. A distinguishing feature of this algorithm is that the expected time spent by this algorithm on junctions which are at the "obstruction level" l, with respect to the viewer, is inversely proportional to l. This provably holds for any input, regardless of the way in which faces are located in the scene, because the expectation is with respect to randomization in the algorithm, and does not depend on the input. In practice, this means that the time complexity is roughly proportional to the size of the *actually visible* output times logarithm of the average depth complexity of the scene (this logarithm is very small generally).

2 Introduction

In this paper we give an efficient, randomized hidden surface removal algorithm, with the best time complexity so far. A basic theory behind this algorithm is a theory of probabilistic geometric games and a theory of a certain θ series, that can be associated with combinatorial arrangements [Mu1,Mu2,Mu3].

The concept of a θ series is essential to the discussion of this algorithm. So let us first see how one can associate such a series with a collection of faces in three dimensions. For the sake of simplicity, we shall assume that the faces are nonintersecting. Intersecting faces are treated in [Mu5]. We, of course, allow faces to share edges. Imagine an observer located at the origin. Assume, for the sake of simplicity, that the origin is located at $(0, 0, -\infty)$; this can be achieved by an appropriate perspective transformation. Project all faces orthonormally in the z direction onto the "view" plane. Abstractly speaking, the problem of hidden surface removal is concerned with finding a suitable partition of the view plane, and labelling each region of this partition with a face

that is visible there. When one projects all faces onto the view plane, this gives rise to several junctions formed by crossings of the xy-projections of the face boundaries. Only a few of these junctions are visible. An efficient algorithm should spend as little time as possible on the invisible junctions. To make this statement precise, we shall associate levels with all junctions. Consider a junction q located at an intersection of the xy-projections of the boundaries of two faces f and g. A face h is said to obstruct q, with respect to the observer o at $(0, 0, -\infty)$, if the presence of h makes q invisible to the observer. This means, that if we consider the line of sight from the observer, corrresponding to the junction q, h occurs on this line of sight before f or g. Define the *obstruction level* of q, $level(q)$, as the number of faces in the scene, which obstruct q. Let V_l be the set of junctions at level $l - 1$, and let $v(l)$ be the size of V_l. Thus V_1 is precisely the set of visible junctions.

For a fixed collection of faces, define a θ series as follows: for every real number $s \geq 0$,

$$\theta(s) = \sum_l \frac{v(l)}{l^s}.$$

A similar θ series can also be associated with a collection of intersecting faces. The main motivation behind associating such a series is that it has a lot of combinatorial information encoded in it. For example, in [Mu3], we showed how a θ series can be associated with an arrangement of hyperplanes in any dimnesion d. It was then shown that the worst case behaviour of this series can be analyzed as a function of s, and that $s = \lceil d/2 \rceil$ is a critical point on the real axis where this behaviour changes abruptly. This has a lot of combinatorial implications. A similar theory can also be developed for the θ series associated with a collection of intersecting faces (in any dimension) [Mu5]. In this paper, we shall restrict ourselves to only an algorithmic implication of this theory in the context of hidden surface removal. The implication is that the running time of our randomized hidden surface removal algorithm depends linearly on the value of the θ function at $s = 1$: $\theta(1) = \sum_{l=1}^n v(l)/l$.

To see what this means, let us first see what $\theta(0)$ is. It is easy to see that $\theta(0)$ is simply the number of all junctions in the view plane, visible as well as invisible. Whether hidden surface removal can be performed in time that depends linearly on $\theta(0)$, in a strict theoretical sense, is itself a nontrivial question. The reason is that, this requires a method to find all m intersections of n segments in a plane in optimal $O(m + n \log n)$ time. This question has been resolved in the affirmative recently in [Mu1,CE,Cl]. The optimal planar partition algorithm in [Mu1] can be easily extended so as to obtain an $O(n \log n + \theta(0))$ hidden surface removal algorithm. Thus, hidden suface removal can indeed be performed in time that is linear in $\theta(0)$. But that is still far from satisfactory, because most of the $\theta(0)$ junctions in the view plane are invisible. We surely do not want to spend equal time on all of them. Linear dependence of the expected running time of our algorithm on $\theta(1)$ achieves precisely that. Note that the expectation is with respect to the randomization used in the algorithm, very much as in Quicksort, and does not depend on the input. So we are assuming nothing about the input.

Linear dependence of the running time on $\theta(1)$ is, in essense, the characteristic feature of the new algorithm. What this means is that the work done by the algorithm on the junctions with level l is inversely proportional to l. Intuitively, the work done on junctions quickly decreases as we move farther from the observer. In practice, sizes of the various sets V_l are comparable. Hence, one approximately gets an harmonic series in the expansion for $\theta(1)$. And it follows that the running time of the algorithm is roughly proportional to the size of the actually visible output, i.e. $v(1)$, times logarithm of the (average) depth complexity of the scene (which is quite small generally). A intuitive explanation for the linear dependence of the running time on $\theta(1)$ is the following. The algorithm proceeds by adding one face at a time in a *random* order. The crux of the algorithm lies in ensuring that if a junction q is computed at some instant, during the algorithm, none of the faces added before that instant could obstruct q. Thus, intuitively, a junction is computed with a probability inversely proportional to its obstruction level. This naive explanation is, unfortunatately, misleading and fallacious, because the dominant part of the algorithm is not the computation of the junctions, but the computation, and the management, of the so called conflicts. Conflict is a transient, imaginary junction, which has no real conterpart. For other uses of conflicts, see [Mu1,CS,Cl,Mu2,Mu3].

Note that $\theta(\infty)$ is precisely the number of visible junctions. Can one perform hidden surface removal in time that is linear in $\theta(\infty)$, or even $\theta(s)$, where $s > 1$? That is an open question. However, it seems plausible that, in the algebraic computation tree model, $\Omega(n \log n + \theta(1))$ is actually a lower bound for hidden surface removal. The only nontrivial bound that has been proved so far in this model is $\Omega(n \log n)$ (for sorting) [Be]. This is essentially based on the Milnor-Thom bound on the number of connected components of a real algebraic variety. To prove an $\Omega(\theta(1))$ bound in this model will definitely require a deeper insight into a similar aspect of algebraic geometry.

Another feature of our algorithm, in contrast to the previous methods [HG,NSS,Sut,Wa,WA,Sc,Mc], is its essential use of randomization. That randomization should help hidden surface removal is only to be expected. This is because hidden surface removal is a kind of sorting, and the power of randomization has already been demonstrated by Quicksort for sorting in dimension one. However, in higher dimensions, the situation is completely different. For example, the divide and conquer stragegy of Quicksort fails to be as powerful in

higher dimensions. The division step of Quicksort is powerful because it results in two problems of a roughly equal size, whereas the division with respect to a geometric element, say a face, in a higher dimension invariably results in an unbalanced division, even if that geometric element were to be chosen randomly. This makes it necessary to follow a different approach in higher dimensions, to be able to exploit the power of randomization. In this approach, Quicksort is to be viewed not as a divide and conquer method, but as a method which exploits the random evolution of the underlying one dimensional configuration. Thus we are led to analyze the nature of a random evolution in higher dimensions, where it is much more interesting and complex than in dimension one. A theory of probabilistic geometric games and θ series in [Mu1,Mu2,Mu3] was developed precisely with the aim of analyzing this random evolution. This theory is a key to the algorithm in this paper. Also of related interest is a theory of random sampling [HW,Cl,CS].

The theoretical time complexity of the new method is much better compared to the previous methods, but can one expect it provide any improvement in practice? This seems quite plausible, because the algorithm is also very simple. With this in mind, we also provide (see the complete manuscript [Mu4]) another related hidden surface removal algorithm. This algorithm makes use of some ideas in the planar partition algorithm of [Mu1]. Its running time is not guaranteed to be linear in $\theta(1)$, but it is quite closely related to the original algorithm. So its observed behaviour might not be too different. Besides, it maintains less auxiallary information than the first algorithm, and this might be significant in practice. Both algorithms make no use of coherence in the image plane. This should make them robust with respect to the rounding errors and degeneracies in the input. This is especially so because randomization is well known for its suppressing the propogation of error.

On the other hand, our algorithm is a general purpose hidden surface removal algorithm, which can not detect cheaply special situations, such as a car in front of a grass field, a box with lots of things inside etc. In fact, if one could prove our above mentioned lower bound conjecture, that would provide a formal proof that a general purpose hidden surface algorithm must take at least $\Omega(\theta(1))$ time to detect such special situations. It is as important to use the usual heuristics, such as clipping and hierarchial comparisons, in conjuction with this method, as with any other method. We shall not deal with the question of heuristics in this paper. We shall, however, mention that [Mu2] gives a new clipping technique called *virtual clipping*, which has all advantages of the conventional clipping, in the amortized sense, but with a logarithmically small overhead in comparison.

For hidden surface removal in the presence of intersecting faces, curved faces etc. see [Mu5].

3   Algorithm

We assume that we are given some standard specification of the scene, which consists of a specification of the faces in the scene together with their edges and vertices. Let n be the number of faces. We assume that the faces are nonintersecting (intersecting faces are treated in [Mu5]), and that the facelengths are bounded by a constant. But the faces are allowed to have arbitrary shapes. We also assume that the usual preprocessing operations such as perspective trasformation, clipping against the view window, culling out irrelevant faces, have already been done. We are thus dealing with only a simple orthographic projection of the scene along the z axis. Given a face f in the scene, we shall denote its projection on the xy plane by $\bar{f}$. The boundary of $\bar{f}$ will be denoted by $\partial \bar{f}$. Similarly the xy projection of an edge e or a vertex v in the scene will be denoted by $\bar{e}$ and $\bar{v}$ respectively. We also assume that there is a special face O in the scene which serves as a background for the whole scene.

The overall organization of the algorithm is as follows. We first form an initial partition H_0 of the (view) window. H_0 is simply the whole window, and thus has just one region. This region will be labelled with the background face O, implying that, in the begining of the algorithm, O is visible throughout the view window. Starting with H_0, we form a sequence of *convex* partitions $H_0, H_1, \cdots, H_n$, by "adding" the faces in the scene *in a random order*. This means that H_{k+1} will be obtained from H_k by adding to it a face f_{k+1}, which is randomly chosen from the set of remaining scene faces. As a convention, we shall let f_0 denote the background face O. By this convention, f_0 is the very first "randomly" chosen face. Each region R in H_k will be labelled with the face $f(R)$, which is "currently visible" in R, among the $k+1$ faces, $f_0, \cdots, f_k$, that have been added so far. This means that the face $f(R)$ would be visible in R, if the scene were to consist only of the faces $f_0, \cdots, f_k$. H_n will be the final *visibility partition* of the view window. H_n tells us which face in the scene is visible at any given location in the view window. Now one can scan H_n from left to right, and paint each region of H_n in accordance with the face visible in that region.

Let us specify in more detail the partition H_k of the window induced by the *randomly chosen* faces $f_0, \cdots, f_k$. For this purpose, imagine that the scene consists only of the faces $f_0, \cdots, f_k$. Consider an edge e of one of these faces. It is clear that, in general, one will only see parts of e – possibly none. The xy projections of these disconnected visible parts of e will be called fragments. Fragments of the edges of $f_0, \cdots, f_k$ induce a partition of the view window. Unfortunately, the regions of this partition can have complicated boundaries. To overcome this difficulty, we pass a vertical attachment through each loose endpoint of a fragment, which extends in upward, as well as downward, direction until it hits either another fragment or a window border. For the input in fig 1a, we have shown in fig 1b the partition that results, if the first three randomly chosen faces are A, C, D. The partition obtained in this fashion is convex, but there is still one theoretical difficulty. A region of this partition, at least theoretically, can have arbitrarily many borders. To overcome this difficulty, we also pass a vertical attachment through every t-junction, where two fragments meet. This vertical attachment will, however, extend in only one direction (see fig 1c). What we have now is the partition H_k. Note that each region of H_k is a trapezoid; a triangle is regarded as a degenerate trapezoid. Hence, H_k can be called a trapezoidal decomposition induced by

the visible fragments of the edges of $f_0, \cdots, f_k$. We point out, however, that in practice, it might be more desirable to impose just a convexity requirement, because a convex partition, as in fig 1b, is less expensive to maintain than a trapezoidal decomposition, as in fig. 1c. Accordingly, the algorithm, we are about to present, can be readily modified. This easy modification will be left to the reader.

We still have to specify, exactly how the trapezoidal decomposition H_k is to be represented. One possibility is an obvious planar graph representation. This has a disadvantage that the representation of a fixed region of H_k can be arbitrarily large, as it can have arbitrarily many vertices on its border. In [Mu1], we presented another representation of a planar partition, which does not have this defect. It is based on the following notion of visibility (this notion of visibility has nothing to do with visibility, as in the context of hidden surface removal):

Definition 1 *A vertex v of the partition is said to be visible in a face R, if ∂R, the boundary of R, has a tangent discontinuity at v.*

In the partition given in fig 1c, u is visible in R_0, R_1 and R_4, whereas it is invisible in R_3. Each trapezoid of H_k will be specified by a circular list of the *visible* vertices on its border. Thus the representation of R_3 in fig 1c is (a_1', a_1, a_2). If v is visible in R, we shall refer to the corresponding entry in the representation of R by v_R. In addition to specifying the faces of the partition, we also need to specify adjacency relationships at each vertex to complete the representation. If a vertex v is visible in R, we shall link v_R to $v_{R'}$, where R' is the next face, in the counterclockwise order, in which v is visible. Thus at the vertex u in fig 1c, we will have links in the order: $u_{R_4} \rightarrow u_{R_1} \rightarrow u_{R_0} \rightarrow u_{R_4}$. To avoid any confusion, we shall, henceforth, reserve the terms faces, edges, and vertices exclusively for those in the scene. Vertices of the partition H_k will be called *junctions*. A junction can be of three kinds: 1) it can be located at an intersection between two fragments, (e.g. the junction u in fig 1c), 2) it can be located at the projection of a scene vertex (e.g. a_0 in fig 1c), 3) or else it can be a point of attachment, i.e. a t-junction, where some vertical attachment meets a fragment or a window border (e.g. a_1', a_1'', u' in fig 1c). Junctions of the first two kinds will be called concrete. A point of attachment, on the other hand, is not concrete. The faces of H_k will always be called trapezoids or regions. A border of a region in H_k is defined as usual. A border in H_k is called concrete if it lies on a fragment (e.g. the border (a_1', a_2) of R_3 in fig 1c). A border which lies on a vertical attachment is not concrete (e.g. (a_1', a_1) of R_3).

As already mentioned, each region R of H_k will also be labelled with the face, among the $k+1$ faces $f_0, \cdots, f_k$ added so far, that is currently visible there. This face currently visible in R will be denoted by $f(R)$. Thus $f(R_3) = A, f(R_5) = C, f(R_1) = O$ etc.

This completes the specification of H_k. Unfortunately, there is still not enough information to make the "addition" of the next randomly chosen face f_{k+1} to H_k easy. The reason is that we have to somehow know which regions of H_k will be affected by the addition of f_{k+1}. With this in mind, we also associate with H_k some conflict information. For the use of conflicts in other contexts see [Mu1,CS,Cl,Mu2,Mu3].

First let us make a few definitions. A face g, other than the added faces $f_0, \cdots f_k$, and a trapezoid $R \in H_k$ are said to be in conflict if

1. $\bar{g}$, the xy-projection of g, intersects R, and

2. $f(R)$ does not obscure g in the region R.

Intuitively, if g is in conflict with R, then g will be at least partially visible in R, if it were the next face to be chosen for addition to H_k. We shall say that $f(R)$ is a background face of this conflict between g and R.

If g is in conflict with $R \in H_k$ then one, or possibly more, of the following kinds of conflicts must occur.

1. **a trapezoid-vertex conflict:** A vertex v of g is in conflict with the trapezoid R, i.e. to say $\bar{v}$, the xy-projection of v, lies in R. This conflict is said to be located at $\bar{v}$.

2. **a border-edge conflict:** An edge e of g is in conflict with a border b of R, i.e. to say $\bar{e}$, the xy-projection of e, intersects b. This conflict is said to be located on b at the intersection of $\bar{e}$ and b.

3. **a junction-face conflict:** a *concrete* junction t of R is in conflict with g, i.e. to say $\bar{g}$, the xy-projection of g, contains t. This conflict is said to be located t. Note that we do not consider conflicts at junctions, which are not concrete.

Each of these conflicts is said to have $f(R)$ as its background face.

Examples:

In fig. 1d, we have overlaid on H_3, for the sake of visualization, those parts of the boundaries of the remaining faces B and E, that are not occluded by the already added faces A, C, D. Referring to this figure, the following observations can be made. Face E conflicts with regions R_0, R_1, R_4, but no other region, as it is occluded everywhere else. E conflicts with the junction u in R_1, R_0, R_4. Because u is "invisible" (Definition 1) in R_3, the question about a conflict in R_3 does not arise. If there were some unadded face, behind C looking from u, it would conflict with u in R_1, but not in R_0 and R_4. The background face of the conflict between u and E, in R_0, is C, whereas the background face of the conflict between u and E, in R_1, is O. These conflicts have the same locations but different backgrounds, hence they are completely different. On the other hand, the conflict between u and E, in R_0, has the same location as well as background as the conflict between u and E in R_4. Indeed, there is no real reason to regard these two conflicts as different. Hence, they can be identified. The vertex e_0 is in conflict with the trapezoid R_0, whereas e_3 is in conflict with R_4. Other vertices of E are all occluded by the added faces, and hence, are not in conflict with any trapezoids. The edge (e_2, e_3) of E is in conflict with the border (u, a_2) of R_4. But it is *not* in conflict with the border (a'_1, a_2) of R_3, which lies on the other side of the fragment (a_0, a_2). On the other hand, the edge of (b_0, b_3) of B is in conflict with both borders, (u, a_2) of R_4, as well as, (a'_1, a_2) of R_3. Though the locations of both these conflicts with (b_0, b_3) are the same, their background faces are different (C and A respectively). Hence, these two conflicts

are to be regarded as completely different. The same edge (b_0, b_3) also conflicts with the vertical attachment (u, u') in R_0, as well as, R_4. Locations, as well as backgrounds, of these conflicts are the same. Again, there is no real reason to regard the border-edge conflicts such as these, which lie on the opposite sides of the same vertical attachment, as different. They too can be identified.

There are various ways to associate conflict information with H_k. Basically, one should be able to deduce in an efficient fashion, the various kinds of conflicts, as defined above, that occur within H_k. The scheme we will choose is not the most efficient, both in terms of memory and time. However, it has an advantage that it simplifies the description of the algorithm. The reader will be able to see many other alternative schemes.

The conflict information associated with H_k will be organized so that:

1. Given any *concrete* junction t in H_k, we know the unadded faces that are in conflict with t, and conversely, given any unadded face f, we know the concrete junctions in H_k that are in conflict with f. Note that we do not store conflicts with the points of attachment in H_k.

2. Given any border b in H_k, concrete or otherwise, we know the scene edges that are in conflict with b, and conversely, given any edge e, we know the borders in H_k that are in conflict with e. Moreover, we assume that the borders of all faces in the scene are oriented so that the corresponding orientations of their xy-projections is counterclockwise. This orients $\bar{e}$, the projection of e, too. We assume that all conflicts of e are kept ordered, by simple links, along the orientation of e.

3. Given any region $R \in H_k$, we know the scene vertices that are in conflict with R, and conversely, given any vertex v, we know the region in H_k that is in conflict with v. Moreover, we assume that all conflicts with a given region R are kept ordered, by simple links, according to the x-cordinates of their locations.

The conflict size of a region $R \in H_k$ is defined to be the total number of conflicts, of all three kinds, that are associated with R.

Now we are ready to describe how the addition of a randomly chosen face $f = f_{k+1}$ to the partition H_k is achieved.

3.1 Preliminary update along the boundary

In this step, we split the trapezoids of H_k that are in conflict with the boundary ∂f, i.e. the trapezoids which conflict with either an edge or a vertex in ∂f. Let us specify this step in more detail. Exploiting the ordering of the border-edge conflicts, we visit these trapezoids along the given counterclockwise orientation of $\partial \bar{f}$. Note that we are not visiting all regions of H_k that intersect $\partial \bar{f}$, but only the ones which conflict. Intuitively, these are the regions where ∂f is not occluded by any of the added faces $f_0, \cdots, f_k$. Assume, for example, that the fourth randomly chosen face to be added to H_3, in fig 1d, is E. In this case, we shall travel on $\partial \bar{E}$ from the conflict on (c'_0, u) to the one on (u, a_2). Here the conflicting part of $\partial \bar{E}$ is connected. In general, the conflicting part of $\partial \bar{f}_{k+1}$ can have many connected components. But that does not cause any problems. As we visit the conflicts on $\partial \bar{f}$ in the counterclockwise direction, we split every conflicting border that we visit. Moreover, when we split a border adjacent to a vertical attachment through some concrete vertex, say v, we retain only that split part which contains v. For example, in the addition of $f_4 = E$ to H_3 in fig 1d, we shall retain only the upper half of the border (u, u'). In addition, we pass a vertical attachment through every new intersection that corresponds to a conflict on a concrete border of H_k. We also create a new junction for every conflict that is located at the xy-projection of a vertex of f_{k+1}. Remember that we perform these actions, *as we travel*. It is possible that, during this travel, we will visit the same region of the old partition H_k more than once. But this should cause no problem. It only means that we have to split sometimes an already added vertical attachment even further.

When we travel in this manner on the conflicting parts of $\partial \bar{f}$, what we obtain at the end is a new trapezoidal decomposition H'_{k+1}, that is obtained from H_k by appropriately splitting the regions of H_k, that conflicted with $\partial \bar{f}$. We also need to label each newly formed trapezoid R' with a face that will be visible in R' after the addition of $f = f_{k+1}$. This is easy to do. Notice that each newly formed trapezoid is either completely covered by $\bar{f}$ or is completely disjoint from $\bar{f}$, except at its boundary. If R' is covered by $\bar{f}$, we label it with f, else R' will retain the old label $f(R)$ of R.

We also have to associate conflict information with each newly formed region R'. R', in general, consists of parts of some old trapezoids in H_k, say $R_1, \cdots, R_l$, that were in conflict with $\partial \bar{f}$. So we have to derive the conflict information, to be associated with R', from the conflict information associated with $R_1, \cdots, R_l$. Notice that an unadded face can conflict with R' only if it was in conflict with one of the trapezoids $R_1, \cdots, R_l$. Moreover, a face g that was in conflict with some R_j, $1 \leq j \leq l$, can be in conflict with R only if 1) $\bar{g}$, the xy-projection of g, intersects R', 2) and, in case R' is covered by $\bar{f}$, the face g is not occluded by f in R'. With the help of these observations, it is easy to derive the conflict information, to be associated with R', in time proportional to the sum of the conflict sizes of $R_1, \cdots, R_l$.

As each $R \in H_k$, that was in conflict with $\partial \bar{f}$, can be split into only a bounded number of trapezoids, the preliminary update along the boundary takes time that is $O(\sum_{R \in H_k} conflict\_size(R))$, where R ranges over the trapezoids that were in conflict with $\partial \bar{f}$. Needless to say, all trapezoids of H_k in conflict with $\partial \bar{f}$ and the conflict information associated with them can now be destroyed.

3.2 A preliminary update in the interior

In this step, we access all trapezoids in the partition, that are in conflict with f, and which are in the interior of $\bar{f}$, but are not adjacent to $\partial \bar{f}$. We update the conflict information associated with each of these trapezoids. At the end of this operation, the new trapezoidal decomposition H'_{k+1}, that was obtained above, will have proper, updated conflict

information associated with it.

It is easy to see that every conflicting trapezoid in the interior of $\bar{f}$ has two *concrete* junctions that are in conflict with f. Hence, using the list of junctions in conflict with f, we can readily access all conflicting regions in the interior of $\bar{f}$. For each region R, accessed in this fashion, we do the following:

1. We label R with f, because f will be the face visible in R after the addition of f.

2. We reduce the conflict information associated with R, by discarding every conflict with a face (or its edge or a vertex) that is occluded by f.

The second step requires us to know, for every face g that is in conflict with R, if f occludes (overlaps) g. The same face g might be in conflict with many of the accessed trapezoids. In this case, it is clearly desirable to carry out the required overlap comparison just once, if that is possible. This is indeed possible if f and g do not overlap cyclically, which is always the case if f and g are convex. In the absense of a cyclic overlap, we carry out the overlap comparison between f and g just once. To expedite this comparison, it is often advantageous to test first if the z-extents of f and g overlap; a complicated test is necessary only if they do [NSS].

At the end of this preliminary update in the interior, we have a partition H'_{k+1}, with the correct conflict information associated with it. However, H'_{k+1} might contain several fragments which have been rendered invisible during the addition of f. These fragments have to be removed from H'_{k+1}; this step is called reconfiguration. After reconfiguration we shall update the conflict information once again. Let us first turn to reconfiguration.

3.3 Reconfiguration

Consider all trapezoids of H'_{k+1} which are labelled with $f = f_{k+1}$ at the end of the preliminary update. The union of these trapezoids form a region $\mathcal{C} = \mathcal{C}_{k+1}$ in the plane. Clearly the trapezoids of H'_{k+1} outside $\mathcal{C}$ need not be considered in reconfiguration. Note that the region $\mathcal{C}$ can have many connected components and the connected components themselves can have complicated, disconnected boundaries (see fig. 2). All these factors have to be taken into account during reconfiguration.

Let $\partial \mathcal{C}$ be the boundary of $\mathcal{C}$. It is easy to see that a vertical attachment can not form a part $\partial \mathcal{C}$. Thus every border of H'_{k+1} that lies on $\partial \mathcal{C}$ is concrete. Moreover, every such border on $\partial \mathcal{C}$ will remain visible after the addition of $f = f_{k+1}$. Thus the fragments which have become invisible after the addition of f must lie strictly in the interior of $\mathcal{C}$. And conversely, every fragment which lies in the interior of $\mathcal{C}$ has become invisible after the adddition of $f = f_{k+1}$. Hence a naive method to reconfigure is the following: remove everything within $\mathcal{C}$, and then find a new trapezoidal decomposition of $\mathcal{C}$. This can turn out to be too expensive for two reasons. First, $\partial \mathcal{C}$ can be very complicated, hence one will need the power of a full fledged triangulation procedure. Second, we also have to "relocate" later the conflicts of the scene vertices, which were located within $\mathcal{C}$. (We need to relocate other kinds of conflicts too.) This means we will also need a full fledged a planar point location algorithm. Obviously, this approach is too costly.

Fortunately, there is a less expensive way to reconfigure. It exploits the fact that what we have at our disposal is not just a boundary of $\mathcal{C}$, but some trapezoidal decomposition of $\mathcal{C}$. It is, of course, true that this trapezoidal decomposition has many unnecessary trapezoids. But it should still be possible to make use of this initially given decomposition somehow. The idea is to remove only a few of the unnecessary trapezoids at a time.

More precisely, let $A_1, \cdots A_h$ be the set of fragments within $\mathcal{C}$. We shall "remove" these fragments one at a time, *but in a random order*. This will be a randomized, decremental algorithm. In contrast, the overall hidden surface removal algorithm is randomized, and incremental. Clearly, the two strategies are complementary.

As we said earlier, we shall deal with the problem of updating conflicts later. So let us consider the removal of a single fragment in more detail. Fig. 3a shows the fragment $l = (l_0, l_1)$, which has been randomly chosen for removal, together with the adjacent trapezoids. Let $a_0, a_1, \cdots, a_q$ be the junctions adjacent to the "lower" side of l and let $b_0, b_1, \cdots, b_r$ be the junctions adjacent to the "upper" side of l. Some of these will be the junctions, where other fragments meet l and the remaining will be the points of attachment. Note that, by our definition 1, the junctions $a_o, \cdots a_q$ are "invisible" on the upper side of l, and $b_0, \cdots, b_r$ are "invisible" on the lower side of l. So we need to merge the two sorted streams $a_0, \cdots, a_q$, and $b_0, \cdots, b_r$ to get a sorted stream $c_0, \cdots, c_{q+r+1}$. Having done this, it is easy to remove l, by extending the vertical attachments ending on the upper side of l in the lower direction, and by extending the vertical attachments ending on the lower side of l analogously. See fig. 3b.

When this procedure is repeated, in a random order, for all fragments lying within $\mathcal{C}$, we obtain, at the end, the desired trapezoidal decomposition of $\mathcal{C}$.

This gives us the partition H_{k+1}, that we sought. But we still have to associate conflict information with the newly formed trapezoids. This is done next.

3.4   Relocating and generating conflicts

In this step, we derive the conflict information, to be associated with the trapezoids formed during reconfiguration, from the conflict information that was associated with those trapezoids in H'_{k+1}, that existed within $\mathcal{C} = \mathcal{C}_{k+1}$ before reconfiguration. We shall proceed by cases.

trapezoid-vertex conflicts

For every scene vertex v, that was in conflict with a trapezoid $R \in H'_{k+1}$ within $\mathcal{C}$, we need to find the new trapezoid $R' \in H_{k+1}$ within $\mathcal{C}$ that contains v. We call this step relocation of the conflict at $\bar{v}$. Relocating this conflict at the end of reconfiguration is a bit difficult. Instead, we shall modify the reconfiguration procedure a little, so that, at the end of reconfiguration, we also know the conflicting trapezoid R' for every scene vertex v, that was in conflict with some trapezoid $R \in H'_{k+1}$ within $\mathcal{C}$. The idea is to perform relocation of these conflicts along with reconfiguration.

Note that, because of the way in which we organize the

conflict information, the vertex-trapezoid conflicts located within any trapezoid of H'_{k+1} are kept ordered by their x-coordinates. We shall ensure that this invariant holds throughout reconfiguration. More precisely, at any stage of the reconfiguration procedure, all conflicts of the scene vertices within any given trapezoid will be kept ordered by their x-coordinates.

So reconsider the removal of a randomly chosen fragment $l = (l_0, l_1)$ as in fig. 3a. We shall perform the following extra steps during this removal. First, we concatenate the lists of the trapezoid-vertex conflicts lying in the trapezoids adjacent to the the upper side of l, and do the same for the lower side of l. Next we merge these two sorted lists. By a simple "interleaving" procedure, one can now split this merged list into various sorted lists of conflicts, corresponding to the new trapezoids formed after the removal of l (fig 3b). Now one is ready for the removal of the next randomly chosen fragment.

border-edge conflicts

Let us see how one can update the border-edge conflicts within $\mathcal{C}$. Note that we do not need to worry about the conflicts which lie outside $\mathcal{C}$, including the ones which lie on the "outer" side of $\partial\mathcal{C}$.

First, let us worry about the update on the inner side of $\partial\mathcal{C}$. Each new border-edge conflict on the inner side of $\partial\mathcal{C}$ is obtained from a similar conflict that existed in H'_{k+1} before reconfiguration. Hence, our task is basically to relocate the conflicts that existed in H'_{k+1}, on the inner side of $\partial\mathcal{C}$ before reconfiguration. Ignoring the vertical attachments in H_{k+1}, that end on $\partial\mathcal{C}$, one sees that $\partial\mathcal{C}$ is a union of many linear segments. Group the above conflicts in H'_{k+1} according to the segments in $\partial\mathcal{C}$ containing their locations. Let l be one of the segments on $\mathcal{C}$, and let S_l be the set of border-edge conflicts located on the inner side l. At the end of reconfiguration, the vertical attachments ending on $\partial\mathcal{C}$ can split the inner side of l into many borders. Hence, for each conflict in S_l, we need to find out the new border that will contain this conflict. We shall find out this border by a simple sequential search along l.

So assume that we have relocated the conflicts on the inner side of $\partial\mathcal{C}$. We also need to generate the border-edge conflicts, that lie on the vertical attachments within $\mathcal{C}$. This will be done next.

If g is scene face, define a *concrete* conflict of ∂g to be a conflict of a vertex on ∂g with some trapezoid, or a conflict of an edge in ∂g with some *concrete* border. At this stage of the algorithm, we know all concrete conflicts within $\mathcal{C}$. Consider a concrete conflict of ∂g within $\mathcal{C}$. This is either a conflict of an edge of ∂g with a border on $\partial\mathcal{C}$, or a conflict of a vertex in ∂g with a trapezoid wihin $\mathcal{C}$. We shall travel from this conflict to the next concrete conflict of ∂g within $\mathcal{C}$, in the counterclockwise direction along $\partial\bar{g}$, if it is possible to do so without leaving $\mathcal{C}$. This travel only involves skipping an appropriate number of vertical attachments in H_{k+1}, until the next concrete conflict is reached. For every vertical attachment encountered on the way, we generate a border-edge conflict. This procedure is repeated for every concrete conflict of ∂g within $\mathcal{C}$.

The same can be done for every ∂g which had a conflict within $\mathcal{C}$. This procedure will generate all border-edge conflicts on the vertical attachments within $\mathcal{C}$.

junction-face conflicts

Fortunately, nothing elaborate needs to generate these conflicts. What makes our task easy is the fact that we store these conflicts only at concrete junctions. It is easy to see that, for every concrete junction t in H_{k+1}, the faces which conflict with t in H_{k+1} are precisely the ones which conflict with t in H'_{k+1}. This makes the updating task straightforward.

At the end of this step, H_{k+1} has been associated with proper conflict information. Now we are ready to add the next randomly chosen face to H_{k+1}.

This finishes the description of the hidden surface removal algorithm.

4   Probabilistic games

A basic idea behind the analysis is to analyze a random evolution of the underlying partition H_k and the associated conflict information. As this global evolution is overwhelmingly complex, we need a tool to break this complex behaviour into tractable parts. The tool, that we will use, is a probabilistic theory of geometric games, which was developed in [Mu1,Mu2,Mu3]. We shall summarize in this section the results from this theory, that we will need in our analysis.

Suppose that we are given a universe set N of some elments. The game we are going to play in this section, consists in drawing the elements of N in a random order without replacement. Fix two disjoint subsets S and R of N throughout this section. Let $r = |R|$, and $s = |S|$. Let us associate an observer with this pair of sets S and R. The following rule will determine the active phase of the observer during the game. The observer is active at any given instant of the game if the following two conditions are satisfied at that instant:

1) all elements from R have been chosen,

2) and no element from S has been chosen so far.

If the observer does indeed become active during the game, he will go into the inactive phase as soon as the second condition is violated. The sets R and S will called the sets of triggers and stoppers respectively.

Now assume that we are given one more subset M of the universe N, and let $m = |M|$. M need not be disjoint from either S or R. But we shall assume that M is linearly ordered. Imagine, just for the sake of visualization, putting elements of M on the positive real axis, according to the ordering of M, with the ordering increasing in the positive direction. Place the observer o, associated with the pair of sets S and R, at the origin. Assume that the observer can "see" only along the positive real axis. We shall soon make this notion precise. We say that an element $b \in M$ was observed by o, at some instant of the game, if b was chosen at that instant and no element $c \in M$, s.t. $c < b$, was chosen before this instant. The idea is that the chosen elements in M are supposed to act as barriers to the sight of the observer. Let O be the number of elements observed by o in his active phase. If the observer never became active in the game, O is defined to be zero.

Theorem 1

$$E(O) = O\left(\frac{1}{\binom{s+r}{r}}\right), \quad for\ t \geq 1$$

$$= O(1 + \ln(m+1)), \quad for\ s = 0,\ t = 0$$

$$= O\left(1 + \ln\left(1 + \frac{m}{s}\right)\right), \quad for\ s > 0,\ t = 0.$$

Now let us define the visibility span of the observer, at any instant during the game, as follows: Let b be the least element in M chosen at or before this instant. Then the visibility span of the observer at this instant consists of all elements in M less than b. Notice that none of the elements in the visibility span at a given instant, could been chosen before that instant. Thus the visibility span at any instant consists of the elements in M, not yet chosen, which lie within the visibility extent of the observer o. Let V be the number of elements in the visibility span of the observer, at the instant he became active. V is defined to be zero, if the observer does not become active at all. We shall define one more random variable W as follows. Charge the observer a cost equal to the length of his visibility span, i.e. V, at the moment he became active. After this, every time the observer observes in his active phase some element of M, say b, we charge the observer a cost equal to the number of elements $\leq b$ in M. (Thus the cost is equal to the length of the visible span at the instant b was observed.) Let W be the total cost charged to the observer. Then it is clear that $V \leq W$.

Theorem 2

$$E(V) \leq E(W) = O\left(\frac{r}{\binom{s+r}{r-1}}\right), \quad for\ t \geq 2$$

$$= O(\ln(m+1)+1), \quad for\ s = 0,\ t = 1.$$

$$= O\left(1 + \ln\left(1 + \frac{m}{s}\right)\right), for\ s > 0,\ t = 1.$$

5   A part of the analysis

We shall first state the expected running time of the algorithm. Let c(f), the coupling coefficient of a face f, be the number of faces g whose projected borders $\partial \bar{g}$ intersect $\bar{f}$. For a fixed point q in the view plane, let $c(q) = max\{c(f)\}$, where f ranges over the faces whose projections cover q. If q is an intersection of $\partial \bar{f}$ and $\partial \bar{g}$, recall from Section 2 that the *obstruction level* of q, $level(q)$, is the number of faces in the scene, which obscure either f or g at q. Intuitively, the presence of any of these $level(q)$ faces will make the junction between the boundaries of f and g invisible at q. If q is the xy-projection $\bar{v}$ of a vertex v of some face f, define $level(q)$ to be the number of faces in the scene which occlude v at q. Let $depth(q)$ be the number of faces whose projections cover q.

Theorem 3 *The expected running time of the hidden surface removal algorithm is* $O(n \log n + n \log(1+c1) \log(1+r) + \theta(1) + \log(1 + c2)\theta(2))$, *where r is the average of the ratio*

$depth(q)/level(q)$ over the projections of the scene vertices, and $c1$ and $c2$ are the averages of the coupling coefficients $c(q)$ over the projections of the vertices, and intersections of the projected boundaries respectively.

The factor $\log(1+c2)\theta(2)$ is smaller than $\theta(1)$ in practice, but in theory, it is a nuisance. This factor can be removed from the running time, at the cost of a considerable complication in the algorithm [Mu5]. On the other hand, we have not been able to remove, so far, the factor $n\log(1+c1)\log(1+r)$. This factor is, in practice, much smaller compared to $\theta(1)$. It is plausible that the algorithm as presented here, or its variant, has $O(n\log n+\theta(1))$ expected running time. That is an open question.

A complete proof of Theorem 3 can be found in the complete manuscript of the paper [Mu4]. Here we shall deal with only a part of the analysis, that deals with bounding the expected number of conflicts created in the algorithm. In this section, we shall prove the following

Theorem 4 *The expected number of conflicts created and destroyed in the whole course of the algorithm is $O(n\log n + \theta(1))$.*

Our prime goal is to illustrate the use of probabilistic games in Section 4. Complete analysis is, in a sense, a long exercise in applying these games over and over again.

Recall our convention to regard two conflicts with same locations but different background faces as different. This makes Theorem 4 more interesting. Thus, if many conflicts with different background faces were created, during the algorithm, at the same location, they are all counted as distinct in the theorem. A created conflict can be destroyed but once, hence we need not worry about the destroyed conflicts anymore. In the proof, we shall treat the three different kinds of conflicts seperately.

Junction-face conflicts

Recall that, in the algorithm, we stored conflicts of this kind at the concrete junctions only.

Lemma 1 *The expected number of conflicts, created in the algorithm, that are located at a concrete junction q is $O(\frac{1}{1+level(q)})$, if q is located at an intersection of the projections of two face boundaries, and $O(1 + \log(\frac{1+depth(q)}{1+level(q)}))$, if q is located at the projection of a vertex. (If a concrete junction was never created at q, during the algorithm, the number of conflicts created at q is defined to be zero.)*

Proof.

We shall only consider the first case, where q is located at an intersection of say $\partial\bar{f}$ and $\partial\bar{g}$. Fix f, g and q. Refer to fig. 4a. Note that, by our Definition 1, q is invisible in the zone Q_0. Thus no conflict located at q can come into existence in Q_0. Also note that among the conflicts located at q, the ones which occur in the zone Q_1, and the ones which occur in the zone Q_2 have different background faces. Hence one has to treat the conflicts in these two zones seperately. We shall only treat here conflicts in the zone Q_1. A similar treatment of the conflicts in the zone Q_2 will be omitted.

The lemma will be derived by applying the probabilistic game of Section 4. The setup is the following. The universe set N will be the set of all faces in the scene. (This will be the choice for the universe set throughout the analysis of the algorithm.) We shall place an observer at q who can "see" only in the positive z-direction. M, the set of objects that the observer can see, is defined to be the set of faces in the scene, whose projections cover q. The set M is linearly ordered according to the increasing z-coordinate of the faces in M at the location q. The sets R and S of stoppers and triggers, that will determine the active phase of the observer, are defined as follows. Let $R = \{f, g\}$, and let S be the set of $level(q)$ faces which obscure f or g at q. Intuitively, the observer remains active as long as the junction q remains visible in the algorithm, and it is easy to see that q is visible iff all elements of R are chosen, and no element from S is chosen. In this setup, it is easy to see that the number of conflicts, created at q in the zone Q_1, is precisely the random variable W defined in Theorem 2. This takes into account the fact that the conflicts located at q, but having different background faces, are to be considered different. Now the lemma follows from Theorem 2. ▯

Trapezoid-vertex conflicts

Let v be a vertex of some face f. Fix f as well as v.

Lemma 2 *The expected number of trapezoid-vertex conflicts, created in the algorithm, that are located at $q = \bar{v}$, is $O(1 + \log(\frac{1+depth(q)}{1+level(q)}))$.*

Proof. Place, as in Lemma 1, an observer at q, who can only see in the positive z-direction. Let M be the set of faces, whose projections cover q, and let S be the set of faces, which obscure v at q. The set of triggers R is now defined to be an empty set. The reason is that the trapezoid-vertex conflicts located at q can come into existence even when the face f has not been chosen for addition by the algorithm, assuming, of course, that no face from S has been chosen. In this set up, it is clear that the number trapezoid-vertex conflicts which are created at q is precisely the random variable O defined in Theorem 1: everytime such a conflict with a background face h is created, the observer at q can "see" the face h that is being added at the time of creation. Now apply Theorem 1. ▯

Border-edge conflicts

Each border-edge conflict, created in the algorithm, is located either on a vertical attachment or on a fragment passing through some concrete junction.

Lemma 3 *The expected number of border-edge conflicts, created in the algorithm, that are located on a vertical attachment or a fragment through a concrete junction q, is $O(\frac{1}{1+level(q)})$, if q is located at an intersection of the projections of two face boundaries, and $O(1 + \log(\frac{1+depth(q)}{1+level(q)}))$, if q is located at the projection of some vertex. (If a concrete junction was never created at q, during the algorithm, the number of conflicts created at q is defined to be zero.)*

Proof. We shall only consider the first case. So suppose that q is located at an intersection of the projected borders $\partial\bar{f}$ and $\partial\bar{g}$ of two faces f and g. Fix f, g, as well as q. We will only estimate the conflicts created on a vertical attachment through q; the ones that are created on a fragment through q can be estimated similarly. Assume, without loss of generality, that f is in front of g at q. Notice that, depending upon how $\partial \bar{f}$ and $\partial \bar{g}$ are situated at q, a vertical attachment through q will either extend upwards or downwards. Assume, without loss of generality, that it extends downwards. Referring to fig.4, notice that a vertical attachment lies either in the region that does not intersect $\bar{g}$ or in the region that intersects $\bar{g}$. We will only consider the first case, and omit the second (easier) case.

Let L be the set of $level(q)$ faces which obscure either f or g at q. Let S_q be the set of faces, other than f and g, whose projections cover q.

Fix a face $h \in S_q$. We shall esimate the expected number of conflicts, created on a vertical attachment through q, which have h as their background face. First notice that h can be a background face for such a conflict only if $h \notin L \cup \{f, g\}$. Assume, henceforth, that $h \notin L \cup \{f, g\}$. Let $level_q(h)$ be the obstruction level of h at q, i.e. the number of faces, other than f or g, which obscure h at q. Obviously $level_q(h) \geq level(q)$.

Claim: The expected number of conflicts created on a vertical attachment through q, which have h as their background is $O(\frac{1}{(2+level_q(h))^2})$.

This will prove the lemma since, by elementary calculus,

$$\sum_h \frac{1}{(2 + level_q(h))^2} \leq \frac{1}{1 + level(q)},$$

where h ranges over all faces in S_q which do not belong to $L \cup \{f, g\}$.

Let $S_h \subseteq S_q$ be the subset of those faces which are in front of h at q. Let T be the semi-infinite imaginary line through q extending downwards. A conflict with a border ∂k of a face k, with h as a background face of the conflict, can come into existence on T, only if k obscures h somewhere on T, *but not at q*. This condition is just necessary, and not sufficient. Let M_h be the set of faces k, which satisfy the above condition. Linearly order M_h by letting $k_1 << k_2$ iff $\partial \bar{k}_1$ intersects T before $\partial \bar{k}_2$, i.e. the intersection between $\partial \bar{k}_1$ and T, that is closest to q, is closer to q than the similar closest intersection between $\partial \bar{k}_2$ and T. The following observation is crucial:

Observation 1 *If $k_1 << k_2$, and k_1 is chosen for addition in the algorithm before k_2, then ∂k_2 cannot conflict with a vertical attachment through q, with the face h in the background. (This does not hold, if the background is allowed to vary.)*

Now let $R_h = \{f, g, h\}$. Letting R_h, S_h and M_h play the roles of R, S, M in Theorem 2, it follows from the above observation that the number of conflicts, that come into existence on T with h in the background, is bounded, upto a constant factor, by the random variable V in that theorem: all faces whose boundaries create these conflicts are in the "visibility span" of the observer located at q, when the face h was added. The claim now follows from that theorem. ☐

Using Lemma 1, Lemma 2, Lemma 3, and summing over all concrete junctions, we conclude that the expected number of conflicts created during the algorithm is $O(n \log n + \theta(1))$.

This finishes the proof of Theorem 4.

References

[Be] Ben-Or M., "Lower bounds for algebraic computation tres", *Proc. of the 15th STOC, 83*.

[CE] Chazelle B., Edelsbrunner H., "An optimal algorithm for intersecting line segments in the plane", *Proceedings of the FOCS, 1988*.

[Cl] Clarkson K., "Applications of random sampling to computational geometry, II", *Proc. 4th Ann. ACM Symposium on Computational Geom., 1988*.

[CS] Clarkson K., Shor P., "Algorithms for diametral pairs and convex hulls that are optimal, randomized, and incremental", *Proc. 4th Ann. ACM Symposium on Computational Geometry, 1988*.

[HG] Hamlin G., Gear C., "Raster-Scan hidden surface algorithm techniques", *Computer Graphics, vol. 11, no. 2, pp. 206-213*.

[HW] Haussler D., Welzl E., "Epsilon nets and simplex range queries", *Proc. 2nd Ann. ACM Symposium on Computational Geometry, 86*.

[Mc] Mckenna M., "Worst-case optimal hidden surface removal algorithm", *ACM transactions on graphics, vol.6, no. 1, 1987*.

[Mu1] Mulmuley K., "A fast planar partition algorithm, I", *Proceedings of the 29th FOCS, 1988, full version to appear in a special computational geometry issue of the Journal of Symb. Logic*.

[Mu2] Mulmuley K., "A fast planar partition algorithm, II", To appear in the Proceedings of the 5th Ann. ACM symposium on Computational Geometry, 89, full version submitted to JACM.

[Mu3] Mulmuley K., "On levels in arrangements and Voronoi diagrams", *Technical report, TR 88-21, University of Chicago, December,88*, submitted to the Journal of Discrete and Computational Geom.

[Mu4] Mulmuley K., "An efficient algorithm for hidden surface removal, I", *a complete manuscript*.

[Mu5] Mulmuley K., "An efficient algorithm for hidden surface removal, II", *in preparation*.

[NSS] Newell M., Newell R., Sancha T., "A new approach to the shaded picture problem", *Proc. ACM. National Conf., 1972*.

[Sc] Schmitt A. "Time and space bounds for hidden line and hidden surface algortithms", *Eurographics, 81*.

[Sut] Sutherland, I. E., R. F. Sproull, and R. A. Schumaker, "A characterization of ten hidden surface algorithms", *Computing Surveys 6: 1–55, 1974*.

[Wa] Warnock J., "A hidden surface algorithm for computer generated half-tone pictures", *computer science dept., University of Utah, TR 4-15, 1969*.

[WA] Weiler K., Atherton P., "Hidden surface removal using polygon area sorting", *computer graphics (Proc. SIGGRAPH)*, July, 77.

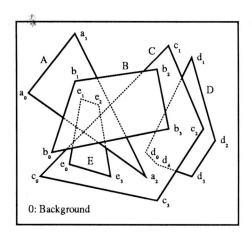

Figure 1a: Input

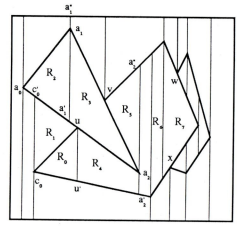

Figure 1c: H_3

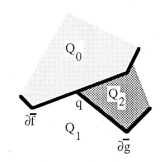

Figure 4a

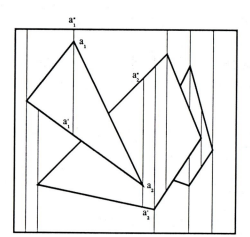

Figure 1b: H_3'

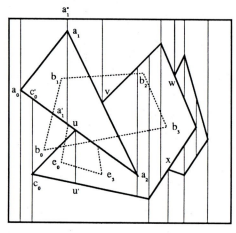

Figure 1d: conflicts in H_3

Figure 4b

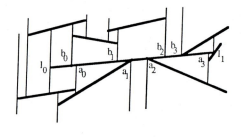

Figure 3: a) Before removal of $l = (l_0, l_1)$

Figure 2: Region $\mathcal{C}$ (shown dotted)

Figure 3: b) After removal of l

Panels

Virtual Environments and Interactivity: Windows to the Future

Chair: Coco Conn, Homer and Associates

Panelists: Jaron Lanier, VPL Research
Margaret Minsky, University of North
    Carolina at Chapel Hill/MIT Media Lab
Scott Fisher, NASA Ames Research Center
Allison Druin, Tell Tale Technologies

Computer-generated virtual environments are the product of human imagination. And as user interfaces become more sophisticated, computer researchers and visionaries are investigating the unexplored realm of virtual environments.

Several projects have recently made progress in integrating force display technology and the use of human sensory simulations into computing-based environments. These projects partake of the spirit of creating virtual worlds, fantasy, or simulation environments that combine the emotional power of touch interfaces with new computational powers of abstraction.

Live demonstrations and videotaped sequences feature the use of head-mounted displays, computer clothing, force feedback joysticks, body motion, tactile environments, and the use of touch sensation.

In this virtual environment panel, people can meet each other, take any form they wish, and experience anything that can be imagined.

Digital Canvas: Artists and Designers in the 2D/3D Marketplace

Chair: Rachel Carpenter, Cinematrix

Panelists: Claire Barry, SuperMac Technology
Peter Conn, Homer and Associates
John Derry, Chromaset
Vibeke Sorensen, California Institute of the
    Arts

With the aid of live computers, slides, and tapes, panelists discuss issues concerning job areas, hardware, creative freedom and compromise, and the merger of art and science leading to new applications. Specifically, the panel focuses on: prepress, the new designer, and today's job market; user interface, creativity, economics and design; animation, broadcast, film and hardware issues; 3D stereoscopic images, music, short films; and future developments.

Special Session: Retrospectives:
The Early Years in Computer Graphics at MIT, Lincoln Lab and Harvard

Chair: E. Jan Hurst, EJH Associates

Panelists: Michael S. Mahoney, Princeton University
Norman H. Taylor, Independent Consultant
Douglas T. Ross, Softech, Inc.
Robert M. Fano, MIT

In 1988, the SIGGRAPH executive committee funded a project to document major milestones in computer graphics history.

Panelists will concentrate on work pursued in the academic environments of the Boston/Cambridge area during the 1950s and sets the stage for panelists comments and enables attendees to understand the environments of that time.

The sessions provide personal perspectives of the problems, excitement, and breakthroughs in the early days of: SAGE, APT, Project MAC, TX-0, TX-2, hidden lines removed, Sketchpad, and curves and surfaces. These sessions are divided into two parts. The second session is in the same location from 3:30 p.m.-5:15 p.m.

Special Session: Retrospectives:
The Early Years in Computer Graphics at MIT, Lincoln Lab and Harvard

Chair: E. Jan Hurst, EJH Associates

Panelists: Jack Gilmore, Digital Equipment Corporation
Lawrence G. Roberts, NetExpress, Inc.
A. Robin Forrest, University of East Anglia,
    UK
Mike Mahoney, Princeton University

This session is a continuation of the Retrospectives special beginning at 1:45 p.m. Refer to description on previous page for more information.

The Multi-Media Workstation

Chair: Dick Phillips, Los Alamos National
            Laboratory

Panelists: Martin Levy, Parallax Graphics, Inc.
            Keith Lantz, Olivetti Research Center
            Paul Vais, NeXT Computer, Inc.
            Steve Perlman, Apple Computer

Workstations now offer more than just text and graphics communication capabilities; video and sound channels are available as well. It is possible, for example, to display a live video window on a workstation screen. Thus, researchers at Los Alamos National Laboratory display supercomputer simulations in a video format and students at MIT are tutored in language study with the aid of videodisk-based lecture fragments.

If equipped with suitable hardware, a workstation can play back voice messages embedded in a conventional document. The NeXT computer has such a capability. The Olivetti Research Center is developing a workstation conferencing system, where text, graphics, and sound can be transmitted in real time among conferees.

This panel explores all of these new multi-media capabilities and how they affect the way workstations are used.

Effective Software Systems for Scientific Data Visualization

Chair: Lloyd A. Treinish, NASA Goddard Space
            Flight Center

Panelists: Robert B. Haber, NCSA University of Illinois
            at Champaign-Urbana
            James D. Foley, George Washington
            University
            William J. Campbell, NASA Goddard Space
            Flight Center
            Robert F. Gurwitz, Stellar Computer, Inc.

Despite advancements, significant problems still exist in bringing today's technology into the hands of the typical scientist. Given the demands of modern research, a scientist rarely has time to learn graphics protocols and standards, data structures, device-specific peculiarities and rendering algorithms. Most technology does not permit straighforward application without expert assistance.

This panel discusses issues associated with building systems for scientists to "visualize," current endeavors, and solutions for solving problems practically.

Physically-Based Modeling: Past, Present, and Future

Co-Chairs: Demetri Terzopoulos, Schlumberger
            Technologies
            John Platt, California Institute of Technology

Panelists: Alan H. Barr, California Institute of
            Technology
            Andrew Witkin, Carnegie Mellon University
            David Zeltzer, MIT Media Lab
            James Blinn, California Institute of
            Technology

Physically-based modeling is an exciting paradigm which made its debut in computer graphics less than five years ago. This paradigm facilitates the creation of complex shapes and realistic motions -- once the sole province of highly trained modelers and animators.

In addition, physically-based modeling adds new levels of representation to graphics objects; embodies physical laws which govern its behavior and control systems to produce desired animation; and synthesizes complex motions automatically, making them responsive to one another and the simulated physical worlds they inhabit.

This panel surveys past results, examines present challenges, and envisions the future of physically-based modeling and its potential impact on related fields. Panelists present video demonstrations of several novel techniques such as deformable models, dynamic constraints, teleological modeling, spacetime control, and physically-based procedural animation.

Hardware/Software Solutions for Scientific Visualization at Large Scientific Research Laboratories

Chair: Linnea Cook, Lawrence Livermore National
            Laboratory

Panelists: Gordon Bancroft, NASA Ames Research
            Center
            Kevin Hussey, Jet Propulsion Laboratory
            John Dragon, Los Alamos National
            Laboratory
            William Johnston, Lawrence Berkeley
            National Laboratory

The emergence of various affordable, high-performance hardware and standardized software for scientific visualization are the most exciting developments in the area of computer graphics today. Many large scientific laboratories are actively pursuing and refuting which graphics hardware to use. Graphics workstations, graphics terminals, frame buffers driven by supercomputers, and distributed graphics are all solutions -- but which solution is best?

This panel focuses on what five scientific laboratories are doing with this hardware. What requirements do these laboratories have in the area of scientific visualization? What strategies are they pursuing to meet these needs? Which hardware/software solutions are they using or exploring? Why is their particular solution the best? Why are other solutions not as good or unworkable?

Panelists will present the merits and drawbacks of each approach, resulting in a lively, informative discussion.

Computer Art-An Oxymoron? Views from the Mainstream

Chair: Dorothy Spencer, Read/Write Press

Panelists: Mark Resch, Rensselaer Polytechnic Institute
Bob Riley, San Francisco Museum of Modern Art
Harry Rand, National Museum of Art
Phillip Pearlstein, Internationally-known painter
Diane Brown, Diane Brown Gallery
Kathy Huffman, Institute of Contemporary Art

The evolution of a novel, new technology to an accepted medium for artistic expression has always been a slow, cautious process. During this special session, museum curators, gallery owners, and artists will discuss the current state of the evolution of computer art as a means for artistic expression from mainstream art world points of view.

Speech and Audio in Window Systems: When Will They Happen?

Co-Chairs: Barry Arons, Olivetti Research Center
Chris Schmandt, MIT Media Lab

Panelists: Michael Hawley, NeXT Computer, Inc.
Lester Ludwig, Bellcore
Polle Zellweger, Xerox PARC

Although multi-media systems are in vogue, the last decade has seen many failed attempts at user interfaces to speech and audio systems. An architecture for sharing audio resources between applications or for integrating audio into graphical interfaces does not yet exist, despite semiconductor advances which have provided low-cost signal processing and audio input/output.

Many applications have been suggested: listening typewriters, voice annotation, computer conferencing, voice mail, speech substitues for mouse and keyboard, and auditory icons. How should these technologies be managed by programmers and users? Will speech be accepted as a command channel and a standard data type? Will voice replace or coexist with the graphical interfaces of today?

Special Session: Bloopers, Outtakes, and Horror Stories of SIGGRAPH Films

Co-Chairs: John Lasseter, Pixar
Bill Reeves, Pixar

Panelists: Philippe Bergeron, Independent Consultant
Eben Ostby, Pixar
Chris Wedge, Blue Sky Promotions
Bill Kroyer, Kroyer Films
Jim Blinn, California Institute of Technology
Craig Reynolds, Symbolics
Loren Carpenter, Pixar
Ralph Winter, Paramount Studios

This special session presents the little-known stories about behind-the-scenes production of the better-known SIGGRAPH films. This session combines fun with informative ideas concerning the tremendous effort required to create films for SIGGRAPH.

Speakers share lessons learned in a storytelling forum, with each having five to 10 minutes for telling a "horror story" and/or show outtakes. Members of the audience are encouraged to add personal experiences, share stories and ask questions.

HDTV (HI-VISION) Computer Graphics

Chair: Hideichi Tamegaya, Japan Broadcasting Corporation (NHK)

Panelists: Ryou Mochizuki, New Video System Research Association
Yoichiro Kawaguchi, Nippon Electronics College
Koichi Omura, Osaka Municipal University
Don Miscowich, Symbolics

Recent hardware developments-with increasingly stronger computational power and higher-resolution display-enable us to use workstations for computer graphics output. However, images must be recorded and transferred properly to preserve their quality. Since HDTV (Hi-Vision) has picture quality comparable to 35mm film, it enables computer graphics to be used for high- quality media such as film, art, publishing, and broadcasting.

Panelists discuss computer graphics applications on HDTV and their impact on the industry. They reveal experiences using computer graphics with various media and discuss issues of quality, expression, and interchangeability.

Future Directions in Desktop Video

Chair: Tim Heidmann, Silicon Graphics

Panelists: Michael MacKay, Diaquest
Gregory MacNichol, *Computer Graphics World*
Floyd Wray, BYTE-by-BYTE

The lowering cost of video equipment and the availability of low- cost personal graphics computers create the possibility of a complete desktop video production system. As desktop publishing is today, some feel this market is the next rage, while others believe the poor quality and complexity of inexpensive video production will prevent widespread practical application.

This panel defines what is happening in the area of low-cost computer graphics and video and discusses the opportunities and shortcomings of those developments. It benefits these people most: hardware manufacturers, who need to respond to upcoming developments in video peripherals; software developers, who must understand the nature and needs of new markets; and, perhaps, nearly all computer users who want to know the practical possibilities and how that changes the way they do business.

Distributed Graphics: Where to Draw the Lines?

Chair: Dick Phillips, Los Alamos National Laboratory

Panelists: Jay Torborg, Alliant Computer Systems
Cleve Moler, Ardent Computer
Michael Pique, Scripps Clinic and Research Foundation
Donald P. Greenberg, Cornell University

There are currently several approaches to producing graphical repersentations of data developed on supercomputers or other compute engines. In one extreme, all data, simulation, and graphics can be developed on a compute engine with the results shown on a vector-oriented "dumb terminal." In another extreme, all work is performed on a compute engine but displayed on a workstation in video format. And, in between, workstations handle various amounts of processing. There are standard workstations equipped with graphics accelerators, 3D workstations, and graphics supercomputers. In addition, there are approaches that use coarse-grained parallelism, where several powerful workstations join forces to solve a complex display problem.

This panel explores many of the approaches to graphics-based distributed computing. Panelists illustrate their contentions with a specific problem, discussing such issues as data volume, data flow bandwidth, and interactivity.

Operating Systems and Graphic User Interfaces

Co-Chairs: J. Paul Grayson, Micrografx

Panelists: T.D. Steele, IBM
Adrian King, Microsoft
Dan'l Lewis, NeXT Computer, Inc.
Larry Tesler, Apple Computer

Microcomputers have tremendously impacted the computer graphics industry. The next generation of personal computers, with their advanced operating systems and graphic user interfaces, promises to accelerate this trend.

Similarly, desktop computers have rapidly become the platform of choice for both users and vendors of advanced graphics solutions. MS-DOS with Windows and Apple Multifinder are the standards newcomers seek to dethrone: IBM launched OS/2 with Presentation Manager; Apple promised new versions of Multifinder, adding multitasking and advanced graphics tools; NeXT captured the industry's attention with a combination of UNIX, Display PostScript, CD-ROM, and object-oriented, end-user programming.

Panelists from IBM, Apple, NeXT, and Microsoft address their offerings and seek to justify their technology as the standard that developers and users should embrace as the next generation of computer graphics products.

Preparing for the Future

Chair: Maria Palazzi, Rutgers University

Panelists: Wayne Carlson, The Ohio State University
Richard Lucas, Bowling Green State Universtiy
Marla Schweppe, School of the Art Institute of Chicago
Mehmet Yanilmaz, Northwestern University

The field of computer graphics education, as no other, combines the disciplines of science and art and in this sense presents computer graphics instructors, in both art and science, with some unique problems not faced by their counterparts in other fields. As computer graphics courses become a standard addition in art and science curriculums, the way we prepare students for this evolutionary field is changing. This panel explores the methods of establishing computer graphics curriculm and maintaining these programs.

With most programs and courses in their infancy, the focus of this panel will be how a program is established from the ground up. Panel members will share experiences pertaining to curriculm developments and goals, intergrating with existing courses, planned growth, raising monetary resources, hardware and software purchasing and other educational issues. Problems, solutions and insights will be addressed. This panel will be helpful for: experienced instructors, who will will find they are not alone with their problems; new instructors, who frequently are not prepared for this challenging position; and for students interested in selecting computer graphics programs that serve their goals.

Computer Graphics Theater

L'Anniversaire/Anniversary

In the midst of frantic preparations for a party, three characters discover to their horror that they have done something unpardonable. Will they be able to restore order in time for the festivities?

Produced in celebration of the 50th anniversary of the National Film Board of Canada.

Contact
Doris Kochanek
Centre d'Animatique, P-36
National Film Board of Canada
P.O. Box 6100, Station A
Montréal, Québec
CANADA H3C 3H5
514-283-9309

Breeze

Seeking an emotive quality via harmony, composition and choreography. Inspired by Henri Fantin-LaTour, 19th century French painter.

Contact
Arthur Schwartzberg
Xaos (formerly Eidolon Inc.)
350 Townsend St. #101
San Francisco, CA 94107 USA
415-243-8467

Complexly Simple

Complex representation using simple object, simple color and simple motion.
Contact
Shinichi Kasahara
c/o Kajima Corporation
Information Processing Ctr., KI Bldg.
5-30, Akasaka 6 chome, Minatoku
Tokyo, 107, JAPAN
03-5561-2111

The Conquest of Form

A computer art film made using constructive solid geometry combined with 3D texturing, lighting and surface qualities. Shows the creation of complex structures.
Contact
William Latham
IBM UKSC
St. Clement Street
Winchester
Hampshire S0239DR
UNITED KINGDOM
0962-844-191

Continuum 1. Initiation

Initiation is the first of four movements in the *Continuum* set. The underlying theme of *Initiation* is the beginning and evolution of consciousness. The goal of this series is to elicit a state of suspension both intellectually and emotionally on the part of the viewer.
Contact

Dean Winkler Maureen Nappi Inc.
c/o Post Perfect 229 W. 78 Street #84
220 East 42nd Street New York, NY 10024 USA
New York, NY 10017 USA 212-877-3168
212-972-3400

Don't Touch Me

"Gaia's dying, can't you see? While you are wasting time on me." --DOZO
Contact
Jeff Kleiser
Kleiser-Walczak Construction Company
6105 Mulholland Hwy.
Hollywood, CA 90068 USA
213-467-3563

Eurhythmy

Eurhythmy, a state of harmony between mind and body, is depicted in a surrealistic, spiritual dance.
Contact
Susan Amkraut & Michael Girard
SCAN, Westerhavenstraat 11-13
P.O. Box 1329, 9701 BH Groningen
THE NETHERLANDS
050-138343

Excerpts from "Leonardo's Deluge"

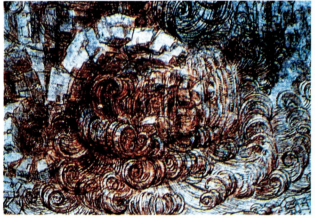

Leonardo Da Vinci's *Deluge* drawings have been put into motion using choreographed image-flow techniques. Leonardo's *Deluge* was produced and directed by Mark Whitney for the Program for Art on Film, a joint venture of the Metropolitan Museum of Art and the Getty Trust.
Contact
Karl Sims
Optomystic
725 N. Highland Avenue
Hollywood, CA 90038 USA

Flora

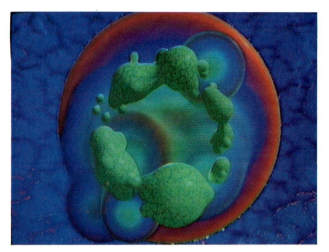

Flora lives in the fantastic Paleozoic seashore or in the visional future.
Contact
Yoichiro Kawaguchi
Nippon Electronics College, Dept. of Art
1-25-4, Hyakunin-cho, Shinjuku-Ku,
Tokyo 169 JAPAN
03-369-1995

Gas Turbine Flowfield Simulation

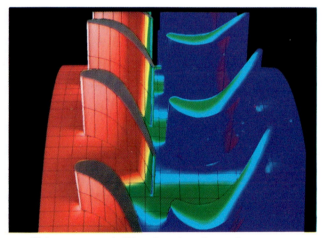

This stereoscopic 3D animation shows the pressure distribution obtained from a full 3D simulation of the flow inside a gas turbine.
Contact
Paul Kelaita
NASA Ames Research Center MS 258-2
Moffett Field, CA 94035 USA
415-694-4453 or 694-4450

Gibbon Event

Gibbon Event was done by a graduate student from the After Hours Group of the UCLA Animation and Design Department.
Contact
Alan Ridenour
UCLA Design Dept.
1300 Dickson Art Center
Los Angeles, CA 90024 USA
213-206-0206

The Hammer Sequence

A king has a contest to find the best gavel with which to rule his kingdom. Computer graphics techniques were used to produce full-character animation from a storyboard designed for traditional animation. Motion control techniques used included standard and parameterized keyframing, procedural descriptions and dynamic simulation.
Contact
Susan Van Baerle
New York Institute of Technology

Computer Graphics Laboratory
Wheatley Road, Gerry House
Old Westbury, NY 11568 USA
516-686-7644

Her Majesty's Secret Serpent

All of the motion was created with simulated dynamics.
Contact
Gavin Miller
Apple Computer Inc. MS60W
20705 Valley Green Dr.
Cupertino, CA 95014 USA
408-974-0186

Imagination

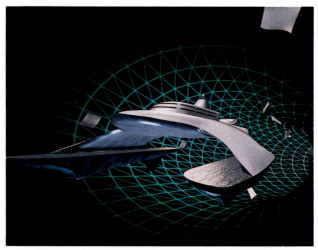

Links Corp. made a 10-minute stereoscopic 3D computer graphics movie for the Yokohama Expo. It took 1 year to make it. Client: Mitsubishi. Planning: Dentsu Inc.

Contact
Shuji Asano
Links Corporation
3-13-6 Higashi-shinagawa, Shinagawa-ku
Tokyo 140 JAPAN
03-450-8181

In Search of New Axis

This research piece explores a way to handle an object's deformation in the most unified manner. X,Y,Z,O combine twisting, bending and diversion, which are the important attributes during deformation.
Contact
Toshifumi Kawahara
Polygon Pictures Inc.
Bond Street T11
2-2-43 Higashi Shinagawa
Shinagawa-ku
Tokyo 140 JAPAN
03-474-4321

Industrial Light & Magic SIGGRAPH '89 Reel

A demo of computer graphic special effects produced for recent theatric-release motion pictures.
Contact
Douglas Kay
Industrial Light & Magic
P.O. Box 2459
San Rafael, CA 94912 USA
415-258-2000

Inforum

Computer-generated representation of a large corporate office facility prior to construction.
Contact
Lisa Berson
Design/Effects
535 Plasamour Dr.
Atlanta, GA 30324 USA
404-876-7149

knickknack

This film has it all! Not just one or two, three full Cartesian dimensions! Not just two or three, but nine heartwarming characters! Not just three or four, but all the known human emotions!
Contact

Ralph Guggenheim
Pixar
3240 Kerner Blvd.
San Rafael, CA 94901 USA
415-258-8100

The Little Death

A visual poem created for HDTV.
Contact
Matt Elson
Symbolics Inc.
150 East 58th St., 34th fl.
New York, NY 10155 USA
212-371-2112

Locomotion

Can a classic children's fable survive in today's world of flashy computer graphics? We think it can. We think it can. We think it can.
Contact
Steve Goldberg

Pacific Data Images
1111 Karlstad Dr.
Sunnyvale, CA 94089 USA
408-745-6755

The Making of *Without Borders*

The story of the design and creation process for the opening of a documentary about saving the world's rivers.
Contact
Lisa Berson
Design/Effects
535 Plasamour Dr.
Atlanta, GA 30324 USA
404-876-7149

Margaux Cartoon

This work sprang out of the immediacy of drawing, direct from my subconscious.
Contact
Beth Warshafsky
Electric Picture Works
24 W 40th St., 3rd floor
New York, NY 10018 USA
212-219-1912 (home), 212-869-2500 (work)

Mars -- The Movie

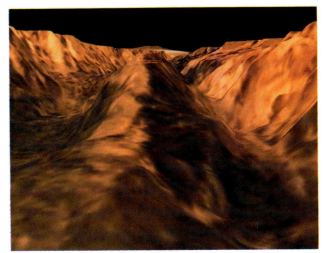

A fly-by over the distinctive Mars' surface using satellite data represents the first animated look at some of the planet's geographically-intriguing regions.
Contact
Betsy Asher Hall
Jet Propulsion Laboratory
4800 Oak Grove Dr, M/S 168-522
Pasadena, CA 91109 USA
818-354-6257

MathematicsΣ

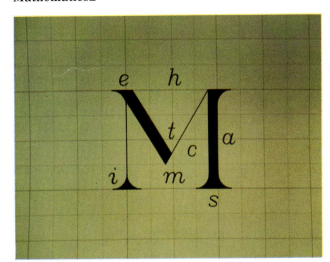

Project Mathematics! is a series of videotapes to teach high school math, funded with seed money from SIGGRAPH and ongoing funds from the National Science Foundation, Hewlett-Packard and Truevision.
Contact
Don Delson
305 S. Hill
Pasadena, CA 91106 USA 818-356-3750

Megacycles

Extensions to constructive solid geometry allowed recursive models. The final scene of this film, showing over 12,000 robot figures, is represented by only a few thousand bytes of data.
Contact
Don Mitchell
AT&T Bell Labs
Rm 3C-446 B
600 Mountain Ave.
Murray Hill, NJ 07974 USA
201-582-5862

A Moonlit Spring Night at Ma-ma Temple

The cherry blossom spirits come out to play among the blossoms on a moonlit spring night.

Contact
Naoko Motoyoshi
4-24-12 Higashikoiwa
Edogawa-ku
Tokyo 133 JAPAN
03-672-4516

NBC 1988 Olympic Open

Contact
Sally R. Kanner
Filigree Films
155 Ave. of the Americas
New York, NY 10013 USA
212-627-1770

Night Cafe

A character piece with the flavor of animation as it might have been created in the thirties. Settings are based on paintings by American painter Edward Hopper to depict the mood of the era. The Wurlitzer jukebox and the Duesenberg automobile were modeled using new 3D Boolean software. Experimental particle software was used to generate a cloud of pepper.

Contact
Sharon Calahan
Cubicomp Canada Ltd.
450, 1550 Alberni St.
Vancouver, British Columbia
CANADA V6G 1A5
604-685-1300

Numerical Experiments on the Interaction of Disk Galaxies

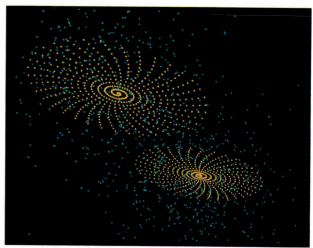

Stereoscopic 3D film.

Contact
Gordon Bancroft
NASA/Ames Research Center
MS 258-2
Moffett Field, CA 94035 USA
415-694-4052

Parfums de Vie

Travel between life, memory and dreams.

Contact
Jean-Luc Ortega
Sogitec
32, Bd de la République
92100 Boulogne
FRANCE
1-46-08-13-13

Paris: 1789

A walk in Paris at the Revolution's dawn.

Contact
Xavier Nicolas
Ex Machina
22, rue Hegesippe Moreau
75018 Paris
FRANCE
1-43-87-58-58

A Public Service Announcement

This work illustrates the use of hierarchical B-splines for character animation.

Contact
Phillip J. Barry
Dept. of Computer Science
University of Waterloo

Waterloo, Ontario
CANADA N2L 3G1
519-888-4421 or 888-4534

Send in the Clouds

Simulation of cumulous cloud development.

Contact
Geoffrey Y. Gardner
MS D12-237
Grumman Data Systems
1000 Woodbury Rd.
Woodbury, NY 11797 USA
516-682-8417

Sio Benbor Junior

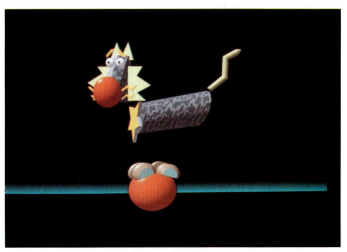

Sio Benbor Junior is a parody of Luxo Junior by
John Lasseter and the second episode of the humoristic
film series. In spite of his young age, ridiculous red
nose and artificial understanding, Sio Benbor was a big
hit at Imagina '89 where he was awarded the European

Grand Prix PIXEL-INA.
Contact
Georges Lacroix
Fantôme
71 rue Ampere
75017 Paris
FRANCE
1-40-53-01-23

Soap Opera

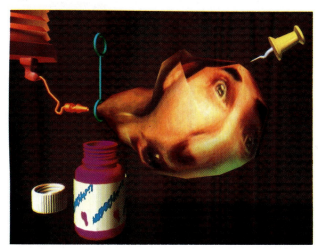

A thin film about a fat head. Stereoscopic 3D.
Contact
Peter Oppenheimer
NYIT Computer Graphics Lab
Wheatley Rd.
P.O. Box 170
Old Westbury, NY 11568 USA
516-686-7644

Study of a Numerically-Modeled Severe Storm

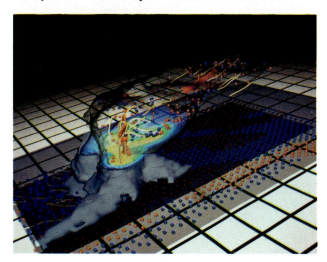

The understanding of severe storms begins by identifying pre-storm conditions. Using this initial environment, a thunderstorm's complexity is modeled with a set of mathematical equations. These equations are solved on a supercomputer, then visualization techniques are employed to simulate the air flow and other features that exist during a storm's lifetime.
Contact
Daniel Brady
NCSA
152 Computing Applications Bldg.
605 East Spring Field Ave.
Champaign, IL 61820 USA
217-244-2003

Tempest in a Teapot

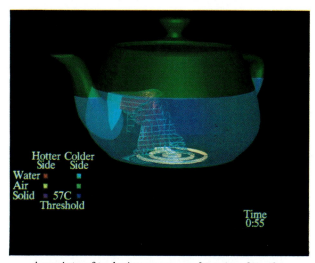

A variety of techniques are used to visualize the results of simulating water being heated in a teapot. Stereoscopic 3D film.
Contact
Thomas D. Desmarais
Mail Stop K1-86
P.O. Box 999
Richland, WA 99352 USA
509-375-2782

Test Scenes from *Echoes of the Sun*

Scenes from the Omnimax stereoscopic 3D film for the Fujitsu Pavilion at Osaka Expo '90.
Contact
Fumio Sumi
Systems Eng. Dep., Expo '90 Promotion Group
Fujitsu Limited
Marunouchi Center Building
6-1 Marunouchi 1-chome
Chiyoda-ku, Tokyo 100 JAPAN
03-216-9243

Tipsy Turvy

The Utah teapot stars in a simulation-driven fantasy.
Contact
Alan Norton
IBM Research 3B-38
P.O. Box 704
Yorktown Heights, NY 10598 USA
914-789-7195

Treadmill

This short piece evolved from being an exercise for a walk cycle to the animation of two men pushing wheels.
Contact
Geoff Campbell
20 George Henry Blvd.
Willowdale Ontario
CANADA M2J 1E2
416-494-8576

Urgence/Emergency

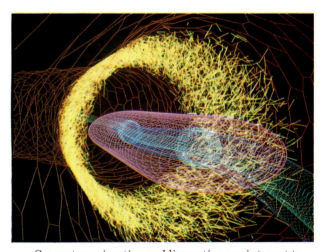

Computer animation and live action are intercut to dramatically illustrate an angioplasty operation to open a partially-blocked coronary artery. Excerpt from a 35-minute drama produced in 70mm Imax™ format.
Contact
Doris Kochanek
Centre d'Animatique, P-36
National Film Board of Canada

P.O. Box 6100, Station A
Montréal, Québec
CANADA H3C 3H5
514-283-9309

The Virtual Lobby

An animated and real-time walk-through of a
realistically-illuminated virtual lobby.
Contact
John Rohlf
307 Sitterson Hall
The University of North Carolina
Chapel Hill, NC 27599 USA
919-962-1827

**Visualization of Simulated Treatment of an Ocular
Tumor**

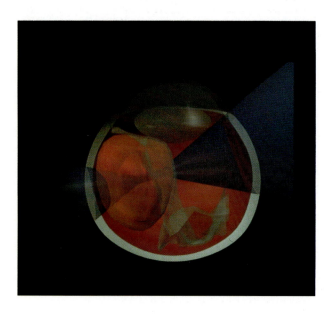

Scientific visualization in action to save life.
Contact
Wayne Lytle
Cornell National Supercomputer Facility
B49 Caldwell Hall,
Garden Ave.
Ithaca, NY 14853 USA
607-255-4162

Voyager: Journey to the Outer Planets

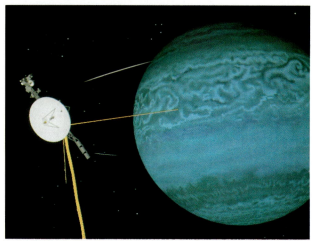

The Voyager Project has supported and reflected
the growth of JPL's Computer Graphics Lab. Neptune
is this year's *star*.
Contact
Sylvie Rueff
Jet Propulsion Laboratory
MS. 510-202
4800 Oak Grove Dr.
Pasadena, CA 91109 USA
818-397-9695

Index

Colophon
and
Credits for Cover Images

Colophon

The SIGGRAPH'89 proceedings are a major collaborative effort to print 22,000 copies of a 408 page full-color high quality book. SIGGRAPH'89 technical program attendees each receive a copy as does the membership of ACM SIGGRAPH. Additional copies are sold by ACM single copy sales to ACM members and for the second year, Addison-Wesley will be distributing these proceedings to bookstores and through mail order as part of their arrangement with ACM Press.

Those involved in the production include Rick Beach, the production editor at Xerox PARC in California; Lois Blankstein, the ACM SIGGRAPH Conference Liason in New York responsible for contracts and liason with ACM publications; Leona Caffey, the document production specialist at Smith, Bucklin and Associates in Chicago who produced the cover type and assembled much of the front matter; Bob Kushner, our print coordinator at Darbert Offset in New York who has printed the SIGGRAPH proceedings each year since 1980 and is responsible for the entire print production effort; Jeff Lane, the papers chair at DEC in Palo Alto who coordinated the selection of the technical papers and wrote the preface; Bob Judd, the panels chair at Los Alamos National Laboratory who coordinated the panel abstracts; Sally Rosethal, the *Computer Graphics Theater* chair at DEC in Palo Alto who coordinated the images for the 12-page catalog; and Bert Herzog, the awards committee chair at the University of Michigan who coordinated the awards.

For the first time, the proceedings include the catalog of contributions to the evening *Computer Graphics Theater*. All of the 38 technical papers (the most in SIGGRAPH history) and abstracts for each of the 16 panel and special sessions are included in the proceedings. The 408 pages are printed in 25 signatures of 16 pages and 1 signature of 8 pages (located in the middle so it will not come apart). These signatures are printed in full-color from separations made from camera-ready copy prepared by the technical paper authors and the production editor. This camera-ready copy greatly reduces the production cost and time for this complex publication. Color separations are made from the camera-ready copy and proofed by the production editor in New York. Three authors provided digital color separations for all of the color images in their papers: Alyn Rockwood *et al.*, p 107 and Dan Baum *et al.*, p 325, both from Silicon Graphics, and Bruce Lindblom, p 117, from Crosfield.

The difficulties with producing the 12-page catalog of the *Computer Graphics Theater* illustrate why we do not encourage submitting slides with camera-ready copy. The catalog includes 44 still images provided on slides by the contributors in all sorts of different aspect ratios, ranging from a square frame buffer image to a 2::1 aspect ratio. Unlike reflective-art mounted on camera-ready copy, these slides must be individually enlarged to fit the page layout during the production process. This requires removing the film from the mount, measuring the image area, calculating the enlargement factor, scanning the slide film, proofing the resulting image, measuring the proof and adjusting the page layout for the actual size and then cropping the images to fit. For the inexperienced designer (like the production editor!), this requires more careful coordination and much more time than dealing with color in camera-ready copy already at the correct size! Furthermore, it requires shipping the slide materials across the country several times with the attendant risks of damage and delays.

Regretably, we did not use the digital color separation process pioneered for the SIGGRAPH'88 proceedings. However, SIGGRAPH has funded some additional development work that will permit us to distribute the color reproduction tools to SIGGRAPH members. Look for more use of this work in future SIGGRAPH publications and in the ACM *Transactions on Graphics*.

At SIGGRAPH'89, look for the SIGGRAPH Interactive Proceedings project demonstration near the SIGGRAPH'90 booth. This project explores the use of multimedia technology to present the SIGGRAPH proceedings as an electronic document using text, mathematics, line art, halftone and continuous tone color illustrations combined with audio sound tracks, dynamic animations and prerecorded video segments. While the initial project concentrated on last year's proceedings, some of the material in this year's proceedings are included in the demonstration.

Front cover:
Bragger Boppin' in Bean Town

Copyright © 1989 The Advanced Computing Center for the Arts and Design, Ohio State University
Artists: John Chadwick, Don Stredney, Scott Dyer, and Jeff Light
Production notes: Character animation software by John Chadwick; rendering software by Scott Dyer; image processing software by Jeff Light; dynamic simulation software by Dave Haumann; beta-generation software by Steve Anderson and Steve Spencer; and shadow software by John Fujii. It was all done with in-house software developed at the Advanced Computing Center for the Arts and Design and the Ohio Supercomputer Graphics Project. It was rendered at 2K X 2K on a Sun 4 workstation and enlarged to 4K X 4K and shot onto 4 X 5 transparency using a Solitaire film recorder.
Reference: *Layered Construction for Deformable Animated Characters*, p 243.

Title page:
Medicine Lake
Copyright © 1988 by F. K. Musgrave, C. E. Kolb, P. Prusinkiewicz, B. B. Mandelbrot
Artist: F. K. Musgrave, C. E. Kolb, P. Prusinkiewicz
Insights: The aesthetics of this image involve the interplay of highly Euclidean geometrics with very natural fractal forms. Thus the image is designed to resemble nature at first glance, but to reveal its composition from regular geometric primitives, such as triangles and cylinders, upon closer inspection.

Extensive use of procedural textures conceals the geometric composition. This camouflage is thorough in the case of the water and the sky, both of which are perfectly flat planes, the first horizontal and the second vertical.

The rainbow model is derived from a simulation of the refraction with dispersion of light through an idealized raindrop. Note the dim secondary arc in the upper right hand corner.

Despite its surreal appearance, "Medicine Lake" was inspired by a similar photograph of a rainbow over a lake of the same name.
Production notes: This is a raytraced image, with "noise-synthesized" terrain, an L-system tree model, and a physical rainbow model.
Reference: *The Synthesis and Rendering of Eroded Fractal Terrains*, p 41.

Back cover, top left:
Architectural Rendering
Copyright © 1989 by Hiroshima University
Reference: *Three Dimensional Terrain Modeling and Display for Environmental Assessment*, p 207.

Back cover, top right:
knickknack
Copyright © 1989 by Pixar
Artists: John Lasseter, Wiliam Reeves, Eben Ostby, Flip Phillips, Craig Good, Ralph Guggenheim, Don Conway, Deirdre Warin, Tony Apodaca, Yael Milo
Production notes: Pixar's *menv* modeling and animation software was used to create this film, running on two workstations, each composed of a Computer Consoles Power 6/32 processor and Evans & Sutherland PS350 display system. The entire film was rendered using Pixar's rendering systems, implementing the RenderMan™ Interface for 3-D scene description, employing such techniques as procedural shading and texturing, self-shadowing, motion blur and texture mapping. A Tektronix 3-D Stereoscopic Display Monitor was used to preview frames of the film. Final animation was recorded on an Agfa/Matrix analog film recorder.
Reference: *Computer Graphics Theater* contributions, p 397

Back cover, middle left:
Attack of the Killer Oyster
Copyright © 1989 by NYIT
Artists: John P. Lewis
Production notes: A sculptured form is created by distorting a sphere with a correlated vector solid noise. This image was rendered on a Vax computer at a resolution of 1024 X 972, using software by the author and NYIT.
Reference: *Algorithms for Solid Noise Synthesis*, p 263.

Back cover, middle right:
Quaternion Julia Set
Copyright © 1989 by John C. Hart
Artist: John Hart, Daniel Sandin, and Louis Kauffman in the University of Illinois at Chicago Electronic Visualization Laboratory
Production notes: This image was created on an AT&T Pixel Machine 964d. Compute time was approximately an hour (one teraflop). The custom ray-tracing software used in this image was designed by John Hart and programmed in C using devtools.
Reference: *Ray Tracing Deterministic 3-D Fractals*, p 289.

Back cover, lower left:
Herbert the Bear
Copyright © 1989 Cal Tech University and IBM
Artist: James T. Kajiya, Timothy L. Kay, and John M. Snyder
Production Notes: Extensions to ray-tracing techniques involving new surface geometry elements and material lighting models produce soft effects. The techniques were developed and the bear was modeled on Hewlett Packard workstations. Herbert the Bear was computed at a resolution of 1280 x 1024 with one ray per pixel on a collection of IBM mainframes.
Reference: *Rendering Fur with Three Dimensional Textures*, p 271.

Back cover, lower right:
Wireframe Joystick
Copyright © 1989 by Silicon Graphics Inc.
Artist: Derrick Burns and Alyn Rockwood
Production notes: Photographed from the screen of a Silicon Graphics 3130 workstation.
Reference: *Real-time Rendering of Trimmed Surfaces*, p 107.